BLASPHEMY

BLASPHEMY

Verbal Offense against the Sacred,

from Moses to Salman Rushdie

LEONARD W. LEVY

The University of North Carolina Press

Chapel Hill and London

First published by The University of North Carolina Press in 1995
Published by arrangement with Alfred A. Knopf, Inc.
Manufactured in the United States of America

Library of Congress Cataloging-in-Publication Data
Levy, Leonard Williams, 1923–
Blasphemy : verbal offense against the sacred,
from Moses to Salman Rushdie / by Leonard W. Levy.
p. cm.
Originally published: 1st ed. New York : Knopf, 1993.
Includes bibliographical references and index.
ISBN 0-8078-4515-9 (pbk. : alk. paper)
1. Blasphemy—Great Britain—History.   2. Blasphemy—United
States—History.   3. Freedom of speech—Great Britain—
History.   4. Freedom of speech—United States—History.   I. Title.
KD8073.L47   1995
342.41'0853—dc20
[344.102853]   94-31365
CIP

Grateful acknowledgment is made to the following for permission to
reprint previously published material:
Jonathan Cape Ltd. and Peters Fraser & Dunlop Group Ltd.:
Excerpt from "New Approach Needed," from *A Look Round the
Estate: Poems, 1957–1967* by Kingsley Amis. Reprinted by
permission of Jonathan Cape Ltd., London, and Peters Fraser &
Dunlop Group Ltd., London.
Macmillan Publishing Company: "A Stick of Incense" from
The Poems of W. B. Yeats: A New Edition, edited by Richard J.
Finneran, copyright © 1940 by Georgie Yeats, renewed 1968 by
Bertha Georgie Yeats, Michael Butler Yeats, and Anne Yeats.
Reprinted by permission.
Seattle Gay News: Excerpts from "The Love That Dares to Speak
Its Name" by James Kirkup, from the *Seattle Gay News* (No. 96,
June 1976), copyright © 1976. Reprinted by permission.

99 98 97 96 95   5 4 3 2 1

To my grandchildren

Aaron Harris

Natalie Glucklich

Adam Harris

Elon Glucklich

Jacob Harris

Nathan Harris

Contents

Preface

THIS book is about the suppression of freedom of expression in the field of religious belief and experience; it is also about an inchmeal progression in the scope of freedom of expression. The past depicted here should not be forgotten or emulated. James Madison stated:

> Whilst we assert for ourselves a freedom to embrace and observe the Religion which we believe to be of divine origin, we cannot deny an equal freedom to those whose minds have not yet yielded to the evidence which has convinced us. If this freedom be abused, it is an offense against God, not against man: To God, therefore, not to man, must an account of it be rendered.

Abuse of freedom as distinguished from its appropriate use, or licentiousness as opposed to liberty, has always been the excuse for suppression. What society deems to be blasphemy—a verbal offense against sacred matters—may differ with time and place, but whatever is condemned as blasphemy is always regarded as an abuse of liberty.

Any definition of the scope of freedom of religious or irreligious expression necessarily requires the drawing of lines and limits. Perimeters against the impermissible, separating blasphemy from the expression of lawful opinion on religion, reveal what society will not and cannot tolerate. Blasphemy is a litmus test of the standards a society believes it must enforce to preserve its unity, its peace, its morality, its feelings, and the road to salvation.

The period covered by this book is approximately thirty-three centuries, from the time of Moses to a 1992 opinion of the Supreme Court. During most of that time, very few blasphemers were irreverent scoffers casting verbal opprobrium upon religion. Atheists and irreligious railers did not become the usual victims of blasphemy laws until the nineteenth century. For most of history, blasphemers have been devout Christians, although obnoxious to the majority of Christians among whom they lived. Even the homosexual centurion of the poem that featured in the

Gay News case of 1977 recognized Jesus as the Son of God. But the centurion, like most blasphemers, offended Christian sensibilities.

The history of the crime of blasphemy raises the question why blasphemers of God should not have been tolerated, if the blasphemer of a pagan god was spared because that god could avenge his own honor (Judges 6:31). My sympathy for Arian and Unitarian beliefs and for Christian victims of persecution is evident.

The first section of this book covers the history of the offense from ancient Jewish thought to the Reformation. Christianity grossly inflated a narrow Old Testament crime until distinctions between heresy and blasphemy disappeared. The first generation of Protestant reformers tended to gag on "heresy," of which they stood accused by Roman Catholicism; they rediscovered the scriptural term "blasphemy" to blacken the dissidents within their own ranks. That early history of the offense provides an essential background to its Anglo-American history, which is the primary subject of this book. Incidentally, for the sake of convenience, I refer to the offense of "blasphemy" without distinguishing blasphemous utterance from published blasphemy. For biblical quotations I use the Revised Standard Version.

The subject of blasphemy forms the basis, at least implicitly, for a study of the struggle for intellectual liberty in general and religious liberty in particular. Freedom of religious opinion, like the origins, scope, and limitations of freedom of expression, have long concerned me. The history of the offense of blasphemy has always lurked in the background. My first book included a chapter on a blasphemy case. When I wrote a study of the origins of the free-press clause of the First Amendment, I focused mainly on seditious libel but discovered that another major category of libel was blasphemous libel. When I studied Jefferson's record on civil liberties, I learned about his lifelong interest in opposing blasphemy laws and the common-law doctrine that Christianity was part of the law of the land. When writing *Origins of the Fifth Amendment*, I learned that persons resorted to the claim that they should not be forced to incriminate themselves in cases of political crimes (seditious libel and treason) and in cases of religious crimes (heresy and blasphemy). The subject of blasphemy has pursued me for nearly forty years. I have written on it before but never whole, as here. For me the subject is a vital aspect of the history of First Amendment freedoms.

A brief word about acknowledgments dictates that I mention Dana Whaley, who for several years was my excellent research assistant when I taught at the Claremont Graduate School, where I did most of the research for this book. She fetched books, typed, proofread, and taught me how to use a word processor. Dr. Ariel Glucklich did the index. I am thankful to him and to Jane Garrett and Paul Schnee of Knopf, who were wonderfully helpful and considerate. In previous books I referred to my daughters, Wendy Ellen and Leslie Anne, but they expressed a monumental uninterest in this book. I expect that Nancy Peterson and her partners at Bloomsbury Books, Ashland's premier bookstore, will earn my thanks when they place pyramids of this book in their window. I have dedicated the book to my daughters' children, so that they will know that I was thinking of them, and I hope that they may one day read the book to learn what their grandfather did when he "worked." Although I wrote this book for myself, to satisfy an urge to master the subject, had I done it for anyone else my wife, Elyse, is that person.

LEONARD W. LEVY
Ashland, Oregon

BLASPHEMY

CHAPTER ONE

Origins of the Offense

B LASPHEMY means speaking evil of sacred matters. Where organized religion exists, blasphemy is taboo. Thus, monotheistic religions have no monopoly on the concept of blasphemy. Any pagan society, whether as civilized as ancient Egypt or as primitive as idol-worshipping natives on Papua, can imagine superior beings or spirits that influence man's destiny; every religious society will punish the rejection or reviling of its gods. Because blasphemy is an intolerable profanation of the sacred, it affronts the priestly class, the deep-seated beliefs of worshippers, and the basic values that a community shares. Punishing the blasphemer may serve any one of several social purposes in addition to setting an example to warn others. Punishment propitiates the offended deities by avenging their honor, thereby averting divine wrath: earthquakes, infertility, lost battles, floods, plagues, or crop failures. Public retribution for blasphemy also vindicates the witness of the believers and especially of the priests; it reaffirms communal norms; and it avoids the snares of toleration.

Toleration of blasphemy poses problems even for a society that can imagine gods sufficiently powerful to defend their own reputations and discriminating enough to do so by a judgment on the offender only. But if vengeance belongs to the supernatural governor of life, why invoke the criminal law? The reasons are that toleration seems to sanction the offense, inviting others to commit it. Toleration also reflects adversely on orthodox truths, shedding doubt on them, since blasphemers escape punishment; moreover, toleration endangers the unity of society. Even if sanctioning blasphemy did not risk divine wrath on the whole community, failure to punish the blasphemer might lead to public disturbances by provoking violence against him and perhaps even against those who tolerate him. Believers whose sensibilities he has injured might seek private retribution when official justice has failed. Fundamentally, however, the blasphemer incurs punishment because society regards his scandalous crime as a form of high treason against the highest powers in the universe. Even societies that cherish liberty have denied it to blasphemers.

Athens in the fifth century B.C. reached cultural peaks that rivaled the finest achievement of mankind for about the next two thousand years. Freedom of expression was an Athenian boast and a source of accomplishment, but the taboo against reflecting on the gods, whom the Greeks invented in their own image, jeopardized even the highest-placed citizens. Impiety was the Greek equivalent of blasphemy. The penalties for impiety circumscribed the prevailing spirit of free inquiry. One could criticize the state but not mock or repudiate its gods, or defile the customary manner of honoring them.[1]

The offense that impinged most on intellectual liberty was expression of disbelief in the gods, their religious servants, or the efficacy of conventional worship. Disbelief or impious opinions challenged the cult by impeaching its foundations. The public honoring of the gods could not be fulfilled unless men accepted their existence. Any act or expression contemptuous of the gods or depraving holy matters was impiety.[2]

Anaxagoras (circa 500–428 B.C.) was the first philosopher to reside in Athens and probably the first freethinker to be condemned for his beliefs. Anaxagoras held that a superior intellect had imposed a purposeful order on the physical world. He regarded the conventional gods as mythic abstractions endowed with anthropomorphic attributes. His writings led him to a dungeon, charged with impiety, probably about the year 450 B.C. Pericles, the pre-eminent Athenian statesman, who had been a pupil of Anaxagoras, defended the frail old philosopher. The celebrated Periclean oratory saved Anaxagoras from a sentence of death. He had to pay a fine and, by some accounts, was banished. He spent his remaining years in exile.[3]

Pericles also defended his mistress, Aspasia, against a charge of impiety. He could not repeat his success when he defended his close friend Phidias, possibly the greatest artist of the classical era. Phidias had designed the interior of the Parthenon and sculpted the colossal statue of the goddess Athena that dominated it. On her shield he carved figures of himself and Pericles as a way of signing his work and acknowledging his patron. Since Athena was the guardian deity of Athens and the Parthenon her temple, Phidias's depiction of himself and his friend was more than a sin of pride; it was a dangerous form of impiety, for any profanation of the protecting gods of the state implicitly attacked the state itself, akin to treason. Phidias probably died in prison, while awaiting trial, in about the year 433 B.C.[4]

Euripides, the tragic poet of the theatre, faced the same charge as Phidias. Several of his plays seemed irreligious and shocking. He questioned some divine legends and exposed the baneful influences that the deities exercised over the lives of mortals. When he seemed to doubt the sanctity of oaths in *Hippolytus*, he passed the threshold of tolerance, for oaths were sacred: they called upon the gods to witness an obligation. Euripides escaped conviction by showing that the oath in his play had lacked divine sanction. Aeschylus, his illustrious precursor, also had to defend himself from the charge of impiety, but the facts of his case have not survived.[5]

During the Peloponnesian War, when Athens and Sparta fought for Greek supremacy, the charge of impiety destroyed many lives and careers. Among the victims were Protagoras, the Sophist philosopher, and Alcibiades, the statesman and general. Both had connections with Pericles, like Anaxagoras, Aspasia, Phidias, and Euripides. With dozens of others, Protagoras and Alcibiades stood accused of impiety for complicity in the mutilation of the statues of Hermes and the profanation of the Eleusinian Mysteries, the holiest of the Athenian sacraments.

In 415 B.C., when Athenians were preparing an expeditionary force against Sparta, the city awoke one morning to an appalling discovery: nearly every statue celebrating Hermes, son of Zeus, the king of gods and men, had been desecrated during the night. Impiety on so vast a scale seemed the work of a conspiracy. The event was taken as a bad omen for the expedition and for the survival of Athenian democracy. Informers, responding to offers of rewards, implicated Alcibiades, and further investigation uncovered a second crime of impiety. If the first was comparable to smashing statues of the Madonna in all the religious shrines in a Catholic town during the Middle Ages, the second was comparable to a Black Mass. One night when the spirits had been high and the flagons low, according to informers, Alcibiades had led a blasphemous parody of the sacred Eleusinian Mysteries, which honored Demeter, the earth goddess. Impersonating the high priest, Alcibiades had revealed and mocked the secret rites.[6]

As one of the commanders of the army, Alcibiades was too important to be condemned summarily, like the others. Moreover, he denied complicity and demanded a trial, which his opponents contrived to postpone. Obeying the Council of Assembly, Alcibiades went off to war. In his absence, he was convicted of impiety and attempting to overthrow the government. He was sentenced to death and forfeiture of his properties. On hearing the verdict, he went over to the enemy and led the Spartans against Athens.

Protagoras was undone by the terror of 415 B.C. He was over seventy in that year, an illustrious philosopher and teacher of rhetoric, who was called the first and the greatest Sophist. At a public reading of the introduction to his book, "On the Gods," while in the home of Euripides, Protagoras confessed that he had become an agnostic: "As to the gods, I have no means of knowing either that they exist or that they do not exist." At a time when Athens was in a frenzy because of the impieties against the hermae and the Eleusinian Mysteries, and was at war as well, Protagoras's philosophy seemed to subvert the public morale. Tolerating him tempted the gods to visit disaster on Athens, which saved itself by confiscating and publicly burning his books. To avoid a trial for his life, he fled the city, but perished at sea.[7]

More dangerous was Diagoras of Melos, a poet whose alleged impieties of belief were so sensational that his very name connoted a repudiation of divine justice. Men spoke of "Diagoras the atheist." When he threw the wooden image of a god into a fire, remarking that the heroic deity should perform another miracle, he drew accusations that he was part of the conspiracy to profane the Mysteries. Sensibly, Diagoras fled for his life. Athens outlawed him and offered a reward for his capture dead or alive. He lived out his life in Spartan territory.[8]

The last of the Pericleans to be tried for blasphemy was Socrates, who, in Plutarch's poignant but misleading phrase, "lost his life because of philosophy." When Socrates drank the cup of hemlock in 399 B.C., he closed a lifetime of intellectual subversion and a long history of associations that contributed to his unpopularity, making him more vulnerable to attack when his enemies gained political power. Socrates had been the teacher and friend of Alcibiades, whom the city drove to treason; no one had done greater damage to Athens than he. If anyone rivaled Alcibiades as Athens's nemesis, it was Critias, who headed the ruling faction during the brief Spartan hegemony. Critias was a close friend of Socrates, as was his next in command, Charicles, a former pupil of Socrates. They and their faction probably executed more Athenians, mostly members of the democratic party, than Spartans had killed in battle. Socrates had no share in their tyranny, but his own lack of sympathy for democracy was well known. The public identified him with its enemies. After the democrats regained power, their tolerance for his corrosive criticism wore out. His enemies would have been satisfied with his exile, but he chose death instead. He died "because of his philosophy" in the sense that it made him uncompromising, religiously different, and politically obnoxious.[9]

Except for that of Jesus, the trial of Socrates is the best known in history. Like Jesus, he upset his universe by his tongue alone, but his method of teaching as much as his teachings did the damage. To be sure, Socrates was the earliest proponent of a morality founded on the compulsions of individual conscience rather than obedience to law even if democratically made. But he was a moralist who professed not to know the path of morality, and he was not religious in the conventional sense. He also sought truth by a pitiless inquisition into accepted beliefs, making him seem abrasive and insufferably superior. He gave the impression of tearing down beliefs without salvaging much. His skepticism shook faith in conventional values, religious and political. His teachings seemed negative, agnostic, and dangerously innovative. The public saw him as a destructive critic and a subversive elitist.[10]

After the treason of Alcibiades, followed by disastrous military reverses and the bloody rule of Critias and the tyrants, Socrates no longer was tolerable. He had to stand trial for impiety. The indictment was that he corrupted the youth, did not believe in the gods of the state, and advocated deities of his own. The charge meant that he taught oligarchy and sedition, as well as unconventional religious beliefs. Socrates was the intellectual leader of a conspiracy that drew its main support from young aristocrats whom he had indoctrinated with a contempt for democracy as well as for the old religious ways. He was a dangerous man, and from a legal standpoint he was guilty as charged. The surprising fact is that the Athenian citizenry who were his jury divided so closely in their verdict. His death was the result of his refusal to accept exile or to be smuggled out of prison.[11]

That the Athens of the fifth century B.C. could drive Socrates, Phidias, and Protagoras to their deaths and drive away Anaxagoras, Alcibiades, and Diagoras proved rather early in the history of the West that religion, when supported by the state, can be hostile to enlightenment and personal liberty. The record does not show that any of the victims reviled the deities. The cases tended to be as much political as religious in character. Treason against the gods was close to treason against the state, but Athens could accept a charge of impiety more easily than it could a political charge. Its targets of attack were mainly intellectual dissidents. Without exception, their cases raised fundamental issues of freedom of expression—literary, artistic, philosophical, religious, and political. Proof of a political charge against the state was harder to come by than proof of deviant religious opinion. Nor did that situation change in later Athenian life. Aristotle, for example, fled Athens in 323 B.C., when he was indicted for impiety; his crime was writing an inscription for the statue of a political patron whom he compared to the immortals, thus insulting religion.[12]

The Athenian character of impiety, mixing religion with politics at the expense of intellectual liberty, was not radically different from that of blasphemy under Christendom. But the West's law on the crime of blasphemy derived from a quite different source. It was a divine ordinance supposedly revealed to Moses for the governance of the Israelites soon after the Ten Commandments.

Exodus 22:28 declares, "You shall not revile God, nor curse a ruler of your people." Jewish history, like Athenian, suggests that a charge of blasphemy reflected politics as well as religion. One case, reported in Leviticus 24:10–23, required a decision by Moses. During a quarrel, a man "blasphemed the Name, and cursed." We do not know exactly what he said, but he apparently pronounced the personal name of God, for which the conventional rendering is "Yahweh," and spoke contemptuously about Him, thereby shocking and frightening people within earshot. The Israelites held the name of God in great awe and probably believed that it possessed some magical properties, because they associated it with the giving of life and the making of miracles. To curse God by name was a horrendous crime that might bring divine wrath down on the people of Israel. The Bible says that they put the offender in custody until God's will could be made known to them, meaning that Moses had to sit in judgment.[13]

A crime had been committed, but the case raised novel questions. The culprit was a visitor whose father was an Egyptian. Was he subject to the same laws as Israelites? Could he be punished for blaspheming a deity in whom he may not have believed? What was the punishment for blasphemy? The ordinance "You shall not revile God" fixed no sentence. The Bible says:

> And the Lord said to Moses, Bring out of the camp him
> who cursed; and let all who heard him lay their hands
> upon his head, and let all the congregation stone him.
> And say to the people of Israel, Whoever
> curses his God shall bear his sin. He who blasphemes
> the name of the Lord shall be put to death; all the
> congregation shall stone him; the sojourner
> (foreigner) as well as the native, when he blasphemes
> the Name shall be put to death.

Leviticus 24:16 fixed the precedent in Judeo-Christian history for punishing blasphemy as a crime.

The method of inflicting the death sentence on a person found guilty of blasphemy had a ritual significance similar to sacrifice. Laying on the hands acknowledged responsibility for the sacrifice and sought atonement for the community's sins, in the hope that God would be forgiving. The sentence and means of carrying it out indicated the way a God-fearing people sought to avert divine wrath. The Bible depicts very few blasphemy cases but many of idolatry, a different crime.[14]

The struggle of Yahweh's adherents against idolatrous foreign cults, which worshipped local deities or Baals, constitutes a major theme of biblical history. Yahweh was forever punishing the Israelites for their idolatry and then, when hearing their contrite prayers, would mercifully raise up a leader to save them. In the twelfth century B.C., Gideon was one of those leaders. The Lord instructed him to pull down an altar of

Baal and to cut down the grove nearby that represented Astarte, a mother goddess, and then to build an altar to the only true God. Gideon carried out his orders, which blasphemed Baal and Astarte. Their supporters demanded his death, but his father saved him from an angry crowd by demanding to know why the people should defend Baal's cause: "If he is a god, let him contend for himself, because his altar has been pulled down" (Judges 6:25–32). The argument was effective, although the Bible does not explain why Yahweh too did not contend for Himself, and why He could not inflict punishment only on his blasphemers rather than on the entire community, or why people must murder one another to avenge an avenging God's honor. His ways were unfathomable to mortals, and they did not dare question His judgment.[15]

By the time of King Ahab, who died about 851 B.C., the Baal cult threatened again to obliterate Yahwism. We learn from the book of Kings that Ahab supported the efforts of Jezebel, his wife, to supplant Yahweh with a foreign deity, Malkart, the Baal of Phoenicia, whom Jezebel, a Phoenician princess, worshipped. Ahab built a great temple to the Baal, while Jezebel desecrated the sanctuaries of Yahweh and killed almost all His prophets. Closely related to the main thread of the narrative is the tragedy of Naboth. Jezebel plotted his death on false charges of blasphemy and treason.

Naboth, an elder of Jezreel, had a vineyard adjacent to the royal summer palace. Ahab, who coveted Naboth's land, offered to buy it, but Naboth refused to sell. Because Ahab, recognizing the right of a subject to hold on to his patrimony, could only sulk, Jezebel corrupted the courts of justice by influencing the elders of Jezreel to accept the perjured testimony of two "base fellows" who accused Naboth of having cursed God and the king. The court summarily found Naboth guilty, and he died by stoning, the punishment for blasphemy. Ahab took possession of his land, after killing Naboth's sons. What follows is one of the Bible's most terrible stories of divine retribution (1 Kings 21:20–24; 2 Kings 9:21–37, 10:6–28).

An episode in 701 B.C., during the Assyrian siege of Jerusalem, became the basis of a peculiar Jewish ritual, the tearing of one's garment on hearing blasphemy. Rab-Shakeh, an Assyrian leader, ridiculed King Hezekiah's ability to save Jerusalem and threatened, "Do not let your God on whom you rely deceive you by promising that Jerusalem will not be given into the hands of the king of Assyria." Rab-Shakeh's speech became blasphemous when he spoke contemptuously against God. The accounts refer to mocking and reviling, although we know only that he compared Yahweh to the gods of various conquered peoples whose deities, by Jewish standards, were "no gods but the work of men's hands, wood and stone," or idols.

Hezekiah's representatives rent their garments as a sign of their grief and horror on being exposed to blasphemy. The king, having also torn his clothes and prayed for divine aid, sent for the prophet Isaiah, who assured him that the only true and living God had heard his prayers and would save the city. According to biblical accounts, Yahweh sent an angel (more likely a plague) who destroyed 185,000 Assyrians. History has known many an army conquered by disease. The Assyrians retreated.[16]

The blasphemy of Rab-Shakeh did not conform to the Levitical requirement that blasphemy consists of cursing God or His name, unless cursing be taken loosely to include abusing, rejecting, and deriding. In the biblical sense, to curse ordinarily means to utter an imprecation or invoke evil, usually by calling on God's power. "God damn," the most familiar curse, is now merely profanity. The Rab-Shakeh story suggests that blasphemy had come to mean a showing of disrespect for God, doubting His powers, even disobeying His commandments. Indeed, we read that as long ago as Moses's time anyone who knowingly sins reviles the Lord. The blasphemous nature of the sin was a considerably less serious offense than that of damning or cursing God by his name, for the punishment was merely that "that person shall be cut off from among his people," or exiled (Numbers 15:31). Similarly, in the time of Ezekiel (about 580 B.C.), the chronicler reports God as saying, "Your fathers blasphemed me, by dealing treacherously with me," and the context makes clear that the offense was worshipping idols (Ezekiel 20:27). By contrast, the verbal crime of blasphemy, which was a capital offense, consisted essentially in speaking evil of God. The Hebrew word for "curse" can mean "show disrespect," which conceivably can be manifested in any irreligious or immoral way, but blasphemy was a crime of utterance. The Rab-Shakeh episode shows that blasphemy encompassed a considerably broader range of offensive utterances than did cursing in a literal sense. Therefore, the episode illustrates a broadened understanding of the crime, though it remained God-centered.[17]

None of the scriptural references to blasphemy actually quote a blasphemous utterance. Those who composed the Old Testament would not dare offend God by repeating the thought, let alone the very words, of such an utterance. Generally, the Hebrew Bible declares that blasphemy, like idolatry, is not to be endured. In Daniel 3:29, for example, Nebuchadnezzar, awed by the rescue of Yahweh's servants from the fiery furnace, decrees that no one shall blaspheme their God on pain of being torn limb from limb. In the original Hebrew version, the decree enjoins against "speaking anything against God," although in the Septuagint, the Greek translation of the Old Testament for Jews in the Diaspora, the verb is "blaspheme." The Hebrew tended to prefer a circumlocution or a more exact word. Thus, Isaiah 66:3 in the Septuagint connects blasphemy with idolatry in a passage where the Hebrew simply compares an abominable offering to blessing an idol. Or, in an Apocryphal text, 1 Maccabees 2:6, the Greek relies on "blasphemy," where the Hebrew more appropriately uses "sacrilegious."[18]

The scriptural term for "blaspheme" in Hebrew is *nakob*, which literally means to specify, enunciate, or pronounce distinctly; but Leviticus 24:10–23 uses *nakob* in conjunction with *killel* or *qillel*, which means "curse." The word's connotations include "pierce" (the name of God), "rail," "repudiate," "derogate," "speak disrespectfully," "denounce," "insult," and "abuse." Although the Septuagint tended to use "blasphemy" as a broad term for offenses against religion, it did not basically differ from the Hebrew Scriptures, nor did the Pseudepigrapha, later extracanonical writings.[19]

In Jewish thought, blasphemy invariably denoted verbal abuse of God. The second book of the Maccabees, which was originally composed in Greek, uses "blasphemy," "blasphemer," or "blaspheme" much more frequently than 1 Maccabees, which derived from a Hebrew version. The second book, dating from about 124 B.C., contains the largest number of references to blasphemy in all the Apocryphal literature. In this chronicle describing how the Hellenizers sought to eradicate Judaism and replace it with idolatrous worship, the text contains various references to offenses against religion—forced apostasy, sacrilege, and "acts of impiety" such as killing mothers who had their sons circumcised, compelling Jews to eat forbidden foods, and building a pagan temple on a sacred Jewish site. Within such a context, described in 1 Maccabees as well, the references to blasphemy suggest that the Hellenizers also reviled the living God in words not fit for quotation. In 2 Maccabees 15:3, Nicanor questions whether there is a "ruler in the sky who has ordered the sabbath day to be observed," giving us the closest approximation to blasphemous words that a Jewish chronicler would permit.[20]

With the exception of Sirach 3:16, no Greek-Jewish text uses "blasphemy" or any variant of it that is not God-centered. The thought in Sirach is that to reject or despise one's father "is like blasphemy." The aberrant analogy recalls the disobedient son of Deuteronomy 21:18–21, who must be stoned. Every other usage of "blasphemy" whose meaning can be inferred occurs in the context of idolatry or a rejection of God. Nowhere in the entire corpus of Greek-Jewish sacred books (Septuagint, Apocrypha, and Pseudepigrapha) is "blasphemy" a synonym for "heresy." Indeed, "heresy" is not a Hebrew term at all, and no equivalent for it appears in the pre-Christian era. Christianity, although greatly influenced by the Septuagint, would use the two terms as equivalents and as more than a God-centered offense. Not until Christianity began did the meaning of blasphemy fundamentally change.[21]

When the rabbis composed the Talmud in the Christian era, they narrowed the meaning of "blasphemy" at the very time, and probably because, Christianity expanded it. The Talmud, a sprawling temple of learning that is a commentary on the Old Testament, contains the ultimate expression of Jewish law on the subject of blasphemy. The Talmud, which would later be burned by medieval Christians as a mountain of damnable blasphemies, contains a discussion of blasphemy that represents a road not taken by Christendom. Scriptural rather than rabbinic law is the source of Anglo-American law on blasphemy, but rabbinic law represents the culmination of the Jewish tradition.[22]

Jewish law avenges God's honor, not that of the Jewish religion. The Old Testament and the Talmud restrict the crime of blasphemy to defamation of the Deity, which has the resonance of high treason against the King of Kings, the Creator and Lord of the universe. The Rab-Shakeh incident and 2 Maccabees reflected an enlarged view of the crime, yet only in relation to God. The Talmud, however, focused on the original injunction from Exodus 22:28, "You shall not revile God," and defined the crime as tightly as possible. It was cursing Yahweh. In the Talmud, as in the Rab-Shakeh incident, blasphemy and idolatry were inextricably related. "Wherein lies the enormity of these offenses? Because they constitute an attack on the fundamental belief of Judaism," the existence and unity of God. Significantly, the reference is to "the" fundamental belief, belief in God, not to "a" fundamental belief, for there was only the one, and it alone could be described as a dogma of Judaism, a religion notably devoid of dogmas. The Talmud condemned the offense of blasphemy for purely religious reasons: blasphemy offended God contrary to His express will as revealed to Moses. Neither scriptural nor rabbinic law actually refers to the need to appease the Deity to avert his wrath.[23]

But the Talmud explicitly confined the offense of blasphemy to cursing God, as in "May Yahweh smite Himself," and additionally restricted it to a particular utterance: "the blasphemer is punished only if he utters [the divine] Name." Thus, to say "God damn" was to curse profanely but was not a curse against God, whereas to say "May God smite Himself" or "Damn God" implied a rejection and reviling of the Deity but did not meet the requirement for the capital crime that God be cursed by His name. Indeed, the Talmud, which often defined a crime in a way that would make its commission nearly impossible or at least extremely unlikely, specified that the blasphemer must curse "the name by the name." Neither cursing God nor saying His name fulfilled the Talmudic requirement for the capital offense.[24]

The actual pronunciation of the name remains a mystery. A four-letter Hebrew word known as the "tetragrammaton," for which the English equivalent of the letters is "YHVH," represents the name. The original Hebrew lacked vowels, leaving doubt as to the sound of the name, although it is commonly rendered as "Yahweh" or "Yahveh," whose meaning, roughly, is "I am who I am." Accordingly, God probably never disclosed His personal name to Moses in Exodus 3:14. A belief that the mere utterance of the name constituted blasphemy drew strength from the fact that the name became more sacred as its use atrophied over the centuries. The tetragrammaton appears only seven times in the last three books of the Old Testament, but commonly before them. Substitutes for the name developed, chief among them being "Adonai" (the Lord) and "Elohim" (God). By the time of Jesus, only the priests in the Temple in Jerusalem used the name, and only during religious observances.[25]

Because superstition and reverence surrounded the name, an assumption arose that its utterance was blasphemous. In fact, however, the Talmud required at the very least that disrespect or contempt must accompany the utterance of the name. So sacred had the name become in the time of rabbinic Judaism that the Talmud employed farfetched euphemisms when describing blasphemy. A witness to the crime could not testify in open court by stating exactly what he had heard: that would repeat the holy name and the abhorrent crime itself. The court instructed witnesses to use a four-letter substitute for YHVH, as in the Talmudic illustration, "May Jose (Joseph) smite Jose." Because the court could not convict on the basis of such testimony, the judges cleared the room of spectators at the end of the trial and commanded the eldest witness, "State literally what you have heard." When he repeated the actual utterance, the judges arose and tore their robes to show their profound grief on hearing blasphemy. Only one witness repeated the blasphemy; the others had only to state, "I too have heard thus," thereby avoiding unnecessary use of the name and repetition of the crime.[26]

So horrifying was the thought that anyone might curse Yahweh by name that the rabbis, when arguing that the name must be cursed by the name, resorted to an antonym for "curse," by saying, "The Name must be 'blessed' by the Name," if the utterance was to deserve death. Some early rabbis taught that reviling God, even without using the name, was a capital crime, although later sages decreed that a blasphemous utterance employing any of the substitutes for YHVH was punishable only by flogging.[27]

For practical purposes, the penalty for blasphemy was flogging, especially after A.D. 70, when the Romans destroyed the Temple. Thereafter, the Sanhedrin, the great rabbinic court with criminal jurisdiction, lost the power to inflict death. In time, the penalty for blasphemy became excommunication.

In sum, the Jewish law on blasphemy remained severely God-centered, but its Talmudic interpretation was a law for a world that had all but disappeared in the late first century A.D. Christian nations would seize upon the scriptural definition of blasphemy as a point of departure for drastically enlarging the definition of the crime.[28] It remained an offense against religion, but its political dimension always loomed in the background.

CHAPTER TWO

The Jewish Trial of Jesus

T HE MOST famous and influential blasphemy trial in history was a religiously inspired fiction. The Jewish Sanhedrin, the great council of seventy presided over by the high priests, neither tried Jesus for blasphemy nor convicted him of any crime. The depictions of the formal trial of Jesus by the Sanhedrin in the Gospels of Mark and Matthew dramatize the Jewish rejection of Jesus. Theologically, the trial scenes in Mark and Matthew are crucial, because they reveal the identity of Jesus as the Christ. Readers understand that he had not blasphemed God and that the blasphemers were those who found him guilty, for they had refused to accept him as Son of God and Messiah.

Although only Mark and Matthew depict a formal trial and condemnation by the Sanhedrin, all four evangelists, the writers of the Gospels, employ the motif that the Jewish rejection of Jesus was blasphemy. The Synoptics—the first three Gospels, whose similarity of viewpoint is especially evident when they are compared in parallel columns—describe a scene in which Jesus forgives a man for his sins and cures him of paralysis, provoking some "scribes" to say, "It is blasphemy! Who can forgive sins but God alone?" (Mark 2:5–8; Matthew 9:2–3; Luke 5:21). In that scene, Jesus relies on his authority as Son of Man to heal and forgive. Thus, he acts from a divinely inspired commission, making the charge of blasphemy warrantless. When Jesus restores the power of speech to a dumb man, Jewish onlookers (Pharisees in Matthew, scribes in Mark, and unidentified members of the crowd in Luke) allege that his miraculous power comes from the prince of demons. Such scenes set the stage for the infamous Jewish trial. They are, like the trial, devices for demonstrating both the Jewish rejection of Jesus and the new meanings of blasphemy. One is rejection of Jesus as Messiah or as Son of God. A second derives from his declaration that to ascribe to the devil a work of the Holy Spirit is an unforgivable blasphemy (Mark 3:22–29; Matthew 12:24–31; Luke 11:15, 12:10).[1]

In reality, Jews in ancient Palestine assumed the omnipotence of God and the commonplaceness of a religious man's having the power to heal and forgive in the name of God. Jesus himself never claimed to act on his own authority. His healing on the Sabbath and his forgiving sins did not violate Jewish law. An assertion by a holy person, relying on scriptural precedents, that he was doing God's will would not likely have been subject to criticism, let alone be called blasphemous. The frequent Gospel assertions that the people, and even Jesus' apostles, were "astonished" show what was probably the Jewish reaction to Jesus.[2]

The Gospels are ambivalent on this point. When, for example, Jesus cured multitudes by the sea and then fed five thousand with five loaves and two fishes, there was no talk of blasphemy. In the fourth Gospel, John says of the feeding miracle that the people took it as a sign that a prophet had come, and they wanted to make him a king (John 6:14–15).

John, however, also uses the theme that Jewish rejection of Jesus was blasphemy. When Jesus performs a healing on the Sabbath, "the Jews" want to kill him "because he not only broke the sabbath but also called God his Father, making himself equal with God." Jesus appropriately silences them by saying, "The Son can do nothing of his own accord" (John 5:18–19). On another occasion, Jesus says, in agreement with John's high Christology, "Before Abraham was, I am," so the Jews began to stone him—a symbolic execution for blasphemy (John 8:59). On another occasion, Jesus declares, "I and the Father are one," and again they stone him. In this scene, Jesus stops them with Old Testament sayings to prove that, far from blaspheming, he acts with divine authority (John 10:30–38).

These episodes in John echo the blasphemy charge in Mark's account of the Jewish trial. Their point, of course, is that Jesus is God or Son of God, as Christian readers of the Gospels, reflecting a Christology that did not exist at the time of the historical Jesus, readily understood. The Gospels broke with the Jewish understanding of blasphemy—reviling God by name—but, from a Christian standpoint, they did not break with its God-centeredness, except for attributing satanism to the work of the Holy Spirit.[3]

The chasm between history and theology separates the historical Jesus, who lived the life of a human being, and the historic Christ, who is the object of Christian worship as God's self-revelation. Each of the evangelists is a "witness" only in a religious sense, expressing Christian faith, in the words of James M. Robinson, as "an inward participant in the history he narrates." But the history he narrates was not intended to be a factual record of what actually happened to the historical Jesus, whose biography cannot be recovered. Religious propaganda is the object of all four Gospels. As one New Testament scholar stated, the evangelists did not even think in historical terms, so "the historian has to treat these sources as he would treat propaganda material." The Gospels Christian-ized the truth of what happened; they are supernatural or superhuman miracle stories, depicting the human life of a divine being. The narrative about Jesus serves the purpose of deifying Christ, making a new religion. Every purported fact has a spiritual or theological motive.[4]

Hans Küng, the controversial Catholic theologian, wrote that the whole Passion narrative is an "absurd story" that "becomes comprehen-sible as the expression of God's mysterious imperative." Because the Gospels are testaments that convey a message deriving from Christian faith, history as a reconstruction of what happened, founded upon veri-fiable facts, cannot get much enlightenment from the evangelists. The chapters dealing with the trials of Jesus—before the Sanhedrin, and then before Pilate—have purposes unrelated to accurate reporting that is founded on original and credible sources. The Gospels are so difficult to comprehend that even Jesus' own apostles did not always understand his message and identity. If Jesus had to rebuke Peter's misunderstanding by saying, "Get thee behind me, Satan" (Mark 8:33; Matthew 16:23), the misunderstanding of the Pharisees, or of the Sanhedrin, or even of Pilate, should not be surprising, and none can be blamed, not even Judas, for fulfilling roles assigned by an inscrutable God.[5]

The chief priests of Judea doubtless collaborated with the Roman occupation authorities and believed Jesus to be guilty of political crimes. They governed the Temple and influenced the Great Sanhedrin, which constituted the supreme religious court of the Jews and as a senate gov-erned Judea, subject to Roman policies. It was a political council even more than a religious or judicial one. The chief priests of the Sanhedrin were implicated in Jesus' fate, but Jesus was a victim of the Romans. As an eminent New Testament scholar, Oscar Cullmann, has declared, "From the beginning the entire action proceeds from the Romans." The inscription attached to Jesus' cross explained the crime for which he died; he supposedly had proclaimed himself to be "King of the Jews." Under Roman law, one claiming to be a king in place of the emperor was guilty of treason, a capital crime. Jesus died by crucifixion, a Roman punish-ment and most certainly not a Jewish one.[6]

According to the four Gospels, however, Jesus never called himself king of the Jews, a title that only non-Jews would use. Jesus was a Jew. He was born a Jew, lived as a Jew, and died as a Jew. The fact that the historical Jesus was Jewish, and a devout Jew at that, means a good deal, most of all that he was not Christian. Christianity did not exist during the lifetime of Jesus. In the words of Rudolf Bultmann, the influential Prot-estant scholar of the New Testament, "Jesus was not a Christian but a Jew, and his preaching is couched in the thought forms and imagery of Judaism, even when it is critical of traditional Jewish piety." The Jews awaited a messiah who would be king of Israel, not king of the Jews. But Jesus did not call himself king of Israel either, nor did he ever use any regal title for himself in a political or temporal sense. In fact, with one exception (Mark 14:61–62), he did not even call himself Messiah, although he did not reject that title. When he asked his disciples whether they realized who he was, Peter replied, "You are the Christ." "Christ" is a Greek translation of the Hebrew word for "messiah." Jesus responded by warning his disciples to keep his identity a secret, and he predicted that he would be killed but would rise again in three days (Mark 8:29–31; Matthew 16:16–21; Luke 9:20–22). At the trial before the Sanhedrin, the high priest asked Jesus point-blank, "Are you the Christ, the Son of the Blessed?" On this occasion only, and nowhere else in the New Testament, Jesus replied directly and affirmatively, "I am; and you will see the Son of man sitting at the right hand of Power, and coming with the clouds of heaven" (Mark 14:61–62).[7]

This was the putative blasphemy for which the Sanhedrin supposedly condemned Jesus. In Matthew, however, Jesus replied ambiguously to the high priest, declaring, "You have said so," and then he continued with the saying about the Son of Man (Matthew 26:63–64). Many New Testament scholars construe his evasive answer as an affirmation, as in "You are right."

According to the Gospels, Jesus never claimed any title for himself except that of "Son of Man." This is a difficult expression, derived from the Old Testament. Of all the titles by which Jesus is known in the New Testament—"Lord," "Son of God," "Prophet," "Rabbi," "Saviour," "Son of David," "King of the Jews," and "King of Israel," among others—the only one he used to describe himself and the only one not attributed to him by others is "Son of Man." A conservative New Testament scholar, Vincent Taylor, said, "It expressed the very idea of lordship, of rule over the messianic community, and its associations are supernatural." As Son of Man, Jesus supposedly felt himself to have divine authorization as a worker of miracles and forgiver of sins. Yet, although the title invoked God's authority, it described a human being.[8]

"Son of Man," in the sense that Jesus used it of himself, if he did, is a term from the book of Daniel, where it is eschatological in character, but carries distinct messianic overtones. Daniel predicts that the Son of Man will come on the Day of Judgment: "And to him was given dominion and glory and kingdom, that all peoples, nations, and languages should serve him; his dominion is an everlasting dominion, which shall not pass away, and his kingdom one that shall not be destroyed" (Daniel 7:13–14). Like Daniel, the New Testament presents the eschatological concept of the Son of Man, but Daniel places the prophecy in a political context, the Babylonian captivity. He was predicting the liberation of the

Jews as well as depicting an apocalypse when the Son of Man would pass judgment on human sins. Old Testament imagery should not be taken in an exclusively religious sense, especially at a time when the Jews were in bondage to conquerors. Politics and religion were inextricably entwined throughout Jewish history from Moses to Jesus—and after. For Mark himself, and in the tradition that he received, Son of Man was a messianic title.[9]

The Gospels preserve the tradition that Jesus believed he would become the Danielic Son of Man after his death. The earliest traditions probably used honorific titles that stressed his extraordinary powers as a teacher and healer, implying nothing about his status after death or his relation to God. Mark, however, found in the obscure term "Son of Man" a useful vehicle for depicting Jesus as Messiah in a way that his readers might understand, while allowing Mark to confound the characters in his story who were closest to Jesus. "Messiah," like "Son of God," "Lord," or "King," would raise false expectations among Jesus' fellow Jews, who would not be able to accept the crucifixion or failure of their beloved leader. When Peter recognized Jesus as the Christ, Jesus taught his disciples that the Son of Man must suffer, be rejected by the Jewish authorities, and be killed. Thus, the "Son of Man" title, which figures prominently in the blasphemy scene in the trial before the Sanhedrin, was a theological device for presenting Jesus as a messianic figure without implying the normative Jewish meaning of Messiah as the Davidic liberator. Indeed, Son of Man became in the Gospels an eschatological heavenly figure divorced from this-worldly political implications.[10]

The Gospels depoliticize all the titles ascribed to Jesus and present each in an exclusively spiritual sense. The evangelists used the titles of "Christ," "Messiah," "Saviour," and "Son of God" to describe a deity. Yet in Jewish thought, which was the only thought that Jesus knew, "Son of God" did not describe a divine being, but referred to a person who had an especially close relationship to God, as in the Danielic usage (Daniel 3:25). Attributing divinity to any human being would be a cardinal violation of the Jewish concept of monotheism. Ascriptions of divinity to "Son of God" or to other titles describing Jesus probably originated in the Hellenistic or gentile world of the postcrucifixion period.[11]

Except in the Gospel of John, Jesus did not claim to be divine in any sense, nor did Peter or any of the other disciples understand the historical Jesus to be divine. When they called him Messiah (Christ), they were using an Old Testament word associated with kings, patriarchs, prophets, priests, and the scion of the House of David. Although Jesus did not use "Christ" or "Messiah" to describe himself, he did recognize and accept the title when used by others to describe him (Mark 14:61–62; Matthew 16:16; John 4:25–26). The Gospels were composed in Greek primarily for a gentile world that would not easily have understood the term "Christ," which is why even the evangelists employed it infrequently.[12]

Whether rendered in Hebrew or Greek, "messiah" was a Jewish concept that referred primarily to the Davidic king, a national deliverer who, with divine assistance, would save Israel from gentile oppressions. The word "messiah" in Hebrew meant "anointed." God figuratively anointed every Jewish king. Most Jews at the time of Jesus thought of the Messiah as a king, favored with the miraculous intervention of God, who would usher in a great kingdom through which God would rule the world. Others thought the Messiah would usher in the Day of Judgment, inaugurating the time when God, assisted by the Son of Man, would judge everyone since Adam's time and raise the innocent dead to heavenly glory. A messiah, no matter how conceived, would preach that the kingdom of God was at hand. That could have here-and-now or otherworldly dimensions, or both in succession. In any case, Roman domination of Israel would be threatened, and so would Sadducean control over the Temple and Jewish affairs. Anyone claiming to be the Messiah or acclaimed as such could expect opposition from the chief priests, and crucifixion by the Romans, as a Zealot or political rebel.[13]

Not only was the Messiah a mortal man of flesh and blood, notwithstanding his special relationship to God, so too was the son of God. Our versions of the Gospels capitalize the word "son," but the earliest manuscripts capitalized no words; where the translation is given as "Son of God," it could equally be rendered as "son of God." In the Jewish world of the historical Jesus, every man was a son of God, who is the Creator of Life. The Jews, as God's chosen people, spoke figuratively of Israel as the son of God (Exodus 4:22; Hosea 1:10). But the Old Testament usage of "son of God" referred in particular to ancient kings—Saul, Solomon, and, above all, David. Yahweh said of Solomon, "I have chosen him to be my son" (1 Chronicles 28:6), and of King David, "You are my son, today I have begotten you" (Psalms 2:7). The Gospels made a point of tracing Jesus' ancestry to David to prove his royal lineage (Matthew 1:1, 9:27; John 7:42). Luke says of the infant Jesus that God "will give him the throne of his father David" (Luke 1:32). The title "son of David" was a Jewish equivalent for "Messiah," conceived of as the royal liberator who combined military prowess, justice, righteousness, and holiness. As Geza Vermes wrote, "the only kind of messianism Jesus' audience would have understood, and the only kind that might have possessed applicability in the world and context of the Gospels, is that of the Davidic King Messiah." Yet the Gospels surely do not depict Jesus as the warrior-king, nor do we have any reason to believe that he thought of himself that way. Indeed, John's Gospel has Jesus say to Pilate, "My kingship is not of this world" (John 18:36). The remark is in keeping with the ordinary understanding of Jesus and with his Galilean ministry.[14]

To the Romans, any claim to kingship conveyed distinct political overtones, as it would to the Jewish authorities of Judea. The Romans, of course, did not understand the metaphysical aspects of Jewish messianism or Jesus' Son of Man claim based on the book of Daniel. But the Romans knew politics. Even if Jesus' message was purely eschatological, concerning only the imminent coming of the kingdom of God and the judgment thereafter, he was preaching that Roman dominion, like all else, would soon pass away. His message, as Luke said in the Acts of the Apostles, "turned the world upside down" (Acts 17:6). The chief priests understood that, just as they understood but did not believe the messianic claim. The Romans, like the Sadducean chief priests, understood the political implications of turning the world upside down.

In John's Gospel, the Sanhedrin never convened to try Jesus. After the Romans arrested him, the high priest, Caiaphas, privately interrogated him and then turned him over to Pilate. But long before the account of Jesus' triumphal entry into Jerusalem, John depicts a meeting of the Sanhedrin to consider the problem of Jesus. One member of the council asked, "What are we to do? . . . If we let him go on thus, everyone will believe him, and the Romans will come and destroy both our holy place and our nation." Caiaphas replied that expediency required Jesus' death so "that the whole nation should not perish" (John 11:47–53). The scene conveys the impression that Jesus somehow threatened the Temple establishment and might even trigger Roman retaliation against the Jews for condoning a treasonous enterprise.[15]

The scene shows no Jewish alarm at any blasphemy on Jesus' part. Indeed, Caiaphas evinced no concern for the *religious* character of Jesus' teachings. Jesus may have advocated radical reforms of the Temple cult and its sacrificial system. He believed in the old prophetic principle that love of God was far more important than burnt offerings and sacrifices (Mark 12:28–33). His hostility to the Temple as a place not fit for worship and as "a den of robbers" may be surmised from his cursing of the fig tree, which is a symbol of the Temple (Mark 11:12–17; Matthew 21:18–19).[16]

The testimony of witnesses before the Sanhedrin about Jesus' supposed threat to destroy the Temple was thrown out, because the witnesses did not agree. That threat was not blasphemous or a capital crime; it echoed Jeremiah 26:1–19. If the Sanhedrin sought Jesus' death, it would have rigged the evidence more effectively, or have accepted the testimony rather than punctiliously following a rule requiring testimony to be consistent in every respect. Perhaps the principal charge failed because the threat to destroy the Temple was not only farfetched; it was erased by the accompanying promise of a miracle: Jesus would rebuild the Temple in three days.[17]

According to Mark and Matthew, the high priest, although defeated on the Temple charge, which was the very reason for the prosecution, next asked Jesus to answer the witnesses. Jesus properly remained silent in face of the improbable request, which defied the Sanhedrin's rejection of the witnesses' testimony. Then Caiaphas asked, even more improbably, "Are you the Christ, the Son of the Blessed?" (Mark 14:61). The question was un-Jewish. None of the Jewish circumlocutions in the Old Testament or in the Greek-Jewish texts refer to God as "the Blessed One." In Matthew, Caiaphas asked the question correctly, although redundantly: "tell us if you are the Christ, the Son of God" (26:63). The Jews circa A.D. 30 would have regarded "the Christ" (the Messiah or Anointed) as God's son, like David.[18]

In Mark 14:62, and only there, Jesus replied, "I am," and continued with his saying about the Son of Man from Daniel 7:13. In Matthew 26:64, the saying is prefaced by "you have said so." At that point, Caiaphas tore his robes and said, "Why do we still need witnesses? You have heard his blasphemy. What is your decision?" Mark added, "And they all condemned him as deserving death" (14:63–65). Matthew's account relies on Mark's (Matthew 26:65–66). The crucial passage in the accounts is Jesus' statement, which is understood by the Sanhedrin to be blasphemous. Thus, Caiaphas tore his garment in horror or grief, an ancient custom. But there are over a score of Old Testament scenes of Jews tearing the clothes in grief over matters that had nothing to do with blasphemy. Josephus also related that leading men as well as the chief priests tore their clothes when they believed that the people would provoke the Roman governor to commit another atrocity.[19]

Jesus had not blasphemed, and if Caiaphas nevertheless tore his robe, his grief or horror had a different cause. Jesus had just admitted that he was the Messiah. To Caiaphas, a Sadducee, that would have no eschatological significance; he would not think that he was gazing at the human embodiment of a deity or that the person before him claimed to be the incarnation. Caiaphas, rather, would have seen standing before him a Davidic pretender. To the high priest, that would mean that the Romans would kill Jesus and perhaps other Jews.

The Jews had not forgotten the mass crucifixions of A.D. 6, which occurred after the Romans had suppressed the Zealot uprising led by Judas of Galilee. According to the Acts of the Apostles, soon after the death of Jesus a member of the Sanhedrin—the great Gamaliel, who was the leader of the Pharisees—spoke of the deaths of the followers of Judas of Galilee and of the four hundred who followed another messiah, Theudas. Significantly, Gamaliel's advice to the Sanhedrin on that occasion, which involved the apostle Paul, was to tolerate such people: "keep away from these men and let them alone." Gamaliel reasoned that if their plan "was of men" it would fail; that is, the Romans would kill them. But "if it is of God, you will not be able to overthrow them. You might even be found opposing God." The Sanhedrin took his advice (Acts 5:33–40), which is probably closer to the truth of what happened in the case of Jesus than the Gospel according to Mark or Matthew.[20]

If Caiaphas tore his robe, assuming that the scene ever happened, he did so not because he had heard blasphemy, but because he had heard a messianic pronouncement that he construed as an omen of catastrophe—more Roman pogroms or crucifixions, perhaps the crucifixion of a Jew honored by the people as a miracle worker, a prophet, or a Davidic king. Despite his own animosity against Jesus, Caiaphas would not welcome his crucifixion, a form of execution execrated by the Jews. Yet Mark 14:64 shows a unanimous judicial verdict: "And they all condemned him." All the Pharisees, including Gamaliel, Joseph of Arimathea, and Nicodemus, supposedly joined with the Sadducees in plotting Jesus' death and then voting for it, against their religious convictions that crucifixion violated the Torah.[21]

The trial of Jesus by the Sanhedrin, as portrayed in Mark and Matthew, leaves a puzzling question. If they condemned him for blasphemy, why did not they execute him by stoning, the prescribed punishment? The Gospels do not answer, or ask, the question, but they present the story as if the Sanhedrin had no power to execute, or as if the conspiracy against the innocent Jesus was diabolical enough to procure his conviction and murder by Pilate. Yet neither alternative can be true. The New Testament also abundantly shows the Sanhedrin acting as if it could try and punish capitally, and it shows Pilate so reluctant to crucify Jesus that the chief priests could not have confidently believed that they could shift the responsibility for his death to the Romans. Indeed, all four Gospels teach that the Jews alone were responsible for the death of Jesus, despite the Roman crucifixion, and despite the fact that Luke 23:2 reports the charges against Jesus as having been exclusively political, not religious.

That the trial before the Sanhedrin never occurred is evident from the Jewish substantive law on blasphemy. The trial was not only impossible as a matter of that law. It was ludicrous. The high priest could not possibly have construed an affirmative reply to his query whether Jesus was the Messiah, in accordance with a later Christian understanding of the meaning of Messiah. Significantly, the trial of Jesus before the Sanhedrin was unprecedented in the sense that the council had never before tried or convicted anyone for blasphemy. Jesus' trial is unique in the New Testament, except for that of Stephen, which is an apparent imitation and is thoroughly misleading if not fictive.[22]

No Jewish court at the time of Jesus would have considered as blasphemous a messianic claim or a claim to be Son of Man or Son of God.
In John, the Jewish officials, immediately on being empowered by Pilate
to execute Jesus, say illogically, "We have a law, and by that law he ought
to die, because he made himself Son of God" (John 19:7). That statement
cannot be taken in the Christological sense of the later church. Moreover,
if the claim to be "Son of God" was the Jewish charge against Jesus, as
John states, then Pilate would have had no jurisdiction or interest in a
purely religious case, and the Jews could not have convinced him to order
the crucifixion. John's depiction of the Jewish charge, that Jesus made
himself Son of God in the Christian sense, or equal to God, is proleptic.

Had Jesus claimed divinity, his crime in Jewish law could have been
false prophecy—leading the people from the one and only God to worship a competing god. Claiming to be the son of God, however, was not
blasphemy or any crime, for the Jews regarded all men as God's sons
(Deuteronomy 14:1). For a Jew at the time of Jesus to claim before other
Jews that he personally was the Deity, or that God or the Holy Spirit was
his biological father in a literal rather than a figurative sense, would have
met with derision. The Talmud preserves a saying: "If a man say to thee
'I am God,' he is a liar; if [he says 'I am] the Son of Man,' in the end
people will laugh at him; if [he says] 'I will go up to heaven,' he saith, but
shall not perform."[23]

Blasphemy, however, was a very special crime to Jews. It was cursing
God by name or, in the loosest Old Testament view of the crime, denying Him or His attributes, honors, or powers. Assuming that Jesus made
a wholly unprecedented claim that he was equal to God or was God's
exclusive natural son, and assuming that the Jewish authorities took him
seriously, they could have believed that he derogated from God's majesty
by breaking the unity or uniqueness of God. But the assumption that
Jesus made such a claim is founded on a serious anachronism. It endows
the historical Jesus with an understanding of himself attributed to him by
Christians of the later first century, and requires the authorities in the
year 30 to receive Jesus' affirmative answer to Caiaphas (in Mark only!) in
terms of subsequent Christian theology. We might as well assume that
Mark understood the Nicene Creed or could distinguish homoousion
(same substance) from homoiousion (similar substance) concerning the
nature of Christ.[24]

Father Gerard S. Sloyan interpreted Jesus' appearance before the
Sanhedrin as a literary composition by Mark enabling him to state a
religious belief, not a historical happening. Mark inserted the entire sequence "as an epiphany or manifestation of him who has come as the
Messiah and will come again as the Son of man." Mark made the Sanhedrin reject Jesus as the Messiah to symbolize Jewish rejection. By

Mark's time, the Jews had rejected a Christianized Jesus. Jesus' answer to Caiaphas should be understood not as something he said but as post-Easter theology. Father John R. Donahue more bluntly and elaborately argued that Mark created the entire trial narrative, including the blasphemy charge and condemnation. Mark's purpose was to explain the Roman destruction of the Temple as evidence of divine judgment on the Jews who had rejected Jesus as the Messiah. The nonhistorical Jewish trial, with its anti-Temple theme, "thus becomes a way for Jewish Christians to come to terms with the destruction of the cult center and to view the [Christian] community as its replacement." Sloyan and Donahue have few rivals in their understanding of the trial of Jesus by the Sanhedrin.[25]

Even Josef Blinzler found little to support the Gospels on the point that Jesus' answer to Caiaphas was blasphemous. Blinzler was the weightiest of the pre–Vatican II Catholic scholars. He wrote on the trials of Jesus as faithfully as possible, completely accepting the historicity of both the high priest's lone inquiry and of the Sanhedrin trial as depicted in conflicting Gospels. Blinzler thought that Jesus' "absolute authority" might have been "incomprehensible and could only be regarded as blasphemous in the light of Jewish religious thought." Blinzler, who did not mean that Jesus claimed to be God, understood that, in the judgment of the Sanhedrin, no blasphemy existed in the utterance about the Temple. "No," Blinzler wrote, "Jesus incurred the charge of blasphemy wholly and solely by His solemn affirmative to the high priest's question, i.e., by His confession of His messianic dignity."[26]

Blinzler acknowledged, however, that the Jews understood the Messiah to mean a Davidic liberator, not a supernatural being. But because Jesus failed in that regard, he blasphemed—or sort of blasphemed. That is, Blinzler conceded that, although his interpretation of the charge of blasphemy was "not quite identical with a charge of blasphemy, it is only a small step from it." Without bridging that step between cursing God by name and failing as Davidic liberator, Blinzler rejected all argument that the blasphemy was a claim to divine attributes, utterance of the sacred name, or anything else. In the end, then, Old Testament law and religion had nothing to do with Blinzler's understanding of the blasphemy charge: the Jews condemned Jesus for blasphemy because they understood him to be a failed messiah. The argument is absurd.[27]

David R. Catchpole, a Protestant scholar who specialized in Jewish accounts of the trial of Jesus, offered an elaborate "evaluation" of the charge of blasphemy. Catchpole reasoned that nothing in the Gospels "suggests that the trial of Jesus hinged on his alleged claim to destroy the temple," but added—without proof—that Blinzler was "probably correct" in saying that such a claim would have been regarded as blasphemous. Blinzler said no such thing; he denied that Jesus' comments about the Temple could have been regarded as blasphemous. Catchpole decided that a messianic claim (not a failed one) would bring about the condemnation for blasphemy, but he added: "Here it must be agreed that Jewish scholars are correct in declaring that a messianic claim is not blasphemous" even under a "looser definition" than the Talmudic one. But, Catchpole believed, Jewish scholars have tended to ignore the possibility that by answering "I am" Jesus pronounced the actual name of God, thus supposedly committing the Talmudic crime of blasphemy.[28]

Catchpole assumed that the Talmudic definition operated in A.D. 30, that "I am" was the name, and that Mark (and only Mark) quoted Jesus verbatim (Mark 14:62). Again, the Talmud, which nearly defined away the capital crime of blasphemy by making it impossible or improbable to commit, required that one must invoke the personal name of God for the purpose of cursing, piercing, or denouncing that name: May YHVH damn YHVH.

Having elaborately considered his "I am" theory, Catchpole finally shelved it, for seven reasons. None dealt with Talmudic definition or the fact that "I am" in Greek, the language of Mark, was not the Hebrew or Aramaic name, or the fact that "I am" is a simple subject and predicate used in daily speech. The "I am" theory of the blasphemy dies hard, because New Testament scholars desperately try to find the blasphemy that the Gospels say existed in the minds of the Sanhedrin's members.

Catchpole relied on a Talmudic saying of about A.D. 300 to show that some rabbis objected to the idea of a man sitting in heaven. Supposedly, this anachronistic saying has the rabbis thinking that such an idea was "sacrilegious," which led Catchpole to conclude weakly "that there is the possibility that such a claim as that in Mark 14:62 [the "Son of Man" saying] might have been regarded as blasphemous." Presumably neither the Sanhedrin, the highest court, nor the later Talmudic rabbis could distinguish sacrilege, the physical desecration of religious precincts or of anything holy, from blasphemy, the cursing of God's name. Jesus' "Son of Man" saying at the trial was part of his answer to the question whether he was the Son of God. On that crucial issue, Catchpole followed Vincent Taylor, Ferdinand Hahn, and many others when he could detect no blasphemy in Jesus' affirmative answer, "I am." Catchpole concluded his analysis by vaguely declaring, "The one place where Jesus can be shown to have caused offense is in matters religious." Luke, for Catchpole, somehow contains the answer, but Luke, who alone stated the charges, made no reference to blasphemy.[29]

J. Duncan Derrett, who took "law in the New Testament" as his subject, rejected the Sanhedrin trial as unhistorical, yet construed Jesus' "Son of Man" saying as "unequivocally blasphemous" to "the dominant school of Jewish law." He did not indicate whether that was Pharisaic or

Sadducean, but he did understand that blasphemy in the Old Testament means "piercing" the name of God or diminishing His honor. Even if this is so, it has nothing to do with the meaning of "Son of Man" in Jewish thought. Derrett reasoned that Jesus, by predicting that he would sit at God's right hand, had usurped the place of Moses, and, still more blasphemously, put himself into a position from which he could gaze upon the face of God, which not even Moses was permitted to do. This explanation botched the facts. Blasphemy was a verbal crime, not looking at God, and the Danielic Son of Man acted for God and did not dishonor Him; moreover, in Isaiah 52:8 the people rejoice "for eye to eye they see the return of the Lord to Zion."[30]

Nevertheless, distinguished theologians and scholars must find the blasphemy somewhere, even if they have to invent it (failed messiah, God-gazer), and even if they do not differentiate crimes. Hans Küng, for example, abandoning the effort to define blasphemy, fixed on heresy. He concluded that the Sanhedrin had heard blasphemy, although he did not say what it was. But Küng repeatedly referred to Jesus as a "heretic" whom the Jewish hierarchy tried to "unmask." They "had to act against the heretical teacher, false prophet, blasphemer and religious seducer of the people. . . ." Their political charge was a "cover" for their "religious hatred."[31]

Küng simply misunderstood Jewish law, history, and ethics. Judaism in the time of Jesus, as now, was monotheistic but not monolithic. It was a syncretistic religion, with a variety of denominations, sects, and factions. Küng assumed that the crime of heresy, which Christians later invented, was known to Jews in the year A.D. 30. It was not. Heterodoxy in religious belief and practice prevailed. Heresy, the crime of wrong or erroneous religious belief, was then unknown. Orthodoxy, which must exist as a standard to determine heresy, was incompatible with Judaism. Orthodoxy surely did not mean correct doctrine. The two major denominations, the Sadducees and the Pharisees, for example, differed on many vital religious matters yet lived together without reference to heresy, nor did they regard as heretical the Nazarenes, the Jews who believed in Jesus as the risen Messiah imminently to return. The Nazarenes, in a sense the first Christians, participated in the Temple cult and were received as Jews by other Jews. The notion of Jesus as a heretic has no basis.[32]

Douglas R. A. Hare showed a better understanding of law and Jewish toleration when he examined whether the Jews hated and persecuted the early churches. Hare believed that, at the time of Jesus, blasphemy had a less technical meaning than the one in Leviticus 24:15–16. He held that "any attack on the Torah or Temple was regarded as blasphemous, but this is not to say that such attacks could be treated as blasphemy in the technical sense and punished as capital crimes." Hare insisted that "some relatively narrow" concept of blasphemy controlled the disposition of prosecutions. Otherwise, "all the Pharisees were liable to capital prosecutions by the Sadducees," because the Pharisees changed the customs of Moses (Acts 6:14). Among the Jews of Jesus' time, only the Essenes believed that Moses could be blasphemed. Nazarene claims on behalf of Jesus, Hare asserted, were blasphemous only in a nonlegal sense. If Jesus had been condemned for capital blasphemy, Hare reasoned, "the profession of Christianity was from the beginning a capital crime from the point of view of the Jewish judiciary." But the Acts of the Apostles shows the contrary, and little evidence supports the view that verbal attacks on the Temple and Torah "constituted blasphemy in the legal sense." Hare concluded that the Jewish charge against Jesus was not capital, but only a "serious" breach of peace. Refreshingly, he discovered nothing that the Sanhedrin could have considered blasphemous, not in the case of Jesus or of Stephen.[33]

J. C. O'Neill vividly illustrated the widespread difficulty of most scholars in capturing the blasphemy of Jesus as the Sanhedrin understood it. O'Neill systematically rejected the Temple charge, the "Son of Man" saying, the claim to forgive sins, the "I am" theory, and the healing on Sabbath. Moreover, he understood that no blasphemy could have been implied or inferred "in calling the Messiah whom God has sanctified and sent God's Son." He showed Old Testament evidence for the Jewish belief that "Son of God" was an acceptable designation for the Messiah.[34]

The blasphemy, according to O'Neill, consisted in Jesus' "temerity of using any title at all before God the Father had himself announced the enthronement of his anointed one." That invented a new Jewish law on blasphemy, but O'Neill abandoned it by saying that Jesus not only did not claim to be the Messiah; he made his claim as Son of Man "in a form that assured that God alone could announce his enthronement." "Jesus," he observed, "took care not to blaspheme" by infringing on divine majesty. Having said all this, O'Neill contradictorily concluded:

> The technical charge upon which Jesus was condemned to death by the Sanhedrin may well have been that he blasphemed in making himself God (John 10:33) by presuming to say he was the Son when the Father alone knew who the Son was (Matt. 11:27, Luke 10:22). He was condemned for making himself the Son of God (John 19:7). The charge was probably false, but the Sanhedrin would regard Jesus's defense as a mere technicality, he behaved with such regal dignity and spoke with such assurance.[35]

In effect, O'Neill said, faith fixed the matter, even if the Sanhedrin could not possibly have decided as it did in accord with the law of the matter.

C. H. Dodd, a major New Testament scholar, advocated much the same view in his mature reflections on "The Historical Problem of the Death of Jesus." What, he asked, was the blasphemy for which Jesus was condemned? All four Gospels take the view, he concluded, "that Jesus was charged with blasphemy because he spoke and acted in ways which implied that he stood in a special relation with God, so that his words carried divine authority, and his actions were instinct with divine power." That, said Dodd, is what the charge of blasphemy "really stands for rather than any definable statutory offense." In the "stylized account" of the trial before the Sanhedrin, the crucial phrases are "Son of the Blessed" and "at the right hand of God," which, for Dodd, constituted a messianic claim "plus." [36]

All these conjectures and strainings derive from the pursuit of a red herring. Jesus had not blasphemed in the opinion of the Sanhedrin. His blasphemy did not exist. It was simply a symbol of the Jewish rejection of Jesus, and was the only capital charge that the evangelists could put in the mouths of Jesus' Jewish opponents. The Sanhedrin trial itself never happened. It was the creation of Mark, imitated by Matthew, but rejected by Luke and especially by John. Even in Mark, the question is not "What happened?" but "What did it all mean?" As Hans Conzelmann said, any attempt to reconstruct the actual course of events is doomed to failure. "Methodologically it is misleading to interpret the present report [the Passion accounts] as such a record. It is a witness of faith." None of the Gospels is reliable as history and none purports to be. They all propagate faith in Jesus. [37]

What happened cannot be separated from its religious meaning, because what happened, in James M. Robinson's phrase, is "theologically understood history." What really happened has been lost forever. Some scholars believe that Mark invented the scene of the formal Jewish trial out of a primitive tradition that the Jewish authorities delivered Jesus to Pilate. Those scholars have speculated that the pre-Markan tradition included no Jewish trial, no Gethsemane story, no references to the Temple, and no apology for the fact that Jesus was condemned by the Romans as a political revolutionary. [38]

Although the Gospels are theology, they had had practical or political functions too. Their pro-Roman stance was intended to protect the early churches from the Romans, by severing those churches from their Jewish origins. The Jews and Romans were military enemies. They were at war from 66 to 73, from 115 to 117, and from 132 to 135. The Romans persecuted the Christians, whom they confused with the Jews, as early as Nero's time (A.D. 64) and long after. The safety of the early churches depended on their identification with a pacifistic Saviour who never opposed Rome and who had been crucified at Jewish instigation. Gentile readers were given to understand that Jesus opposed the Pharisees, the Temple, and the Jewish cult, and above all that his real crime was not treason but blasphemy before the Sanhedrin. The Gospels also taught that the rejection of Jesus as Messiah or Son of God is blasphemous. At first the story sought to protect the Christians by appeasing the Roman world. It also proved enormously helpful in softening gentiles for conversion. Along the way, Jesus became Christ, the Jews the villains, and blasphemy a new sort of crime under Christianity.[39]

CHAPTER THREE

Christianity Transforms Blasphemy

U NDER Christianity, "blasphemy" became so bloated with meanings that it burst all bounds, becoming almost meaningless. By the year 400, "blasphemy" was hardly more than a vile epithet, and in a confused way similar to the concept of "heresy." The word "heresy" originally meant factionalism, which was a form of blasphemy to early Christians because it exposed the true faith to contention, even scorn. Eventually, "heresy" became the more encompassing term. Not until the time of Thomas Aquinas in the thirteenth century did the church coherently define blasphemy, although even then it continued as a peculiar species of heresy. Long before—before there was a Roman Catholic church, or a formally canonized New Testament, or an authorized creed on the Holy Trinity, or a body of doctrine that could be described as orthodox, or a secular power that could enforce the church's wishes—blasphemy was the cardinal sin. The Shepherd of Hermas, an early-second-century patristic work, referred to "blasphemy or treason" against God.[1]

Christianity in the pre-Nicene period, before the fourth century, was heavily Greek in language as well as thought. Accordingly, "impiety," the Greek equivalent of "blasphemy," rivaled "blasphemy" as the name of the crime. To the Greeks, blasphemy meant any sort of speaking evil, verbal abuse, or defamation, especially profane speech. Although the English word "impiety" has a soft sound, meaning a lack of piety or something irreverent, in Greek the word signified shocking and abhorrent ideas about religion. In early Christian thought, "impiety," like "blasphemy," gathered numerous and complex meanings. Blasphemy became more than just cursing or reproaching God. It rapidly came to signify breaking the unity of Christianity. Any viewpoint or utterance that deviated from the true faith was blasphemous or impious.

Early Christians, however, understood the true faith differently.

They embraced Jewish monotheism and accepted the Old Testament as divinely inspired Scriptures, which they reinterpreted in the light of Jesus. He was the risen Christ through whom salvation became possible for all humanity. Beyond that, Christianity was protean, heterodox, and fluid. In the absence of orthodoxy, distinctions between blasphemy and heresy became difficult, if not impossible; both offenses blurred in meaning and blended with faction, sedition, schism, apostasy, and sacrilege.[2]

The main problem of early Christianity was to define itself even as it had to establish itself. To do either, it required an authority or a standard for its faith. The earliest traditions were oral, Jewish, and varied. The writing of gospels preserved traditions, but the four Gospels presented different theologies as well as different histories of Jesus, and so did the other writings that ultimately became canonized as the New Testament.[3]

The twenty-seven books of the New Testament spoke differently among themselves and to different people. What one person took as a cardinal reproach to the Christian religion or to a particular doctrine or to Christ himself, and called blasphemy, was another's sacred belief. Heresy to one was orthodoxy to someone else. Jesus' own apostles did not always agree with him, understand him, or concur among themselves. Christianity had to establish itself against rivals from without and against dissident proclamations of orthodoxy from within. It had to establish and define itself even as it continually evolved.

Until at least A.D. 325, when the Council of Nicaea formulated the first creed (at least for the Eastern division of the Roman Empire), there were Christian churches but not a Christian church, not one that was catholic, or universal. Nor did Nicaea settle anything. The dissident parties, who were condemned as blasphemers and heretics by the emperor and council, soon became dominant, won the support of the state, and controlled most of the churches. That reversed the definition of orthodoxy until another emperor made possible a reaffirmation of the Nicene Creed at the Council of Constantinople in the year 381. The Trinitarian victory was not secure until confirmed by the council of Chalcedon in A.D. 451. Not until the fifth century did the Roman Catholic church have the power to enforce its theology as orthodox.[4]

As long as Christianity remained decentralized, many Christianities existed within the Roman Empire. Religious beliefs based on Jesus as the Christ had fanned out across the Mediterranean into Asia Minor, Europe, and North Africa. Judaism, paganism or Hellenism, and Gnosticism successively affected Christian thought in different ways in different places at different times. Credal lines of evolution veered and clashed. Orthodoxy in one place was heterodoxy and heresy in the same place at a later date, and the orthodoxy of one place was heretical in another at the same period of time. In 359, councils of bishops in the East and the West reached contradictory declarations on the Christian creed. In Rome, Constantinople, and Alexandria in the 350s, what would become the Nicene orthodoxy thirty years later was condemned as heretical, schismatic, and blasphemous. The orthodoxy that finally prevailed at the close of the fourth century was syncretistic in character but Nicene. It controlled most people's minds, the writing of history, the making of theology, the understanding of the New Testament, and the definitions of offenses against religion.[5]

After the crucifixion, Jesus joined God as a divine majesty in Christian thought. Cursing, reproaching, criticizing, mocking, rejecting, or denying Jesus Christ became the offense of blasphemy. Doubting his miraculous powers, his teaching, or the true Christian faith also became blasphemous. Posing as Jesus, claiming to be equal to him, or asserting the powers or attributes that belonged to him constituted blasphemy too. Matthew 12:31–32 makes blasphemous the attribution of evil or immoral inspiration to any work of God or of the Holy Spirit that moved Jesus. Luke 12:10 regards as blasphemy speaking evil of the Holy Spirit.

As components of the Holy Trinity, Jesus and the Holy Spirit were received as divine in their natures, making the step from God to them logical. One more step, however, had to be taken to elevate the Christian religion to such sacrosanctity that criticism of it could be thought of as blasphemy. Yet another step thrust particular doctrines beyond dissent by anyone but blasphemers. Paul and the author of the Acts of the Apostles took those extra steps. Paul confessed that he was guilty of blasphemy because he had once persecuted Christians by trying to force them to renounce their faith in Jesus. The tradition taught that for a Christian to deny Jesus or his teaching was blasphemy (Acts 26:9–11; 1 Timothy 1:13).

The case of Stephen depicted in Acts is special and would be unique but for that of Jesus, which it seems to echo. The charge against Stephen was "blasphemous words against Moses and God" (Acts 6:11), although the only evidence of the alleged blasphemy is the statement attributed to Stephen that he had seen Jesus as the Son of Man at the right hand of God. The charge of blasphemy makes no sense, because in Jewish law only God could be blasphemed, not Moses (except among the Essenes), and God had to be cursed by name. Stephen's crime probably was preaching an inflammatory speech in a synagogue, repudiating the entire Mosaic law, the Torah. That too was a strange crime, because Jesus himself had announced that he had come "to fulfill the law, not to destroy it" (Matthew 5:17). Stephen's denunciation of the law made his offense an extravagant antinomianism. The crime was not preaching Jesus as Saviour, but preaching Jesus as a divinity who superseded the Torah.[6]

That was not the crime of blasphemy. Moreover, at the time of

Stephen's case, the Jerusalem church of Jesus' disciples was still part of
Judaism, kept the Torah, participated in sacrificial rites, observed the
Sabbath, and practiced circumcision (all condemned as heresies by Christians a century later). Stephen's use of a synagogue to condemn Judaism
wholesale, by demanding repudiation of its fundamental religious code,
was comparable to Luther's using the pulpit of St. Peter's to censure
Roman Catholicism with all his prodigious invective.

Paul shared Stephen's antinomianism, but suffered no prosecution on
that account. The Paul of the book of Acts, written by the author of
Luke, claimed that the Jews persecuted him, although, if Paul's own
epistles are true, Acts is unhistorical. Neither the authorities in the Jerusalem church nor those in the Temple excommunicated Paul or prosecuted him for his deviant beliefs. The word *minim*,[7] loosely construed in
the post-Temple era as a Hebrew usage to describe "heretics," was not
leveled at Paul. The Sanhedrin sought to prosecute him only after he had
defiled the Sanctuary by bringing a gentile into it (Acts 21–28). At no
time in Paul's career, despite all his anti-Judaic and anti-Torah pro-
nouncements, was Paul charged with an offense against religious belief.
The reports of Stephen's prosecution for blasphemy, Paul's supposed
role in it, and the subsequent persecutions are inexplicable and unbeliev-
able. Whatever Stephen's crime was, it was not blasphemy to the Jewish
authorities. But after Luke's description of Stephen's case, blasphemy in
Christian thought became any attempt to persecute Christians, and any
denial or renunciation of the faith by Christians.

In a deutero-Pauline epistle, "Paul" instructed Timothy, a disciple, to
uproot everything "contrary to sound doctrine." He himself had had to
excommunicate two congregants, "that they might learn not to blaspheme." Although baptized in the true faith, they had undermined it by
spreading divergent beliefs (1 Timothy 1:3, 10, 19–20). "Paul" also commanded that the name of God "and his doctrine be not blasphemed" (1
Timothy 6:1 K.J.V.).[8]

The belief that dissent from or defamation of Jesus' teachings was
blasphemy laid the basis for a nearly limitless expansion of the concept,
particularly because Paul and his disciples had a habit of distinguishing
"truth" or "true" faith from counterfeit versions. To Titus, whom he
counseled to reject heretics, "Paul" wrote that sound doctrine inspired a
moral life and thus avoided blasphemy or the discrediting of the word of
God (Titus 2:2–5, 3:10). That, like the blasphemy against doctrine, allowed any difference in the interpretation of "the word of God" to be
considered blasphemous. Recalling that the penalty for violating the Mosaic code was death, "Paul" declared that a person who profaned the
covenant of the faith deserved still worse (Hebrews 10:28). He also declared that any behavior that made enemies of Christianity calumniate it

by blaspheming the name of God was tantamount to blasphemy (Romans 2:17–24). Similarly, "Peter" warned that heretics blasphemed Christianity (2 Peter 2:1–3, 15). The connection between heresy and blasphemy continued in Christian thought for at least fifteen centuries.

Clement, reputedly an associate of Paul and head of the church in Rome during the 90s, showed the continuity between New Testament authors and the church fathers. To a rebellious group that had overthrown the presbyters of the church in Corinth he wrote, "you bring blasphemy on the name of the Lord." About fifty years later, "Clement II" made the same point. He regarded as blasphemous anything that contravened the wishes of ecclesiastical authority. Blasphemy, he announced, consisted in that "you do not do what I desire." This view, that blasphemy consisted of any religious belief contrary to the policy of the church or its leadership, became a fixed position in Christian thought.[9]

The purpose of an early Christian apology by "Mathetes" was to differentiate Christians from Jews at a time when Jews had again rebelled against Rome. The author, a Greek Christian, equated impiety with speaking falsely of God. He meant that Jewish practices like circumcision and observing the Sabbath showed impiety. Christians were scarcely better off when the Romans finally learned to distinguish them from Jews. Sporadically, and usually on a local basis, the Romans continued their persecution of Christians. The Romans disliked Judaism but tolerated it as an ancient religion of a nation. Separated from Judaism, Christianity became a stateless and atheistic novelty to Romans. They executed Polycarp, the bishop of Rome, for spurning a Roman offer of freedom conditioned on his reproaching Christ. Polycarp declared that he would never "blaspheme my King and Saviour." To the Romans, that sounded like treasonous rejection of the emperor, and blasphemy in a wholly different sense: Polycarp's teaching went against their gods. He said, for example, that anyone who did not confess the testimony of the cross "is of the devil." Justin Martyr, whom the Romans executed in 165, about a decade after Polycarp's execution, explained that Christians looked like atheists to their persecutors, because they rejected Roman gods. Their crime was atheism, or blasphemous insult to the gods.[10]

From the time of Ignatius, who was martyred about 110, to the time of Eusebius, the fourth-century historian, Christians regarded their persecution and anti-Christian charges as blasphemy. Ignatius of Antioch condemned Docetism and Judaism as heresies. By "Judaism" he may have meant Ebionism, which was a form of Jewish Christianity. Judaism was still regarded as a heresy as late as the time of Hippolytus of Rome, who wrote *The Refutation of All Heresies* about 220. He included many forms of paganism as well as Judaism, showing that heresy was not yet understood as a Christian deviation from some orthodox standard. As for the Docetists, who called themselves Christians, they thought of Jesus as so purely divine that he could never have lived, suffered, and died as a man. Ignatius wrote that they "blaspheme my lord by not admitting He carried living flesh about Him." Ignatius also censured as blasphemous those who, at the other extreme, denied the divinity of Christ. Anyone who said that Jesus was a mere man was a blaspheming Jew, no better than a murderer of Christ.[11]

The varieties of Christianity before the fifth century were probably as numerous as those of today. They included, among others, Paulinists, Johannines, Gnostics, Marcionites, Docetists, Montanists, Samosatans, Sabellians, Meletians, Arians, Semi-Arians, Nicenes or Athanasians (Catholics), and Donatists. They also included varieties of so-called Jewish Christians, most of whom were not Jewish but agreed with Jews on circumcision, the Sabbath, diet, and the humanity of Jesus. The real Jewish Christians, the members of the first Jerusalem church, who were the closest to Jesus, held beliefs that by the second century were regarded as heretical and blasphemous, as the writings of Justin prove.[12]

Despite the rift between Jews, Jewish Christians, and varieties of Christians, the Gnostic Christians constituted most of the "false" and blasphemous Christians of whom early fathers like Ignatius, Justin, Irenaeus, Tertullian, and Hippolytus wrote so vitriolically. Gnosticism (from "gnosis," the secret knowledge of mysteries of the universe) might have originated in Zoroastrianism a millennium before Christianity. Gnosticism expressed itself in many cultural forms, but it was always bafflingly complex and fantastic in its mythology; it was also formidable, because it confronted the problems of existence, evil, and salvation. Usually, Gnosticism depicted an unknown, ingenerate, transcendent supreme being and a polytheistic pantheon of numerous lesser deities in a dualistic universe of opposites—spirit against matter, good against evil, heaven against hell, light against dark, divine against demonic. To the Gnostic, life on earth was hell, but not hopeless if an individual could reawaken the spirit deep within him which was the part of his nature that linked him to the pure cosmic Spirit. The solution to the human dilemma was to seek redemption from this world, but redemption could only be found in the form of revelation or self-knowledge, gnosis, which could be assisted by a divine messenger. The Gnostic knew he would be saved, because he had discovered his true inner self or spirit. One who knew had no need of faith. On his death, he would be released from demonic bondage and his soul would ultimately yield up his spirit, allowing it to unite with the primal Spirit.[13]

In the second century, Gnostics who were exposed to Christianity, and Christians who were exposed to Gnosticism, spawned an extraordinary variety of theosophies. Their common nexus was Jesus as the Saviour who brought revelation and salvation, thus rescuing people from this hellish world. But Gnosticism blasphemously held that God did not create earth and its life; that Jesus was a lesser deity, about thirty times removed from the Supreme One; that Jesus had not been resurrected, because only the spirit could be resurrected, not the body or the soul. Additional Gnostic blasphemies included the belief that only those who had gnosis, not those who had faith or lived by the Law, would be saved, and that the Old Testament was, on the whole, irrelevant. The possibilities within Gnosticism for blasphemous opinions were limitless. Still worse, by the mid-second century the number of people who blended Gnostic and Christian elements into a new religion possibly exceeded the number who reinterpreted the Old Testament in the light of the Gospels and the Pauline epistles. Gnostic Christians and Christian Gnostics "style themselves Christians," Justin bitterly objected, but, because they taught such "impious and blasphemous things," Christians called them by the name of the particular doctrines of their leaders—Simonians, Basilidians, Saturnilians, Marcionites, Valentinians, and the like.[14]

Irenaeus, the most formidable Christian antagonist of the Gnostics, was bishop of Lyon in the last quarter of the second century. His huge polemic, *The Detection and Refutation of False Knowledge* (Gnosis), is usually called *Against Heresies*. To call it *Against Blasphemies* would be as accurate, for Irenaeus used "heresy" and "blasphemy" interchangeably and with about the same frequency. Valentinus and Marcion, who were both active in Rome in the 140s and 150s, received Irenaeus's fullest attention and exhausted his pejorative vocabulary. He thundered against vile heresies and hideous blasphemies, but those offenses were merely epithets to signify the countless heterodoxies of which he disapproved. He was intelligible as to the specific doctrines that he condemned, but never as to the differences between schism, atheism, apostasy, impiety, blasphemy, sacrilege, and heresy.[15]

Tertullian, a presbyter of the church in Carthage in the early third century, had legal training, but he mixed concepts with the same ease as Justin and Irenaeus. At one point in his "Prescription Against Heretics" he seized a fundamental idea. Speaking of "false doctrines," he said they were "called in Greek heresies, a word used in the sense of that choice which a man makes when he either teaches them [to others] or takes up with them [for himself]." Unfortunately, Tertullian lost the thought when he denied that there was a difference between idolatry and heresy and when he said that every lie against God was "a sort of idolatry." And when he wrote that the teachers of false doctrine were blasphemers, without demonstrating the blasphemy and explaining how it differed from heresy, he had lapsed into the epithetical theology of Irenaeus. To Tertullian, every heretic was a blasphemer, every blasphemer a heretic.[16]

By the middle of the third century, no change was discernible, although the early stages of the Trinitarian Controversy had begun. The task of Christianity was to define itself by explaining the Holy Trinity as well as by differentiating itself from blasphemers, schismatics, and heretics. Any continued inability to see the differences among religious offenses showed that the identity of the true church had not yet been established.

Before the Council of Nicaea in 325, every offense against Christianity of whatever stripe affected only local churches. Until an international council fixed a creed, a body of religious dogma bearing the stamp of recognized ecclesiastical authority, no orthodoxy existed. Accordingly, the Novatians, who remained most steadfastly Christian in the face of Roman persecutions, confronted the censure of Dionysius, the bishop of Alexandria. He charged them with having "rent the Church" by not recognizing sacraments performed by lapsed clergymen, and having drawn brethren "to impiety and blasphemies." Novatians returned the sentiment.[17]

At about the same time, A.D. 250, another Dionysius, the bishop of Rome, condemned Sabellius, a Libyan priest, for numerous blasphemies in his theory of the Holy Trinity—a theory that would persist for centuries. (From the sixteenth through the nineteenth century, people were still being prosecuted for "Sabellianism.") Sabellius tried to preserve the unity of God by subordinating the Son and the Holy Spirit to the Father. He divided "the holy unity into three different substances, absolutely separated from one another," declared Dionysius. The doctrine of the Trinity was moving to the forefront of Christian differences as the focal point of blasphemies.[18]

Historically, the Holy Trinity was not the basis of a creed. The simple reference in Matthew to the Father, the Son, and the Holy Ghost and to other "slogans and tags" became consecrated by usage in Christian liturgy. Jesus was the man in whom the pre-existent Logos, or the Spirit, or the Christ, or the Father dwelt. There was no consensus on the right way to make the point. Although all believed that Jesus was finally exalted and possessed godlike honor, some thought he was merely human, others that he was a heavenly spirit who had assumed a human body. The problem posed by his existence was that Christians worshipped one God and Jesus Christ. Some theologians called "adoptionists," trying to preserve the monotheism of Christianity, understood Jesus to be divine in some way but not as God Himself. Jesus was subordinate to Him; God the Father, they said, had adopted him. They were trying to avoid the "blasphemy of three gods" or, equally bad, the "blasphemy" of two gods, which they thought resulted from acknowledging Jesus Christ as God or as a divine Son who was a separate person. The crisis in Christian thought in the third and fourth centuries turned on the need to retain the unity of God without sacrificing the divinity of Christ.[19]

In the end, the authority of the church, when backed by the coercion of the state, fixed the creed that became the test of orthodoxy. It also became the tests of heresy and blasphemy, yet did not settle the controversy. The acrimonious debate among Christians viciously denouncing one another for blasphemy and other offenses against religion continued. In the long run, anti-Trinitarians came to be regarded as the worst blasphemers, worthy of criminal punishment.

"Monarchianism," meaning the rule of one God, was a type of anti-Trinitarianism. Some "modal monarchists" depicted God as having revealed Himself in different modes at different times. They believed that Christ was God, but only one God existed. Therefore, the Father and the Son were the same. That, however, led to "patripassianism," the absurd idea that God the Father died on the cross, but it preserved the unity of God by denying the existence of any persons in the Godhead but God Himself. An indivisible single God divided into three persons is as paradoxical as an immortal God dying. Sabellius led a faction of modal monarchianism that avoided patripassianism and also took the Holy Spirit into account. He described the Father, the Son, and the Holy Spirit as the same person or essence who by different modes revealed himself successively as Creator and Lawgiver, then as Redeemer, and finally as the Spirit to inspire and bestow grace. This was the view that Hippolytus of Rome called a blasphemous folly, that Bishop Dionysius of Rome denounced as the highest blasphemy, that Peter, who held the same chair in Rome in 306, called an impiety, and that Athanasius still later coupled with Arianism as the worst of blasphemies. Yet, during the lifetime of Sabellius, some bishops of Rome supported him; the fundamental of his doctrine, that God is the only person in the Trinity, lived on.[20]

Another form of anti-Trinitarianism that reverberated through the centuries derived from the ideas of Paul of Samosata, who was condemned by a synod in Antioch in 269. He was even more uncompromisingly unitarian than Sabellius. Before his condemnation, Paul of Samosata was the bishop of Antioch, the highest see in the East. He sought to restore the earlier view of Christianity that Jesus was a mere man, although exercising the divine office of the Redeemer. Unfortunately, the Samosatan's writings, like those of Sabellius and their successor, Arius, did not survive. We know of them only from the writings of their enemies. Somehow most of the work condemned by the church disappeared, despite the survival of a huge body of pre-Nicene work by "church fathers." Denying the incarnation and calling the Son of God a creature, as Paul did, remains blasphemous in the Roman Catholic world today, and was so in the Protestant world until this century.[21]

In the fourth century, Christians were still trying to understand the idea of God, which they made phenomenally complex by the worship of a being who was once a man; more mystical still, Christians added a third dimension of divinity, the Holy Spirit. They had to protect their faith in Father, Son, and Spirit, yet maintain the integrity of one God. The chance of establishing an orthodox church and creed came when Constantine united the entire empire after winning the victory that allowed Christianity to become the official state religion in 313. Eusebius, the bishop of Caesaria in Palestine and the most famous ecclesiastic of his time, ended his great history of the church with a rhapsody: Christians, he wrote, were at last freed from tyrants and worshipped together in harmony. But the harmony did not last long, because Christians were soon accusing one another of blasphemy.[22]

In Alexandria, where the see ranked in importance with Rome and Antioch, and where the bishop was called "pope," the church knew neither peace nor unity. In 318, Arius of Alexandria accused his bishop of Sabellianism for having used a Greek term referring to "the same essence" of the persons of the Trinity. Arius used "Sabellianism" as an epithet; soon "Arianism" also became an epithet, and the name of Arius became the most execrated in Christendom as the heresiarchical blasphemer for about fourteen centuries.[23]

Arius began with the proposition that God was the Father—one, infinite, and indivisible. He was uncreated, existed forever, and ruled as sole sovereign and judge. No other God existed but He. Given His nature, He could not impart it to any other being. He had no equals. Accordingly, the other elements of the Trinity had to be subordinate. The Son could not be "true God." Bishop Eusebius, the historian, held the same view. It was an extrapolation of the words ascribed to Jesus: "The Father is greater than I" (John 14:28).[24]

Arius regarded himself as a devout Christian whose theology was orthodox in the sense of being "our faith from our forefathers." He rested his case exclusively on Scriptures, claiming that he restored the primitive church of Jerusalem. But most Christians took Christ's divinity as axiomatic and therefore found Arianism un-Christian. Bishop Alexander of Alexandria, whom Arius had denounced, reported that Arius had drained the dregs of impiety by his "unscriptural blasphemy against Christ." A synod of bishops condemned Arius for apostasy, schism, and heresy, as well as blasphemy, and anathematized his views as those of the Antichrist. Although excommunicated and exiled, Arius spread his doctrines with the sympathetic support of other bishops, including the powerful Eusebius of Caesaria, the historian, and Eusebius of Nicomedia, who was related to the imperial family.[25]

Arianism was an atavistic reversion of Christianity to its primitive apostolic age, but the clock could not be set back. Although Catholic Christianity had not yet fully emerged, the time had long since run out when it could recognize and accept its past. Alexander and his successor as bishop of Alexandria, Athanasius, projected the Catholic future. The Arian or Trinitarian Controversy was a turning point in the history of Christianity, the most decisive since Paul had undertaken to preach the Gospel to gentiles. Although the fourth century can be termed the age of the Trinitarian Controversy, it can with equal validity be called the age of blasphemy, judged by the incessant use of "blasphemy" and "impiety" to describe the advocacy of doctrine that for a time threatened to overwhelm what became Roman Catholicism.

The reason for the intensity of the conflict seems clear. Not only was the future development of Christianity at stake; the right road to salvation was at issue. It was a matter on which the slightest mistake or deviation from the "true" faith, as the contestants variously understood it, could mean the damnation of all the souls of Christendom. Thus, "Antichrist," "atheist," "blasphemer," and other epithets of similar force seemed appropriate characterizations for those who had made a misstep in understanding the meaning of words for "same," "similar," and "different" in relation to substances, consubstantiality, natures, hypostases, existences, properties, persons, coessentiality, essences, and subsistences within the Trinity.

Emperor Constantine, valuing a unified church as a bulwark of his domains, called the first ecumenical council in Christian history, inviting Arius and all eighteen hundred bishops of the empire to meet in the summer of 325 at Nicaea, then a thriving town not far from the imperial residence at Nicomedia, near the Bosporus. Only a sixth of the bishops attended, including but two from the West. Bishop Eusebius, the historian, introduced a creed used in his church, to which the Arians could have subscribed by construing its meaning their way. The emperor assented on condition that a Greek term meaning "of the same essence" or "consubstantial" be added to show the relationship of the Father and the Son. And the emperor demanded a unanimous vote.[26]

The Nicene Creed, as modified to please the Alexandrians, defined the faith as belief in God the Father and in Jesus Christ, "the Son of God, begotten of the Father, Only-begotten, that is from the essence of the Father; God from God . . . begotten and not made, One in essence with the Father," who came to earth for the salvation of men, "was made flesh," suffered, and ascended to heaven to judge the quick and the dead. Almost as an afterthought came the terse affirmation of belief "in the Holy Ghost." The Logos disappeared, the Holy Spirit shriveled, and the Son of God ranked "in essence with the Father." [27]

Eusebius managed, however, to secure the emperor's approval for an interpretation by the council to the effect that the Son was not "a part" of the Father. Eusebius took that to mean that "the Son was from the Father, not however a part of His essence." Thus, he construed away the objectionable albeit ambiguous provision. Yet Arianism was defeated, because, although it recognized Jesus Christ and the Holy Spirit as divine by the Father's grace, it did not regard them as being of the same essence. Arius was excommunicated, and the emperor himself ordered Arius's books to be burned. The council spoke of Arius's "pestilential error" and referred three times to his "blasphemy," thrice more to his "impiety." Eusebius of Nicomedia and Theognis of Nicaea, the leading Arian bishops, were deposed, and the emperor decreed that anyone caught with Arian books would be treated as a "criminal" and suffer "capital punishment."[28]

Thus, for the first time, Christians began to persecute one another for differences of opinion and faith. Constantine's edict fixed the precedent for temporal punishment of offenses against the true Christian faith. Yet the Council of Nicaea did not establish Catholic orthodoxy. That was impossible without unity between the Eastern and Western churches. The Latin churches of the West had not committed themselves in 325— indeed, had absented themselves from the council. Moreover, the Nicene Creed allowed Semi-Arians, if not Arians, to read their own meanings into it and Alexandrian or Athanasian meanings out of it.

The wily bishops of Nocomedia and Nicaea, pretending to recant, reingratiated themselves with the emperor. They controlled a majority at a succession of councils held in Caesaria, Tyre, Jerusalem, and Constantinople during Constantine's last years. They arranged the condemnation and exile of Athanasius and several other bishops who had championed the Nicene Creed. The Nicomedian even managed to restore Arius to communion with the church. By Constantine's death in 337, the Nicene party had lost the emperor's confidence and its major sees. For forty years, the Arians won the battle on whose outcome depended the definition of orthodoxy. Arian bishops censured the blasphemies of Nicene or Athanasian bishops.

By 350, the Arians were completely triumphant. The Emperor Constantius II reunited East and West under the Arian banner. Several church councils endorsed Arian views. The Council of Sirmium in 357 was noteworthy, because exclusively Western bishops brought Arianism as far as it could go, rejecting both "of one essence" and "of like essence." The Sirmium Creed expressed belief in Jesus as Lord and Redeemer, the only Son of God, "but two Gods may not and shall not be taught." That, according to the Council of Sirmium, was "the blasphemy of Nicaea." Jerome, the great scholar in Rome, would lament, "The whole world groaned and marvelled to find itself Arian."[29]

For reasons of state, however, Constantius changed his mind and his theology. Arianism, he discovered, jeopardized the peace and unity of his empire. Above all, worshippers believed in the divinity of Christ, despite Sirmium. Semi-Arians joined with the old Nicene party, with the result that new church councils in 359 and 360 condemned the Arian heresy for having reached "beyond every pitch of blasphemy." The newest creed, abandoning the term "essence" as unscriptural and provocative, declared in Semi-Arian style that "The Son is like the Father in all things."[30]

Athanasius, who three times was deposed as bishop of Alexandria, was Arianism's foremost enemy, and he finally triumphed in his defense of the Nicene Creed. He was convinced that a "blasphemous conspiracy" masterminded by Eusebius had prejudiced Constantine against him and inspired his removal, which he also thought to be an act of blasphemy. As a Greek scholar, Athanasius usually preferred "impiety" to "blasphemy," although he used the terms synonymously. Indeed, he used synonymously and interchangeably all words that described any offense against religion, although they might be as different as "idolatry" and "schism." Sabellianism and Arianism, he said, were "both heresies equal in impiety." The worst crime of the "godless heresy of the Arians" was their "blasphemous" rejection of Christ, for which the guilty deserved the "hatred" of all Christians.[31]

Preserving two credal statements by Arius himself, Athanasius headed them "Blasphemies of Arius." The great Nicene also described his enemies, by no means all Arians, as "Arian heretics" or, synonymously, as "Jewish blasphemers." He called even some Nicene bishops with whom he disagreed on some points "Jews," "heathens," "antichrists," and "blasphemers," as if the terms were without differences in meaning. Athanasius debased the language by censuring any non-Athanasian viewpoint as blasphemous and heretical. The deluge of his vituperation, which opponents reciprocated, registered the tremendous importance that creedmakers attached to their task. The true faith was at issue, and on it depended the road to salvation as well as the road to power.[32]

In the end, the bishops of the fourth century deserve no credit for fixing a creed. An emperor and especially ordinary priests and Christian worshippers settled the most important issue before the Reformation. No creed that diminished or derogated from the sovereign divinity of Christ had a chance of remaining dominant. Athanasius won not because his invective was stronger or his theology more persuasive; he won because Christians worshipped Jesus Christ as God from early times. People wanted a divine Saviour. Neither grace nor salvation could emanate from one who had a nature different from the Father.[33]

Theodosius, who became emperor in the East in 379 and subsequently reunited East and West for a time, was a devout Athanasian and a merciless ruler. The Council of Constantinople in 381 reaffirmed the Nicene

Creed but expanded on the section describing the Holy Spirit. In 451, the Council of Chalcedon, concerned with combatting the new heresy of Monophysitism, and supported by Pope Leo of Rome, fixed the Nicene-Constantinople Creed as the authoritative one. By that time, the pope was a temporal as well as a spiritual leader.[34]

Although Theodosius and Christian liturgy settled the creed of the church, establishing Catholic orthodoxy, the fourth-century bishops prepared church and state for persecuting heterodoxy. By popularizing the heinous character of blasphemy and heresy, the bishops made those transgressions against the faith acceptable as crimes against church and state. Hebrews 10:28 had first pointed the way, when its anonymous author declared that profaning the faith deserved worse than death. Constantine, backed by Nicene bishops, set the precedent for burning heretical books, commanding death for blasphemy, and banning deviant Christian worship. Athanasius's litany of hate and his references to the "crime" of heresy and the "crime" of blasphemy also helped fix a course for the future. Theodosius followed that course with legislation. Christian truth did not yet come from an executioner's torch or ax, for the ordinary penalty consisted of the imposition of civil disabilities. First the church anathematized the offender, then turned him over to the state. Heretics lost their property and their civil rights.

The union of church and state made secular punishment possible. The Theodosian legislation enthroned Catholic Christianity as the exclusive religion of the empire and punished dissent. Religious intolerance soon became a Christian principle, contrary to the Scriptures. Within fifteen years of 380, imperial edicts deprived all heretics and pagans of the right to worship, banned them from civil offices, and exposed them to heavy fines, confiscation of property, banishment, and in certain cases death. By 435, there were sixty-six laws against Christian heretics plus many others against pagans. The purpose of persecution was to convert the heretics and heathen, thus establishing uniformity.[35]

The first instance of capital punishment for heresy occurred in 385, when the pious Bishop Priscillian of Spain and six of his followers were tortured and decapitated with the approval of a synod in Trier. Never before had ecclesiastical authorities resorted to the ultimate secular power against a dissident. In Alexandria, Christians under the patriarch Cyrillus engaged in murderous attacks against Novatian schismatics and, in 415, kidnapped the foremost Platonic philosopher of her time, Hypatia, stripped her in a church, and tore her limb from limb. Rome did not approve of lynch law, which lacked the obligatory formalities. The Theodosian code, by contrast, had official sanction, both secular and ecclesiastical.[36]

From the time of that legislation, "heresy" became the formal name of the great crime against Christianity. The idea of false doctrine or willful error of opinion covered much more ground than "blasphemy," because "blasphemy," however loosely used, retained a core connotation of scorning or cursing, rather than disagreement. "Heresy," which emerged as the generic term, being unfreighted with Old Testament origins, was intrinsically more flexible and spacious. "Blasphemy" had been used as the equivalent but was best reserved as an epithet that conveyed ultimate abhorrence. The one "unforgiveable sin" according to Jesus himself was a particular blasphemy: "blasphemy against the Holy Spirit," or attributing to demonic forces a saving work of God or the Spirit (Matthew 12:31).

Nevertheless, the term "blasphemy" had lost meaning by becoming invective to describe a difference of religious opinion. About the year 400, for example, Rufinus, a presbyter and founder of monasteries, engaged in a dispute with his former friend Jerome, the incomparable Christian scholar and translator of the Scriptures. Offended by something Jerome had said, Rufinus countered by describing a remark of Jerome's about the "bride of Christ" as heathenism, sacrilege, and a "blasphemy" so "great and foul" that it was "worthy of death." Rufinus's use of "blasphemy," which once described an exact crime, closed an era that had begun with the Gospel stories of the trial before the Sanhedrin.[37]

CHAPTER FOUR

Compelling Heretics

OR TWELVE centuries after the Trinitarian Controversy, blasphemy had almost no history, because Christianity confronted a
"crime" with a different name: heresy. From the standpoint of the church,
it was substantially the same crime; only the name was different. "Blasphemy" merely signified its most reprehensible expression. "Heresy"
superseded "blasphemy" as the description of the offense against religion,
because the church faced a proliferation of competing doctrines about the
faith, challenging its mastery. The preoccupying problem of the church
was not abusive speech about religion but different interpretations of the
faith.

With the state supporting its standards of orthodoxy, the church was
in a position to enforce its will wherever the writ of the state was en-
forceable. Only Christian deviants could commit heresy. No matter how
devoutly they believed in Christ, heretics suffered because their beliefs
differed from the church's. By remorselessly persecuting them, the
church attained and long kept its catholicity. Its monopoly as the only
recognized or established religion was built on murder as well as on the
exclusivity of its control of salvation.

The first Catholic theologian who advocated systematic persecution
was Augustine, the bishop of Hippo Regius (now in Algeria). His
contributions to the church made him the most revered figure in its
postapostolic history from his death in 430 to the time of Thomas Aquinas in the thirteenth century. No person except Paul had such a shaping
influence on Christianity. Augustine also became the most authoritative
name in the history of the theory of persecution. Although he did not
originate that theory, he gave it substance and the force of his extraordinary imprimatur. He led the way to the medieval mentality and to the
Inquisition.[1]

For the church to have had a direct hand in murder would have been un-Christian. Augustine understood that. Although he opposed the death penalty, he justified it. The church had to maintain the appearance of charity, but the state had to inflict death when necessary. The church merely turned offenders against religion over to the secular authority. That required the cooperation of the state. Indeed, it required an elaborate rationalization for church-state cooperation against dissenters. Its premise was that the offender against religion, by being a rebel against God, rebelled against the state. The state protected itself and society by using force against the heretic.

Augustine's theory of persecution developed in connection with the Donatists, a schismatic group in North Africa that passed itself off as the orthodox Catholic church. The Donatists, who constituted a large majority of the Christians of North Africa, Augustine's home, were stricter than the Church of Rome, whose authority they rejected. To be in communion with the church, the Donatists believed, required rebaptism or rebirth as a Christian under Donatist auspices. Donatists regarded communicants of the Church of Rome as defiled Christians, and the Church of Rome believed the Donatists to be blaspheming heretics, because they knew the absolute truth yet rejected it from the one true church.[2]

Before the empire condemned Donatists as heretics in 405, Augustine described their schism as both heresy and blasphemy. The state had no alternative but to use force against the Donatists. "How otherwise should they [Christian kings] give an account of their rule to God?" Nebuchadnezzar had provided a model for Christian kings when he decreed that any who blasphemed God should be "cut off." The Donatist blasphemers, Augustine declared, "slay souls," and for that must suffer physically. They caused "everlasting deaths." Coercing them by exerting the temporal powers of Catholic princes inflicted mere "bodily suffering, not the suffering of spiritual deception."[3]

In Augustine's thinking, schism, heresy, blasphemy, and treason were strands in a twisted cable. Recognizing two spheres of jurisdiction, the spiritual and the temporal, he contended that the temporal was subordinate to the spiritual in any matter concerning the unity of the church. The Church of Rome taught that life on earth is a fleeting moment compared with the future life, which is in Christ's charge acting through the church. Salvation came from Rome alone. As long as the church could sustain its claim to exclusive power over salvation, it controlled the policy of the state on any issue concerning an offense against religion.[4]

The theory of the church was that a society forfeits the protection of heaven by offending the divine powers that protect against disasters. A wrathful God could inflict droughts, famines, plagues, poverty, and military defeat. Rulers, said Augustine, used the sword well as "ministers of

God, avengers unto wrath against those who do evil." Having established the church by law, rulers recognized it as possessing the only true faith and the sole jurisdiction over the state, thus ensuring the possibility of future rewards. The heretic, standing athwart the path of salvation, constituted an immortal danger to himself, and a mortal one to state and church. As a public enemy, the heretic had to be corrected by force for his own benefit and society's, or be removed. His contagion was worse than that of a plague, because carnal death counted for nothing compared with the everlasting life of those saved by their adherence to the church. It alone administered divine grace; thus, the power of kings and the health of the body politic depended on spiritual unity.[5]

The purity of the faith was incomparably more important than the "coercion of exile and loss of goods." Even rape, torture, and temporal death were nothing compared with rejection of the faith. The death to be feared was "not a temporal death, which is bound to happen sometime; we fear their eternal death, which can happen if we do not guard against it and can be averted if we do guard against it."[6]

Salvation was the strongest trump of the church and the fount of persecution. Because salvation did not exist outside the church, the state had to cooperate with the church in compelling everyone to worship in the one true faith. To those like the Donatists who argued that no one should be forced to do right, Augustine preached his favorite text: "compel them to come in" (Luke 14:16–23). Force could free a man from destructive error. The shepherd called his wandering sheep back to the fold "by using the lash." The mother was "harsh and stern" with her children, using punishment "to heal by love, not to injure by hatred." So too with the mother church. Her intentions made all the difference. Paul had damned men eternally, "that they may learn not to blaspheme." From this Augustine reasoned that it was "a good work to correct evil men by evil."[7]

He taught that Christians, when persecuted, had to plead conscience and the obligation of wicked magistrates to tolerate Christian truths, but that when Christian magistrates were in power their duty was to sustain the church by persecuting errors of faith. In the same vein, Augustine argued, "there is an unjust persecution which the wicked inflict on the Church of Christ, and there is a just persecution which the Church of Christ inflicts on the wicked." The church persecuted "out of love," he reminded, "to reclaim from error to save souls."[8]

Toleration was no mercy to the heretic, for it merely intensified his damnation. Still worse, it passed his guilt to church and state for allowing him to contaminate others. Thus, more than the vindication of God's honor was at stake, because toleration of the heretic multiplied his eternal fate among the faithful. Augustine's reasoning was simple. Those who

absolutely knew the revealed truth and accepted it, yet permitted disloy-
alty to it, committed a greater crime than those who did not know it or
rejected it. Thus, toleration could bring a curse to state and church;
indulging willful error in a matter of salvation betrayed the revealed faith
and risked the worst calamities that could befall mankind in this life and
the afterlife. From the standpoint of the state, no one who betrayed the
faith could be a dutiful subject. The heretic stirred up wars and treasons.
How much worse, then, for society was a blasphemy against God, or
Christ, or his church, for blasphemy was the most "diabolical heresy."
The traitor betrayed only his king, the heretic and blasphemer the King
of Kings.[9]

Augustine argued that "it has been a blessing to many to be driven
first by fear of bodily pain, in order afterwards to be instructed." Experience showed that persecution was successful, but the strongest argument for it came from the model of Christ himself, as Augustine
understood him. Donatists claimed that Christ had not used force on
anyone. Augustine repudiated them first by recalling the case of Paul.
Christ not only compelled him by words "but used His power to strike
him prostrate." Christ also blinded him, because Paul, as Saul of Tarsus,
seeing nothing through his open eyes, was filled with dark unbelief. "Paul
was forced by Christ; therefore, the Church imitates her Lord in forcing
them [heretics], although in her early days she did not expect to have to
compel anyone in order to fulfill the prophetic utterance."[10]

In the same way, Augustine reasoned, "the Lord Himself commands
the guests first to be brought in to His great supper, but afterwards to be
compelled." When there were empty seats at the banquet, the Lord
commanded: "Go out into the highways and hedges and whomsoever you
find, compel them to come in" (Luke 14:16–23). Augustine concluded
that, if those who are found in the highways and hedges—that is, in
heresies and schisms—were compelled to come in, the church was guiltless for compelling them, but they were to be blamed "for waiting to be
compelled." He opposed the death penalty, favoring lashings, exile, and
confiscation of worldly goods. Thus, he recommended that the devout
Christian emperor should prefer a reformation of "impious aberrations"
by stringent laws short of death, but should "force those who carried the
standard of Christ against Christ to return to Catholic unity, under stress
of fear and compulsion, rather than merely . . . leave them free to go
astray and be lost."[11]

Augustinian thought represented the final stage of Roman Catholicism under the old Roman Empire. Even as Augustine completed the
writings that made him the most popular of the church fathers for over a
thousand years, the empire was crumbling under the onslaughts of Germanic invaders, the "barbarian" Goths and the Vandals, who were, in

fact, Arian Christians. Roman Catholicism triumphed in Europe, despite the capture of the Eternal City in 476 by the Goths and the end of the old empire in the West. Germanic Arians had little capacity for theology or ecclesiastical organization, but the church in Rome had a genius for both, plus the prestige of being the residual legatee of ancient Roman culture. In time, the church "civilized" and converted the Arians, while its allies conquered them.[12]

In Byzantium, the eastern half of the old empire, where the Greek Orthodox church dominated, Emperor Justinian I sponsored a massive codification of the laws, called the Corpus Juris Civilis. It greatly influenced subsequent legal developments in Europe. Its provision on blasphemy, dating from 529, alleged that "famine, earthquake, and pestilence" occurred because a failure to punish blasphemy "provoked God's wrath." Although blasphemers would ultimately lose their souls, the code fixed the punishment in this world as death, in order to bring offenders into "anguish." Imperial officers who were slack in enforcement would be damned by God and subject to the emperor's displeasure. Charlemagne, who in 800 founded what became the Holy Roman Empire in Central Europe, endorsed this provision in Justinian's code, as did successors.

What blasphemy meant and the frequency of its punishment during the Middle Ages cannot be easily determined. Penalties short of death also existed, including imprisonment on bread and water (then a lingering substitute for death), cutting off the lips or slitting them, burning through the tongue, and tearing it out or cutting it off. From the early Middle Ages to the outset of the Reformation, Christian thought on heresy and blasphemy remained static. Theologians who discussed blasphemy in the times of Bede, Gratian, Aquinas, Bernard Gui, and Bellarmine said nothing significantly different from Augustine. Blasphemy engaged their attention hardly at all. Heresy was the offense against religion that progressively preoccupied them and the energies of the church in crushing dissidence.[13]

Punishments for heresy became increasingly common; for blasphemy, rare. No pattern of punishment for obdurate heresy existed before the thirteenth century, nor is there any way to differentiate heretics from blasphemers, especially if the facts showed no cursing or reviling. Even in the thirteenth century, when the death penalty for obstinate heresy became routine, the Christian habit of identifying blasphemy as heresy, or of equating the two as one, persisted. Heresy, long the generic crime, supplanted blasphemy as the offense for which the state was obligated to punish those condemned by the church. Blasphemy, in fact, nearly disappeared as a legal concept or a separate crime; heresy engulfed and superseded it. Theologians scarcely distinguished the two offenses, even when this would have been possible.[14]

The Albigensian Crusade of the early thirteenth century, followed by the Inquisition, had a genocidal effect upon the Cathars of southern France. Although the Cathars could have been condemned as blasphemers and were called blasphemers, the church condemned them as heretics. Cathars believed that God was the primal Spirit but that Satan created the world. Christ, to them, was a deity, one of many, whose pure spirit could not have been born of Mary or crucified. He had a human appearance only to fool Satan while he rescued human spirits. As Docetists, the Cathars also rejected incarnation. They were a neo-Manichaean version of Gnostic Christianity that regarded Roman Catholicism as the church of Satan. The church waged war on them.[15]

Thomas Aquinas (1225–74), the greatest of the medieval theologians and philosophers, laboriously expounded on the various offenses against religion. He started with Tertullian's definition of heresy as a deliberate choice of "false or new opinions" on matters of faith. The authority to define "what Christ really taught" rested in the "Sovereign Pontiff." One who defied that authority adopted "a species of unbelief."[16]

To Thomas Aquinas, several "species of unbelief" existed, among them heresy, paganism, Judaism, apostasy, and blasphemy. Some people thought that, because "blasphemy" referred to the utterance of an "insult against the Creator," it did not refer to untrue beliefs. On the contrary, maintained Aquinas, blasphemy opposed "the confession of faith" and therefore was a species of unbelief. "Blasphemy" denoted "disparagement"—not just of God but of the true faith. To Aquinas, a distinction between the faith and God as "the object of faith" misled. Leviticus 24:16 taught that the blasphemer should suffer death. Aquinas maintained that a person who asserted "something false about God" took His name in vain even more than one who knowingly perjured himself under oath. Given the extraordinary sanctity with which oaths were regarded in the thirteenth century, Thomas Aquinas's finding that "blasphemy is worse than perjury" is startling until his reason becomes clear: the perjurer did not "say or think something false about God"; the blasphemer did.[17]

But to "say or think something false about God" was heresy as much as blasphemy. Indeed, both were species of unbelief or deviance from the faith. Both sprang from a willful or evil intent, and both asserted a falsity about God. Both were mortal sins, and neither could be tolerated. Heresy could not be tolerated even though executing the heretic deprived him of the opportunity of repentance. The obstinate heretic deserved not only the excommunication which separated him from the church; he had to be "severed from the world by death." Aquinas employed similar reasoning against blasphemers. Other evildoers, such as forgers of money and murderers, were executed. Heresy and blasphemy were worse than counterfeiting coins and committing murder; therefore, heretics and blasphemers too must be executed. Thomas Aquinas not only defined blasphemy in terms of heresy, he condemned all heresies as blasphemy. Heretics, he declared, "by right . . . can be put to death and despoiled of their possessions by the secular [authorities], even if they do not corrupt others, for they are blasphemers against God, because they observe a false faith. Thus they can be justly punished [even] more than those accused of high treason. . . ."[18]

In the thirteenth century, such logic was irrefutable, because temporal crimes were insignificant compared with spiritual crimes. Thomas Aquinas, like Augustine, was concerned with the issue of the death penalty not just as a punishment for wrong opinion but as a matter of salvation everlasting. The heretic who remained pertinacious was beyond salvation; he was lost to the church. The church had to look "to the salvation of others" by delivering the heretic to "the secular tribunal to be exterminated." The heretic really intended "the corruption of the faith," endangering all souls: "eternal salvation takes precedence of temporal good, and . . . the good of the many is to be preferred to the good of one." The obstinate heretic could not be given another chance, because he might infect others, tempting them to join his heresy.[19]

The reasoning about the blasphemer was similar. Blasphemy was "the most grievous" and "the greatest sin." By conflicting with the "confession of faith," blasphemy reflected unbelief, like heresy. Comparing murder with blasphemy, Thomas Aquinas held that "blasphemy, which is a sin committed directly against God, is more grave than murder, which is a sin against one's neighbor." The gravity of the sin depended on the intention of the doer. Since the blasphemer "intends to do harm to God's honor," he was the worst sinner. "In comparison with blasphemy, every sin is slight." But Aquinas admitted that blasphemy "can do no harm to God." Although he was really concerned about the harm it would do by infecting others and tempting them to the blasphemer's damnation, he advocated the death penalty even if heretics did not in fact infect others and blasphemers could not hurt God; his reason for such severity was that "heretics . . . blaspheme against God by following a false faith."[20]

Thus, having begun with the element of disparagement as the basis of a distinction between blasphemy and heresy, Thomas Aquinas ignored it thereafter and left heresy and blasphemy as interchangeable as ever. Disparagement itself turned out to be nothing more than heresy or false doctrine. Because blasphemy and heresy were different aspects of the same thing—a deviation from the faith as defined by the church—calling the Cathars heretics rather than blasphemers apparently did not matter, although they regarded Satan as the Creator, scorned the Old Testament, denied Jesus' humanity, and vehemently reviled the church. What did matter was that the Cathars had to be exterminated.[21]

Because only Christians could be heretics, the Jews were the only group officially regarded as blasphemers rather than heretics in the late Middle Ages. Beginning in the thirteenth century, popes habitually described Jews as blasphemers. The church identified Jesus Christ as God. No greater blasphemy existed than rejecting him, except the greatest blasphemy of all, deicide. The Jews were considered guilty of both.[22]

The blasphemy of the Jews posed a special problem for the church. Alexander of Hales (d. 1245), the theologian of the University of Paris whom contemporaries called "the Unanswerable Doctor," confronted the Jewish problem. "On the face of it," he argued, "it appears that they should not be tolerated." Their blasphemies against Christ and the Virgin Mary were notorious; their very religion persecuted Christianity and its sacraments. By their own law, blasphemy was a capital crime; it was immeasurably worse when committed against the true faith. Logic seemed to require the extinction of the Jews. But, Alexander counterargued, they were unique. Jesus himself had prayed for them, and both Testaments spoke of them as the saving remnant. Therefore, their survival was necessary as a testimony to the Christian faith. The existence of Jews proved the truth of the story of the Gospels. What stronger testimony for the faith than from its enemies? Although they did not understand their Scripture, they were its guardians, and it predicted Christ's advent. Their conversion must be awaited; its occurrence would be Christianity's triumph. But their blasphemies could not be publicly tolerated; the church was obligated to urge princes to suppress them without mercy and burn the books that nourished them. On the other hand, their religion must be tolerated, for "we have accepted the Old Law from them, Christ issued from their seed, and the promise was given of their ultimate salvation." Thomas Aquinas agreed. Judaism foreshadowed the true faith and bore witness to it. "For this reason," Aquinas concluded, "they are tolerated in the observance of their rites."[23]

Judaism was tolerated, but not the Jews. Because of their perpetual blasphemies, they had to be systematically degraded. The Fourth Lateran Council of 1215 stripped Jews of civil rights and forced them to wear special marks of identification so that no Christian would unknowingly deal with them. They were technically the serfs of the Christian princes in whose lands they resided by sufferance. They were subject to boycotts, confiscation of properties, expulsion, and mass murders, not by the church but by a populace taught to hate. For centuries, the church taught that all Jews bore a hideous hereditary guilt. The Gospel was witness that they themselves had crucified Christ and cried, "His blood be on us and on our children!" (Matthew 27:25). The massacres began with the First Crusade, in 1096, and continued without end. During the Shepherd's Crusade, in 1251, almost every Jew in southern France was slaughtered.

In 1348–49, when the bubonic plague wiped out one-third of Europe's population—including its Jewish population—religious fanatics blamed the Jews; in German cities, entire communities were murdered on a scale not exceeded until modern times. Bishops and popes who had poisoned the minds of the people with hatred of Jews could not stop the mobs bent on revenging the Jewish blasphemies against Christ.[24]

Book burning was part of the church's campaign against Jewish blasphemies. The church took the matter with the utmost seriousness, and the Jews lamented the loss and desecration of their holy books. Gregory IX ordered the Talmud to be burned throughout Christendom for its alleged blasphemies against Christ and Mary. Tens of thousands of copies of the Talmud and other rabbinic writings were burned, especially in France.[25]

In 1415, a papal bull forbade Jews to have, study, or read the Talmud. In 1442, Eugene IV ordered magistrates to fine Jews and impose "more severe penalties as they may see fit," because Jews "blasphemed God, the most glorious Virgin his mother, or some saints, or else in some other way commit transgressions of this kind." The charge of blasphemy was also used by authorities to extort Jews into paying a fortune into the royal treasuries to escape the penalties. The worst burnings occurred during the Roman Inquisitions in Italy in the sixteenth century, by which time the invention of printing presses had simplified the manufacture of books. In the 1550s, Jewish books as well as rare rabbinic manuscripts were burned by the hundred thousand in Italian cities. A bull of Clement VIII in 1593 forbade Jews to have not only "impious talmudic books or manuscripts" but even writings that "tacitly or expressly contain heretical or erroneous statements against the Holy Scriptures of the Old Law and Testament." As late as 1629, an Italian cardinal boasted of having collected ten thousand outlawed Jewish books for destruction.[26]

Real blasphemies existed in the late Middle Ages, although not in the crude sense of reviling God. The church did not have to look to the Jews if it wanted to find blasphemy. Periodically, religious psychopaths cropped up who claimed to be divine. For over two hundred years, beginning in the thirteenth century, the Free Spirit movement existed throughout Europe. Next to Arianism, it was the longest-lasting, most widespread blasphemy in Christian history. In the seventeenth century, a muted form of it called Ranterism appeared briefly in England. Adherents of the Free Spirit movement sometimes joined together, but they were rarely organized as a sect, and they differed from place to place; not all members even of the same group in the same place agreed on all the various doctrines associated with the Free Spirit. But its adepts, sharing a core of common beliefs, circulated freely among brethren from place to place, even across national borders. Zealous vagabonds, dependent on alms, were the most common carriers of the Free Spirit. They were called Beghards, from which we derive the words "beg" and "beggar." Their female counterparts were Beguines, laywomen who devoted themselves to good works among the poor. Probably only a small fraction of Beghards and Beguines were committed to the doctrines of the Free Spirit, although many were infected with some of those doctrines.[27]

They were particularly interested in the nature and powers of the soul. Soul liberty or spiritual liberty (liberty of the spirit, in a Gnostic sense) became the fundamental characteristic of the movement. About a dozen members of the earliest Parisian Free Spirits were burned for heresy. Innocent III, in 1215, denounced their impieties but added that their doctrines seemed "not so much heretical as insane." The pope probably referred to the doctrine that "all things are One, because whatever is, is God," from which later adepts of the Free Spirit concluded that they were God. Some claimed to be each member of the Trinity. They perverted the doctrine of incarnation by claiming that incarnation occurred within each of them.[28]

During the next two centuries, as Free Spirits traversed Europe and spread their beliefs, the church ordered the Inquisition to capture, interrogate, and condemn them. Occasionally, the church spoke of their "blasphemy" or "impiety," but believers in the Free Spirit were burned for the crime of heresy. The heresy seemed to be a compound of blasphemies that derived from religious lunacy. Free Spirits claimed that, because a person's spirit or soul was "one with God," God or Christ dwelt within him. The Free Spirit regarded himself as "perfect." The Gnostics had preached that eventually every spirit would find its way back to God and become reabsorbed in His essence or substance. The Free Spirits taught that they had made that great leap in this life—indeed, that there was no afterlife, no heaven and no hell, except in man's imagination. Having received direct revelation and self-understanding, they believed that heaven was here and now for the liberated soul. Life itself was the incarnation and the resurrection. "The divine essence is my essence and my essence is the divine essence," said a Free Spirit. Another said he was "wholly transformed into God," so that not even the Virgin Mary could tell the difference. "Rejoice with me, I have become God," announced a third.[29]

A French abbot described as "supreme madness," not blasphemy, "that such men should not fear nor blush to say that they are God." Some Free Spirits disavowed Christ and the Holy Spirit as being less perfect than they, and some diminished and even debased Christ for not being perfect. A perfect man could lie, cheat, steal, and even kill without the least remorse, because he was emancipated from conscience. All that he did was perfect and godly. Adultery before the altar, or, still better, incest with mother or sister, reaffirmed the Free Spirit; they called the act the divine sacrament of "Christerie." They also believed that intercourse with a Free Spirit increased a woman's chastity, even her virginity.[30]

Popes issued bulls against the Free Spirit and sometimes called it blasphemous, but rarely. Some archbishops and inquisitors spoke in passing of blasphemy, and a chancellor of the University of Paris said that the doctrines of the Free Spirit were "the most impious and foolish since the world began." Clearly, they had to be punished. Some adepts of the Free Spirit were allowed to die in jail because they were regarded as insane, but most, when caught, were burned as heretics. Blasphemy was not a threat to the church.[31]

Heresy was. A blasphemer had to be killed, of course, for his crimes against God, but the heretic, although called a traitor against God, was executed by the state for his crimes against the church. God could not be harmed, although He might avenge Himself on those who tolerated blasphemers. The heretic, however, could harm the church by dividing it and winning away its adherents. Free Spirits, even if psychopathic zealots, created envy because of their emancipated and immoral life outside the church. In all probability, the church concentrated on them as heretics rather than blasphemers for that reason; similarly, it had condemned the Cathars as heretics, although they too held blasphemous doctrines, because they had captured the affections of most of southern France. Since the church was capable of recognizing blasphemy when confronted by it, only this quasi-political interpretation explains why the Cathars and Free Spirits were condemned for heresy. What surprises is that their condemnation was not reinforced by the church's calling attention to the blasphemous character of their doctrines.

Throughout the history of the Inquisition, the church turned blasphemers over to the secular arm to be burned at the stake for "heretical pravity," a practice in keeping with Thomas Aquinas's teaching that, although all heretics blasphemed God, blasphemy was not in principle different from heresy. Actually, most heretics were not blasphemers at all, because they were as reverent in their beliefs and worship as the pope. From the late twelfth century to the Reformation, the Waldensian heresy, so named after its originator, Peter Waldo, flourished despite persecution. The Waldensians were proto-Protestants, precursors of the Reformation. So too were the followers of John Wycliffe in England and John Huss in Central Europe. The church unquestionably considered them to be blasphemers. A papal bull of 1418 against the sects founded by such "archheretics" denounced them because they "blaspheme the Lord God," although in fact they disparaged only the church. Jerome of Prague, a Hussite, was burned for heresy even though he allegedly taught "very blasphemous" doctrines such as denial of the Real Presence in the

Mass. His doctrines, like those of most proto-Protestants, came from a different reading of the New Testament. That his doctrines did not come from Rome was the real nature of his heresy—and of his blasphemy. In the sixteenth century, the church began to speak of "blasphemous heresies" and "heretical blasphemies." When doing so, the church followed the practice of the heretics themselves, the Protestants, who would, in a sense, reinvent the crime of blasphemy. Condemned as heretics, Protestants sought a different term and found it in "blasphemy," but they really followed Paul, Augustine, and Thomas Aquinas, in the sense that they used "blasphemy" to censure "false" religious doctrines.[32]

CHAPTER FIVE

Protestantism Rediscovers Blasphemy

THE MAJOR Protestant denominations of the Reformation—Lutheranism, Calvinism, and Anglicanism—repudiated the Roman Catholic church but quickly established their own standards of orthodoxy and ecclesiastical polity in the areas they controlled. However, the Reformation, once unleashed, could not be contained. To a minority of sixteenth-century Protestants, the Reformation was a deformation. They believed that the rebirth of the simple church of the Gospels had died aborning under Luther and Calvin. With the assistance of the printing press, the Reformation made the Bible available to every person who could read or listen to his own language; it taught the supremacy of the Bible over hierarchies and theologies, and it offered the saving grace of God directly to every individual without the intervention of any church or religious officials. In effect, the Reformation gave to every Christian the hope, however illusory where establishments of religion existed, that he could serve as his own priest by finding Christ his own way. Schisms, sects, and heresies were inevitable as individuals reinterpreted the Bible for themselves, whether mystically, literally, allegorically, or rationally.

Although the varieties of religious experience within Protestantism's dissidence ranged from divinely inspired ecstasies to withdrawn pietism, two main streams of belief diverged from the officially sanctioned Protestant churches. One was Arianism, the other Anabaptism, both names imposed by derisive enemies. Arianism, which later called itself Socinianism and, ultimately, Unitarianism, referred loosely to any species of anti-Trinitarianism, and was named after the hated fourth-century heretic Arius. Lutheranism, Calvinism, and Anglicanism followed the Nicene or the Athanasian Creed: "God the Father, God the Son, and God the Holy Spirit." Accordingly, Arianism was as execrable to Protestant establishments of religion as to Rome.

Arians tended to be rationalistic scripturalists who pointed out that the standard creeds were extrascriptural, and that the injunction of Jesus to baptize in the name of the Father, the Son, and the Holy Spirit (Matthew 28:19) said nothing about the three persons of the Trinity sharing the same essence. Arians accepted Jesus as serving a divine office on behalf of God, but they denied his divinity or identity with God, believing that God was one and indivisible. Other Christians, even most Anabaptists, found this denial and the Arian rejection of the doctrine of the Trinity to be atheistic and blasphemous.[1]

Only the Anabaptists were as loathed as the Arians by the rest of Christendom. "Anabaptism" meant "rebaptism," a term rejected by those to whom it was applied. Referring to themselves simply as "the Brethren" or by some other nondescript term, the Anabaptists disagreed on many points and eventually split into several sects, although the name stuck to the bulk of them in the form of "Baptists." They believed that children, being in a state of innocence, would be received into the kingdom of heaven without baptism. Baptism was therefore reserved for persons of maturity who understood and accepted the Gospel. Such persons were regenerated by their faith before baptism. Infant baptism, rather than baptism of believers, was to the Anabaptist an abomination invented by Rome to keep everyone within fealty to the pope. The Bible taught Anabaptists that Jesus received baptism as an adult; he had commanded, "He that believeth and is baptized shall be saved" (Mark 16:16).[2]

Anabaptism, which spread faster than Arianism and attracted far more adherents, emerged in the 1520s in Central Europe. In Germany, a few atypical Anabaptists incited a class war in 1525, and others, in 1533, briefly captured the city of Münster to make it their New Jerusalem. Those freak incidents associated seditious conspiracies against governments as well as against established churches.

Yet the overwhelming number of Anabaptists were peaceable, righteous, hardworking, pious, and humble folk. They shared with other Protestants an abhorrence of Rome, its sacerdotal hierarchy, its administration of sacraments, its worship of relics, its veneration of Mary and the saints, and its worldliness and corruptions. To Catholics, therefore, Anabaptists were revolutionary Protestant heretics.[3]

Protestant establishments regarded Anabaptists with fear and loathing too, although the Anabaptists sought to emulate the primitive church of the original apostles as they imagined it to have been. They were despised for their virtues. They believed that no true Christian should serve the state, which they considered a necessary evil administered by sinful men. They would not take any oaths, not even oaths of allegiance. As pacifists, they would not kill, countenance the death penalty, or serve in armies. They passively resisted any form of coercion as contrary to the love which man owed his fellows. Believing that the state had no religious duties, they refused to pay tithes or ecclesiastical taxes for the support of established churches. For them, religion was a wholly private and voluntary affair. They wanted only to be left alone to worship as they pleased and live apart from an un-Christian world. They asked of government only that it keep peace for the pious. Their apparent rejection of civil officers, courts, the military, taxes, and established churches made them seem as dangerous to Lutherans and Calvinists as to Catholics.

Usually, Catholics punished unrepentant Anabaptists as heretics and burned them alive. Protestant localities tried to avoid condemning them as heretics, because heresy was a papist description for Calvinism and Lutheranism. Protestants preferred imprisonment, mutilation, and exile as punishments. They executed when Anabaptism was compounded by sedition or blasphemy. In 1530, a year after an imperial decree had capitally condemned Anabaptists, Martin Luther (1483–1546), once an advocate of religious toleration, endorsed the death penalty. He considered Anabaptists to be blasphemers, because they taught doctrines contradicting articles of faith believed by all Christians. He also believed that anyone who taught that Christ is not God should be punished for blasphemy; likewise anyone who taught that Christ did not die for the sins of mankind, or that there was no resurrection of the dead, or that there was no heaven and hell. All such people, Luther urged, should be condemned "out of hand." By 1536, he advocated capital punishment for Anabaptist blasphemers.[4]

Luther fixed upon the term "blasphemy" and invested it with his enormous prestige. The Protestant reformers were being killed by the Catholic church as heretics, and he himself was called a heretic; so he tended to choke on the word "heretic." He had written and preached for years about the futility and evil of punishing heresy. Accordingly, he preferred not to use "heretic" as a description of his Protestant enemies, although in fact he did call them heretics. But the word that came easily to him was "blasphemy," as if it differed from "heresy." It did not, especially not as Luther used it. He used it indiscriminately to describe anything that he disliked or disagreed with, just as the church had used "heresy."

Luther always believed that the Jews were blasphemers. Initially, he was tolerant toward them. As he aged, however, he became their vicious persecutor. For their infinite blasphemies against Christ, he insisted that they could not be tolerated. He urged that their synagogues, Talmuds, and prayer books be burned, their houses destroyed, their monies confiscated, their rabbis forbidden to teach, and that no Jews be allowed to use the name of God under penalty of death. All must be put to forced labor or, better still, exiled. Had he the power, he said, he would cut out their tongues because of their blasphemies and force them to accept

Christianity. A Jewish historian observed that, thanks to Luther's anti-Semitism, "Protestants became even more bitter against Jews than Catholics had been."[5]

Luther also raged against Catholicism as a blasphemy against God, although he hesitated advocating the use of the Mosaic law on blasphemy against Catholics; he did not hesitate in the case of Anabaptists and Jews. On the other hand, he so vehemently despised Catholics that in his ranting against them he even called them heretics, but, more characteristically, blasphemers. Their Mass was blasphemous. Their popes were blasphemers and Antichrists. Their church was a synagogue of Satan, "full of blasphemous lies" and "terrible idolatry." They must be compelled to worship in Lutheran churches, and if they failed to attend, their very absence was blasphemy and should be met with excommunication and exile. By 1536, he finally endorsed imprisonment and death for Catholic blasphemies to prevent the spread of their contagion. He ranted endlessly against the Catholics, using the words "blasphemer" and "blasphemy" with such frequency that they lose all meaning and become impossible to count.[6]

Impartially, if promiscuously, Luther condemned Anabaptism, Arianism, and Catholicism as blasphemies, Judaism and Islam too. Any denial of an article of Christian faith as he understood it was blasphemy, as was speaking against the faith; also, sin was blasphemy, opposing Luther was blasphemy, questioning God's judgments was blasphemy, persecution of Protestants by Catholics was blasphemy, Zwinglian dissent from Lutheranism was blasphemy, missing church was blasphemy, and the peasantry's political opinions were blasphemy. Luther abused the word but revived and popularized it. It became part of the Protestant currency.[7]

In Geneva, Protestantism's greatest theologian, John Calvin (1509–64), also revitalized the concept of blasphemy, although, like Luther and the other reformers, he still clung to the concept of heresy and did not clearly differentiate the two. As he aged and achieved power in Geneva, becoming that little republic's civil as well as ecclesiastical dictator, his bigotry and inhumanity intensified. His Mosaic fierceness and his doctrine of predestination (only the saints, whom God unfathomably chose, were destined for the life everlasting) allowed him to say of the children killed in the destruction of an impious city, "We may rest assured that God would never have suffered any infants to be slain except those who were already damned and predestined for eternal death."[8]

Not surprisingly, Calvin abhorred all offenses against religion. Impartially, he called both heretics and blasphemers "traitors to God." Yet Calvin distinguished various degrees of blasphemy. Swearing by the name, blood, or body of Christ, taking frivolous oaths, engaging in impious imprecations and incantations, and calling on a divine power to assist in magic or sorcery were not nearly as serious as denying, defying, or renouncing God. Dishonoring God, Calvin thought, was the worst crime anyone could commit, and teaching false doctrine (any doctrine but his own) dishonored God. Traditionally, of course, false doctrine was heresy, not blasphemy, although Calvin did not make such fine distinctions.[9]

In the 1547 case of Jacques Gruet, who was accused of blasphemy and treason, the punishment was death. Calvin wrote of Gruet, "Not only did he oppose himself to our holy religion, but he poured forth such blasphemies that they make the hair stand on end." At the time, Calvin confronted opposition from a party in Geneva that he described as the Libertines. They included well-to-do burghers like Gruet, who disliked Calvin because he sought to impose the letter of the Decalogue on everyone. Geneva's Libertines were basically a political faction, but their religious opinions made them seem kin to the Spiritual Libertines, notoriously dissolute antinomians of Western Europe; they espoused doctrines reminiscent of those of the Brethren of the Free Spirit, whom the Inquisition had not quite extinguished after more than two centuries of persecution and executions. In 1544, Calvin wrote a tract against the Spiritual Libertines, whom he identified with his Genevan enemies. Condemning their licentious behavior as subversive of Christian liberty, he characterized their "heresy" as the embodiment of "wretched and horrible blasphemies."[10]

The Protestant preference for describing opponents as blasphemers, compared with the Catholic preference for condemning religious deviants as heretics, represented a distinct tendency. But neither side was consistent. Desiderius Erasmus, the great Catholic humanist, wrote, "What does it matter if there be no blasphemy of the tongue, if the whole life breathes blasphemy against God?" Erasmus deplored the excesses of the Inquisition, but was orthodox when he declared that no more "detestable blasphemy" existed than calling the Beatitudes a lie. He believed that it was "heretical" to question any point that the church had authoritatively decided. When Erasmus seemed too tolerant and was criticized for it, he demanded, "How could anyone infer . . . that I do not approve of killing heretics?" There was heresy that was "manifest blasphemy" and heresy that was "sedition," Erasmus declared. "Shall we sheath the sword of the magistrate against this? To kill blasphemous and seditious heretics is necessary for the maintenance of the state." Thus, Luther and the Protestants were not alone in urging death for blasphemers, but, interestingly, Erasmus the Catholic spoke of "blasphemous . . . heretics." In the Catholic world, blasphemy was a form of heresy.[11]

Catholic practice was to convict for the crime of heresy even though the criminal charges might include articles on blasphemous utterances. In

1529, for example, Ludwig Hatzer was charged with blasphemy by the magistrates in a small town in southern Germany. As an anti-Trinitarian, he believed that Christ was not equal to God and was of a different essence—the conventional Arian belief—and he excoriated the worship of images as idolatry. He was burned for heresy. In 1539, the bishop of Cracow tried Katherine Weigel, one of the first anti-Trinitarians of Poland, on charges of apostasy and blasphemy when she was eighty years old. She denied that Christ was begotten from the substance of God and that he was the Son of God in the Catholic sense, and she protested against the Mass. Such ideas were commonly described as Jewish or Arian or both. Cracow burned her as a heretic. In 1546, Paris burned Etienne Dolet, who, by adding levity to anti-Trinitarianism, seemed so dangerous that he was widely reputed to be an atheist. These rare cases of blasphemous heresy in the Catholic world scarcely have significance compared with the frequency of the death penalty for ordinary heresy. Countless thousands died for religious beliefs that the church deemed ordinary heresy.[12]

Etienne Dolet, the anti-Trinitarian, had been a friend of the Spaniard Michael Servetus (1511–53), probably the most celebrated martyr of his century. Servetus was a Protestant victim of Calvin's Geneva, which burned him at the stake in 1553 for both blasphemy and heresy. He was also the precursor of Unitarianism. The tradition of anti-Trinitarianism preceded Arius, but Servetus was the first systematic anti-Trinitarian theorist. He challenged the established churches, Catholic and Protestant, to return Christendom to its pre-Nicene purity. He became notorious throughout Europe as an Arian heresiarch. The systematic suppression of his masterwork, *Christianismi Restitutio* (*Christianity Restored*), minimized even his posthumous influence on religious thought. Faustus Socinus (1539–1604), an Italian of the next generation who lived most of his adult life in Poland, became the principal influence on anti-Trinitarian thought. Although Servetus was not forgotten, men remembered his death, not his accomplishments. His martyrdom triggered the first great controversy over toleration.[13]

Servetus believed that Luther, Calvin, and Zwingli were not revolutionary enough, because they accepted the doctrine of the Trinity. He discovered that "not one word is found in the whole Bible about the Trinity, nor about its Persons, nor about an Essence, nor about a unity of the Substance, nor about one Nature of the several beings." In language often offensive, he tried to re-educate the leading scholars and theologians of the Reformation. Having failed to engage Erasmus in debate, Servetus sought out Johannes Oecolampadius in Basel, only to be driven away with the warning, "By denying that the Son is eternal you deny of necessity also that the Father is eternal. . . . I will be patient in

other matters but when Christ is blasphemed, No!" Oecolampadius
alerted other Protestant leaders, and Zwingli urged that they convert or
silence the young Spaniard or risk the danger that his "false and evil
doctrine, would, if it could, sweep away our whole Christian religion."
Do everything possible, Zwingli urged, to end "such dreadful blasphemy." Rebuffed in his efforts to persuade the reformers, Servetus determined to write a book that would reveal the truth of his discoveries to all
Christians. In 1531, only fourteen years after Luther had posted his
theses on the church door in Wittenberg, Servetus published *De Trinitatis
Erroribus* (*On the Errors of the Trinity*). It made him a despised and hunted
man, although he was not yet twenty-one. The Inquisition sought him in
Spain and France. The Protestants banned his book and closed their cities
to him. Martin Bucer, from his pulpit in Strassburg, thundered that
Servetus should "have the guts torn out of his living body."[14]

Servetus "disappeared" and assumed a new identity. In a few years,
Catholic France was talking about a brilliant young humanist and scientist named "Michel de Villeneuve." At the University of Paris, he ranked
with his colleague Vesalius as an anatomist. As Dr. Villeneuve, a Catholic, Servetus the heretic became personal physician to the archbishop of
Lyon, who had been fascinated by his lectures on comparative ethnology
and geography. On the side, the doctor resumed his biblical scholarship.
He was at work on a new book.[15]

His ambitions for the book were boundless. It would, he hoped,
rejuvenate Christianity by restoring it to the innocence and simplicity it
had had in the time of the Gospels. Restoration, not mere reformation,
was Servetus's objective. The very title of the book, *Christianismi Restitutio*, would be a reproach to the Reformation. It had failed because it had
not sought a return to Christianity as it was before becoming corrupted
in the early fourth century by pagan doctrines, by the church's possession
of temporal power, by the state's encroachments on the spiritual realm,
by the Council of Nicaea's dictation of an erroneous Trinitarianism, and
by the un-Christian practice of infant baptism. Servetus would purge all
the corruptions. The Reformation had repudiated the papacy but not its
teachings or its sacraments that had no biblical foundation. The Reformation had failed to confront Trinity, incarnation, and redemption, essential matters of Christian theology. Servetus's theology became
increasingly radical. He accepted the Anabaptist tenet that one became a
Christian by being baptized after experiencing Christ and repenting one's
sins. Becoming a Christian meant sharing a spiritual communion that no
infant could understand. Christ himself was not baptized until he was an
adult.[16]

Servetus's soul burst with his rediscovery of Christianity. He could
no longer withstand the spiritual torment of suppressing his secret reli-

gion. After fourteen years as Villeneuve the Catholic, he had to find someone, if only a correspondent, to whom he could reveal himself and with whom he could discuss religion. In his desperation, he convinced himself that John Calvin would understand and encourage him. Calvin and Servetus were about the same age, considerably younger than the Protestant leaders whom Servetus had encountered before being forced to flee from them. Geneva, during Servetus's fourteen years in France, had become the new center of Protestantism, and Calvin, its foremost theoretician, had dominated Geneva since 1541. In 1546, Servetus opened a correspondence with him.

Signing his real name, Servetus wrote letter after letter. At first, Calvin tolerated him, answering at length, correcting his errors. Servetus, never deferential, became increasingly condescending and critical. Calvin was wrong on the Trinity, wrong on regeneration, wrong on baptism. Servetus dared to instruct him on theology and, for Calvin's better guidance, sent him a manuscript copy of part of his book-in-progress, *Christianismi Restitutio.* Calvin had recommended his own book, the monumental *Institutes of the Christian Religion,* only to be sent an annotated copy of it by Servetus with the errors exposed in marginal comments. "Servetus seizes my books," Calvin wrote a friend, "and defiles them with abusive remarks." Not a page was free from his "vomit." Servetus did not understand that he had roused in Calvin a murderous hatred. Servetus, Calvin wrote, had offered to come to Geneva, "but I shall not pledge my faith to him; for if he did come here, I would see to it, in so far as I have authority in this city, that he should not leave it alive." Servetus in a final letter told Calvin, "Your gospel is without God, without true faith, and without good works. Instead of a God you have a three-headed Cerberus." Prophetically, he added that he knew he would die for his beliefs.[17]

Servetus finished his anonymous book in 1552. Calvin got hold of a copy, recognized it as the work of Servetus, and betrayed Servetus to their common enemy, the Inquisition, which was responsible for the deaths of so many Protestants. Servetus was imprisoned and held for trial, but he tricked his jailor and escaped. The Inquisition condemned him *in absentia,* sentenced him to be burned, and carried out the sentence using a picture of him as an effigy. Bales of copies of his book were burned with the effigy. Calvin also urged that the book be destroyed in Protestant countries. Its pages, he warned, were "prodigious blasphemies against God." Only three copies of the *Restitutio* survived.[18]

Servetus decided to start a new life in Italy but made the fatal mistake of choosing the route through Geneva. On the day after his arrival, he attended church there, heard Calvin preach, was recognized, and at Calvin's instigation was imprisoned. The trial of Servetus dragged on about two and a half months. During that time, he was kept in solitary confinement in sickening conditions. As the weeks wore on and his physical condition worsened, he became angry, frenzied, and abusive, calling Calvin every epithet his crazed, frightened mind could summon. The judges were aghast at his tirades against their Christian leader, who sat there in his starched black robes, frostily watching his victim discredit himself. Twenty-five judges, the City Council of Geneva sitting as a criminal tribunal, tried him for his "infinity of blasphemies."[19]

Servetus was no Anabaptist. He did not advocate separation of church and state, reject the authority of the magistrates, or oppose oaths. He did not exalt the inner light above the Scriptures. He did not contend against ceremonies. For Protestants to put such a man to death was unprecedented. Geneva needed support. So a copy of the theological records of the trial, a copy of the prisoner's *Restitutio*, and a request for advice went to Bern, Basel, Schaffhausen, and Zurich, and Calvin paved the way with his own letters. Not one of the cities openly advocated death, although some of their ministers did. All agreed, however, that Servetus was guilty, and they expressed their confidence that Geneva would defend the faith. Basel, for example, declared that he had exceeded all the old heretics by spewing their combined errors in one blasphemous mouth. Shaffhausen said, "We do not doubt that you, in your wisdom, will repress his attempts lest his blasphemies like a cancer despoil the members of Christ."[20]

The verdict of Geneva was that Servetus had spread "heresies and horrible, execrable blasphemies against the Holy Trinity, against the Son of God, against the baptism of infants and the foundations of the Christian religion." He had confessed to calling the Trinity a three-headed monster of the devil, and believers in the Trinity Trinitarians and atheists. He had blasphemed by saying that Christ was not the Son of God. "His execrable blasphemies are scandalous against the majesty of God, the Son of God and the Holy Spirit. This entails the murder and ruin of many souls." Because he had maliciously infected the world with his "stinking heretical poison," he was burned to ashes with his book. His last recognizable words were, "O Jesus, Son of the Eternal God, have pity on me." They took that as final proof of his guilt, for he had not referred to the "Eternal Son of God."[21]

Sixteenth-century Europe was hostile to religious toleration. On both sides of the Reformation, political and religious leaders believed that the safety of the state and the preservation of the faith required the execution of obstinate and blasphemous heretics. They saw nothing un-Christian in punishing capitally for a crime against the majesty of God. Had an epidemic among livestock annihilated as many pigs and sheep as the number of people slaughtered for their religious opinions, governments would have bemoaned the loss. But they would have thought themselves traitors to their faiths if they had not rid the world of its Servetuses.

One man's heresy was another's blasphemy. Although men differed on heresy, no one would champion a blasphemer or the right to blaspheme. Still, Calvin felt the need to defend the execution. He demanded implacable severity to show "devotion to God's honor." When he threatened, "Those who would spare heretics and blasphemers are themselves blasphemers," he meant to silence dissent. The teachings of Servetus, he complained, were spreading; he knew too that the execution had stirred up an undercurrent of criticism. Even among the faithful there were formal requests for information about the crime that merited burning. Accordingly, Calvin justified his views on the case and on crimes of religious opinion generally by publishing, in 1554, a book, *Defense of the Orthodox Faith Against the Prodigious Errors of Michael Servetus*. In the Lutheran world, Alexander Alesius of Leipzig published *Against the Horrible Blasphemies of Servetus*.[22]

Theodore Beza, Calvin's confederate, grumbled that Servetus's ashes were not yet cold when a dispute arose on the question whether heretics should be executed. The dispute occurred because one man, and he alone, had the courage to protest in print against the bloodletting in Christendom over points of doctrine, and even he, Sebastian Castellio of Basel, did not dare put his real name to his book. Those who agreed with Castellio discreetly kept their thoughts to themselves.[23]

Castellio's book, *Concerning Heretics*, which he published in Latin, French, and German under different pseudonyms, appeared immediately after Calvin's *Defense*. A professor of Greek, Castellio wrote epic poems in classical languages and did translations of the Bible. His preface to one edition, in 1551, contained an unprecedented argument against persecution. Calvin pestered the authorities at Basel to punish him as an enemy of religion. In the manuscript of another volume by Castellio, which Calvin managed to suppress, Castellio said there were three professors at Basel "whom the Calvinists openly regard as followers of Servetus," and he named himself as one. His *Concerning Heretics* was the sixteenth century's first book on religious liberty, and, although not as analytical or systematic as Jacobus Acontius's *Satan's Stratagems* of 1565, Castellio's book deserves praise as "the most important work favouring religious toleration to be published on the Continent during the century." The modernity of much of his argument is striking, and for that reason much of it seems pedestrian. We take for granted what was then incisive, original, and even shocking. To conventional Christians, the argument was both heretical blasphemy and blasphemous heresy.[24]

Castellio wrote to "stanch the blood" so wrongfully shed by those called heretics. After carefully investigating the meaning of "heresy," he concluded "that we regard those as heretics with whom we disagree." Each sect looked upon others as heretics, "so that if you are orthodox in one city or region, you must be held for a heretic in the next." Persecution derived from the diversity of religious opinions, the certainty of each sect that it was right, and the arrogant desire of each to rule the rest. In fact, however, the points of religion over which Christians disagreed and persecuted one another were intrinsically uncertain. The persecutor might be as mistaken as his victim, if the issue that divided them was the Lord's Supper, free will, justification, baptism, the Trinity, predestination, or other mysterious matters on which the Scriptures are unclear. Were these matters obvious, as that there is one God, all would agree. The course of wisdom, then, was to condemn no one—Jew, Turk, or Christian—who believed in God.[25]

Conduct alone, Castellio concluded, was punishable, but never religious belief or worship. (Jefferson reached the same conclusion over two centuries later.) Men could agree, Castellio reasoned, that robbery, murder, and treason are crimes; they would never agree on religious matters. That a Christian believed in God, in salvation through Jesus, and in the Bible was "enough." Religion, to Castellio, did not consist of "dubious or ambiguous doctrine," of ceremonies, of "indifferent matters," or of points that transcended human understanding and for which there was no indisputable scriptural authority. On all such matters, like the doctrine of the Trinity, "each may be left to his own opinion and the revelation of the Savior." Thus, no one should be molested for religion, "which above all else should be free, since it resides not in the body but in the heart, which cannot be reached by the sword of kings and princes." Since faith could not be compelled, coercion was futile. To claim that loyalty to a true faith demanded coercion of those who differed confessed a lack of confidence in that faith. A ruler ought to content himself with the punishment of injury to persons and their property. If anyone disturbed the public peace by an assault under the color of religion, "the magistrate may punish such an act not on the score of religion, but because he has done damage to bodies and goods, like any other criminal." But the punishment of a religiously motivated offense ought to be limited to fines, imprisonment, and banishment—never death. The church should restrict itself to admonition and, in the last resort, excommunication.[26]

One danger in prosecuting heresy was that the victim might not be a heretic. Christ and his disciples, Castellio claimed, died as heretics and seditious blasphemers. "This ought to fill us with fear and trembling when it comes to persecuting a man for his faith and his religion." Another danger in prosecuting heresy was that the punishment exceeded the crime. There was, moreover, a real danger of letting loose a war of extermination among Christians. Some people argued, said Castellio, that to suffer heresy caused sedition and disseminated false doctrine. Persecution, he answered, caused those evils. "Seditions arise from the attempt to force and kill heretics rather than from leaving them alone, because tyranny engenders sedition." He admitted the danger of dissemination of false doctrine, but maintained that the remedy should not be worse than the disease. Here too persecution spread the evil to be averted. People saw the constancy of heretics in martyrdom and joined their faith. Servetus, for example, had fought with "reasons and writings" and should have been answered the same way. His books could have been sold without disturbance, "but now that the man has been burned, everybody is burning with a desire to read them."[27]

Castellio emphasized that the sword and the stake did not and could not protect sound doctrine. For him, sound doctrine was that which made men good, endowed them with love, and gave them a conscience. He judged religion by its fruits, not by the names of sects or by their appeal to authority. "Take a good Papist, one who fears God and does not swear, commit adultery, bear false witness, or do to another what he would not have done to him. I say that such a man should by no means be called impious and killed. He worships idols. Well? He does so in error and not with malice, just as we all worship." Not even Milton or Locke over a century later tolerated "Papists."[28]

Distinguishing heresy and blasphemy, Castellio found that the first was mere error of opinion and should be exempt from the law: "To err is not to blaspheme." Blasphemy, as far as the law is concerned, should be governed by its definition in the Mosaic code: it was consciously reviling God or His Scriptures. Had Servetus said that God is the devil, that would have been "real blasphemy," meriting punishment. But he had merely expressed an opinion about religion. His having said that the Calvinists did not know God and worshipped a false god was a comment against men, not God. He had simply interpreted the Bible differently, as was his Christian right. The greatest blasphemers, Castellio declared, "are those who confess God with their lips and deny him with their lives." But not even Castellio would tolerate "real blasphemy." Nor was he consistent in his Mosaic definition, for he regarded the denial of God or Christ as blasphemous. "I do not classify under the name of heretic the impious, the despisers of sacred Scriptures and blasphemers," Castellio wrote. "These in my judgment are to be treated as impious. If they deny God, if they blaspheme, if they openly revile the sacred teaching of Christianity, if they detest the holy lives of godly men, I leave such offenders to be punished by the magistrate, not on account of religion—they have none—but on account of irreligion."[29]

To Calvin and Beza, Castellio was a blasphemer and deserved Servetus's fate. They quickly uncovered his authorship of *Concerning Heretics* and tarred him with the vilest epithets. He replied in a stinging, satirical polemic, *Against Calvin's Book* (1555), in which he answered Calvin's *Defense* point by point. His enemies suppressed his book by seeing that no publisher would print it; it circulated only in manuscript until about 1612, when it was published for the first time, in Holland. For a decade, the Calvinists hounded Castellio, and in 1563 managed, at last, to institute a proceeding against him. His death intervened to deprive them of a triumph.[30]

Concerning Heretics initially influenced liberal Protestants, who stood to gain most from a policy of toleration. Among them was a band of refugees from the Italian Inquisition who had founded an Italian church in Geneva. Some were sympathizers of Servetus and friends of Castellio. In 1558, the orthodox among them enlisted Calvin's assistance in stamping out the spread of heresy among the Servetians and Socinians. All persons under suspicion had to sign a confession of faith repudiating opposition to the Trinity, predestination, the divinity of Jesus, and the sacraments. Six who resisted finally subscribed, under coercion. Among them was Giovanni Valentio Gentile, a teacher of Latin who was a bold advocate of anti-Trinitarianism. Gentile was arrested for heresy in Geneva in 1558, but he recanted on realizing that Servetus's fate awaited him. He promised that he would sooner die than repeat his blasphemies against the Trinity.[31]

After escaping from Geneva, Gentile advocated the beliefs that he had renounced. In 1566, he returned to Switzerland. Because Calvin had recently died, Gentile mistakenly believed he would be safe. He had become either fanatical or demented. In a town near Bern, he challenged all the Protestant ministers to debate him on religion, the loser to suffer death for false religion. The authorities held him in prison for trial in Bern. He remained obstinate, defending his religious opinions, though claiming lunacy.

The evidence against him was conclusive. Benedictus Aretius of Bern, a supporter of Beza, published a book against Gentile to justify Bern's course of action to the world. The prisoner had condemned himself in a scurrilous libel against the doctrine of the Trinity, calling it a "mere human invention," for which Bern charged him with having "impiously blasphemed God." Another count in the indictment was that Gentile had adopted "the Blasphemies of Arius." Aretius's account reads as if Bern thought it was trying that fourth-century enemy of Athanasius. The trial of 1566 ended in a sentence of death by beheading for "most horrid Blasphemies against the Son of God, and the Glorious Mystery of the Trinity."[32]

In the Low Countries, which Spain controlled and which instituted an Inquisition rivaling Spain's itself for severity, the duke of Alva's armies and the Inquisition murdered about eighteen thousand Protestants between 1567 and 1573. Individual cases seem inconsequential against the numbing total. One case that both Mennonite and Unitarian martyrologists remembered, probably because an account of the inquisitional proceedings against him survived, was that of Hermann Van Flekwyk. He stood accused of having "blasphemed against the true body and blood of God, by speaking against the Mass," and by professing anti-Trinitarian beliefs. He acknowledged the Trinity in a Servetian sense—"One God, the Son of God, and the Holy Spirit"—but refused a demand that he subscribe to the Athanasian Creed of "God the Father, God the Son, and God the Holy Spirit." The inquisitor pelted him with epithets—"blasphemer against the Holy Ghost" as well as against God and Christ, "diabolical Antitrinitarian," and "enemy of the Mother of God." Van Flekwyk died at the stake for heresy in 1569, in Bruges.[33]

Of all the blasphemy cases of the sixteenth century, that of Francis David was the strangest and least likely: his persecutors were Socinians, the most rational and tolerant of sects, and he was the head of their church. The locale, moreover, was the most liberal in Europe, the eastern region of Hungary known as Transylvania. A decree of 1557, intended to promote religious peace, provided that "every one might hold the faith of his choice, together with the new rites or former ones, without offense to any." Re-enactments benefited Calvinists and even anti-Trinitarians or Unitarians, as they came to be known. Transylvania was the only place on the continent where the Socinians would call themselves Unitarians. It was also the only place where Unitarianism became an established religion, and the only place ever to have a Unitarian monarch. The man mainly responsible for the Unitarian triumphs in Transylvania was a charismatic minister named Francis David (David Ferencz).[34]

David, who never reached a theological stasis, kept embracing innovations. The most controversial was his rejection of the invocation of Christ. David believed that there was no scriptural authority for invoking Christ's name in prayer. Royal admonitions against repudiating the invocation did not silence David. At a general synod of the Unitarian churches of Transylvania in 1578, he opposed prayers to Jesus because he was not divine. Unitarian leaders worried whether Unitarianism might be discredited by David's heresy. Faustus Socinus, the foremost divine of Unitarianism in Europe, came to Transylvania and stayed as a guest in David's home for months, but could not sway him. In 1579, conventional Unitarians denounced David to Prince Blathory for innovations and blasphemy. Socinus framed a document which became the basis of an indictment; its theme was that to imply that Christians could not find salvation through Jesus Christ was blasphemous.

Prince Blathory summoned David under armed guard to be tried before the Hungarian Diet at the capital. The trial lasted two days, with the prince himself presiding. Denying the charge of blasphemy, David contended that to worship anyone but God was unscriptural. The members of the Diet, with some Unitarian nobles dissenting, returned a verdict of guilty. Blathory sentenced David to life imprisonment in a dungeon for execrable blasphemies and innovations. He died of illness in prison, probably within a year, an eccentric quester denied the religious liberty he had won for so many. The Unitarians who were responsible for his persecution doubtless acted to save the reputation of their church and defend its faith. In that regard, they were little different from their counterparts in Geneva or Rome.

Rome burned the foremost philosopher of the Italian Renaissance, Giordano Bruno, in 1600. Neither a scientist nor a theologian, he sought to reconcile science and religion, but his philosophy subverted basic theological premises. Bruno never became a Protestant, nor was he a practicing Catholic. He found all denominations mean and narrow, preoccupied with rituals, dogmas, and petty disputes. His business was to get at the truth of the cosmos.[35]

Bruno derived from the Copernican revolution a wholesale assault on the prevailing Aristotelianism and the basis for constructing a "New Philosophy," as he called it. He was a metaphysicist, not a physicist. He knew Copernicus's work; intuition and imagination led him the rest of the way.[36]

Bruno's massive assault on Aristotelianism brought him into direct conflict with the church. It was concerned with how to go to heaven, not with how the heavens go. One heaven and one hell was all that it could conceive, whereas Bruno speculated about an endless number of celestial worlds. To the church, that violated Scripture. Although Bruno undermined some conventional premises of religion, he was a God-intoxicated man. He believed that the infinite universe was the result of an infinite divine power, whose work was manifest in a grain of sand, in all life, in human reason, and in the endless stars. God caused all and was in all, and He alone was Absolute, Infinite, the One, the soul of the world, the spirit of the universe. On and on Bruno went, rhapsodizing the Supreme Being who brought unity to the seeming chaos of human existence and nature. To the church it seemed like heresy.[37]

The Inquisition seized Bruno in 1592, when he was denounced for having uttered numerous blasphemies against the Trinity and the majesty of God. On being asked whether he believed in the Trinity, he construed it in terms of metaphysical abstractions: creative power, intellect, and love. When asked whether he believed that the Father, Son, and Holy Spirit were one in essence but distinct persons, he admitted, "I have never been able to grasp the three being really Persons and have doubted it." His inquisitors at Venice made him beg for mercy and repent his errors, yet kept him in prison.[38]

The chief inquisitor at the Holy Office in Rome demanded that Bruno be delivered there for trial. No ordinary heretic, he was an apostate monk who praised Protestant princes, and he was a "heresiarch"—an originator and leader of heresy. Venice extradited him to Rome, where he was kept in the dungeon of the Roman Inquisition for seven years. Then, in 1599, several cardinals examined him on heresies they had extracted from his books. At a final interrogation, Bruno declared that he would recant nothing. In January 1600, a meeting presided over by the pope decreed that Bruno be turned over to the secular arm to be burned at the stake for "many various heretical and unsound opinions." A Catholic witness who described the burning concluded, "he is gone, I suppose, to recount to those other worlds imagined by himself the way in which the Romans treated blasphemous and impious men."[39]

During the seventeenth century, blasphemy increasingly became a secular crime on the continent. It remained, as always, a religious offense, but the state began to supplant the church as the agency mainly responsible for instigating and conducting prosecutions. The association of religious crimes with political ones such as sedition and treason had its roots in Exodus 22:28, which declares, "You shall not revile God, nor curse a ruler of your people." The intimacy between *laesa religio* and *laesa maiestas*, crimes against religion and crimes against the state, was a feature of Athenian law, and then of Roman law, both before and after Christianity became the state religion of Rome. The Reformation, especially in Protestant countries, reinforced the belief of sovereigns that they were "the images of God, representing in the governance of their several States that authority which is exercised by God in the governance of the Universe." In the seventeenth century, the belief that a nation's religious unity augmented its peace and strength accounted, at least in part, for the rising dominance of the state in policing serious crimes against religion. The connection of religious dissent with political subversion was old, but governments intervened more frequently to suppress nonconforming intellectuals and sectarians. Political considerations began to supersede religious ones in justifying persecution, first in Protestant countries and then in Catholic countries, where the sovereign was not the head of the church and the Inquisition still prevailed. Even when bigotry motivated a prosecution for blasphemy, rather than concern for security, unity, or peace, the state led the church. In earlier times, the state had usually followed the church or cooperated with it. The cases of Tyszkiewicz and Vanini are examples of fanatic zeal by secular authorities.[40]

In Poland, the scene of Socinus's major mission, Iwan Tyszkiewicz became an ardent Socinian. His abandonment of Catholicism, his pros-

perity, and his spirited advocacy of his new faith in an area dominated by
Catholics made him a marked man. His refusal to swear an oath by the
Trinity or on a crucifix led to his conviction by a local court. On an
appeal that went all the way to the royal court in Warsaw, in 1611, the
public prosecutor pressed the charge of blasphemy. The Catholic sovereign influenced the judges to return a verdict of death. The executioner
cut out Tyszkiewicz's tongue, because of his blasphemy, before burning
him for blasphemous heresy.[41]

The case of Julius Caesar (originally Lucilio) Vanini in 1619 carried
echoes of the Bruno affair. Vanini, who earned his doctorate at the University of Naples, was a wandering monk, like Bruno. For several years,
he too visited the capitals and university towns of Europe, supporting
himself as a teacher. He too wrote books on philosophy, touching religion, science, literature, and all the subjects of interest to a learned,
skeptical-minded humanist. Vanini, however, for all his independence of
spirit, was a minor figure in his time and would be forgotten but for his
martyrdom. The secretary of the City Parliament of Toulouse instituted
before that body a blasphemy proceeding against Vanini. He is supposed
to have written mockingly about religion and made the mistake of calling
nature "Queen of the Universe," thereby derogating from God's sovereignty. The charges against him made no mention of heresy, although the
entire trial consisted of an examination of his religious beliefs. He insisted
that he believed in the Trinity, as defined by the church, as well as in
God, whom he described as the Creator of nature. He was convicted on
the testimony of a witness who swore that Vanini had privately confided
his disbelief in God and really credited natural laws for the governance of
the physical world. The Toulouse Parliament found him guilty of "atheism, blasphemies, impieties and other crimes," unstated, and ordered
that he be taken to his place of execution wearing a placard with the
words "Atheist and Blasphemer of the Name of God." After his tongue
was pulled out with pincers and severed, he was garotted and his body
burned at the stake.[42]

Although Bruno had been charged with blasphemy and sentenced for
heresy, Protestant precedents were not without some influence. When
the Catholic states of Poland and France prosecuted Tyszkiewicz and
Vanini, the sentences were for the crime of blasphemy, contrary to conventional Catholic precedents. The church condemned for heresy, the
state increasingly for blasphemy. Blasphemy prosecutions continued in
continental Europe into the present century, although the death penalty
for the crime died out during the eighteenth century.[43]

CHAPTER SIX

The Fires of Smithfield

UNTIL the later fourteenth century, England was so isolated from the heresies of the continent that punishments for religious offenses were unusual. Catholic orthodoxy peacefully reigned over the English church, which escaped the Waldensians and the Cathars, the Albigensian Crusade, and the Holy Inquisition. The instances of heresy that cropped out in England were isolated and rare; always excepting the Jews, religious persecution did not exist, because there was no need for it. When that need arose, the response of the ecclesiastical courts was decisive.

In 1166, for example, about thirty people from Flanders, probably Cathar heretics fleeing from persecution, sought refuge in England. Their proselytizing brought them to the attention of the authorities at a time when Henry II, having broken with Thomas à Becket, was eager to prove his orthodoxy. With the king himself presiding, a council of bishops convened at Oxford and condemned the heretics, whose religion seemed un-Christian enough to be blasphemous. The heretics rejected baptism, matrimony, and the Eucharist, disparaging the church. Innocent III and Frederick II had not yet made pertinacious heresy a capital crime, even on the continent, although cases of burning alive were known in 1166. In England, however, no legal basis for the death penalty existed for any offense against religion—not until 1401. The Oxford ecclesiastical court of 1166 met the heretical challenge by ordering that the heretics be branded, flogged, stripped to the waist, and sent out into the winter fields to die, "and they perished miserably." By royal command, "if any one shall have received them, he will be at the mercy of the lord king, and the house in which they have been shall be . . . burned."[1] This, said the historian of the Inquisition, was "the first secular law on the subject . . . since the fall of Rome."[2]

Ecclesiastical courts, with their canon law, had taken root in England in the aftermath of the Norman Conquest, and they eventually achieved control over offenses against religion. They reached into the daily lives of the English people, regulating their beliefs as well as their conduct. Ecclesiastical jurisdiction glutted itself with all sorts of cases. One category covered the various sins of the flesh; "immoralities" of a wholly different kind, as disparate as breach of contract, disorderly conduct, usury, and defamation, constituted another category. Still another was "spiritual" affairs, reaching cases on matrimony, wills, clerics, and church properties. Offenses against religion encompassed a variety of sins, from desecration of the Sabbath and failure to attend church to profanity, sacrilege, and witchcraft. The gravest offenses against religion, touching the security of the church and the salvation of souls, were errors of religious opinion. As on the continent, "heresy" was the generic name for such errors. It included within its spaciousness everything from a trivial difference on some point of faith to speaking evil of God. Defamation of God's church, its sacraments, its sacerdotal hierarchy, its discipline, or any of its doctrines or saints was a form of heresy—blasphemous heresy, but heresy nevertheless. Distinguishing one kind of heresy from another did not matter. Any heresy, blasphemous or not, was high treason against God. Its punishment was intended to keep believers in uniformity and the church in power, rich and influential.[3]

The orthodoxy of England during the thirteenth century was unsullied except for tantalizing glimpses of heresy. In 1210, there is a reference to a solitary Albigensian being burned in London; nothing more is known about the case, which would be unprecedented in English history if true. A dozen years later occurred the strange case of the deacon who, having converted to Judaism for the love of a Jewess, was condemned for apostasy by an ecclesiastical court presided over by Stephen Langton, the archbishop of Canterbury. In consonance with a canon-law pretense of the church that it never stained itself with blood, the prelates turned the victim over to the sheriff for execution by burning. The same court in the same year, 1222, also decided a peculiar blasphemy case. A couple who represented themselves as Jesus and Mary, thereby assuming divine attributes, were condemned to solitary imprisonment for life, on a diet of only bread and water. Before the middle of the century, a Jew who converted to Christianity relapsed; although the outcome of his trial is not known, anyone baptized as a Catholic was liable to the church for his religious errors. Another Cathar heretic refused to attend church, declared that the devil was loose, and said "blasphemous" things about the pope. There is a reference, finally, to the Dominican fathers of Yorkshire hunting for heretics but thwarted by a sheriff who thought the power of arrest belonged to him. At the close of the century, the author of *The Mirror of Justices*, a lawbook of questionable repute, described heresy as the crime of high treason against God, and its punishment as excommunication and cremation; but the author was theorizing about what should be done in the event that heretics turned up in England.[4]

Ireland's first experience with heretics occurred in 1325, when Richard Lederede, the bishop of Ossory, armed with a decretal of Boniface VIII as his authority, introduced the Inquisition. The bishop discovered an arcane form of heresy, the blasphemous belief that demons have power attributable only to God. The criminals, who were reputed to be sorcerers or practitioners of witchcraft, confessed under torture, and the bishop had the satisfaction of burning some as heretics. The confusion in styling their crimes—heresy, blasphemy, sorcery—was enormous. So great was the secular opposition to the bishop, because of his methods and the fact that some of his victims were kinsmen of powerful chiefs, that he himself had to flee into exile to escape a countercharge of heresy. A more conventional case was that of Adam Duff O'Toole, who in 1327 was burned alive in Dublin as a heretic and blasphemer. He is supposed to have denied that the person of Jesus embodied the divine spirit, and he rejected the doctrine of the Trinity. He also made improper remarks about the mother of Jesus and called the stories in the Bible fables. O'Toole was possibly the first anti-Trinitarian in Ireland or in the British Isles to die for blasphemous heresy.[5]

Heresy as an organized movement did not exist in England until the late fourteenth century, the time of John Wycliffe and his followers, the Lollards. That name of contempt signified mumblers at prayers. Wycliffe was the pre-eminent English heretic before the Reformation. Although he meant to purify, not divide, the church, his teachings led to a sect that plagued it ever after. Wycliffe attacked the authority of the pope and the priesthood, repudiated auricular confession, and denied the doctrine of transubstantiation, according to which, by the teachings of the church, the bread and wine used in the holy communion literally became the body and blood of Christ. Wycliffe also advocated the translation of the Bible into English, on the theory that men, without the intervention of the clergy, should read and understand the holy book for themselves. Although he did not advocate freedom of conscience, he believed that the church should not have prisons to punish transgressors. In many respects, he anticipated fundamental Protestant convictions. His heresy was clear; the pope himself, Gregory XI, condemned him for "heretical pravity, tending to weaken and overthrow the status of the whole church, and even the secular government." According to the papal bull, William Courtney, archbishop of Canterbury, presided over an ecclesiastical convocation that enumerated all the damnable opinions of Wycliffe and his adherents. One of the beliefs ascribed to him without supporting proof, and of which he was doubtlessly innocent, was plainly blasphemous:

"That God ought to obey the devil." That he blasphemed Christ's vicar on earth was clear to the church, for he implied that the pope could be "a reprobate and evil man, and consequently a member of the devil," without power over the faithful of Christ. The prelates, faced with such heresies, called upon the secular authorities to assist in their extirpation; those heresies were infecting many Christians, causing them to depart from the faith, "without which there is no salvation." An earthquake, which occurred at that very time, proved to the heretics that divine judgment sided with them. Wycliffe, although hounded, had the support of a powerful duke, and so died peacefully in 1384. Forty years later, his remains were dug up on the orders of the church, his memory reviled, and his bones given to the flames.[6]

Wycliffe's followers paid the penalty of his heresies. England was a devoutly Catholic nation in an age that was convinced of the duty of the state to support the church's infallible judgments on spiritual matters. As a partner of the church, the state too was responsible for protecting the souls of its subjects against heresy. Its existence threatened eternal damnation for all who were victims of its contagion; as Archbishop Courtney declared, heresy could "destroy the tranquility of the realm," as well as subvert the church.[7] There was one fixed body of revealed and absolute truth. To permit deviations reflected doubt on the purity of the faith and the sincerity of the convictions of true believers. The sovereign must, therefore, obey the command of the church on matters of faith or be excommunicated as a heretic and have his people be absolved from their allegiance to him. The trouble, however, was that the hazy precedents on heresy in England showed no lawful authority for the prelates or the prince, acting separately or together, to order anyone burned for a religious crime.

Courtney and his bishops audaciously rose to the occasion; they forged a statute of Parliament providing that, on certification by the prelates, sheriffs should arrest and imprison heretics, holding them for "the law of the holy church." In 1383, the House of Commons asked the king to annul the law "never assented to nor granted by the Commons." By 1386, however, the spread of Lollardy at last provoked Parliament to outlaw heretical writings and make their teaching a crime, punishable by forfeiture of properties and imprisonment. The prelates, not satisfied, sought fuller cooperation from the state and, on the advice of Pope Urban VI, vainly asked for the death penalty. Meanwhile, Lollard leaders, especially at Oxford, the seat of Wycliffe's influence, suffered from the archbishop's inquisitions. Much later, John Foxe, the indefatigable Elizabethan martyrologist, complained that, although the church quickly condemned for heresy, "In times past [before the Lollards] it was not accounted as a heresy, except it did contain blasphemy, and did bring in some great peril to the faith, or where the majesty of Christ was hurt: such as were the Donatists, Manichees, Apollinarists, and Arians." But those heresies of the early church were no more blasphemous than the Lollards'.[8]

William Swinderby, the foremost Lollard priest in Lincoln, faced an accusation in 1391 of having preached "many heretical, erroneous, blasphemous, and other slanderous things contrary and repugnant to the . . . holy catholic church." Unfortunately, the charges against him did not distinguish which "things" were heretical and which blasphemous. Swinderby denied transubstantiation, claiming that Christ was only figuratively, not really, present in the sacrament of the altar. He described as the "very Antichrist" any doctrine, even if taught by a pope or a cardinal, that was against Christ's scriptural laws. He denied too that the pope had power to remit any man's sins, for only God could do that, and he claimed that the pope's assumption of such power "makes himself Christ, and blasphemeth in God as Lucifer did. . . ." When sentenced for heresy—the sentence always referred to the generic crime, "heretical pravity"—Swinderby appealed to king and council.

The king's courts, he claimed, were above those of the bishop; an ecclesiastical court could put no man in jail without a writ from the secular authority. Heresy, Swinderby conceded, was punishable by death, but not without justice from the king's courts. Christ's law, he reminded, bade us to love our enemies, whereas "the pope's law gives us leave to hate them and slay them." Denying that he was a heretic, Swinderby complained, in a remarkable confusion of concepts, that the sentence of excommunication against him, by damning him to hell, was "a foul heresy of blasphemy." So too John Purvey, a close associate of Wycliffe and the probable author of the Lollard Bible, accused Innocent III, "the head of Antichrist," of having "invented a new article of our faith," transubstantiation, which Purvey ridiculed and damned as "blasphemy" as well as heresy. Purvey recanted and was imprisoned. Swinderby, edified by the spectacle of dry wood being gathered for his burning, also recanted for "dred of death." Soon afterward, he relapsed into heresy, but when cited to appear for an inquisition he escaped to Wales.[9] The authority for his death sentence was so baseless as a matter of law that both church and state determined to resolve once and for all that the power to punish capitally for heresy was beyond dispute.

The case of William Sawtre, a parish priest, provided the occasion for legislation. Sawtre, having recanted his Lollard heresies and sworn to be faithful to the church, began preaching the very criminal doctrines he had renounced. Thomas Arundel, the archbishop of Canterbury, meant to make an example of Sawtre, who had not only flaunted his religious convictions but also mocked his inquisitors at his trial in 1401. Arundel condemned Sawtre as a relapsed heretic and committed him to the secular power for burning. The archbishop was aided in his policy by the accession to the throne of Henry IV, whose orthodoxy was beyond question. Henry made a tacit agreement with the prelates to persecute the Lollards in return for the church's support of his dubious claim to the throne. During Sawtre's trial, Parliament had been considering a bill, long urged by Arundel and his predecessor, that would make heresy a capital offense. Papal decrees and precedents notwithstanding, there was still no law in England that authorized the execution of heretics. Before Parliament could enact its bill, Henry IV hurriedly issued a writ that ingratiated him with the church. Proclaiming himself "a cherisher of the Catholic faith, willing to maintain and defend Holy Church . . . and to extirpate radically such heresies and error from our kingdom of England," the king commanded that Sawtre "be burnt in the flames, according to law divine and human, and the canonical institutes customary in that behalf." The writ was dated February 26, 1401; Sawtre was roasted alive on March 2, before Parliament passed its act. The king and the archbishop hurried to burn their victim to show that they could send a heretic to the stake whenever they wished, without relying on statute; Parliament could neither give nor take the authority to burn a heretic. If the scepter supported the miter, canon law prevailed.[10]

Parliament, far from objecting, assisted the church by belatedly passing the statute, De Haeretico Comburendo (On the Burning of Heretics), which neglected to define heresy because it was a canonical offense. Consequently, the ecclesiastical courts had a blank check to condemn as heresy anything they pleased. In addition, Parliament did not require the ecclesiastical courts to seek a royal writ for the execution of their judgment, as was the practice for other capital crimes; church authorities could arrest, imprison, try, and condemn as they pleased for the crime of heresy, and oblige the sheriff to execute the victim without further delay or formality. Burning was the mandatory sentence for an obstinate or relapsed heretic, "to the intent that this kind of punishment may strike a terror on the minds of others." An act of 1414 reinforced that of 1401 and extended the punishment to "lollardies."[11]

The church's victory in 1401 extended the Inquisition into England, although neither on the scale nor of the severity as on the continent. From 1401 to 1534, when Henry VIII ended Rome's spiritual supremacy in England, about fifty persons were burned as obstinate heretics. For every one who was burned, many recanted and suffered lesser penalties, which ranged from long sentences of imprisonment to a peculiar form of penance—carrying fagots, or firewood, to symbolize their deaths by burning. For every one who was punished, there were undoubtedly thousands who were put to an inquisition for their religious beliefs. The ecclesiastical courts functioned as accuser, prosecutor, judge, and jury; they met in secrecy and compelled self-incrimination. Between 1518 and 1521, in just the diocese of Lincoln, those courts convicted 342 people of the crime of "not thinking catholickly", five relapsed heretics were burned, forty-six were sentenced to life imprisonment, and the remainder were burdened with lesser forms of penance.

The extant records show that the crime of blasphemy almost disappeared without a trace, swallowed by the crime of heresy which it had spawned in the days of the apostolic church. That many of the heretics must have been accused of blasphemy is highly probable. In 1418, for example, a papal bull against the "sectaries and followers" of those "archheretics" John Wycliffe of England, John Huss of Bohemia, and Jerome of Prague declared that they "cease not to blaspheme the Lord God," yet the bull focused on the need to extirpate their "heretical pravity." Huss's case shows no charge of blasphemy, although in Jerome's there is an accusation that he taught heretical doctrines, "some being very blasphemous." Yet Jerome was burned for heresy, the generic crime that encompassed the more specific one of blasphemy. The two crimes were confusingly treated as the same offense and, indeed, overlapped. Transcripts of the trials hardly mention blasphemy. Early in the reign of Henry VI, a woman named Joan was accused of being "a diabolical blasphemeresse of God," but her blasphemy took the form of sorcery.[12]

Soon after, about 1432, Bishop William Lyndewood, the foremost expert on the canon law of England, finished his great compilation. He warned of the penalties for anyone who observed any sacrament "otherwise than it is found discussed by the Holy Mother the Church," or doubted anything decided by the church, or spoke "blasphemous words about the same," or engaged in any heresy. Lyndewood defined none of the crimes, nor did he distinguish them. Yet their seriousness is evident from his saying that, "though there be a certain likeness and equalness in divers laws between the crime of heresy and treason, nevertheless the offense is unlike, and it requireth greater punishment to offend the majesty of God than of man."[13]

The English reformation of religion began with the heresies of Wycliffe and the Lollards. The Henrician Reformation was chiefly political; the king substituted himself for the pope as the head of the church in England but was otherwise as orthodox as the pope. On matters of heresy, Henry VIII differed from other Catholic rulers of his time, if at all, only in his greater severity and intolerance. He meant to make himself undisputed sovereign of the English church as well as the state, and to that end encouraged measures that turned the people against the pope's supporters. He also welcomed to England antipapists from the continent if they were industrious subjects and supported the crown. They began to stream in, especially from Holland. Dutch Protestants saw England as a refuge from Spain, which ruled the Low Countries, and from the Spanish Inquisition.

In England under Henry, anyone who kept his mouth shut and attended the English church was tolerated, but not Protestants who wished to worship in their own way, and certainly not the proselytizing, anti-Catholic foreigners, whose bizarre notions about religion set them apart from most Christians. The unwanted were promiscuously denounced as Arians or Anabaptists, whose beliefs were said to blaspheme Christianity, but they were not an organized sect, nor deemed as dangerous as the Lollards seemed to have been in the early fifteenth century. On the other hand, Lollardy, although persecuted, still seethed among the lower classes and would become the seedbed of Puritanism; but, fragmented and undisciplined, it was hospitable to novelties like the alleged power of personal revelation over scriptural literalism, or the aspersions cast on the doctrine of the Trinity, or the claims that the bread and wine of the holy sacrament were no more than a remembrance of Christ's sacrifice, and that infant baptism was a practice of the Antichrist. These "blasphemies" and others were received with abhorrence by Henry's church, their carriers designated as heretics.[14]

As early as 1528, under Henry, the "Defender of the Faith," the church imprisoned seven Dutch "Anabaptists," a term of reproach which at that date could signify any antipapal Christian who differed from Luther. Two of the seven burned. There is no knowing whether they were anti-Trinitarians, who denied the divinity of Christ or his coessentiality with the Father, or were "Donatists new-dipped," who rejected certain sacraments, like infant baptism. The government issued edicts against "Anabaptists and Sacramentaries, being lately come into this realm," and warned against their heresies. But they kept coming, Rhinelanders and Dutchmen, who were said to dispute in taverns yet lurked in secret places, stirring the king's subjects to their opinions about baptism and the holy sacrament of the altar.[15] According to a sixteenth-century chronicler:

> The five and twentieth day of May, was in S. Paules church at London examined nineteen men and six women borne in Holland, whose opinions were: first, that in Christ is not two natures, God and man: secondly, that Christ tooke neither flesh nor blood of the Virgine Marie: thirdly, that children borne of infidels shall be saved: fourthly, that baptisme of children is to none effect: fiftly, that the sacrament of Christs bodie is but bread onely; sixtly, that he who after his baptisme sinneth wittingly, sinneth deadly, and cannot be saved. Fourteene of them were condemned, a man and a woman of them were burned in Smithfield, the other twelve were sent to other townes there to be bernt.[16]

Two more were burned in 1538, and others, who repented in time, bore fagots for their penance. At least half of the people burned as obstinate heretics under Henry VIII were "Anabaptists," reputed throughout Christendom to be the most despicable blasphemers. Their doctrines and reputations aside, the crime for which they died was heresy, or "blasphemous heresy." The name of the crime scarcely mattered. They died for their religion.[17]

The government made distinctions of a different sort. The king, having become supreme head of the English church, took any deviation from his new religious order as a threat to royal supremacy. Whether loyalty to the former "bishop of Rome" or conscientious belief in any of the deviant new Protestant doctrines, the expression of dissent blended heresy and treason into almost indistinguishable crimes. The government branded Protestant heterodoxy as seditious and traitorous, but only those who continued to support the authority of the pope went to a fiery death to avenge God's honor. The form of execution differed with the belief. The crime was essentially the same—disagreeing religiously with the king—but one offense was called treason, the other heresy.

Thomas Bilney, a London priest who prematurely became a Protestant—before Henry VIII did—was arrested on suspicion that he was a Lutheran. He "blasphemed most perniciously the immaculate flock of Christ, with certain blasphemies," "blasphemed the efficacy of the whole church," and affirmed, "blasphemously, that the bishop of Rome is the very Antichrist." Bilney repeated good Lutheran belief when he declared that papal "miracles" came from Satan rather than God, but his remark was taken as another blasphemy. He abjured and did penance, but two years later, in 1531, he openly preached all that he had renounced, and so died as a relapsed heretic.[18]

In that year, James Bainham, a lay scholar and lawyer, was prosecuted by the lord chancellor, Sir Thomas More, for the same offense as Bilney. Bainham too identified the pope as the "Antichrist." He also rejected transubstantiation as "idolatry to the bread," mocking the possibility that Christ "should dwell in a piece of bread," when he was sitting in heaven, on the right side of God. More had Bainham whipped, racked in the Tower of London, and kept in the stocks in irons for a fortnight before burning him, yet More does not seem to have multiplied the heinousness of Bainham's offense by calling it blasphemous. Although More verbally scourged Protestants in his writings, he thought "heresy" was sufficient as the word with which to condemn them. "Treason" was the word that Thomas Cromwell, More's prosecutor, later used to condemn More, although Cromwell conceded that the difference in the crime was the difference between beheading and burning.[19]

Elizabeth Barton, known as the nun of Kent, together with twenty-four coconspirators, also died for treason, in 1534, although the government denounced her for blasphemy as well. Under the pretense of a direct communion with God, she had trances during which she revealed prophecies, carefully schooled by a papal faction, inimical to the crown. If Henry VIII divorced Catherine of Aragon, the nun predicted, he would die the death of a villain. When the conspirators confessed their fraud, the nun's feigning a divine commission struck some of her judges as a blasphemous imposture, but the offense against the king's majesty took precedence over that against God's.[20] There was, however, no shortage of obstinate heretics. Fifty-one were burned between 1534, when Henry VIII began his reformation, and his death in 1547—as many as were burned in the whole period from 1401, the date of the statute De Haeretico Comburendo, to 1534. In that latter year, Parliament abrogated the act of 1401 and other laws connected with the bishop of Rome, but the king, as a matter of royal prerogative, authorized his sheriffs to issue the old writ for burning.[21]

The death of Henry VIII in 1547 passed the crown to his young son, Edward VI, and to the Protestant cause, although Thomas Cranmer, who had been an obedient archbishop of Canterbury since 1533, continued in office. In an age of unspeakable cruelty, the short period of Edward's sovereignty, 1547 to 1553, was notable for its comparative mildness. Religious persecution, which was taken for granted and even counted a duty on the part of believers of whatever persuasion, hardly existed by any comparison with the immediately preceding and succeeding reigns. Foxe, the anti-Catholic martyrologist, lightly skipped over the Edwardian burnings. "Briefly," he wrote, "during all this time, neither in Smithfield nor any other quarter of this realm, were any heard to suffer for any matter of religion, either papist or protestant, either for one opinion or another, except only two, one an Englishwoman, called Joan of Kent, and the other a Dutchman, named George, who died for certain articles not much necessary here to be rehearsed."[22] During the Marian burnings of the next reign, the Catholics delighted in citing those two cases as precedents that justified their roaring fires. A modern Catholic historian searching for evidence of real persecution under Edward discovered only the heresy provisions of a proposed canon-law revision that was never enacted, two burnings that he admitted would have occurred under Henry or Mary, and the plunder of Catholic properties.[23] He might have added that ecclesiastical inquisitions into religious belief slowed but did not abate.

One inquisition under Edward VI uncovered the remarkable heresy of John Assheton, a cleric. His views were even more repugnant than those of the execrated Arians, who accepted the eternal divinity of Christ, although assigning him an inferior station beneath God. The later Socinians, whose blasphemies were notorious, agreed that Christ was less than God but saw him as a human being whom God made divine. Assheton's anti-Trinitarianism was still more radical; he anticipated Unitarianism. Recognizing only one God and no divine persons, neither Christ nor the Holy Spirit, Assheton thought of Christ as a holy prophet, beloved of God, but only a man. Assheton was probably the first Englishman to be charged with such opinions. They were surely blasphemous, more so than Servetus's, but Assheton's timely recantation, saving him from the fire, referred only to "detestable errors, heresies, and abominable opinions." That clearly showed the demise of "blasphemy" as the legal designation of the crime.[24]

Joan Bocher, whom Foxe called Joan of Kent in his history of martyrs, was a "lady of quality" who was received at Edward's court. Archbishop Cranmer protected her for a while, but her opinion of the incarnation became too fantastic for him to tolerate. She denied the humanity of Christ by claiming that because his mother's own flesh "was sinfully begotten" he did not get his body from her but passed through her as light through a glass. Cranmer and his ecclesiastical commission condemned her as an obstinate heretic, but kept her in Newgate Prison for a year, mercifully hoping she would recant. She could not be persuaded to abandon her "Anabaptisicall opinion." Before her execution at Smithfield in 1550, she told the bishops that not long ago they had burned Anne Askew, her friend, "for a piece of bread"—that is, for denying transubstantiation—"and yet you came yourselves soon after to believe and profess the same doctrine for which you burned her. And now forsooth you will needs burn me for a piece of flesh. . . ." When Cranmer finally sought a writ for her execution, he argued from the Mosaic law that blasphemers must be stoned to death, and that this woman was guilty of capital impiety.[25]

Denying that a divine Christ could have been human was unusual; denying his divinity was not. That had been Assheton's heresy in 1548, and others shared it. Immigrants were thought to be responsible for its introduction into England. London in Edward's reign had about three thousand Protestant refugees, mostly from the Low Countries. The majority were Lutherans and Calvinists, but an alarming number were reputedly Arians—the word then common for any sort of anti-Trinitarians. In 1549, the discovery of an Arian manuscript led to the publication of the first book in English defending the faith from attacks on Christ's divinity; it was the beginning of a literary genre of works against anti-Trinitarianism. The author believed that Arianism was "rife," so many were the people who impiously held that Christ "is not true god, but a mere creature, a passable man only."[26] George van Parris, a Dutch physician who belonged to London's Church of Strangers (foreigners), held that view; his reverent beliefs notwithstanding, he scandalized his own congregation. The government ordered an inquisition; Archbishop Cranmer himself was in charge. Van Parris, who knew little English, defended himself through an interpreter, one of the bishops who accused him. Relying on his reading of the New Testament, Van Parris held that Christ was not divine and that calling the Father the only God could not be heresy. When informed that it was heresy, he stubbornly refused to retract. The king's journal includes the laconic entry, "In 1551, April 7. A certain Arian of the strangers, a Dutch Man, being excommunicated by the congregation of his country men, was, after long disputation, condemned to the fire." Van Parris's inquisitors, calling him "a child of the Devil," felt obliged to burn a foreign Arian as an example to others. Their victim's constancy to his faith and his devoutness to God awed those who had come to Smithfield to jeer.[27] No reference to blasphemy appears in the superficial accounts of the case. When Calvin burned Servetus for blasphemy two years later, he showed Protestants how to describe heresy in the most horrific way.

Mary's accession to the throne in 1553 ushered in a Catholic restoration and a persecution unique for its ferocity and extent, at least in England. A distinguished Catholic historian, Philip Hughes, declared:

> The facts are, that in the last four years of Mary's reign, between February 4, 1555 and November 10, 1558, something like 273 of her subjects were executed by burning, under laws which her government had revived, for the capital crime of obstinately adhering to beliefs that contradicted the teaching of the Catholic Church, of which Church they were all presumed to be members. In this respect alone, namely of so many executions for this particular offense in so short a time, the event is a thing apart, in English history; never before, nor ever since, was there anything at all quite like it.[28]

According to Hughes, the revulsion that one feels must be tempered by the understanding that the Marian period differed, in the main, only quantitatively. Heresy everywhere in Christendom was accounted the greatest crime. The foremost leaders of the Reformation—Luther, Zwingli, Calvin, Melanchthon, Beza, and Bullinger on the continent, and Cranmer, Knox, Latimer, Ridley, and Coverdale in England—believed that the failure to persecute betrayed God's true faith, the version they professed. In England, however, the Protestants under Edward burned only two people, both of whom were regarded as fanatical extremists. Even the Edwardian inquisitions were not directed against Catholics. Under Mary, in less time, the 273 included not only Arians and

Anabaptists, who by Hughes's count may have accounted for a maximum of 111 of the victims; the rest were Anglican Protestants, and among them were the leading bishops of the Edwardian reformation. As for the 111 supposed extremists, Hughes does not prove a single case, although undoubtedly there were some, including blasphemy cases.[29]

The case of the first victim, John Rogers, who had been the prebendary of St. Paul's Cathedral under Edward, is typical of the Marian persecutions. Rogers denounced the Church of Rome as "false and antichristian," and he denied the doctrine of transubstantiation. He was burned alive at Smithfield for "heretical pravity and execrable doctrine."[30] The "sentence definitive" from the pope for the condemnation of Thomas Cranmer, primate of England, was also restricted to heresy in accordance with conventional practice. But his trial began with the pope's representative announcing: "Thomas archbishop of Canterbury! appear herre and make answer to that shall be laid to thy charge; that is to say, for blasphemy, incontinency, and heresy." Cranmer, although denying the charges, threw them back at the Church of Rome. He even accused the pope of having "brought in gods of his own framing, and invented a new religion. . . . O Lord, whoever heard such blasphemy?" Cranmer's own blasphemy, as defined by his prosecutor, was his denial that, in the sacrament of the altar, "Christ's body is there really."[31] John Philpot, who had been archdeacon of Winchester under Edward, also denied the "real presence" of the body and blood of Christ during the sacrament, but in his case, as in many others, the crime was designated as heresy. The other charge against Philpot was that he had "blasphemously spoken against the sacrifice of the mass, calling it idolatry and abomination." In this case, at least, the distinction between blasphemy and heresy was that the former involved reviling, the latter only a denial. But this distinction held only for the statement of charges, because Philpot repeatedly, during the trial, reviled the Catholic view of the sacrament as blasphemous. Indeed, he defamed the Church of Rome more openly than Cranmer.[32] Several Protestant prisoners denounced their persecutors for blasphemy. They reviled Roman Catholicism and died for heresy.[33] Philpot was freer than most with his abuse. When he claimed to speak in the spirit of God, one of his inquisitors replied, "All heretics do boast of the Spirit of God, and every one would have a church by himself; as Joan of Kent and the Anabaptists." Philpot retorted, "As for Joan of Kent, she was a vain woman (I knew her well), and a heretic indeed, well worthy to be burnt. . . ."[34]

In prison, while awaiting his execution, Philpot had an argument with a fellow prisoner who declared that God was not in Christ. Philpot reacted by spitting in the man's face. On being criticized by one of his own church for conduct unbecoming a Christian, he wrote a tract explaining that he had spit for the honor of Christ, whom the other prisoner blasphemed. Philpot made his tract "an Invective against the Arians." They were the Antichrists "whom the Devil hath sh—— out in these days to defile the gospel." By robbing Christ of his "infinite majesty," the Arians were blasphemers who cut themselves off from Christian fellowship. Philpot reminded his readers of biblical examples of pious people tearing their garments to express grief on hearing blasphemy. So too he had spit to show his sorrow and to demonstrate to other prisoners who were present that a blasphemer is to be abhorred by all Christians. Philpot, who was more learned than most on the subject of blasphemy, was, not surprisingly, an admirer of Calvin, whose books he recommended to his inquisitors. When one of them replied with a criticism of Calvin, Philpot declared, "I am sure you blaspheme that godly man, and that godly church where he is minister; as it is your church's condition, when you cannot answer men by learning, to oppress them with blasphemies. . . ."[35] His inquisitors sentenced him as an obstinate heretic, as he might have sentenced them, given the chance; doubtless he would have aggravated the offense by adding the offense of blasphemy to it.

Elizabeth's accession to the throne in 1558 began an era of relative tolerance. Men like Philpot honeycombed the church, but reasons of state, not of church, prevailed. England had not embraced an official policy of toleration. That was still impossible in an age that could not conceive of a state without an established church to which all, without exception, must conform—if not for the greater glory of God, then for the greater security of the monarch, national independence, and public order. By subordinating religion to politics, Elizabeth's government quenched the fires of Smithfield. Treason against the state, not against God, was the crime for which nonconformists died under the Elizabethan establishment. The distinction, however nice, theoretically advanced the cause of toleration; and the government, in fact, repealed all the laws against heresy. It professed to abhor even the appearance of persecution for the cause of conscience. Yet the inquisitions continued against Catholics and Puritans as well as some Arians and Anabaptists, whom Catholics, Puritans, and Anglicans alike loathed murderously. But only Arians and Anabaptists suffered for their religion alone. All others suffered because their religion, in the eyes of the state, led them into political offenses. The church under Elizabeth was remarkably latitudinarian; it included men whose beliefs ranged from Catholicism to Calvinism. For over a decade, an astonishing variety of practices prevailed within the church, despite official disapproval, and when Parliament finally, in 1571, adopted a binding body of doctrine, the Thirty-nine Articles, the laws were not rigorously enforced. Some clergymen conducted authorized public services and then privately celebrated Mass. Catholic laymen, for the most part, attended the established church on Sundays and holy days, or paid the small fine for recusancy, and went to Mass in private. The government scarcely knew the names of recusants—and did not want to know them. All that was required, however much it injured Catholic or Puritan consciences, was an outward conformity. Although the openly contumacious put themselves in jeopardy, the law demanded only a *pro forma* obedience—not for spiritual reasons, but to sustain the political supremacy of the crown.[36]

In that state of affairs, heresy began to die as a capital crime in England. In fact, heresy as any erroneous doctrine of faith or any departure from a prescribed religion died with Mary. Under Elizabeth, heresy became what the vast majority of people regarded as so monstrous a contradiction of the cardinal principles of religion that the guilty party must be deemed anti-Christian and irreligious. He might profess a belief in God and appear pious and law-abiding, but if he denied the fundamentals of Christianity, he was a heretic. In effect, there was no such thing as a heretic under Elizabeth or ever after in English history unless blasphemy suffused his heresy, so aggravating it that most outraged Christians felt that the state had no choice but to rekindle the fires with fresh fagots. When that happened in Elizabethan England, the victim always was an accursed Arian or Anabaptist of the sort that provoked Philpot to spit on the blasphemer. The state saw such a person as a blasphemous heretic who had to be "cut off" from the flock of Christ lest he infect it with a contagion and sicken the realm.

John Knox, who introduced the Genevan system into Scotland, revealed the new-dawning Protestant understanding of heresy. He had read the work of an Anabaptist who relied on Castellio to reproach all religious persecution as un-Christian, and in particular to castigate the burnings of Joan of Kent and Servetus. The Anabaptist condemned the cruelty of all who affirmed "it to be lawfull to persecute and put to death such as dissent from them controversies of Religion, whome they cal blasphemers of God." He would say no more about such persecutors, the Anabaptist wrote, because God had already revenged the blood of the true martyrs by serving some of the persecutors "with the same measure where with they measured to others." To Knox, this aspersion on the memory of Cranmer, Ridley, and Latimer was "horrible blasphemie in the eares of the godlie." In 1560, he published *An answer to a great number of blasphemous cavillations written by an Anabaptist*. With Proverbs 17:15 as his text—"he that justifieth the wicked, and he that condemneth the innocent, are alike abominable before God"—Knox justified the persecution of blasphemers. One who had the lawful authority to kill, he reasoned, yet allowed a murderer to live, was a murderer. As with the murderer, so with the blasphemer. The Anabaptists justified Servetus, a blasphemer; "therefore ye are blasphemers before God, like abominable as he was."[37]

That blasphemers must be executed was clear from the Mosaic law. Blasphemy, Knox wrote, providing a complex definition that did not even refer to heresy, "is not onely to denie that there is a god, but that also it is lightly to esteme the power of the eternal God." Although distinguishing blasphemy from heresy, he defined blasphemy in a way that corresponded to the conventional definition of heresy. Blasphemy also consisted in spreading such opinions "as may make his Godhead to be doubted of" and departing from the religion of God "to the imagination of man's invention's," which was Knox's characterization of the Anabaptist doctrine of grace from inner light. Blasphemy, additionally, was the obstinate defense of "diabolicall opinions plainely repugning to God's truth; to judge those things which God judgeth necessary of our salvation, not to be necessarie; and finally, to persecute the trueth of God, and the members of Christes bodie."[38] On the final point alone, Knox and his Anabaptist adversary agreed, although they were as night and day on "the trueth of God." From both Old and New Testaments, Knox garnered examples to illustrate each category of blasphemy and then explained Servetus's guilt under each. Significantly, Knox found blasphemous only those opinions of Servetus, and of Joan, concerning "the Godhead."

> For what is more blasphemous, then to affirm that such as beleve in the Godhead three distinct Persons, have no true God, but the illusion of the Devilles: that Christ Jesus is not the Eternal Son of the Eternal Father: That there is no distinction betwixt the Father and the Sonne, but in imagination onely: that Christ hath no participation of man's nature, but that his flesh is from heaven; yes, that it is the flesh of the Godhead: That in stockes, stones, and all creatures, is the substantial Godhead?[39]

Drawing on bloody stories of the prophets' endorsing the murder of Baal and the children of Moloch, Knox defiantly justified persecution; "convict us if ye can by Scriptures," he demanded.

> We say [he concluded] the man is not persecuted for conscience, that, declining from God, blaspheming his Majestie, and contemning his religion, obstinately defendeth erroneous and fals doctrine. This man, I say, lawfully convicted, if he suffer the death pronounced by a lawful Magistrate, is not persecuted, (as in the name of Servetus ye furiously complain,) but he suffereth punishment

according to God's commandement, pronounced in Deuteron-
omie, the xiii. chapter.[40]

As blasphemy, the reviling of God, had ballooned into heresy and
nearly disappeared under the influence of the Roman Catholic definition
of heretical pravity, so, in Knox's thinking, heresy almost vanished as it
was absorbed into the definition of blasphemy that had emerged in the
days of the apostolic church. To differ on doctrine of a much later date,
such as transubstantiation, was no crime; to deny any aspect of the
Trinity, or any matter involving the Godhead, was blasphemous.

Elizabeth's church rejected the fierce Calvinism of Knox as well as his
zealous hatreds, but was influenced by his definition of blasphemy. Characteristically, compromise, the middle road between Catholicism and
Calvinism, was the Elizabethan response. Heresy became blasphemous
heresy, which was directed against the Godhead. Five times under Elizabeth, possibly a sixth time, and twice again under her successor, blasphemers were executed. The first two victims were foreigners, Dutch by
birth. They were among the thousands who fled from Spanish atrocities
in the Low Countries. Probably fifty thousand Dutch refugees sought
asylum in England during Elizabeth's reign. Most were Calvinists, but
some belonged to lesser Protestant sects and others to no recognized
communion at all. Among these were the Anabaptists and the Arians,
religious eccentrics who met in secret conventicles and lacked the organization of a sect, and also the Familists or members of the Family of
Love founded by Hendrik Niclaes (or Nicholas). In 1568, the queen
ordered an inquisition in London, which at that time had over five thousand Dutch refugees, to find any who held "heretical opinions, as the
Anabaptists do hold." Those detected were banished, but more refugees
took their places. In 1574, the government captured and banished another
batch of Anabaptists. A conventicle of Familists was discovered in the
same year; some publicly recanted and others were imprisoned.[41]

On Easter Sunday, 1575, the government uncovered an Anabaptist
meeting in a private home. Of the twenty-seven people arrested, eleven
were at first condemned to the flames. Terror tactics succeeded in bringing some to abjure. The form of recantation by which they renounced
their "Anabaptistical" errors gives us a glimpse of their beliefs. The first
was Joan of Kent's blasphemous heresy: Christ did not take flesh of the
Virgin Mary. The second was that infants should not be baptized. The
others were more in the nature of affronts to the state than to religion:
Christians should not serve as magistrates, bear arms, or swear oaths.
Those who would not recant were kept in prison, where one died. Ministers of the Flemish church in London and the queen's ecclesiastical
commissioners tried unsuccessfully to convert the prisoners. The queen

regarded the Anabaptists as atheists, opposed to all religion and government, but she and her council eventually consented to the banishment of the women, children, and those who had recanted, leaving five intransigents in the dungeons. Two of them, Jan Peeters, a wheelmaker, and Henry Turwert, a goldsmith, the leaders of the conventicle, proved to be so contumacious that the queen and her council would not spare them. Turwert wrote a petition for clemency, which was denied. It was a plea for toleration, based on the commandment "Thou shalt love the stranger as thyself," and on Jesus' teachings. Persecute none, Turwert wrote, "who have the one true gospel doctrine"; but the government thought his doctrine was worse than wrong. The writ De Haeretico Comburendo, which had not been used for seventeen years, directed the sheriff of London to burn the two men at Smithfield for their wicked, corrupting Anabaptist heresies, as an example to others.[42]

John Foxe, the martyrologist, whom Elizabeth favored, interceded in behalf of the condemned men. Pleading for their lives, he argued that to "roast the living bodies" of those who erred in judgment "is a hardhearted thing, and more agreeable to the practice of the Romanists, than the custom of the gospellers." Reminding the queen that she had punishments short of death, Foxe suggested imprisonment, banishment, burning just the hand, whipping, "or even slavery." "This one thing I most earnestly beg; that the piles and flames of Smithfield, so long ago extinguished by your happy government, may not be revived." Elizabeth, relentless, allowed only a month's reprieve to see if the two would recant. They did not. The queen said that her severity was necessary, because she had already executed men for treason, so, if she spared "these blasphemers, the world would condemn her, as being more in earnest in asserting her own safety than God's honour."[43] At the scene of the execution, an Anglican preacher told the crowd, "These people believe not in God," yet Peeters's reply was an orthodox confession of the Trinity. Turwert, in his petition, also embraced Christ and the Holy Ghost as divine. The wonder is that such reverent believers could have been so execrated. Bishop Edwin Sandys believed that the Anabaptists were "of no religion, of no church, godless and faithless people," yet their real offense, one is tempted to say, was, in Sandys's words, that they were people who "condemn all superiority, authority, and government in the church." Similarly, John Whitgift, the master of Trinity College, Cambridge, and later the archbishop of Canterbury, declared that, although the Anabaptists pretended the glory of God, "they assert, that the civil magistrate has no authority in causes of religion and faith, and that no man ought to be compelled to faith and religion." Their religion led them to treasonous opinions, but church and state saw them as blasphemers and burned them as heretics.[44]

Turwert proved to be right in arguing that the execution of a man for his religion would convince no one. The number of Anabaptists continued to swell. Their offshoot, the Familists, grew so numerous that by 1579 the Privy Council redoubled efforts to suppress them. Nicholas, the founder of the sect, was a disciple of David Georg, reputed to be one of the great Anabaptist heresiarchs. In his youth, Georg's tongue was bored with an awl, because he had blasphemed by publicly criticizing the church for idolatry. Georg fled from Münster to Amsterdam and then, under an alias, to Basel. He spent his last years there quietly, risking discovery only once, when he wrote a letter eloquently pleading for Servetus's life. The authorities discovered Georg's real identity soon after his death in 1556, dug up his corrupted body, and burned it with his writings as punishment for his blasphemous heresies. Nicholas, his follower, fled from Amsterdam to England, where he somehow escaped detection. His disciple, a Dutch carpenter named Christopher Vittel, had spent several years in prison for professing Arian doctrines, but on recanting was released. Vittel, who had a good knowledge of English, translated several of Nicholas's books, which had been written in German. The appearance of the translations, from 1574 to 1578, alarmed both state and church. In 1578 and the following year, several tracts appeared by orthodox writers who exposed the Familist connection with Georg and denounced Arian and Anabaptist principles, in livid language, as both heresy and blasphemy. The Familists supposedly denied both the doctrine of the Trinity and the divinity of Christ. Vittel's natural death in 1579 and Nicholas's in 1580 denied the government the chance of burning these leaders, but their books were burned. They had many followers, especially in the Norfolk area of East Anglia.[45]

Matthew Hammond (or Hammante), a plowmaker of Dutch origins who lived in a village near Norfolk, may have been a member of the Familists. The authorities, who did not know what to make of his religious convictions, also called him an Anabaptist or an Arian or an atheist, as if the names did not differ. Hammond was certainly no atheist, nor did he fit the other categories. Unlike the Anabaptists, he dismissed the need for baptism; and unlike the Arians, he repudiated not only the doctrine of the Trinity but Christ and the Holy Spirit as well. The little we know of Hammond—all of it from hostile sources—makes him seem something like a precursor of the deists. Whatever his sect, he was a religious man. William Burton, an Anglican minister who witnessed his execution, remarked:

> I have known some Arian heretiques, whose life hath beene most strict amongst men, whose tongues have beene tyred with scripture upon scripture, their knees even hardened in prayer, and their

faces wedded to saddnesse and their mouthes full of praires to God, while in the meanetime, they have stowtly denied the divinity of the Sonne of God. . . . Such were Hammond, Lewes and Cole heretikes of wretched memorie lately executed and cut off in Norwich.[46]

John Lewes and Peter Cole, artisans of the same locality, may have been members of the same Familist conventicle as Hammond. We know scarcely more than that they shared his religious views and, later, his fate.

Hammond first got into trouble for seditious and slanderous words against the queen. He probably came under suspicion as a foreigner, was questioned about his religious beliefs, and boldly claimed that they were not the queen's business. That led to an inquisition by Edmund Freake, the bishop of Norwich, acting for the Court of High Commission for Ecclesiastical Causes. Hammond openly professed the following convictions, each of which the bishop condemned as blasphemy and heresy:

That the new Testament and Gospell of Christ are but mere foolishness, a story of men, or rather a mere fable.

That man is restored to grace by the meere mercy of God, without the meane of Christ's blood, death and passion.

That Christ is not God, not the Saviour of the world, but a meere man, a sinfull man, and an abhominable Idoll.

That all they that worship him are abhominable idolaters; and that Christ did not rise againe from death to life by the power of his Godhead, neither, that he did ascend into heaven.

That the holy ghost is not God, neither, that there is any such holy ghost.

That baptisme is not necessary in the Church of Christ, neither the use of the Sacrament of the body & blood of Christ.[47]

The bishop, having found Hammond guilty, turned him over to the secular authority of Norwich. For his utterances against the queen and her council, Hammond was sentenced to stand in the pillory and have his ears cut off. For his denials of Christian beliefs, he was taken to a ditch and burned at the stake. That was in 1579. Lewes and Cole, who are also supposed to have denied Christ, were burned in the same ditch, the first in 1583, the latter in 1587.[48]

The case of Francis Kett, who suffered the same fate in 1589, was different. He was a native Englishman of good family and well educated. He had a Master of Arts degree from Corpus Christi College, Cambridge, and was elected a fellow in 1575. For at least ten years, his religious convictions were orthodox; he may even have served as an Anglican

minister. About 1586, he returned home to Norwich, where he underwent a conversion, perhaps under the influence of the Familists or from
reading the works of Hendrik Nicholas. The Reverend William Burton,
who regarded Kett as another Arian heretic, like Hammond, described
him as a "holy" man, "the sacred Bible almost never out of his hands,
himselfe alwayes in prayer," yet Burton found his opinions "more monstrous" than those of Hammond. That charge seems strange, since Kett
embraced rather than rejected Christ—but not a Christ who is God. Kett
mixed a mystical chiliasm with Unitarianism. Utterly rejecting the
Church of England and its authority, he believed that Jesus had suffered
only as a man for his sins, but had returned to Jerusalem as the high
priest, with his apostles, and was gathering the true church. He would
suffer again as Christ and then be without sin. No man could find salvation unless he was first baptized as a believing adult and visited Jerusalem before he died. Such preaching made Kett notorious in Norwich.[49]

In 1588, Edmund Scambler, Freake's successor as bishop of Norwich,
summoned Kett for an examination of his beliefs. Scambler condemned
Kett as a heretic whose "blasphemous opinions" merited an order from
the Privy Council that he be executed at once as a "dangerous" person.
The "Blasphemous Heresyes of One Kett" include the following charges,
of which he was found guilty:

> That the Holie Goste is not god, but an Holyspirite.
> That there is no such persone and that God is no person.
> That Christ is only man and synfull as other men are.
> That no Children ought to be baptized before their full age and to
> knowe what they should beleave.
> That no man ought to be put to death for heresies, but that the
> wheate and tares should both growe together.
> That no man as yeat doth preach the trewe Gospel of Christ.
> That he is even gatheringe his people togeyther at Jerusalem in his
> owne personne.[50]

Burton, who witnessed the execution in 1589, thought that Kett acted
like "a devil incarnate." He went to his death in the flames leaping and
dancing, clapping his hands, and blessing God, "and so continued until
the fire had consumed all his neather partes, and untill he was stifled with
the smoke."[51]

Kett was the last Protestant executed for his religious opinions during
the reign of Elizabeth. Like Hammond, Lewes, and Cole, he died for
heresies of a blasphemous nature. Many other Protestants, like those
implicated in the Marprelate Controversy, as well as scores of Catholics,
died for their religion in the late sixteenth century, but they were con-

victed because their religious beliefs made their political opinions trea-
sonable. Again, essentially secular considerations, rather than spiritual
ones, dictated Elizabethan policy. When nonconformity or recusancy
was unobtrusive and respectful, the government preferred, as the queen
herself reputedly said, to look the other way, rather than make windows
into men's souls and their secret thoughts. Those whom she burned for
their blasphemies were guilty of such heinous crimes, by sixteenth-
century standards, that they might have been burned almost anywhere in
Christendom. To believers, the denial of the divinity of Jesus seemed so
execrable an outrage that exceptions to a comparatively mild policy
seemed necessary to avenge God's honor. In general, the gallows of
Tyburn and the executioner's ax replaced the fires of Smithfield. They
would flare again for the last time in 1612, when James I executed two
more people for reasons of religion alone. The two last martyrs were, like
those of Elizabeth's time, radical Protestants whose crimes included the
blasphemous Unitarian heresy, refusal to regard Jesus as on a plane with
God.

The first of the two was Bartholomew Legate, a cloth merchant from
Essex whose business took him to Holland, where exposure to advanced
Unitarian thought turned him to religion. Convinced that there was no
true church to be found anywhere, Legate began preaching in London.
His views were similar to those of Francis David in his last years. Legate
believed that Jesus was "a meere man," not literally the son of God, yet
born free of sin because he was God's anointed one—that is, the Messiah.
Specifically rejecting the Nicene Creed, Legate argued that Jesus was not
divine in essence or substance; his office, rather, was divine, for through
it he represented God's righteousness and gave salvation. But there were
no persons in the Godhead. Thus, prayers must be directed only to the
one God. Legate explicitly repudiated the invocation of Christ. The
Church of England might tolerate a man of such "Arian" beliefs, as they
were inaccurately described, if he conducted himself quietly. But Legate
had a mission. His preaching denied the authority of the established
church and its doctrines. In effect, he forced himself on the attention of
the church.[52]

King James, a man of enormous conceits and considerable learning,
fancied himself to be a skilled dialectician and theologian. He told Parliament that kings were not only God's "lieutenants upon earth, and sit
upon god's throne, but even by God himselfe they are called Gods. For
if you will consider the attributes to God, you shall see how they agree
in the person of a King."[53] Nothing Legate believed was as blasphemous.
Since James's bishops obsequiously backed his assertions of divine right,
James, who had been a Presbyterian in Scotland, embraced Anglicanism
and took its enemies to be his. His favorite aphorism, "No Bishops, No

King," reflected his conviction that the fortunes of church and crown were the same. On hearing about Legate, James decided that he would personally convince him that his religion was founded on errors. He summoned Legate several times in 1611 and engaged him in debate, hoping to convert him. Although Legate apparently had never gone to college, he was "of bold spirit, confident carriage, fluent tongue, excellently skilled in the Scriptures." The king got nowhere with him. On one occasion, James, not realizing that his heretic opposed the invocation, tried to trick him into a tacit confession of the divinity of Jesus by asking whether Legate did not pray to him daily. When Legate replied that he used to pray out of "ignorance, but not for these last seven years," the king kicked at him in a fury and turned him over to the bishop of London for trial.[54]

The bishop too tried persuasion to exact from Legate a confession of his errors, but failed. The prisoner came to trial in 1612 before "many reverend bishops, able divines, and learned lawyers" at St. Paul's. Legate steadfastly held to his opinions, while denying that the church had any authority over him. The formal charge of heresy was based on thirteen "blasphemous opinions" advanced by Legate. They included his contentions that the Trinity was not a true Christian profession, that Christ was not God, and that he was not to be prayed to. Both the indictment and the sentence treated heresy and blasphemy as if they were synonymous. The sentence closed by describing him as a "blasphemous heretick."[55]

The king wanted Legate burned and ordered that a writ be issued authorizing the sheriff to execute the fiery sentence. Some of the common-law judges, however, doubted whether the old statute De Haeretico Comburendo was still in force and, even if it was, whether the consistory, the ecclesiastical body that tried Legate, properly had jurisdiction over him. Punctilious on the legal points in this case, James commanded the archbishop of Canterbury to tell the lord chancellor to appoint a commission of a few judges to settle the issues; the chancellor was to make certain that he appointed judges "who make no doubt that the law is cleere to burne them ['blasphemous heretikes']."[56] Legate was reduced to ashes at Smithfield before a huge crowd, "for the manifest example of other Christians, lest they slide into the same fault."[57]

Within a month, Edward Wightman of Burton-on-Trent was burned at Lichfield "for far worse opinions (if worse might be) than Legate maintained," as an Anglican minister said.[58] How Wightman came to his opinions, some of which were bizarre, is unknown. He had been a member of the established church, and as recently as two years before his trial his opinions were orthodox. Then, after questioning the doctrine of the Trinity and the sacrament of the Lord's Supper, he underwent a strange conversion from which he emerged with a religion that was, in part, a rational Unitarianism mixed with the equally rational tenet that only adult believers should be baptized; but he also thought that he was the prophet spoken of at different points in the Old Testament and that he was the Holy Ghost. He even claimed to be the Holy Ghost of whom Jesus spoke when saying that the one unpardonable and eternal sin was blasphemy against the Holy Ghost—attributing to the devil a miracle by Christ, or charging Christ with being the devil incarnate. To believers, Wightman blasphemed by claiming that he was himself of a divine nature. Wightman did not believe that the Holy Ghost was divine, but that surely was a distinction that James I and his episcopacy could not understand.[59]

Given Wightman's message, that he alone professed the only true Christianity, nothing but a maniacal zeal could explain his presentation to the king of a manuscript revealing his beliefs. The result was inevitable. James ordered that Wightman be imprisoned, and instructed Richard Neile, the bishop of his diocese, to examine him. Neile, assisted by numerous divines—including his chaplain, William Laud, the future archbishop—held many conferences with the prisoner "to make him see his blasphemous heresies, and to reclaime him." But, Neile later reported, Wightman "became every day more obstinate in his blasphemous heresies." On learning of his obstinacy, the king ordered the bishop to take his prisoner to Lichfield, where a consistory, the same kind of tribunal of divines that had tried Legate, should condemn him formally.[60]

The articles against Wightman charged him with holding that there is no Trinity, that Jesus was not the natural son of God and "of the same substance, eternity and majesty with the Father in respect of his Godhead," that Jesus was only a man, that the Holy Ghost was neither divine nor equal to the Father, that the Nicene Creed is un-Christian, that the Lord's Supper should not be a sacrament, and that infants should not be baptized. In addition, there were a series of charges relating to Wightman's belief that he was the Holy Ghost and the Comforter spoken of in John 16:7–8. Bishop Neile, who conducted the trial in the Lichfield Cathedral, decided not to pass sentence before giving the prisoner a final chance to recant. The bishop himself delivered a sermon confuting Wightman's blasphemy against the Trinity, with a different divine assigned to each of the other blasphemous points, so that collectively they covered the sixteen counts of blasphemy in the articles. "To all which," Neile reported, "He no way relenting, but p'sisting in his blasphemies, I read ye sentence against him to be a blasphemous heretique, and to be accordingly certified to ye secular power, whereupon his matie's [majesty's] writ was directed to ye sheriffe of ye county . . . to burn him as a heretique." The king's writ, commanding that Wightman be burned, at one place described him "as a blasphemous and condemned heretic," as if blasphemy were a form of heresy, and at another place condemned him for "heresies and other detestable blasphemies," as if heresy were a form of blasphemy.[61]

Neile's report of the case almost concludes with a respite from the gruesome end. As the flames began to burn Wightman, he cried out in pain that he would recant. "The people thereupon ran into the fire, and suffered themselves to be scorcht to save him." The authorities kept him chained to the stake until he signed a hastily framed recantation. They then escorted him back to prison. A couple of weeks later, the consistory court reconvened and required Wightman to make a proper recantation. He surprised them with his bold refusal. James, on being informed, commanded that the execution be carried out at once. On April 11, 1612, Wightman "died blaspheming," the last person in England to be executed for his religious beliefs.[62]

Not that England embarked on a new policy of toleration. Hardly. The seventeenth century witnessed Laud's persecutions of nonconformists, a civil war of religious character, and Presbyterian persecution of dissenter sects; in 1698, Parliament passed an act against blasphemy, and prosecutions under statute or common law continued for more than two centuries. The burnings ceased after 1612 in deference to the public reaction against them. A "Spanish Arian" condemned about the same time as Legate and Wightman was allowed to live out his remaining years in prison, because James did not wish to risk stirring up public sympathy for him by a burning. Besides facing the growing revulsion against the hideousness of the punishment, the government learned that it had little to gain from making martyrs. The people, being unable to distinguish between obstinacy and constancy of faith, "were ready," said Bishop Thomas Fuller, "to entertain good thought even of the opinions of those heretics, who sealed them so manfully with their blood." Consequently, James shrewdly preferred that "heretics hereafter, though condemned, should silently, and privately waste themselves away in the prison."[63]

The burning of Legate and Wightman ended an era during which English law showed a distinct movement from heresy to blasphemy. In 1553, when Geneva burned Servetus, Archbishop Cranmer proposed the first Protestant codification of the ecclesiastical law in England. It was the first, ever, to have a separate title on blasphemy.[64] The Calvinists, those zealous students of the Old Testament, were responsible for reviving blasphemy as a crime distinct from heresy. In Elizabethan England, where a middle way between Catholicism and Calvinism prevailed, blasphemy did not displace heresy; rather, it supplemented and modified it, giving rise to confusion in usage. Thus, we read of convictions for the simultaneous crimes of blasphemy and heresy, or for blasphemous heresy, or for heresy resulting from blasphemous opinions. The nomenclature of the crime was of slight importance compared with the character of the crime. The infliction of death was restricted to denials of "the God-head," generally speaking to some form of anti-Trinitarianism, as in the cases involving those called Arians, Anabaptists, or Familists; all were regarded as atheists. They did not deny the existence of God, but "athe-ism" at that time meant also denial of any person of the Trinity. About 1607, Sir Francis Bacon, who was more sophisticated than most of his contemporaries, wrote, "All that impugn a received religion, or super-stition, are, by the adverse part, branded with the name of atheists."[65] As late as 1632, Thomas Richardson, the lord chief justice of England, remarked, "I say they are Atheists that scoffe at religion in others."[66]

From the time of Elizabeth, however, the law did not inflict death merely for holding different Christian opinions, no matter how obsti-nately. One had to reject the divinity of Christ or some other principle equally fundamental. Sacramental differences, which led to the deaths of most of the Marian martyrs, were no longer capital offenses under Eliz-abeth and her successors. In a peculiar way, the renaissance of Old Testament studies in Protestant England assisted the cause of toleration: the Old Testament renewed interest in the crime of blasphemy yet re-stricted its application. If Elizabeth had emulated her father and sister by burning people for heresy, which was defined as any deviation from her church, multitudes of English Catholics and Protestants would have died for reasons other than political crimes against the crown. Elizabeth and James inflicted the ultimate penalty for crimes against religion only upon those regarded as loathsome by Catholics, Anglicans, and Puritans alike.

CHAPTER SEVEN

Socinian Anti-Trinitarians

PROSECUTIONS for blasphemous heresy or for any sort of erroneous religious opinions all but expired in England after 1612 and did not revive until the 1640s, when the Presbyterians rose to power. The burning of Legate and Wightman occurred when James I was passing through a phase of Calvinist righteousness. It soon subsided, and he became the most tolerant monarch England had known. James never abandoned his belief "that it is one of the principall parts of that deutie which appertaines unto a Christian King, to protect the trew church within his owne dominions, and to extirpate heresies," but he resorted to extirpation of anti-Trinitarians only when his very belated discovery of Arminianism in Holland provoked in him a rage for orthodoxy.[1]

England and Holland were allies, bound together by Protestantism, trade, and common enemies. Holland was England's doorway to an extraordinary diversity of reformationist currents from Calvinism to Socinianism. Dutch Protestants of every sect fled from Spanish tyrants to England. After the Dutch gained independence with England's aid, English nonconformists, persecuted at home, found refuge in the Netherlands. There were English churches in Holland, and Dutch churches in England. The cultural connections between the two countries were so close that, when the Arminians solidified their control of the endowed chair of divinity at the University of Leyden, the Dutch Calvinists turned to the Church of England for support, and James I presumed to interfere in the affairs of the Dutch church. The king had never heard of Jacobus Arminius, the pre-eminent leader of religious liberalism in Holland, until the excitement surrounding the appointment of his successor, Konrad van den Vorst. Vorst espoused the Arminian heresy of free will in opposition to the basic Calvinist doctrine of predestination.

James read Vorst's books and those of Arminius—and erupted. He denounced Arminius as "an arch Anabaptist," "a blasphemer," and "the enemy of God," reserving equally choice epithets for his successor at Leyden. The king burned Vorst's books as "monstrous blasphemie" and called his followers "Atheisticall Sectaries." Through his ambassador at the Hague, James presented a list of the Arminian blasphemies suckled by "the Disciples of Socinus." Graciously conceding that the professor need not be sent to the stake if he recanted his blasphemies, although none "ever deserved it better," James demanded Vorst's expulsion. The tolerant Dutch allowed him to retain his emoluments but moved him to a different university. The controversy occurred in 1611–12. By the end of James's reign, in 1625, the Arminian heresy had infected the Church of England, setting it on a collision course with Puritanism.[2]

James acted as God's avenger again on discovering the existence of the Racovian Catechism. The Latin edition of 1609, which Faustus Socinus and his Polish brethren wrote as an explanation of their faith, was dedicated to England's Protestant monarch. When the book came to his attention in 1614, he assailed it as "satanic," and Parliament ordered the public hangman to burn it. Socinianism—or Unitarianism, which it later became—was the seventeenth century's scapegoat for almost everything that Trinitarians deemed detestable in radical Protestantism.[3]

In the sixteenth century, Christians execrated Anabaptism; in the next century, Socinianism. The two were alike in some respects, yet very different in others. Both believed in the primacy of the Scriptures, but the Socinians professed to construe the Bible in the light of reason, whereas the Baptists, as one offshoot of the Anabaptists came to be known, preferred the guidance of an inner light derived from the promptings of God and private conscience. Notwithstanding their stress on reason, the early Socinians accepted a great deal of biblical supernaturalism, such as the virgin birth and miracles. The Baptists remained literalists in such matters, whereas the Socinians evolved in the direction of rationalism and eventually toward the abandonment of a formal creed. In the seventeenth century, however, the Socinians had as little in common with modern Unitarianism as the English Baptists with the Anabaptists of revolutionary Münster. The distinguishing tenet of Socinianism was anti-Trinitarianism, or rejection of the doctrine of the Trinity and the deity of Christ, on which the Baptists were orthodox Christians. Socinianism inconsistently emphasized both the humanity of Jesus and the divinity of his office, but distinguished divinity from deity. One God and no incarnation was the tenet, yet Socinians invoked Christ's name in prayer, as did the Baptists. Socinianism disavowed the Christian theory of atonement and the doctrine of original sin, which Baptism embraced.[4]

The distinguishing tenet of Baptism was that the church is a voluntary congregation of believers who signify their acceptance of Christ as Saviour by undergoing the rite of immersion. Socinianism agreed with Baptism on the sovereignty of private judgment and the voluntary character of church membership, but regarded baptism, whether of infants or of believing adults, as unnecessary for salvation. Both Socinianism and Baptism looked upon most sacraments as superfluous, the Lord's Supper as a mere commemorative service. Except for the Particular Baptists, a later faction that reconciled Calvinist theology with adult baptism, Baptists and Socinians rejected predestination in favor of free will. The most important tenet common to both was that religion is a private matter between the individual and God. Thus, no external authority, political or ecclesiastical, could impose a church or any beliefs upon a Christian; Christian liberty meant freedom to worship as one pleased. The Baptists were the only sect to advocate the free exercise of religion not only for themselves but for everybody, without exception. The Socinians shared the same principle, but in seventeenth-century England lacked organization as a sect. The Baptists were intensely evangelical, believing in the efficacy of individual efforts to achieve a state of grace and the promise of salvation. By the end of the seventeenth century, English Socinianism, which tended to avoid proselytizing, was still a movement, both within and outside the established church, rather than a separatistic group or church. The Socinianism of which James I read in the Racovian Catechism was, like early Baptism, pacifistic, against capital punishment, democratic in church organization, and utterly opposed to the interference of the state in matters of spiritual concern; unlike Baptism, Socinianism repudiated Christ as God.

The king hated Socinianism and Baptism alike, but he grew to distinguish one from the other. Always excepting those like Legate and Wightman, whom he did not regard as Christians, James understood that persecution could not create Christians or a body of unified church doctrine. Like Thomas Aquinas and Calvin, he declared that heresy was much more dangerous than a plague, by the same degree that the soul was more important than the body. Yet, his imprisonment of separatists notwithstanding, he gradually turned a blind eye and deaf ear toward all but the most aggressive and vociferous who insisted on worshipping outside his church. He preferred to believe that the Church of England would become national in fact as well as name by ignoring most differences within it. He hated the Puritans—not because of their theology, which for the most part he accepted, but because they insisted on exaggerating differences and demanded that their way be imposed on everybody else. James wanted as many Christians as possible to embrace his church. Believing that compulsion could control behavior but not conscience, he realized that he could force a subject to attend the established church or imprison him for attending another, but could not make him have faith in anything against his will. The sovereignty of church and state could not prevail over private judgment in matters of faith.[5]

James did not realize, however, that England already had such a diversity of religions that uniformity was a hopeless objective. The Cath-olics, whose suppression James wished to ameliorate for reasons of for-eign as well as domestic policy, were an unpopular but strong minority. Religion in England also included Arminians and Calvinists within the Protestant establishment, plus a bewildering variety of sects, some of which, like the Baptists, wanted to withdraw peaceably from the national church and form their own congregations, with permission if it was forthcoming, without it if necessary; others, like the Puritans, sought to control the national church and persecute any who differed. Sectarianism had become a permanent force in England, irreconcilable with the prin-ciple of one nation, one church. The government would not tolerate the separatists, because they seemed subversive: they rejected the king as head of their churches. They suffered harassment and imprisonment not because they endangered the souls of true believers, but because as non-conformists they challenged the royal prerogative. But James's persecu-tion, however harsh to its individual victims, was sporadic; it was certainly not systematic and suppressive.

As early as 1615, James and his archbishop of Canterbury, George Abbot, demonstrated their understanding that even a separatist, if he acknowledged Christ as his Saviour, was not a heretic. Bishop John Jegon of Norfolk, having captured a separatist named William Sayer, asked permission to burn him for denying Christ and the Holy Ghost. Abbot refused. He replied, in effect, that Sayer espoused Barrowist, Baptist, Brownist, and other separatist opinions, but he was not an Arian or an atheist deserving the stake. The moderates who controlled the government distinguished between those who agreed on fundamen-tals and those who did not. The godly, all of whom the Church of England claimed, included anyone who accepted Christ as the divine Son of God offering salvation. That included, by orthodox reckoning, all Christians except Arians and Socinians, deniers of the Trinity. This view of the matter allowed the separatists to exist, certainly not free to worship as they pleased with official toleration, but free to survive and grow.[6]

Thus, as early as 1611, Thomas Helwys, perhaps more with a spirit of martyrdom than with good sense, returned to England from his exile to Holland to bear witness to his Baptist convictions. Helwys established the first permanent Baptist church in England—and in London, no less. He sent King James a copy of his book, personally inscribed: "The King is a mortall man and not God, therefore hath no power over the immortall soules of his subjects to make lawes and ordinances for them to set spirituall Lords over them." That got Helwys a term in Newgate Prison, and John Murton, who took his place as the head of the congregation, followed him there. But Baptism won converts; by the close of James's reign, the first Baptist church in London had about 150 members, and there were several other Baptist churches in southeastern England.[7]

Helwys's book, *A Short Declaration of the Mistery of Iniquity* (1612), was the first work in England to claim religious liberty for all subjects. Castellio's *Concerning Heretics* (1554) and Acontius's *Satan's Stratagems* (1565) were Latin works that were later republished in various languages—including Dutch, which the early Baptists knew—but neither of those pathbreaking books on toleration existed in English during their time. Helwys presented their thesis in English. No state, he argued, had a lawful authority to force conscience or even to foster religion; church and state should be separated. Christ's domain must be protected from temporal authority, no matter how beneficent, because every individual is responsible to God for his own salvation. Erroneous opinions on religion were no concern of anyone, least of all the state and its established church, except the individual who held them. "For men's religion to God, is betwixt God and themselves; the king shall not answer for it, neither may the king be judge betweene God and man. Let them be heretikes, Turcks, Jewes, or whatsoever it apperteynes not to the earthly power to punish them in the least measure." Much as Helwys abhorred the Church of Rome, he made no exception to his principle: Catholics must be as free as any to worship as they pleased. Leonard Busher, a Baptist layman who wrote *Religion's Peace; or, A Plea for Liberty of Conscience* (1614), presented the same argument. Busher systematically summarized every reason that religious liberty was beneficial to believers and unbelievers, and to government and society as well as individuals.[8]

John Murton's *Objections Answered* (1615) also sought to prove that government had no jurisdiction in matters of religion. Murton stands out because he fully developed a point not adequately treated by Helwys and Busher. In opposing secular punishment of erroneous opinions, they advocated the "spiritual sword" of excommunication as the punishment of last resort for heretics. They did not address themselves to the problem of blasphemy. Nor had Acontius. Castellio's tolerance had withered when he faced the problem of blasphemy that took the form of atheism. Murton not only opposed secular punishment for heresy and blasphemy; he even questioned ecclesiastical punishments. He treated blasphemy as a special problem. It was the worst of all offenses against religion: the atheist merely denied God, whereas the blasphemer reviled Him, and the Old Testament explicitly prescribed death for the blasphemer. Murton believed, however, that Christ's law had abrogated the Mosaic law. Excommunication, like death, sent a condemned soul to hell. Accordingly, it was a punishment not rightfully available to ecclesiastical authority, any more than the temporal authority could rightfully imprison or harm a person for his religious beliefs. Christ taught gentleness and charity, reserving to himself the punishment even of those who blasphemed him or his Gospel. God's way, Murton believed, surpasses human understanding. We must, therefore, leave blasphemers to the mystery of His divine purpose. Moreover, every person, no matter how unregenerate, possessed within him the potential for grace. To expel anyone from the church shut him off from possible salvation. St. Paul himself had blasphemed before he discovered the light. Had he been cut off, God's purpose would have been thwarted. The Jews were "fearfull blasphemers of Christ and his Gospel," but by Christ's commandment were to be persuaded by the power of spiritual truths. So too all blasphemers. Later libertarians of the seventeenth century, such as Roger Williams and William Penn, sound derivative when compared with Helwys, Busher, and Murton.[9]

The early Baptist theorists were pathetically out of joint with their time. Persecution increased after the death of James I. His successor, Charles I, gave a free hand to the one formidable man in his government, William Laud, who, after the death of Abbot in 1633, became archbishop of Canterbury. Abbot had grown tolerant and neglectful with age. While Abbot lived, Laud, then bishop of London, was kept on a leash; after he died, Laud's repressive temper knew no restraints, and the Puritans felt its full severity. Under Laud, the Church of England was never more influential in molding government policy. He dominated the Privy Council, the Court of High Commission, and possibly the Court of Star Chamber; he even managed to get one of his bishops appointed lord treasurer. Although he tended toward Arminianism and rationalism in matters of theology, his interests in theology were perfunctory. He had no drive for certainty in religious truths and therefore lacked the theological bigotry and fanaticism of his Puritan antagonists. They could not conceive of more than one true religion, which they must force on everyone else; Laud could not conceive of anyone's being sure about the mysteries of divine truth.[10]

Although Laud knew he could not coerce uniformity of belief, he held that if all men worshipped in the same way, using the same words and ceremonies, a spirit of communion might unite them. Laud, like the Puritans, believed in uniformity, but he thought that it derived from external conformity. He was, above all, an obedient servant of the law, and it required uniformity of worship. Laud ruthlessly enforced its letter and spirit. He had resolution of purpose, incredible energy, and a sense of mission in exacting the last jot and tittle of obedience to the Book of Common Prayer and the Thirty-nine Articles of Faith. He could allow no exceptions, and so drove thousands of his countrymen out of the national church, many more to America, and others toward revolution. His enforcement of High Church Anglicanism had the unintended effect of causing people to think that Puritan nonconformity represented English Protestantism and national independence from Rome. To Laud's victims, most of whom were far more narrow and mean-spirited than he, he was dissolving the Reformation in England. His religious policies were unrepresentative of his church as well as his country. Yet he knew, rightly, that the Puritans matched his zeal; they meant, if given the chance, to remodel the national church in the image of Calvin's Geneva, destroying the episcopacy and derogating from the royal supremacy, whose obedient servant he was.

One difference between Laud and his Puritan victims was that he controlled the ecclesiastical powers of the government and mightily influenced the civil. Another difference was that the Puritans professed obedience to the letter of the Mosaic law. Laud was too enlightened and shrewd to prosecute for erroneous opinions, heretical or blasphemous. To have done so would have staggered public opinion, which knew that men who accepted the divinity of Christ could not be enemies of God or religion. Laud did not persecute for the high purpose of saving souls from contagion or preserving the purity of doctrine. He persecuted because the peace, order, and uniformity which he cherished derived from obedience to the law. The crimes of the dissenters, he believed, sprang from their willful opposition to the laws of church and state. Nonconformity was the crime, and nonconformity he meant to extirpate—because it was factious, not erroneous.

Thus, in the 1639 case of John Trendall, a Dover separatist who held conventicles in his home and rejected the national church, Neile, the archbishop of York, and members of the Privy Council considered whether he should be sent to the stake as a "blasphemous Heritique." Laud, however, would not burn him. Trendall's crime was nonconformity, not blasphemy, and his punishment was fine and imprisonment. The government severely treated nonconformists of every kind—Baptists, Brownists, Congregationalists, Familists, and Presbyterians—for reasons of state. They were, Laud knew, seditious people who, given the opportunity, would overthrow the established church and undermine the royal prerogative.[11]

Laud's engines of repression were the Court of Star Chamber and the Court of High Commission for Ecclesiastical Causes. The Star Chamber, although it was the judicial arm of the Privy Council, which could do as it pleased, deferred to the High Commission in cases of offenses against religion. In 1596, when the Star Chamber heard a case of "blasphemous heresy" arising from a man's statement "that Christ was no savioure and the gospell a fable," the court declined jurisdiction and turned the prisoner over to the prelates for punishment. In 1606, when considering the case of a person accused of a variety of misdemeanors, the Star Chamber heard evidence of his "great blasphemye"; he had declared that, if God came down from heaven and threatened him, he would not obey. The court took notice of the fact that its own jurisdiction did not extend to matters of religion, but sentenced the defendant to three years for his misdemeanors in order to punish his blasphemy. Vicar's case of 1631 was also unusual. The High Commission, in this instance, described a separatist's Calvinist doctrines as "hereticall blasphemous and scandalous," and then punished him for his "seditions." Generally, the Star Chamber had discretionary jurisdiction over any acts that it chose to regard as offenses, excepting treason and felonies. It could imprison, fine, and punish by mutilation short of dismembering a limb, but it could not inflict death, which was the sentence for treason and felonies; jurisdiction over those crimes belonged to the regular common-law courts.[12]

The common-law courts deferred to the High Commission in cases involving religious offenses. The law, as summarized by Sir Edward Coke, was that, "in causes ecclesiastical and spiritual, as namely blasphemy, apostasy from Christianity, heresies, schism and others (the conusance of whereof belongs not to the common laws of England,) the same are to be determined and decided by ecclesiastical Judges." In Attwood's case of 1617, however, the King's Bench, which was the highest common-law court on felonies and treason, took jurisdiction for the first time in a matter belonging to the ecclesiastical judges. Attwood had declared that the established religion was a recent innovation and that preaching was but prattling. The King's Bench sustained his conviction by the lower trial court, because his words were "seditious against the state of our Church and against the peace of the realm." Since the king was the head of the church, an attack on it was an attack on him as well as on the law establishing the church. Nonconformity and erroneous opinion could, therefore, be converted into sedition, either in the common-law courts or in the Star Chamber, whenever the judges of either were so minded. Normally, however, offenses against religion belonged to the High Commission.[13]

That court, which emerged by royal authority in Elizabeth's time, had jurisdiction over violations of any statute enacted on the subject of religion, of all cases within the cognizance of ecclesiastical law, and of cases dealing with religious errors, recusancies, schism, and any preaching contrary to the Book of Common Prayer and the Thirty-nine Articles defining the Anglican establishment. In addition, the High Commission shared jurisdiction of cases on seditious utterances, conspiracies, and contempts. The High Commission was a formidable prerogative court, not only because its authority was so broad and it operated throughout the realm, but also because it employed inquisitorial procedures and had an array of effective punishments. Although it could not torture, it could force a party to incriminate himself or find him guilty as charged if he refused; it acted as his accuser, prosecutor, judge, and jury. Its powers of search and seizure, like those of the Star Chamber, were unfettered, and it could fine and imprison for indefinite terms. The High Commission also exercised powers of censorship, granted by the Star Chamber, against all heretical, schismatical, and seditious works, offensive to state or church, and against any works published without prior license. When the Star Chamber prosecuted a clergyman, it first turned him over to the High Commission to depose him from the ministry; the Star Chamber, in turn, inflicted gory physical punishments for the High Commission. In theory, an ecclesiastical court should not shed blood. The Star Chamber and High Commission operated in such close collaboration, especially under Laud, that the two became indistinguishable to the public.[14]

When Laud was archbishop of Canterbury, the High Commission decided no cases of blasphemy. He preferred, for reasons of expediency, to prosecute on other charges. Under his lax predecessor, the High Commission had only one blasphemy case, in 1631. Richard Lane, a tailor, stood accused of blasphemy, wholly apart from heresy, because he supposedly claimed divine attributes. Laud, then bishop of London, menacingly said to Lane, "I hear you are a high Familist, and you hold it very lawful to equivocate. Did you not say you were as Christ was God and man?" The prisoner explained that he thought Christ dwelt in every believer; God, through Christ, accepted him as perfect. Archbishop Abbot replied that, if Lane did not fall to his knees and ask forgiveness for his blasphemy, he would receive a sentence that would make him an "example to all the world." Laud thought Abbot was too lenient in allowing Lane to escape by offering him a chance at repentance. Laud preferred the "*ultimam poenam*," the ultimate punishment, but if Lane tasted the severest discipline of Bridewell Prison until the last day of the court's term, he could then make his submission. The High Commission agreed. As Abbot's successor, Laud arranged that the charges against dissenters should be brought for nonconformity and seditiousness.[15]

The cases of Bastwick, Burton, and Prynne demonstrate how Laud treated his enemies and gained the odium of the populace. Dr. John Bastwick, a Puritan physician; the Reverend Henry Burton, a Puritan preacher; and William Prynne, a Puritan lawyer, were tried together in 1637 for seditious libel. Each of the defendants had committed the crime by publishing vitriolic attacks against Laud, his prelates, and the established church. Bastwick and Prynne were violent extremists who would have inflicted death for heresy and blasphemy not only on Anglicans and Catholics but even on Baptists and the independent Puritan sects that opposed a Presbyterian establishment. Burton would have exempted the Calvinist sects from the ultimate penalty. Both Bastwick and Burton had

composed their seditious tracts while in prison under sentence from the
High Commission. Prynne also had a conviction record. The Star Chamber had punished him in 1633 by disbarring him, exorbitantly fining
him, and ordering the hangman to hack off his ears. In 1637, the Star
Chamber pronounced the three Puritans guilty of the offense charged
and imposed a punishment meant to terrify others who might repeat
their offenses. They were fined £5,000 each and sentenced to life imprisonment in distant fortresses, and the hangman cut off their ears.
Prynne had already suffered that grisly punishment, but the court
discovered that he had stumps which could be severed—and they were.
The hangman also branded Prynne's cheeks with the letters "S.L."
for "seditious libeler"—"*stigmata Laudis*," the scars of Laud, Prynne
said. When he had been mutilated in 1633, few people had cared. By 1637,
Laud's policies had created popular sympathy for his victims. Hundreds
watched their bloody torment and, with tears and cries, shared the
religious ecstasy of their martyrdom.[16]

Three years later, the country was on the edge of rebellion. The Short
Parliament, the first in eleven years, dissolved after three weeks, having
achieved nothing; the king refused to redress grievances, without which
the House of Commons refused their approval of new revenue measures.
Laud's attempt to force Anglicanism on Presbyterian Scotland had led to
war with the Scots, and riotous crowds in London cheered Presbyterian
victories as their own. Laud convened a synod that adopted new canons
for the church, reinforcing his policy of uniformity. One canon, taking
aim at "the spreading of the damnable and cursed Heresie of Socinianism," sought to curb its "blasphemous errours" by strengthening censorship decrees. Another canon, directed against "Sectaries," described
Baptists, Brownists, and Familists as destroyers of the church. Late in
1640, a mob of "2000 Brownists," as Laud called the separatistic Calvinists, tore apart the High Commission's courtroom as one of their number
was about to be sentenced. The Privy Council was afraid to prosecute the
ringleaders, and a grand jury refused to indict them. The government
was breaking down. When the Long Parliament met in November 1640,
the Puritans dominated it. They repudiated Laud's recent canons, emp-
tied the jails of dissenters, imprisoned the archbishop himself and executed him in 1645, and abolished the Star Chamber and the High
Commission. By the summer of 1642, the civil war between royalist and
parliamentary forces had begun.[17]

A majority of the House of Commons favored Presbyterianism. They
had the strength to destroy the episcopacy and suppress Catholicism
within the area controlled by their armies, but they could not muster a
majority to establish their own religion. They disagreed among themselves on the question of whether Parliament or the presbyters should

control the new church. The politicians, who championed their own prerogatives against the ministry, realized too that a narrow establishment could lead to their own overthrow: the hodgepodge of dissenting sects that had mushroomed within the Puritan movement made up the rank and file of the army. The sects feared any uniformity of religion; their dedication to the principle of congregational independency made them gravitate toward the Baptist position of separation of church and state.

Thwarted in their foremost aim to make Presbyterianism a lawfully established system of exclusive, infallible truths, the emulators of Geneva vented their suppressionist tendencies in books and tracts. Francis Cheynell's *The Rise, Growth, and Danger of Socinianism* (1643) regarded the case for persecution as unanswerable. The author was able to discover Socinianism in any opinion the least different from Presbyterianism. Adam Steuart conceded that persecution could not alter religious beliefs but pressed the obligation of the state to ensure that God's name and honor were not outraged by heretics and blasphemers. The magistrate could "cut away an ill tongue," even if an ill-will could not be prevented. Error must perish or the godly would be exposed to its infection. "God in the Old Testament granted no toleration of divers religions, or disciplines." Because the New Testament established a much holier covenant, it required a firmer union among Christians than the Old Testament did among the Jews. Ephraim Pagitt's *Heresiography* (1645), demanding death for blasphemous opinions, reasoned that, if a man should be executed for poisoning drinking water, death was all the more necessary for those who "poyson mens soules." He was speaking not just of Socinians but of the congregationalist sects as well. John Bastwick, one of Laud's martyrs, who had returned to London from his distant prison amid the roars of an approving crowd, also recommended persecution for any who disagreed with Presbyterianism. The Bible, Bastwick argued, expressly prohibited toleration; God himself demanded death for "atheism, blasphemy, profanation of the Sabbath, and all manner of impiety and toleration of all religions." That many of the sects who opposed God's true church professed Calvinist doctrine only veiled the dangers of their heresies. Thus, the Presbyterians, knowing that there could be no prosecutions for nonconformity when there was no established religion with which to conform, sought to revive prosecutions for erroneous opinions.[18]

Presbyterian threats alarmed the sects, but they had the army's protection—indeed, they were the army, in a large sense. Socinianism, however, was vulnerable. Socinian books were being imported into England; their importers and disseminators had been the target of Laud's abortive canon of 1640. Parliament's rejection of it did not reflect sympathy for Socinians. The House of Commons had rejected the anti-Socinian canon only because, by its failure to define Socinianism, it allowed the prelates to decide who was guilty of it: Parliament reserved that decision to itself. Having removed the prelates, it was free to punish advocates of that "most vile and damned heresy." In 1645, both houses of Parliament condemned John Archer's *Comfort for Believers*, a treatise whose thesis was that true believers, although weak in faith, "should not be opprest, or perplext in heart." Both houses agreed that the book was "blasphemous Heresy." There being no way to reach its author, a London preacher who had recently died, Parliament had to content itself with a search for its printers and an order to the common hangman to burn copies of the book at various places in London, with ministers present "to declare to the People the Abominableness of it."[19]

The imprisonment of Paul Best in 1645 was the first blasphemy case in many years, and the first of many during the Puritan hegemony. Best, a man of mettlesome intellect and spirit, was the first Englishman to write a Socinian work, although he had to smuggle the manuscript out of prison to get it published—and Parliament summarily ordered that the hangman burn it in public. A country gentleman educated in theology at Cambridge, he had money enough to indulge his intellectual interests. For over a decade, he had traveled on the continent, searching out people and books that exposed him to new religious ideas. No Englishman before him had studied Socinianism firsthand in Poland and Transylvania, its places of origin. On his return to England, Best, who had had experience as a soldier abroad, joined the parliamentary army. He also began writing on the subject of religion. Renewing an old friendship with his former roommate at Jesus College, Cambridge, Best showed him a manuscript on the doctrine of the Trinity and some Socinian books imported from abroad. The former roommate, who had become a Puritan minister, was horrified by what he read and reported Best to the military authorities. In early 1645, Best was in prison, probably in York. He soon became notorious.[20]

The ministers of York complained about Best's "blasphemous opinions" to the Westminster Assembly of Divines. That body, a ministerial group established by Parliament in 1643 to recommend and supervise a new religious settlement for England, determined to make a test case of Paul Best. The Presbyterians, who dominated the Westminster Assembly, admired the Scottish church as a model of ecclesiastical organization and discipline. They abhorred sects, of course, and saw in religious diversity a threat to the success of their objective, the imposition of Presbyterianism on all England. People like Best stood in their way. If they could make an example of him, they might snuff out the rising demand by the autonomous congregationalists for a policy of toleration. Best was proof, to the Presbyterians, that toleration led to defilement of the true church, opened the door to soul murder, and resulted in schism, satanism, and sedition. Lord Fairfax, in whose army Best had served, sent him to London for interrogation by the Westminster Assembly. Its committee examined his books and writings and recorded his replies to its interrogatories.[21]

On June 10, 1645, the Westminster Assembly, "vindicating the honour of God and of Jesus Christ," condemned Best's "horrid blasphemies" and demanded the speedy suppression of the "liberty of all opinions and religions, under the pretence of liberty of conscience, maintained in books and otherwise . . . which hath been the occasion of those and the like blasphemous opinions." On the same day, the entire assembly appeared before the House of Commons to press their case. They accused Best of blasphemies "against the Deity of our Saviour, Jesus Christ, and of the Holy Ghost," produced their evidence, and requested Parliament to execute "condign punishment" on so terrible an offender. The Commons, promising condign punishment, turned the matter over to a committee to investigate Best's blasphemies. The committee was enjoined not to "meddle with any other Business, until they have dispatched this," and to bring its recommendations to the house "with all Speed." The matter was much too complex to be settled speedily, though, and Best remained a close prisoner, not permitted to speak to anyone except members of the committee. Despite the naggings and promptings of the Westminster Assembly, which complained that Best still vented his "blasphemous heresies," the committee did not report till seven months had passed.[22]

An unprecedented legal predicament explained the delay, and also the reason that the House of Commons in September added lawyers to the committee in charge of Best's case. When the committee reported at the end of January 1646, its chairman told the House that Best was guilty, yet the law did not provide for his punishment. The man continued pertinacious in his opinions. He denied the Trinity, rejected the deity of Christ and of the Holy Ghost, and engaged in "several other monstrous and unheard-of Blasphemies." In "former Ages," the punishment was clear; the chairman reminded the House of the fate of Bartholomew Legate. But in those times the jurisdiction over offenses against religion had belonged to the ecclesiastical courts. Parliament, however, had abolished them all in 1641, when it demolished the Laudian system. Thus, "the former Course of Proceeding against Hereticks is, by the Taking away of the Power of Ecclesiastical Courts, defective," leaving no way of punishing the crimes of a man like Best. No statute reached him, and the common-law courts had always denied that their jurisdiction extended to such matters. The committee lamely asked Parliament for guidance. The House of Commons ordered that Best be kept under close restraint and resolved that an ordinance be framed "for punishing with Death Paul

Best, for his abominable, prodigious, horrid Blasphemies." The course of procedure, at least at that stage, was to be a bill of attainder: Parliament would outlaw the crime, apply its statute retroactively to Best, and then conduct the trial against him in order to provide a semblance of due process of law. To work out the details, the Commons augmented its committee by adding "all the Lawyers of the House." They were to report in one week.[23]

They did not report, however, for two months, and still the proceedings foundered. A bill was introduced demanding Best's death by hanging for his denials of the Trinity and of the deity of Christ and the Holy Ghost, and for other "execrable Blasphemies, not fit to be named," but the bill was merely read twice—not thrice and enacted—"and nothing more done at this Time." Uncertainty is evident from the fact that the House of Commons also voted to examine Best and at the same time deputized a committee of ministers to visit him in jail "to make him sensible of his Errors." He remained obdurate.[24]

On April 4, 1646, Best's jailer brought him to the House of Commons. It was the day appointed for his trial, but they condemned him first and tried him next. The chairman of the committee which had been deliberating his case for nearly a year read the charges "proved against him," and then Best got his chance to speak. Adroitly defending himself, he claimed to acknowledge the Holy Trinity, by which he hoped to be saved. He had simply denied "the Tripersonality of Athanasius" (who in the fourth century contended against Arianism), which he denounced as "Popish," and he would hold to his opinion unless otherwise convinced. Most members of the Puritan House, who opposed anything "Popish," knew little about ancient heresies. Best baffled them, even after he conceded that he did deny that Jesus Christ "is co-equal, co-eternal, and co-existent, with the Godhead of the Father." After the House sent him back to jail, the members indecisively resolved to deliberate "what shall be done with him." Not knowing, they appointed a new committee to bring in a recommendation. At least two of its five members opposed Presbyterianism, and one of them, Sir Henry Vane, had argued "for a full libertie of conscience to all religions." Five members of the Westminster Assembly were commissioned to assist, if need be. Although they included two Presbyterians who believed that blasphemy merited death, another member was the foremost Independent leader in the assembly, Thomas Goodwin, who could not tolerate intolerance.[25]

The reason for the inconclusive deliberations on Best is that he had become a pawn on a chessboard in a match between those who sought a uniformity of religion and those who saw in uniformity a threat to themselves. The religious situation in England had swiftly changed during the 1640s. Once the Puritans pulled down the Church of England under

Laud, the persecutions, which had kept them fraternal, ended, and they split apart. As a minister who supported the Presbyterians complained, "Every one that listeth turneth preacher, as shoo-makers, coblers, button-makers, hostlers and such like, take upon them to expound the holy scriptures, intrude into our pulpits, and vent strange doctrine, tending to faction, sedition and blasphemie." Sectarianism had rampantly spread throughout the country and in the army and Parliament as well. Although the Presbyterians had gained the upper hand by the middle of the decade, they were not strong enough to impose their will on all the other Protestant sects. By one Presbyterian count, the sects had multiplied from three to forty within a couple of years. Collectively, they were known as the Independents, because they insisted on their own tenets, congregations, and governance. All shared some Calvinist beliefs, but they differed among themselves. Only a common dread of Genevan rigidity held them together, and of necessity they rallied around the principle of toleration of religion for all but the Catholics, Socinians, and atheists. Cromwell supported the Independents. After his victory at Naseby, he wrote a famous letter to the speaker of the House of Commons, demanding liberty of conscience to anyone who served in Parliament's army against the king. When choosing men to serve, said the general, the state took no notice of their opinions.[26]

To the Presbyterians, if Best, a "blasphemer," could not be convicted, no one could. The Presbyterian author of *Hell Broke Loose* complained that Best was a source for the opinion that the doctrine of the Trinity was "a mystery of Iniquity," and Thomas Edwards, that fierce Calvinist, singled Best out as the man responsible for numerous other blasphemies. Edwards's huge and abusive book, *Gangraena*, purported to be a "catalogue and discovery of many of the errours, heresies, blasphemies and pernicious practices of the sectaries of this time." The prevailing toleration, he complained, was Satan's work, resulting in innumerable sects and no fewer than 176 heresies and blasphemies, about twenty-five of which were of the worst kind, Arian or Socinian. As the recorder of the Westminster Assembly lamented, while blasphemous heresies spread in England with unprecedented velocity and variety, the army and the Independents had become "pleaders for liberties almost to them all." Even the House of Commons, the greatest pulpit in England, invited Independents to preach before it. For the time being, the best the Presbyterians could do was to keep Best imprisoned; the chessboard was in a position of stalemate.[27]

Intermittently through 1646, the House of Commons fretted about its prisoner, examined him, returned him to jail, and failed to reach a decision. That he had influential supporters is evident from the fact that he was able to publish a brief tract addressed to the Westminster Assembly.

Someone who had access to the closely guarded prisoner supplied the pen, ink, and paper, and arranged for the printing. In his tract, Best cleverly argued against the death penalty: only a live heretic could repent, and "Paul Best (what-ever his errours be at present), as well as Paul the Apostle, once a blasphemer, may one day become a convert." He also wrote a petition to Parliament, which he managed to get published, requesting that he be given a speedy judgment or be set free. Parliament resolved at the end of 1646 to fix the death penalty for anyone tried and convicted "by the judges of the land" for the crime of saying anything against "the attributes of God." The ambiguity of this purported condemnation of atheism showed the continuance of the stalemate; the reference to a regular judicial trial showed that the House of Commons had abandoned its attainder procedure. Meanwhile, the committee in charge of Best's case complained that he had access to pen and ink, and his jailer had to answer for that.[28]

Notwithstanding security procedures, Best somehow published a little book, *Mysteries Discovered*, which did not reveal the mystery of how he did it. That was in mid-1647. He did, however, take note of the fact that over one hundred petitions in his behalf had been sent to Parliament. Although Parliament was debating passage of a bill to punish blasphemy, the army submitted proposals that would have guaranteed religious liberty to all but Catholics. Important people openly supported Best. John Selden, the foremost legal scholar and parliamentarian of the age, reportedly said, on hearing Best, "that he was a better man than he understood himself to be." Another eminent member thought that Best showed himself to be a moderate man willing to reason. Outside of Parliament, the Levellers, who were the first group in modern history to battle for libertarianism and democracy, opposed all coercion of conscience. William Walwyn, one of the Leveller leaders, answered the Presbyterians by saying that, if they could not convince Best's conscience, they should not punish his person. Edwards, the Presbyterian leader who collected such remarks in his *Gangraena* as evidence of blasphemy, also reported that John Goodwin spoke on behalf of Best. Goodwin, one of the leading Independent ministers, reputedly demanded "a full liberty of conscience to all sects, even Turks, Jews, Papists." He claimed that Best's imprisonment did "no good at all," and that no force should be used against him, "even should he gather a church and vent Arian opinions."[29]

Despite the gathering support for Best and for toleration, Best's illicit book was a challenge Parliament could not ignore. The Presbyterians, still the majority party, were enraged by his open Socinianism. He subordinated Christ to God, condemned the Nicene multiplication of the Deity, and even claimed that to detract from its Unity was "blasphemy." Acknowledging the Father to be God "essentially," the Son "vicentially," and the Holy Spirit "potentially," Best argued that "to make Christ coequall to his Father, is to make another or false Christ, or . . . an Idoll Christ, or two Gods." To regard Christ as both God and man, Best believed, conflicted with both "reason and Scripture." His reliance on "reason" was characteristically Socinian. Refusing to make the "creature" equal to the Creator, he rejected the Nicene Creed as a "semi-Pagan" innovation of ancient times "made Catholike by Imperial decree." Real blasphemy, which he compared to treason, consisted in multiplying the Deity or detracting from His Unity. Arius, Best contended, had a much better understanding of Christianity than Athanasius. Best also argued that the experience of Holland and Poland showed that toleration was beneficial, and he showed esoteric learning when he described the 1560s in Transylvania, Lithuania, and Poland as a "reformation of the Reformation" and a time of liberty.[30]

The House of Commons condemned Best's work as blasphemous and ordered that copies be "burnt by the Hands of the common Hangman" on three separate days at different points in London. An inquiry to determine "by what Means this blasphemous Pamphlet came forth" got nowhere. Best himself suffered no additional punishment. The last reference to him in the House of Commons was in September, when his case was joined with that of a man named Biddle. John Biddle would become "the father of the English Unitarians," and his "blasphemies" troubled England for many years. Best, however, simply faded out of the picture. Sometime before the close of 1647, he was quietly released. Cromwell is supposed to have been influential in securing his liberty. In all likelihood, Best had to promise never again to publish his religious opinions. He retired to his estate in Yorkshire, where, unmolested, he wrote voluminously about religion until he died ten years later, leaving many manuscripts. He had no disciples, although he probably influenced Biddle.[31]

Biddle too was a lone intellectual. Although he had a congregation for a short time during the few years he was left at liberty, he did not found a church or lead a sectarian movement. He was very much the creation of his persecutors. His enduring reputation as "a very conspicuous Heresiarch," a characterization that follows the judgment of his contemporaries, seems unmerited. His martyrdom more than his own contributions to Unitarianism accounts for that reputation. Although his publications attracted attention even on the continent, he owed far more to the continental Socinians, whose writings he introduced to English readers, than he gave in return. His own writings were remarkably independent-minded and restrained in doctrine and tone. That so mild, moderate, and scholarly a person could have aroused such hatred as a reputed blasphemer is evidence of the bigotry of his time. Many hundreds of his contemporaries, especially among the frenzied Ranters, who did blaspheme by cursing, reproaching, or repudiating God, Christ, or religion—crimes with which Biddle had no remote connection—suffered comparatively mild harassment. They seemed to be more crazy than dangerous. The extraordinary response to Biddle suggests that England's leaders in government and religion saw in him a man of awesome intellect and character that made him capable of subverting received religion, if not of leading a new reformation. We cannot know whether their estimate of him was exaggerated, as it appears, because the seventeen years of his persecution succeeded in quashing him. On the one hand, persecution drove him further into opposition and gave him a name; on the other, it denied him the opportunity of commanding a reform movement, if ever that was his desire.[32]

In 1644, when Biddle first got in trouble, he was twenty-eight. Nothing in his previous life indicates any departure from orthodoxy. He was still a teenager when his English translations of Latin poets stimulated predictions that he would be a gifted scholar. At Oxford, where he earned an A.B. in 1638 and an M.A. in 1641, he specialized in classics and philosophy, and he knew the New Testament so thoroughly that he could repeat it verbatim, through chapter 4 of Revelation, in both Greek and English. He continued his scriptural studies after he became master of a grammar school in Gloucester. In 1644, he reached the conviction, based entirely on his own reading of the New Testament, that the Holy Ghost of the Trinity was the principal angel but not divine. His views, expressed in conversation, were reported to Presbyterian authorities, who accused him of "dangerous opinions," but he subscribed to a confession of faith that satisfied them. That was the only occasion on which Biddle, who was a quiet but extremely obstinate man, backed down.[33]

In the following year, to clarify his own thinking on the subject of the Holy Ghost, he composed a short treatise and indiscreetly showed the manuscript to some friends. Again, one betrayed him, and parliamentary commissioners in Gloucester arrested him. Another friend bailed him out of jail, pending his being summoned before the House of Commons for an examination. In the spring of 1646, James Ussher, the lord archbishop of Ireland, stayed in Gloucester on his way to London and decided to convince the bright young scholar that he was in "damnable Error" or else all Christendom "had been guilty of Idolatry." Ussher relied only on the church fathers, whereas the sole authority Biddle relied on was the New Testament. In London, Ussher reported his opinion that the presumptuous schoolmaster believed that everyone else was guilty of idolatry. Soon after, Parliament summoned Biddle to London. When examined by a committee, he admitted that he had denied the divinity of the Holy Ghost but refused to express an opinion on the divinity of Christ. In June

1646, they sent him to the Gatehouse Prison in Westminster, where Paul Best was locked up. The two probably met in prison, and Best, the most learned Socinian in England and twenty-five years Biddle's senior, may have awakened him to a literature that he had not known to exist. Biddle's unorthodoxy up to that time had been limited to his own idiosyncratic interpretation of the third person of the Trinity. Whereas Best's case agitated and perplexed the House of Commons, Biddle's was ignored. His "crime," like Best's, was not punishable under the law as it then stood. So the Commons neglected him. He tried to get a hearing by petitioning Sir Henry Vane, the parliamentary tolerationist. Biddle related the facts of his case, explained his beliefs about the Holy Spirit, and concluded that he had relied solely upon "the principles of reason and scripture." His placing reason before Scripture showed a Socinian characteristic. Vane was unable to get Biddle discharged or even bring his case before the attention of the House.[34]

Over a year after his arrest, in May 1647, the Commons at last resolved that a committee which had been drafting an ordinance against blasphemy should look into the case of "one Biddle, a Schoolmaster of Gloucester, that has written a Treatise against the Divinity of the Holy Ghost." Nothing further happened, though, and Biddle continued in jail, with neither bail nor trial. Desperate to capture attention, he resorted to a daring strategy. He published the manuscript that was responsible for his plight. The little tract appeared in September 1647 under the title *Twelve Arguments drawn out of the Scripture; Wherein the commonly received Opinion touching the Deity of the Holy Spirit is clearly and fully refuted*. It got him the attention that he wanted but gravely worsened his situation. The House condemned the tract as blasphemous, ordered that it be publicly burned, authorized a search for its printers, and instructed the committee on Best's case to examine Biddle. When he would not renounce his opinion, a committee of the Westminster Assembly was deputized "to remove him from his blasphemies and dangerous opinions," but no one could satisfy him that he was wrong. So they kept him where he was, without trial; he was too dangerous to let loose and impossible to prosecute.[35]

The order to burn Biddle's tract had the effect of advertising it. Its secret printers ran off a second printing for sale later that year. The orthodox rushed into print to refute Biddle. In 1647, *God's Glory Vindicated and Blasphemy confuted* was on the streets. Biddle, of course, had not questioned God's glory. *A Testimony to the Truth of Jesus Christ*, which attacked the blasphemies of both Best and Biddle, received the signatures of fifty-two London ministers. Almost as many from York in the next year signed *Vindiciae Veritas (Truth Vindicated)*. Two Presbyterian tracts of 1648 bore the same main title, *Blasphemoktomia*. One was subtitled *The*

Blasphemer Slain; or, a Plea for the Godhead of the Holy Ghost vindicated from the cavils of J. Biddle; the other too purported to be a vindication of the Holy Ghost. While the pamphlet warfare was in progress, a Presbyterian board of visitors at Oxford discovered and seized Socinian literature in the possession of John Webberly, the subrector of Lincoln College, leading to his ouster and imprisonment.[36]

The seeming spread of Socinianism, the most detested heresy in Christendom, spurred Parliament to legislate. First Best's case, then Biddle's and Webberly's, showed the absence of any lawful course against alleged blasphemers. For about two years, the Independents, fearing that the Presbyterians might use legal sanctions against them, had blocked passage of an act. But by 1648 the situation had changed. The Congregationalists were undergoing the transformation whereby a heretical sect becomes a respectable church alarmed by religious anarchy. And the threat of a monolithic, bigoted Presbyterian establishment was vanishing. Even moderates of that denomination had come to realize that a uniformity of religion was simply no longer possible in England. The country was too divided religiously. Independents who stood closer to Calvinism than to the heterodox fringe sects had reached high places and had the support of the army; they were no longer afraid of a bill that would outlaw the most reprehensible of religious offenses. Secure in the knowledge that they had achieved toleration for themselves, they believed that they could vote against blasphemy without installing presbyter in place of priest or prelate as inquisitor of heretical pravity. If an occasional Socinian as well as outright atheists had to be sacrificed, the price seemed well worth paying to secure toleration of most religious differences. There was no chance that the punitive character of the bill would intrude upon the consciences of any recognized Protestant communion. A sop to placate Presbyterian moderates, moreover, would prove the fitness of the bill's Independent supporters to share the reins of government; they favored neither toleration for blasphemers nor the extreme sectarianism of the lower classes. On May 2, 1648, Parliament, without serious Independent opposition, passed "An Ordinance for the Punishing of Blasphemies and Heresies."[37]

The act of 1648 had two sections. The one on blasphemy fixed the death penalty, to be determined by regular judicial procedure, for anyone advocating "that there is no God, or that the Three are not one Eternal God, or that . . . Christ is not equal with the Father," or that Christ did not rise from the dead and ascend to heaven or was not the Son of God, or that Holy Scripture is not the word of God, "or that the Bodies of men shall not rise again after they are dead, or that there is no day of Judgment after death." But for the clause against atheism, the capital provisions of the act focused primarily on Socinian doctrines. The heresy section of the act was far milder in its punishment but more comprehensive in its coverage. It reached Arminians, Baptists, and most critics of Calvinism by declaring unlawful the advocacy of any of the following beliefs: that all men shall be saved, that man has free will, "that man is bound to believe no more than by his reason he can comprehend" (another Socinian belief), that the moral law of the Ten Commandments is not a rule of Christian life, that believers should not pray for pardon of sins, that the sacraments of baptism and the Lord's Supper are not "commanded by the Word of God," that infant baptism is wrong and that only believers should be baptized, that the Churches of England are not "true churches," or that "the Church government by Presbytery is Antichristian or unlawfull." These provisions against heretical "errors" were, in the main, concessions to Calvinist church discipline. Anyone convicted of any of these errors by the testimony of two or more witnesses had to recant or be sent to jail until he found two "suffient Sureties" who would be liable in the event that he maintained the same errors.

The chief sect that denounced the act of 1648 was the Baptists. The argument that complete religious liberty would inundate England with pernicious heresies and corrupt the faith did not convince them. To them it showed little faith in true religion, which in time would prevail over error. Erroneous opinions, they thought, were inevitable. God permitted them, and He alone reserved judgment over them. The Baptists did not condone blasphemy but believed that the persecution of anyone professing God was evil. To the claim that blasphemy was irreligious, thus not deserving the protection afforded religion, they answered that persecutors always saw truth as blasphemous, thus justifying their coercion of conscience. Christianity flourished when men were left alone to advocate whatever religious views they wished. Christ had not planted his church by force. To exact an unwilling and hollow conformity was the real blasphemy. Persecution convinced no one; it only hardened souls. Any limitations on religious belief or any punishment for it destroyed the foundations of liberty, opening the way to further persecution. The Baptists acutely sensed the possibility that they stood next in line if Socinians or papists or anyone suffered for conscience' sake. They remembered history and knew that "blasphemer" was, like "papist," a term of reproach which men with bitter hearts indiscriminately used to assail their opponents. They recalled that Christ himself suffered reproach as a blasphemer, and that his followers were accused of sedition and heresy. The most awful sin of the Christian churches was persecution. Baptists genuinely believed that the church should use only spiritual weapons, ranging from persuasion to excommunication, and that the civil magistrate had no business with anything touching religion. They would spare even blasphemers from molestation if only because no one, civil or ecclesiastical, was sufficiently infallible in his judgment to justify punishment. If the government could punish even a Socinian for religious reasons, rather than because he had created a civil disturbance, anyone dissenting from a prescribed religion could suffer the same fate.[38]

The same tolerationist arguments came from a motley group of thirty autonomous congregations in London who published their petition to Cromwell, urging that he declare the Blasphemy Act of 1648 "Null and Void" and liberate John Biddle. The petitioners maintained that "the most mistaken Christians," if peaceable, should be protected in the "exercise of their Religion." Biddle, "though differing from most of us in great matters of faith," deserved "liberty of Religion." If he could be punished under the "Bloody Ordinance" of 1648, so might anyone who had "begun already to reject the Traditions of men, the unscriptural words and notions of Trinity in Unity, & Unity in Trinity, of three persons in one essence, of the hypothetical union of two natures in one person." All should be free to profess their faith, or dissenters would be "left out" of the liberty Cromwell had promised to "godly men of different judgment." If Biddle did in fact differ on vital points of faith from the petitioners, they had taken a principled stand on the right of every peaceable Protestant to freedom of religion, while anxiously warning that Biddle's fate foreshadowed that of any heterodox believer.[39]

The act of 1648, despite the provocations that led to its passage, remained dormant on the books, but not because tolerationist arguments prevailed. At the close of 1648, Pride's Purge cleaned the Presbyterians out of Parliament, quelling the demand for enforcement. The Independents now controlled the government.

Shortly before the purge, however, Biddle defied the penalties of the "Draconic Ordinance" against blasphemy by smuggling out of prison for publication his *Confession of Faith touching the Holy Trinity* and, soon after, his *Testimonies* [of the Church Fathers] *concerning the One God and the Persons of the Holy Trinity.* How he got the necessary materials for his research is unfathomable. The new books revealed that he had become a convinced Socinian, familiar with the literature of which he had been ignorant when first imprisoned. He believed "the Father only to be One God" and contended that the leaders of the Reformation had failed to go far enough by having failed to reject the "Idolatrous Pollutions of the Romane Antichrist" on the subject of the Trinity. Repudiating the Nicene Creed, he declared that it introduced "three Gods, and so subverteth the Unity of God." To Biddle, Christ was the Son of God and of divine nature, but was not God. Prison was radicalizing him. His views tempted death; he could not know that he was safe because enforcement of the act of 1648 would have brought within its penalties officers of Cromwell's army.[40]

The expulsion of the Presbyterians from Parliament eased Biddle's treatment. At one point, he briefly got out, when a Staffordshire justice of the peace, who admired his work, posted bail. Biddle returned with him to Staffordshire in his first position as a preacher to a congregation. But John Bagshaw, the head of the Rump Parliament's Council of State, secured from the House an order for Biddle's reimprisonment. He stayed in jail, more closely confined than before and on the verge of starvation, until February 1652, when an act of "oblivion," dictated by Cromwell, freed him. He had spent five and a half years in jail, without ever having seen a judge, for the crime of denying the divinity of the Holy Spirit. Three years later, he would again be charged with blasphemy.[41]

During Biddle's long incarceration, the House of Commons discovered an anti-Trinitarian in its midst. The House had difficulty enough coping with an eccentric Yorkshireman, Best, who had been to Transylvania, and with a young Gloucester teacher, Biddle. John Fry was a tougher antagonist. A seventeenth-century antiquary described him as "a man of more than ordinary parts." He was an army captain, a prosperous gentleman with friends in high places, and, since Pride's Purge, a member of Parliament, sufficiently important to be appointed one of the commissioners to try King Charles. He could be blunt on his feet and satirical with a pen.[42]

In 1649, a fellow member of Parliament asked Fry to help free Biddle. Another member, overhearing Fry consent, objected that Biddle deserved to be hanged. In the argument that ensued over the Trinity, Fry admitted that he was "dissatisfied with those expressions of three distinct Persons or Subsistences in the God-head." He denied that there could be any persons in the Godhead, meaning that God is not a "person"; the word, he said, referred only to people. If God is a person, he added, "I might be said to be God too, as well as Jesus Christ, and the like might be affirmed of all other creatures whatsoever." The remark sounded like double-barreled blasphemy; Fry's adversary took him to mean that Jesus was not divine and that he, Fry, and everyone else had divine attributes. The charge of blasphemy led to Fry's suspension from the House until an investigating committee reported. His denial that he claimed to be as much God as Christ was, satisfied the committee, leading to his reinstatement. He would not, however, let the matter rest.[43]

To clear his name from the charge of blasphemy, Fry published a detailed account in which he repeated his rejection of the "Persons or Subsistences" of the Trinity, and he denounced that doctrine as a "chaffy [worthless] and absurd Opinion." Finding no scriptural basis for the doctrine of the Trinity or for "the forcing of a man's conscience by civil Power," he favored toleration for anti-Trinitarians. In the course of his argument, he ridiculed and condemned the Westminster Assembly, adding that he would sooner put a sword in the hands of a madman "than a high-flying Presbyter."[44]

Before its final session, the assembly asked Francis Cheynell, one of its highest flyers, to answer Fry. Cheynell was one of those Presbyterians who specialized in seeing Socinians under the bed. In 1643, he had published *The Rise, Growth, and Danger of Socinianism*, and in 1648 he had found Socinian books under John Webberly's bed. As a reward for his labors, Cheynell was appointed to the most richly endowed professorship of divinity and became president of St. John's College, Oxford. His response to Fry became a huge book, *The Divine Trinity* (1650), but before it could reach print, others rushed out tracts against Fry. One had the title *Mr. Fry: his blasphemy and error blown up and down the kingdome* (1649). Cheynell's theme was that, for the past century, "there have been many blasphemous bookes to the great dishonour of the blessed Trinity printed in England." He classified Fry with "Atheistical Libertines," with whom communion should not be held. Socinians, like Fry, he claimed, maintained that Jesus was a mere man, "and therefore they are blasphemers," as were all who claimed to be as much God as Christ was. Fry "had too much acquaintance" with such "high swelling blasphemies." If he thought that Christ was a mere man to be worshipped as divine, he was an idolater; if he thought Christ should not be divinely worshipped, he was a blasphemer.[45]

Fry promptly replied in a second tract, *The Clergy in their Colours* (1650). He confessed that he had been adequately answered if "foul-mouthed language be a sufficient confutation." He made his defense of his views on the Trinity an assault on the clergy. They taught many things as truth that were not. People who took their religion on faith or authority were no wiser than parrots. He commended men who did their own thinking and rejected clerical teachings "if after a careful and con-scionable search, they find no footing for such things in the Scripture." A rational man, especially a Christian, should profess nothing without first determining its truth for himself. The clergy were full of tricks, and if you put a hard question to them, they answered, "tis a thing above reason, and yet you must believe what the received opinion is of it." Fry would have none of that. "Every man that knows anything, knows this," he answered, "That it is reason that distinguisheth a man from a beast: if you take away his reason you deny him his very essence." That Socinian passage would be quoted against him in Parliament. Fry concluded by writing: "I drive at this, that men may reflect upon those things which are taught, not believing anything, because their teachers say so; but because what is taught, is rational and grounded upon the Scriptures."[46]

Fry's attack on the clergy was so provocative that not even his friends in the House of Commons could down the clamor against him. Early in

1651, both his little books were cited against him and went to a committee for examination. The committee reported that the first one, by denying the Trinity, contained blasphemous matter. The second was scandalous and tended to the "Overthrow of the Preachers and the Preaching of the Gospel." Both books, "throughout," were against the doctrine of "the true Religion." Substantial quotations from both were introduced in evidence to support the charges. Fry got no chance to defend his position; the only questions asked of him concerned his authorship. Two days later, the House debated Fry's case from morning to night. On the "Matter of Blasphemy," the House resolved that Fry's first book was "erroneous, profane and highly scandalous." The book against the clergy was similarly condemned. Both were ordered burned. Fry himself, however, was not molested. His punishment was limited to expulsion from Parliament. He was too important a person to be imprisoned for a crime that Cheynell advertised as infecting high places in the realm. The last word in print came from Cheynell. His tract *A Discussion of Mr. Frye's Tenets lately condemned in Parliament* purportedly proved Socinianism "to be un-Christian Doctrine." Proof does not exist for the tradition that Fry joined John Biddle's congregation. A few years after being expelled from Parliament, Fry died.[47]

Biddle, the former schoolteacher, had begun preaching the Gospel in London after being pardoned in early 1652. His congregation was small, but his notoriety occasionally attracted Sunday crowds, causing the orthodox to complain that he vented his blasphemies in public. The government, which was committed to a policy of toleration for anyone who publicly worshipped God through the Christian religion, preferred to take no notice. No loyal subject of peaceable deportment was molested. Biddle's literary productions attracted attention, but, not bearing his name, drew only suspicion. In 1652, he published the first English translation of the Racovian Catechism, with a preface containing a plea for religious toleration.[48]

Biddle's edition of the Racovian Catechism was an especially bold project. The name came from the city in Poland, Rakow, which was once the "capital" of Socinianism, with a flourishing religious press that distributed anti-Trinitarian books throughout Europe. The Racovian Catechism, although in question-and-answer form, was scarcely for children. It was a systematic manual of Socinian doctrines whose Latin edition James I had ordered burned. All orthodox Europe knew Rakow as a source of spiritual contagion until Poland cauterized it. In 1638, the Polish government, under the influence of the Jesuits, abolished Rakow's press, college, schools, and churches; dispersed its congregations; and exiled its ministers under penalty of death. So died a remarkable center of intellectual liberty and religious liberalism. For a short time, John

Biddle made London the new Rakow—or so his hysterical enemies said. In 1652, the secret presses in London turned out a new Latin edition of the Racovian Catechism. What an Anglican king saw as heresy in 1614, a Parliament of Independent Puritans condemned to the flames as blasphemy in 1652. Unfazed, Biddle freely translated the Latin into English a few months later, interspersing his text with his own unmistakable emendations. He followed with unsigned translations of several Socinian tracts and a biography of Faustus Socinus.[49]

Biddle's works reached readers as far away as Danzig. A Calvinist scholar in Holland, after studying Biddle, concluded that London seemed to be "snatching the palm from . . . Rakow." In London a Presbyterian wrote "that Socinianisme hath fixed its metapolitical seat here in England, and displayed openly the Banners of its Impiety." The "prime man" behind it all was John Biddle. John Owen, a pre-eminent Independent minister, and vice-chancellor of Oxford University, devoted hundreds of pages to a refutation of Biddle's works, and even Owen, a sensible man, panicked before Biddle's supposed influence: "the evill is at the doore; there is not a Citty, a Towne, scarce a village in England, wherein some of this poyson is not poured forth." The Reverend Matthew Poole, who kept bringing out revisions of his book, *The Blasphemer Slain*, in order to keep up with Biddle's productions, found it all "most lamentable to rehearse":

> . . . the whole body of Socinianism, that hydra of Blasphemies, that Racovian Catechism (which walked only in the dark, and in the Latine tongue in the Bishops times) is now translated into English, for the more speedy corruption of the people; many bold Factors for these Blasphemies, which in those times durst not appear, do now both publickly, and from house to house, disseminate their Heresies without fear: amongst these is Mr. John Biddle.[50]

In 1653, Biddle brazenly published an anthology of his own works, including those burned earlier as blasphemous. His final work and masterpiece was *The Twofold Catechism*, which appeared in 1654, exasperating even a Parliament of Independents. The newest book was probably the most radical assault on conventional Christianity ever seen in England. Biddle, following Fry's suggestion, simply threw out sixteen hundred years of theology, council edicts, and church confessions; he went back to the source of Christianity. Not even the Racovian Catechism satisfied him. It was too marred, like all its sectarian counterparts, by running commentaries on early church fathers and disputes with authorities. Biddle determined to rediscover "the chiefest things" concerning Christian belief and practice, "whilst I myself assert nothing (as others have done before me) but onely introduce the Scripture faithfully uttering its own assertions." He restricted his own commentary to an introduction, saying he wrote for "meer Christians" rather than for one sect or another; the paradoxical result was that, in his effort to avoid sectarianism, he wrote the ultimate sectarian catechism. It covered the whole field of Christian doctrine.[51]

In effect, by distilling Christianity from the New Testament, Biddle produced an epitome of what later would be called Unitarianism. Although he urged that the Scripture should be taken "in its plain straightforward sense" with no twisting or construction, where doubt arose in meaning he relied on "Reason." On the whole, he stayed with a literal interpretation, even to the point of describing God as a person with anthropomorphic features and dwelling in a particular place. In an attempt "to reduce our Religion to its first principles," Biddle discarded all glosses on the Bible, as well as the "Babylonish confusion of language" and "intricate expressions" that had accumulated with the "traditions of men." By speaking of original sin, the Trinity, hypostatical union, and transubstantiation, theologians had abandoned the Bible and "common sense," making religion unintelligible to the ordinary man for whom Biddle wrote. The Bible, Biddle held, was "plain enough to be understood, even by the simple." It taught the unity and love of God, salvation through God, the sonship of Jesus Christ, who was a mortal, and the free will of man. It taught nothing about original sin, predestination, the coessential divinity of Christ, justification by faith alone, the resurrection of the body, or much else that passed for Christianity.[52]

Parliament, on receiving complaints about Biddle's last two books, which bore his name, resolved "to suppress his School" and arrest him. The first book, anthologizing his earlier works, was familiar. Again the House condemned it for "blasphemous Opinions against the Deity of the Holy Ghost" and ordered it burned. On December 13, 1654, the House examined Biddle, who admitted writing both books, but said that he had no congregation and refused to identify his printers. "The Law of Christ," he explained, enjoined him "not to betray his Brethren." He denied the divinity of the Holy Ghost, as earlier, and, when asked whether Jesus Christ was God "from Everlasting to Everlasting," he denied that the Bible said so. The House committed him to the Gatehouse Prison, as before, ordering close confinement "without Pen, Ink, or Paper," in order to initiate a further Proceeding against him. *The Twofold Catechism* was, of course, burned.[53]

A month later, the House adopted the report of its committee, which had studied Biddle's last two books. The House condemned each as "full of horrid, blasphemous, and execrable Opinions; denying the Deity of

Christ, and of the Holy Ghost." The thirteen "Particulars" cited from *The Twofold Catechism* and the half-dozen more from the other book contained many flat denials but no reviling; John Biddle was a temperate, reverent, and rationalistic Christian. The list of his blasphemies concerning Jesus Christ were, in Parliament's language, as follows: He claimed Christ had a "divine Lordship, without a Divine Nature," that he was not "a Priest, whilst he was on Earth," and that he did not die "to reconcile God to us." He claimed that "Christ is the Second Cause of All Things pertaining to our Salvation, And that the Son is not equal with the Father." He claimed that Christ had "no other than a human Nature," was "not the Most High God, the same with the Father, but subordinate to him," and finally that "Christ is not the supreme and independent Monarch Jehovah."[54]

Parliament's prosecution of Biddle was lawless. The proceedings against him awaited a report from "the Committee on Printing," which the House ordered to "bring in a Bill for the Punishment of the said John Biddle." He had published the books without prior license, in violation of the censorship law, but the proper course for prosecuting such an offense was trial before a magistrate, and the maximum sentence was a fine. In exceptional cases, the Council of State had jurisdiction. Even if Biddle had committed a capital crime—indeed, especially if he had committed such a crime by violating the act against blasphemy passed in 1648— jurisdiction over the offense belonged, by the terms of that act, to the ordinary courts of justice. Conviction by a legislative attainder was the only purpose of ordering a bill against him. Revolutionary oppression often takes the form of an improvisation that has the color of law.[55]

In the late 1640s, when Parliament had first jailed Biddle, he was an unknown. At that time, only the Baptists and a few Independents like John Goodwin would have exempted anti-Trinitarian beliefs from sanctions against blasphemy. By 1655, Biddle was a celebrity with a congregation, some influential friends, and the support of many who believed that, if so reverent though misguided a man could be punished for his religion, so might they. On the other side were those, like the majority of Parliament, who believed that toleration should go far, but not far enough to protect "blasphemy." Those favoring Biddle's prosecution by Parliament also demanded severer penalties for breaking the act of 1653 against unlicensed "scandalous" publications "to the great dishounour of God . . . and insufferable contempt of all good Order and Government." One faction that demanded stronger press regulation to prevent blasphemies like the Racovian Catechism complained that prosecutors had "no standing penal Law" on which to rely. As the public awaited Parliament's disposition of Biddle's case in January 1655, the question of censorship and that of toleration linked together.[56]

John Goodwin, who had spoken up for Best's liberty, saw the connection between censorship and toleration. Although he deplored Biddle's anti-Trinitarianism, Goodwin believed that "liberty of the Press" permitted no censoring of any religious opinions. In a *Fresh Discovery of the High Presbyterian Spirit*, he opposed censorship laws as unscriptural, dangerous, and ineffective; they hampered learned men like Goodwin himself from rebutting Biddle. Although none of Biddle's publications had been licensed, Goodwin perversely blamed the censors for them. The printing of Biddle's "most enormous and hideous notions, and conceits about the nature of God," wrote Goodwin, was the fault of those who sought to suppress the liberty of the press. Blasphemous writings had to be publicly exposed "to become the loathing and abhorring of all men." Error, he reasoned, flourished in "spiritual darknesse" but died in the light of open controversy. "The Gospel and the truth never flourished, prospered, and triumphed at a higher rate in the world, than when errors and heresies were not otherwise restrained, punished, or opposed, than by those spiritual means, which God himself hath sanctified . . . as *viz.*, by effectual preaching of the Gospel." Opposition to the liberty of the press was "AntiChristian," an inheritance from priests and prelates, preventing the learned and godly from having free access to printed opinions like Biddle's so that he could be rebuked and confuted.

Licensing laws, Goodwin claimed, worked either to the benefit of the "Orthodox," who authorized only their own version of religious truth, or to the benefit of men like Biddle, who had to resort to secret presses. The Bible clinched Goodwin's argument. He found "neither footing nor foundation in the Scriptures" for licensing laws, and he demanded to know where Christ or the Holy Ghost had authorized anyone to decide what "shall publickly go forth into the world. . . . What ground is there in the Word of God . . . to stifle or slay what books they please?" No one, civil or ecclesiastical, could be trusted with a sovereignty over the press; censorship was inconsistent with the interests of a free government and true religion. Licensing laws inevitably tended toward the establishment of "a State Religion." Goodwin saw no reason for "a power of gagging the Press." It did no good, did a lot of damage, and did not even work. It was like coercion of conscience. Punishments and restraints were no answer. "If you saw the Books [by Biddle] that you speak of burnt by the hand of the hangman, do you think that the Errors, Heresies and Blasphemies, contained in them, would burn with them?" Goodwin concluded that the ashes of Biddle's books would propagate his opinions more than the books themselves.[57]

Biddle, although not fortunate enough to have Goodwin as his judge, had a momentary stroke of luck. Cromwell, for reasons of his own, dissolved Parliament before its attainder process got far. A few weeks later, on February 10, 1655, he allowed a court to fix bail for Biddle, pending his appearance at its session next May. At that time, on finding that Biddle was not under indictment, the court dismissed the case against him. He returned to his congregation, which began to grow. Some of the converts came from a Baptist congregation whose jealous minister challenged Biddle to an old-fashioned theological dispute. On June 28, 1655, the rival sectarians before an audience of about five hundred people disputed the question "whether Jesus Christ be the most High or Almighty God." Biddle denied the divinity of Christ throughout several hours of debate, scandalizing a faction of Presbyterians who were present. They reported the affair to the Council of State, complaining about Biddle's argument and the fact that the debate was scheduled for continuation a week later. The Council of State, with Cromwell himself in attendance, ordered the lord mayor of London to prevent the intended meeting, if necessary by arresting Biddle. The Presbyterians took their testimony to the mayor, who promptly jailed Biddle.[58]

The mayor, in concert with his alderman and recorder, who was a magistrate, reluctantly consented to a hearing. The prisoner had the support of a small group of his friends, who included a lawyer. Because Biddle was held without a warrant, his friends demanded a specification of the charges against him. The mayor, equivocating, replied that the Council of State had ordered his commitment, to which Biddle's counsel replied that not even the council could imprison someone without a transgression of the law. The mayor asked Biddle whether he had denied Christ to be "the most High God." This time, Biddle equivocated, and when the recorder handed him a copy of his *Twofold Catechism* and asked whether he had written it, Biddle refused to answer the incriminating question. He would answer no questions against himself, he declared, "because we finde, that even Jesus Christ himself, when he was questioned before the High Priest, refused to answer in this sort." When an alderman retorted, "What Christ?," Biddle replied, "My Lord and Saviour Jesus Christ, that sitteth at the right Hand of God in the Heavens." A report of the case, written by one of Biddle's partisans, asserted that Biddle acknowledged Christ "to be his Lord and God," which sounds unlike the Biddle of 1655. Notwithstanding Biddle's conformity, the recorder produced a copy of the 1648 act against blasphemy with certain passages marked that were pertinent to the case.[59]

Biddle was the first victim of the act of 1648, because it had never been enforced. Not even Parliament's proceedings against Biddle had referred to that act. Biddle "desired the Recorder, if that were a Law, to shew him how he was liable to it." The recorder replied that many passages reached him, but refused to specify which. Biddle replied with a quibble that the act did not cover his denial that "Jesus Christ was the Almighty, or the most High God." In fact, his *Twofold Catechism* at many points violated the prohibitions against advocating that "the Son is not God, or that the Holy Ghost is not God, or that they Three are not one Eternal God, or that . . . Christ is not God equal with the Father." Nor could Biddle have taken the negative position in the public disputation of June without having violated the same provisions of the act. If it was still law, his guilt seemed clear to the authorities, although the recorder conceded that Biddle had not used the "very words" proscribed by the act; yet his words were "tantamount," and that was enough to bring them within the intentions of Parliament. The mayor then recommitted Biddle by a warrant dated July 10, 1655, "for publickly denying, That Jesus Christ was the Almighty or most High God." Biddle's friends tried to post bail for him, but the city authorities ruled that the accusation, being a capital felony, was not bailable. They sent him to Newgate Prison, where he awaited trial in the dreaded Old Bailey criminal court.[60]

Biddle's reimprisonment, this time under the act of 1648, caused consternation among the sectarians and tolerationists. Within two weeks, hawkers were selling unlicensed tracts denouncing the government and spreading alarm. Two tracts in particular, vividly describing the proceedings against Biddle, sent a shiver through sectarian readers. Their very titles attracted attention. One was *A True State of the Cause of Liberty of Conscience in the Commonwealth of England, Together with a true narrative of the Cause, and Manner, of Mr. John Bidle's Sufferings*; the other was *The Spirit of Persecution Again broken loose, by An Attempt to put in Execution against Mr. John Biddle Master of Arts, an abrogated Ordinance . . . for punishing Blasphemies and Heresies.* The anonymous author of *The Spirit of Persecution* observed that Biddle's exact words did not match those prohibited by "the Draconic Ordinance" of 1648. If he could be brought within its terms of death by inferences, as the recorder claimed, then by the same reasoning "all Christians" breached it, "for thus we argue, he that saith Christ dyed, said that Christ was not God, for God could not dy. But every Christian saith that Christ dyed, therefore every Christian saith that Christ was not God, and so become guilty of death by this ordinance."[61]

Less contrived was the argument that the Instrument of Government, which was the constitution that established Cromwell's First Protectorate in December 1653, guaranteed religious liberty and rendered the act of 1648 obsolete. Article 37 of the Instrument of Government provided that Christians (anyone believing in God through Jesus Christ), "though differing in judgement from the Doctrine, Discipline, and Worship, publickly held forth, shall not be restrained from, but protected in the profession of their faith and exercise of their religion." Article 38 provided that "all acts and ordinances to the contrary are to be esteemed null and void." The catch was that article 37 did not conflict with the orthodox contention that blasphemy was antireligious; the liberty granted was not to be abused to the injury of others or disturbance of the peace, and it did not extend "to Popery or Prelacy, nor to such as, under the profession of Christ, hold forth and practise Licentiousness."[62]

The popular understanding, however, was that Cromwell had promised liberty of conscience to all Christians. "Oh! what miserable desolations would be made in this Land, were not Liberty of Conscience allowed! It had been better for us, never to have seen a day of Liberty, than now again to return to Bondage." If Biddle suffered for his conscience, "the old Presbyterian designe of persecution" would again prevail, forcing all people to be of their opinion. That would destroy the Commonwealth and Cromwell by sapping "the foundation of our Government . . . libertie of conscience in Religion a fundamentall."[63]

A True State of the Cause of Liberty of Conscience considerably amplified the argument of *The Spirit of Persecution*. The anonymous author of *A True State*, who claimed to know Biddle well, described him as a peaceable and righteous Christian, although quite mistaken on some "high points" of the doctrine of the Trinity. Biddle's differences notwithstanding, he was no heretic or blasphemer. *A True State* vividly reminded readers that, under the episcopacy, the grossest errors had passed for religious truths, and opinions once persecuted were now taken as orthodox. If Biddle suffered for conscience' sake, "let no man, differing from the multitude, think to go free; nor let those that now, by reason of their consent with those in power, enjoy present Liberty, dream of keeping it, except they resolve to change with the changeable Spirits of men, or the vicissitude of times." The only proper course was to emulate the example of Jesus, who fought error with argument even among those mistaken in the "highest points of Religion."[64]

From prison, Biddle wrote letters in his own behalf, first to Cromwell himself, then to the president of the Council of State. He described his religious opinions and stated his reliance on the Instrument of Government for his freedom. His letters were read to the council and, for the time being, ignored. One night in the middle of August, a few weeks after, copies of an incendiary pamphlet were scattered about the streets of London: *A Short Discovery of His Highness the Lord Protector's Intentions Touching the Anabaptists in the Army*. Amid its main argument, that Cromwell was weeding the Baptists out of the army, was the claim that the Instrument of Government had become a worthless piece of paper. If it could not save Biddle from prison, might not Cromwell, a "dissembler" and a "persecutor," lock up all sectarians? The lord protector replied to the libel with a stringent new order against "Dangerous, Unwarrantable, Seditious, Blasphemous, and Scandalous" publications. Clearly, Cromwell did not regard his Instrument of Government as having abrogated the act of 1648 or as having extended protection to blasphemy.[65]

On September 5, after Biddle was indicted, his case came to trial in Old Bailey. He refused to plead to the indictment unless granted counsel, but the court threatened to take him as a standing mute. That meant that he could be spread-eagled on the ground, pressed with more weights than he could bear, and starved—until he pleaded. The purpose of that punishment was to extort a plea, not a confession; the law did not care whether the prisoner pleaded guilty or not guilty. Biddle pleaded not guilty and, without counsel, attacked the indictment, using the arguments his friends had employed against the lord mayor and in their tracts in Biddle's behalf. The exact words used in the charge against him, he argued, did not coincide with the language reached by the act of 1648; anyway, the Instrument of Government had abrogated that act. At that point, the court belatedly granted the prisoner counsel and took the case under advisement. Until the court met the next month, Biddle was remanded to Newgate.[66]

In the middle of September, Parliament reconvened, which raised the possibility that, if the court freed Biddle, the House of Commons, not having finished with him, would again arrest him. A week later, a group of his supporters, including some of his congregation, Baptists, and a few other sectarians, got an audience with Cromwell and the Council of State in order to present a petition in the prisoner's behalf. The petition described Biddle as "a man, though differing from most of us in many great matters of faith, yet by reason of his diligent study in the Holy Scripture, sober and peaceable conversation, which some of us have intimate good knowledge of, we cannot but judge every way capable of the liberty promised in the Instrument of Government." Cromwell's reply was that, because the Instrument "was never intended to maintaine and protect blasphemers from the punishment of the lawes in force against them, neither would hee." He rebuked them for defending a man who had held that Christ was "but a creature." Thomas Firmin, who had given Biddle room and board and paid for his lawyer, was one of the petitioners. Later he would become a great merchant-philanthropist and the leading Unitarian layman in England. In 1655, he was only twenty-three. When he pleaded for Biddle's release, Cromwell is alleged to have retorted, "You curl-pate boy you, do you think I'll show any favor to a man who denies his Saviour, and disturbs the government?" The petitioners got the last word: they published their statement for all London to read.[67]

About a week later, a tract entitled *The Protector, so called, in Part Unvailed* appeared on the streets. It was the work of an anonymous ex-soldier who claimed to be a witness to the events he reported. He accused Cromwell of having "cheated and robbed his People of their Rights and Priviledges." He told how the protector had treated the petition for Biddle, who lay in prison, his books burned, with none allowed to see him and death around the corner. The author blamed Cromwell for having chosen a persecuting Parliament and for having allowed "the doing of such things." Then Biddle's friends added to the public's excitement by publishing his letters of the preceding July to Cromwell and the president of the Council of State. The campaign of agitation against the government was becoming unbearable as the day for Biddle's trial in Old Bailey approached.[68]

On October 5, immediately before the court was scheduled to give its opinion on the question whether the indictment against Biddle was defective, Cromwell took the case out of the hands of the court and decided it for himself. He banished Biddle for life, sending him under armed guard to a castle-fortress on one of the Scilly Islands, about forty miles off the southwesternmost point of England. There Biddle received mild treatment, had an allowance of 100 crowns a year for his subsistence, and had the privilege of books and writing materials.[69]

Biddle's exile was the best solution for the government's dilemma. If the court freed him, Parliament would get him. If the court convicted him, he would face the death penalty. Cromwell could not afford to have him acquitted or convicted, nor did he welcome a formal ruling on whether the Instrument of Government abrogated the act against blasphemy. If the case continued, its outcome, no matter what, would antagonize loyal subjects. Cromwell could neither jeopardize his support in Parliament nor alienate the sectarian tolerationists. He himself hated persecution and drew his strength from the sects, yet could not tolerate what he believed to be Biddle's excesses. Making him a greater martyr for the cause of conscience risked demoralization of the radical Protestants and tempted sedition. Freeing him would outrage the conservatives and many moderates who drew distinctions between liberty and licentiousness. Biddle at liberty on a faraway prison-island satisfied no one but infuriated none.

His friends continued to work for his freedom, he periodically petitioned the protector, and for a time tracts in his behalf were published. After almost three years, when Biddle was all but forgotten, Cromwell relented. Liberated but chastened, Biddle returned to London. Although he continued preaching, he published no more, and when Parliament was in session he prudently sought the safety of the countryside. A parliamentary committee, soon after Cromwell's death, sought to revive his persecution, but no report was ever made on the inquiry "how Biddle came to be released, being imprisoned for blasphemy." After the Stuart Restoration in 1660, Biddle did not dare preach in public. The prelates were once again in power, as if Laud had returned from his grave to Canterbury. The Act of Uniformity in 1662 prescribed the Anglican Book of Common Prayer for every pulpit. No one might lawfully preach contrary to it, or preach at all except following ordination by the epis-copacy. Two months after the passage of the act, agents of the crown burst into Biddle's home while he was conducting religious service for some friends. All were arrested, tried, and fined. Nonconformity, not blasphemy, was the issue. There was nothing special about the episode. During the Stuart Restoration, thousands of nonconformists, ranging from Quaker to Presbyterian, died in jail. Biddle was merely one of them. Unable to pay his £100 fine, he was kept in prison under sickening conditions. He caught a fatal malady and died in 1662 at the age of forty-seven. His congregation did not survive him, and Socinianism, once supposedly raging in every nook and corner of the realm, almost disappeared from it.[70]

CHAPTER EIGHT

The Ranters: Antinomianism Run Amok

REMINISCING about the years 1649 to 1651, when he was called "Captain of the Rant," Laurence Clarkson wrote:

> I brake the Law in all points (murther excepted:) and the ground of this my judgement was, God had made all things good, so nothing [was] evil but as man judged it; for I apprehended there was no such thing as theft, cheat, or a lie, but as man made it so; for if the creature had brought this world into no propriety [property], as *Mine* and *Thine*, there had been no such title as theft, cheat, or a lie; for the prevention hereof *Everard* and *Gerrard Winstanley* did dig up the Commons, that so all might have to live of themselves, then there had been no need of defrauding, but unity one with another.

The reference by the Ranter Clarkson to Everard and Winstanley, the Digger leaders, showed a kinship. They did not believe in private property or in sin as organized religion taught it, although they differed radically about the meaning of sin. In the spring of 1649, the Diggers, those religious mystics who sought to establish a Christian communist community, had occupied St. George's Hill in Surrey. They dug the ground and planted vegetables, because, as Winstanley explained in *The True Levellers Standard*, "the great Creator Reason made the Earth to be a Common Treasury" for all mankind. The government fined them for trespass and prosecuted them for both unlawful assembly and disorderly conduct; soldiers destroyed their little utopian community.[1]

"Digger," like "Ranter" and "Leveller," was a term of contempt. In a political tract of 1647 advocating the sovereignty of the common people, Clarkson spoke of the "True Levellers," a name which the Diggers adopted. Cromwell despised them all—Levellers, True Levellers, and

Ranters. "Did not the levelling principle," he asked, "tend to reducing all to an equality . . . to make the tenant as liberal a fortune as the landlord?" Winstanley, knowing that poor people worked for only four pence a day and that the price of flour was high, remembered the prediction "The poor shall inherit the earth," and he added, "I tell you, the scripture is to be really and materially fulfilled. . . . You jeer at the name Leveller. I tell you Jesus Christ, who is that powerfull Spirit of Love, is the Head Leveller."[2]

Men of the "true" leveling principle, Diggers and Ranters, were a tiny minority who posed no military or political threat, but their theory resonated subversion of Christian society. Even the Socinians, as well as the Baptists and other autonomous congregational sects, could agree on that. If Paul Best, John Fry, and John Biddle had converted much of the nation to their anti-Trinitarianism, England's momentum toward intellectual freedom and an open society would have accelerated, but the future would not have significantly differed. If the Levellers, the constitutional radicals led by John Lilburne, Richard Overton, and John Wildman, had triumphed, political democracy would have come swiftly, followed by some amelioration of the injustices of the class system and the economic order. If Winstanley, Clarkson, and Abiezer Coppe had prevailed, law and order, the Protestant ethic, private property, the class system, and even Christianity itself might have disintegrated in a revolutionary and blasphemous upheaval. Although the threat of such an upheaval remained rhetorical, the government summarily squashed it. The Ranters could not be ignored; they were too blatantly offensive, deliberately going to extremes to shock, to show contempt for society, and to scorn its right to judge them. As political radicals, the Ranters had the clout of pipsqueaks, but as antinomian libertines, they stirred envy, disgust, and hostility, as did their late-medieval precursors, the Brethren of the Free Spirit.

Antinomianism defies definition even more than Puritanism or Independency. The word in its narrowest sense means being against the law—generally, the moral law; specifically, the Ten Commandments. But antinomianism need not be taken in its narrowest sense except, perhaps, in the case of those who, like the Ranters, wholly repudiated the concept of sin. Too narrow a definition of antinomianism misses its religious argument—namely, that, God's grace being unbounded, eternal salvation is open to all, that salvation begins here on earth and not beyond the grave, and that the righteous or moral man does not, or cannot, sin. A world of difference exists, of course, between "does not" and "cannot." The antinomians lived in that contradictory world and could not consistently resolve its contradiction.

Antinomianism begins with the proposition that human nature is perfectible and is perfected even in this world through the gift of divine grace. God makes the moral law subordinate to His grace or love, just as He makes the spirit of the Bible transcend its letter. Antinomians such as Behmenists, Familists, Grindletonians, Seekers, and Quakers believed that divine inspiration and spiritual regeneration perfected the soul, making the acts of a righteous or perfected man correspond with and even supersede the moral law. In Christ none can sin; sin is a temporary aberration pardonable through spiritual regeneration. Antinomians magnified the compelling nature of grace. They emphasized man as redeemed, not man as the fallen and depraved Adam. They focused on Paul's doctrine that salvation is attained not by observance of the Law but by faith inspired by the divine spark within the soul. Christ, Paul proclaimed, lived within him (Galatians 2:20). "The Father is in me" is also a doctrine of the Gospel of John 10:38. An Epistle of John reinforced antinomianism's mystical principles: "No one born of God commits sin; for God's nature abides in him" (1 John 3:9), and "God abides in us and his love is perfected in us" (1 John 4:12).[3]

Antinomian readings of such texts were intensely exalting, personal, and liberating. Antinomianism was not easily communicable or understandable to someone not on the same spiritual wavelength. Antinomians scarcely agreed among themselves. Perhaps there were as many brands of antinomianism as there were inner selves. The Ranters reflected an extreme: antinomianism run amok into religious anarchism. Not that there was a different sort of rant for every Ranter, but Ranters differed sharply. Joseph Salmon, George Foster, Laurence Clarkson, William Franklin, and John Robins were dissimilar Ranters but definably Ranters. A former Ranter fancifully classified seven types of schools of Ranters and to each gave an exotic name—Familists, Shelomethes, Clements, Athians, Nicholartanes, Marcions, and Seleutian Donatists. The Ranters themselves made no such distinctions, did not worship in churches of any sort, and never organized into sects.[4]

The conduct and opinions of Abiezer Coppe suggest why he became the most notorious of the Ranters, although he was no more "typical" than any other Ranter. The repressions of Coppe's early life suggest reasons for his later libertinism. So puritanical was his upbringing that thoughts of hell consumed him; he kept a daily register of his sins and "did constantly confess." His tears, he wrote, were his drink; ashes, his meat; and his life, "zeal, devotion, and exceeding strictness." At seventeen, he entered Oxford as a "poor scholar" to study for the ministry, but the Civil War ended his formal education. An enthusiast for the parliamentary cause, he became a preacher to an army garrison. Drifting from Presbyterianism to Baptism, he continued his search for religious satisfaction. The histrionic powers that Coppe later displayed as a Ranter must have been at his command as an itinerant Baptist preacher, for he claimed to have "dipped" about seven thousand people.

In 1649, a year that began with the execution of Charles I and ended in the sudden emergence of Ranterism, Coppe underwent a spiritual conversion that was not at all uncommon at the time. He heard terrifying thunderclaps and saw a light as dazzling as the sun and as red as fire; "with joy unspeakable in the spirit, I clapt my hands and cryed out, *Amen, Halelujah, Halelujah, Amen.*" Trembling and sweating, he felt divine grace sweeping over him. "Lord," he shouted, "what wilt thou do with me," and the "eternal glory" in him answered that he would be taken into the everlasting kingdom after first being thrown into "the belly of hell." He was among all the devils, he reported, but "under all this terrour, and amazement, there was a little spark of transcendent, transplendent, unspeakable glory . . . triumphing, exulting, and exalting itself," till at last he was the "Eternal Majesty" and heard a voice saying, "The spirits of just men made perfect." It was the antinomian message: a pure or sanctified man can do no evil. After four days and nights of revelations, Coppe received his divine commission: he must go to the great city of London to spread his new gospel. Thus, he explained his conversion to Ranterism as a spiritual experience, although by conventional standards of morality and religion Ranterism was obscene, blasphemous, and seditious.[5]

In London, Coppe preached his antinomian version of the doctrine of the Free Spirit: Christ's death liberated mankind from sin, God dwells within everyone, and all shall be saved, all except perhaps the prosperous and powerful. Coppe's theology was saturated with a hatred of the rich. He assaulted "men and women of the greater rank" in the city streets, ranting and gnashing his teeth at them, while proclaiming that the day of the Lord, the "great Leveller," had come. He embraced the poor and the diseased, and he became a libertine. "Twas usual with him," recorded an Oxonian biographer who knew him, "to preach stark naked many blasphemies and unheard-of Villanies in the Daytime, and in the Night to drink and lye with a Wenche, that had been also his hearer, stark naked." He was imprisoned for fourteen weeks, possibly for similar conduct. In London, he fell in with Laurence Clarkson and an orgiastic group of Ranters who called themselves "My One Flesh," probably to symbolize their unity with all God's creatures. A 1650 vignette of "Ranters ranting" depicts Coppe, "their Ring-leader," as having drunkenly "bestowed an hours time in belching forth imprecations, curses, and other such like stuffe, as is not fit to be once named among Christians." He was supposed to have retired that night with two of his "she-Disciples." The rumor was that "he commonly lay in bed with two women at a time." The cursing, nudity, adultery, drunkenness, and generally immoral behavior (none of it sinful to Coppe) reflected the Ranter repudiation of Puritan middle-class conventions.[6]

Coppe's eloquent and cadenced biblical rhetoric was a mix of mystical ravings and social radicalism. Antinomianism (a repudiation of the moral law), pantheism (the doctrine that God dwells within all creatures), and a repudiation of private property suffused Coppe's utterances. In late 1649, he wrote his sensational tract *A Fiery Flying Roll* [of Thunder] and its successor of the same title. The two tracts purported to be Coppe's witness to a divine warning issued against "all the Great Ones of the Earth." Their dreadful day of judgment was at hand. God would save England with a vengeance. The gospel, according to Coppe, was "I overturn, overturn, overturn." The bishops, lords, and king had had their turn, and the surviving great ones would be next. Although Coppe identified God as "Universal Love," served by "perfect freedome, and pure Libertinisme," the love did not extend to those who could not endure "levelling." "Behold, behold, behold, I the eternall God, the Lord of Hosts, who am that mighty Leveller, am comming (yea even at the doores) to Levell in good earnest . . . putting down the mighty from their seats; and exalting them of low degree." God would level riches and bring "parity, equality, community" to avenge the deaths of the army Levellers who had been shot for mutiny. Coppe himself was a pacifist who repudiated "sword levelling, or digging levelling"; rather than fight, he preferred to be drunk "every day of the weeke, and lye with whores." The real sins, he declared to the great ones, were wealth, pomp, and property—and taking the "enslaved ploughmans money from him." Coppe would rather starve than do that, although stealing from the rich was not sin.

> Mine eares are filled brim full with cryes of poor prisoners, Newgate, Ludgate cryes (of late) are seldome out of mine ears. Those dolefull cryes, Bread, bread, bread, for the Lords sake, pierce mine eares, and heart, I can no longer forbeare.
> Werefore high you apace to all prisons in the Kingdome,
> Bow before those poore, nasty louisie, ragged wretches, say to them . . . we let you go free, and serve you,
> Do this or (as I live saith the Lord), thine eyes (at least) shall be boared out, and thou carried captive in a strange Land.
> . . . undo the heavy burdens, let the oppressed go free, and breake every yoake. Deale thy bread to the hungry, and bring the poore that are cast out (both of houses and Synagogues) to thy house. Cover the naked: Hide not they self from thine own flesh, from a creeple, a rogue, a begger, he's thine own flesh. From a Whoremonger, a thief, &c. he's flesh of thy flesh, and his theft, and whoredome is flesh of thy flesh also, thine own flesh.[7]

In an anticlerical passage, Coppe represented God as demanding that branding with the letter "B" for "blasphemy" be ended. The clergy could not judge "what is sinne, what not, what evill, and what not, what blasphemy, and what not." They served God and Jesus for money, and for all their learning could not understand the real meaning of sin: oppressing the people. Coppe reversed orthodox values when he declared his belief that what was called good was evil, "and Evill Good; Light Darknesse, and Darknesse Light; Truth Blasphemy, and Blasphemy Truth." To the pure, all things are pure. Cursing by some was more glorious than praying by others. What God cleansed should not be called unclean.[8]

The second *Fiery Flying Roll* warned those who had "many baggs of money" that the Great Leveller would come "as a thief in the night" with sword drawn, and say "deliver your purse, deliver sirrah! deliver or I'll cut thy throat." The rich should turn over their wealth to the cripples, lepers, rogues, thieves, whores, and to all the poor, "who are flesh of thy flesh, and every whit as good as thy self in mine eye." The "fat swine of the earth" would soon "go to the knife," if they did not obey the command to "give, give, give, give up, give up your houses, horses, goods, gold, Lands, give up, account nothing your own, have ALL THINGS common, or els the plague of God will rot and consume all that you have." In other chapters, Coppe explained how he had found "unspeakable glory" in the basest things, how he had found God in gypsies and jailbirds ("mine own brethren and sisters, flesh of my flesh, and as good as the greatest Lord in England"), and how the path to salvation lay in abandoning "stinking family duties," biblical laws, and personal possessions. The presence of God within him filled his life with joy and beauty, not to mention "concubines without number." In his final chapters, Coppe returned to the theme that kings, princes, and lords, "the great ones," who pleaded "priviledge and Prerogative from Scripture," must yield to "the poorest Peasants" to fulfill the grand design: "equality, community, and universall love." His closing jeremiad (from James 5:1)—"Howl, howl, ye nobles, howl honourable, howl ye rich men for the miseries that are coming upon you"—revealed Coppe's utopian vision: "For our parts, we that hear the APOSTLE preach, will also have all things in common; neither will we call any thing that we have our own. . . . Wee'l eat our bread together in singleness of heart, wee'l break bread from house to house." The same thought is in Winstanley.[9]

Abiezer Coppe was a religious eccentric and a spiritual anarchist, but he was not demented and, judged by his time, was not a capricious sport. Millenarian and mystical traditions reached back into the Middle Ages. The foremost doctrine of Ranterism, that God lives within every creature, was an old heresy bolstered by scriptural evidence. That heresy thrived in the thirteenth and fourteenth centuries in most of Europe as the Free Spirit movement, and it cropped out in an entirely different form in Elizabethan England when Dutch and German immigrants imported Hendrik Nicholas's Familist beliefs. Christopher Vitell, a disciple of Nicholas, translated his works into English. The Familists survived royal persecution and the libels of even radical sectarians. Henry Ainsworth, a Separatist, in 1698 said that no one wrote "more blasphemously" than Nicholas; and Edmond Jessop, who despised English Anabaptists, described the Familists as "the most blasphemous and erroneous sect this day in the world." Yet Nicholas explicitly repudiated libertinism and preached that personal righteousness bears witness to a new life, which showed that one has experienced the inward revelation that God or Christ is within one's spirit. Such mystical knowledge led to the Familist belief that regenerated people, in whom Christ dwells, have reached perfection and cannot sin; that belief opened Familists to the antinomian charge. They also invited denunciation by exalting the spirit above Scripture. Anabaptists advocated similar principles, and so did the Behmenists. Others, called Seekers, believing that there was no true church yet, wandered in search of a revelation of God's glory. Even John Murton, the tolerant Baptist leader, condemned Familists and Seekers (although he would not silence them) for advocating the "libertine doctrine" that people need not hear preaching or read the Bible. Gilbert Roulston, who was once a Ranter, designated a particular school of them as Familists or members of the Family of Love, which he traced to a German of Elizabeth's time. Another anti-Ranter writer entitled his tract *The Bottomless Pit Smoaking in Familisme*.[10]

Familism influenced Coppe and the Ranters. In 1649, the turning point in the history of Ranterism, four of Nicholas's English books were reprinted. But Ranterism was more directly a product of the Civil War of the 1640s and of the revolutionary upheavals that accompanied it. The period was both disruptive and creative. The overthrow of the episcopacy and of their ecclesiastical courts, which had maintained law, order, and status, and helped keep people in subjugation to state and church, snapped religious restraints. People formed "gathered churches" or voluntary congregations and separated from society. They advocated universal grace and took up all sorts of old heresies as if they were new revelations. The inner light in the soul of the individual believer, whatever he believed, became the highest standard of authority in spiritual matters. Judging what was sinful was left to personal conscience, and men were saying that the clergy, with the support of the rulers, had invented sin as a means of suppression. People felt emancipated. They were free from sin and from prosecutions for sin; they were free to form their own congregations, to preach as they pleased, or to choose lay preachers. They felt free to argue against and reject the orthodoxies of the past. In the absence of effective censorship, those who dreamed of new worlds freely expressed themselves. Infinite liberty and utopia seemed within the realm of possibility, especially in religious matters. Next to instinctual needs, religion was still the most important aspect of life—and of death. John Biddle, the Socinian, rationally rejected original sin and eternal damnation, while uneducated people—herdsmen, tinkers, soap makers, and weavers—instinctively came to the same conclusions.

In 1644, a conservative identified "Antinomians and Familists" as "enemies of civil government, who seek to overthrow the eternall Law of God, on which the civil law is built. . . ." He was saying, in effect, that religious questions contain or mask political and social issues. That inference can also be drawn from a sermon preached before the House of Commons by Thomas Case in 1647. Case warned that, if liberty were granted to sectaries, people would claim their birthright to be free from parliaments and kings and even rebel against them. "Liberty of conscience, falsely so called," Case added, "may in good time improve itself into liberty of estates and liberty of houses and liberty of wives." Within a year, Levellers mutinied in the army, and in the next year a king was beheaded, while Diggers, Ranters, and others proclaimed that property should be shared in common and that there should be free love. The free exercise of religion, coming almost all at once in the 1640s, after the sudden breakdown of the usual controls, burst forth in a torrent of exotic and eccentric religious opinions, many of which were precursors of Ranterism. And many openly or implicitly expressed political positions.[11]

In that, nothing was new. When there was a dispute, provoked by Laud, within the Church of England on the placement of the altar, the issue was as much over who should control the church as it was theological. If the altar was at the far end of the church, above the congregation and railed off from them, the people received the sacrament from the priest on their knees before the railing; if the altar was a table within the nave, on a level with the congregation, they could take the sacrament closer to God, seated, and on equal terms with the priest. Presbyterians wanted the elders to select the minister, whereas the Independents said that the whole congregation should choose him: the theological issue pitted ecclesiastical oligarchy against congregational democracy. So did the sectarian demand for lay preachers, especially because the pulpit was a public rostrum for the expression of political and social ideas. Thomas Edwards, the Presbyterian cataloguer of the heresies and blasphemies that infected England in 1646, believed, rightly, that many disorders attributable to wrong opinions and practices derived from "mechanics taking upon them[selves] to preach and baptize, as [did] Smiths, Taylors, Shoo-makers, Peddlars, Weavers," and even women.[12]

The Calvinist doctrine of predestination was obviously theological but was as surely political in its implications. Sin having corrupted human nature, eternal damnation was the just reward for all mankind. God in His mercy, however, had for His own reasons predestined some people for salvation; they were the elect. Although they could not know they were the saints, their spiritual rigor and material prosperity were a sign, which made them best qualified to govern church and state. But if Christ had died for all mankind and all were saved, then all were equally qualified to govern. Amid the "gangrene" in Protestantism, Edwards reported, was the common doctrine "That by Christs death, all the sins of all the men in the world, Turks, Pagans, as well as Christians committed against the morall Law and first Covenant, are actually pardoned and forgiven, and this is the everlasting Gospel," meaning universal salvation. Edwards listed corollary doctrines that the Ranters would popularize. The Creator was responsible for people's sins and for the "Pravity, Ataxy, Anomy" which is in them. God loves them whether they pray or sin, do good or evil. It could not stand with the goodness of God to damn His own creatures eternally, "nor would he pick and choose" among people in showing mercy, for if He manifested His love to only a few, "it is far from being infinite."[13]

Two other "errours" in Edwards's catalogue concern Ranterism. One was the argument for religious liberty made by Roger Williams in a book of 1644 which Parliament ordered burned. Some "eminent sectaries" endorsed the argument, Edwards said, and they added that, where conscience was concerned, "the Magistrate may not punish for blasphemies, nor for denying the Scriptures, nor for denying there is a God." The second "errour," in Aesopian language, was "That God the Father did reign under the Law, God the Son under the Gospel, and now God the Father and God the Son are making over the Kingdom to God the holy Ghost, and he shall reign and be poured out upon all flesh." That was remarkably like the message of *A Rout, A Rout*, the first Ranter tract, which appeared in early 1649. Its author, Joseph Salmon, believed that God had progressively manifested himself: first when he gave the Law to Moses, then when he revealed himself through Jesus, and finally in the present age, when he destroyed the monarchy and was spreading his spirit upon all the people of England. But Parliament and the army, Salmon wrote, had made themselves "as absolute and tyrannicall as ever the King"; the "Grandees," he warned, should watch out, "for the Lord is now comming forth to Rip up your bowels." If the grandees laid down their swords and sought deliverance, they would replace oppression with "a blessed Freedom."[14]

Salmon wrote shortly after Charles had been beheaded, when the Rump Parliament—the approximately fifty Independents who survived Pride's Purge of the Presbyterians—and the Council of State governed

England. For people like Salmon, Clarkson, and Coppe, "the fall of the monarch," as A. L. Morton observed, "was only the first stage in vast changes by which the whole social order would be turned upside down." Radicals versed in the Bible expected that "the world would be turned upside down" (Acts 17:6). England had become a republic; even the House of Lords had been abolished. Yet the country was governed as autocratically as ever. The government represented substantial property owners and the generals of the New Model Army. "We were before ruled by King, Lords, and Commons," said a Leveller leader, "now by a General, A Court Martial, and House of Commons: and we pray you what is the difference?"[15]

Ranterism probably developed because the difference was so very little, blasting the expectations of many people and leading them back to religious expression as their only consolation—and their only way of venting defiance against everything their rulers stood for. The "tyranny" of the generals and of Commons was a Ranter theme. For a time there had been a reasonable expectation that a New Jerusalem would arise in England. The constitutional radicals, the Levellers under John Lilburne, demanded popular sovereignty, a genuinely democratic government, and civil and religious liberty. The common soldiers of the New Model Army constituted the rank and file of the Leveller movement and of the gathered churches of the sectaries. The Civil War seemed to them a revolution signaling the reconstruction of society. William Dell, one of the leading preachers of the army, told his congregation of soldiers, "the power is in you, the people; keep it, part not with it." He said of them, after a victory over royalist forces, "Poor illiterate, mechanic men turned the world upside down." Leveller leaders encouraged the vision that the ordinary people were on the threshold of inheriting the earth. Richard Overton, in his *Appeale . . . to the . . . free people in general*, wrote, "I am confident that it must be the poor, the simple and mean things of this earth that must confound the mighty and strong." But the Levellers miscalculated their strength when negotiating with the generals, "the Grandees," for a united front in securing their program from Parliament. The people, a Leveller despairingly wrote, grieved; "they are deceived, their expectations . . . frustrated, and their liberty betrayed." A royalist commentator pointed to the reason: "The Grandees and the Levellers can as soon combine as fire and water; the one aim at pure democracy, the others at an oligarchy."[16]

When the generals rejected the Leveller program, the radicals had no choice but to submit or rebel. Their leaders repudiated the government and the generals in a manifesto calling for the abolition of the Council of State because it was a front for military despotism. The House of Commons condemned that seditious tract as tending to cause mutiny in the

army and branded its authors as traitors. On the next day, Cromwell
arrested Lilburne, Overton, and two others, sending them to the Tower
of London on a charge of treason. From the Tower they published further incitements, including the third Agreement of the Free People, the
climax of Leveller thought. A week later, mutiny broke out in the army,
but Cromwell responded with overwhelming force. His defeat of the
Levellers at Burford destroyed their military power. By no coincidence,
Ranterism soon became prominent. "You have killed the Levellers,"
Coppe accused the "Great Ones," and "Ye have killed the just." That
refrain, like his assault on the rich, was an echo from James 5:6.[17]

Ranterism was a religious phenomenon among the defeated and dis-
illusioned political left. Politics had failed, pamphleteering had failed,
mutiny had failed. Only religion remained. When the Stuart tyrant was
beheaded in January 1649, there had been talk about King Jesus succeeding King Charles. Regicide, the defeat at Burford, and the dispersion of
the Diggers later the same year were shattering events that provoked a
crisis of faith. If the time of deliverance was at hand, millenarian expectations and social radicalism required further revelations. George Fox
began his travels throughout England in 1649, proclaiming his "Quaker"
message of love and the divinity within all persons. Those who became
Fifth Monarchists first insisted in 1649 that the kingdom be turned over
to them, to be governed by officers appointed by the power of Christ.
Others survived their despair by becoming Ranters.[18]

The Ranter message was a peculiar one to be cast in religious terms;
but religion was then the universal language, and Ranterism was an
expression of religious conviction, not a loss of religion. The Ranters
shared the universal craving for a communion with God, although they
understood Him differently. Ranters saw the inhumanity of man to man,
and they could not stand their pain. They lost their revolution and could
not stand their grief. And they reacted extravagantly in a form of religiously inspired surrealism, which was anchored in the familiar Familist
heresy of the immanence or indwelling of God as the activating force of
the universe.

What set the Ranters apart, though, was the surrealistic way they
translated their visions. They acknowledged no authority but their own
intuition and emotional satisfactions. They allowed their subconscious to
reveal itself in their theology and in the uncensored conduct of their daily
lives. Their imagery was nonrational, their style frenzied, their subjectivity intense. They exaggerated everything for emotive purposes. Their
fantasy that they were truly liberated people led them from spiritual
ecstasies to crude and energetic sensationalism. They made a principle
out of unsocial conduct, sexual promiscuity, and even madness. And, of
course, they raved vehemently and interminably, giving rise to the name

by which they were called. They smoked tobacco even as they preached, drank and cursed heavily, fornicated lustily, ate gluttonously, tended to shiftlessness, and in every way imaginable tried to be shocking. If a Ranter had known French, his motto would have been "Epater les bourgeois!"

Their extravagant flouting of normative conduct also reflected the Ranters' belief that the normative principles were no longer right and authoritative. Depression, war, revolution, and betrayal led to an erosion of confidence in the guides that conventionally defined conscience. The Fifth Monarchist, the Familist, the Behmenist, the Leveller, the Digger, the Seeker, the Quaker, and other radicals were not libertines, although each in his own way, like the Ranter, was a symptom of and a response to widespread social breakdown. Only the Ranter greedily practiced a rejection of the moral law. The values and institutions of England no longer commanded the respect of tens of thousands of people, but all radicals except the Ranters belonged to the overwhelming majority who still professed the conventional standards of morality. The majority determined what was eccentric, crazy, and dangerous; the same majority defined blasphemy. By every standard but their own, the Ranters were blasphemous. A basically Puritan society had to prosecute them. Yet Ranter blasphemy, although calculated, perverse, and threatening, was usually harmless defiance. Its harmlessness did not mitigate its offensiveness. But its offensiveness was chiefly a matter of sensibility. Cursing, whoring, and theft appalled moralists, but war, profit making, and poverty were at least as shocking to Ranter sensibilities as Ranter blasphemy was to Puritan sensibilities. Ranter blasphemy—which is to say, Ranter theology—was a symptom of anomie, unlike Socinian blasphemy, which was a reflection of rationalism. Ranters believed that people were not responsible for the "Pravity, Ataxy, Anomy" within them. In that belief they were not wholly wrong. But they did not blame society for their abnormal convictions and behavior. They blamed no one. They gave credit where credit was due: all that is in man, all that he feels, all that he does, is God-given, for God is the Creator, omnipotent and all-wise.

God was that and much more to the Ranters, because they carried every principle to its logical extreme—and beyond. John Holland, "an eye and ear witness" who wrote a reliable description of their theology, not surprisingly condemned their "Atheistical blasphemies." They maintained, he wrote, that God is as much in a leaf as in an angel. He heard one Ranter say that God did not exist except in creatures and that men should pray to no god "but what was in them." They called God "the Being, the Fulnesse, the Great motion, Reason, the Immensity," and one Ranter said that, if there was any god, he was it. When Holland called that blasphemy, because man could not create as God could, the Ranter replied, "he was not The God, but he was God, because God was in him and in every creature in the world." Jacob Bauthumley, who spoke reverentially for a Ranter, had their usual pantheistic view; he saw God in every flower—indeed, in "Man and Beast, Fish and Fowle, and every green thing from the highest Cedar to the Ivey on the wall." God was the life and being of all, "doth really dwell in all," framed men's thoughts, and was in all their acts—all of them. Like other Ranters, Bauthumley abandoned an anthropomorphic concept of God as well as a God who favored an elect of any sort. His god was little more than a divine spirit suffusing everything alive. To some Ranters, God was even in inanimate things, incarnate in the furniture in the room. Edward Hide reasoned logically that, if God was in all things, "then he is sin and wickedness; and if he be all things, then he is this Dog, this Tobacco-pipe, he is me, and I am him." Bauthumley said that man could not know, believe in, or pray to God. Richard Coppin concluded that, if God was perfect and was in every man, each person was perfect—so none could sin. To Abiezer Coppe, God was not only the great Leveller; He was base things, unspotted beauty, and the Divine Being. "My spirit dwells with God," said Coppe, "sups with him, in him, feeds on him, with him, in him."[19]

Whatever God was to the Ranters, he was never evil to them, or connected with evil. They attributed God to everything useful or enjoyable—a table, sex, children, a daisy, comradeship. They did not find godliness in the things they opposed—war, disease, wealth, inequality, churches. Yet they insisted, illogically, that God created everything and dwelt in everything. Christ had no significance for them, except as a rarely used synonym for God; the Christ of the Bible meant as little to them as the Bible. Laurence Clarkson "really believed [in] no Moses, Prophets, Christ or Apostles, no resurrection at all."[20]

The Bible laid down the moral law, the Ten Commandments. To Ranters, it was merely the work of men, a human invention, a figment of the imagination. Some Ranters construed the Bible as a collection of allegories. The Resurrection, for example, was spiritual, not of the body. Christ's coming meant the saving of all men, or free grace. For others, who rejected the Bible altogether, scriptural truths had no meaning. The sense of God within man should be his guide, not the Bible. It was, they said, a "dead letter," a "piece of Witchcraft," and "but a meer Romance." One said that it consisted of tales "to keep People in subjection," and had as much truth in it as the history of Tom Thumb. The commandments of both Old and New Testaments were "fruits of the curse" from which the grace of God freed mankind. Heaven, hell, the afterlife, and sin were fictions, said the Ranters, to enslave people and make them content with their lot. Clarkson thought there was nothing after death. He would "know nothing after this my being was dissolved." Even as a stream was distinct from the ocean till it entered the ocean, he said, so he was distinct from God until death returned his spirit to God and he "became one with God, yea God it self." He spoke too of death as no more than rot and corruption. Heaven was pleasure in this world; hell was poverty, sickness, or, in Bauthumley's phrase, "an accusing conscience." The Ranters had fun with the concept of the devil. He was, they said, just an old woman stuffed with parsley, or the rear end of God, and not really a bad fellow, because he too was a creation of God.[21]

Sin, another fiction, was the invention of churches to make a living for priests. Ranters were fond of the royal motto "Evil to him who evil thinks," and insisted, like Coppe and Clarkson, "To the pure all things are pure." "Whatever I do," said Clarkson, "is acted by that Majesty in me." From this he concluded that "Scripture, Churches, Saints, and Devils are no more to me than the cutting off of a Dog's head." God was good; He was in every act; therefore, every act was good. Clarkson applied his simple logic to swearing, drunkenness, adultery, and theft. He drew the line at murder and, perhaps, at praying in church. All else was the product of God and perfected by His wisdom. The very name "sin," Clarkson said, was but "a name without substance, hath no being in God, nor in the Creature, but only of the imagination." Men reached perfection and grew closer to divinity if they could commit "sins" with no remorse or shame. None could be free from sin "till in purity it be acted as no sin." Clarkson clinched his point by claiming that a man would continue to feel sin until he "can lie with all women as one woman, and judge it not a sin." In an anti-Ranter tract by "a late fellow-Ranter," an eyewitness described a Ranter meeting in a tavern as affirming

> that that man who tipples deepest, swears the frequentest, commits adultery, incest, or buggers the oftenest, blasphemes the imprudentest, and perpetrates the most notorious crimes with the highest hand, and rigedest resolution, is the dearest darling to be gloriously placed in the tribunal Throne of Heaven, holding this detestable Opinion, (equalizing themselves with our blessed Redeemer) that it is lawful for them to drink healths to their Brother *Christ*, and that in [drinking] their liquor, each Brother ought to take his Fellow-Female upon his knee, saying Let us lie down and multiply. . . . *O most horrible blasphemy!*

People believed that Ranters regarded sexual intercourse as the highest sacrament and, therefore, that they supposed it was no sin for "hundreds of Men and Women (savage like) to lie with each other, publickly all together, either in Houses, Fields, or Streets, which is their constant course." Pornographic woodcuts depicting lascivious conduct by Ranters illustrated *Strange Newes from Newgate and the Old Baily*, a tract that retailed the sensational evidence given at the trial of two Ranters charged with blasphemy. Ranters were amusing as well as repellant. One of them took a candle and in broad daylight began hunting about the rooms of a tavern, saying "that he sought for his sins, but there were none, and that which they [the police] thought so great unto him, was so small, that he could not see it."[22]

Ranters liked to meet in taverns—houses of God, Clarkson called them. Ephraim Pagitt, in a clever phrase, called Ranters "the merriest of devils." They sang bawdy songs, often to the tune of church hymns; they whistled, danced, clapped hands, and reputedly enjoyed orgies. One critic spoke of their "prodigious pranks, and unparalleled deportments," and another entitled his comic, anti-Ranter play *The Jovial Crew, or the Devill turn'd Ranter* (1651). Dining was a ritual that some Ranters turned into a travesty on the Christian Mass. One police informant testified that he saw a group in a tavern eating a piece of beef and "one of them took it in his hand, tearing it asunder said to the other, *This is the flesh of Christ, take and eat*. The other took a cup of Ale and threw it into the chimney corner, saying, *There is the bloud of Christ*." They discussed God over their meal, and one said he could go to the outhouse "*and make a God every morning*, by easing his body."[23]

Some Ranters were undoubtedly scatological and coarse, and much in Ranterism was outrageous and deliberately disrespectful. But by pushing the doctrines of free grace and human perfection to the outermost limits of antinomian practice, the Ranters seized upon what was for them an enormous truth—organized religion stifled human expression. They blamed religion for muzzling people's emotional lives. Using theological terms disabled the Ranters from saying that religion had failed man; they intended what Freud meant when he said religion was the universal neurosis. Their intense subjectivity, which was based on hopelessness, was no program, but it was no more unrealistic than the Diggers' economics or the Levellers' politics, both of which had failed. By vomiting away moral repressions, Ranters sought to emancipate the inner lives of people. Their life-style was an invitation for all to live out relatively harmless but socially disruptive fantasies; Ranterism was a purge for sickening anxieties and for an oppressive sense of guilt, especially about sex. Coppe and Clarkson, wild as they were, spoke to the alienated person, alienated from his own inner life as well as from his "fellow Creatures."

The Ranter fantasy was that man could return to Eden, the godly inheritance which religion denied. Before the Fall, God was a benefactor, the world was good, and man did not know evil. After the Fall, the Ranters were saying, the God of theology appeared, vengeful and arbitrary; it was He whom they rejected. Orthodox theology represented Adam as the sinner and Eve as temptation, not as love or fulfillment. The Ranters offered an alternative theology as well as an alternative life-style. Unfortunately, we have no Ranter statements by women, but the sexual content of the writings of the Ranter men and even of the anti-Ranter writings implies that Ranter women were willing believers and partners. The first Ranter sermon that Clarkson heard was preached by a Mary Lake. In a titillating pamphlet, *The Ranters Last Sermon,* "Mistress E.B.," in mixed company, went to one of the men and offered "to unbutton his Cod-piece." When her partner asked why, she is supposed to have replied, "For sin: whereupon . . . in the sight of all the rest, they commit Fornication." If she did reply "For sin," she was jesting, because, as the author of the pamphlet acknowledged, Ranters believed that "whatsoever they did was Good and not Evill, there being no such thing as sin in the world."[24]

The England of the Ranters was a Puritan society in which the foremost connotation of sin was sexual. John Holland, an accurate though hostile reporter, depicted women as equal beneficiaries of free love. "They say," he wrote, "that for one man to be tied to one woman, or one woman to one man, is a fruit of the curse; but, they say, we are freed from the curse, therefore it is our liberty to make use of whom we please." The lack of contraceptives doubtless robbed women of that equality. Gerrard Winstanley, the Digger, warned women to "beware this ranting practice." It burdened them with excessive childbearing. The mother and the children were likely, he said, "to have the worst of it, for the man will be gone and leave them . . . after he hath his pleasure." Winstanley was probably right, but he missed the point that the Ranters hungered for an emotional expression, of which sex was a part, that religion inhibited. Nor did he understand that the Ranter advocacy of extreme individual freedom represented a desperate search for psychological health. It was present even in Jacob Bauthumley's attempt to understand God: "If I say I love thee, it is nothing so, for there is in me nothing can love thee but thy self; and therefore thou dost but love thy self: My seeking of thee is no other but thy seeking of thy self: My delighting enjoying thee, is no other but thy delighting in thy self, and enjoying thy selfe after a most unconceiveable manner." Bauthumley's narcissistic illusion that he loved the God within him expressed a drive to fulfill himself through someone else.[25]

The Ranters fed a hunger in people. John Taylor wrote in 1651 that heretics used to emerge one by one, "but now they sprout by huddles and clusters (like locusts out of the bottomless pit). They now come thronging upon us in swarms, as the Caterpillers of Aegypt." He was speaking of the Ranters. Samuel Sheppard, who thought the devil had turned Ranter,

claimed that same year, "All the world now is in the Ranting humour."
In 1652, Durand Hotham, a justice of the peace, told George Fox, the
founding Quaker, that "all the justices of the nation" could not have
prevented England from being "overspread with Ranterism." These were
no doubt exaggerated statements; although Ranters existed throughout
England, in both town and country, their strength lay in London among
the teeming poor. They attracted unskilled workers, petty artisans, the
unemployed, vagabonds, former soldiers, and underworld elements.
Ranterism had a lower-class character. Coppe romantically identified
with thieves, whores, and beggars. Salmon addressed *A Rout, A Rout* to
fellow soldiers "of inferior rank and quality." The caterpillars of Egypt
notwithstanding, Ranters usually congregated in small groups. Even before the government launched its campaign to suppress them, they tended
to be a secretive, underground movement. When Clarkson first tried to
meet the Ranters who called themselves "My One Flesh," he had to be
given introductions to one intermediary after another. In London, the
Ranters probably numbered thousands, but their constituency never
competed with the organized denominations or with the gathered
churches. Ranterism was more boisterous and articulate than truly dangerous. Focusing on what their leaders said can make them sound dangerous. A. L. Morton observed that leveling, as the Ranters understood
it, "involved a far greater social upheaval than the political changes advanced by Lilburne and his associates, or Winstanley's quite limited
proposals for a joint cultivation of the commons and waste land." But for
all their militancy, Ranters were pacifists and appealed "only to the defeated and declassed, the lower strata of the urban poor, and upon these
no substantial movement could possibly be built." They were also badly
organized, if organized at all, and schismatic. They did not even have a
program. Men who left the movement revealed that a "Ranter's Parliament" in London lost half its attendance of three hundred when the
speakers could not satisfactorily answer questions about the problems of
poverty. People should borrow money without paying it back, the leaders
said, and steal, and "not only make use of a Man's wife, but of his Estate,
Goods, and Chattels also, for all things were common." Even the poor
understood that the "stratagem" was "no wayes feasible."[26]

Most people perceived the Ranters as spiritual fanatics and libertines.
Their critics usually lambasted them as "Atheistical blasphemers," but a
few who condemned them for having abandoned all religion spoke con-
tradictorily. One referred to their "irreligious Religions." The titles of
some anti-Ranter tracts show the same ambivalence: *The Ranters Religion*,
The Ranters Creed, and *The Ranters Bible*. One writer, noting the dualism in
Ranter thought, perceptively defined a particular gang of Ranters as
"Marcions," an allusion to second-century Christian Gnostics; the "Mar-

cions," like the old Gnostics, believed in two deities, one of which was
the creator of all evil. Another writer, appalled by the "horrid" blasphemy that sin was imaginary, said, "These Ranters are but the Gnosticks of former Ages brought backwards among us." Yet the Presbyterian
divine Richard Baxter, although esteemed for his learning and his attempts to be tolerant, discerned in Ranterism no more than its run-of-
the-mill opponents did. The Ranters, Baxter claimed, made it their
business, "under the Name of Christ in Men," to dishonor all churches,
the Bible, the clergy, and worship. They demanded that men and women
should "hearken to Christ within them," Baxter wrote, but

> they conjoyned a Cursed Doctrine of *Libertinism*, which brought
> them to all abominable filthiness of Life: They taught, as the
> familists, that God regarded not the Actions of the Outward Man,
> but of the Heart; and that to the Pure all things are Pure, (even the
> most forbidden): And so as [if] allowed by God, they spoke most
> hideous Words of Blasphemy, and many of them committed
> Whoredoms commonly . . . and this all uttered as the Effect of
> Knowledge, and a part of their Religion, in a Fanatick Strain, and
> fathered on the Spirit of God.

Quakers and Presbyterians agreed on Ranters, although the early Quakers often suffered the indignity of being confused with Ranters. George
Fox first encountered Ranters in a Coventry prison in late 1649. When he
met them, "a great power of darkness struck me," and they said they were
God. Fox asked them whether it would rain tomorrow; they did not
know. God knew, he rejoined, and after reproving them for their blasphemies, he left, because "I perceived they were Ranters, and I had met
with none before."[27]
    Although Gerrard Winstanley and the Ranters shared some fundamen-
tal tenets, he publicly repudiated them to still the slanders that Diggers and
Ranters were indistinguishable. Winstanley believed that man should earn
his bread by the sweat of his brow; labor, hard and productive, was a virtue
with him. He scorned the Ranters as slothful and condemned them for
cheating others of their earnings. Winstanley, who was very Quaker-like,
condemned libertinism. Righteous and quietistic, he spurned the Ranters'
materialism. Theirs, he wrote, was the "Kingdome that lies in objects; As
in the outward enjoyment of meat, drinke, pleasures, and women; so that
the man within can have no quiet rest, unlesse he enjoy those outward
objects in excesse." They believed, he complained, only in the life of the
senses, "which is the life of the Beast." Overindulgence, he warned, im-
paired the "Temple" of the body and brought eventual "sorrow of mind."
He thought too that "excessive copulation with Women" broke up fami-

lies, caused quarrels, and burdened women with childbearing. Winstanley was the only critic of the Ranters who did not castigate their theology, nor would he suppress them. Let him who was without sin, he wrote, "cast the first Stone at the Ranter." He counseled patience and righteous living, "and thou shalt see a returne of the Ranters."[28]

The government pursued a different policy. Coventry was probably the first town to jail its Ranters. Among the group that George Fox visited in prison there in late 1649 was Joseph Salmon, the former soldier and itinerant preacher who had written *A Rout, A Rout*. Abiezer Coppe, who had just written the two installments of his lurid *Fiery Flying Roll*, was probably in the same Coventry prison with Salmon and his group. The charge against them may have been based on a provision in the Blasphemy Act of 1648 for punishing the heretical belief that the moral law of the Ten Commandments is not a rule of Christian life. Too little is known about the Coventry case to be certain. In January 1650, the two *Fiery Flying Rolls* were republished as one, adding to their notoriety. The authorities in Coventry did not know they had the book's author in custody, nor did the House of Commons know that Coventry had him when, on February 1, the House directed that a search be made for him. The House censured the book for its "horrid Blasphemies" and ordered that all copies be seized throughout the realm and burned by the public hangmen. According to George Fox, the Coventry Ranters won their release by recanting their beliefs "not long after" he encountered them. Salmon had to promise to put his recantation into public print. Coppe, who was probably using an assumed name to escape detection, recanted orally; he and Salmon were at liberty in mid-1650.[29]

Ranters had not the stuff of which martyrs were made. They renounced their beliefs with comparative ease. Believing in neither heaven nor hell, that even the soul died with the body, and that there was no afterlife, they had nothing to win if they stood fast by their beliefs and nothing to lose by repudiating them. Life was to be enjoyed here and now, rather than be wasted in prison. Anyway, the Ranters were amoral enough to say what had to be said to gain their freedom. As Justice Hotham told Fox in 1652, they would have said and done as the magistrates commanded "and yet kept their principle still." Salmon, in his book of recantation, professed a "sincere abdication of certain Tenets, either formerly vented by him, or now charged upon him." The very title of his *Heights in Depths and Depths in Heights* was a clue that he had not fundamentally changed. Ranters were fond of oxymorons, rhetorical figures that joined contradictory and incongruous meanings, as when Coppe spoke of his "filthy, nasty holiness," or said that one could not know unspotted beauty without knowing base things. The oxymorons reflected Gnostic dualism.[30]

Salmon recanted after he suffered "above halfe a years imprisonment under the notion of a blaspheamer; which through want of air and many other conveniences, became very irksome and tedious to my outward man." Those are Ranter sentiments. Similarly, Salmon, supposedly repentant, defined God as "one simple, single, uncompounded glory: nothing lives in him or flows from him, but what is his pure individual self." A minister, commenting on the Ranter practice of using Aesopian language, declared that Ranters say "one thinge and mean another. . . . They will say and unsay in one breath." Their expressions had "wayes and windings, to keep themselves from being known, but to their owne."[31]

In 1650 Clarkson published his libertine manifesto, *A Single Eye All Light, no Darkness; or Light and Darkness One*. The "Devil is God, Hell is Heaven, Sin Holiness, Damnation Salvation, this and only this is the first Resurrection," Clarkson announced. The House of Commons, in June 1650, after listening to a reading of *A Single Eye*, empowered a committee that was investigating "a Sect called Ranters" to find and imprison them. The House also ordered the committee to prepare a bill to suppress such blasphemies "and to make the same Offences capital."[32]

New legislation was needed because the Blasphemy Act of 1648, having been passed before the emergence of the Ranters, did not speak to their principles or conduct. The heresy clause on the denial of the Ten Commandments, the only one applicable to the Ranters, allowed recantation as an alternative to a prison term. The act of 1648, a Presbyterian product, required death for a conviction of any of the blasphemies it proscribed, and in the main they were Socinian in character. The heresy clauses of the same act were so broad that, if enforced, they would have ensnared Cromwell, members of the Rump Parliament, and a large part of the army. The Independents, who controlled the government, were reluctant to enforce a Presbyterian measure, especially at a time when Presbyterian Scotland was engaged in a war against England for the purpose of placing Charles II on the throne. As the House of Commons debated a new measure on offenses against religion, Scottish divines charged that the English Independents were guilty of blasphemies and heresies. Repudiating that charge, Cromwell declared that he abhorred the detestable blasphemies "lately broken out amongst us," and he called attention to the fact that "We have already punished some among us for blasphemy, and are further ready to do it." On the same day in July when the House of Commons received a copy of Cromwell's declaration, it voted against death as the punishment for Ranter blasphemy by accepting a six-month prison term for the first offense. The House also voted against a proposal that punishment for the second offense should be boring through the blasphemer's tongue with a hot iron. Banishment was to be the recidivist's sentence; death was reserved only for those who, having been banished, returned to England without permission from the House.[33]

On August 9, 1650, the house passed its "Act against several Atheistical, Blasphemous and Execrable Opinions, derogatory to the honor of God." By comparison with any previous standard in English history, this was not an enactment into law of bigotry; it was carefully framed to cover only Ranter professions and practices. No persons whose religious beliefs were recognizably Christian, not even the Familists, who upheld the teachings of Hendrik Nicholas, or any of the novel and recent sects such as the Quakers and Fifth Monarchists, came within its terms. From the standpoint of its framers, the target of the statute was not the unorthodox but the irreligious, or those who made a religion of immorality. John Milton supported the act of 1650 because, he said, blasphemy "or evil speaking against God" was not a reflection of religious conscience. He offered the act of 1650 as a definition of blasphemy that was plainer and more judicious than the clergy had produced "in many a prolix volume." Actually, all the act did was to catalogue Ranter precepts and call them blasphemous.[34]

The act applied to anyone who maintained any of the following opinions: that he or another living person was God, was equal to God, or possessed His attributes; that God dwells within man "and no where else"; that unrighteousness or sinfulness was not immoral; or that heaven and hell, or salvation and damnation, did not exist or could not be distinguished. The act also applied to anyone who denied or blasphemed God, cursed Him, or swore falsely or profanely in His name; and to anyone who claimed that it was not sinful to speak obscenely, or steal, cheat, and defraud, or commit adultery, fornication, incest, or sodomy, or that any of the enumerated sins were as holy as praying or preaching. In addition, the act covered anyone who professed that whatever he did, "whether Whoredom, Adultery, Drunkenness or the like open Wickedness," could be done without sin or expressed the God within him; and anyone who professed that heaven consisted in acting out the things that were sinful, or that one committing them was closer to God or reached perfection by feeling no remorse, or that sin had God's approval, or that there was no such thing as sin.

A month later, the same House of Commons passed an act that repealed all enactments requiring uniformity in religious belief and practice, or establishing any form of religion in England. That statute of September 1650 also advanced the cause of religious liberty by implying that no establishment of religion should exist and by allowing every variety of Christian worship. As an alternative to Sunday worship, one might privately preach, pray, read the Bible, or discuss it. In effect, toleration existed for anyone not subject to the provisions of the Blasphemy Acts of 1648 (Socinianism) and 1650 (Ranterism). The Toleration Act was fittingly denoted an act for the relief of "religious and peaceable people."[35]

On the very day of the passage of the Toleration Act, the House tried two Ranters who had been arrested, Laurence Clarkson and Major William Rainborough, a former Leveller. Clarkson was a great prize, for his *Single Eye* was the immediate provocation of the Blasphemy Act of 1650, although Coppe claimed credit for it. He too had been captured and awaited his turn to be examined. The House's committee on Ranters had already examined Clarkson. He was a difficult witness, for he admitted nothing, demanded that his accusers prove that he wrote the book whose title page bore only the initials "L.C.," and refused to answer incriminatory questions. The committee, however, reported that he had confessed, and the House summarily condemned him as guilty and ordered the burning of his book. They sentenced him to a month in jail, following which he was to be banished "and not to return, upon Pain of Death." The sentence of banishment was not carried out, probably because it was illegal. Indeed, the entire trial of Clarkson by the House of Commons was illegal. By the terms of the Blasphemy Act of 1650, the accused was to be held for trial before a judge, a justice of the peace, or a mayor, and the sentence of banishment could be imposed only after a second lawful conviction. Clarkson was released from prison after about fourteen weeks. Rainborough, for his Ranter conduct, was simply stripped of his rank and discharged from the army.[36]

When the same committee of the House examined the author of the *Fiery Flying Rolls*, "the wild deportment of Mr. *Copp* the great Ranter" made news. He disrupted the proceedings by acting like a lunatic—talking to himself and flinging fruit and nuts about the room. His having "disguised himself into a madnesse" was rational, because the act of 1650 exempted persons "distracted in brain," and Coppe apparently believed that appearing mad was the appropriate response of a sane man in an insane world. The tactic failed; they returned him to Newgate Prison and left him there. Although the statute of limitations had run out on Coppe's offense, the House of Commons did not stick at a legal nicety. Like Biddle, he received no trial, not even a formal condemnation by the House, and they had already done him the honor of burning his book.[37]

In Newgate, Coppe was as feisty as ever, at first. He received visitors with éclat and converted some fellow prisoners. But he had little of Biddle's courage and consistency. Ranters were not cut out to suffer for a cause. A few months later, Coppe published a hemidemisemiquaver of a recantation; it was a protest, denying that he held blasphemous opinions and complaining that he had been defamed. The government paid no attention to him. After fourteen months of incarceration, Coppe published his *Return to the wayes of Truth*, begging Parliament's pardon. He renounced his blasphemous opinions, although he retained his social radicalism. While damning the conventional sins, he emphasized hypocrisy, a lecherous heart, and tyranny over the poor as the worst sins. If a "fellow creature" hungered, Coppe would feed him: "If I have bread it shall, or should be his, else all my religion is in vain. I am for dealing bread to the hungry, for cloathing the naked, for breaking of every yoak, for the letting of the oppressed go free." Doing otherwise was sinful. But he was on the side of the angels on the issue of righteous living, so the government set him free. As part of the bargain, he had to preach a recantation sermon at Burford, where Cromwell had suppressed the Leveller mutiny. A minister who heard Coppe's sermon remained unconvinced. Coppe, he wrote, used "melting words, Honey-sweet, smooth as oyle, but full of poison."[38]

The act of 1650 punished the Ranter conviction that, if God was in man, man was God. Some Ranters took that literally, among them William Franklin, a ropemaker of London. His spiritual adventure and apprehension occurred before the passage of the statute. Its "Franklin clause" was intended to remedy a gap in the law. Franklin had been a pious Congregationalist, but, on recovering from an illness that affected his mind, he announced that he was God and Christ. In 1649, he fell in with Ranters, abandoned his wife, and began practicing free love. One of his women, Mary Gadbury, was a religious eccentric given to visions. That Christ had been reborn in Franklin came to her in a revelation, and she spread the glad tidings. When a minister questioned the morality of her living with Franklin, she replied that Adam and Eve had lived naked in their innocence and had been unashamed till sin brought shame into the world; but Christ had taken sin away. She called herself the spouse of Christ and claimed to be equal to God. In late 1649, Franklin and Gadbury left London to bring their gospel to the Southampton countryside. They made converts and even found disciples. "Now," wrote an eyewitness, "doth this poysonous infection begin to amaine [at full speed] to spread itself, having gotten many, and these also very active persons, to be the Preachers, Spreaders, and publishers of it abroad to the people. . . . They perswade others to imbrace and entertain also, that . . . this Franklin is the Son of God, the Christ, the Messiah." Millenarians expected King Jesus but not that he would spout Ranter doctrines. Franklin, Gadbury, and their disciples were arrested in 1650. At first, they all claimed, and Franklin agreed, that he was literally Christ. The disciples, having been reborn when they met him, dated their ages from that event. They were steadfast in their new beliefs until their leader betrayed them. Confronted with prison, he recanted, angering his disciples and causing them to abandon him. Mary Gadbury, unrepentant, was sent to Bridewell Prison, where she was whipped intermittently for several weeks. The men received prison sentences but were released on giving sureties for good behavior. Franklin, who was penniless, joined Gadbury in Bridewell. When the next impostors came along, the law was readier to deal with them.[39]

The act of 1650 and the imprisonment of Salmon, Clarkson, Coppe, and Franklin did not intimidate some Ranters. George Foster published his *Sounding of the Last Trumpet*, apocalyptically restating the social doctrines of the early Coppe. Foster presented God as the Great Leveller who would usher in King Jesus' communist utopia after overthrowing the rich, the clergy, and Parliament—all oppressors of the poor. Jacob Bauthumley's *Light and Dark Sides of God* was quietistic but anti-Trinitarian and pantheistic. Bauthumley, once a cobbler from Leicester, wrote his little book when he was a soldier. The army, following its own law, made an example of him: he was punished by being bored through the tongue with a hot iron. The army suppressed its Ranters remorselessly. Cromwell himself cashiered one Ranter officer for denying that man could sin. Ranter officers lost their commissions and, like rank-and-file Ranters, were publicly whipped. Some soldiers were suspended by their thumbs, and one, a "W. Smith," was hanged by the neck at York, at the close of 1650, "for denying the Deity, Arianlike," and for other, unnamed Ranter practices. Following the act of 1650, the police cracked down on civilian Ranters. Systematic raids resulted in scores of arrests. In one case, eight Ranters, taken in a London tavern, were sent to Bridewell to beat hemp, and the two who were the most offensive were put on trial at Old Bailey, the seat of the central criminal court in London, and sentenced to six months in prison. Other Ranters, a gang of them, were sentenced to be whipped at Bridewell. The police raids continued into 1651. We may disbelieve one report that a Ranter, supposedly in league with the devil, escaped after he "called for . . . a pissepot, and in an instant, upon a great flash of fire, vanished, and was never seen more."[40]

Undoubtedly, some Ranters were mentally deranged. One writer classified "these Atheistical Creatures" as either Free Will Ranters or "your mad Ranters, for they are lunatics very often." They were punished anyway, because of the enormity of their blasphemous conceits. Two women, both named Elizabeth Sorrell and related to each other, were arrested for blaspheming the "Holy Trinitie" and claiming the power to raise the dead. Four of their followers were also arrested, and at least one of the Sorrells was sent to jail. Messianic delusions were not uncommon among Ranters. In the same year, 1651, Richard King was imprisoned for the blasphemous claim that his pregnant wife was about to give birth to the Holy Ghost. Mary Adams also went to jail for claiming that her unborn child was Jesus Christ, although Joan Robins contested that claim by saying the same about her own child; she too earned a sentence for blasphemy, also in 1651. It was a vintage year for messiahs. The two most notorious were Joan's husband, John Robins, and Thomas Tany.[41]

John Robins was a blasphemer who inspired blasphemy in others. Thomas Tilford, first arrested as a follower of the Sorrells, transferred his allegiance to Robins and, like Robins, whom he called "God the Father, and the Father of our Lord Jesus Christ," landed in jail for blasphemy. Robins, as well as the Sorrells, claimed the power to raise the dead, but he went further. By his own statement, he had already raised Cain, Benjamin the son of Jacob, the prophet Jeremiah, and Judas; he had not only raised but redeemed them. Lodowick Muggleton, then an associate of Robins and later a great heresiarch, recorded that he had had "nine or ten of them at my house at a time, of those that were said to be raised from the dead. For I do not speak this from a Hear-say from Others, but from a perfect Knowledge, which I have seen and heard from themselves." Robins, whom an enemy called "the Shakers god" and "the Ranters' god," allowed his followers to worship him. He was fluent in the Scriptures, claimed to have been Adam and then Melchizedek in previous incarnations, and came by his Hebrew, Greek, and Latin, he said, "by inspiration." He had a plan to lead 144,000 people out of England to the Mount of Olives in the Promised Land. Joshua Garment, his Moses, would part the waters of the Red Sea for the pilgrims, and Robins would feed them with manna from heaven. In May 1651, Robins, his wife, and eleven disciples, including the Kings and the Sorrells, were imprisoned. After a year in jail, Robins addressed a letter of recantation to Cromwell, which won him a discharge.[42]

Thomas Tany, an associate of Robins, spent six months in Newgate for his blasphemies. He had abandoned his business as a goldsmith to proclaim that God had personally spoken to him, giving him to understand that he was a Jew of the tribe of Reuben whose mission was to lead the Jews back to the Promised Land and rebuild the Temple. By divine command, Tany changed his name to Theaurau John and, according to Muggleton, circumcised himself. Tany had many silly ideas, some of them sublime. He claimed to be the earl of Essex, heir to the throne of England, and in a pamphlet of 1651 debated Magna Carta "with the Thing called Parliament." He ranted madly in the streets about his mission as high priest of the Jews and the indwelling of God. Following his prison term, he was quiet for several years, but in 1654 he was claiming that, as a descendant of Charlemagne, he was entitled to the crown of France. As that year closed, he publicly burned the Bible and then assaulted the House of Commons while it debated the fate of John Biddle.

With a long, rusty sword, Tany hacked away at the doors of Parliament, slashing at people nearby. After he was subdued and brought before the bar of the House, he explained, irrationally, that the people were ready to stone him (the Old Testament punishment for blasphemy) because he had burned the Bible. Asked why he had burned it, he said it had deceived him: it was only letters and idolatry, not "Life" and "the word of God." But he "did it not of himself: And being asked, Who bid him do it; saith, God." The House, taking him for a Quaker, resolved that, for drawing his sword, burning the Bible, and declaring that it was not the word of God, he be committed to the Gatehouse Prison. After his liberation some months later, he revived his project for restoring the Jews in Jerusalem. There being no Jews in England, Tany sailed to Amsterdam, but perished at sea.[43]

Robert Norwood, a friend of Tany, was a more conventional Ranter, if Ranters of any stripe can be said to have been conventional. A former army captain, he came to the Ranter way of thinking by abandoning belief in the immortality of the soul, the physical existence of heaven and hell, and the literalness of the resurrection. Convicted in Old Bailey in 1652 for the crime of blasphemy, he was sentenced to six months' imprisonment under the act of 1650. Richard Faulkner of Petersfield was lucky that Parliament did not get him before the criminal courts did. He not only drank a toast to the devil; he said "our saviour Christ was a bastard," and, with the class consciousness of a Ranter, added that Joseph was only a poor carpenter. He too got six months.[44]

When Parliament got hold of William Erbury in 1652, it was scraping the barrel. Although Erbury's record made him a likely suspect, he was no Ranter. After attending Oxford, he had been an Anglican priest frequently in trouble with the Court of High Commission. In 1640 he became a Puritan, later an Independent. During the Civil War, he was a chaplain in the army. Thomas Edwards charged that he vented antinomian doctrines, which could mean merely that he advocated universal salvation. Cheynell, another Presbyterian, debated Erbury publicly and accused him of Socinian blasphemies. Like Biddle, Erbury denied the divinity of Christ while preaching the "inner Christ," a doctrine of universal incarnation in believers. He defied all labels, except that of Seeker. His politics were as radical as his religion. Although he flirted with Ranterism and shared some of its views, much in Ranterism offended him. When examined by the parliamentary investigating committee, he denounced the Ranters, but that occurred in 1652, after the law had turned against them and the craze had subsided. That the committee examined Erbury is proof that by that date the Ranter heresiarchs had been silenced or driven underground. There were still some Ranters around, but if they did not keep to themselves they risked being caught, like Henry Walker, a tavern keeper who pronounced "a poxe on Jesus Christ" and said he would rather be in bed with his girlfriend than in paradise with Jesus.[45]

The prosecution of John Reeve and Lodowick Muggleton under the act of 1650 was as misdirected as the investigation of Erbury. Worse, their prosecution, like that of Biddle, reflected religious prejudice against mere doctrinal novelty. Reeve and Muggleton were upright men with exceedingly strange ideas, too strange to countenance. These two cousins were not Ranters, although Reeve had briefly consorted with John Robins and Thomas Tany, and Muggleton had been fascinated by them. Muggleton had also avidly read the works of Jacob Boehme, one of the mystics who believed in the indwelling of God and in universal salvation. By 1653, however, when Reeve and Muggleton were arrested, they had completely repudiated Ranterism; indeed, they felt so repelled by it that they cursed its advocates—and when they cursed anyone, he was damned everlastingly.[46]

Thomas Babington Macaulay amusingly referred to a "mad tailor, named Lodowick Muggleton, [who] wandered from pothouse to pot-house, tippling ale, and denouncing eternal torments against all those who refused to believe, on his testimony, that the Supreme Being was only six feet high, and that the sun was just four miles from the earth." Muggleton, who knew nothing of astronomy, was more sober than Macaulay and no madder. His logic told him that, if God made man in His own image, God was human in form and size, exactly like Jesus Christ. Muggleton, like Reeve, was only a tailor. If the Old Testament prophets could have been herdsmen, and Christ's apostles fishermen, he asked, then why couldn't tailors be the two witnesses mentioned in Revelation 11:3? Reeve and Muggleton, like the new faith they had the boldness to imagine, were Interregnum period pieces fashioned by the religious turbulence of their time, but "Muggletonianism" survived it. Of all the sects spawned in that period, only two have endured, Quakerism and Muggletonianism, the two which in the seventeenth century hated each other. The Muggletonians are doubtless the most obscure and tiny sect in all Christendom.[47]

Reeve and Muggleton no more advocated sin than a believing Presbyterian did. No Ranter shared their fantastic opinion that Eve, the Ranter's sex symbol, was the devil come to flesh. The two witnesses, Reeve and Muggleton, thought that prosecuting them for their beliefs was blasphemous. The act of 1650 aimed at those who made a religion out of immorality or who justified sin by blasphemous opinions. Reeve and Muggleton, by contrast, were puritanical; as men of rectitude, they were industrious, believers in Christ, faithful to their wives, and opposed to drunkenness and gambling. Muggleton, who died at the patriarchal age of eighty-nine, proudly recorded that he had never lived off the Gospel as the apostles had; he had always earned his livelihood from his craft as a tailor, accumulated property, paid his taxes, and had no debts. Although he was not given to religious enthusiasm, spiritual fires smoldered within him. He had lost his zeal as a Calvinist after the Civil War fractured Puritanism into squabbling factions, and he stopped the habit of praying. If anything followed death, he wrote in his autobiography, he would leave it to God to do "what He would with me." God did not wait for Muggleton's death. In 1651, he began getting revelations that opened to him "the Paradise of heaven, within man upon earth," and he began reading the Bible again. Reeve, long envious of Muggleton's serenity, finally experienced similar revelations. Reaching a state of peace, the two thought they would never again dispute with anyone about religion. Then, in 1652, Muggleton recalled, "we were made the greatest meddlers in Religion of all Men in the World. Because our faces were against all Mens Religion in the World, of what Sect or Opinion soever."[48]

Reeve got the message first. As he recorded in a tract of 1652, the one that got them into trouble for blasphemy,

> . . . the Lord Jesus, the only wise God, whose glorious person is resident above or beyond the stars, . . . spake to me Reeve, saying, I have given thee understanding of my mind in the Scriptures, above all men in the world. . . . I have chosen thee my last messenger for a great work unto this bloody unbelieving world; and I have given thee Lodowicke Muggleton to be thy mouth. . . . I have put the two-edged sword of my Spirit into thy mouth, that whoever I pronounce blessed through thy mouth is blessed to eternity, and whoever I pronounce cursed through thy mouth is cursed to eternity.

Reeve and Muggleton had a divine commission to teach the Word as they understood it, and they were armed with a unique power. In compliance with other messages from the Lord Jesus, they pronounced curses of damnation upon Theaurau John Tany and John Robins. The curse on Robins, a marvel of hellfire and brimstone, damned him eternally as the Antichrist. Robins, who was in Bridewell Prison at the time, put his hands on the grates of his cell and uttered, "It is finished; the Lord's will be done," and soon after he recanted. The new prophets began attracting the crowds that had thronged around Tany and Robins.[49]

In their revised version of Christianity, Reeve and Muggleton renounced the Trinitarian principle. No point was clearer at the time of their arrest in 1653. Reeve, until his death in 1658, and Muggleton thereafter continued to develop their theology without ever resolving some contradictions. From the beginning, though, they believed that the Father, the Son, and the Holy Ghost were synonymous expressions for one real person, the God Jesus Christ. In the beginning, when He was the Creator, He was Spirit, but He came to earth as Jesus the man, to die so that He would understand the human predicament. On the cross, He cried out to Elijah, whom He had left on the throne of glory as His representative while He was mortal. When Jesus died, God died, but rose again body and soul, and thereafter paid no further attention to man. Having set everything in motion, God would not concern Himself with the human race again until Judgment Day. So wars, plagues, famine, and human cruelty were the work of the devil, a fallen angel who had planted his seed in Eve and lived in all her descendants through Cain. God, having fixed a conscience in man's heart, allowed him to work out his own destiny. Thus, every person had within him both the spirit of God and that of the devil; as the voice heard by Reeve had said, the kingdoms of heaven and hell were in man's body. On Judgment Day, God would resurrect the righteous, body and soul. Till then, He would do nothing. After that time, this earth would become hell, inhabited by the damned. One need only believe and live righteously. All else was pointless: worship, churches, sacraments, ceremonies, clergyman, and their ordinances. Anyone who heard the message of God's last prophets, Reeve and Muggleton, and willfully disbelieved was damned.

Some angry readers delivered copies of Reeve's book to the lord mayor of London and demanded an arrest. Reeve and his "mouth," Muggleton, said that God had died, repudiated the doctrine of the Trinity, and claimed that the soul was mortal. It was too much. The mayor ordered their arrest. When the two witnesses appeared before him, he had a copy of their book and copies of their letters to the Presbyterian ministers of London ordering them to quit preaching or be damned eternally for the unpardonable sin of blasphemy against the Holy Spirit. Reeve admitted writing the book, Muggleton the curses. "You are accused," the mayor said, "for denying the three Persons in the Trinity: You say there is but one Person Christ Jesus, you deny the Father." Reeve replied that they accepted the Trinity as "all but one person." When the mayor answered that the devil had spoken to Reeve, the prisoner damned his lordship and demanded an explanation of God. He was an "infinite, incomprehensible Spirit," the mayor said, with "no Body or Person at all." Reeve insisted that Jesus had a body "in form like Man, Sin excepted." Then the mayor read from the act of Parliament "newly made against Blasphemy," which condemned any man who said that he was God and that God was nowhere else. Reeve and Muggleton had not, of course, made that claim. Muggleton informed the mayor that, as a mere temporal magistrate, he was "not to judge of Blasphemy against God; not those that made this Act neither." And, with stupefying arrogance, Muggleton added that God had chosen only his two witnesses to be judges of blasphemy. The mayor sent them to Newgate.

After a month in jail, they were tried before a jury, with the mayor presiding, at Old Bailey. The charge of blasphemy was based on the denial of the Trinity in Reeve's book. After a few questions and direct answers, the trial was done, "and the Jury laid their Heads a little together" and found them guilty. They were sentenced to six months in Bridewell. When they got out, they wrote *A Remonstrance from the Eternal God*, which they addressed to the government. They restated their mission as the Lord's messengers and lamented their unjust sentence, but in the main they pleaded for liberty of conscience. They did not understand that the power they claimed, to damn willful disbelievers, conflicted with conscience, "which belongs not to man to judge, but to God only that knows the heart." But they made a ringing plea in behalf of "the free people of England, that they should not only enjoy their civil liberties, but the liberty of consciences towards God."[50]

The government, which paid no attention to their demand, did not understand that in Reeve and Muggleton it had had behind bars a pair of heresiarchs whose opinions violated the act of 1648, not the one of 1650. When Reeve died four years after coming out of prison, Muggleton took command of the new sect, and he survived until 1698. He would be troubled three times more with the charge of blasphemy, but he was a witness with a divine commission. He could not be stopped by a government that did not impose crippling sentences and could not distinguish a Muggletonian from a Ranter.

The government never did stamp out all the Ranters. In time, they faded away; they were never more than a passing craze. Coppe changed his name, became a physician, and was buried in the town church. As late as 1655, he reciprocated a visit that George Fox once paid him in a Coventry jail; when Fox was in jail, Coppe and Bauthumley and a company of Ranters visited him. Fox called Bauthumley a "great Ranter" in 1655, but Bauthumley too lapsed into respectability; he became keeper of the library in Leicester. Salmon emigrated to Barbados. Coppin became a Seeker, and Clarkson a Muggletonian. That Ranterism survived throughout the 1650s is evident from occasional glimpses of it. In 1655, R. Forneworth, a Quaker, published a denunciation of blasphemous Ranterism in this sketch of Robert Wilkinson of Leicester:

> . . . he said he was both God and Devill, and he said there was no God but him, and no Devill but him, and he said whom he blest was blest, and whom he curst was curst, and he said he was a serpent, and so he is, and he said the Apostles were lyars and

deceivers, and I gave him a Bible to prove that, and he said the
Bible was a pack of lyes, and there was neither heaven nor hell but
here, and yet he was both in heaven and hell, and had as lieve be
in hell, as in heaven, and he said he was a serpent, and a whore-
master, and before he said he was born of God, and could not
commit sin.

That is Ranterism, straight and pure. As late as 1659, Richard Hickcock,
another Quaker, also published a tract "against the People call'd Ranters,"
in which he complained about those who cursed, lied, fornicated, believed that one sinned only if he thought so, and contended that God is
the author of sin.[51]

When Ranters surfaced publicly, the government prosecuted. Richard Coppin, a founding Ranter, would never have served time for blasphemy if he had shunned publicity. His first tract, *Divine Teachings*
(1649), for which Abiezer Coppe wrote the preface, became a source that
other Ranters looted for ideas and imagery. After the act of 1650, Coppin
was quiet for a while. He claimed later that he had never abandoned his
beliefs of 1649, although he explicitly repudiated Ranterism as well as
Quakerism and every other religion but his own. Coppin the Seeker was
an antinomian but no libertine. For him, Scripture had become "dead
letter" unless understood through the revelation that God had given to
the Christ in Coppin. Yet his God was as much in everyone as in Christ,
and made every person perfect. Coppin also denied the physical existence
of heaven and hell. A Worcester jury convicted him of blasphemy in
1652, but the judge, noting that the beliefs proscribed by the act of 1650
did not precisely correspond with those charged against Coppin, bound
him over for retrial. A jury in Oxford found him guilty too, but again a
judge, disagreeing, persuaded the jury to reconsider its verdict; it divided
indecisively. That was in 1653. In the next year, Coppin was again
arrested for blasphemy because he preached in violation of the act of
1650, but once more a judge strictly construed the statute in his favor.
Coppin had clearly repudiated Ranterism, but few conventional Christians could tell the difference.[52]

In 1655, Coppin foolishly agreed to a public debate in Rochester on
theological matters—against a Presbyterian, no less. Major General
Thomas Kelsey heard Coppin. Assisted by justices of the peace, Kelsey
accused him of blasphemy for having declared that Christ as a human
being had been defiled by sin, that all men would be saved, and that
heaven and hell existed only in man. Kelsey recommended to Cromwell
that Coppin should be banished like Biddle, but Cromwell let the law
take its course. Belatedly, Coppin received the statutory six-month sentence.[53]

The same fate awaited two weavers in the village of Lacock in Wilt-shire. William Bond and Thomas Hibbord rantingly maintained in pub-lic that there was no God, no Christ, only the sun overhead. Bond said that his friend Tom Lampire of Melksham could write better Scriptures than the Bible. Heaven was good fortune in this world, and hell was poverty. Hibbord, who believed that God was in anything thought sin-ful, said he "would sell all religions for a jug of beer." That was in 1656. The grand jury that indicted them deplored the fact that there were "many" people wandering about spreading such blasphemies.[54]

Ranterism could persevere in a free and disordered society like that of the England of the Interregnum, but not in Presbyterian Scotland. The Scots did not have the problem that Kelsey described to Cromwell after Coppin's arrest: "people are ready to cry out for liberty of conscience, and not backward to say it's persecution worse than in the bishops time, and the like." Uniformity in religion and severe persecution flourished in Scotland like heath and thistle. To a Scot of the established church, a sentence of merely six months for treason against God was coddling blasphemers. Alexander Agnew of Dumfries, a vagrant known as Jock of Broad Scotland, found that out. He was an atheist with the Ranter habit of talking too much and too offensively, but without sense enough to know when to shut up. His blasphemies, as his indictment stated, were frequent, uttered wherever he went. When asked whether he desired to attend church, he replied, "Hang God." God had given him nothing, and he was just as indebted to the devil, whom he thought the more powerful. When asked how many persons were in the Godhead, he replied only one person, God made all; Christ, a mere man, was not God. He denied that he was a sinner, scorned God's mercy, and mocked all worship. Declar-ing that he never had any religion and never would, he flatly said "there was no God, nor Christ." Only nature reigned. Heaven and hell did not exist, the Bible was false, and man had no soul. On that evidence, the jury found him guilty. On May 21, 1651, Jock of Broad Scotland was hanged from a gibbet.[55]

CHAPTER NINE

The Early English Quakers

IN THE 1650s, the Ranter and the Quaker were allied in antinomian-ism and opposed in all else. One was the libertine Antichrist, self-indulgently reveling in sin, the other the primitive Christian self-righteously overcoming sin—and demanding, in the shrillest possible tone, that everyone else must find Christ exactly his way and no other. To the Quaker, no other way was possible. Linking Quakers with Ranters and even with blasphemy sounds preposterous to modern ears, but the Quakers of the mid-seventeenth century were not like their descendants. The first Quakers had the fiery temperament of Old Testament prophets, and they trumpeted the message of the New Testament as if no one had done so since Christ's apostles. They made extravagant claims that of-fended and infuriated people. In conduct and belief, the first Quakers had about the same effect upon their contemporaries as Holy Rollers would have in a quiet Friends' meeting today.

The Quaker founder, George Fox, and his captains, James Nayler, Francis Howgill, and William Dewsbury—all condemned for blas-phemy—were pentecostal, puritanical, proselytizing zealots. Quakers obeyed no sacrament, no law, no ministry, and no custom that conflicted with the indwelling Light of Christ that guided their lives. They were militant, intolerant, and vituperative; they invited persecution, and they gloried in it as a sign of their witness to Christ. They saw themselves as the only true, infallible church and saw all Christians of the preceding sixteen centuries as apostates. The Protestants of England, whether An-glican, Presbyterian, Congregationalist, or Baptist, belonged, Fox said, to the "Synagogues of Satan."

> And therefore in the name & power of the Lord Jesus was I sent
> to preach the everlasting gospell which Abraham saw & was
> preached in the Apostles days. . . . And since has the Apostacy
> gonne over all nations. . . . Nowe wee haveinge the false prophetts
> antichrists deceivers whore false Church beast & his worshippe in
> the dragons power betwixt us and the Apostles . . . I say the

everlastinge gospell must bee preacht againe to all nations & to every creature: which bringes life & immortality to light in them that they may see over the Devill & his false prophetts & antichrists & seducers & deceivers & the whore & beast & before they was. And in this message of this glorious & everlastinge gospelle was I sent foorth to declare & thousands by it are turned to God & have received it & are come Into the order of it.[1]

Fox and his Quaker preachers engaged in "the Lamb's War." The Lamb, of Revelation 5:1–14, is the victorious Christ, exalted by God to govern the world after conquering the Antichrist. Edward Burrough, one of Fox's soldiers for Christ, proclaimed that the Lamb "hath called us to make War in righteousness for His name's sake, against Hell and death, and all the powers of darkness. . . . And they that follow the Lamb shall overcome. . . ." Dewsbury spoke of the Lord's gathering a mighty host exalting Christ as King of Kings. The Quaker army raised in the north of England would march southward, reinforced by the mighty power of the word of God, as sharp as the two-edged sword, to cut down anyone, rich or poor, who disobeyed the righteous law. England would be conquered, but the victory would come "neither by sword or spear, but by the Spirit of the Lord." Although the message was purely spiritual, its military coloration made the Quaker preacher, as Burrough acknowledged, look like a "sower of sedition, or a subverter of the laws, a turner of the world upside down, a pestilent fellow." No wonder the members of Parliament thought that Theaurau John, the demented Ranter, was a Quaker when he flailed his sword against the great doors of the House of Commons.[2]

Quakers were not yet thoroughgoing pacifists, although they were incapable of harming anyone. While Fox was in Darby Prison for his blasphemy conviction, he demonstrated such charismatic qualities of leadership that he won the devotion of the common soldiers who heard him preach from his cell; the army offered him a captaincy if he would take up arms for the Commonwealth, but he declined, saying his was "the covenant of peace." His celebrated "flaming sword" was the sword of the Spirit, forged, he said, in the "pure fires" that lit up his soul. Still, he later censured the army for discharging Quakers as unreliable, and he lamented the army's failure to attack Spain, end the Inquisition, march on Rome itself, and continue into the lands of Islam, everywhere planting the true religion. Nayler, who had extensive military experience, presented the militant Quaker message most disarmingly when he wrote in his tract, *The Lamb's War*, that everyone should discover Christ the Quaker way and so find a life of gentleness, faithfulness, and truth. The war was not directed against the government or the social order, and was only indirectly aimed against all the churches and sects of England. The war was, rather, directed at everyman; it was an inward war, exhorting the individual to crucify his spirit by confronting the Spirit of God within him and to find salvation.[3]

The Lamb's War was a full-time occupation for Quaker preachers. They were not Sunday Christians. Indeed, the Sabbath day had no special significance for them. They abominated even the pagan names of the days of the week and months; when they redesignated the months and days as numbers (e.g., fourth day, second month), they were acting religiously. Matters of indifference to most people were for Quakers suffused with religious meaning. They rejected all oaths, on the theory that a religious man would not perjure himself or affirm falsely; an oath implied that he spoke the truth only when he was sworn. But their first reason was that Jesus had said, "Do not swear at all" (Matthew 5:34). Quakers would not even swear an oath abjuring papal authority and the doctrine of transubstantiation, which they hated as they would the Antichrist.[4]

"Moreover," Fox wrote, "when the Lord sent me forth into the world, he forbade me to 'put off my hat' to any, high or low; and I was required to Thee and Thou all men and women, without any respect to rich or poor, great or small." Quakers, who in the first generation almost invariably came from humble origins, enraged the gentry and magistrates by refusing "hat honor." Uncovering was the usual mark of deference or respect, but to the Quaker it was the sin of vanity. Similarly, they used "thee" and "thou" in addressing any individual, no matter how high his station, at a time when "thee" and "thou" were customarily used by superiors toward inferiors as marks of command, and between equals as a mark of familiarity. "Plain speech," as the Quakers called it, was not a symbol of class warfare, or a thing indifferent. Their refusal to kneel, remove their hats, use titles, or say "you" to a gentleman were deliberate acts of insubordination that conscience prompted. The Quakers were not really "levelers" in a political or social sense. Rather, they acted in the belief that God, before whom all were equal, was no respecter of rank. "Thee" and "thou" did not exalt the humble; the usage, like other Quaker customs, was an assault on the sin of false pride before God. Quakers owed loyalty only to the Spirit and to other "convinced" Quakers as signs of the Spirit. Every Quaker affront to a judge, a member of the gentry, a "priest," a government official, or an army officer was a self-testing by the regenerate against the unregenerate, and a purposeful provocation of the unregenerate to see his own sins and thus become receptive to the Light of God within. Plain speech, plain clothing, and plain manners rebuked the world's vanities, set righteous standards, and, if necessary, led to the cross.[5]

Quakers eagerly exposed themselves to martyrdom and suffered cruelly—needlessly, in the minds of others—as proof that the Spirit within conquered one's own spirit or willful bent. "Being faithful to the Light," instructed John Audland, ". . . will lead you to the Death upon the Cross, and Crucifie you unto the World and worldly things, and raise you up into the pure Life, to follow the Lamb whethersoever he goeth." Self-crucifixion, figuratively, was a Quaker specialty—"follow the Lamb whethersoever he goeth . . . and therefore all come to the Cross and love it, and rejoyce in it." Prison became an almost normal form of Quaker self-crucifixion. Addressing a magistrate as "thee" instead of "your honor," or refusing to uncover before him, could be taken as contempt of court. Quakers conscientiously opposed tithes for the support of an ungodly ministry, refused to pay fines, and failed to put up sureties for good behavior, and so they were jailed. They were stoned—the biblical punishment for blasphemy—and beaten by mobs so frequently and put into the pillory or flogged by court order so often that self-crucifixion became a way of life. In 1656, Fox estimated that "there were seldom fewer than one thousand in prison in this nation for Truth's testimony,—some for tithes, some for going to the steeplehouses, some for contempts, as they called them, some for not swearing, and others for not putting off their hats, etc." Included in Fox's "etc." was the woman who went to the "steeplehouse"—that is, challenged the parish minister for un-Christian teachings; she was tried for blasphemy and acquitted, but preferred to spend the winter in jail rather than promise that she would not disturb the worship of others.[6]

"Going to the steeplehouses" was probably the most provocative Quaker witness to the Spirit. Fox introduced the practice in 1649, when a steepled church in Nottingham appeared to him as an "idolatrous temple." The Lord instructed him, he reported, to "cry against yonder idol, and against the worshippers therein." On entering, he heard the minister say that the Scriptures decided all matters of religion, and Fox "could not hold, but was made to cry out and say, 'Oh, no, it is not the Scriptures,' and was commanded to tell them God did not dwell in temples made with hands." The Holy Spirit, he declared, had inspired the Scriptures and was the source of all religion. For disrupting divine service, Fox was jailed, the first of many such occasions. Thereafter, Fox and his converts to the indwelling Light invaded churches to denounce the preachers and their sinful congregations. God, the Quakers said, dwelt in the Spirit and the Spirit dwelt within every individual. The true church was a congregation of believers, not a building. Houses of worship, with or without steeples, became abominations to the early Quakers, as did ministers who taught falsely, or were ordained, or preached for money. Even the gathered churches of the separatist sects and their lay preachers, if paid, became targets of Quaker disruptions. "The disturbance of ministers in their sermons and alleged blasphemies," wrote William C. Braithwaite, the foremost historian of the early Quakers, "were the most usual grounds of complaint—the Quaker was frequently guilty of the first, and his innocence of the second, though clear to himself, was not easy of proof to a prejudiced and unsympathetic judge, who put the worst construction possible on unguarded statements about the indwelling life of Christ."[7]

William Penn entitled one of his books *Primitive Christianity Revived* (1696). That was Quakerism, or, rather, primitive Quakerism. Fox sought a return to the primitive church, as he understood it, purified of the accretions of sixteen centuries. Christianity in England was false and vain, and did not lead to the Cross, Fox preached. His mission was to bring the "pure religion" of Jesus to the people. One way of doing it was crying down and disrupting false worship, which the Quakers could not tolerate. There being so many souls that must be saved, errors in worship or in points of faith, "contrary to or different from the perfect Truth of the Gospel of Christ," required direct exposure and censure. Since the Lord accepted only His own worship, "here all Indifferency hath an end." Although the first Quakers were among the foremost advocates of liberty of conscience, it was not for them an end in itself but a means of propagating their faith. Their claim to infallibility matched that of the Roman Catholic church or of Calvinism. In the 1650s, the Quakers enjoyed freedom of worship among themselves only; their faith compelled them to be missionaries among Christians worshipping falsely.[8]

Belief and action were inseparable to the Quaker. He must damn the Antichrist in others and bring about conversions. "Hireling priests," the Quaker name for any ordained or paid ministers, were too tolerant of sin and swollen with ceremonies and sacraments. Presbyterians and Independents won the particular contempt of Quakers, because many of their ministers, having graduated from Oxford and Cambridge, knew less about the Spirit than common folk did. Herdsmen and fishermen, Quakers said, understood that the Spirit within man governed the interpretation of the Scriptures. Read literally, without the indwelling Light for guidance, the Bible became the "letter that killeth the Spirit." Fox liked to say that a believer needed no man to teach him, but only "an anointing within man to teach him, and that the Lord would teach his people himself." A Puritan preacher interrupted in his service could easily take such a statement as a rejection of the Bible, Christian sacraments, and Christian ministers.[9]

For all their talk about the love of God, Quakers used billingsgate, laced with biblical epithets, against other Christians. After spewing jeremiads, Fox would deny that he was railing; he spoke out of love, he said, while there was still time for repentance. Richard Baxter, the leading Puritan clergyman in western England, and no stranger to bitter religious controversy, wrote in 1657 that hardly a common scold in the past seven years had used against base people so many railing words as the Quakers used "against the faithful servants of Christ. . . . And no servant of Christ who hath learnt of Him to be meek and lowly can believe, if he be well in his wits, that this is the language of the Spirit of Christ." Long after, when Penn was succeeding Fox as the leader of the Quakers, Baxter noted their "extream Austerity," but insisted that their doctrines were

> mostly the same with the Ranters: They make the Light which every Man hath within him to be his sufficient Rule, and consequently the Scripture and Ministry are set light by: They speak much for the dwelling and working of the Spirit in us; but little of Justification, and Pardon of Sin, and our Reconciliation with God through Jesus Christ: They pretend their dependance on the Spirit's Conduct, against Set-times of Prayer, and against their due esteem of Scripture and Ministry. They will not have the Scripture called the Word of God: Their principal Zeal lyeth in railing at the Ministers as Hirelings, Deceivers, False Prophets, &c. . . .[10]

Cromwell, who could tolerate almost any Protestant opinion and did in fact tolerate Fox's refusal of hat honor and his use of the familiar "thee," condemned the Quaker practice of violating the Christian worship of others. In 1655, he issued a proclamation of religious liberty "for all to hold forth and profess with sobriety, their light and knowledge therein, according as the Lord in His rich grace and wisdom hath dispensed to every man." The government would uphold liberty for "all persons in this Commonwealth fearing God, though of differing judgements," by protecting them against any who "abuse this liberty to the disturbance or disquiet of any of their brethren in the same free exercise of their faith and worship which himself enjoys of his own." Lately, declared the proclamation, "Quakers, Ranters, and others" had vilified and interrupted ministers and "daily" reproached congregations of Christians in public and private meetings. Hereafter, they would be prosecuted as disturbers of the peace. Until 1655, the law had been that one might question a minister after his sermon, although the Quakers did far more.[11]

Driven by religious exaltation and devotion to the cross, they reproached other Christians by going naked in public "for a sign." Baxter acknowledged that it was "a Prophetical act," but he did not realize its significance. As Fox told the vicar of Ulverston in 1652, God made a Quaker "goe naked amongst you a figure of thy nakedness . . . before your destruction cometh . . . that you might see that your [you're] naked from the truth." The Quaker leaders did not reprove the practice, rooted in Isaiah 20:3, for it also showed a central trait of early Quakerism: the denial of self-will or the evidence of humility before the cross. Each Quaker had to find God through Jesus Christ by learning to "give up self to die by the Cross. . . . Therefore keep in the daily cross, the power of God, by which ye may witness all that to be crucified which is contrary to the will of God, and which shall not come into his kingdom." To become a member of the "Children of Light," as the Quakers first called themselves, an individual must know his depravity by confronting the Light within. Conversion required a psychologically painful and prolonged encounter with self and God. Before one could be transformed as a person and become reborn as guiltless as Adam before the Fall, he must acknowledge his sins, layer after layer, and personally experience divine wrath until it turned into love for the purified one.[12]

The very name "Quaker" reflected the fear and trembling a believer showed in the presence of the God of Jeremiah. The inward suffering produced intense physical agitation. "At first," Baxter recalled, "they did use to fall into Tremblings and sometimes Vomitings in their Meetings, and pretended to be violently acted by the Spirit; but now that is ceased; but now they only meet, and he that pretendeth to be moved by the spirit speaketh; and sometime they say nothing but sit an hour or more in silence, and then depart." Robert Barclay, writing at about the same time, said in his book *Apology for the Quakers* (1675) that in the early Quaker meetings the "painful travail found in the soul" affected the body, so that "oftentimes, through the working thereof, the body will be greatly shaken, and many groans, sighs, and tears, even as the pangs of a woman in travail, will lay hold of it; yea, and this not only as to one, but . . . sometimes the power of God will break forth into a whole meeting," everyone quaking, shaking, and groaning as he struggled with the evil in himself, until the Spirit brought serenity and thanksgiving. "And from this the name of *Quakers*, i.e., *Tremblers*, was first reproachfully cast upon us; which, though it be none of our choosing, yet in this respect we are not ashamed of it, but have rather reason to rejoice therefore. . . ." Fox himself attributed the origin of the name to a magistrate who scornfully used it while examining Fox for blasphemy in 1650, although the name in fact existed as early as 1647 to describe the spiritual behavior of others. After Cromwell's victory at Dunbar in 1650, an officer rode back from his troop to discover the reason for a great commotion among his soldiers.

> When I came thither, I found it was James Nayler preaching to the people, but with such power and reaching energy as I had not till then been witness of. I could not help staying a little, though I was afraid to stay, for I was made a Quaker, being forced to tremble at the sight of myself. I was struck with more terror before the

preaching of James Nayler than I was before the Battle of Dunbar, when we had nothing else to expect but to fall a prey to the swords of our enemies. . . . I clearly saw the cross to be submitted to. . . .

The curious aspect of this account is that Nayler, himself a veteran of the battle, had not yet met Fox and was not yet a Quaker.[13]

Primitive Quakerism was very much an embodiment of the youthful experiences of George Fox. In effect, he demanded that others re-enact his tormented conversion. He was born in 1624 in a tiny village in Leicestershire, the son of a weaver whom neighbors called a "Righteous Christer." The nickname more properly belonged to his son, who at nineteen, after his apprenticeship to a cobbler, left home to wander through the Midlands and learn more about religion. He listened to people of every Protestant persuasion, although he quickly abandoned "the high professors," the university-trained clergy, and consorted mainly with varieties of separatist sects, from whom he probably absorbed many ideas. He saw a turbulent and evil world. Finding no hope in institutions or men, he began receiving "openings" or insights directly from God. Between 1646 and late 1648, he shunned people as much as possible: he was "a stranger to all." So great was his misery that he could not express it. But his description of his conversion and his commission to preach is one of the most agonizing and rapturous in English prose. By early 1649, he had "come up in spirit through the flaming sword into the paradise of God," relived the Creation, and by the indwelling Light reached Eden before the Fall. "But I was immediately taken up in spirit, to see another or more steadfast state than Adam's innocency, even into a state in Christ Jesus, that should never fall." His mission was to take others on the same journey. It was a dangerous mission, because being taken "into a state in Christ Jesus" could be construed as antinomian blasphemy.[14]

Fox had little schooling and no formal divinity training; education would probably have ruined his ministry. No theologian, he expressed himself carelessly and overbluntly. He was a mystic, a firebrand, an inspired prophet, and, later, an organizer of a sect. But he had nothing new to offer in religious doctrine. Belief in the indwelling Christ who offered universal grace and perfection was certainly commonplace. Henry Lawrence, the president of the Council of State, told the House of Commons during a debate concerning Nayler's declaration that Christ was in him: "I wonder why any man should be so amazed at this. Is not God in every horse, in every stone, in every creature? Your Familists affirm that they are christed in Christ, and godded in God. . . . If you hang every man that says Christ is in you . . . you will hang a good many." Even the Ranters had that "convincement," as Fox conceded, although he said they "fled the Cross." Edwards's *Gangraena* and Pagitt's *Heresiography* were filled with examples of antinomian heresies. Behmenists, Familists, early Baptists, Diggers, Grindletonians, and many Seekers like William Erbury preached the Light within, the godded man, the reborn innocent. Fox grew up in that religious milieu, which was strongest in the north and the west, where he began his mission. Unsophisticated rural folk on the geographic fringes of Puritan centers were most receptive to Fox's preaching. They found in it a way to salvation that was direct and familiar, and they discovered a range of emotional expression that was not otherwise permitted in daily life. Fox was a fundamentalist who suited their wants, and he conducted a great awakening in the style that later revivalist preachers copied.[15]

But Fox's extravagances in statement led him into trouble. In 1650, while traveling through Derby, he stopped with some followers at a "steeplehouse" where many "priests" congregated for "a great lecture." Fox waited for all to finish, then rose to speak about Christ's dwelling within. He and two friends were promptly arrested and brought before "Collonels and Justices and Priests," who examined them for eight hours. Fox told them that all their preaching, sprinklings, and sacraments would never sanctify a man. They asked whether he was sanctified. "I said, sanctified? yes, for I was in the Paradise of God, and they said had I noe Sinne? Sinne said I Hee hath Taken away my sinne (viz. Christ my saviour) & in him there is noe sinne . . . & soe They committed mee upon That as a Blaspheamer. . . ." He was sentenced to six months' imprisonment for violating the provision of the act of 1650 against anyone claiming to be God or equal to God, or to have God's attributes, or to have God within him.[16]

The act of 1650 was framed for Ranters, whom Fox despised as filthy beasts. But the early Quakers were frequently mistaken for Ranters. A tract of 1652 condemned "Enthusiasts, Seekers, Shakers, Quakers, Ranters, etc." Ranterism and Quakerism were rival antinomian movements, and after the severe suppression of the Ranters in 1650–51, many were converted to Quakerism; but old habits kept cropping out. A magistrate, Durand Hotham, told Fox in 1652 that the Quakers were saving England from being overrun by Ranters, but Hotham was a friend of Fox's and privately admitted to him that he had believed in the indwelling Spirit for ten years. Others found blasphemy in such a belief. When Henry More, the Cambridge scholar, wrote that "Ranters and Quakers took their original from Behmenism and Familism," he was connecting the Quakers with blasphemy. Their enemies connected them with much more that was despicable—anarchists of the spirit, "levellers against magistracy and property," and the Anabaptists of Münster. One grand jury denounced "Ranters, Levellers and atheists, under the name of Quakers." Levelling might be inferred from Quaker plain speech and refusal to defer to rank, even though the Quakers had no political program. To call them political radicals was absurd. But that Fox should have been condemned under the act against Ranters was not at all strange.[17]

When Fox's term in the Derby jail ended, the magistrate who had sentenced him demanded a steep bond of more than £200 for his release on good behavior. Relatives and friends raised the money, but Fox refused to pledge that he would not return to Derby and proclaim against its "priests." The magistrate, Gervase Bennett, who soon after became a member of the Council of State, furiously struck Fox and ordered him back in jail, this time in the dungeon, and there Fox stayed for over five months more. Immediately after his release, he was preaching again.[18]

In Wakefield, to the north, he converted James Nayler, who became a leader of the early Quaker movement. Nayler, who was eight years Fox's senior, had left home in 1643 to serve in the army. After extensive combat experience, he rose to become quartermaster of General Lambert's regiment. He left the army in late 1650 because of illness and took up farming. When Fox met him, he was a member of an Independent congregation whose minister had been trained in Boston by John Cotton. Shortly after Nayler's conversion to Quakerism, he was "at the plow," he said, "meditating on the things of God, and suddainly I heard a Voice." It commanded him to leave his family and become a wandering Quaker preacher. Before Nayler left, Fox returned to his community and disputed Nayler's minister; there was a fracas, during which Fox was physically beaten by the congregants, although Nayler supported him. When Nayler left home to preach Quakerism, his minister excommunicated him for blasphemy. Fox and Nayler became intimate friends and remained so until 1656.[19]

That was the year of Nayler's disgrace, after the greatest blasphemy trial of the century. His death in 1660, shortly after his release from prison, and Fox's survival to 1691 dimmed the memory of Nayler's contribution to Quakerism. Within a few years of his conversion, he rivaled Fox. He was an equally powerful preacher, a superior prose stylist, and a prolific writer of tracts; and, unlike Fox, who was abrasive and imperious, Nayler was gentle and considerate. When Baxter later reminisced about the Quakers, he mentioned Penn as their rising leader, did not refer to Fox at all, and said that Nayler had been "their chief Leader." Braithwaite, the leading Quaker historian, called Nayler "the most brilliant of the Quaker preachers," and a non-Quaker authority wrote that he was "a spiritual genius of a high order," whose "depth of thought and beauty of expression deserve a place in the first rank of Quaker literature."[20]

In 1652, Fox and Nayler preached together in northern Lancashire. On one occasion, they were both nearly beaten to death by an enraged mob. They recovered at Swarthmore Hall in Ulverston. There Fox con-

verted Margaret Fell, the wife of Judge Thomas Fell, who had been a
member of the Long Parliament. Although Fell never converted, he used
his influence to protect the Quakers and allowed his home to become their
headquarters. Margaret Fell became one of the foremost Quaker missionaries and martyrs after the Restoration; following an imprisonment of
four years, she married Fox in 1668, although he was ten years younger.
She treated him adoringly as the Messiah from the time they met, believing that he was possessed of the living Christ. If her early letters to
him had fallen into the wrong hands, Braithwaite wrote, they would have
"confirmed the belief that Margaret Fell was bewitched and that Fox was
a blasphemer." Others addressed Fox with the same divine submission.
He did not reprove them, but years later, when arranging his papers, he
crossed out some idolatrous phrases. Even Nayler wrote, "Geo. Fox was
denied as dust, but the Spirit that spoke in him is equall with God." Fox
himself did not deny that, although on one occasion, when asked whether
he was Jesus Christ, he replied, "No, I am George Fox."[21]

For their preaching around Ulverston, Fox and Nayler were charged
with blasphemy in October 1652. Judge Fell managed to see that the
warrant was not served, but Fox, accompanied by Fell and Nayler,
insisted on riding to the Lancaster sessions to answer the warrant. Forty
"priests" appeared as witnesses against Fox, but only three testified. The
offense was serious, because under the act of 1650 a second conviction for
blasphemy required banishment from the country. Shortly before, Fox
privately told a friend that he was "the Sonne of God," although someone
later changed Fox's manuscript account to read "a sonne of God." There
is no doubt that he made unguarded oral statements. Fortunately for Fox,
Fell was not the only sympathetic magistrate at his Lancaster trial, and
the witnesses offered conflicting testimony about the defendant's exact
words. To the first charge, that he had said he "had the divinity essentially in him," Fox denied having said "essentially," although he defended
the doctrine of the indwelling Spirit. He also denied the charge of having
said "he was equal with God," explaining that "He that sanctified and
they that are sanctified are all of one in the Father and Son," and that all
who were sanctified were the sons of God. He denied having claimed that
he was "the judge of the world," although the testimony against him on
that point was clear. To the charge that he had claimed to be as upright
as Christ, he argued that "the saints," the true believers, "are made the
righteousness of God" and shall be "like him"; Christ brought the saints
to "perfection." One of the magistrates declared that Fox had blasphemed
while presenting his defense in court. Another asked, directly, "Art thou
equall with God?" Fox replied, "My Father and I are one, and as hee is,
soo are wee in this present world." Nayler, quickly perceiving the danger
in that reply, asked, "Dost thou ask him as a Creature or a Christ

dwellinge in him?" When Fox insisted that Christ dwelt in him, Nayler added that nothing was sanctified but the Son, "and the Sonne being one in all, then the thinge sanctified is equal in all."[22]

Judge Fell, relying on the requirement that two witnesses must agree, said they had not; consequently, he quashed the warrant for blasphemy, leaving the issue unresolved. Orthodoxy sought satisfaction from a higher authority. Some Lancashire ministers, supported by a few local magistrates, petitioned the Council of State in London against the blasphemies of Fox and Nayler. All the old charges were repeated, and the Quaker leaders rushed an answer into print. Even as they denied the accusations, they exposed themselves more by saying, contrary to the act of 1650, "that God will dwell in man and walk with man." Braithwaite concedes that their vivid sense of personal union with Christ led them to identify with the Divine and advocate their own perfection. Tract writers replied and censured Fox and Nayler for blasphemy, but the busy Council of State took no notice.[23]

Nayler and Fox split up after the Lancaster trial, Nayler going into Westmorland, where he met with violence and hatred, especially around Kendal. For blasphemous preaching about the resurrection, a warrant was issued against him. He was taken by force and tried by a lynch mob, presided over by a justice of the peace who struck off Nayler's hat with a pitchfork when he refused to uncover. For a while, he submitted to theological questions put to him by local ministers. "I witness that Christ [is] in me," he said, but one minister answered that Christ was physically in heaven. He is in heaven spiritually, Nayler answered, not in the flesh. The armed mob was growing ugly, so the justice of the peace decided to remove the trial to a nearby tavern. There Nayler again refused to take off his hat and "thou"ed the magistrate, who immediately jailed him for contempt and vagrancy. When the Quaker preacher Francis Howgill gathered a group of Friends to protest the treatment of Nayler, Howgill was locked up with Nayler. The next day, the two were transported under guard to the prison in Appleby, farther north, to await trial.[24]

In January 1652, two months later, their case came to trial under the act of 1650. But the prisoners were in luck. One magistrate, Gervase Benson, was a local dignitary of great authority who had recently become a Quaker, and another, Anthony Pearson, was sympathetic. Others on the bench were hostile, but Benson and Pearson prevented a verdict of guilty. Pearson instructed the prisoners to remove their hats. They refused, Nayler explaining that they had no contempt for authority but honored God, who did not respect temporal distinctions in people. On a direct command from Pearson to uncover, Nayler pleaded "Conscience sake. . . . Where God commands one thing, and Man another, I am to obey God rather than Man." Benson called for the indictment to be read:

the blasphemy consisted in Nayler's having preached "that Christ was in him, and that there was but One Word of God." Pearson asked, "Is Christ in thee?" "I witness him in me." "Spiritual you mean?" "Yea, Spiritual . . ." "What difference then between the ministers and you?" They, Nayler answered, affirm that Christ rose with "a carnal body, but I with a spiritual." A colloquy ensued on the distinction between the Bible and "the Word of God." Nayler explained his doctrine that "the Word" is spiritual, not seen by the eyes of men but experienced by the Light within. At length, the magistrates fell to disputing with one another. Benson favored a directed acquittal on the ground that there was no blasphemy in Nayler's teaching. Others disagreed. In the end, the court decided not to put the case before the jury but to render no verdict, and to keep Nayler and Howgill in prison indefinitely until they answered fresh accusations from local clergymen. The prisoners were not released until five months later. While they were still in the Appleby jail, Anthony Pearson, whose Puritanism had been unsettled by his encounter with Nayler, visited Fox at Swarthmore Hall; he left shaken but unconvinced. When Nayler was released, Pearson invited him to his home, and Nayler brought his judge into the Quaker fold. Pearson traveled with Fox that summer of 1653 and helped save him from another blasphemy charge.[25]

Fox was accused for the third time in Carlisle that summer. He was near the border of Scotland, in a Presbyterian stronghold, and had provoked disturbances on his way north. In Carlisle, despite warnings from the magistrates, he "stood a-top" the cross in the middle of the market at midday and preached his gospel to a curious throng. Soldiers in the audience "were convinced" and protected him. He went to their garrison and convinced more, and on the next day, Sunday, he went to "the steeplehouse," the cathedral church. When the minister finished, Fox rose to speak. People "trembled and shook," he said, "and they thought the very steeplehouse shook and thought it would have fallen down." Friendly soldiers prevented a riot and surrounded Fox. Some were imprisoned for protecting him. But the town hall filled with "officers and justices" and "many rude people" that swore evidence against Fox, "for they were Independents and Presbyterians." Fox was summoned by a warrant.

And one sware one thing and one sware another thing against me. They asked me if I were the son of God. I said, "Yes." They asked me if I had seen God's face. I said "Yes." They asked me whether I had the spirit of discerning. I said, "Yes. I discerned him that spoke to me." They asked me whether the Scripture was the word of God. I said, "God was the Word and the Scriptures were writings; and the Word was before writings were, which Word did fulfil them." And so after a long examination they sent me to prison as a blasphemer, a heretic, and a seducer. . . .[26]

Fox was being held until the Assizes, when the county judges held trials with a jury. The news in the county was that Fox was to be hanged. The lord high sheriff, Sir Wilfrid Lawson, according to a letter from Margaret Fell, wanted to execute him at the first opportunity and spread the word that he would be tried for his life. Fox reported that "great ladies" and "bitter Scottish priests" came to Carlisle "to see a man they said was going to die." In fact, however, when the Assizes convened, the judges refused to try Fox, leaving him to the local magistrates, who had no power to condemn capitally. The judges who had that power probably believed that Fox was guilty of blasphemy; if he was convicted at the Assizes by a jury in a hostile town, the act of 1650 required banishment for the second conviction, and the expectation was that Fox would refuse, allowing no alternative under the act but execution. The judges of the Assizes did not want the responsibility of being the first civil officers to hang a man for his religion since the executions in 1612 of Legate and Wightman. So Fox languished in jail without a trial.[27]

He reported that the judges of the Assizes reviled him, left him to the town magistrates, and encouraged the latter to treat him cruelly, but in fact those whom he blamed probably saved his life. Anthony Pearson and Gervase Benson assisted him too. The two Quaker magistrates from Lancaster traveled to Carlisle, but the jailer refused to let them see Fox. He was transferred from a locked room to a foul dungeon with felons of both sexes and no toilet; the prisoners were "exceedingly lousy . . . almost eaten to death with lice." Pearson formally complained to the Assize judges, defending Fox from the accusations against him and protesting that he should not be left "to the rulers of this town who are not competent judges of blasphemy." Fox himself advertised his situation in letters to Friends and to the town magistrates, as did Pearson and Benson. Weeks passed, enough time for word to reach London. Cromwell and the Nominated Parliament then in session favored broad toleration. Parliament, Fox recorded, "hearing that a young man was to die for religion at Carlisle . . . writ down to the sheriff and magistrates." Carlisle set him free even before the writ arrived from London. After seven weeks of near starvation and brutal clubbings by his jailers, Fox returned to Swarthmore to recuperate, although on the way he turned "thousands" to Christ.[28]

During the next few years, Quakerism penetrated southward throughout most of England, as its indomitable preachers worked county by county in pairs. The persecutions that followed them were severe but sporadic and local. By 1654, Fox was in London for the first time, preaching to huge crowds. Nayler, who joined him, was also received as a heroic figure. When Fox departed, he left Nayler in charge. For the first time, the Quakers were winning converts from better-educated, prosperous city people. With eloquence Nayler coupled wit and warmth, and he had the civility of a gentleman, with Fox's personal magnetism to boot. Quakerism almost became a London fashion; Nayler was lionized at parties attended by leading politicians and ministers as well as titled ladies. On a trip out of the city, Nayler bested more than half a dozen "priests" in a public debate, and the crowd shouted, "A Nayler, a Nayler hath confuted them all." But hints of spiritual travail within Nayler began peeping through his triumphs. He could not quash the sin of vanity. Some Quaker women were so smitten with him that they began to reverence him as more than a great preacher, and Nayler did not rebuke them. Nor had Fox when he received adoration. With Nayler, though, the problem became far more serious.[29]

Meanwhile, the growing popularity of Quakerism made it the focus of rumors, some vicious, others absurd. William Prynne, the old mutilated Puritan martyr, was one of several who published the libel that the Quakers were really Jesuits and Franciscan friars in disguise, sent by Rome to subvert the English people. The government flinched at plots, real and fancied. An officer arrested Fox on suspicion; when Fox would neither swear an oath abjuring Rome nor promise to return home and quit preaching, he was sent under guard to London and imprisoned. Cromwell required from him a pledge that he would not take up the sword against him or his government. Fox complied in a letter unlike anything Cromwell had ever seen. Calling himself "the son of God who is sent to stand a witness against all violence," Fox added, "My weapons are not carnal but spiritual, and 'my kingdom is not of this world.' " The lord protector read the letter, interviewed its author, and set him at liberty. As Fox left, Cromwell shook his hand and tearfully said, "Come again to my house; for if thou and I were but an hour in a day together we should be nearer one to the other." That was three weeks after Cromwell's declaration against Ranters and Quakers for disturbing Christian worship.[30]

As 1656 opened, Fox and his companions in Cornwall were thrown into Launceston Prison "till the Assizes" in nine weeks. There was talk that the Quakers would be hanged, although their crime was not defined. The lord chief justice of England, John Glynne, presided when the sessions convened, but Glynne aborted the trial by furiously ordering the Quakers back to prison because they would not uncover before him. At a rehearing, Fox managed to get the charges read—vagrancy, disturbance of the peace, refusal of the oath of abjuration, and perhaps sedition for that refusal. Once again, though, Glynne imprisoned them without trial for their contempt in refusing hat honor. They rotted in Launceston under horrible conditions—excrement was poured on their heads, and the jailer beat them—until word reached London. Cromwell promised them liberty if Fox and his companions would go home. They refused; they also refused to pay court and jail costs. Hugh Peters, Cromwell's chaplain, observed that the government could not perform a greater service to the spreading of Quakerism than by making martyrs at Launceston. After eight months, Fox and the others were freed.[31]

While Fox was at Launceston, Nayler's friends worried that Nayler's head was being turned by reverential admirers in London; they persuaded him to travel to Bristol for a religious fair, but his worshippers followed. In Bristol, Nayler decided to visit Fox at Launceston. Fox had already heard about the strange goings-on around Nayler. In a letter of warning, Fox wrote, "Thou became a shelter for the unclean spirits, the beasts of the field, they made thee their refuge." In his *Journal*, Fox recorded that Nayler and his companions "ran out into imaginations." A short distance from Launceston, the Nayler group was arrested for vagrancy and jailed at Exeter. On Fox's release, he visited Nayler at Exeter and "saw he was out and wrong." At prayers, as Fox admonished the Exeter prisoners, Nayler and his followers left the room—evidence, said Fox, of a "wicked spirit risen up among Friends." He spoke to Nayler the next day. Nayler, remorseful, would have kissed Fox in the Quaker fashion, but, "seeing he [Nayler] had turned against the power of God," Fox extended his foot for Nayler to kiss: "the Lord God moved me to slight him and set the power of God over him." So ended the Fox-Nayler relationship. In Exeter Prison, Nayler was moody, ill, and exhausted; he scarcely ate for weeks at a time.[32]

Letters from admirers intending to comfort him aggravated the growing delusion, which he found disturbing, that he, James Nayler, was a special sign from God. A Quaker, when impelled by the Light within to serve as a sign, experienced spiritual torment and exaltation. To reject the sign implied self-will, a reproach to the divine prompting that betokened the sign. Nayler read the admiring letters, and although they sent a fear through him, he kept them. One follower described him as "King of Israel and Son of Most High." The writer of another letter wished she could present him with gold, frankincense, and myrrh. Still another called him the "son of Zion, whose Mother is a Virgin, and whose birth is immortal." One woman saluted him as the "Prince of Peace" and "fairest of ten thousand, thou only begotten Son of God," and her husband added the postscript, "Thy name is no more to be called James but Jesus."[33]

The "miracle" in Exeter Prison involving Dorcas Erbury magnified tenfold Nayler's overpowering sense that the God in him had chosen him for a special mission. Dorcas, the daughter of William Erbury the Seeker, had fallen into unconsciousness and seemed dead for two days. Nayler entered her cell, placed his hands on her, and commanded her to rise—and she did. Fox himself had exercised healing powers. Once he cured a deformed boy by laying his hands on him, and on another occasion he claimed that he "raised up" a woman and her child who were dying. Francis Howgill had once called upon the power of God that raised Jesus to make a lame boy walk, and when the miracle failed, Howgill was surprised. No Quaker had raised a person from death until Nayler seemed to do so in Exeter. His success intensified the hysteria among his worshippers. Fox wrote, "James, thou must bear thy owne Burden, and thy Companyes with Thee, whose Iniquity doth increase, and by thee is not cried against."[34]

In late October 1656, Nayler and the Exeter Quakers who had been arrested for vagrancy were freed. He and eight of his followers traveled from Exeter to Bristol. Their sensational entrance into the city drew crowds even in a downpour. Nayler sat on his horse as if in a trance, while the others, bareheaded, surrounded him and led him through the mud, singing, "Holy, holy, holy, Hosannah, Lord God of Israel." They spread their sodden cloaks for his horse to walk upon as he passed through the city streets. The deliberate re-enactment of Jesus' entry into Jerusalem on Palm Sunday was intended as a symbol of the imminent coming of Christ—a common enough millenarian belief. The whole group was arrested and sent to the Guildhall for an examination. Ordinarily, local Quakers—Bristol had a thousand—turned out to show sympathy for a Friend in trouble, but Fox had passed through Bristol and sent letters there warning the Quakers not to support Nayler's extravagances. Not one appeared at the Guildhall.[35]

There, before the mayor, the local magistrates and ministers, and the townspeople, Nayler and his followers were searched. The "incriminating" letters of adoration were found on him, used as evidence, and published in lurid accounts. One of the women in his company had in her pocket a description of Jesus that fit Nayler closely; a formal report of Parliament later took notice "how much he resembled . . . the picture usually drawn for our Saviour." During the examination in the Guildhall, the women prisoners sang and cried hosanna, and one kissed Nayler's hand before the horrified magistrates. If any were guilty of blasphemy, they were the Quakers offering worship to Nayler. Whether they believed that he was Christ incarnate is uncertain, but they worshipped the Christ whom they believed to be patently manifest within him. Nayler himself was neither an impostor, as many then believed, nor a fool, nor was he crazy, as some historians have thought. He was guilty of bad judgment, excessive zeal, and an incapacity to see himself as others—Fox as well as non-Quaker Christians—saw him. He was the reluctant Jesus in a Passion Play, because he had become convinced by the agony of his spirit that God intended him as a sign, both of Immanentism and Immanence.[36]

The Quakers of the 1650s saw their time as the edge of the Apocalypse. They expected the Lamb's victory over everybody during their lifetime. Much of Quaker preaching was a gloomy prediction that the wrathful day of the Lord was near. "Who waits upon the Lord in his Light," wrote Margaret Fell, ". . . shall see this fulfilled and shall be preserved." Naturally, the Second Coming would be preceded by signs of all sorts; Nayler, in a judgment misrepresented by his worshippers, thought he was such a sign, because the strong Light within him made him God's instrument. But he did not believe he was the only sign, the only instrument, the only man through whom the Light worked its mysterious wonders. His interrogators at the Bristol Guildhall, not understanding, quite reasonably saw blasphemy. The misunderstandings between Nayler and them are clear from his examination.[37]

In response to questions, he said that he made his extraordinary entrance into Bristol at the command of the indwelling Christ. He did not rebuke those who sang praises, because they were praising the Lord, not him as a man. Promptings from God were not his to rebuke; people about him heeded the Spirit within. No, he was not the "Fairest of Ten-Thousand." He could not help looking as he did, but he denied that his physical appearance was an "attribute" of any sort.

Q. Art thou the only Son of God?
A. I am the Son of God, but I have many brethren.
Q. Have any called thee by the name of Jesus?
A. Not as unto the visible, but as Jesus, the Christ that is in me.
Q. Dost thou own the name of the King of Israel?
A. Not as a creature, but if they give it to Christ within, I own it, and have a kingdom not of this world; my kingdom is another world, of which thou wotest not.
Q. Whether or no art thou the Prophet of Most High?
A. Thou hast said, I am a Prophet.
Q. Dost thou own that attribute, the Judge of Israel?
A. The judge is but one, and is witnessed in me, and is the Christ, there must not be any joined with him: if they speak of the spirit in me, I own it only as God is manifest in the flesh, according to God dwelleth in me, and judgeth there himself.[38]

The answers were pure Quakerism. Fox had said the same things to Cromwell. The only Christological note that Nayler introduced was his answer "Thou has said [it]." But pure Quakerism was blasphemy to those who believed that Christ was not within people but physically in heaven. And Nayler's replies lent themselves to misinterpretation. When, for example, they asked him whether he was "the everlasting Son of God," he replied that any in whom Christ dwelt was the everlasting Son, "and I do witness God in the flesh; I am the Son of God, and the Son of God is but one." He meant, as he had said earlier, that he had "many brethren." For Nayler, Christ was the only Son of God, and the Son "is but one" dwelling in many. When asked whether he or any of his followers blasphemed, he declared, "What is received of the Lord is true."

> Q. Was Dorcas Erbury dead two days in Exeter, and didst thou raise her?
> A. I can do nothing of myself: the Scripture beareth witness to the power in me which is everlasting; it is the same power we read of in the Scripture. The Lord hath made me a sign of his coming: and that honour that belongeth to Christ Jesus, in whom I am revealed, may be given to him, as when on earth at Jerusalem, according to the measure.

They called that blasphemy, and his answer, "Who made thee judge," also reflected his own refusal to judge his worshippers: "I ought not to slight anything which the spirit of the Lord moves." The entire examination made him seem arrogant beyond belief, if not worse, yet for his part he was reflecting the humility he felt before his God. Any miracle he had performed he attributed to the indwelling Christ; any worship directed at him he had received on the same behalf. Only at the end of the examination did he lose his self-control and violate Quaker precepts. Nayler had offered excessive tenderness to a woman whom Fox had rejected as unclean in spirit; on learning that Nayler favored her, Fox reproved him for treating her like "the mother"—that is, the Virgin Mary. The Bristol examiners asked Nayler why he had called her "mother, as George Fox affirms." Nayler exclaimed, "George Fox is a lyar and a firebrand of hell; for neither I, nor any with me called her so." Long after, Nayler declared that that was the only answer he regretted.[39]

Nayler's worshippers, when examined, did not make the distinctions that he did, and their testimony did him harm, as if he were guilty of their blasphemies. One woman acknowledged that she should worship him on her knees, because "James Nayler will be Jesus, when the new life is born in him." If there was any ambiguity in her statement, she resolved it when she added that Nayler had the spirit of Jesus in him "above all men." Dorcas Erbury's evidence was the most damaging. She insisted that Nayler had raised her from the dead and therefore was Jesus. When they asked whether Jesus Christ did not sit at the right hand of God, she replied, "He, whom thou callest Nayler, shall sit at the right hand of the Father. . . ."[40]

The Bristol magistrates, believing that they were confronted by more than they could cope with, sent a transcript of the proceedings under seal to their deputy in the House of Commons. He reported it to the House, which appointed a committee of fifty-five to investigate and propose action. The committee summoned Nayler, three women including Dorcas, and the man who had called Nayler Jesus. Five members of the committee interrogated them in even greater detail than had the Bristol officials. Nayler, of course, was the center of attention. In the end, the committee of fifty-five agreed on two charges against him: that he assumed "the gesture, words, honour, worship, and miracles of our blessed Saviour," and that he had assumed Jesus' "names and incommunicable attributes."[41]

Nayler replied to the committee as candidly as he had in Bristol, yet the committee took every point as "proved" against him by his own words. They reported that he did not deny being "the only begotten Son of God," although he insisted, "I am the Son of God, but I have many brethren." When the question was asked whether he was the "only begotten Son," he replied, "Thou has said it. . . . Do not ensnare the innocent." The committee resolved that he claimed the title of "the Prophet of the most high God," although he declared, "There be other Prophets besides me." Similarly, the committee resolved that he claimed to be king of Israel, when in fact he denied all titles "as a creature," although he acknowledged that the Christ in him was king. When he conceded that others gave the name Jesus "to the Christ that is in me," they resolved that he had assumed the name; yet he denied that he ever used the name for himself. They insistently misconstrued his meaning. At one point, he stated, "Nay, do not add to my words; I speak as plain as I can, that all the glory may be given to God, and none to the creature . . . and none to me, as you look upon me as a creature." If his companions attributed anything to James Nayler that belonged to God, "then it is reprovable." He took their remarks as honoring the Lord; otherwise he would have "utterly denied" them. After the committee had examined him for the third and last time, they allowed him a final statement. It was a sockdolager:

> I do abhor that any of that honour which is due to God should be given to me, as I am a creature: But it pleased the Lord to set me up as a sign of the coming of the righteous one; and what hath been done in my passing through the towns, I was commanded by the power of the Lord to suffer such things to be done to the outward as a sign. I abhor any honour as a creature.

Thomas Bampfield, a man respected enough to become the next speaker of the House, reported to the House of Commons on behalf of the committee that Nayler was guilty of blasphemy and various misdemeanors.[42]

From the moment the House of Commons had taken jurisdiction of Nayler's case, his conviction was certain and Cromwell's policy of toleration was in jeopardy. Under the 1653 Instrument of Government, by which Cromwell had become protector, most Christians were free to worship as they pleased. The protectorate was a Puritan commonwealth tempered by a very broad measure of toleration, even more in fact than in law. Article 35 of the Instrument "recommended" the Christian religion as the religion of the nation and provided for its support, but article 37 protected anyone professing faith in God through Jesus, "though differing in judgment from the doctrine, worship, or discipline publickly held forth." At the time of Nayler's case, no doctrine, worship, or discipline had been defined. The Instrument of Government provided that, except for "popery or prelacy" and "licentiousness," no one should be restrained in his religion who did not use his "liberty to the civil injury of others" or "actual disturbance of the peace." The Instrument, which reflected the wishes of Cromwell, his Council of State, and the army, was imposed upon a reluctant Parliament. From the outset, Parliament sought to narrow Cromwell's policy of toleration. Members of the House were appalled by his courtesies toward Quakers, his talks with Fifth Monarchists, his dignifying Anglican priests, and his refusal to enforce laws against both Roman Catholic worship and Anglican use of the Book of Common Prayer. Cromwell's policy prevailed because the army backed him. He would have liked the Protestant clergy to agree on a national church comprehensive enough to take in all Protestants, from the sectarians to peaceable Anglicans like Archbishop Ussher. Cromwell drew the line at Socinians, who repudiated the divinity of Christ, and at Ranters, whom he believed opposed to all religion.[43]

Cromwell's hope for a comprehensive national church foundered on sectarian divisions. The Protestant clergy of England bitterly disagreed among themselves; they could not even concur on the fundamentals of the Christian faith. Not even the Presbyterians and Independents could agree, though they were all Puritans; indeed, members of the same sect conflicted among themselves. As time passed, the Congregationalists had emerged as the strongest Independent sect, and they grew increasingly conservative. The Independents opposed a national church and uniformity in religion. By the time of the protectorate, the Congregationalists, like their counterparts in New England, favored state support of religion and religious guidance of the state. Gradually, the Congregationalists grew closer to the Presbyterians than to the separatistic and voluntary churches of the sects from which Congregationalism had sprung. But even the Presbyterians were divided between latitudinarians like Richard Baxter and those like Samuel Rutherford who looked to Scotland. The principal difference between Congregationalists and Presbyterians was that the former believed that the individual churches should be self-governing, whereas the latter preferred a centralized ecclesiastical polity of church synods. Both Congregationalists and Presbyterians, who dominated Parliament in the 1650s, strongly favored an establishment of Trinitarian Protestantism along Calvinist lines, and they supported the continuation of tithes. Cromwell too favored tithes, till some better substitute might be found.[44]

Cromwell's toleration policy, by seeking to please almost everyone, antagonized the most powerful alliance in Parliament—Congregationalists and Presbyterians. The protector's settlement allowed each parish to choose its minister from lists approved by committees that certified ministerial fitness. Congregationalists, other Independents, Presbyterians, and a few Baptists controlled the committees of certification. In effect, England had a multiple establishment of various Puritan churches that was wedded, reluctantly, to a constitutional policy of toleration for the numerous gathered churches that supported themselves and existed outside the establishment. It was a strange and divided confederation of Protestant denominations, plus the sects, without doctrines or rites beyond profession of Christ. Anglicanism labored under repressive legal disabilities, but in practice the government in the 1650s—Cromwell and his council—connived at allowing religious liberty for them and any Christians (Socinians always excluded) who did not disturb the state or the worship of others. The persecution of the Fifth Monarchists was centralized but motivated purely by political considerations. The persecution of the Quakers was locally inspired, not centrally, but only because Parliament could not dominate the religious settlement of the Commonwealth, try as it might. Catholics, a despised and untolerated minority, to Parliament's alarm were left unmolested even in London, as were Anglicans, if they worshipped quietly, although the worship of both violated the law. The Venetian ambassador in 1655 reported that the English were "divided into as many faiths as there are heads, and the number of religions equals the number of men." The protector, he observed, favored no sect, and it "suits his policy that 246 religions should be professed in London . . . differing greatly from each other and incompatible. This division into so many sects makes them all weak, so that no one [sect] is strong enough to cause his apprehension."[45]

Most Puritans in and outside of Parliament abhorred the sects, abhorred tolerating them officially, and abhorred the *de facto* toleration of Anglicans and Catholics. And Parliament represented, in the main, the Puritans. They divided on religious matters but not radically on the issue of toleration, and on this issue Parliament probably represented the nation more accurately than did the executive branch and the army. If Cromwell's first Parliament had had its way, it would have produced what the quarreling divines could not—a confession of faith that subverted the Instrument of Government. If Parliament had had its way, it would have disposed of John Biddle under the Blasphemy Act of 1648. If Parliament had had its way, it would have excluded from the scope of toleration many of the self-supporting churches that used lay ministers. Parliament was particularly rabid in condemning "atheism, blasphemy, damnable heresies, popery, prelacy, licentiousness, and profaneness," all of which it moved to bring exclusively within its jurisdiction and definition. Parliamentary intolerance, representing a Puritan phalanx of conservative Independents, Congregationalists, and Presbyterians, plus a few Particular Baptists (Calvinists), was deadly opposed to the toleration policy of the executive and the army. In a blistering attack on their bigotry, Cromwell dissolved his first Parliament in January 1656, after it had sat for five months. By dissolving Parliament, he saved Biddle and prevented the formation of a national or uniform confession of faith determined by the Commons.[46]

Cromwell's second Parliament, which met in September 1656, was even more conservative than the first on religious matters. Of 460 who were elected, approximately one hundred were so objectionable that the Council of State, under a power wrested out of the Instrument of Government, excluded them. About fifty more failed to take their seats. The remainder were loyal to Cromwell, but not to the latitudinarian religious provisions of the Instrument. This was the Parliament that passed by a two-to-one majority a severe recusancy act intended to disable the practice of Roman Catholic worship. The same Parliament, which offered the crown to Cromwell, forced a change of the constitution of England by altering the religious provisions of the Instrument. The new constitution of 1657 provided for a "Confession of Faith," to be jointly approved by the protector and Parliament; "no other" professions or worship should "be held forth and asserted" as the public profession, but orthodox Trinitarians who believed the Scriptures as the revealed word of God would be tolerated. Socinians, irreligious persons, "Popery," and "Prelacy" would not be tolerated, nor would any who should "revile or reproach the Confession of Faith," or blaspheme, or behave licentiously. By implication, Quakerism and dozens of obscure sects, including Familists, Sabellians, Muggletonians, Seventh-Day Baptists, Fifth Monarchists, and Ranters, were proscribed.[47]

And this was the "Nayler Parliament," in the words of the historian Thomas Carlyle, who floridly satirized it as follows:

To Posterity they sit there as the James-Nayler Parliament. Four-hundred Gentlemen of England, and I think a sprinkling of Lords among them, assembled from all the counties and Boroughs of the Three Nations, to sit in solemn debate on this terrific Phenomenon; a Mad Quaker fancying or seeming to fancy himself, what is not uncommon since, a new Incarnation of Christ. Shall we hang him, shall we whip him, bore the tongue of him with hot iron, shall we imprison him, set him to oakum [making hemp]; shall we roast, or boil, or stew him;—shall we put the question whether this question shall be put; debate whether this shall be debated;—in Heaven's name, what shall we do with him, the terrific Phenomenon of Nayler? This is the history of Oliver's Second Parliament for three long months and odd.[48]

Carlyle's parody lacked understanding, because the Nayler case raised fundamental constitutional questions that received serious consideration by Parliament. Moreover, the case really tested the limits of tolerance in a Christian commonwealth that enjoyed a greater degree of free exercise of religion than England had ever known, and many members of Parliament, including some rabid ones, sought to rationalize their positions. Not since the Servetus case had there been so important a blasphemy trial, and this one produced the greatest debate on the meaning of blasphemy, and thus on the limits of toleration, in English history. In the end, Parliament exercised its *judicial* powers to condemn Nayler for "horrid blasphemy" and sentenced him to grisly corporal punishments followed by an indeterminate period in prison. But the end was not a foregone conclusion. The key votes were close, and the issues so complex that many members could not make up their minds; almost one-third of the House abstained from voting.

From the beginning, there was no certainty that Nayler had violated any law or, if he had, what the law was. Was it parliamentary law, common law, natural law, moral law, or biblical law? Was his crime, if he had committed one, divine impersonation, seduction, idolatry, or blasphemy? Was an offense against religion an offense against the state when the head of the state was not the head of a national church? In the absence of ecclesiastical courts, which had been abolished since 1641, was an offense against religion merely a sin, which was cognizable only by God? If Nayler had committed blasphemy, and it was a high crime against God, comparable to treason, could or should the state vindicate the honor of God? What did blasphemy mean? Were there differing degrees and kinds of blasphemy, some capital in nature and others not? If blasphemy was a crime punishable by the state, did jurisdiction over it lie with the regular criminal courts, or could Parliament intercede? A trial court had sentenced William Franklin for claiming to be Jesus, in 1650, prior to the enactment of the statute against the Ranters; but no determination had ever been made by the King's Bench, the high court of criminal jurisdiction, that blasphemy was an offense at common law. That did not happen until 1676. The House had tried and convicted Paul Best for blasphemy in 1646, but they had no law for their action, and even after imprisoning him they never reached a formal decision of a judicial or legislative nature. The House kept John Biddle in jail without even trying him. During the debate on Nayler's case, no one dissented from those who pointed out that Parliament had not judged Biddle in a legal sense. As Lord Chief Justice Glynne told the "Nayler Parliament," "This is a new case before you, and it will be a precedent." He and many others would have let the courts decide the precedent. For Parliament to decide it, some legalists believed, was "dangerous."[49]

Under the Instrument of Government of 1653, which was the Constitution of Great Britain, "the supreme legislative authority" was vested in the lord protector, assisted by a Council of State whose approval he required. Parliaments were to be called every third year, consisting of one house only. Bills enacted by Parliament required the consent of the executive, who might dissolve any Parliament after it had sat for five months. The Instrument vested no judicial authority in Parliament. The House of Lords, before its abolition in 1649, could act as the highest court of the land. Did its judicial authority somehow devolve upon the Commons, authorizing them to take jurisdiction of Nayler's case? If so, what law had he broken? A judicial body can apply only the standing law; it cannot otherwise punish. Did Nayler violate the Blasphemy Act of 1648? Significantly, no one during the entire debate on Nayler's case relied on that statute; it was a dead letter. Some members tried to wrest precedents against Nayler from the Bible and even from the act of 1401 for the burning of heretics, De Haeretico Comburendo, but not a member even referred to the act of 1648. They seemed to assume that the Blasphemy Act of 1650 against the Ranters had superseded that of 1648. Francis Rous, a member of Cromwell's council, sought Nayler's death, but declared, "The laws against blasphemy and Ranters are in force, and you may proceed upon them," forgetting that the courts had jurisdiction under that statute and that the penalty for a first offense was only six months. John Thurloe, the secretary of state, declared, "I know no law in force this day against blasphemy; unless it be that of the Old Parliament"—the act of 1650.[50]

Could Parliament proceed against Nayler under its *legislative* authority? If so, Cromwell could veto any bill. Parliament might pass a bill of attainder—that is, a legislative declaration of guilt against the accused— and fix a sentence against him; but all the precedents seemed to show that attainders had been based on some standing law—that, at least, was the legal theory. Alternatively, Parliament might proceed by an *ex post facto* law, making criminal an act committed earlier and not at the time illegal. Some declared that any attainder in this case must be retroactive, but many warned against the injustice of *ex post facto* laws. "You are launching into a matter of great consequence," warned Major General Howard. "Whatever you do in this, it may be of ill consequence to posterity." "To take away a man's life by a subsequent law, it is of dangerous consequence," warned Colonel William Sydenham, a councilor. Another councilor, Walter Strickland, urged, "I would have every Englishman be careful in this case. It has been our happiness to be governed by a known law." One theme that ran continually throughout the debates was that Parliament had no law for what it was doing. Yet some took the view that "Parliament is so sovereign, that it may declare that to be an offence, which never was an offence before." When, however, Major General Thomas Kelsey said, near the end, "This is a new business. . . . You have no law for what you do," he was technically correct.[51]

Because the case was unprecedented, there was no certain knowledge how to proceed or what to call the crime. Government spokesmen had no fixed position, except perhaps that death was too severe a punishment. Those who insisted that Nayler had committed a "horrid" blasphemy demanded death; avenging the honor of God required an exemplary vindication before the whole nation. That too was a major theme of debate, reiterated monotonously. One of the revengers was Bampfield, who chaired the committee report. He called the moderates the "merciful" party. Although Cromwell was the leader of the merciful party, he kept aloof from the affair until after Parliament rendered its judgment. Only then, when demanding to know by what authority the members had acted, did he reveal that not even he could extenuate Nayler's conduct. He detested giving the least countenance "to persons of such opinions and practises, or who are under guilt of such crimes as are imputed to the said person. . . ." But he did not want Nayler executed. Yet his oldest surviving son and successor, Lord Richard Cromwell, announced at a state dinner, well before Parliament voted against capital punishment, that "Nayler deserves to be hanged." The members of the Council of State who held seats in Parliament, although tending to oppose death, reflected a spectrum of opinion ranging from broad toleration to bloodthirsty prejudice.[52]

The lord president of the council, Henry Lawrence, was the one who declared that God was in "every horse, in every stone, in every creature," and added, "If you hang every man that says, 'Christ is in you the hope of glory,' you will hang a good many." Every Quaker said that, he observed. He understood and accepted as tolerably Christian Nayler's distinction between the historical Christ who died in Jerusalem and the Christ that was "in him in the highest measure." Lawrence thought it was a "sad" opinion, no more. He could not call it blasphemy of any sort. "It is hard to define what is blasphemy," he remarked. Doubtless, members thought Arianism was blasphemy, and so too was denying the divinity of Christ, but people's private opinions were not an affair of Parliament. Lawrence acknowledged that he knew Quakers, discoursed with them about religion, and read some of their books. He hoped that most Christians knew "the mystery of Christ manifest in the flesh." Still, he thought that Quakers tended too much toward Arminianism and he would restrain them. But not by punishing for blasphemy.[53]

Major General Philip Skippon was also a member of the council. He called himself "the Christian Centurion," although one scholar called him a bigot and a typical Presbyterian. Skippon recommended that Nayler be "hanged, drawn, and quartered." His views represented nearly half the members that voted. The "growth of these things," he said of Quaker practices, "is more dangerous than the most intestine or foreign enemies. I have often been troubled in my thoughts to think of this toleration. . . . Their [Quakers'] great growth and increase is notorious, both in England and Ireland; their principles strike at both ministry and magistracy." Skippon was jealous of God's honor and zealous for it. Nayler's blasphemy was "horrid." The Mosaic law governed the nation, Skippon held, and all who blasphemed should be accountable under it. He raged against "these Quakers, Ranters, Levellers, Socinians, and all sorts" who "bolster themselves under [articles] thirty-seven and thirty-eight [of the Instrument] of Government, which, at one breath repeals all the acts and ordinances against them." Nayler was the product of the Instrument's liberty of conscience, and so were the sects. "If this be liberty, God deliver me from such liberty. It is to evil, not to good, that this liberty extends." God's glory had been trampled enough by it.[54]

Major General William Boteler, an Independent, agreed with Skippon, and backed his case with biblical precedents, many farfetched, to prove that Nayler should be stoned to death. As if they were theologians, soldiers and lawyers vied in construing arcane passages from the Scriptures to support their arguments that Nayler had committed horrid blasphemy, or ordinary blasphemy, or some other offense. The Bible carried more weight by far than the common law, even more than parliamentary law, because the offense was against religion; Puritans knew their Bible, and it yielded more precedents to construe than their secular law. George Smith, one of the judges who hanged Jock of Broad Scotland earlier that year, offered the case of several who were hanged in the sixteenth century for speaking against the Book of Common Prayer; and, he reminded Parliament, its laws imposed death on a man who stole a shilling. "Yet we make nothing of robbing God of his glory." If the secular law failed, Judge Smith proposed, the Bible showed the way: death by stoning.[55]

Skippon's rant against Quakers, other sects, and liberty of conscience mirrored a theme of the revengers. They used Nayler's case to discredit the burgeoning sects generally and Quakerism in particular, which they found execrable. As of 1656, Nayler loomed larger and more dangerous than George Fox. Skippon believed that only "Biddle and his sect" were as dangerous as Nayler's. In and outside Parliament, Nayler was described as "the chief of the Quakers," "a most eminent Ringleader," and "worst of all the Quakers." His prominence—especially in London, where he had proselytized so successfully—marked him as a target. After Parliament had sealed Nayler's fate, Colonel Sydenham of the council marveled at how zealous members were against Nayler, yet how merciful they were to his four companions whom Parliament also held in the Gatehouse Prison. Bampfield, who had brought in the committee report, recommended that the four be sent "to the House of Correction for three months, and [you] rid your hands of them." And yet, Sydenham declared, they were the greater offenders; they had actually committed idolatry, whereas Nayler "denied all honour to himself." With "no law at all for it," Parliament had "opened a gap to prostitute both life, member, and liberty" as a result of the "arbitrary" power of men who had the votes to do whatever they wanted.[56]

The reason for the distinction in treatment between Nayler and his companions is obvious: he appeared to be the great leader. "Cut off this fellow, and you will destroy the sect," one member urged. Anthony Ashley Cooper of the council sensibly replied that, if Parliament killed Nayler, it would make him a martyr and multiply Quakerism. Although Cooper was one of the merciful party and spoke abstractly for toleration, his Presbyterianism surfaced when he urged, "I would have you use some endeavour to suppress the growth of them in general." Griffith Bodurda, who found no blasphemy in Nayler, believed that "Millenaries" of "this sort of Quakers" should be "suppressed" as dangerous. Major General William Goffe, a prodigious Bible expert who advocated "amity, love, and charity" while urging death for Nayler as a horrid blasphemer, charged that all the Quakers "go about and revile the ordinances and ministers of Christ, and would tear the flesh off the bones that profess Christ." They were all "beasts" and deserved to die. Judge Smith lamented that England had the reputation among nations as "the great nursery of blasphemies and heresies." Colonel Briscoe too was sure that Quakers "are destructive to human society. . . . Do not they all hold against the essence of Government?" Sir George Downing, alarmed because Ranters and Quakers had increased by the "thousands," recommended that Parliament should "take them all off by a law," if it did not execute Nayler. "It is high time to take a course with them," chimed in Glynne, the chief justice; he knew from his experience that they contemned magistracy, and now "they grow to a great number."[57]

Whether the sects should be tolerated was the broad issue of the Nayler case. A few speakers, including Councilors Walter Strickland, Gilbert Pickering, and William Sydenham, like Henry Lawrence, the head of the council, defended toleration of the sects, Quakers included. "If Nayler be a blasphemer," said Sydenham, "all the generation of them are so, and he and all the rest must undergo the same punishment." Yet "The opinions they hold," he declared, "do border so near a glorious truth, that I cannot pass my judgement that it is blasphemy." Those who defamed the sects and spoke alarmingly about their growth used the instance of James Nayler to reproach the Instrument of Government's toleration. His blasphemy, they claimed, proved that its lax policy easily degenerated into spiritual anarchy, fanaticism, and gross immorality. The result threatened the safety of the nation and of the Protestant religion. Skippon was correct about article 38, for it held "null and void" all laws against religious freedom that conflicted with article 37; but article 37 only roughly defined that freedom. Captain Adam Baynes, one of the tolerationists who did not believe that Nayler had blasphemed, declared, "the Instrument of Government says, all shall be protected that confess faith in Jesus Christ, which, I suppose, this man does." But Colonel Francis White, in support of the same cause, corrected Baynes by quoting the Instrument to show that article 37 set a proper limit on religious freedom by restricting it to those who did not injure others or practice licentiousness. Downing, a revenger, hoped that the Instrument would not stand in the way of death for a horrid blasphemer; and Goffe claimed that, although he would give his life for the Instrument, "Yet if it hold out anything to protect such persons I would have it burnt in the fire."[58]

Lord Strickland, a tolerationist, called attention to the fact that, wherever the Gospel flourished, "most prodigies of heresies and opinions" will be found, "which will happen always, unless you restrain the reading of the Scriptures." The right of each person to think for himself about the Scriptures was at stake, and that was what the Instrument protected. Banish Nayler if you must, Strickland observed, but nothing more. Even banishment would be a "dangerous precedent to posterity. It is against the Instrument to proceed. . . ." Bodurda, on the same side, objected to admitting the power of the civil magistrate in matters of religion. Those who demanded Nayler's death, he declared, kept claiming that the mind of God was clear in this matter, and they repeatedly resorted to biblical texts for various proofs; but, said Bodurda, he was sure that Nayler "would also say, 'The mind of God was clear to him,' and it may be proved just, by as many texts." Colonel Holland summed up the tolerationist view: "Consider the state of this nation, what the price of our blood is. Liberty of conscience, the Instrument gives it us. We remember how many Christians were formerly martyred under the notion of blasphemy; and who can define what it is."[59]

Many definitions were offered and applied to the case, but every member shaped his argument to suit the outcome he sought. By no means were all of the "merciful" party tolerationists. Not that anyone opposed toleration in the abstract. Even Skippon and the other revengers favored their brand of it. The real tolerationists were those who opposed finding blasphemy in the case and construed the Instrument and anything else at hand—the Bible, the examples of Holland and Poland, natural law, moral law, common law, and parliamentary law—to prove their point. All the tolerationists were merciful men, but not all the merciful men were tolerationists. Indeed, most who opposed the revengers opposed death or a brutal sentence, but not a lighter sentence. Few openly claimed that Nayler was guiltless or deserved no punishment whatever. The revengers took the lead, from the moment Bampfield presented the committee's report, and the others resorted to all sorts of maneuvers to oppose whatever motions the vengeful recommended.

At the very beginning, when the committee reported on December 4, 1656, the revengers wanted to condemn Nayler on the basis of the report, while their opponents demanded witnesses, sworn testimony, and a fair trial. For two days Parliament debated whether Nayler should be given an opportunity to speak out against the charges, although they had not agreed on what the charges were. Those who argued for due process voted with many who confidently expected Nayler to hang himself by confessing his guilt. Most members had never seen him and were curious. Major General John Lambert, a councilor, had known Nayler well. "He was two years my quartermaster," Lambert recalled, "and a very useful person. We parted with him with great regret. He was a man of unblameable life and conversation, a member of a very sweet society of an independent church. How he comes . . . to be puffed up to this opinion I cannot determine."[60]

On December 6, Nayler was brought before the bar of the House. He refused to kneel or remove his hat; they had expected that and agreed that he might stand, but the sergeant-at-arms took off his hat. The clerk read to Nayler the main sections of the committee's report. Thomas Burton, who recorded the parliamentary debate, was one of the vengeful. He recorded that Nayler, "in effect, confessed," and some historians accepted Burton's judgment. However, Nayler's words show only an admission that the committee had accurately reported what he had said. Nayler hoped that Parliament would not misconstrue his meaning. Questioned for less than half an hour, he told the same story as before, denying any worship paid to him. "I abhor it, as I am a creature." If Christ was in him, they asked, how did he pray to the Christ who died at Jerusalem? To questions on this problem Burton recorded none of Nayler's answers, noting only that he "answered pretty orthodoxly."[61]

After Nayler withdrew and awaited judgment in the Gatehouse Prison nearby, the debate rambled and raged for nine long days before the decisive voting. The revengers demanded and won immediate acceptance of the committee's report. "Seeing Nayler must die," one member promptly said, "I desire to know what manner of death it must be." Members roared objections. Questions of procedure and jurisdiction remained to be resolved, let alone the character of the offense; talk of punishment was quite premature. On the evening of December 8, the revengers won another victory when Parliament resolved, without a vote count, that Nayler, "upon the whole matter, in fact, is guilty of horrid blasphemy." Not even that was conclusive, because they continued to argue as if every question were still open; often more than one question was before the House at a time, and members, on getting the floor, addressed several issues. Everything—procedure, jurisdiction, the offense, its punishment—seemed interwoven. But the overriding issue was clear to all: would death be the punishment?[62]

When the revengers recommended the use of Parliament's legislative power by passing either an attainder or an *ex post facto* law, the merciful and the tolerationists demurred at the injustice as well as the danger to posterity. When the revengers recommended Parliament's judicial power as the basis for its sentence, the others claimed that no such power existed, or, if it did, it could not extend to life or limb. When a vengeful Ashe located the source of parliamentary judicial authority in De Haeretico Comburendo, the act of 1401 for the burning of heretics, the reply shot back: We will never rake out those ashes; under that law we must all burn as heretics and blasphemers. When the revengers claimed that Nayler had blasphemed and that Parliament should not trifle about the law that authorized the death penalty, the others looked to lesser offenses.[63]

When the revengers insisted that Nayler's blasphemy was "horrid," the others ridiculed the distinction between blasphemy and horrid blasphemy, although they adeptly made distinctions of their own to suit their purposes. Those distinctions between blasphemy and lesser offenses saved Nayler's life. The vengeful claimed that Nayler's offense was the "crime that deposes the majesty of God Himself, *crimen laesae maiestatis*, the ungodding of God," as Major Beake said. The vindictive Downing asserted that blasphemy was the highest offense: "treason against Heaven." No one commented on the blasphemous irony in his reminding the House that

Nayler would not remove his hat, "though you be gods in one sense." But the other faction denied that Nayler had blasphemed at all. He had exalted himself, Councilor Strickland admitted, but neither he nor any of his followers claimed that he was Jesus or Christ. He did not allege that "the essence of Christ is in him." He was scandalous, overproud, and sinful, but not a blasphemer, because he honored God; a blasphemer would curse or revile Him. All the mercifuls and terationists agreed on that point. Leviticus 24:15–16 proved that capital blasphemy consisted only in reviling God.[64]

Bulstrode Whitelocke, the lord commissioner of the treasury and an eminent jurist, studied the Hebrew text and patiently explained it. He defined the Hebrew words, concluding that this was not a case warranting death. Indeed, if those lusting for Nayler's blood had understood the very text that they claimed as the basis for their judgment, they would have known that in Hebrew law the crime of blasphemy could not be committed at all unless the very name of God was cursed. Some divines, Whitelocke conceded, disagreed whether the sacred name must be the express object of the curse, but all agreed that, without speaking evil of God and making imprecations against Him, there was no blasphemy. At worst, Nayler's offense came within the fifteenth, not the sixteenth, verse of Leviticus 24, and so merited only a whipping. With a lawyer's fine sense for punctilios, Whitelocke noted that the motion to condemn Nayler for "horrid blasphemy" did not specify that it was blasphemy "against God." In any case, God's mind in the matter was not knowable, and His law did not require death. Nayler's claim that Christ dwelt within him did not constitute blasphemy. That claim, Whitelocke observed, was not uncommon, for even the Lutherans believed in "the ubiquity of Christ." Whitelocke recommended that Parliament turn the case over to the Upper Bench: let the highest judges grapple with the problem. Parliament ought to do nothing more. "One Parliament may count one thing horrid blasphemy, another parliament another thing. The word blasphemy may be as far extended as was heresy." Whitelocke hoped not. Once opposition to tithes had been heresy, and now some said that having compulsory tithes was heresy. Learn from past mistakes, Whitelocke urged. If Nayler died, no man might be safe in the future. Whitelocke's long speech was a marvel of erudite learning in law, religion, and history. If any of his listeners had been undecided, they must have been influenced by his proofs that no law—Mosaic, Gospel, moral, natural, national, or international—supported the death penalty in such a case.[65]

But Whitelocke persuaded no one whose mind was already convinced. The vengeful members, challenged time and again to define the particular nature of Nayler's blasphemy, replied that Nayler had assumed the honors and attributes of God or Christ; they misstated the facts by claiming that he had passed himself off as Christ. Every misstatement provided the others with a chance to correct the record. Those who worshipped Nayler were idolaters, said Pickering, but not Nayler. "Take well what he said for himself as well as against." Pickering recalled that the late John Selden, the greatest parliamentarian, after listening to Paul Best the Socinian, had remarked that Best was a better man than he thought himself to be. "That may be this man's case," Pickering added. Nayler simply gave himself out to be "a prophet, a type, a sign, to warn men of the second coming of Christ. . . ." Samuel Highland stressed that Nayler not only did not revile God; he worshipped Christ. Where was the blasphemy?[66]

To that the revengers replied that, because Nayler was a Christian, his assuming the attributes of Christ magnified the offense. The tolerationists responded that he did not say Christ dwelt wholly or exclusively in him, and one member reminded the others that Christ himself said that blasphemy should be forgiven (Matthew 12:31). To the revengers, however, the doctrine of the indwelling Christ was blasphemous in and of itself. Blasphemy, they admitted, might in its literal sense mean speaking evil of God, but its commonsense meaning was that no person could call himself Christ. Major General Packer replied that, if the crime was against God, no man could decide for Him. Many of us, like Job, are blasphemers, he said. As for Nayler, he adored, not vilified; he believed in the Father, the Son, and the Holy Spirit. Let him repent, even if it was only a "show" of repentance. Those wanting his death misinterpreted his words in such a way as to require the destruction of all the sects. The Christian way was moderate and tolerant. "You may as well condemn a Papist," said Packer, "for worshipping Christ in the bread and wine, as in this case of Nayler's." Cooper saw in Nayler a dark carriage and a strong delusion, but not blasphemy, surely not horrid blasphemy. If there was horrid blasphemy, did that mean there was blasphemy "more horrid, and most horrid? I offer it to you, whether it were not a greater blasphemy to say he were very Christ." Cooper dared not say it was blasphemy at all. Nayler, he noted, made a "nice distinction, a vast difference between Christ Jesus dwelling in us, and being worshipped in a creature." Still others seeking to save Nayler said he acted without malice, was only a seducer or an impostor, merely disturbed the peace, had high delusions, or set up signs like an idolater. But he was no blasphemer, let alone a horrid one.[67]

On December 16, the members were finally ready for a conclusive vote. A motion that Nayler be executed lost by a vote of ninety-six to eighty-two. The debate suddenly collapsed. Rapid motions were introduced on lesser punishments—that his long hair be cut, that he be branded with a "B," that his tongue be slit—and were voted up or down.

Finally, the motions that passed, all without recorded vote, were stitched together to produce a sentence:

> Resolved, that James Nayler be set on the pillory, with his head in the pillory, in the New Palace Westminster, during the space of two hours, on Thursday next, and be whipped by the hangman through the streets of Westminster to the Old Exchange, London; and there, likewise, to be set upon the pillory, with his head in the pillory, for space of two hours, between the hours of eleven and one, on Saturday next; in each of the said places, wearing a paper containing an inscription of his crimes: and that at the Old Exchange, his tongue shall be bored through with a hot iron, and that he be there also stigmatized in the forehead with the letter B.; and that he be, afterwards, sent to Bristol and conveyed into and through the said city, on a horse bare ridged, with his face back, and there also publickly whipped, the next market-day after comes thither: and that from thence he be committed to prison in Bridewell, London, and there restrained from the society of all people, and kept to hard labour till he be released by the Parliament: and during that time, be debarred of the use of pen, ink, and paper, and have no relief but what he earns by his daily labour.

The boring of the tongue implicitly, and the branding with "the letter B." explicitly, signified the crime of blasphemy. The sentence was entered as a judgment of Parliament—that is, a judicial sentence not subject to review by the courts, thus preventing appeals, bailing, or release on habeas corpus.[68]

Debate resumed on the question whether Nayler should be recalled to the bar to hear the sentence. The vengeful members opposed that, although Chief Justice Glynne had never heard of a case in which a convicted man was not given an opportunity to say why judgment should not be passed against him. A compromise was arranged: they voted to call him back to hear their judgment but not to let him speak against it. Sir Thomas Widdrington, the speaker, told Nayler he had escaped death: "They desire your reformation rather than destruction." Nayler asked what his crime was; he tried several times to say more but was cut off. The speaker pronounced the sentence. As Nayler was led away, he said, "God will, I hope, give me a spirit to endure it." Some members were bitter that an Englishman should have been denied his right to speak about the judgment against him.[69]

The first part of the sentence was executed on December 18. "The eyes of the whole nation are upon you in this business," revengers had repeated during the debate. Now the eyes of London were on Nayler. He stood in the pillory near Parliament with a paper pinned to his hat, inscribed: "For horrid blasphemy and being a Grand Imposter and Seducer of the People." Although the weather was unusually cold, the bailiff stripped him to the waist after they took him down from the pillory, and bound him to the back of a cart which they drew to the Exchange. The executioner, using a whip of seven cords, each knotted, lashed Nayler at every step. He took 310 lashes. Colonel Holland reported to Parliament that the women who later nursed Nayler's wounds told Holland "there was no skin left between his shoulders and his hips." A Quaker who watched the punishment and walked alongside the cart reported that Nayler did not cry out.[70]

In Parliament that day, members presented petitions against Quakers from various cities and counties. The revengers wanted a statute against them generally, and also a new act against blasphemy. The Quakers were all "levellers," said one, against authority and property. Whitelocke opposed either bill. Sydenham agreed: "It is like the word Lollards or Puritans, under the notion whereof, many godly people are now [buried] under the altar, their blood being poured out. It is of dangerous consequence." Strickland would have no act against blasphemy: punish only disturbers of the peace, he argued. "We may all, in after ages, be called Quakers." Laws against papists, he reminded them, had been turned against "the best Protestants." The proposed bills were consigned to a committee which let them die, although in the following year, 1657, Cromwell accepted from Parliament a new constitution that constricted the liberty of conscience guaranteed by the Instrument of Government.[71]

Londoners, having watched Nayler receive the first part of his punishment, petitioned Parliament to suspend the rest of it. General Lambert, affirming that Nayler was too sick to undergo the remainder, urged that a physician be sent to him. Parliament decided to send "some godly ministers" instead, but postponed the next dose of the punishment for another week. On December 20, crowds were at the doors of Parliament with petitions in behalf of Nayler. After a debate whether to receive some prosperous burghers, the house by one vote allowed thirty to enter. They represented about one hundred; their spokesman had once been a chaplain in the New Model Army. They were honest, godly persons who disowned the crime, Lambert said. None was a Quaker. Their petition spoke for "Conscience-Liberty." They claimed that the state should not pass judgment on religious error or blasphemy, and that corporal punishment in such a case was wrong. They had signed the petition, they said, out of "tenderness to the cause of spiritual and civil liberty." Resting their case on article 37 of the Instrument, they requested that the remainder of the sentence be canceled. When they withdrew, a debate flared anew on the basic question of whether liberty of conscience meant protection for blasphemers, but, "being weary of it," the house adjourned for lunch.[72]

The same petitioners, joined by many others, turned to Cromwell. One petition forwarded to him at this time came from George Fox; it was less a petition than a theological statement of the Quaker position on Immanence written when Parliament first took custody of Nayler. Fox did not mention Nayler by name. The only point of pertinence was a cryptic postscript: "If the seed speake which is Christ . . . it is not blasphemie but truth, but if the seed of the serpent speake and say he is Christ it is the Liar and the blasphemie and the ground of all blasphemie. . . ." Cromwell offered no support to the petitioners for "spiritual and civil liberty." He intervened only with a terse letter to Parliament asking for their grounds in passing the sentence against Nayler. That provoked a two-day debate on constitutional issues bearing on the adjudicatory powers of Parliament and touching only incidentally on the issue of blasphemy. In the end, Parliament proved incapable of formulating a response to the protector. But some of the mercifuls tried to use the issue to obtain a decision on the petition to cancel the rest of the sentence. They lost overwhelmingly, 113 to 59. Members knew that, when the deputation of ministers had met with Nayler on Christmas Day, he had still defended his beliefs. Downing shouted, "We are God's executioners. . . . Had you anything from himself, of recantation, it were something. But, as the case is, if ten thousand should come to the door and petition, I would die upon the place before I would remit the sentence you have already passed." Even some of the mercifuls made much of the fact that Cromwell had not asked for a remission of the sentence. And Nathaniel Fiennes, a councilor who had stood with the mercifuls, argued that the petition for remission was "dangerous," because it would "debar the civil magistrate in matters of religion. . . . That is too much liberty."[73]

On December 28, Nayler underwent the second part of the sentence. Burton, one of the revengers, was present among the crowd of "many thousands." They were strangely quiet and sympathetic, and those who were closest and could see the spectacle stood bareheaded. Burton recorded that he went

> to see Nayler's tongue bored through, and him marked in the forehead. He put out his tongue very willingly, but shrinked a little when the iron came upon his forehead. He was pale when he came out of the pillory, but highcoloured after tongue-boring. He was bound with a cord by both arms to the pillory. Rich, the mad merchant [a Quaker] sat bare at Nayler's feet all the time. Some times he sang and cried, and stroked his hair and face, and kissed

his hand, and sucked the fire out of his forehead. Nayler embraced
his executioner, and behaved himself very handsomely and patiently. A great crowd of people were there. . . .

A week later, Nayler still could not speak.[74]

The final part of the sentence was executed in mid-January in Bristol,
as a burlesque of Nayler's entrance there about three months earlier.
They transported him to that city sitting on a horse, with his face to the
rear. In Bristol, they stripped him for the whipping. This time, however,
the Quakers turned out en masse to support him; many wept. Bristol had
more compassion than Westminster. The authorities allowed one of Nayler's friends to hold the executioner's arm to check his lashes. From
Bristol, soldiers conveyed him back to London's Bridewell Prison to
begin a perpetual imprisonment. He was put to hard labor in solitary
confinement and denied a fire to keep him warm in winter.[75]

In February 1658, Nayler, who had been gravely ill, repented by
acknowledging that he had been possessed by a dark spirit and had
received idolatrous worship. The Spirit of Jesus in him now dictated
"lowness, meekness, and longsuffering." He wanted Fox's forgiveness,
but Fox was unyielding. On September 8, 1659, after nearly three years,
the Rump Parliament released Nayler. The army had by then deposed
Richard Cromwell as the second protector, and it freed many Quakers.
Nayler, subdued, returned to preaching. At a London meeting arranged
by common Friends, he and Fox appeared on the same platform, but Fox
was distant. In 1660, thirteen months after his liberation from Bridewell,
Nayler, at the age of forty-four, a sick and broken man, died—the victim
of a system that could not allow "too much liberty." In that year,
the Stuart Restoration began. Soon after, the Puritan "priests" who
had shrieked for Nayler's life, as well as the Quaker preachers who
had reviled those priests, were jailed by the tens of thousands, fellow
prisoners.[76]

CHAPTER TEN

Christianity Becomes the Law of the Land

A FTER the Restoration of 1660, England's grand political design nourished persecution of conscience, but the term "blasphemy," like "heresy," passed out of style as the formal designation of most offenses against religion. During the foregoing period of the Interregnum, the Puritans, who found Old Testament precedents attractive, saw blasphemy in those who repudiated the moral law, rejected the doctrine of the Trinity, impersonated Christ, or worshipped the Christ within. English Protestants of the seventeenth century, confronted with some form of the age-old crime of erroneous religious belief, shied from calling it "heresy." That conjured up the stench of burning flesh at Bloody Mary's Smithfield, and the image of mangled bodies under the Spanish Inquisition. Even the Anglican church under Laud and the High Commission had avoided "heresy" as the crime *de jure*. "Nonconformity," the principal usage under the early Stuarts, once again became the generic name for the crime under the later Stuarts. "Nonconformity" differed little in substance from "heresy" or "blasphemy"; yet it somehow implied that, although conscience was free, seditious subjects obstinately violated the nation's laws requiring uniformity of religious worship. Calling the crime "nonconformity" avoided the appearance of bigotry, at least in the minds of the persecutors.

The Restoration of the Stuart monarchy revived the English constitution as it had existed prior to the civil wars of the 1640s. Acts of Parliament to which the crown had consented were law once again; all subsequent acts and ordinances were null and void. Thus, the High Commission, the Star Chamber, and the oath *ex officio* were dead, but so was all law from 1642 to the restoration of Charles II. Thus, the Restoration meant that the Church of England was by law established, that the House of Lords sat as a second chamber, that the Anglican bishops were members of the Lords, and that the House of Commons and the common-law courts might thwart the royal prerogative.[1]

The Restoration also meant that persecution rode booted and spurred once again. The tragedy of the Stuart Restoration consisted in that fact, but it was a tragedy compounded by paradox. Parliament, which represented the nation, was more Anglican than the Anglican church, and both Parliament and the church vigorously advocated intolerance, while Charles II (1660–85) and James II (1685–88), who had the audacity to violate Parliament's customary legislative powers, championed toleration. Indeed, they went further by advocating the free exercise of religion for all peaceable and loyal subjects, without exception. Thus, the later Stuarts outdid Cromwell and matched even the Baptist theorists, the most consistent friends of religious liberty. The phenomenon was novel: royalist policy was enlightened as to conscience but politically autocratic, while Parliament and the church supported persecution and constitutional government.[2]

Charles II immediately declared himself in favor of "a liberty to tender consciences . . . [so] that no man shall be disquieted or called in question for differences of opinion in matter of religion, which do not disturb the peace of the kingdom." Although the king would consent to "such an Act of Parliament," Parliament, dominated by Anglican gentry who had suffered during the Puritan regime, was in a vengeful mood. Anglican gentlemen meant to even the score with the Puritans and did not bother to distinguish Presbyterians from Fifth Monarchists, Quakers, or gathered churches. Anyone not a member of the Church of England was considered a potential subversive. Parliament at first singled out the Quakers for special treatment, although the king had promised a Quaker group that none would suffer for religion "so long as you live peaceably." The Quaker Act of 1662 inflicted fines and imprisonment on the supposedly dangerous opinions and practices of those who met in great numbers and maintained the illegality of all oaths; for five or more such people to assemble for worship not authorized by law became criminal. The Quakers, of course, conscientiously persisted in their worship and suffered the consequences.[3]

The only official road of Protestantism led to the Church of England. In 1662, the Act of Uniformity reinstated the episcopacy, Anglican rites, the Anglican prayer book, and Anglican ordination; any minister refusing to give his "unfeigned consent" lost his living. Uniformity and conformity were intended to end the "factions" of "the late unhappy troubles." The Conventicles Act of 1664 extended the principle of the Quaker Act: religious assemblies other than Anglican were outlawed, to prevent the growing and dangerous practices of "seditious sectaries and other disloyal persons" who met under pretense of conscience to "contrive insurrections," as the "late experience hath showed." The Five Mile Act of 1665 fixed penalties for any nonconformist minister who refused to swear an oath that he would seek no alteration in the ecclesiastical policy. The act took its name from the fact that it excluded a nonjuror from teaching, preaching, or living within five miles of a place where he had served as a minister. The Test Act of 1673 required any person holding government office or receiving money from the government to swear an oath against the Catholic doctrine of transubstantiation and to receive the sacrament of the Lord's Supper according to Anglican usage. Without doubt, this body of legislation reflected the intense dislike of Englishmen for Catholics, whom the Anglicans outnumbered 170 to one, and for Puritans and sectarians of any sort, whom Anglicans outnumbered twenty to one. Charles II, who was wholly dependent on Parliament for money, consented to all the legislation.[4]

On the whole, the Anglicans in church and state simply reinforced conventional anti-Catholic policies and reversed the laws enacted by Puritan governments against Anglicanism. All dissenters suffered—the Quakers disproportionately, because their faith compelled them to refuse even to pay fines or give sureties for what the courts called "good behaviour"; in effect, "good behaviour" meant apostasy from Quakerism, if not conversion to Anglicanism. Between 1660 and 1688, one-fourth of the sixty thousand nonconformists who suffered for conscience' sake were Quakers. Estimates of the number of nonconformists who died in prison because of the hideous penal conditions of that era range as high as five to eight thousand. Those figures are no doubt exaggerated, but by any reckoning the persecution was widespread and appalling. Richard Baxter, the Presbyterian moderate who himself became a victim of the persecution, conceded that, after the Conventicles Act,

> . . . the Fanaticks called Quakers did greatly relieve the sober People for a time; for they were so resolute, and gloried in their Constancy and Sufferings, that they assembled openly . . . and were dragged away daily to the Common Jail; and yet desisted not, but the rest came the next day nevertheless. So that the jail at Newgate was filled with them. Abundance of them died in prison, and yet they continued their Assemblies still. And the poor deluded Souls would sometimes meet only to sit still in Silence. . . . And it was a great question whether this Silence was a religious exercise allowed by the liturgy, etc.[5]

In 1672, Charles II, having concluded that persecution bore only bitter fruit, brazenly exercised his "inherent" royal prerogative as the "supreme power in ecclesiastical matters." He summarily suspended the execution of all penal laws "against whatsoever sort of nonconformists, or recusants," and ordered all his officers to obey. In his "Declaration of

Indulgence," the king commanded that, to avoid illegal conventicles, all Protestants should be free to worship as they pleased publicly, Roman Catholics privately. Charles went as far as he dared for the "Papists," and he did not mind winning the loyalty of the nonconformists. Religiously indifferent himself, he said nothing about the religious value of freedom of conscience. His reasons for the Declaration of Indulgence were realistically based on secular, if not political, grounds. Twelve sad years of experience, he said, showed that coercion settled none of the religious differences among his subjects and did not prevent "seditious conventicles." Exempting dissenters from the penal laws would diminish the political dangers from religious discord, bring peace to the realm, and encourage both commerce and immigration. Parliament, enraged by a renewal of the old Stuart propensity to legislate unilaterally, compelled Charles to revoke his declaration. The church, obsessed by its own ecclesiastical concerns, supported Parliament against the king, although one of the intriguing aspects of the persecution is that secular considerations motivated church and Parliament, as well as Charles.[6]

The growing prevalence of secular considerations, as contrasted with theological, explains why prosecutions for blasphemy were so infrequent during an era of persecution. The church, although controlled by vengeful Anglicans under Gilbert Shelton, the archbishop of Canterbury, had sound historical reasons for hating sectarians. Yet the church was no monolith. It was hospitable to any Christian who could accept conformity on matters of rites, ordination, and the prayer book. Many churchmen thought such matters concerned only externals. Ever since Elizabeth's time, the church had sought to be comprehensive and national; during the Restoration period, it harbored a wide spectrum of religious convictions, ranging from Calvinism to Arminianism to Anglo-Catholicism. Although intensely antipapal and nationalistic, Anglo-Catholicism was a movement within the church that approached as closely as possible the pageantry and ceremonials of Roman Catholicism. The Anglo-Catholic or "High Church" movement composed a distinct minority within Anglicanism, but a politically powerful one. The church also included latitudinarians, who favored the broadest comprehensiveness. The most tolerant of the Anglicans, the latitudinarians were satisfied with subscription to the fundamentals of the Christian faith: acceptance of the Apostles' Creed, which included belief in the doctrine of the Trinity and in the Scriptures as divinely inspired. The diversity within the Anglican church produced a decline in a distinctive Anglican theology.[7]

Not even the High Church men claimed theological infallibility or the absolute truth of their beliefs. The episcopacy, with notable exceptions, had practical, not theological, reasons for supporting Parliament's persecution policy. Personal and institutional considerations outweighed theological ones. Bishops no longer persecuted to redeem lost souls or even to save uncontaminated believers from the contagion of heretical opinions. Anglicans rarely disputed with one another on the overweening issue of how to achieve salvation; Anglicanism conceded that religious truth could not be known with certainty. The theological motive for persecution was still triumphant only when anti-Trinitarians—Socinians, Muggletonians, deists, freethinkers, or "atheists"—came to official notice or entered as topics of abstract debate. The institutional motive to persevere in the attack on nonconformity was fundamentally secular. At issue were good order and the power to govern the church and to reap the benefits of patronage and perquisites.[8]

The Anglican church had become the true church not because it was right but because it was in power. If it was right, the reason was that it contributed to good order, dignity, the political influence of the episcopacy, and the livings of episcopally ordained priests. If it was right, the reason also was that it was the church established by law: to defy it was wrong because illegal. Anglicanism seemed congruent with the constitution and security of the realm, as well as the good of the great majority of Englishmen, who were faithful communicants. The theological basis of persecution, the saving of souls, dramatically waned even as the persecution itself reached new peaks. Few Anglicans believed that uniformity was really possible; religious diversity had gone too far for that. The trouble was that external conformity, which was all the church hoped for, had passed the threshold of possibility too; but few Anglicans understood that. Some realized that even external conformity, which barely touched the conscience (as they saw the matter), could be achieved only by extreme measures that England refused to undertake: the physical extirpation of dissenters, Protestant and Roman Catholic, by a terrible and systematic exercise of power comparable to the Inquisition and lasting over several generations.[9]

But death for religious differences was no longer an acceptable English way. The Nayler case had proved that, even when the crime was "horrid blasphemy." Despite its panoply of repressive measures, Charles's Cavalier Parliament inflicted moderate penalties for violations. Non-Anglicans could not hold political or religious offices and endured other civil disabilities, such as the loss of the right to sue in the courts, or be guardians and trustees, or receive legacies and deeds. The maximum imprisonment under the Act of Uniformity was three months. The Conventicles Act imposed only fines until the third offense, which required "transportation" or banishment for seven years. The Five Mile Act provided for fines and a maximum sentence of six months' imprisonment.

In practice, the courts, when confronted with the obdurate recalcitrance of a Quaker or of a principled Baptist like John Bunyan, could keep a man in jail indefinitely for contempt, but he had his own key: he could get out anytime he agreed to sureties for good behavior. The statutes required civil disabilities, fines, and light imprisonment. Conscientious objectors, like Bunyan, who spent twelve years in jail, embarrassed the government and the church. The magistrates who enforced the laws had to choose between ignoring prescribed penal sanctions and increasing them by punishing for contempt. Englishmen could make fine distinctions between punishing for contempt, sedition, or nonconformity, and punishing for conscience. But England did not like making the exercise of conscience a felony. Even the few Cromwellians who fell back on De Haeretico Comburendo during the debate on Nayler's case would not have burned anyone. Indeed, it was the Cavalier Parliament of 1677, no less, that repealed the act of 1401 that had established the writ for burning obdurate heretics. Criminal prosecution for "heresy" really died as a result of the reforms of the Long Parliament of 1641. The act of 1677 belatedly recognized that fact. Ecclesiastical courts had returned to business in 1660, and the act of 1677 authorized them to punish for "atheism, blasphemy, heresy, schism, or other damnable doctrine or opinion," but those courts had neither fang nor claw. At most they could only excommunicate.[10]

Parliaments of the Restoration did not argue that conscience should be punished; their position was that conscience pushed to external disobedience of the law raised the specter of seditious conspiracy. To Parliament, nonconformity suggested regicide, treason, revolution, civil war, and the persecution of Anglicanism. Thomas Tomkins, the archbishop of Canterbury's chaplain, wrote that "gathered churches," the backbone of Cromwell's army, "are most excellent materials to raise new troops out of." Samuel Parker, Tomkin's successor and later bishop of Oxford, warned that toleration of different sects meant that, if the "grandees" took control, "there is an army." An order for the suppression of nonconformists, in 1683, spoke of the "seditious and rebellious practices of the sectaries" and blamed the nonconformist preachers as the authors of "the late execrable treasons."[11]

The anomaly of the great persecution of 1660 to 1688 is that the theory of toleration grew while the theory of persecution for the sake of religion waned. In state and church, those who argued for persecution outside the church hatched subversive plots. The persecutors demanded law and order—obedience for its own sake as a Christian virtue and a political virtue. The church, for them, was the cement of a safe and sane society. Their persecution policy mirrored their conviction that the state had an obligation to preserve the church so that the church could buttress the state.[12]

Theological reasons for persecution are blind to reason; secular reasons for persecution disintegrate when experience proves them to be unfounded. Religious reasons for toleration meet with prejudiced repudiation; secular reasons for toleration become acceptable when experience validates them. During the Restoration period, excellent tracts were published by Baptists, moderate Independents, Socinians, and Quakers, making the argument for toleration on religious grounds. Even Fox spoke for toleration, although William Penn had no superior among the Quakers. His *Great Case of Liberty of Conscience* (1671) put the religious argument in imperishable terms, but *England's Present Interest Discovered* (1675), his next tract, reached the same conclusions on the basis of political and commercial considerations, and it would eventually prove to be more persuasive. Toleration, however, waited on a second revolution against the Stuarts.[13]

Until then, the government prosecuted nonconformists because they subverted church and state. Most prosecutions—and there were thousands—were for violations of parliamentary enactments, but prosecutors abetted by magistrates developed the theory that at bottom the criminality of nonconformity consisted in its seditiousness: subversion of church and state. No court would concede that mere difference of religious opinion *per se* was a crime. That difference had to take on a dangerous political coloration before dissenters were subjected to penalties.

When John Bunyan was arrested in 1660 for preaching Baptist doctrine, no law existed for prosecuting him until ingenious local magistrates invoked Elizabethan acts against conventicles and for uniformity in religion. The magistrates offered Bunyan his freedom in return for sureties for his good behavior, but he was as intractable as a Quaker. Indomitably he pledged to resume his preaching from the moment prison did not prevent him. The government indicted him for unlawful sermons and conventicles "to the great disturbance of the . . . Kingdom." The magistrate told him that his sort of nonconformity led to "insurrection" and "the ruin of the kingdom." Bunyan's three-month sentence turned into an imprisonment for twelve years; his refusal to abandon his ministry amounted to perpetual contempt, and his mounting fines and jailer's fees made his liberation seem impossible. The law had no way to cope with his spiritual steadfastness, which it had converted into a political crime. Only Charles II's Declaration of Indulgence provided a means of releasing Bunyan. His name and those of others like him were added to a list of pardons, including the remission of fees, intended mainly for the benefit of Quakers. Bunyan had the same experience as the Puritan minister Matthew Mead, who was also arrested in 1660. Mead wrote: "I have been charged with faction and sedition, nay that I preached rebellion and treason is charged on this sermon, though I mentioned not either the King or his government."[14]

Most of the famous "state trials" of nonconformist ministers were, similarly, prosecutions for seditiousness, which became the common-law synonym for nonconformity. Although seditiousness can be defined in technical terms, the crime, if judged by actual prosecutions, consisted in criticizing or differing from the government—its form, constitutional officers, laws, symbols, conduct, and policies. In effect, any comment was seditious that could be construed to have the bad tendency of lowering the public's esteem for the government or of disturbing the peace. When the head of the state was the head of the church, nonconformity or criticism of the church became virtually indistinguishable from sedition.

Field's case of 1662 was a turning point in the law, because the King's Bench, the highest criminal court of the realm, resolved the legal issue. Field was indicted for seditious words, because he said from the pulpit "the government of the Church of England is popish, superstitious. . . ." His counsel argued that the matter was "spiritual and ecclesiastical," not against the government, and not within its criminal jurisdiction. The prosecutor argued that Field had, in effect, said that the king was a heretic or a papist, "to the disturbance of the Government now established." Field denied that, and denied speaking with malice. On conviction, he was disabled from all civil and ecclesiastical offices, fined £500, and jailed until he paid the fine. His motion to arrest the judgment failed, on the ground that, although he spoke only against the church, "The government of England is all one, and all from one foundation, though in several parts. . . . The ecclesiastick is the prime part of the Government." Lord Chief Justice Robert Foster pronounced the judgment. A precedent of 1618 had laid down the same rule, that criticism of the church was "*seditious parolls encontre le State de nostre Eglise & encontre le peace del Relme*," but the precedent had been forgotten until published by a court reporter, using manuscript records, in 1668, six years after Field's case.[15]

After Field's case, nonconformity constituted one form of the crime of seditiousness at common law, even in the absence of any parliamentary enactments. Two years later, in 1664, Chief Justice Robert Hyde, Foster's successor, mercilessly browbeat a Baptist preacher, Benjamin Keach, and bulldozed the jury into convicting him for seditious libel. Keach's crime was publishing a book in which he said such things as "Believers only are the right subjects of Baptism" and "Infants are not to be received into the Church." Keach was pilloried twice, fined £20, and imprisoned for two weeks. Trials like Keach's continued throughout the Restoration.[16]

One of the cruelest and most sensationally publicized cases was that of Thomas Delaune, a London Baptist who made his living by teaching and translating. In 1683, he published (without imprimatur) a small book entitled *A Plea for the Nonconformists*. His argument was reasoned and temperate, free from the scurrility that characterized partisan writings at that time. The attorney general prosecuted him for seditious libel before the King's Bench presided over by Chief Justice George Jeffreys, whose ferocity earned him the nickname "Bloody Jeffreys." Delaune was convicted, fined, and forced to watch the burning of his book by the hangman. Unable to pay the fine, Delaune was imprisoned in Newgate. Wealthy Baptists could have paid his fine of £67, but he preferred to suffer as a witness for his religion. His wife and child joined him in Newgate and soon died there; after fifteen months, he too died from the foul conditions. The secret presses turned out four editions of his book while he was in Newgate, and they also printed his *Narrative of the Sufferings of Thomas Delaune* (1684). In 1706, Daniel Defoe wrote the introduction to the seventh edition of the book for which Delaune gave his life.[17]

The most celebrated of all the nonconformist ministers who were prosecuted for seditious libel was Richard Baxter. In 1685, at the age of seventy, Baxter was Puritanism's gray eminence. Six lawyers defended him against the prejudiced Jeffreys, who had instigated his trial on learning that Baxter's latest book supposedly criticized the bishops of the Anglican church. Baxter had denounced Roman Catholic bishops, but court and prosecution wrested innuendos from his words and called them seditious libel. Jeffreys maligned Baxter throughout the trial, obstructed his lawyers, and harangued the jury on the theme that he was "the main incendiary" in a nonconformist "design to ruin the king and the nation." The packed jury whispered a moment and agreed on a verdict of guilty. Jeffreys fined Baxter 500 marks (about £333) and ordered him to prison until he paid it. Baxter's friends who had hired his counsel could have paid the fine, but they realized that Jeffreys would get revenge sooner or later if Baxter did not suffer some disgrace. Influential friends managed to arrange for his imprisonment in a private home, where he lived comfortably while they pulled strings for him. After seventeen months, James II pardoned him and remitted his fines, leaving Baxter to preach until his death in 1691. The ordinary nonconformist minister was not as fortunate.[18]

Since seditiousness comprehended offenses against religion in cases from Bunyan's to Baxter's, as well as offenses against the temporal government, blasphemy, which was most obviously an offense against religion, became in legal theory a form of seditiousness. In the first Restoration case involving blasphemy, Sedley's case of 1663, the issue of blasphemy was tangential. That crime is basically verbal in character.

Sedley's immoral words and conduct provoked a riot, overwhelming the blasphemous aspect of his crime. We have no record of what he said, and his intoxication probably mitigated the verbal offense. Nevertheless, his case is significant because the common-law courts took jurisdiction over what formerly had been a matter exclusively within the authority of the ecclesiastical courts.

Sir Charles Sedley (1639?–1701) became a dramatist and "one of the best gay lyric poets of the century." In his youth, he was a notorious rake. He was about twenty-four on the day when he and some friends got roaring drunk at an inn near Covent Garden. According to one account by a contemporary, the revelers went out onto the balcony of the inn in broad daylight "and putting down their Breeches they excrementiz'd in the Street: which being done, Sedley stripped himself naked and with Eloquence preached Blasphemy to the People." Samuel Pepys, the diarist, based his account of the young aristocrat's escapade on the remarks of a friend who observed the trial before the King's Bench. There Sedley stood, Pepys wrote, naked on the balcony, "acting all the postures of lust and buggery that could be imagined, and abusing of the scripture, as it were, from thence preaching a Montebank sermon from that pulpitt, saying that he hath to sell such a pouder as shoud make all the cunts in town run after him—a thousand people standing underneath to see and hear him." After his speech, Sedley "took a glass of wine and washed his prick in it and then drank it off," and then he took another and toasted the king.[19]

The brief notes of the court reporters speak mystifyingly. One primly recorded that Sedley did "such things, and spoke such words" as were misdemeanors against the public peace, "to the great scandal of Christianity." Thus, the offense, in part at least, was verbal and against religion, although the reporters did not mention "blasphemy." In passing sentence against Sedley in 1663, Chief Justice Foster told him that the King's Bench, being custodians of the public morality, meant to punish "profane" actions against Christianity. Foster imposed a fine of 2,000 marks, a week's imprisonment, and sureties for good behavior for three years. When asked whether he had anything to say, Sedley is supposed to have remarked that he thought he was the first person "that paid for shitting." He was also the first person (whose case was reported) to be punished by the common law for a crime later called "obscenity" and, possibly, he was the first to be punished for the common-law crime of blasphemy. In later cases, the courts would develop the implications of *Rex* v. *Sedley*. During the Restoration, the common-law courts began extending secular control over various offenses against Christianity. The law of blasphemy developed in that broad context, connected with crimes such as seditious libel, obscenity, public immorality, profanity, and perjury. But blasphemy always remained a distinct crime.[20]

Very likely the first person to be charged with blasphemy after the Sedley case was Lodowick Muggleton, in 1664. Muggleton had suffered imprisonment for that crime in 1653, under the act against Ranters, after he and John Reeve publicly announced their divine commissions as the two witnesses. By 1664, Muggleton was the sole prophet of an obscure sect, hardly known outside of London, that bore his name. The Muggletonians discussed the Bible but did not believe in prayer and had no rites. They believed in a deviant but harmless version of Christianity that produced tolerant, morally upright, and industrious people. But they were nonconformists of a type that most Christians then loathed as anti-Christian, because they repudiated the doctrine of the Trinity. Muggleton himself also claimed a power to damn eternally, which might be construed as a divine attribute. That the Muggletonians were few in number, lacking in religious enthusiasm, almost unknown, and not given to worship in any conventional sense probably saved them from blasphemy prosecutions. Their leader, however, was an eloquent man who knew his Bible but had not yet learned to fear man's law.

While traveling in the vicinity of Nottingham, Muggleton got into a religious dispute with some nonconformists, mainly Quakers and Independents. He pronounced the sentence of eternal damnation on several people, who complained to the parish priest. The priest got him arrested and taken before the mayor's court in Chesterfield. During the examination, the priest asked Muggleton whether he believed in the Trinity. "I answered, No, I did believe there was three Names, or Titles, of Father, Son, and Holy Ghost, but one Person, the Lord Jesus Christ." At the conclusion of the examination, they charged him with blasphemy for denying the Trinity, claiming to be one of the Witnesses referred to in Revelation 11:3, claiming the power to damn and save and saying that "the Scriptures would do them little good now." On the latter point, Muggleton believed that God would not intervene in the affairs of men until Judgment Day. He was imprisoned in Derby to await trial before the Assize. Muggleton's prosecutors made the mistake of taking his horse. The earl of Newcastle, the local magnate, knew nothing about the religious issue, but he placed a high value on the sanctity of private property. He reproved the mayor and the town recorder for their offense against Muggleton. When the Assize met, the judge allowed Muggleton bail for his appearance at the next session. Muggleton might have sued the town officials, but they arranged to let him disappear, ending the matter. He had spent only nine days in jail. The next time he was charged with blasphemy, he did not get off so easily.[21]

Thomas Hobbes, the political theorist, found himself in a risky situation in 1666, because he had saturated his enduring monument, *Leviathan* (1651), with his skepticism about Christianity, leaving the faint odor
of atheism. Hobbes, in fact, strongly supported a state church, although
for political reasons exclusively; he considered only the safety of the state,
not the intrinsic values of religion. In October 1666, the House of Commons talked about reviving the writ De Haeretico Comburendo to cope
with Hobbes. The great fire that had burned London in that year, following the terrible plague of the preceding years, seemed to some of the
devout a visitation of divine wrath that ought to be appeased. The House
of Commons established a committee to which it submitted for consideration a bill "touching such books as tend to atheism, blasphemy, and
profaneness, or against the essence and attributes of God, and in particular . . . the book of Mr. Hobbes called the *Leviathan*." The bill failed,
however, making Hobbes, in the words of Sir James Fitzjames Stephen,
"the last person of eminence who went in fear of it [the writ for burning
heretics]." Parliament permanently abolished the writ in 1677, as has
been noted.[22]

The first person during the Restoration to get into serious trouble for
blasphemy was William Penn. In 1668, he had been a Quaker for only a
year. His father, Admiral Sir William Penn, who professed whatever the
Church of England required, never understood how his son could be so
obsessed by religion. Oxford expelled young William after two years for
his nonconformity, and he finished his education among the Huguenots
in France. After a year of law, he tasted the military life and was a
courtier. An accidental encounter with a Quaker preacher in 1667 ended
in Penn's conversion, conscripting his prodigious talents into the Quaker
and tolerationist causes. A year later, when he was twenty-four, Penn
published *The Sandy Foundation Shaken*, a tract intended to answer Presbyterian tenets. Pepys called it "Penn's book against the Trinity," indicating why it immediately became notorious. John Evelyn, in his diary,
paraphrased a public gazette which reported that Penn had written "a
blasphemous book against the deity of our B[lessed] *Lord*." Penn called
the Presbyterian version of the Trinity, which was identical to the Anglican, "a fiction." Relying on Scriptures for his argument, he sounded
like a Socinian. One passage, intended to reveal the illogic of the doctrine
of the Trinity, dangerously verged on ridicule: "And since the Father is
God, the Son is God, and the Spirit is God, then unless the Father, Son
and Spirit are three distinct nothings, they must be three distinct substances, and consequently three distinct Gods. . . . If each person be
God, and that God subsists in three persons, then in each person are
three persons or Gods, and from them three, they will increase to nine

and so ad infinitum." Penn's Presbyterian opponent Thomas Vincent replied to "the Quaker's hideous blasphemies, Socinian and damnably-heretical opinions."[23]

When the printer of Penn's book was arrested, Penn turned himself in to Lord Arlington, the secretary of state. Arlington consulted the Privy Council. The "Helm of the Church," Penn mistakenly wrote, procured his imprisonment. Arlington and the king himself were responsible. The council ordered Penn to be committed to the Tower of London as a "close" prisoner, meaning that he was to be kept in solitary confinement and denied the usual amenities that political prisoners of his class enjoyed in the Tower. The order of the council explicitly stated the cause of imprisonment: "a blasphemous treatise." The council did not even state that it was unlicensed. While Penn froze in his attic room in the winter and smothered in the summer, the council took its time investigating. It had no power to convict and sentence, but it could hold a person indefinitely while it investigated his offense against the government.[24]

Penn was never formally charged or tried. "That which I am credibly inform'd to be the greatest reason for my Imprisonment," he wrote, "and that noise of Blasphemy, which hath pierced so many Ears of late, is, *my denying the Divinity of Christ, and divesting him of his Eternal Godhead*." Admiral Penn petitioned the council for clemency to no avail, but managed to send a family retainer to see his son in the Tower. "Thou mayest tell my father . . . these words: That my prison shall be my Grave, before I will budge a Jot; for I owe my Conscience to no Mortal Man." Those brave words were spoken on Christmas Eve, 1668, after less than two weeks in the Tower. Soon after, the king sent his chaplain, Dr. Edward Stillingfleet, the archdeacon of St. Paul's, to convince Penn that he held "blasphemous and heretical opinions."[25]

The choice of Stillingfleet as the king's emissary proved to be fortunate for Penn, for Stillingfleet was then close to the latitudinarians within the church; he would grow more conservative as he rose to a bishopric. Although Stillingfleet could not budge Penn from Quakerism, Penn convinced Stillingfleet that he had never meant to reject the divinity of Christ. He asked Stillingfleet to inform the king that "the Tower is the worst argument in the world to convince me." He also addressed letters to the secretary of state, complaining of his harsh treatment, the fact that he had never had a judicial hearing, and his being held "without legal cause or just procedure, contrary to the privileges of every Englishman." Neither king, bishop, nor council relented. Stillingfleet suggested that Penn put in print a clarification of his views on the Trinity. Penn promptly published *Innocency with Her Open Face Presented by way of apology for the Book Entitled the Sandy Foundation Shaken*, thereby vindicating himself and winning his release. He had suffered in the Tower for eight and a half months. Later, when James II sat on the throne, Penn credited him with using his influence as duke of York to gain Penn his freedom.[26]

While he was in the Tower, Penn's cause was taken up by the Socinians—doing him no good, nor the Quakers either. Excluding the handful of Socinians and Muggletonians in England, no Christian then conceded that anti-Trinitarianism was Christian; all, rather, agreed that it was blasphemy. Yet Penn's seeming lapse into Socinianism suggests that more Englishmen were drifting toward it. Thomas Firmin, one of Biddle's converts whom Cromwell once dismissed as a "curl-pate boy," was becoming London's greatest merchant and earned the nation's gratitude for his philanthropy during the great plague of 1665 and the London holocaust of 1666. Firmin never abandoned or hid his anti-Trinitarianism, although he joined the Anglican church, which required external conformity only. Inquisitions into men's beliefs really had died with the abolition of the High Commission in 1641. Firmin, who was on good terms with nonconformist leaders and Anglican bishops alike, welcomed Penn as a Socinian, but their friendship cooled when Penn wrote the apology that was the price of his freedom.[27]

Penn explicitly declared that, although he denied a Trinity of three separate persons in one Godhead, "yet I do not consequentially deny the Deity of Jesus Christ." Penn admitted having read Socinus, and courageously he praised Socinus's wisdom; "if in anything I acknowledge the verity of his Doctrine, it is for Truth's sake, of which, in many things, he had a clearer prospect than most of his contemporaries." That was a risky acknowledgment, but Penn emerged from the incident as a Sabellian, not a Socinian: for him, the three persons of the Trinity expressed different manifestations or aspects of God. That Penn continued to deny the Athanasian Creed is unquestionable. Many Anglicans, however, also rejected what Penn called the "Popish School" on the doctrine of the Trinity.[28]

Although Penn repudiated Socinianism, he had unwittingly opened what later became a major theological controversy in England, leading to a new act against anti-Trinitarian blasphemy in 1698. By 1672, Penn was in the vanguard against the "Biddlean or Socinian Cause," while Henry Hedworth, a follower of Biddle and a friend of Firmin, from the safety of anonymity defended the opinion on Christ of Christians "who for distinction sake call themselves Unitarians, being so called in those places [Holland], where by the Laws of the country they have equal Liberty of Religion with other men." Hedworth was the first Englishman to call himself a Unitarian. By the end of the century, there were many.[29]

A "unitarian" of a different sort, but as thoroughgoing as any in his outright denial of Trinitarianism, had been plaguing the Quakers for years with his denunciations of their "bodiless God," the Inner Light.

Lodowick Muggleton had published *The Neck of the Quakers Broken* (1663) and *A Looking Glass for George Fox* (1668). Those books attracted more attention than Muggleton bargained for: in 1670, he was a wanted man. His heterodoxy on the Trinity caused his book to be seized and publicly burned as blasphemous, but he went into hiding, evading capture for six years. Penn, having taken on the Socinians, challenged Muggleton too, and his attack, *The New Witnesses proved Old Heretics . . . the Doctrines of John Reeve and Lodowick Muggleton . . . Proved to be Mostly Ancient Whimsies, Blasphemies, and Heresies* (1672), did nothing for the cause of toleration. Muggleton, it is true, had been overgenerous in sentencing Quakers to eternal damnation for their unpardonably "blasphemous" sin of denying his commission. More than half of all his curses were against Quakers, including Fox and Penn. But Muggleton made no exception to his principle of equal practice of conscience for all. To Fox he had written:

I have always loved the persecuted better than I did the persecutor, and I always had compassion upon the afflicted for conscience-sake, though I knew they suffered for a mere lie, as all you Quakers do. Yet I say, whoever doth persecute you for conscience in meeting and worshipping an unknown God (as you Quakers do), I say those men that do persecute willingly, will be every man of them damned to eternity.

Penn did nothing to reciprocate the sentiment of tolerance toward the Muggletonians or the Socinians. It was Firmin, the Socinian, who financed the relief of the French Huguenots (Calvinists), the descendants of those who had burned Servetus, when hundreds of them fled to England for their lives.[30]

In 1675, John Taylor, a yeoman from Guildford in Surrey, uttered words so blasphemous that not even a Socinian tolerationist would defend his liberty of opinion. The magistrates in Guildford kept Taylor in jail while they forwarded a statement of his case to the House of Lords at Westminster. The Lords, perceiving that they might be confronting the most horrendous case of blasphemy since James Nayler's, summoned Taylor under heavy guard, and also all the officials and witnesses from Guildford. Three days later, Taylor was brought to the bar of the House, and his words, as taken down by the mayor of Guildford, were read to him. He admitted that he was the author of the blasphemies. His confession so startled the Lords that they ordered the keeper of the Bethlem Royal Hospital (Bedlam) to lock him up "and take Care that the said John Taylor be kept there with Bread and Water, and such Bodily Corrections as may conduce his recovery from Madness wherewith at present he seems possessed." The keeper of Bedlam was under orders to return

Taylor in the event that he "shall not be proved to be mad, but persist in the said Blasphemies." Six days later, the keeper reported that his treatment proved that Taylor, although persisting in his blasphemies, was not mad. The Lords wisely decided to refer the matter to the highest judges of the land for a recommendation on procedure.[31]

Six months later, the judges advised that, although the ecclesiastical courts should proceed against Taylor for his "horrid" words, "We are also of the opinion, That inasmuch as many of the said words tend immediately to the Destruction of all Religion and Government," Taylor should be prosecuted in the "King's Temporal Courts, as for a high Misdemeanor." That decision marked a watershed in English law. Never before had the common-law courts taken jurisdiction in a case of blasphemy *per se*.[32]

In early 1676, Taylor went to trial before the King's Bench, presided over by Lord Chief Justice Matthew Hale, England's greatest jurist since Coke. The accusation against Taylor was that he had defamed Christianity by blaspheming God and Christ, having loudly said in public:

> Christ is a whore-master, and religion is a cheat, and profession [of Christianity] is a cloak, and they are both cheats, and all the earth is mine, and I am a king's son, my father sent me hither, and made me a fisherman to take vipers, and I neither fear God, devil, nor man, and I am a younger brother to Christ, an angel of God, and no man fears God but an hypocrite, Christ is a bastard, God damn and confound all your gods, Christ is the whore's master.

With embellishment, the king's attorney described the words as great blasphemy and scandal to the ruination of Christian "government and society."[33]

Taylor pleaded not guilty, although he acknowledged having said all the words except "bastard." His defense was that he meant the words in a different sense from that placed on them by the prosecution. By calling Christ a whoremaster, for instance, he meant Christ was the "master of the whore of Babylon," a standard Puritan allusion to the Church of Rome. Taylor, according to the report of the trial, used "such kind of evasions for the rest," but the jury believed the prosecution. Chief Justice Hale sentenced Taylor to stand in the pillory in three different places, wearing a paper saying, "for blasphemous words, tending to the subversion of all government." Taylor also had to pay a fine of 1,000 marks and find sureties for good behavior for life.[34]

Before passing sentence, Hale delivered the opinion that made Taylor's case the most important from the standpoint of jurisprudence that had ever been or ever would be decided in England on the subject of blasphemy. Two brief versions of Hale's opinion exist, in the notes of the same reporter. In one, Hale acknowledged that, although Taylor's words were "of ecclesiastical cognizance," the common law could punish them, because they tended "to the dissolution of all government." As in the cases of nonconformist preaching or publishing, the words here were akin to seditious libel, although Hale did not use that term. He defined blasphemy as "contumelious reproaches of God, or the religion establisht," and reasoned that blasphemy, by "taking away religion," left no basis for obligations to government as by oaths. In stating the rule of the case, he said that "injuries to God" are punishable by the criminal courts, because the "Christian religion is part of the law itself." In the other, similar report, Hale said:

> And . . . such kind of wicked blasphemous words were not only an offence to God and religion, but a crime against the laws, State and Government, and therefore punishable in this Court. For to say, religion is a cheat, is to dissolve all those obligations whereby the civil societies are preserved, and that Christianity is parcel of the laws of England; and therefore to reproach the Christian religion is to speak in subversion of the law.[35]

The sentence against Taylor was lenient compared with Nayler's and with the near victory of those who had demanded his death. In that sense, Taylor's case showed that abhorrence of the crime had diminished. In England at that time, people were still being hanged for stealing a shilling or for being witches. Hale himself ordered the executions of two women convicted for being witches, a capital felony. A fine of 1,000 marks against Taylor, a simple farmer, ensured his imprisonment for life; thus, the sentence was not as merciful as it sounds, but it was devoid of the cruelty that characterized Nayler's punishment. The enduring significance of Taylor's case lies in the comprehensive definition of the crime, "contumelious reproaches" against God or the established religion, and in the doctrine, which long survived in England, that Christianity is part of the law of the land. No other case on blasphemy had such far-reaching effects, neither in America nor in England. It reverberated down the centuries in many cases in which freedom of religious opinion or separation of church and state was at issue.[36]

Even if Christianity were the law of the land, Hale did not explain why it could not be criticized or reproached. The law is always subject to criticism, even in the severest terms. Such criticism or reproach of the law constitutes no crime. The only reason that Hale could sensibly describe Christianity as part of the law of the land was to legitimate common-law jurisdiction over what had been a crime previously cognizable by ecclesiastical courts or, in extraordinary cases under the Commonwealth, by Parliament itself. But Hale went much too far in Taylor's case. He assumed that civil society could not exist without religion, in particular the Christian religion. Moreover, he assumed that society and Christianity had been started on the path to dissolution by Taylor's language. Actually, his language had no influence on anyone. In order for it to dissolve the obligations whereby civil societies are preserved, Taylor must first have convinced nearly everyone to share his opinions. Hale's poorly reported opinion should never have had such phenomenal influence, given its weak reasoning.

In the year following Taylor's case, the King's Bench convicted another blasphemer, Lodowick Muggleton. He had been in hiding since a warrant was issued for his arrest in 1670. As time passed, he became incautious. A lawsuit involving him as the executor of a friend's estate brought him into an ecclesiastical court in 1676. He was recognized and arrested on a charge of blasphemy. The indictment referred only to Muggleton's book of 1663, *The Neck of the Quakers Broken.* An act of 1674 had immunized against prosecution any illegal publications more than three years old. Accordingly, the only book by Muggleton that could lawfully be the basis of an indictment was his *Answer to William Penn*, published in 1673. It contained abundant evidence of his denial of the doctrine of the Trinity and his assumption of the divine attribute of bestowing eternal blessing and damnation; yet neither the indictment nor the prosecutor mentioned the book of 1673. Apparently, the government did not know about its existence. The fact that it had been published anonymously meant nothing; so had the 1663 book. Muggleton's theology and style were unique, and his 1673 book, like the one of a decade earlier, revealed him as surely as if he had put his name on the title page.[37]

At the trial in 1677, Muggleton's court-appointed counsel rested his defense by pointing out that the 1663 book was written "before the act of grace." That should have ended the matter. But Hale, a fair man who had been chief justice for six years, had recently died. His successor, Richard Rainsford, was only a cut above Jeffreys as a tyrant. Jeffreys himself was then the recorder of London. Rainsford took over the prosecution, declaring that anyone capable of writing such blasphemy had the subtlety to antedate its publication. The contention was specious—Fox had replied to Muggleton's 1663 book in 1667—but the defense counsel did not know that, and Rainsford would not let Muggleton speak. A witness stated that Muggleton had acknowledged his authorship of the 1663 book before the lord mayor of London, when he was arrested in 1676. Rainsford took that as proof of guilt. Judge Robert Atkins protested that Muggleton's confession of authorship proved nothing about the date of publication. The witness said that the lord mayor had had a hard time making Muggleton confess his authorship. "We have no law to make a man accuse himself," Atkins replied; "can you make it appear that Mr. Muggleton has writ these books since the Act of Grace?" When the witness said "no," Atkins told the jury that the crown had no case against Muggleton.

Rainsford, however, when charging the jury, harangued them about Muggleton's guilt for many blasphemies, concluding: "And who knows what design this villain had both in church and government: and therefore, Gentlemen, if you do not bring him in guilty, yourselves will be sharers in his curst apostasy." The jury took half an hour to convict. Rainsford then poured abuse on Muggleton, ending with the epithet "murderer of souls." Atkins left the bench, saying audibly, "things are not fairly carried on here." But William Montague, the chief baron of the exchequer, presided over the trial and endorsed everything said by Rainsford, ending by thanking the jury for "so just and pious a verdict" against such a blasphemer. When the judges left the bench, Recorder Jeffreys— "Pilate," Muggleton called him—lashed the prisoner with vile epithets, and then pronounced sentence upon him: to stand in the pillory at three places in London, with a paper pinned to his chest announcing him to be a blasphemer, and at each place to witness the burning of his book, and to pay a fine of £500.

Muggleton, unable to pay the fine, was sent to Newgate. At each place where he stood in the pillory, the crowds "pelted" the sixty-eight-year-old man "with clay, rotten eggs, and dirt in abundance." On the third occasion, they stoned him "thick as hail"; his friends who witnessed the event and reported the trial recorded that one stone "broke" the head of the "prophet," making his blood gush. After he had spent six months in Newgate, Muggleton's fine was reduced to £100; he paid it and went free. Although he wrote his autobiography in 1677, he kept it from publication until after his death; nor did he publish anything else during the twenty remaining years of his life. The Muggletonians ever after celebrated July 19, the day of his liberation from Newgate in 1677, as a religious festival. His trial and conviction were illegal, but, again, only because his 1673 *Answer to William Penn* was not the basis of the indictment. As a matter of law, denial of the Trinity was blasphemy.

In Old Bailey, the scene of Muggleton's trial, at least three more convictions for blasphemy occurred between 1678 and 1698. In addition to those three, there may have been up to sixteen more, plus an unknown number of other convictions outside of London. All were run-of-the-mill cases, showing no movement in the law, nothing unusual in the nature of the crimes, no extraordinary punishments, and no defendants of distinction. To distinguish prosecutions for blasphemous opinions from prosecutions for seditious ones is not possible in many of the cases, but some cases of seditious libel, such as Delaune's and Baxter's, had nothing to do with blasphemy. A legal historian, G. D. Nokes, who attempted to chart all the cases after Taylor's, refused to distinguish blasphemy from seditiousness in any case involving an offense against religion. He reasoned "that when the word blasphemous was first used judicially [in 1676] it was employed to describe an extension of the offence of seditious words. For more than a hundred years after that decision the intimate relationship between seditious and blasphemous offences seems to have been maintained." Nokes's point on the relationship between seditious and blasphemous opinions is valid, but relatedness is not identicalness. Although all blasphemy in a state that has an established church is a form of seditiousness, not all seditiousness that is an offense against religion is blasphemous.[38]

During the Restoration and after, blasphemy was a distinctive crime. When nonconformity as seditious libel died in consequence of the Toleration Act of 1689, blasphemy remained an offense against religion punishable by the state. The law made distinctions, even when it punished blasphemy as a crime against the state. The law of criminal defamation fanned out into different branches, including obscene libel, seditious libel, and blasphemous libel, or, if the blasphemy was spoken instead of printed, blasphemous utterances. The Toleration Act, followed by the Blasphemy Act of 1698, spurred the demarcation between blasphemousness and seditiousness.

The Toleration Act, a direct consequence of the Revolution of 1688–89, was a reward by Parliament and the Anglican church to the nonconformists for throwing their support against James II. To put the same point another way, the Toleration Act was a sop to the nonconformists for remaining staunchly anti-Catholic. Few Protestants, except some Baptists and Quakers, advocated religious liberty for Catholics. Few Protestants did not hate Catholics. Memories of Bloody Mary, Torquemada, the St. Bartholomew's Day Massacre, the ravages of the duke of Alva, Guy Fawkes, the revocation of the Edict of Nantes, and other outrages countless in number fixed Catholicism in the Protestant mind as a threat to Protestant and national liberty. Rome, Spain, and France were the leading enemies of England. The very real fear of Catholicism always underlay the fear of granting toleration to Protestant nonconformists. Charles II's Declaration of Indulgence was intended to be an opening wedge for tolerating Catholics and was understood as such by Parliament and the church. James II's policy pushed open the doors to Catholic freedom in England.

James, who succeeded his brother in 1685, openly practiced Catholicism and had a Catholic wife who in 1688 bore him a son and successor.

The Stuart dynasty seemed to be leading England back to Rome and to the possible extinction of the English Reformation. James not only gave preference to his coreligionists at the highest levels of government; he formed a standing army that included many Catholics, both officers and men, as a bulwark of his regime. Yet James, although less interested in the Protestant nonconformists than in his Catholic countrymen, really favored religious liberty. His Declaration of Indulgence of 1687 suspended all penal laws related to religion, and pardoned all "nonconformists, recusants [chiefly Catholics], and other our loving subjects for all crimes and things by them committed or done contrary to the penal laws, formerly made relating to religion."[39]

James's policy of religious liberty looked like a means of overthrowing Anglicanism and reviving papistry. Among the Protestant nonconformists, only the Quakers supported James; Penn and the king were good friends. Most others, fearful of relying on the royal prerogative for their freedom, and more fearful still of finding themselves allied with Catholics and thus in a sense allied with the Church of Rome, joined with the Anglicans, their recent persecutors, in condemning royal tyranny. Like Charles before him, James had acted without Parliament by unilaterally abrogating its laws. Unlike Charles, James did not back down. In 1688 he reinforced his Declaration of Indulgence with a command that it be read from the pulpits throughout the realm. When the episcopacy refused, James declared that they had raised the standard of "rebellion." The archbishop of Canterbury and six of the leading bishops pleaded loyalty, but they still refused on good constitutional grounds. James sent them to the Tower of London. While they awaited prosecutions for seditious libel, the Catholic queen of England gave birth to a male heir. At the trial of the Anglican divines, the royal judges divided in their instructions to the jury; the jury's verdict of not guilty was celebrated as a national holiday. The bloodless revolution soon followed, bringing stalwart Protestants, William and Mary of Orange, to the throne of England—and bringing a promised reward to the Protestant nonconformists.[40]

The Toleration Act, which belied its name in form but not in effect, was the product of political necessity—"a nauseous necessity," as a Quaker historian has said. The new king, Parliament, and the church agreed to the act to restore peace to the country. No act more liberal than the very peculiar one passed could possibly have been adopted. A few intellectuals, like Penn and Locke, favored the right to worship as one pleased, and the historical position of the General Baptists had been that religion, being a private affair between man and God, transcended the state's concern. England overwhelmingly abhorred such principles. The Toleration Act reflected no principle at all, not even that of toleration. Yet, despite the name by which it came to be known, the act was entitled

"A Bill of Indulgence." It exempted most nonconformists "from the penalties of certain laws." Parliament did not repeal any of the persecutory laws of the Restoration, thus leaving persecution the rule of the law, but in a state of suspended animation. It was the English way of walking forward into the future—facing backward to the past. In much the same way, prior censorship died in England, not because Parliament passed a bill establishing the principle of freedom of the press, and not even because it passed a bill repealing the old licensing laws, but simply because those laws expired and were not renewed.[41]

Under the Toleration Act, laymen who took the requisite oaths to support the new king and to reject transubstantiation were allowed to worship as they pleased in the church of their choice, because they were exempted from the penalties for doing otherwise. Clergymen who subscribed to most of the Anglican Thirty-nine Articles received exemption too from the laws that had suppressed them. Because the articles to which they had to subscribe were not the controversial ones, their consciences went unconstrained. Baptists received a special indulgence: they alone were exempted from the article that required infant baptism. Quakers too received a special indulgence, by being allowed to swear that they professed the doctrine of the Trinity and thereby to prove that Unitarianism had not infected them. Not until an act of 1696 were Quakers allowed to affirm rather than swear. The Toleration Act had the effect of making nonconformity lawful if it conformed to the requirements of the act. Nonconformists still had to pay tithes for the established church, and they still endured many civil disabilities. The act was a compound of contradictions and exceptions wrought out of the prevailing system of persecution. Yet secular considerations had triumphed, with the result that, whereas hundreds of thousands had suffered before for conscience' sake, the number fell to a few hundred Protestants and a few thousand Catholics.

Section XVII of the act excluded from its benefits "any papist or popish recusant whatsoever, or any person that shall deny in his preaching or writing the doctrine of the Blessed Trinity, as it is declared in the aforesaid articles of religion." The exclusion of Catholics was to be expected, given the recent revolution against their religion. Yet Protestant monarchs, being above suspicion, found the means, unavailable to their Restoration predecessors, to mitigate the severities against peaceable Catholic subjects. By 1710, the Vatican received from an English agent a report declaring that the English Catholics "enjoy the exercise of their religion totally free"; in fact, they felt the sting of double taxation and civil disabilities. Catholics did not actually come within the terms of the Toleration Act until 1778.[42]

The exclusion of anti-Trinitarians from the act indicates that they were regarded as covert blasphemers. Most clergymen could not accept their opinions as Christian. Some anti-Trinitarian intellectuals considered themselves freethinking "deists"; they composed the vanguard of a growing movement, which by 1689 rivaled the Muggletonians in numbers. The Muggletonians, however devout in their Protestantism, still seemed loathsome fanatics. The far more numerous and growing Unitarians fell into a related category. The exclusion of these Protestants from the Toleration Act conclusively shows that most of England still deemed them as execrable as atheists and hardly distinguishable from them.

The Jews constituted a special case. Not more than four hundred of them lived in England at the time of the Toleration Act, none longer than about three decades. They enjoyed freedom of religion, thanks to the Stuarts, although they enjoyed no other civil rights. In 1664, after the Conventicles Act came into force, a movement to bring the Jews within its terms was cut off by Charles II and his Privy Council. Again, in 1673, when leaders of the Jewish community of London were indicted for a "riot," which consisted in their praying in their synagogue, another order of the council quashed the indictment. Later, when thirty-seven Jews were arrested in 1685 for failure to attend the Church of England, James II, the Catholic king, personally ordered his attorney general to allow the Jews "quietly [to] enjoy the free exercise of their religion, whilst they behave themselves dutifully." Thus, the Jews, never having come within the terms of the Restoration's penal statutes on religion, did not need to be exempted in the Toleration Act from the penalties that had been inflicted on Protestant nonconformists. The Jews continued to suffer long after 1689 from severe disabilities and discrimination, but Protestant England never prosecuted a Jew for blasphemy, nor a Catholic either. The Toleration Act left the Unitarians, however, in a class with blasphemers.[43]

Paradoxically, Unitarianism was surging in strength, mostly within the Anglican church. Not till much later did it become a separate sect. After the suppression of Biddle's little congregation, Unitarianism seemed to survive only among the few whose minds he had touched. They were, however, exceptional minds, and they found secret presses to perpetuate anti-Trinitarian principles. The movement—or, rather, the drift—centered around Thomas Firmin, the merchant. His splendid home in Lombard Street was a meeting place for his close friends. Among them were high-placed latitudinarian Anglicans and some dissenters. Most, like Firmin, became or remained communicants of the established church. They had no serious quarrel with its mode of worship or its discipline except on the issue of toleration. In all England, none were more advanced proponents of religious liberty. They also completely rejected the doctrine of the Holy Trinity, but their dispute with the church remained in the church. Although most of them kept their vocal opinions within the group, they published a staggering number of tracts. With rare exceptions, however, they wrote anonymously. To place one's name on the title page of an unlicensed anti-Trinitarian tract would have been as foolhardy as organizing for independent worship. Secrecy among the Unitarians was the rule. Although they differed from their church on a cardinal doctrine, they believed Anglicanism to comprehend every opinion on the Trinity from the most Catholic to the deistic. They believed too that the episcopacy included a growing number of "nominal" as opposed to "real" Trinitarians. Unitarianism cropped up in unexpected places. When, for example, Milton died in 1674, he left a secret cache of unpublished Unitarian manuscripts.[44]

Firmin's circle included Henry Hedworth, a gentleman scholar and author of many Unitarian tracts; John Locke, the philosopher; Gilbert Clerke, the mathematician and scripturalist, who also wrote Unitarian tracts; Stephen Nye, an Anglican rector, the best and most productive of all the Unitarian writers; and Isaac Newton, the scientist. Remarkably, the three greatest intellectuals of seventeenth-century England—Milton, Locke, and Newton—were covert Unitarians. Hedworth, the literary antagonist of Penn, argued that "the Trinitarians ought to own the Unitarians for Christian Brethren." Most Trinitarians thought otherwise. As early as 1672, Andrew Marvell, the metaphysical poet, complained that "Socinian books are tolerated, and sell as openly as the Bible." A similar complaint issued in 1680 from George Ashwell, an Anglican priest who thought that the Socinians were making headway with the Church of England.[45]

Ashwell was correct, and events seemed to justify his complaint. When William III called a church convocation in 1689 to reform the church, the doctrine of the Trinity divided the Anglican divines so severely that the convocation was paralyzed. While it was in session, Stephen Nye published a withering assault on the Athanasian Creed, triggering a controversy that lasted the remainder of the decade—and after. It had begun, in a way, much earlier, with Penn's *Sandy Foundation* of 1668. By the 1690s, the Sabellian views which had put Penn in the Tower were common within the church, and at its highest levels. The Trinitarian Controversy began as a purely Anglican affair, first with Nye's anonymous book, then with another by Dr. Arthur Bury, the rector of Exeter College, Oxford. His book of 1690, like Nye's, made many an orthodox minister goggle-eyed. In *The Naked Gospel*, Bury intended to show that during the church's first few centuries of existence it had preached one God and no Trinity. Sympathizing with the doctrine of the primitive church, Bury argued that Christians had perplexed and persecuted one another too long because of bitter differences about the doctrine of the Trinity. When Bury's identity as author of the book was uncovered, a convocation of the entire university consigned *The Naked Gospel* to the flames as heretical and blasphemous, deposed him from office, and fined him. Bury was not, however, without articulate supporters—in print.[46]

Stephen Nye, who was tireless in behalf of the Unitarian cause, rejected the Socinian label, because he did not agree on all points with Faustus Socinus or John Biddle. Nye called himself a Christian, thought of himself as a Sabellian, and in print argued for Unitarianism. In 1687, at Firmin's commission, Nye published *A Brief History of Unitarians, commonly called Socinians*. The book was less history than Unitarian propaganda. Firmin distributed free copies of many of Nye's productions, and between 1691 and 1697, Nye, assisted by several others and by Firmin's money, wrote and compiled three substantial volumes, the *Unitarian Tracts*. The first volume reprinted a life of Biddle, several of Biddle's tracts, and Nye's *Brief History*.[47]

The superorthodox, who heatedly replied to every Unitarian tract, inadvertently aided their opponents' cause by overstating their own position on the doctrine of the Trinity. Some, like William Sherlock and his disciple Joseph Bingham, so exaggerated the distinct persons or substances of the Holy Trinity that they exposed themselves to the charge of polytheism or tritheism. Bingham suffered the same fate as Bury for the opposite reasons. Oxford pronounced a tract by Bingham to be false, impious, and heretical, because of its tritheism. That was in 1695. A year earlier, a Unitarian who signed his name to his tract was caught and punished. He was William Freeke, an Oxonian, who foolishly sent copies of his tract to members of both houses of Parliament. The Lords condemned it as an infamous and scandalous libel, without indicating whether it was of the seditious or the blasphemous type, and ordered the hangman to burn the tract. Freeke was prosecuted, heavily fined, and forced to make a public recantation. In 1696, someone put into an English translation Aretius's Latin book of 1567, which was published in Bern in justification of the Calvinist execution of "Valentinus Gentilis, the Tritheist"; what made the English edition significant is that its translator wrote in the preface that he thought the book should edify Dr. Sherlock. It was a form of gallows humor. Robert South, a middle-of-the-road Anglican priest, ridiculed Sherlock's tritheism so unmercifully that Nye welcomed South to the rational creed of Unitarianism.[48]

Some Anglican clergymen found the Trinitarian Controversy so unsettling that they embraced the views advocated by Nye. In the course of counterattacking extremists on the right, like Sherwood and Bingham, some moderates and latitudinarians found themselves driven by the force of their logic to the fringes of Sabellianism, if not beyond. John Tillotson, who was the archbishop of Canterbury, and Bishop Gilbert Burnet had that experience. Tillotson published some sermons in 1693 in which he praised his friend Firmin and commented favorably on Socinianism, thereby subjecting himself to criticism that compelled him to deny the accusation that he covertly harbored the dreaded unorthodoxy on the Holy Trinity. Tillotson, who deplored the Athanasian Creed, wrote to Burnet, "I wish we were well rid of it."[49]

Unitarians could never dominate the Anglican church, however, or even become a major force within it, because the church used a prayer book that conditioned worshippers and priests to accept the three persons of the Godhead. Dissenters, who were more familiar with addressing the One Almighty God, found their theological divorce from the doctrine of the Trinity easier to come by. In 1693, Dr. Edmund Calamy, the famous Presbyterian, noting the growth of heterodoxy on the Trinity within his own denomination, saw one side of the disputants "verging toward Arminianism, or even Socinianism." Thoughtful and unprejudiced people, incited to study the literature of the Trinitarian Controversy, underwent a change of opinion. Their number is indeterminable, but the fallout of the controversy continued well into the eighteenth century and led to the "Arian movement" within the Church of England and among the dissenters' churches. Indeed, the first dissenter minister who publicly adopted the Unitarian name was Thomas Emlyn—a Presbyterian, no less. "Socinians," said one orthodox writer, "under the name of Unitarians," grew bolder and "fill'd the nation" with their writings.[50]

The controversy was infinitely complex because of its metaphysical focus, making any labeling of its contestants controversial. John Locke, for example, explicitly denied being a Socinian, but he told only a half-truth. When his *Reasonableness of Christianity* was published in 1695, the orthodox raked him with obloquy. John Edwards, a worthy son of the author of *Grangraena*, called Locke a "Socinian," a "Racovian," a "criminal," a "casuist," and a "dissembler"—and Edwards was not all wrong. Locke replied that he had not read Socinus or the Racovian Catechism. In fact, his work showed their influence plainly, and his library included both as well as the works of Dutch and Polish Socinians, those of Biddle and Nye, and the *Unitarian Tracts*. Locke's closest friends were Unitarians. He may not have been a Socinian; Nye, one of Locke's friends, also denied being a Socinian. But Locke, like Nye, spoke only in a very technical sense. By the mid-1690s, the anti-Trinitarians, who collectively and explicitly called themselves Unitarians, had divided into differing shades of opinion on the Trinity. All, however, shared the opinion that the Bible as construed by human reason led to the conclusion that Jesus, although the Messiah, the Son of God, was human, not God. Scripturalism taught them one God and no Trinity in the Godhead. Arians, Sabellians, Socinians, and deists—unitarians all in the 1690s—rejected the Nicene and Athanasian Creeds. They rested on the Apostles' Creed as sufficient, fundamental, and scriptural. They were literal scripturalists, to the core. In 1698, when Locke replied to the bishop of Worcester, who tried to draw him out on the subject of the Trinity, Locke declared: "My Lord, my Bible is faulty again, for I do not remember that I ever read in it either of these propositions, in precise words, 'there are three persons of one nature, or, there are two natures and one person.' " God was One.[51]

The Toleration Act, the excesses of the superorthodox, and the leavening influence of the Enlightenment, then beginning, impelled many Anglicans toward a rejection of the traditional doctrine of the Trinity. Gilbert Clerke once told Baxter that he should not malign Socinians, because they were "the best sort of Christians." Clerke's was a growing opinion, and it frightened the orthodox. They feared that the controversy had gotten out of control, becoming more dangerous with each passing year. Calamy said the "world was wearied out with pamphlets and creedmaking." The presses kept disgorging disputatious books and tracts on the Trinitarian Controversy. The interminable theological dispute would have glazed the eyes of medieval scholastics. The orthodox sensed that they were being bested in the analyses of primitive heresies and on such metaphysical points concerning the Trinity as hypostatical union, essences, persons, modes, names, incarnation, attributes, substances, and faculties. Every tract provoked several responses, and the number grew geometrically; the writings multiplied themselves like their long-winded titles, until they would, if piled on the dome of St. Paul's Cathedral, have crushed it by their weight. As the controversy wore on, the orthodox hammered on the theme that the realm was being infected with the pestilence of heterodoxy.[52]

Events in Scotland suggested that a statute against blasphemy might prove necessary or useful in England. In Scotland, where the Church of England dispossessed Presbyterianism at the Restoration, blasphemy confronted much harsher laws than in England. The English Puritans had treated Ranter blasphemies mildly; although they came close to killing Nayler, at the time he loomed as a heresiarch. Shortly before, in Scotland, the Puritans had hanged Jock of Broad Scotland. When the Scottish Anglicans regained control of state and church in 1661, they were fiercer than their English counterparts in their persecution and their legislation. The Five Mile Act in England was the Twenty Mile Act north of the Tweed. In 1661, the Parliament of Scotland enacted its first statute against blasphemy. The English act of 1648 against Socinianism had fixed capital punishment for the crime, but the statute never came to life; the Scots enforced their law. It had two independent sections. The first applied to any sane person who reviled or cursed God or any of the persons of the Trinity. Cursing or reviling presumably showed deliberate malice. The second part of the act of 1661 applied to those who "obstinately continue" to deny God or any person of the Trinity; since denial might derive from ignorance of momentary passion, the blasphemer might repent. Consequently, the act of 1661 made blasphemy against God or the Trinity unrepentant denial or malicious reviling.[53]

Sir George Mackenzie, a Scot who was the king's advocate and formerly a supreme justice of the criminal courts, declared in a book of 1678 that blasphemy was also a crime by the Scottish common law. Mackenzie defined the crime as "divine lease majesty, or Treason"—that is, treason against God. The offense consisted in denying to God that which belonged to Him, or attributing to Him that which was inconsistent with His divine nature, such as sin. More than a century later, after Scotland had abolished its blasphemy statutes, another Scottish jurist remarked that to describe blasphemy as treason against God contained "more fancy than propriety."[54]

The first accusation under the act of 1661 occurred twenty years after its enactment, when Francis Bortwick, a Christian who had converted to Judaism, supposedly railed against Christ and his divinity. Bortwick had to be condemned *in absentia* and declared a doomed outlaw, because he managed to escape to the continent. In 1695, when the Presbyterians were again in control of Scotland, the Scottish Parliament supplemented the earlier statute, because it was too tight to cover some opinions that had become current on account of the Trinitarian Controversy. The act of 1695 extended blasphemy to the obstinate denial of, or reasoning against, not only the persons in the Godhead but the literal authority of the Bible and the providence of God in the governance of the world. However, the act of 1695 deferred the death penalty to a third conviction, making it seem an unlikely eventuality. On the first conviction the blasphemer had to make public atonement in sackcloth, and on the second to pay heavy fines and remain in prison until his parish was satisfied.[55]

Statutory law and its enforcement by courts sometimes bear slight correspondence when pious shock, bigotry, and the lack of assistance by counsel work against a defendant, as the case of Thomas Aikenhead showed. He was arrested in 1696, imprisoned for several months while awaiting trial, and at the end of the year faced the lord barons who composed the highest criminal court. Aikenhead, still a legal minor, was a medical student at the University of Edinburgh when he caught the "plague of blasphemous Deism"—the phrase of one of the ministers who visited him several times in his prison cell. Later that minister, William

Lorimer, faced denunciation as one responsible for Aikenhead's death. At the time of the prosecution, Lorimer had preached before the prisoner's judges on the theme of blasphemous deism. Later, when defending himself against the opinion that he had abetted a judicial murder, Lorimer insisted that Aikenhead had remained obstinate for months. Yet Lorimer also declared that, on his first visit to the prisoner, "he [Aikenhead] immediately confessed that he . . . was sorry for what he had said, and he desired my prayers."[56]

In fact, before his trial, Aikenhead addressed a petition to the court that tried him, in which he made an elaborate orthodox confession of faith. He not only repeatedly professed to "abhorre and detest" the opinions for which he had been indicted; he also embraced the Trinity, the Old and New Testaments, infant baptism, the sacrament of the Lord's Supper, and everything else that Calvin or Knox might have wanted. He repented each specific "atheistical" opinion ascribed to him, saying that he had repeated them only as the views of authors (unnamed) whom he had read, not as opinions he personally held. That he may have lied about that point is irrelevant; he recanted and was not obstinate. Indeed, Lord Anstruther wrote: "We had lately an anomely, and a monster of nature, I may call him, who was execut for cursing and reviling the persons of the Trinity, he was 18 yeers of age, not vicious and extreamely studious. Fountionehall [one of the judges] and I went to him in prison, and I *found a work on his spirit*, and wept that he ever should maintained such tenets." Anstruther petitioned on the prisoner's behalf for a reprieve but learned that, unless the ministers interceded, clemency was impossible. The "ministers," he reported, "out of a pious, though I think ignorant zcal spok and preached for cutting him off."[57]

Lorimer said that George Meldrum, another minister involved in the case, solicited a pardon for Aikenhead and, when that failed, requested a reprieve, "and I joined with him in it." That was the day before the execution. The chancellor took the petition to the Privy Council, the judges attending. After a debate, a plurality of the council sustained the judges' sentence, "that there might be a stop put to the spreading of that contagion of blasphemy." This concurs with Lorimer's final judgment. Although he conceded that Aikenhead finally recanted his opinions, Lorimer concluded: "I am far from thinking that the Socinians who deny the Holy Trinity and the etcrnal Deity of Christ, are such Deists as that poor man was; yet I think the mention of this may serve as a warning to them, to others likewise; for there seems to be but a short passage from Socinianism to Deism." That does not square with Lorimer's statement that Aikenhead died "very penitent, pouring out his soul to Christ . . . and taking shame to himself, and humbly and earnestly begging of God mercy and pardon for Christ's sake."[58]

The Aikenhead case posed two difficult legal questions, though these seem trivial compared with the decision to execute him as an example to terrorize others. Was Aikenhead guilty under the law? Under what law? The indictment referred, in part, to the crime of blasphemy against "our holy religion," which was not a crime under either of the two statutes of the Parliament of Scotland, both of which the indictment restated. Five witnesses appeared against Aikenhead, all acquaintances of his age. That he denied the persons of the Trinity and the authority of the Bible is unquestionable. But the act of 1695 made death the punishment only for a third offense, and Aikenhead's was a first offense. That act could not have been the basis of his conviction and execution. Nor could the second part of the act of 1661, which required obstinate denial. Abundant proof shows that he recanted often—in prison, before his trial, after his conviction, and at his execution.[59]

The only alternative legal bases for the proceedings were the common law of Scotland or the first part of the act of 1661, which required proof of cursing. Even Mackenzie's definition of blasphemy protected God only, not "our holy religion." Moreover, the king's advocate, Sir James Stewart, never referred to the common law in his prosecution. He stressed Aikenhead's scoffing, ridiculing, railing against, and cursing the Bible, the doctrine of the Trinity, and the deity of Christ. The five witnesses agreed that Aikenhead, over the period of a year, had denied them all, but only one witness swore the defendant had reviled and cursed. That witness's testimony brought Aikenhead within the terms of the first part of the act of 1661, which imposed death for a first offense even against a defendant who was not obstinate. The key witness was the one who had given Aikenhead the unknown books that led to his blasphemies. The same witness immediately recanted and turned state's evidence to avoid prosecution. His testimony alone convicted Aikenhead under the first part of the act of 1661. Aikenhead confessed to much, but he denied railing, cursing, and ridiculing. In London, John Locke, who gathered the documents of the case, stressed the fact that the prisoner was denied counsel; Locke concluded that the jury that had returned the verdict of guilty had committed perjury.[60]

The only other blasphemy case in Scotland that might have influenced England to enact its own statute against the crime occurred in 1697. Later in the year in which Aikenhead twisted on the gibbet, Patrick Kinnymount escaped that fate; Aikenhead became the last man in Great Britain to die for his opinions on religion. The same bench that condemned Aikenhead tried Kinnymount, who had able counsel. His utterances were certainly blasphemous, for among other things he called Christ a bastard. But Kinnymount's ingenious counsel argued that Kinnymount, who repented everything, had uttered the words when drunk.

The court rejected the defense of temporary insanity under the influence of whiskey, but committed the prisoner for a first offense only. Long after, Baron David Hume, in his treatise on Scottish criminal law, criticized the judgment in Kinnymount's case. Hume reasoned that intoxication in a case of impetuous and repented blasphemy should be a valid defense against the charge, because the defendant stood to gain no profit from his crime, unlike a drunken thief. Kinnymount's utterances and relatively light sentence showed that Aikenhead's case was all the more a miscarriage of justice, the victim being nothing more than a sacrifice to make a precedent during the Trinitarian Controversy.[61]

The example of Scotland and the unceasing Unitarian barrage during the Trinitarian Controversy finally prodded England into action. Although the censorship laws had expired, in 1697 some dissenting clergymen petitioned William III to stop the Unitarian presses. The year before, in 1696, John Toland, a young friend of John Locke, published his first book, *Christianity not Mysterious*. It triggered a new controversy, "the first act of the warfare between the deists and the orthodox which occupied the next generation," wrote Leslie Stephen. The book infuriated the orthodox, some of whom presented it to the grand jury of Middlesex. Toland prudently left for Ireland, but a grand jury there presented the book, and in 1697 the Irish Parliament, which had not yet learned that "heresy" was archaic as a legal term except in ecclesiastical courts and convocations, condemned the book to the flames as heresy. The Irish also ordered Toland's arrest. He fled back to England, where he remained under cover until the furor over him died down.[62]

In 1697, John Gailhard published *The Blasphemous Socinian Heresy disproved and confuted*, which he dedicated to the Parliament of England. Gailhard recommended that Parliament take notice of the Scottish Parliament's salutary statutes against blasphemy. Although William III prorogued Parliament before it could enact any sanguinary legislation, the king had wearied of the ceaseless Trinitarian Controversy. He interceded, at last, on the side of religious peace and orthodoxy, commanding the archbishops and bishops, "for the sake of preserving unity in the Church and the purity of the Christian faith concerning the Holy Trinity," to see that theologians muted their publications and preaching. Henceforth, no clergyman could employ invective or scurrility in controversial matters, or write against the Christian faith by attacking the Holy Trinity. The king promised that his criminal courts and sheriffs would execute all laws against laymen who scandalized or disturbed the peace of the realm by their religious opinions. In Old Bailey in 1698, Susan Fowls was convicted of blasphemy and was pilloried, fined, and jailed; she had passed the bounds of decency by cursing the Lord's Prayer and verbally abusing Christ.[63]

Parliament, which convened again in 1698, was, as usual, more orthodox than the church. The House of Commons beseeched the king to
suppress "all pernicious books and pamphlets" that contained "impious"
doctrine against the Holy Trinity and "other fundamental articles of our
faith, tending to the subversion of the Christian Religion." The king
consented to the passage of a new blasphemy statute, Parliament's real
objective. The act of 1698 remains law to this day, although rarely enforced. The courts, using their common law, needed no assistance from
Parliament against blasphemy, but a statute carried greater weight than
a court decision in forming the public mind. Parliament, with the assent
of the king, spoke for the nation and laid down the supreme law. A court
merely decided particular cases.[64]

The act of 1698 "for the more effectual suppressing of Blasphemy"
provided that any person who had professed the Christian religion should
be convicted for blasphemy if he should say anything, in conversation, in
the pulpit, or in the press, to deny "any one of the Persons of the Holy
Trinity to be God," or deny "the Christian Religion to be true," or deny
the divine authority of the Bible. The punishment for a first offense was
disablement from any civil, military, or ecclesiastical employment. For a
second offense, the punishment was loss of all civil rights, in effect rendering the culprit a nonperson with respect to any suits, legacies, deeds,
and trusts; in addition, conviction for a second offense carried the penalty
of three years' imprisonment "without bail or mainprize." As usual, England was more lenient that Scotland.[65]

The act of 1698 was intended to thwart the spread of Unitarianism in
any of its forms and, more broadly, to protect the Christian religion
against harsh criticism. As the century ended, then, blasphemy in England had a variety of meanings, judicial and statutory. John Godolphin,
a legal scholar skilled in canon-law matters, had summarized the law of
blasphemy in 1678, three years after Taylor's case. Blasphemy consisted
in injuring God with contumelious words, "which is when they detract
from God the honour due to him, or attribute any evil to him." Mackenzie had provided a similar definition for Scotland in the same year. By
coincidence, Godolphin too characterized the crime as "speaking Treason
against the Heavenly Majesty" by execrable words that reproached the
Deity. Distinguishing heresy from blasphemy, Godolphin wrote that
heresy "is an opinion repugnant to the orthodox Doctrine of the Christian
Faith, obstinately maintained and persisted in by such as profess the
Name of Christ."[66]

In effect, the act of 1698 converted heresy into blasphemy by including as part of the crime of blasphemy denials of the truth of the Christian
religion. Similarly, Chief Justice Hale, in Taylor's case, when ruling that
Christianity was part of the law of the land, found blasphemy in any

contumelious reproach against God or against the established religion. Denial of the doctrine of the Trinity, the blasphemous crime in Muggleton's case, also attained statutory endorsement in the act of 1698. Receiving the honors due only to God or claiming divine attributes also fell within the common-law definition of blasphemy. The Toleration Act of 1689 had in effect excluded from the realm of blasphemy criticism of the established religion, such as denying Anglican doctrines, the episcopacy, the sacraments of the church, and the prayer book, unless that criticism was accompanied by what the courts might call contumelious reproach or cursing.

Now, by the act of 1698, a simple denial of Christianity or the Bible was blasphemy. In effect, the statute was a signal to the courts to cast their nets wider in order to repress criticism that reached the level of an explicit denial of anything Anglican. If prosecutor, judge, and jury concurred, dissident Anglicans like Firmin and all Protestant nonconformists could be exposed to conviction for blasphemy. That law had been forged by the end of the century as a weapon for subverting the Toleration Act as well as intellectual and religious liberty of opinion. And where blasphemy might not prove the easier crime to prosecute, the law of seditious libel concerning offenses against religion stood as an additional and alternative bulwark of orthodoxy.

CHAPTER ELEVEN

Early Colonial America: Gorton and the Quakers

THE HISTORY of blasphemy in colonial America is intriguingly skimpy. In seventeenth-century Britain, the offense of blasphemy, from the burnings of Legate and Wightman to the hanging of Aikenhead, was richly detailed and kaleidoscopic in variety, as well as deadly. It encompassed kooky new religions like Ranterism and Muggletonianism, which petered out, as well as Baptism, Socinianism, and Quakerism, which had staying power. In America, Englishmen could not be found in so many dissentient variants, and appear by comparison to have been impossibly pious or law-abiding. The history of blasphemy prosecutions in America, from Puritan New England to the Anglican Deep South, is just a bit more voluminous than a history of the sex life of the steer—notwithstanding ferocious laws against the offense of blasphemy.

In Virginia, the first law in the code of laws of 1610–11, usually called Dale's code, commanded that God be daily served and that anyone not attending prayers twice daily would be "duly punished." The second law provided for death to anyone who maliciously spoke against the doctrine of the Trinity, any person of the Trinity, or the "Articles of the Christian faith." The next law tersely fixed death as the penalty for blasphemy against God. The code did not distinguish blasphemy from profanity but promised lesser penalties for the use of unlawful oaths, taking the name of God in vain, or cursing—that is, calling on God to damn someone. For the first offense, the penalty was "severe punishment," probably a whipping but no mutilation; a bodkin or a stiletto through the tongue was the punishment for a second offense; death was reserved for the third. The same law spoke of these offenses not as profanity but as blasphemy. For good measure, another law added that any word or act tending to derision or contempt of the Bible would result in death.[1]

Dale's code expired in 1619, and no further laws against blasphemy appeared on the statute books until 1676. Yet Virginia harshly punished criminal offenses with or without statutes. In 1624, for example, for the offense of divulging the correspondence of the governor's council, the clerk of the council was put in the pillory, to which his ears were nailed before being cut off. In the same year, another man who aspersed the governor had his arms broken and his tongue bored through with an awl. But blasphemy was an offense that was either not committed or not punished. No prosecution of blasphemy occurred in Virginia until 1642, when there were suddenly four cases of "swearing a blasphemous oath," one of "prophaning gods holy name"; in 1643, another case involved a "blasphemous oath." What constituted a blasphemous oath and differentiated it from profanity is an enigma. Whatever those people said, their oaths did not likely insult, scoff at, or defame God, because convictions resulted in minor fines.[2]

Amazingly, no other blasphemy case occurred in the mother dominion until 1670, when an Anglican priest blasphemed, but he also committed forgery and mutiny. We do not know what he said. For his crimes he was defrocked and banished. Six years later, Thomas Miller, an apothecary, was tried for both blasphemy and treasonous remarks but was acquitted. In the next year, however, he committed the crime again in North Carolina, by declaring that the sacrament of the Lord's Supper was "hogs wash putt in a piggs trough." He escaped punishment by breaking out of prison and returning to England. In 1683, a man who spoke "in derogation of the bible," declaring that much of it was false, was held by the council for trial on a charge of blasphemy, but the records of his case seem to fizzle out.[3] The blasphemy enactment of 1676 contained little to show the meaning of the offense, but a re-enactment in 1699 extended the offense to denial of God, the doctrine of the Trinity, or the truths of Christianity or the Bible. By then, the rigors of the law had softened, because the maximum sentence was three years in prison for a third conviction.[4] There is no record of anyone committing the crime a third time, and hardly any record of its commission at all.

The meager history of blasphemy prosecutions in Virginia during the seventeenth century and still more so in the eighteenth raises the question why blasphemy cases were rare. Virginia was a representative colony, so the question persists for all the colonies. The other Southern colonies had even fewer blasphemy cases than Virginia. One reason there were so few is that in the South, the established church, the Church of England, was not a thriving institution. It dominated in the coastal areas, where the planters who held political power tended to be broad-minded and abhorred prosecution for religious differences as a form of persecution. In the interior of the southern colonies, especially in Virginia, Scotch-Irish Presbyterians, and Germans who were Lutherans or members of pietistic sects like the Mennonites, grew in number. The Episcopalians of the tidewater enforced their privileges when they could by prosecuting dissenters for having administered sacraments without a license, for unlicensed preaching, for unlawful assembly, for preaching contrary to the Anglican Book of Common Prayer, or for refusal to pay taxes in support of the establishment. In 1774, young James Madison exploded, "That diabolical Hell conceived principle of persecution rages among some and to their eternal Infamy the Clergy can furnish their Quota of Imps for such business." The cause of his outburst was that in the next county "not less than 5 or 6 well meaning men [were] in close Gaol [jail] for publishing their religious Sentiments which in the main are very orthodox."[5] By then, blasphemy was a crime ritualistically denounced from time to time in sermons or statutes, but the cases were isolated, sporadic, and minor.

The middle colonies enjoyed considerable religious freedom, tolerated the existence of many denominations, and never had establishments of religion. Accordingly, they were inhospitable to prosecutions for blasphemy. Excepting maverick Rhode Island, the Congregationalists, who overwhelmingly dominated in the New England colonies, were the beneficiaries of the laws providing for establishments of religion; not surprisingly, the offense of blasphemy was most prevalent in New England. But the differences between Virginia and Massachusetts are easy to exaggerate. Not even in Massachusetts was the number of cases considerable.

Massachusetts in particular was infamous for its religious intolerance. The Puritans knew that their religion was the true faith. As the Reverend John Cotton, the popular minister of Boston's First Church, declared in reply to Roger Williams's argument for religious liberty, the New England way was the way that would exist "if the Lord Jesus were here himselfe in person."[6] Tolerating religious differences would merely broadcast religious error, contrary to God's word. Religious uniformity was needed, because dissent presented genuine dangers to the public peace and the peace of God's churches. Wherever toleration existed, it produced, said Nathaniel Ward, "a multimonstrous maufrey of heteroclytes and quicqudlibets." Ward believed that whoever tolerated any religion "besides his owne, unlesse it be in matters meerly indifferent, either doubts of his owne, or is not sincere in it."[7] On fundamentals, "without right belief," declared Cotton, "a man cannot be saved." If a minister instructed a misguided individual in the truth and that person still rejected it, he was a pertinacious heretic who could not be tolerated. He might contaminate others with his errors and so deny them eternal salvation. Punishing the obstinate heretic did not violate his conscience or persecute him; rather, his obstinacy made him sin against his conscience. Thus, the heretic should be punished for his own good. Because Puritan

Massachusetts—or Connecticut or New Hampshire—cared deeply about obstreperous religious error, it did not normally confuse error with blasphemy.[8]

Massachusetts lacked statutory provisions against blasphemy until the Body of Liberties, the colony's first adopted code, in 1641. Yet an elaborate system of courts had existed for over a decade, adjudicating criminal cases with rigor. The magistrates preferred to operate without a code and without fixed penalties that might limit their authority; they also exercised a wide degree of discretion in the administration of the law after, as well as before, the codification of the law. In 1644, the General Court, which was the colonial legislature, requested the church elders to explain whether magistrates should be able to prescribe different penalties for offenses that admitted varying degrees of guilt, and whether capital crimes could be punished by lesser sentences than death. The elders, ministers acting in conjunction with influential church members, were highly respected for their knowledge of religion. They acknowledged that the degree of guilt could vary with the person. He might be a first offender or a recidivist. He might be the principal or an accessory. He may have acted with malice or premeditation. Therefore, magistrates might properly consider mitigating factors and vary penalties in accordance with their sense of the individual's guilt. Puritan courts sought to be rehabilitative and were by no means bloodthirsty. Their flexibility in fixing penalties aided them in their objectives. They never executed anyone for blasphemy as such. The "as such" provides for the situation in which an offender returned to Massachusetts after having been banished on pain of death. The infliction of the death penalty in such a case was, in a technical sense, for the crime of returning, not the crime for which the banishment had been imposed.[9]

The 1631 case of Phillip Ratcliffe is evidence of judicial aggressiveness in the absence of statute. Ratcliffe, who may have been the Bay Colony's first blasphemer, was tried in Boston before a court consisting of the governor, his deputy, and several magistrates. The record shows that he was sentenced to be whipped, have his ears cut off, pay a heavy fine, and be banished for the crime of "uttering mallicious and scandalous speeches against the government and church of Salem." Therefore, the crime, not named as such, seems to have been seditious utterance.[10] Governor John Winthrop's *Journal* describes the offense as the "most foul, scandalous invectives against our churches and government." But another contemporary reported to a member of the Privy Council in England that he had been "credibly informed" that Ratcliffe's crime was "horrible blasphemy." Still another, who reported the case in detail, named the crime as "blasphemy against the Church of Salem," and described Ratcliffe as having said that the devil was the founder of the Salem church. The same writer accurately noted that Ratcliffe was originally sentenced to a punishment considerably more barbarous than the one inflicted. He was to have had his tongue bored through, his nose slit, and his forehead branded, and he was to have been whipped in every town—a sentence worthy of the Star Chamber.[11]

"Blasphemy" as a word meaning "speaking evil" can in the loosest sense apply to defamation of a church—that is, one may speak evil about a church or its ministers—but the history of the matter is that blasphemy meant speaking evil of God, Christ, the Bible, or Christianity, not a church or its minister. Winthrop did not designate Ratcliffe's offense as blasphemy. A careful use of the word by the Massachusetts authorities would account for the paucity of blasphemy cases. That they did use the word with care appears from the earliest definition of the crime in the various codes of law that were proposed.

The first code, the work of John Cotton, was called by Winthrop "Moses His Judicials." In 1636, Cotton, relying heavily upon the Old Testament, defined the capital laws. The first of these was blasphemy, "which is a cursing of God by atheisme, or the like, to be punished with death," citing Leviticus 24:15–16. In a second version, of 1638, Cotton altered the definition to read "a cursing of God, or wicked denial of God by Atheism." The original version displayed a Hebraic understanding of "blasphemy," using the word in its narrowest sense. Cursing God—in ancient Hebrew law, only cursing Him by His name—was blasphemy and nothing else. The Puritans were religiously and intellectually attached to things Hebrew. The influence of the Old Testament on the Bay Colony in matters of church and state, especially in the area of criminal justice, is more than a twice-told tale. The Body of Liberties of 1641 and the General Laws and Liberties of 1648, like Cotton's "Moses His Judicials," drew heavily upon the Mosaic code. Four years of Hebrew study was a requirement for all students at Harvard College, and the college library possessed an excellent collection of Talmuds and works of rabbinical exegesis. Not surprisingly, the ancient Jewish understanding of blasphemy thrived in the Puritan colonies.[12]

Cotton's addition of "wicked denial" of God to the definition of blasphemy in the 1638 revision of "Moses His Judicials" reflected a Christian understanding but one that fell quite short of extending the offense of blasphemy to a denial or reviling of Christianity, the Bible, or Jesus Christ. If the authorities in New England had Cotton's understanding of blasphemy, or even if such an understanding merely played an important part in their thinking about that crime, the number of blasphemy prosecutions would inevitably be few. Cursing God was a crime in New England. Even denying God was an uncommon crime in the colonial period of America. Atheism, in the sense of denying the existence of

God, was really a nineteenth-century development, although many sorts of dissent had for generations been promiscuously described by the orthodox as atheistic.

Cotton understood the difference between blasphemy and heresy. In his fifth capital law, he described heresy as the "maintenance of some wicked errors, overthrowing the foundation of Christian religion." Thus, the error had to be a fundamental one, and the heretic merited death only if he remained obstinate, persisting in his error after having been corrected by a minister, and if he had sought to persuade others to his viewpoint.[13] Distinguishing between heresy and blasphemy meant that having severe religious differences would not be understood as constituting the offense of blasphemy.

Cotton's "Moses His Judicials" did not receive the General Court's approval, probably because of their excessive severity and their incompleteness as a codification. Nevertheless, many of Cotton's provisions, including his capital punishment for blasphemy, influenced the framing of the Body of Liberties of 1641 and the General Laws and Liberties of 1648. Moreover, a copy of "Moses His Judicials," called "An Abstract of the Laws of New England," was reprinted in England in 1641, and copies circulated in America too, becoming the basis of early laws in New Haven and elsewhere. It is important that the published version of "Moses His Judicials" was the original one restricting blasphemy to cursing God.[14]

In 1641, however, the General Court adopted the Body of Liberties framed by Nathaniel Ward, later the author of "A Simple Cobbler of Aggawam," which called for the suppression of heresy. An English barrister who became a minister at the age of forty and settled in Massachusetts, Ward was the most knowledgeable legal authority in the colony. The provision on blasphemy, the third of the capital laws in the Body of Liberties, declared: "If any man shall Blaspheme the name of God, the father, Sonne or Holie Ghost, with direct, expresse, presumptuous or high handed blasphemie, or shall curse god in the like manner, he shall be put to death."[15] Presumably, "Blaspheme" here means cursing or speaking evil of. This provision of 1641, repeated in the Laws and Liberties of 1648, reflected a considerably broader concept of blasphemy than Cotton's "Moses His Judicials," yet a fairly tight one compared with the English understanding of blasphemy, which regarded certain religious doctrines and mere denials of God as blasphemous. That is, in England the distinction between heresy and blasphemy remained obscure, as was shown by the conviction of devout Christians for the crime of blasphemy. In America the distinction was more meaningful, thus accounting for a paucity of blasphemy cases. And in America most colonies did not punish heresy, even if pertinacious.

In 1646, Massachusetts enacted a statute "Against Blasphemy of the Name of God." In the course of extending to Indians and pagans as well as Christians the penal law against blasphemy, the General Court restated its understanding of the crime. Blasphemy of God's name must be obstinate denial of Him, cursing Him, or reproaching His "holy religion" of Christianity. The same enactment punished heresy, defined as obstinately held errors of opinion that tended to subvert Christianity and destroy people's souls. The enactment offered, as an example of a heresy, the denial of the soul, of the resurrection of the body, or of the belief that Christ died to redeem people's sins. Heavy fines constituted the punishment for a "damnable" and pertinacious heresy; the death penalty for heresy disappeared in 1646. At the same time, the penalty for profanity, in the form of swearing "rashly and vainely" by any oath or the holy name of God, was reduced to a moderate fine or, alternatively, one to three hours in the stocks. Profaning the Sabbath by working or playing resulted in a similar punishment.[16]

The punishment of heresy depended on the existence of an orthodox religion established by law. In the absence of an established church, no standard for heresy existed. The established church in the Southern colonies was entrenched only in the tidewater areas. In any event, after the abolition of the Court of High Commission and the Star Chamber in England in 1641, the punishment of ecclesiastical offenses such as heresy ceased during the Interregnum. After the Stuart Restoration, prosecutions for reasons of religion became politicized, with the result that the crime of heresy in effect died out, replaced by the crimes of nonconformity and seditious libel. After the Toleration Act of 1689, any Trinitarian Protestant conducting himself peaceably was exempt from the criminal laws. By then, even Massachusetts had abandoned the prosecution of heresy, the colony was becoming more religiously pluralistic, and persecution seemed like a relic of a different age.

The demise of heresy as a criminal offense against the state meant that blasphemy had necessarily become restricted. It could no longer accommodate prosecutions for religious differences under the rubric "blasphemy." What remained as blasphemy became something other than sectarianism. Blasphemy had come to be understood as irreligion or atheism, the vilification of Christianity, or the cursing of God. The blasphemer became the truly uncommon person whose opinions on religion were morally repulsive because of supposed atheism or outrageous assaults on Christian belief. Yet the village atheist was seen as a harmless eccentric, because, his opinions notwithstanding, everyone knew him to be just a curmudgeon. Accordingly, punishment, as actual cases show, was mild or suspended.

The first blasphemy prosecution after Ratcliffe's case occurred in

1635, in the separatist colony of Plymouth, against Thomas Williams, a servant who had the indiscretion to claim that he feared neither God nor the devil. The accusation against him was for blasphemy and profanity. Although the words were proved by witnesses as well as by his confession, the court judged that he spoke in "passion & distemper." After he acknowledged his offense, he was dismissed with merely a reproof.[17]

In the same year, Massachusetts banished Roger Williams for "dyvers newe & dangerous opinions" against the magistrates, but, significantly, none of his opinions was described as blasphemous. Williams's insistence on his separatist views would have compromised the Massachusetts authorities in their relations with England if they had not demonstrated their disapproval of separatism in a striking manner. In 1639, Ambrose Marten called the church covenant "a stinking carryon" and wondered at God's patience for allowing the ministers to "dethrone Christ" and set themselves up in his place. For that crime, which was not described as blasphemy, he was merely fined £10 and required to present himself to a minister for instruction. One James Brittane, who committed a similar crime, failed to appear when summoned; his punishment was censure and a whipping. For his "athisticall carryage" Henry Faine was jailed, but the court did not call him a blasphemer. After ten days, he was dismissed with an admonition. In 1640, Hugh Buet was found guilty of some serious heresy, not explained; because the court feared that he might infect others, he was banished and ordered not to return or he would be hanged. Francis Hutchinson, in the following year, libeled the church of Boston by calling it "a whoare." For that and other "corrupt" beliefs, none described as blasphemy, he was heavily fined, ordered to be kept imprisoned until the fine was paid, and then banished on pain of death.[18] Ruben Guppi, for various crimes including profanity, wife abandonment, lying, and stealing, as well as blasphemy, was severely whipped. The nature of his blasphemy is unknown.[19]

The failure of the records to describe someone's blasphemy may be attributed to an emulation of the ancient Jewish aversion to repeating the offense against God, but that explanation is, alas, inadequate; rather, the records are just too sparse. They are brief minutes that most often do not detail the nature of a crime, whatever it was.

The records are ample, however, concerning the Antinomian Controversy, which convulsed Massachusetts between 1636 and 1638. The resolution of the controversy in favor of the prevailing orthodoxy constituted a watershed in the colony's history: it preserved the government and the Congregational church by banishing religious dissidents thought to be subversive. The controversy centered mainly on the opinions of Anne Hutchinson and her brother-in-law the Reverend John Wheelwright. He was convicted of sedition and contempt, she for having "troubled the peace of the common-wealth and the churches." Their offense consisted of popularizing beliefs that in a considerably modified form had once represented Puritan orthodoxy.

Calvinists had differentiated themselves from the Church of Rome by stressing a covenant of grace rather than the covenant of works associated with Rome because of its emphasis on obedience to the church as a means of salvation. Advocates of a covenant of grace believed that salvation was not dependent on righteous behavior or "deeds of law." They opposed the church—its discipline, its clergy, and its sacraments. All that was superfluous; one could not earn salvation, because God by His grace had ordained whom He would save. What was once a Protestant orthodoxy when the Puritans were a persecuted minority in England, contending with the episcopacy, had become a heresy when they were the majority in control of the government and the churches in New England. The corporate decision, not the individual's, came to matter. Church and state had an obligation to exert discipline over the individual so that his or her conscience was properly educated to be loyal to them. The antinomians, however, were ineducable; they rigidly insisted on the supremacy of individual conscience when in communion with God.

What mattered to them was personal revelation directly from God, a mystical knowledge that His spirit had entered one's soul. If God had decided whom to save, intimacy with Him rather than the intermediation of ministers was sufficient. But institutionalized Congregationalism undergirded both civil and ecclesiastical polities. Neither could survive soul religion or antinomianism, which made obedience to law seem unnecessary because being in tune with God meant everything. If the person of the Holy Ghost dwelt within an individual—a view that later on in England was regarded as blasphemous—even the Bible became subsidiary to a covenant of grace. If the Almighty directly communicated with Anne Hutchinson, giving her revelations as true as the Bible, she could believe herself to be unfettered by the commandments—hence, antinomian or against the law. "Antinomianism," when used to justify libertinism, was an opprobrious term meant to stigmatize those who advocated a covenant of grace. Yet Anne Hutchinson was as correct in her conduct as the most righteous Puritan.

She would scarcely have merited prosecution if she were just an eccentric crank at whom people laughed. Rather, she seemed to be converting a significant part of Boston at a time when the magistrates and ministers were already under political attack because people were dissatisfied with their authoritarianism. The magistrates already had to agree to the framing of a code of laws "in resemblance to a Magna Charta" to fix limitations on their powers. Antinomianism seemed to be a religious manifestation of a similar sense of public restiveness. It was a threat to the security of the establishment. Winthrop feared that almost the whole church of Boston were becoming Hutchinson's converts. The ministers asserted that her heresies were "manifestly dangerous to the state." The clergy, making hysterical analogies with the 1535 Anabaptist uprising and anarchy in Münster, warned of the dangers of a new Münster in Massachusetts. Accordingly, Hutchinson's religious errors were treated as if they were politically subversive. Sedition, a political crime, not blasphemy, was the issue for the Massachusetts authorities. However, when the Reverend John Wilson pronounced the sentence of excommunication and banishment from the church of Boston, he delivered Hutchinson to Satan, so that "you may learn no more to blaspheme." In England, where antinomians, whether Ranters or Quakers, never threatened the state, their religious views were deemed blasphemous, not seditious.[20]

The first major blasphemy case in Massachusetts occurred in 1643. The culprit was Samuel Gorton, described by the legislature of the colony as "a man whose spirit is starke drunke with blasphemies and insolencies, a corrupter of the truth, a disturber of the peace where ever he comes."[21] Gorton was unquestionably a heretic. Whether he was a blasphemer is unclear, despite the official certainty. It was true, though, that he was an altogether impossible man. Irascible, pugnacious, presumptuous, and offensive in the extreme, he was constitutionally incapable of living with authority.

Once a clothier, Gorton had become a preacher or "Professor of the Mysteries of Christ." In England, self-proclaimed preachers were common, but not in New England, where the ministers were college graduates and were often learned. Gorton hated "hireling" ministers of any sect. Though he was a devout Christian, his religious views seemed to be in perpetual flux. He was something of an antinomian who accepted the indwelling Christ; he seemed touched by Ranterism; he surely was a Baptist; he welcomed Quakers as brethren. But his religious views seemed as unfathomable as his prose, which was prolix, ponderous, and opaque. That he was a mystic is clear enough, one for whom Christianity began and ended with Jesus Christ and the New Testament. To say that he was Christocentric does not make the point strongly enough. To an orthodox Trinitarian, Gorton seemed to make Christ supplant God. He thought the doctrine of the Trinity was "pernicious," because, by positing a trinity with one divine essence, it derogated from Christ as a human being, the form in which he became Saviour. Yet Gorton believed that God created Adam in Christ's image, and that the loss of Adam's image signaled the death of Christ. Gorton sometimes seemed to have Docetist notions about the Christ of the cross, who seemed a "semblance" or a "shadow." If on occasion Gorton seemed confused or contradictory, perhaps he was.[22]

His religious opinions were eccentric and hard to understand. He was forever claiming to be misunderstood. His prime antagonists, the ministers of Massachusetts, summed up what they thought he said, frequently provoking him to assert that they had distorted his meaning. When he wrote, he used marginal annotations "to help the Reader to understand our true meaning." When he was on trial for his life and had to write answers to questions on his religious beliefs, he insisted on reading aloud what he had written, so that he could "pronounce the Phrases and words according to the true meaning, and intent," having previously experienced a court misreading his words. What was clear enough was his vitriolic anticlericalism. He believed that every individual should commune with Christ directly, not through priestly mediations. The clergy to him were the Antichrist, minions of the devil. The sacraments, church ordinances, rites, and observances he thought to be nonessential if not devilish.[23]

Gorton in his way was an advocate of religious liberty—not that he tolerated differences, but, like Roger Williams, he believed that government and civil society were too corrupt for the true faith and, therefore, for the sake of the faith, magistrates had no right "to intermeddle between God and the consciences of men." God's kingdom being of another world, the magistrate possessed no authority over "spiritual" matters; his lawful authority extended only to matters between "creature and creature" or "civil things," not to religious ones. On the other hand, much that Gorton said gave the impression that he thought magistrates had no legitimate authority at all. He was as radical politically as religiously. When *Hypocrisie Unmasked*, a 1646 tract devoted to exposing Gorton's "manifold Blasphemies," went into a second edition, the revised title was *The Danger of Tolerating Levellers in a Civill State*; the title page still promised to reveal Gorton's "blasphemous speeches."[24]

Gorton had left London to seek religious freedom. He arrived in Boston in 1637, when the Antinomian Controversy was raging, and settled in Plymouth. In short order, his argumentativeness and opposition to authority, clerical and civil, led to charges of heresy and stirring the people to sedition. After being fined and banished, Gorton emigrated to Portsmouth, where he again conducted himself insubordinately. He was whipped and banished for seditiousness, having had the nerve to call the magistrates "great asses" who were "corrupt." Gorton next went to Providence, where he tangled with Roger Williams, renowned for his religious tolerance and graciousness. Williams described Gorton, in a letter to Winthrop, as one who, having "foully abused" the authorities elsewhere, was "now bewiching and madding poor Providence," where the people "suck in his poison" as he berated their ministers with "unclean" censures. Williams also called Gorton an advocate of "familisme," a pejorative description of radical enthusiasm that has little meaning. People from Providence, when complaining in 1640 to Governor Winthrop about Gorton and his supporters, condemned their "licentious lust," claimed that they acted like "savage bruite beasts," and alleged that they "put no manner of difference betweene houses, goods, lands, wives, lives," a description that sounds remarkably like Ranterism.[25] However, because Ranters were unknown in New England, the remark revealed merely prejudice.

With a dozen disciples, Gorton left Providence for a place to the south on Narragansett Bay, later called Warwick. They had bought the land from Indians, but several Englishmen in Providence, who claimed the same land, asked the governor of Massachusetts for assistance against the Gortonites. After they placed themselves under the jurisdiction of Massachusetts, Winthrop dispatched a warrant to the Gortonites asking them to produce their title to the disputed land. Gorton's reply became notorious and put him in jeopardy.[26]

He filled a twenty-two-page letter to the government of Massachusetts with outrageous invective. Massachusetts found twenty-six blasphemous passages, Gorton later observed as if surprised. He reviled and ridiculed the government of the colony, its officers, its ministers, its churches, and their beliefs, becoming a marked man. For the time being, Massachusetts ignored the provocation. It later issued a warrant to the Gortonites informing them that, some Indians having complained of injuries at their hands, they ought to answer to the legislature in Boston under a pledge of safe passage in and out of Massachusetts. The Gortonites defied the warrant and sent an amazingly insulting letter to the legislature, addressing it not by its title as the General Court but as the "Idol General," a device of "Satan." At that point, Massachusetts dispatched commissioners to the Gortonites to hear their answers to the charges against them. A small army of forty soldiers accompanied the commissioners. Defiance by the Gortonites led to shooting. No one was killed, but Gorton and his disciples were arrested and transported back to Boston. When some citizens of Providence complained to Winthrop about the episode, Winthrop replied, in justification of Massachusetts, that, apart from the land dispute, it had captured men who "have subscribed their names, to horrible and destestable blasphemies, against God, and all Magistracie, who are rather to be judged as Blasphemers" if they persisted in their opinions.[27]

The twelve were jailed and held for trial before the legislature, which was the highest court of the colony. The prisoners were examined by the court for several weeks in an effort to make them incriminate themselves. That failing, Winthrop instructed Gorton to answer several questions in writing "speedily upon life and death." Gorton, in effect, was charged with capital blasphemy. The questions required Gorton to summarize his basic religious beliefs about God and Christ. His orthodox replies astonished Winthrop, who told Gorton "that they were one with him, in those answers; for they held as he did." Nevertheless, the court convicted him as "a blasphemous enemy to the true Religion of our Lord Jesus Christ, and all his holy Ordinances, and also to all civill authority among the people of God, and particularly in this jurisdiction, as appeareth by writings and speeches." Gorton's companions were also found guilty. None would retract. The magistrates, by a vote of nine to three, favored the death penalty, but the "greatest number of the deputies," who numbered about forty, opposed a death sentence. The court sentenced seven who had signed the letters to hard labor, to wear irons to prevent their escape, "and so to continue during the pleasure of the Court." If any of the seven repeated the "blasphemous or abominable heresies" contained in the letters to Massachusetts, they would be executed. The other five got off lightly.[28]

What were the blasphemies, and why did the court also refer to heresies? Gorton never denied or reviled God, Christ, or the Bible. Most of his targets were not protected by laws or precedents dealing with blasphemy. The term "blasphemy" did not apply to officials or to churches; nothing Gorton had said about the magistrates or even the ministers could have been blasphemous. Most of the statements reflected his own religious deviance, even when he assaulted the sermons of the ministers. That he was a heretic is beyond dispute, judged by the standards of conventional Puritan Trinitarianism. However, by the standards of blasphemy prevailing in Massachusetts at the time, he had scarcely blasphemed.

When Massachusetts presented its case against Gorton for the benefit of England, to demonstrate that it had not violated liberty of conscience, its spokesman, Edward Winslow, three times governor of Plymouth, illustrated Gorton's blasphemies. Gorton, he wrote, had declared

> that in the Church now there was nothing but Christ, so that all our Ordinances, Ministers, and Sacraments, &c. were but mens inventions, for shew and pomp. . . . He said also, that if Christ lives eternally, then he died eternally, and other speeches of like kinde. And indeed it appeareth both by his speeches and letters, that it was his opinion, that Christ was incarnate in *Adam*, and was that image of God, wherein *Adam* was created; and that his being borne after of the Virgin Mary, and his suffering &c. was but a manifestation of his suffering, &c. in *Adam*.

All this was heresy. Winslow added other supposed blasphemies. Gorton, he wrote, believed that the image of God, "wherein *Adam* was created, was Christ; and *Adams* loosing that Image was the death of Christ," whereas his resurrection restored his image.[29] That too was heresy. To call Gorton's beliefs blasphemous, notwithstanding his devotion to Christ, revealed that the Massachusetts authorities had lost control because of an unendurable man. They had abandoned their tight understanding of blasphemy.

Despising the clergy and their religious views, Gorton had also claimed that they made "a nullity" of Christ and crucified him. Against the word of God, said Winslow, Gorton had called the sermons of the ministers "lyes and falshoods." Inasmuch as the ministers' sermons reflected Puritan beliefs, to call them lies surely was reproachful, and, to the Puritans, blasphemous.[30] Winslow also instanced Gorton's denunciation of infant baptism as an "abomination." And Gorton had ridiculed the Lord's Supper by calling it "your disht up dainties, turning the juice of a sillie grape that perisheth in the use of it, into the blood of the Lord Jesus, by the cunning skill of your Magicians." He had also asserted that a Christian should not seek consolation in Christ, for that made the Son of God "the devill himself." Gorton reviled and ridiculed the religion espoused by the ministers of Massachusetts.[31] In that sense, he had blasphemed. In all probability, the authorities had been so incensed by Gorton's unprovoked and outrageous assaults on them that their good sense was jostled; they exaggerated Gorton's blasphemies. They did not seek out Gorton to persecute him for his religion, but they overreacted to his intolerable provocation.

Imprisoning Gorton and his followers did not stop their tongues: they had sympathizers and they proselytized. By the end of the winter, Winthrop acknowledged, "Gorton and his company did harm in the towns where they were confined, and not knowing what to do with them," the authorities decided to release and banish them from Massachusetts and even from their village in Narragansett. Return meant death.

Gorton sailed to England to obtain satisfaction for his grievances against the Bay Colony. In London, some people denounced him to Parliament as a blasphemer, causing a committee of Commons to examine him; they acquitted him of the charge. England at the time, 1646, was far freer for heterodox religious opinions than New England. The grant of a charter to Roger Williams helped Gorton's cause too, because Rhode Island obtained jurisdiction of the Narragansett village where the Gortonites had lived. The earl of Warrick, head of the Commission on Foreign Plantations, granted a warrant of safe conduct to the Gortonites. They returned home to Shawomet and renamed that village Warwick. There, safely among his own kind, Gorton lived out his life.[32]

The next blasphemy case in Massachusetts, in 1645, was a trivial affair resulting in a fine. The first case in Connecticut occurred in 1646, involving an Indian. An earlier case had arisen in New Haven in 1641, but the blasphemy issue was buried in the still greater charge of bestiality, which resulted in the individual's execution. The Indian, Pawquash, had declared that Jesus was nothing and that his bones had rotted. For that blasphemy he was severely whipped and warned that a repetition of the offense could cost him his life. A Mrs. Moore, who stubbornly denied the charge that she had said that the ministers were "inventions of men," was warned that the magistrates would not tolerate blasphemy or the reviling of the holy ordinances of Christ's church. She was admonished. In 1647, George King was charged with blasphemy because he cursed by the name of God, an offense that would later be regarded as merely profanity. With semi-Hebraic understanding, the court declared that blaspheming God meant piercing his name, although the ancient Hebrew crime consisted of piercing his personal name, "YHVH," not "God." The court warned King that for his rash oath he might have his tongue bored through, but sentenced him to be whipped instead. In the same year, Richard Smoolt was severely whipped for scoffing at the Bible.[33]

The first blasphemy statute of Connecticut, enacted in 1642, had copied the blasphemy provision of the Massachusetts Body of Liberties. Connecticut's code of 1650 retained that provision unchanged. The crime was cursing God or vilification of any person of the Trinity. However, New Haven, which was not incorporated into Connecticut until 1662, enacted in its capital laws the Massachusetts provision of 1646, defining the crime as obstinate denial of God or the persons of the Trinity, cursing any of them, or reproaching the true religion of God.[34] But for the provision concerning reproach of religion, New Haven and Connecticut, like Massachusetts, operated under a fairly strict understanding of the offense of blasphemy. Plymouth and Rhode Island had no blasphemy acts in this period.

Maryland, in 1649, adopted "An Act Concerning Religion," an extraordinary code on the subject. It contained a clause guaranteeing that anyone who professed a belief in Jesus Christ should not be troubled because of his religion or "the free exercise thereof." That was the first use of the phrase that eventually became part of the First Amendment. The same act criminalized religious name-calling; to describe anyone as a heretic, schismatic, idolater, Puritan, independent, Presbyterian, papist, Jesuit, Lutheran, antinomian, Separatist, or any other name in a reproachful manner would result in a fine or a whipping. Profaning the Lord's Day was also a crime. But the only religious crime punishable by death was blasphemy. A Maryland act against felonies adopted in 1639 had properly defined blasphemy as "acursing or wicked speaking of God," and provided execution by burning. The act of 1649, however, extended the capital crime to denial of Christ as Son of God, denial of the Trinity, or denial of any person of the Trinity. A lesser offense of blasphemy, punishable by fines and severe whipping, consisted of reproaching the Virgin Mary or Christ's apostles; repetition of the offense resulted in banishment.

This statute of 1649 is usually known as the Maryland Act of Toleration. It did not extend toleration to Jews or anti-Trinitarians of any sort, but for its time it was remarkably comprehensive. Nowhere else in America did the law protect Catholics and Protestants of every Trinitarian sect; nowhere else did they live together in comparative peace if not amity. Cecil Calvert, the shrewd and tolerant Catholic proprietor of Maryland, understood that the protection of Roman Catholics, who would necessarily become a minority, depended on a comprehensive declaration.[35]

Maryland's first blasphemy case occurred in 1652. The defendant "much dishonoured God" by her statements, but her case was complicated in that she also confessed to fornication. She was severely whipped. In Maryland, as elsewhere, the harsh statutory law was administered with discretionary mitigation. At this time in New Haven and Connecticut, where blasphemy was also a capital offense, cases were tried in courts that had no authority to impose the death sentence. That suggested that the cases were not thought to constitute capital blasphemy, or that the authorities refused to permit the ultimate punishment. New Haven flogged the daughter of Captain Howe for her speeches about the Bible "tending to Blasphemy," and warned that the punishment would be greater if she repeated the offense. In Boston in 1657, John Crossman was severely beaten for his blasphemy (which the records do not describe), a letter "B" for "blasphemy" was burned into his forehead, and he was banished forever from the colony.[36]

In 1652, Plymouth gave two men the choice of a fine or a whipping for speeches that derided the Bible. A more serious case occurred in 1656, when Plymouth sentenced Katherine Aines. For lascivious behavior, she was whipped; for her blasphemous words, she was required to wear a capital "B" on her sleeve and warned that if she were ever found without it she would be whipped again. The "B" was a symbolic branding. This was a lenient sentence, as was New Haven's admonishment of Jeremiah Johnson in 1657 for his "profane scoffing against the Scriptures"; similarly, the same jurisdiction merely fined and denied intoxicating drinks to William East, who had blasphemed the name of God when drunk. New Amsterdam was more severe when fining and banishing someone whose supposed "scandalous blasphemies" were aimed at his magistrates.[37]

A major case concerned Benjamin Saucer, a soldier, who committed blasphemy in Boston in 1654 by saying that Jehovah was the devil and that the only God he knew was his sword. The court wanted to try him capitally, but a grand jury refused to indict because the evidence showed he had blasphemed when drunk. The magistrates rejected that verdict, and tried and convicted him, but before they could impose sentence, he escaped from prison. A year later, another man's blasphemy was deemed not capital; he was fined and imprisoned.[38]

In 1654, the General Court banned and consigned to the flames any copies that might be found of the "hereticall and blasphemous bookes" by Lodowick Muggleton and John Reeves. The records do not indicate that any were ever found. Muggletonians were unknown in Massachusetts or, for that matter, anywhere in America. Much more surprisingly, Socinians did not constitute a problem either. William Pynchon, one of the founders of the Bay Colony and a prosperous merchant, in 1650 published in London a book that caused a sensation in Boston. The General Court deemed it heretical and ordered that copies be burned. Pynchon was called to answer for his heterodoxies. Significantly, he did not deny the Trinity, and he was not accused of blasphemy. His prosecution ended when he returned to England. A historian of Socinianism conceded Pynchon's aberrant views but described him as a Trinitarian. Anti-Trinitarianism, a common form of blasphemy in England, was rare if existent at all in seventeenth-century America.[39]

Baptists were plentiful and were feared, especially in New England, but not even in Massachusetts were they proscribed as blasphemers. Anyone condemning infant baptism was regarded as a heretic, even if a threat to the basis of the established church. Early Baptists vehemently denounced infant baptism. One called it a "badge of the whore," meaning the Church of Rome, and censured its believers as worshippers of the devil. A special act of the Massachusetts legislature in 1644 made denial of the validity of infant baptism a crime punishable by banishment, but the crime was heresy, not blasphemy. In 1651, when John Clarke and Obadiah Holmes preached against infant baptism, the governor, speaking for their court, declared that they made Congregational worship "a nullity" and deserved death; but the Baptists were merely fined and banished. Holmes was also whipped when he refused to allow his fine to be paid. Hated though he was, he was not tarred as a blasphemer.[40]

In 1652, Massachusetts modified its laws against those who offended religion. Denial of the truth of any part of the Bible, though thought to be a heinous crime overthrowing true religion and salvation, was punishable as heresy only, and the penalty was reduced to a heavy fine or severe whipping. Death, once the only prescribed punishment, was reserved for a repetition of the offense of obstinate heresy, and banishment was made an alternative punishment, as the court saw fit.[41] No one was ever executed for heresy in Massachusetts or anywhere in America.

In Maryland, the chief problem was not the denial of religious freedom to heretics but to Catholics. When Puritans migrated into Maryland, chiefly from Virginia, they evinced hostility toward Catholics, and when the Puritan party constituted a majority, in 1655, they excluded Catholics from the protections of the 1649 Act of Toleration. In 1660, the proprietor managed to secure a restoration of the policy of freedom of conscience for all Trinitarian Christians who were peaceable.[42]

A unique blasphemy case occurred in Maryland in 1658, when a prominent Jewish physician, Jacob Lumbrozo, foolishly allowed himself to be trapped by unfriendly Protestants into revealing his opinions about Christ. In 1633, when the first ship had sailed into Chesapeake Bay, a few Sephardic Jews were aboard. Not until Lumbrozo's case were any molested, and he got into trouble only because the Catholics, at the time, had lost control of the colony to the Protestants, who opposed toleration. In a conversation that turned to religion, one man asked Lumbrozo whether Jews looked forward to the coming of the Messiah. When Lumbrozo said yes, he was asked who had been crucified in Jerusalem, and he replied that Christ was a man. Another declared that Christ was more than just a man, as his resurrection proved. Lumbrozo replied that Christ's disciples stole the body. To the remark that no one had ever performed such miracles, Lumbrozo declared that one who knew "Art Magick" might have done them.

Called before the provincial court, Lumbrozo admitted his statements but claimed that he had said nothing scoffingly or in derogation of Christ. The court declared that his words had been blasphemous and that he would have to stand trial for the crime at its next meeting. Lumbrozo then had an extraordinary stroke of good luck. Richard Cromwell, on succeeding his father as lord protector of England, issued a general proclamation of amnesty, and the Catholics regained power in Maryland. When Governor Philip Calvert extended the pardon to Maryland, Lumbrozo was released. He avoided going to trial, became a naturalized citizen, and prospered.[43] No other Jew was accused of blasphemy anywhere in America.

Quakers confronted accusations of blasphemy, which triggered events that led to the deaths of four of them and the infliction of inhuman punishments on many. In England, of course, Quaker blasphemy was a familiar and frequent phenomenon. On both sides of the Atlantic, English-speaking people in authority loathed the first generation of Quakers, who were fanatically militant and provocative. Their conduct was boisterous, disruptive, and in some respects indecent. They were a people possessed by their acute sense of an indwelling Christ, who seemed to compel them to witness to him in ways that offended and repulsed peaceable folk. Having a Quaker break into a religious service and berate the minister and congregation for their satanism, or watching a Quaker "go naked for a sign" to reveal the religious nakedness of those who called themselves Christians, shocked staid Puritans. Quakers dumbfounded them by glorying in persecution, inviting it as an additional proof of their witness. Quakers experienced religious ecstasy when they were punished. They felt duty-bound to seek crucifixion, secure in the belief that God would accept them for eternity. After 1655, when Cromwell issued a proclamation against those who invaded peaceable religious worship, the English in America were alerted to the Quaker menace. Anti-Quaker tracts had already circulated in New England. Events in England involving Quakers were common knowledge on the other side of the Atlantic.

The Puritans feared and expected exactly what they got by reading into the Quakers their worst suspicions. No Congregationalist could understand a religion that was completely internalized, attuned to the indwelling Christ. Congregationalists were appalled that Quakers repudiated their church, ministers, sacraments, and rites as irrelevant to Christianity, and repudiated too their government. Some mystical, direct communion with God infused Quaker souls, but Congregationalists had no understanding of a religion that was all inward experience. They knew only that the Quakers believed that their way was the way of Baal, no better than the idolatry of the ancient Hebrews who had turned from God. Quakers reputedly used foul language to describe every institution and idea cherished by the Puritans. Before one Quaker set foot in Massachusetts, the authorities had determined to see that none did. Quaker missionaries would be treated like the devil's offspring.

When two Quaker women arrived in Boston harbor in mid-1656, they were arrested before they could debark. Their books were seized and publicly burned. They were imprisoned, stripped naked, searched for signs of witchcraft, and held incommunicado for five weeks before being deported. Two days after their departure, eight more Quakers arrived by ship, with similar results. Excepting Rhode Island, commissioners of the New England colonies, meeting in Plymouth, proposed that the legislature of each should enact a law "that all quakers Ranters and other notorious heretiques" be prohibited, and that any who arrived should be banished. Massachusetts responded with an enactment that Plymouth, New Hampshire, New Haven, and Connecticut adopted. The act of 1656 denounced the "cursed set of heretickes" known as Quakers, who "speak and write blasphemous opinions" against government and "the order of God in the churches and common wealth." Quakers also reviled magistrates and ministers and sought to gain proselytes. Accordingly, the master of any ship bringing in Quakers "or any other blasphemous haereticks" would be steeply fined and obligated to return them. Any Quakers who managed to arrive would be jailed, severely whipped, forced to work at hard labor, and held incommunicado. Their books and writing would be burned.[44]

The Quakers learned that the best way to enter Massachusetts to do battle for the Lord was to infiltrate through Rhode Island. They obtained their own ship and went to that colony, whose boast was its flourishing freedom of conscience for every peaceable inhabitant. Anne Hutchinson's followers and Samuel Gorton's were sympathetic to the indwelling Christ of the Quakers, whom they welcomed. The authorities left the Quaker missionaries alone. The rest of New England, alarmed at this development, requested Rhode Island to deport the Quakers. Rhode Island replied that it had no law to punish people for declaring their minds concerning religion. Skeptical of the damage Quakers might do, Rhode Island added that her experience showed that, where Quakers were "suffered to declare themselves freely, and are only opposed by arguments in discourse, there they least of all desire to come, and we are informed, that they begin to loathe this place, for that they are not opposed by civil authority." Rhode Island observed that "they delight to be persecuted by civil powers, and when they are so, they are like to gain more adherents by the conceit of their patient suffering, than by consent to their pernicious sayings."[45]

Unfortunately, Massachusetts could not understand this splendid advice, and in 1657, to cope with Quakers spilling across its borders, enacted a law authorizing the cutting off of a male Quaker's ear and the flogging of female Quakers, as well as imprisonment at hard labor; those of either sex who returned after banishment "shall have their tongues bored through with a hot iron." The statute also applied these punishments to subjects of Massachusetts who joined the Quakers. And it was savagely enforced. One man suffered 117 strokes from a corded whip and was left for dead. Three men had their right ears severed. One was branded. Five were kept fifteen days without food. Many were imprisoned without bedding or heat during the Massachusetts winter.[46]

Yet the Quakers kept coming, and their conduct became more outrageous as the persecution increased their exaltation. One man broke empty bottles in a church to show how the Lord would cut persecutors to pieces. Women smashed bottles in church as a sign of the minister's emptiness. In court a man vilified the magistrates to their faces and simply would not be silent. A woman appeared in Boston in sackcloth and ashes as a sign of the plagues that the Lord would bring to that city. Another woman showed up with her face blackened to warn Boston that the pox awaited it. One woman walked stark naked into a church service, and still another paraded that way in a street in Salem. Both naked women witnessed to the spiritual nakedness of Congregationalism. Their brutal punishments by the saints of the Bay Colony pass belief. In desperation, Massachusetts enacted another statute that fixed death as the punishment for any person who returned after having been banished.[47]

Humphrey Norton's case illustrates. He disrupted a church service in New Haven by inveighing against the minister, was arrested for disturbance of the peace, heresy, and "some degree of blasphemy." He denounced the government, the magistrates, the church, and the sacraments. The Reverend John Davenport sought to answer his denunciations in court, but Norton would not shut up to let him talk. He was severely whipped, branded with an "H" for "heresy," and banished. He went to Plymouth, where he was scourged and expelled. Then he turned up in Boston, in the Reverend John Norton's church. For his remarks, he was charged with blasphemy, was kept some weeks in prison, and was savagely whipped again and again.[48]

The legislature asked John Norton, Boston's leading clergyman, to reply to Quaker tracts, reaching England, which claimed that Massachusetts persecuted freedom of conscience. Norton produced a tract intended for the outside world, entitled *The Heart of New-England Rent at the Blasphemies . . . of the Quakers, Demonstrating the destructive nature thereof, to Religion, the Churches, and the State* (1660). Norton explained why he thought Quaker doctrine blasphemed the Trinity, Christ, and the Bible. Even Roger Williams, the champion of toleration, despised the Quakers because of their beliefs. He called Quakers "Anti-Christians." To Williams, Jesus the human being, who had been crucified in Jerusalem, was the center of Christianity. God, Williams thought, was the eternal Creator whose essence was immortal, and the Bible was God's word, laying down the rules for a visible church. The Quakers, by contrast, knew only a mystical, nonhuman Christ; they prated about invisibilities, the indwelling Christ, yet rejected his church. They "acknowledge a God and Christ within them, that is in English, that themselves are God and Christ . . . and can rail and curse all that oppose them . . . and they are free from Sin, born of God and cannot sin." Even Williams accused the Quakers of "monstrous *Blasphemies*," but he never recommended that they be punished.[49]

Massachusetts, sharing the view that the Quakers were heretics and blasphemers who took on the attributes of God, enforced capital punishment. In 1659, two men were hanged in Boston, and Mary Dyer, once a follower of Anne Hutchinson, stood there, a noose around her neck, and watched them die, expecting to be next. She was released at the last moment and banished again. In the spring of 1660, Dyer returned to Boston, in obedience to God's will, she said, ready to die. Reluctantly, Massachusetts accommodated her. Soon after, a fourth Quaker was hanged.[50]

The authorities murdered the four because of their religion. Technically, the four were executed because they defied a banishment decree on pain of death; technically, they were condemned for their "rebellious and seditious" defiance. But they had been banished because Massachusetts understood their religion to be both "blasphemously heretical" and blasphemous. Massachusetts explained to the new king, Charles II, that the four had virtually committed suicide. Although they were "capitall blasphemers, open seducers from the glorious Trinity . . . the Quakers died, not because of their other crimes, how capitoll soever," but because they returned knowing that death awaited them.[51]

The executions ended, and for a while the other punishments ended too, only because of an order from King Charles. But the Quakers kept coming into New England. Massachusetts responded in 1661 with a new statute that censured the "absurd & blasphemous doctrines" of Quakers and provided that, in order to prevent the intrusions of "rogues & vagabonds," any "wandering Quaker" would be stripped to the waist, tied to a cart's tail, whipped through the town until he arrived at the next town, where the punishment would be inflicted again, town after town, until the Quaker was outside of the Bay Colony's jurisdiction. Indigenous Quakers were subject to earlier statutes providing for imprisonment and banishment on pain of death. Numerous Quakers of both sexes were stripped and flogged from town to town. The king intervened no more: though he favored freedom of conscience, he did not favor indulgence for people who opposed government authority. As late as 1676, Massachusetts was still flogging Quakers. In time, the fury on both sides diminished, although Quakers did not enjoy toleration until the charter of 1692 provided liberty of conscience for all Protestants. In England, by that time, Quakers had long been accepted and prospered. In New England, always excepting Rhode Island, other Protestants despised Quakers for decades after they were left alone.[52]

CHAPTER TWELVE

America from 1660 to 1800

AFTER the execution of the four Quakers by Massachusetts, no blasphemy cases of comparable importance occurred in America. During the 1660s, there were eleven prosecutions, all in New England—five in Connecticut, four in Plymouth, and two in Maine. None of the defendants threatened church or state. All received discretionary leniency from their trial courts, although the offense of blasphemy was indisputable in several cases: describing oneself as being as holy as God, calling Christ a "bastard," saying that the devil was as merciful as God, and asking whether God was man or beast. One woman whose guilt was clear could have been hanged. Instead, she was symbolically executed by being taken to the place of execution with a rope about her neck, made to climb the ladder to the gallows, and required to stand in view of spectators so that "all Israill may hear and feare." In a similar capital case, the defendant, who had wished she were in hell so that she could curse God and "break him in peeces," was whipped thirty times and then made to stand on the gallows. She was lucky to escape with her life. In two separate cases, the atheistical blasphemies, so called, of two men whose statements were the product of drunkenness resulted merely in fines. A woman whose blasphemy was compounded by a charge of witchcraft, or "familiarity with Satan," was acquitted on both counts. In another case, the defendant was forced only to acknowledge the evil of his blasphemous statements, after the court determined that they were not such high blasphemy as to warrant his execution. Still another person, a clergyman, was merely corrected for his "horrible blasphemy," though his crime, saying that Christ as God was equal to the Father, hardly sounds blasphemous at all.[1]

In the 1670s, there were only six cases—four in Massachusetts, one in Plymouth, and one in New York. The heaviest punishment in these cases was meted out to Samuel Forman of Oyster Bay, Long Island, convicted for having disrupted church services, abused the word of God, and blasphemed His name. As an example to others, he was severely flogged with rods, fined the costs of prosecution, and banished forever. New Haven imposed a similar sentence on one defendant, but his blasphemy was compounded by other crimes. The case of a Massachusetts surgeon, Phillip Reade, involved a capital blasphemy: the charge was that he had said that the devil could take Christ and prayers. However, on finding that his blasphemy was "not fully proved," the court acquitted him with an admonition and the imposition of costs. A student at Harvard College, for having said something aspersive about the Holy Ghost, was publicly whipped before the student body by the town jailer and suspended. In this period, Plymouth, which had been punishing blasphemy in the absence of a statute ever since 1635, passed its first blasphemy statute, a copy of the Massachusetts act of 1646. New Hampshire enacted its first blasphemy statute in 1679, which also copied the same act.[2]

There were six blasphemy cases in the 1680s, three of them in Massachusetts. In New Hampshire's only case, the defendant was heavily fined for saying that Christ was just a carpenter. For "rash inconsiderate words tending to blasphemy," Maine also fined its malefactor. An Albany, New York, case involved an unspecified "Godless blasphemy" as well as a denial of the virginity of Mary. The defendant was probably whipped and fined. These cases did not involve a capital blasphemy, but two of the Massachusetts cases did. Each revealed judicial discretion. In one, William King, a Quaker, regarded by his neighbors as "crazey in his head" on matters of religion, had claimed to be a person of the Trinity and to have godly attributes. He declared himself to be the eternal Son of God, holy and pure as God Himself and able to walk on water. Although the defendant behaved "like a mad man" in court, his judges probably assumed that, because most Quakers were mad, he was not entitled to much mercy. It sentenced King to twenty lashes and imprisonment at the pleasure of the governor's council. In the other capital case, a Marblehead man declared that Christ was "an imperfect Saviour & a foole." He also denied the existence of God, of heaven and hell, and of the devil. After the jury convicted him, he received a harsh punishment, yet his life was saved. He was sent to the pillory, where he was to have "his toung drawne forth out of his mouth & peirct with a hott iron." He was then imprisoned until he paid court costs. Pennsylvania during this period enacted its blasphemy act, broadly defining the crime as profaning the Bible or any person of the Trinity; but the penalty was merely a 5-shilling fine or five days in jail on bread and water. Other colonies retained the death penalty in their statutes without enforcing it.[3]

In Massachusetts in 1686, Francis Stepney's blasphemy led to a judicial reaffirmation of the discretionary administration of criminal sentencing. A man with a flair for the impractical, Stepney, a dancing master, settled in Boston and opened a dancing school without permission. The town promptly closed it and hauled him into court, where he made some testy remarks against the government, followed by some animadversions about the local religion. One of his comments was that there was more divinity in some theatrical productions than in some of the Old Testament. That earned him a charge of blasphemy, for which he was convicted. The sentence for his blasphemy and his reviling the government was a heavy fine of £100 plus a like amount in sureties for his subsequent good behavior. Outraged, Stepney appealed his sentence to the Court of Assistants, which ruled that, because blasphemy could be punished capitally, a lesser sentence was lawful. The court upheld its discretion in sentencing, in effect justifying decades of its practice of imposing *ad hoc* justice.[4]

In 1694, Connecticut confronted John Rogers in a blasphemy case comparable in importance to the cases of Samuel Gorton and of the Quakers. Rogers was no more a blasphemer than Gorton or the Quakers, whom he resembled in many respects. On fundamental matters, he was a devout Christian and orthodox in theology. His problem was not that he lost his temper and spoke against God. Rather, he reviled tenets, clergymen, and sacraments of the prevailing religion. A nonconformist who insisted that all others conform to his nonconformity, he was that impossible person: a zealous Christian round the clock, seven days a week, who proselytized, condemned, and provoked relentlessly. In 1674, at the age of twenty-two, he underwent a conversion experience and joined the Seventh-Day Baptists, whose strict observance of Saturday as the Sabbath brought them into direct conflict with the Sunday laws of Connecticut and all other colonies. Any activity on the Sabbath deemed by church elders and magistrates as inappropriate could result in prosecution. Fines, brief imprisonment, and whippings were common punishments for such violations. Rogers and the Seventh-Day Baptists were in constant conflict with the authorities on this matter, because Sunday was a working day to them. Rogers did not merely work on Sundays. He railed against those who failed to observe the Saturday Sabbath, and on Sundays tumultuously interrupted the religious services of those whom he regarded as serving the devil. He could not control his obsession to witness his faith.

Within four years of his conversion, Rogers was not only the pastor of his own church but the head of his own sect, a breakaway group that differed with Seventh-Day Baptists on the question of when prayer was justified. Quaker beliefs strongly influenced Rogers, but he differed with them on rebaptizing born-again adults who experienced Christ, on observing Saturdays as Sabbath days, and on observing the Lord's Supper.

He did accept the Quaker doctrine of the indwelling Christ, which eventually was the pretext for charging him with blasphemy. But the charge was provoked by more than a theological point.

Rogers was truly subversive of church and state. He opposed the established church and any church supported by secular authority and taxation. He unsparingly denounced not just Sunday laws but also a professional clergy and ordination, infant baptism, the swearing of oaths, and service in secular positions. He favored complete separation of church and state in order to protect religion from the state. For persistent violation of Sunday laws and baptizing adults, he was regularly fined £5 monthly—a pittance to him, because his father was one of the wealthiest men in the colony. He used the imagery of Revelations against the Congregationalists in much the same way they used it against the Roman Catholic church. The man reveled in epithetical theology. To him, the Congregationalists represented the Antichrist, the church of Satan, the idolaters. He spent frequent periods in jail for disrupting church services. In 1685, he and his followers, who were called "Rogerenes" or "Rogerene Quakers," invaded the New London Congregational Church during Sunday service and behaved "as if possessed with a diabolical spirit, so affrighting and amazing that several women swooned and fainted away." Rogers was flogged on that occasion.[5]

In 1691, Gurdon Saltonstall became the minister of the New London church and suffered persistent harassment from Rogers. In 1694, Rogers pushed a wheelbarrow full of shoes into the church during Sunday services and in front of the pulpit tried to sell the shoes. Imprisoned, he hung a proclamation out of his window reviling Saltonstall's church. The minister charged him with blasphemy as well as disturbing the service. The blasphemy count was founded on a reply Rogers had made to Saltonstall's question whether Rogers believed, as he said, that his body was the body of Christ. Rogers replied: "Yes, I do affirm that this human body is Christ's body; for Christ has purchased it with His precious blood, and I am not my own, for I am bought with a price."[6]

Rogers was removed to the jail in Hartford to stand trial. Upon conviction, he was fined £5 and sentenced to symbolic execution on the gallows. Refusing on grounds of conscience to pay the fine, Rogers was returned to prison. Connecticut had had all of him that it could stand. One cold day in 1695, because of his contumaciousness, he was taken from prison, tied to a cannon, and flogged seventy-six times with a whip that had knots at its end as large as walnuts. He was then thrown in his cell without bed or bedding, not even straw, and chained to the wall.[7]

On that occasion, he was kept in prison three and a half years. Altogether, during the forty-seven years he lived after his 1674 conversion, he spent about eighteen years locked up. As he aged, he lost none of his irascibility, militancy, or conscientiousness. Rogers, who thought of himself as a Christian like the Christians of the primitive church, was both a persecutor and a victim. His violations of peaceable religious services would earn him prison time today, but he was also a victim of the law of blasphemy. It was used against him not because he cursed God or reproached Christ or denied scriptural truths, but because it was a pejorative way of condemning his beliefs and a pretext for revenge. The Rogerenes, a tiny sect, lasted until World War One.[8]

In 1696, Massachusetts tried its last Quaker for blasphemy. He was Thomas Maule, a Salem merchant who published a book entitled *Truth Set Forth*, which described Massachusetts's persecution of Quakers and Salem's witchcraft trials. A grand jury indicted him for slandering church and state, but he exploited Salem's guilty feelings about the witchcraft excesses and appealed over his judges' heads to the trial jury. He cleverly rested his case on technical errors of the prosecution as well as freedom of conscience. One of his three judges informed the jury that Maule should be convicted for his blasphemies, but the jury acquitted.[9]

The next accusation of blasphemy was against John Coode of Maryland, a Protestant planter who had led a rebellion against the Catholic proprietary authorities in 1689. The rebellion led to Maryland's becoming a royal colony with the Church of England as its established church. In 1696, the governor charged Coode with blasphemy against the Trinity. He had called religion lies and a sham, denied that Jesus ever existed, and doubted God's ability to generate a son. That, as the governor said, was blasphemy "in the highest degree." Coode escaped trial by fleeing to Virginia. Maryland asked that colony to seize and return him. After a couple of years in hiding, Coode made an abject apology and received a Maryland pardon. Once again, mercy won, rather than the letter of the law. Coode was the last blasphemer of the century.[10]

In the eighteenth century, the number of prosecutions sharply diminished. Prosecutions were so sporadic and isolated as to show no patterns; it remains an enigma why they occurred at all. A blasphemy case in Connecticut in 1701, with the most substantial manuscript record of all colonial cases, ended in an acquittal. The defendant should never have been charged with blasphemy; he had cursed a neighbor. When New Hampshire modified its blasphemy law in 1702, it provided for punishments far short of death: six months in prison, boring through the tongue with a hot iron, the pillory, or whipping, at the discretion of the court. In a blasphemy act of 1703, South Carolina made the punishment for the offense on the first occasion merely disability from holding any public position, on the second offense disability from having access to the courts, and on the third offense imprisonment for three years. South Carolina defined the crime as defaming any person of the Trinity, denying the truths of Christianity, or denying the divine authority of the Bible.[11]

In the same year, 1703, Lord Cornbury (Edward Hyde), the governor of New York, ordered the prosecution of John Tallman, a justice of the Queens County court. Cornbury was attempting to force recognition of the Church of England as the established church, and Tallman was in his way. Although Tallman was bailed on payment of £100 until his trial at the next session of the Supreme Court, no further record of his case exists. He was probably never tried, and Cornbury's efforts failed.[12]

Delaware's first blasphemy case, which occurred in 1705, ended in an acquittal. The indictment against Gabriel Jones, a laborer, claimed that he had said in a loud voice, "Cursed be My God for Suffering me to live to be so old to be abused." A jury found the testimony of his accusers to be unconvincing. In 1710 occurred a Maryland case that resulted in the severest punishment meted out for blasphemy in the colonies. Charles Arabella, the master of a sloop at dock in Maryland, had the misfortune of spilling some scalding pitch on his foot. In sudden pain, he uttered (unknown) words for which he was convicted of blasphemy. In accord with a Maryland statute he had his tongue bored through with a hot iron, was fined £20, and was sentenced to six months' imprisonment. Unable to pay, he was kept in prison over a year. The Privy Council, on a petition to Queen Anne, ordered his release. The Maryland statute that governed his case derived from the Act of Toleration of 1649, which included provisions against blasphemy. Those provisions were re-enacted in 1694 without reference to the saints or the Virgin, and then re-enacted periodically without alteration. The penalty for a second offense was a £40 fine, boring through the tongue, and one year in prison; for the third offense, the penalty was death.[13]

Maine's first eighteenth-century case consisted of a charge of blasphemy that ended in a conviction of profanity—swearing—and a fine of 10 shillings. New Hampshire, which had no more blasphemy cases, modified its law in 1717, reducing the punishment for the offense to imprisonment of not more than six months, the pillory, whipping, boring through the tongue with a "red hot iron," or symbolic execution on the gallows, at the discretion of the court. North Carolina's sole case occurred in 1721, when John Hassell, a debtor, was convicted for saying that he was not beholden to God for anything, because he had had to work for everything he had. He was merely fined £5. But shortly after, when he said something profane and scandalous, he was severely whipped and held in prison until he posted sureties for good behavior in the amount of £50.[14]

In a 1757 Massachusetts case, a farmer was found guilty of blasphemy for having said, "God was a damned fool for ever making a Woman." He stood on the gallows with a rope about his neck for one hour, and then was whipped twenty-five strokes. The last case in Massachusetts occurred in 1770; its defendant escaped from the colony.[15] That the jurisdiction with the greatest number of, and most important, cases in America concluded its prosecution of blasphemy with a case that fizzled out seems symbolic of the history of the offense in the eighteenth century.

Connecticut, the only rival of Massachusetts as a blasphemy-conscious jurisdiction, prosecuted John Green of Norwalk because he shouted, "Damn the being who made me such a miserable creature. . . . Damn God to hell." The words were uttered when Green was drunk. Witnesses described him as a raving madman when in a whiskey frenzy. Green was convicted, and pleaded with the Superior Court judges not to sentence him to death. Before sentence could be passed, a merciful legislature found mitigating circumstances in his case and instructed the court to fine and pillory him. The last case in Connecticut involved a Thomas Baldwin, whose words are unknown; upon conviction, he underwent symbolic execution on the gallows and then suffered ten lash strokes.[16]

In Virginia, which prosecuted no one for blasphemy in the eighteenth century, a newspaper reported in 1769 that, before Parliament adjourned, a bill would be brought in to disqualify from a seat "all Gentlemen who behave unkindly to their wives, every man who keeps a whore, every man who speaks or writes blasphemy and every man who is not willing and able to pay his debts." That gave the topic of blasphemy its appropriate due for the times. And yet colonial legislatures periodically enacted and revised blasphemy statutes as if dealing with a crime that occurred with regularity. In 1782, for example, Massachusetts re-enacted its blasphemy statute, omitting the punishment of boring through the tongue and reducing the penalty to imprisonment for not more than a year, the pillory, whipping, or sitting on the gallows with a rope about the neck, the sentence in each case to be decided by the discretion of the court. In 1784, Connecticut reduced its penalty from death to severe whipping and the pillory. That left the independent state of Vermont with the only statute that still imposed death as the punishment for blasphemy on the first offense. But Vermont soon made the penalty forty lashes and pillorying, and by the close of the century reduced that to a fine of not more than $200. New Jersey had a similar statute, which defined the crime as denying, cursing, or reproaching any person of the Trinity, Christianity, or the Bible.[17]

Independence and statehood meant that the former colonies, except Rhode Island and Connecticut, adopted their first written constitutions. All guaranteed religious freedom, although as of 1791, when the Bill of Rights was ratified as part of the United States Constitution, seven of fourteen states then in the Union had or permitted laws establishing religion. All seven had plural or multiple establishments—the only sort that existed in the United States at the time. Not a single state favored one sect or denomination over others as a matter of law. In all seven, the establishments were nonpreferential, in the sense that no church was preferred by law. Public taxes could be used to support religion, but each person's taxes, for the most part, were supposed to go to the church of his choice. In actuality, where Congregationalists dominated because of numbers, they rigged the system to benefit their own churches, although even in Massachusetts there were towns where Baptists, Quakers, and Unitarians benefited from public taxes.[18] On the other hand, even the 1780 constitution of Massachusetts specified that "no subordination of any one sect or denomination to another shall ever be established by law." Presumably, the laws of blasphemy could not operate in a way that favored a particular religion. In Europe, all establishments of religion favored one church above others. Nowhere in Europe did an establishment of religion comprehend all Christian churches. In America, the establishments that existed included either all Protestant churches in states where Roman Catholics did not exist, or all Christian churches.

Pennsylvania's constitution of 1790 guaranteed religious liberty, banned public support of any place of worship, and declared "that no preference shall ever be given by law, to any religious establishments or modes of worship." That could have been construed to mean that blasphemy laws were unconstitutional as violations of religious liberty or the ban against preference. A blasphemy law protects and favors Christianity over other religions. Pennsylvania, founded by Quakers, had never had an establishment of religion of any kind, or a prosecution for blasphemy—until 1799. In that year, the aberration occurred in a Dauphin County court. A tobacconist was indicted for blasphemy because of his shocking remarks, made in "High Dutch," about Christ and the unlikelihood of Christ's having been the Son of God. The report expunges the actual words. At first, the individual pleaded not guilty, but he switched his plea and submitted to the court. He received a moderate fine and a sentence of three months in jail.[19] This case in a trial court, leaving no judicial record, closed the eighteenth century yet heralded the nineteenth, which would witness a resurgence in the law of blasphemy.

In the eighteenth century, however, blasphemy all but disappeared as an offense that was actually prosecuted. The law governing the offense remained clear, like a warning. Everywhere but in Rhode Island, there were statutes against blasphemy. They were reinforced by the vade mecums or printed handbooks of the local magistrates. A 1722 Philadelphia guide for justices of the peace contained a formulation on the law of blasphemy that was common in the colonies. That formulation derived verbatim from a Virginia statute of 1699 on blasphemy. Blasphemous words were condemned not only as an offense to God and religion but as a crime against the laws of the local government and of the kingdom. Any person raised as a Christian who by any words denied any of the persons of the Trinity, or asserted that there was more than one God, or denied the truth of Christianity or the divine authority of the Bible was guilty of the crime. On the first offense, he was to be disabled from holding any public office; on the second offense, he would be banned from use of the courts and would face three years' imprisonment. Throughout the colonies, this formulation was uniform in the magistrates' manuals. In 1764, a manual printed in Woodbridge, New Jersey, reprinted the same definition of blasphemy and provided the same penalty but added that denying God's being or providence, reproaching Christ, profanely scoffing at the Bible, or exposing any part of it to contempt or ridicule constituted a blasphemous crime to be punished as the court deemed appropriate, "according to the heinousness of the crime." Thereafter, both the Philadelphia and the Woodbridge formulations appeared in manuals published everywhere in America.[20]

In 1700, Maryland had passed an act for repealing laws "which time and experience have rendered useless and not agreeable to the present constitution to the State of Affaires as they are now Settled."[21] Why were blasphemy laws not so regarded? Why were they repeatedly enacted in Maryland and elsewhere? Why did manuals for justices of the peace instruct magistrates to institute prosecutions of blasphemers? Why, indeed, was the number of prosecutions so very low during the century?

Not because Americans were astoundingly law-abiding and religiously observant. As a matter of fact, they were not. A very large majority of Americans were not church members; only a minority were even churchgoers. The author of *Religion in Colonial America* wrote that the largest proportion of unchurched people in Christendom lived in America. At the time of the American Revolution, perhaps only 4 percent of the population of the country belonged to churches.[22] Because many people were irreligious or indifferent to religion, we might assume that their language would be blasphemous—surely more so than the language of the devout. Accordingly, we might expect a large number of prosecutions for blasphemy. But it would be wrong to assume that the unchurched were irreligious: frontiersmen did not have access to churches or even to ministers, yet many of them were evangelicals or pietists. Still, religious indifference as well as an extraordinary multiplicity of sects promoted religious freedom, which in turn reduced the provocation felt by criticism of religious beliefs.

America in the eighteenth century became increasingly more tolerant of aberrant beliefs once thought to be offensive and actionable. "Indifference" is, indeed, perhaps more accurate than "tolerant." Religious liberalism came to dominate American thinking. It took various forms—Christian rationalism, natural rather than revealed religion or religion that conformed with reason and science, Unitarianism or some other form of anti-Trinitarianism, and deism—but all tended toward indulgence of language revealing beliefs that might have shocked evangelicals.

Until the 1780s, only intellectuals and the well-to-do in larger towns or on big plantations repudiated divine revelation, biblical inerrancy, miracles, the doctrine of the Trinity, virgin birth, and the divinity of Jesus. The repudiation, however, was expressed privately; in public, they tended to evince no more than skepticism. Almost half the signers of the Declaration of Independence were skeptics who believed in natural religion. Although conservative clergymen complained in every generation about the decline of religion, a change was occurring. In 1783, Ezra Stiles, the president of Yale and a devout Christian but a tolerant one, explained that change. Regretting the opposition to liberal establishments of religion, he observed that "it begins to be a growing idea that it is mighty indifferent, forsooth, not only whether a man be of this or the other religious sect, but whether he be of any religion at all; and that truly deists, and men of indifferentism to all religion, are the most suitable persons for civil office."[23]

Nothing better signified the change than the fact that Massachusetts, once the center of intolerance, became most indulgent of religious liberalism. Nowhere else did so many reject Jesus Christ as God. Harvard College and Boston brimmed with skeptics, anti-Trinitarians, and the deistically inclined. Leading Congregational clergymen, including Ebenezar Gay of Hingham, who headed his church for nearly seventy years; Charles Chauncy, for sixty years the minister of the First Church of Boston; and another brilliant Boston clergyman, Jonathan Mayhew, repudiated the doctrine of the Trinity and championed individual judgment. More extraordinary still, James Freeman, who became head of King's Chapel, the oldest Episcopalian church in New England, converted his congregation to Unitarianism in 1784. In Salem, where William Bentley preached Jeffersonianism as well as Unitarianism, twenty of the twenty-four most important families were members of his church.[24]

Foreign radicals were attracted by the intellectual freedom of America. Joseph Priestley, the English Unitarian philosopher, was driven from his country and sought refuge in the United States in 1794. He lived his last ten years as an honored celebrity whose lectures in Philadelphia drew many congressmen and officers of the executive branch of the United States government. Comte de Volney, whose anti-Christian history was enormously popular in America, lived there for two years in the 1790s. Tom Paine returned in 1802. America was the freest nation by far, and irreverence flourished where liberty did.[25]

In his autobiography, John Trumbull, the artist, reported being at a "freethinking dinner party" in 1793 at the home of Thomas Jefferson. Senator William Branch Giles of Virginia ridiculed Jesus, much to Trumbull's consternation, while Jefferson smiled and nodded approval. Finally, David Franks, a bank official, took up the argument on Trumbull's side. Trumbull turned to Jefferson and said, "Sir, this is a strange situation in which I find myself; in a country professing Christianity, and at a table with Christians, as I supposed, I find my religion and myself attacked with severe and irresistible wit and railery, and not a person to aid in my defense, but my friend Mr. Franks, who is himself a Jew." Giles returned to the attack with "new virulence," ending up with a rejection of God. Similarly, William Dunlap, the playwright who praised Elihu Palmer's deistic orations, recorded in his diary in 1797 that, at a meeting of his club attended by various luminaries, James Kent, the future chancellor of New York, "remark'd that men of information were now nearly as free from vulgar superstitions or the Christian religion as they were in the time of Cicero from the pagan superstition."[26]

Intellectuals and well-to-do skeptics, even if privately deistic, supported Christianity rather than see deistic beliefs spread among the common people. Religion was a hedge against radicalism and a bulwark of law, order, and stability. Kent would write an opinion in 1811 adopting the common law of blasphemy for New York. When Ethan Allen published his *Reason, the Only Oracle of Man* in 1784—the first deistic anti-Christian book by an American aimed at converting ordinary Americans—prosperous merchants, professionals, and large planters withheld support. They strongly opposed the even more militantly irreligious books of Tom Paine and Elihu Palmer at the turn of the century. *The Age of Reason* was immensely popular and, according to conservative clergymen, "unchristianized" nominal believers by the thousands. *The Temple of Reason*, a deist weekly, doubtless exaggerated when it declared in 1802 that there were more deists in the country than Christians.[27]

Paine, Palmer, and other anti-Christian deists probably would have had far less influence if the evangelicals had not addressed so many denunciatory sermons and tracts against them. But they could not succeed in driving out Christianity without the support of the prosperous and influential. Palmer did all he could to spread deism as a religion among ordinary people. He organized deist societies, delivered popular lectures, founded and edited deist journals, and wrote the deist book *Principles of Nature* (1802), which ranked in importance next to Paine's *Age of Reason* as a systematic and influential exposition of deism. The tone of Palmer's work is indicated by his description of "the pretended Saviour" of Christianity as an "imposter" and "an illegitimate Jew" whose offer of salvation rested "on no better foundation than that of fornication or adultery." Palmer castigated the Bible with similar vehemence. Although he was a target of hatred from evangelicals, Palmer never was threatened with prosecution. Neither he, nor other deist spokesmen, nor Volney, nor Paine himself, worried about laws against blasphemy. They were completely free in their expression, and the law ignored them. In England, meanwhile, those who published or sold Palmer's book were prosecuted for blasphemy.[28]

The reason that Palmer and the deists were as free as evangelists might be discerned in a letter of 1759 by Ezra Stiles. Disagreeing with his predecessor at Yale, who rejected a gift of deistic books, Stiles wrote: "Deism has got such Head in this Age of Licentious Liberty, that it would be in vain to try to stop it by hiding the Deistical Writings: and the only Way left to conquer & demolish it, is to come forth into the open Field & Dispute this matter on even Footing." In short, prosecution in Enlightenment America seemed unthinkable, probably because, like censorship, it was ineffective.[29] And yet, if that were true and Americans understood it, there would have been no further prosecutions. But there were. Freedom of expression explains little. America in the nineteenth century was equally free, yet politically conservative jurists who were religious liberals—James Kent and Lemuel Shaw—endorsed the common-law principle that Christianity is part of the law of the land, and they sustained the constitutionality of blasphemy laws despite explicit state-constitutional guarantees of nonpreference and religious liberty. The fact is that the reason for particular blasphemy prosecutions is usually inexplicable, as is the reason there were so few. The records mystify.[30]

CHAPTER THIRTEEN

England's Augustan Age
of Toleration

T HE FIRST dissenting minister in Great Britain courageous enough
to describe himself publicly as a Unitarian was Thomas Emlyn,
who mustered his candor when confronting a charge of blasphemy. Emlyn had abandoned Emmanuel College, Cambridge, to finish his education for the pulpit in a Presbyterian academy. While ministering to a
Presbyterian congregation in Suffolk, he fell under the influence of a
Socinian. Not rationalistic enough to accept the Socinian conviction that
Jesus had no previous existence before Mary bore him, Emlyn nevertheless began to lose his faith in the doctrine of the Trinity. He kept his
doubts to himself when, in 1691, he agreed to officiate at a Presbyterian
church in Dublin whose members were orthodox.[1] Presbyterians at the
time tended to be Trinitarian and intolerant. In 1697, after the licensing
system had died, they petitioned King William to restrain "the licentiousness of the press, in relation to the Unitarian books."[2] In that same
year, Emlyn privately wrote that he was thinking of openly declaring his
anti-Trinitarianism and breaking with his congregation, but he kept silent. In 1702, an influential member of his church noticed that he never
referred to the doctrine of the Trinity or to Christ as God. Questioned
about his silence, Emlyn finally confessed his belief that "the God and
Father of Jesus Christ is alone the Supreme Being," and he offered his
resignation.[3] The matter might have ended there, but it soon became a
public scandal.

A presbytery of Dublin's dissenting ministers, fearful that Emlyn
might dissemble in another post, deposed him.[4] He responded with a
pamphlet giving his side of "the Case of Mr. E——."[5] The theological
question, as Emlyn defined it, was whether "God and the Man Christ
Jesus should be one and the same person?" To believe the affirmative, he
argued, conflicted with the Gospels, because Jesus himself had distinguished himself "from God his Father whom he thought greater than

himself." The Dublin ministers replied in print that a refusal to assent to "the Supreme Deity of Jesus Christ, is such a crime that no one suspected thereof . . . is to be allowed to preach, or so much as to be tolerated among them."[6] Emlyn, unable to restrain himself, at last published his Unitarianism; he replied in a major tract, *An Humble Inquiry Into the Scriptural Account of Jesus Christ* (1702), a sustained argument against the doctrine of the Trinity. Emlyn relied wholly on scriptural evidence to prove that Jesus could not be God or equal to God.[7] Jesus had spoken of a God other than himself and conceded that he lacked God's omnipotence and omniscience. Emlyn believed that Jesus was not more than a man who possessed a divine commission and exercised miraculous power derived from God. Contending that Jesus deserved worship not as God, and not as one sharing God's essence, but as an intercessor, Emlyn saw "no reason . . . to oppose Unitarians, who think him to be a sufficient Saviour and Prince, though he be not the only supreme God."[8] That statement, though made in the context of a pedant's scriptural argument, proved to be blasphemous.

On a complaint against Emlyn by two zealous dissenters, the lord chief justice of Ireland, Sir Richard Pine, issued a warrant to seize Emlyn and all copies of his book. In 1703, a grand jury, which included a deacon of the congregation that Emlyn had served for eleven years, indicted him for having been "moved by the instigation of the devil" to publish blasphemous libels against Christ.[9] Emlyn's trial was a farce. The established church and the government, as well as dissenting churches, united in the prosecutions. Several lawyers whom Emlyn sought to retain turned him down, and one, Sir Richard Levins, later the lord chief justice of the Court of Common Pleas, candidly warned Emlyn that he would be "run . . . down like a wolf, without law or game," and without a chance to defend himself. At least half a dozen Anglican bishops attended the trial, and the two leading ones—William King, the archbishop of Dublin, and Hugh Boulter, the archbishop of Armagh, who was the primate of Ireland—took the bench with Chief Justice Pine.[10] The prosecution, having failed to prove that Emlyn wrote the blasphemous book, fell back on the argument that strong presumption was as good as evidence; the court permitted that argument and even repeated it to the jury as law. Although Emlyn had in fact written the book, finding a verdict against the defendant without proof was unjust.

The chief justice also allowed the prosecution to assume that the book was blasphemous, even though it contained nothing scornful, reproachful, or contemptuous. In Taylor's case in 1676, when Chief Justice Matthew Hale had originated the rule that blasphemy was a crime punishable at common law, the defendant had publicly declared that "Christ is a whore-master, and religion is a cheat."[11] Emlyn's was the voice of sweet reason by comparison; in fact, he had said nothing more shocking than had some eminent churchmen in England, including Bishop Gilbert Burnet and Archbishop John Tillotson. Emlyn's incompetent counsel failed to produce evidence rebutting the blasphemy charge, and when Emlyn tried to speak on his own behalf, the court silenced him; Pine did not even allow him to say anything at the conclusion of his trial. In a prejudicial charge to the jury, Pine menacingly told the jurors that, if they acquitted, "my Lords the Bishops were there."[12] The jury found Emlyn guilty, and the chief justice sentenced him to serve one year in prison, pay an exorbitant fine of £1,000, and remain in prison until the fine was paid. Pine informed Emlyn that his sentence was merciful, because in Spain he would have been burned at the stake.[13] Indeed, only six years before Emlyn's trial, in 1697, Scotland had hanged Thomas Aikenhead for making some innocuous remarks.[14]

After Emlyn had served a little over two years in prison, his fine was reduced to £70, which he paid. On his release, he returned to England, where he eked out a living fearlessly publishing Unitarian tracts. Although all of them were reverential, he risked the law's vengeance, because the Blasphemy Act of 1698 subjected Unitarian beliefs to prosecution. The statute was not enforced, however, because of London's permissiveness and the extraordinary latitudinarianism within the English church. Emlyn himself won the friendship of such distinguished latitudinarians as Samuel Clarke and William Whiston.[15] Bishop Benjamin Hoadly sarcastically summed up Emlyn's case when he wrote in 1715, "I must do the Dissenting Protestants the justice that they have shown themselves on occasion, very ready to assist us in so pious and Christian a work, as bringing Heretics to their right mind." Hoadly added, "The Non-conformists accused him, and the Conformists condemned him, the Secular power was called in, and the cause ended in an imprisonment and a very great fine; two methods of conviction about which the Gospel is silent."[16] In 1719, when the Irish Parliament passed a Toleration Act, one clause, inserted at the instigation of the dissenters, excluded from the benefits of the statute all persons who by preaching or writing denied the doctrine of the Trinity.[17]

Dublin was provincial compared with London, but both had their limits, and John Asgill passed the limits of both. In 1703, the year when the crown prosecuted Emlyn in Dublin, the Irish House of Commons expelled Asgill from its membership and ordered the public hangman to burn his book. That book of 1700 bore a strange title: *An Argument Proving, That according to the Covenant of Eternal Life revealed in the Scriptures, Man may be translated from hence into that Eternal Life, without passing through Death, altho the Humane Nature of Christ himself could not be thus translated until he had passed through Death*. Asgill—who, after the book, was derisively called "The Translated"—had experienced a revelation after reading the Gospels, especially the passage in John 11:25–26: "I am the resurrection, and the life; he that believeth in me, though he were dead, yet shall he live; and whosoever liveth and believeth in me shall never die." Taking that literally, Asgill argued that a believing Christian could conquer death, and be "translated" directly to eternal life through Christ. Adam, he claimed, had brought death upon himself and his descendants by his sin, but Christ's death, which was as miraculous as his birth, overcame the law of death as if by satisfying a debt. Moreover, by his resurrection the "Law of Death is taken away." Asgill stated his thesis concisely in his conclusion: "we are not only ransomed from that Law under which we fell in Adam, but are delivered over into . . . that absolute and indefeasible Estate of Eternal Life, in which Christ was installed by his Resurrection."[18] Asgill's book was bizarre and eccentric and, to the Irish House of Commons, blasphemous.[19]

After his expulsion from that august body, Asgill, a London lawyer, returned to England, stood for Parliament, and won election. Although his book and Irish experience were notorious, he served uncontroversially as an M.P. until late 1706, when his imprisonment for a debt inexplicably triggered an investigation of his 1700 book by the English House of Commons.

The supposition that the book reflected on Christianity rested on various passages yanked out of context. For example, after his quotation of John 11:25–26, Asgill had written that, if Christ's words were "words only, then was he an imposter and the doctrine false."[20] A House committee turned that into an allegation that Christ was an impostor who preached false doctrine, although Asgill had built his entire thesis on the reverent belief that Christ canceled man's need to die. The committee compiled a ten-point list of offenses, the last of which consisted of Asgill's remark that, if he should die like other men instead of exiting by translation, "I declare myself to die of no religion."[21] He made an elaborate defense against each accusation, expressing resentment that he should have been charged with blasphemy, a crime "higher than High Treason," and insisting that he had written the book "under a firm Belief of the Truth of the Scriptures."[22] Asgill did not rely on freedom of religion or on liberty of the press as a justification for his expressions; he simply insisted that the Scriptures warranted his beliefs. Nevertheless, the House formally resolved to adopt its committee's report finding the book to be a blasphemous traduction of the Christian religion. The hangman received orders to burn the book, and Asgill was expelled, probably the only man to have been expelled from both the Irish and English Houses of Commons.[23] But he was not criminally prosecuted, an indication that church and state were fairly complacent about their safety and therefore did not regard his crime as "heinous." Asgill "translated" in his seventy-ninth year.

The blasphemy of Dr. William Coward in 1704 was not heinous either. His tract, *Second Thoughts concerning Human Soul*, sought to prove that the soul was a "heathenish Invention" that conflicted with reason and religion, and he assailed prelates for exploiting the concept of a soul. According to a resolution of the House of Commons, his views clearly conflicted with "the doctrine of the church of England" and contributed "to the Subversion of the Christian Religion." Called to the bar of the House for explanation, a contrite Coward denied that he meant to subvert Christianity or blaspheme it; he eagerly expressed a willingness to recant. The House generously allowed him to escape prosecution and punishment, other than having to watch the public burning of his blasphemous works.[24]

The prosecutions of Emlyn, Asgill, and Coward in the early eighteenth century, when viewed from the perspective of the entire century, seem atavistic or, at the least, like extensions of the seventeenth century. Book burnings, however, were as typical of the eighteenth century in character as of the seventeenth. But a proceeding against an author's writings instead of against the author represents a leap in toleration. A century before the Emlyn case, England burned both people and their books. The Toleration Acts of both England and Ireland kept the practice of book burning alive by excluding anti-Trinitarians from their protection; denying the Trinity, the classic expression of blasphemy, remained blasphemous, which is why Emlyn could be imprisoned for his religious convictions. His imprisonment, however, was less significant than the fact that on his release he fearlessly and freely published his Unitarian books and tracts in Dublin and London.

It is of enduring importance that, throughout the remainder of the eighteenth century, Ireland did not convict and imprison another anti-Trinitarian, and the efforts to prosecute were few and weak. In 1713, the clergy of the established church, acting in convocation, recommended prosecution of a prominent Whig member of the Irish House of Commons for remarks they considered to be "an indictable profanation of the Holy Scriptures," but neither the Commons, the Lords, nor the courts took notice, and nothing further happened. In 1726, Ireland tried two men for having blasphemed by drinking a toast to the devil and "Confusion to Almighty God," but the jury acquitted, because of the lack of a reliable witness. In 1756, an Irish bishop, in the midst of a tract pleading for greater toleration, examined the doctrine of the Trinity, found it scripturally wanting, and recommended that the Irish House of Lords should omit the Nicene and Athanasian Creeds from the liturgy of the Church of Ireland (Episcopal). Devout Trinitarian bishops sought a prosecution for blasphemy, but the death of the offending bishop ended the proceeding—and ended blasphemy cases in Ireland in the eighteenth century.[25]

There were a few English cases, some important. But the law remained pretty much an empty threat, a means of displacing the resentment of righteous orthodoxy and a warning that the law served Christianity. Believers might take satisfaction in knowing that. What mattered most, however, was that a new age of toleration had begun.

Although the idea of toleration had developed with harrowing slowness, government sponsorship of toleration became a swift success. Religious dissensions of nearly two centuries, accompanied by wars and revolutions, had created a yearning for peace. We do not know whether the persecutions of the Stuart Restoration (1660–88) sickened Anglicans, but sustaining the hatreds and righteousness that must fuel persecution— the imprisonment of tens of thousands of dissenters and the deaths in prison of over five thousand—had to be exhausting and, maybe, repelling. In any case, the Toleration Act, which brought relief and tranquillity, was enormously popular. Toleration even brought a rapid cooling in evangelical ardors, because dissenters no longer felt compelled by conscience to give witness to their faiths by nonconformism that invited criminal penalties. Even Quakers—especially Quakers—shed their aggressive and obnoxious conduct. Toleration proved the wisdom of the sly principle that the best way to cope with heretics is to indulge and ignore them. Toleration allowed Protestants to become reconciled with one another; it had a healing character. The fact that it was also good for business, as William Penn had predicted, helped considerably. Religious peace and economic prosperity made an unbeatable combination, and the popularity of toleration and of the politicians who supported it benefited as a result.

In 1728, Archbishop William Wake, the primate of England, expressed a new dilemma when he wrote: "This is our misfortune; we are so afraid of the least tendency to persecution, that we cannot bear the least restraint. It is a sad case that we cannot keep in the middle way, and allow what is fit to be published . . . but at the same time both restrain and punish what is openly blasphemous and tends to the ruin of all religion."[26] Wake had defined the dilemma not only of his age but of his century and of a free society in any age: must verbal outrages, even on the most sacred matters, be ignored by the law as the price for maintaining liberty, or can the religious sensibilities of the great majority be avenged by suppression of the offenses without significant damage to freedom of conscience?

That Wake, a good Whig, could express the dilemma indicates how triumphant had become the policy of toleration, which had been inaugurated so begrudgingly in 1689—begrudgingly because the Toleration Act had merely abrogated criminal penalties on Protestant dissenters who complied with its terms, and although it indulged their open worship, it did not abrogate universal taxation for the benefit of the established church, and it did not suspend the Test Acts. In order to prevent the possibility of government measures against the establishment, those acts monopolized political offices for persons who received the sacraments according to Anglican rites.

Despite the narrowness of the Toleration Act, Tory clergymen who opposed the revolution fanatically opposed the policy of toleration. About four hundred of them, having refused to swear allegiance to William and Mary, suffered deprivation of their livings. Compliant divines who praised the settlement of 1689 received their offices. As Whigs gained preferment within the Church of England, the church became increasingly liberal or "latitudinarian." Tories in the church who conformed by subscribing to the settlement of 1689 tended to sympathize with the political and ecclesiastical views of the nonjurors. The word "Tory" came to connote intolerance and the High Church party. Tory clergymen who subscribed to the oath of fealty to King William despised the Toleration Act, which they believed responsible for having alienated the nonjurors and having divided the church. They would have restricted the Toleration Act to utter irreconcilables among the Protestant dissenters, in the hope that most of the others could be coerced into conformity with Anglicanism. Church politics became as intense, bitter, and divisive as parliamentary politics. Anglican Tories were High Church men, who longed for the divine right of kings and believed in the equality of church and state. They regarded the established church as the only true church, whose doctrines and rites led to salvation. The Low Church, or latitudinarian party within the church, seemed subversive to them, and the Whig bishops the foremost menace. High Church men preached obedience to the Blasphemy Act of 1698 and would extirpate heresies within the church as well as blasphemers.

Edmund Gibson, the Whig bishop of London, declared in 1733 that the "distinguishing characters of a whig" were the settled principles of "maintaining the Protestant succession, the church establishment, and the Toleration."[27] Whigs and Low Church men, who became indistinguishable, were Erastians: they believed in the subordination of the church to the state, and since they were latitudinarians, their religious dogmas were not too stiff. The Whigs reached supremacy in politics and within the church, buoyed by the enthusiastic support of dissenters, who grew rich and numerous. Whigs believed in the oath of allegiance, but otherwise rejected the Tory principles of coercion and conformity. Prosecution for divergent religious opinion or practice struck Whigs as akin to persecution. They even preferred to indulge Roman Catholics as well as the most deviant Protestants, including the various anti-Trinitarians— Sabellians, Arians, Socinians, and Unitarians. Latitudinarian Low Church men indulged even deists and atheists, who were rarely distinguished. If England really had any atheists, they were not publicly trumpeting their arguments against God; no atheistical tracts appeared. The term "atheist" was little more than a dirty word to stigmatize freethinkers among deists and even among latitudinarians.[28] Deists did exist, but they possessed almost no significance religiously; they did not constitute a sect or a church or even an organization. As believers in God, deists repudiated atheism. Indeed, some deists professed themselves to be Christians, and most—surely the noted ones—were members of the Church of England. So were the anti-Trinitarians of various kinds.

All deists were anti-Trinitarians, but few deists and anti-Trinitarians existed. The writings of about a score of intellectuals created a heavy tempest that frightened the wits of the orthodox, who thought of all deists and anti-Trinitarians as blasphemers. Every radical or freethinking tract that speculated about theological matters and criticized Christianity confronted dozens and dozens of tracts by defenders of Christianity, both Anglicans and dissenters. Arians, Socinians, and other anti-Trinitarians also squabbled with one another in print on fine distinctions. Unitarianism or anti-Trinitarianism—the two were the same—preceded Nicene Christianity and once represented a conventional or orthodox view that became the most common form of blasphemy from the late fourth century and after. For that reason, anti-Trinitarianism requires further explanation.

Orthodoxy came to depend on fine distinctions that made all the difference to an understanding of Christianity. Christians sought to comprehend the persons in the Trinity. The Bible offered no assistance, because the doctrine of the Trinity had no scriptural basis other than the mere reference, in the final verse of Matthew, to baptism in the name of the Father, the Son, and the Holy Spirit. Christians understood Christ to be divine in some way but disagreed intensely on the nature of his divinity and on the question whether Christ was God Himself in some form. They worshipped God *and* Jesus Christ and tried to reconcile their belief in one God with the worship of two and the belief that the Holy Spirit also shared God's essence.

Anti-Trinitarians, especially Arians, believed that God the Father in effect adopted Jesus—that is, that Jesus was not God Himself but was subordinate to Him. Their belief derived from scriptural authority and from an effort to retain the unity of God without sacrificing the divinity of Christ; they sought to reconcile that divinity with the fact that Jesus, having lived and died, was a creature of the Creator; and, they believed, no creature should be worshipped. Seeking to define the sovereignty of the Supreme Being, they confronted the paradox that, if the Father and the Son were the same, God the Father had died on the cross. By definition, however, an immortal God, God the Father, cannot die. And an indivisible God cannot be divided into three persons. Arians believed that the Trinity was figurative as well as unscriptural, an invention of the later church. All anti-Trinitarians indulged the belief that they were resurrecting the truths of the primitive or pre-Nicene church.

All Christians understood that the issue of the Trinity, however complex, was crucially important to Christianity; it was a matter on which the slightest distinction or deviation from the "true" faith could mean the damnation of all the souls of Christianity. At stake was the right road to salvation. The complexity of the matter issued from the confrontation of a problem that surpassed human understanding. As a result, differing interpretations of the same words led to centuries of controversy about the doctrine of the Trinity; whether the persons of the Trinity had the same or similar or different substances was a question that resulted in answers that had multiple shades of meaning, depending on the way one defined or understood such key words in the dispute as "substances," "consubstantiality," "natures," "hypostases," "existences," "properties," "persons," "coessentiality," "essences," and "subsistences" with respect to the Trinity. In effect, Arianism recognized Jesus Christ and the Holy Spirit as divine by the Father's grace, although not in actuality of essence. If God did not give His only begotten son as a ransom for mankind, the Christian doctrine of salvation became groundless. Thus, even a mild Arianism undermined Christianity by denying the doctrine of the Trinity—and therefore it seemed blasphemous.[29]

Socinianism, which was far more radical, regarded Jesus as human only, the greatest moralist but a mere creature. If his mission was divine, he was not. Socinians, like Arians, believed that some matters of faith could transcend reason but could not conflict with it. They rejected any mystical belief that was unintelligible or incomprehensible to reason, such as three being equal to one, or one being equal to three. And they preferred human reason to faith. If reason was sufficient, revelation was really superfluous. That point brought Socinians closer to deism than Arians would travel.

Although Arians and Socinians thought of themselves as scriptural literalists, deists, who construed the Bible allegorically, tended to reject faith, mystery, revelation, and the divine inspiration of the Bible. Some claimed to be Christian deists, but they probably identified with Christianity and the Church of England for ulterior purposes, to ward off the law's penalties for denial of Christian truths, and to enhance their rejection of the Judaism of the Old Testament, which they despised. They relished showing how ridiculous were the myths and prophecies and mysteries of the Jewish Bible, thereby undermining the New Testament. They also relished showing how ridiculous was the idea that God would have revealed Himself to an obscure, tiny tribe in the Near East. If God the Creator was responsible for all human life, deists believed, He was the Father of all peoples and races, in all nations and on all continents, not merely a chosen few. Deists also loved to ridicule the diversity of sects, denominations, and churches within Christianity. The Bible could not be the revealed word of God, because He would not have revealed Himself so discrepantly to the many different kinds of heretics and of Christians. They disagreed over fundamental matters other than the Trinity. Did the Bible reveal the truth of free will or predestination, infant or adult baptism, the real or symbolic presence in the Eucharist? That Christians clashed over which creed and which interpretation of the sacraments constituted truth convinced deists that truth did not depend for its meaning on a document of such ambiguities concerning the character of divine purposes.

Deism, which was a religious expression of Newtonian science, promulgated a different sort of deity, a God whose existence could be inferred from the design, order, and harmony of the universe. Creation and life itself testified to His existence. And the universe ran like clockwork, according to natural laws that God had ordained. Through those laws, which were fixed, natural, and scientific, the universe operated in perpetuity, and through those rational laws and only those laws God had revealed Himself. Nothing He did was unnatural or supernatural, nor was it superstitious or miraculous in the Christian sense.

Unlike forms of Unitarianism, which purported to be scripturally based and had historic roots as old as Christianity, deism was a recent development. Deism seems a product of the Age of Reason, although Lord Edward Herbert of Cherbury (1583–1648), the first Englishman to advance ideas later associated with deism—a term he never used—long preceded the dawn of that age. Change is usually incremental; cause and effect are not always apparent. Deism could not have flourished but for the widespread and rapid acceptance of Newtonianism, but other developments helped make deism possible. Among them were the end of press censorship, the beginnings of scholarly criticism of the Bible, geographical discoveries that disclosed the existence of an astounding variety of religions other than theistic ones, and a disgust for the zealotry and persecutions that characterized the seventeenth century. Spinoza and Locke, even Copernicus, had as large a hand in creating free thought as Newton. In any case, deism was probably the logical result of a fissiparousness that is inherent in Protestantism: if every person interprets the Bible for himself, some will come to conclusions regarded as deistic.[30]

Charles Blount (1654–93) was the first Englishman to acknowledge himself to be a deist; his *Summary Account of the Deist's Religion*, published in the year of his death, was followed by dozens of deist publications. Some of the authors eschewed the word "deist." None followed a party line; they differed considerably with one another. Some attacked prophecies, some miracles, and some the divinity of Christ. Deist authors tended to disparage the Bible by indirection—by circumlocutions, by irony, by allegory, by satire—in order to shrink the target they constituted for those who wished to avenge the honor of God or the reputation of religion. In fact, deists confronted not the restraints of the law but bales of refutations by believers, who represented the case for Christianity quite strongly. The sole deist argument that escaped much damage concerned morality. Deists effectively contended that morality did not depend on revelation, was not unique to Christianity, and even flourished in pagan and monotheistic societies.

Although a reflection of Newtonianism, deism had no monopoly on being "scientific." Arians, Socinians, and latitudinarian Anglicans claimed the authority of science as a bulwark for their beliefs. Science was rational. Religion, everyone seemed to believe, was rational. Therefore, religion was scientific. A Tory High Church man, Francis Atterbury, declared that the Church of England desired "nothing more than to be tried at the bar of unbiased reason, and to be concluded by its sentence."[31] Even orthodoxy believed that no conflict existed between science and religion. No Christian doubted that Christianity was rational. Robert Boyle, the great chemist, who was a devout Anglican although a latitudinarian one, endowed an annual lectureship "for proving the Christian religion, against notorious Infidels, *viz.* Atheists, Theists, Pagans, Jews, and Mahometans, not descending lower to any Controversies, that are among Christians themselves."[32] The Boyle lectures were given by major clerics, including Samuel Clarke and William Whiston, both of whom were subsequently accused of blasphemy. The lecturers were invariably followers of Newton, and they boasted that natural philosophy or science enhanced natural theology, a latitudinarian view of Christianity. Newtonianism was "the articulation of a mechanical philosophy that required God's active participation in the workings of nature," or a "Christianized philosophy of science."[33] It contributed to the swift success of the government's policy of toleration.

IN LITTLE more than a decade, the Toleration Act had become so cardinal a part of government policy that direct and malicious opposition to it seemed subversive. Daniel Defoe, the journalist who would invent the novel, learned to his misfortune that an attack on toleration, exposing the government to acute public embarrassment and lowering the public's esteem of its rulers, could result in criminal punishment. Defoe himself was a dissenter and a champion of dissenters' rights, who in 1702 reached a point of desperate exasperation after all rational arguments against an intolerant measure pending in Parliament had failed. Anne had become queen in that year, and for political reasons relating to the costs of a war with France, the Tories won a majority of the House of Commons. Although Anne declared herself to be a supporter of the policy of toleration, she informed Parliament that she would give her most unstinting support to those who displayed the "truest zeal" for the Church of England. Tories and High Church men responded with an assault on the practice of "occasional conformity," which they detested.

Occasional conformity permitted dissenters to evade the Test Acts of 1673 and 1678, whose purpose was to disqualify Roman Catholics from holding civil and military offices. The statutes required certain oaths, which only Protestants could take, and also required that officeholders must receive the sacrament of the Lord's Supper according to the usage of the established church. Because the acts were directed against "Popish Recusants," Protestant dissenters—including Presbyterians, Baptists, Congregationalists, Quakers, and even those who disbelieved the doctrine of the Trinity—felt that they violated no principle by occasionally attending their parish church and taking Anglican communion; that display of Christian fellowship qualified them for office. The bill of 1702, which Whigs and dissenters opposed, would have disqualified from civil and military offices any person who attended any religious services other than "according to the liturgy and practice of the Church of England." Whig bishops in the House of Lords managed to defeat the bill, which had passed in the Commons.[34]

Defoe got into trouble because of the way he responded to Tory demands for Parliament to enact that bill disqualifying dissenters from office. Shortly after the queen announced that those who were most zealous on behalf of the Church of England would "have the greatest share in Her Favour," Dr. Henry Sacheverell, an Oxford divine, delivered an inflammatory sermon against all dissenters, which soon appeared in print as *The Political Union* (1702). Sacheverell called the dissenters "apostates and renegades to their oaths," "false traitors" to their trusts, and "avowed enemies to our communion," against whom everyone who supported the church "ought to hang out the bloody flag."[35] Defoe had consistently criticized fellow dissenters for the practice of occasional conformity, and as consistently opposed any measure against the practice. He believed that dissenters were entitled as of right to enjoy all places of profit and preferment, without any sort of discrimination; dissenters paid taxes for the support of church and state, and they served in the armed forces; they should, therefore, qualify as officeholders, civil and military.

The failure of such arguments as well as the queen's speech and Sacheverell's violent sermon prompted Defoe to resort to a hoax in order to make the public and the government understand that measures against dissenters stood on principles of bigotry and persecution.

He therefore wrote *The Shortest Way With the Dissenters: Or Proposals for the Establishment of the Church*, published in 1702; he wrote it ironically, as if its author were someone who shared Sacheverell's opinions. The Church of England could best be served, Defoe wrote anonymously, "by extirpating her implacable Enemies." Acknowledging that some people might object to "renewing Fire and Faggot," Defoe made his Tory author reply that killing a snake or a toad was necessary because "the Poyson of their Nature makes it a Charity to our Neighbours to destroy those Creatures, not for any personal Injury receiv'd but for prevention; not for the Evil they have done, but for the Evil they may do." He did not propose that "all the Dissenters in England shou'd be hang'd or Banish'd," only that the shortest way to obtain the compliance of the multitude, as in cases of rebellion, was to make a few ringleaders suffer as an example to the rest.[36]

Some High Church men were so gulled by the imitation of their sentiments that they applauded *The Shortest Way*, until the government discovered that its author was a prominent dissenter. Then the ultra-rightists considered Defoe's tract as "a blasphemous attack on Mother Church."[37] Government ministers recognized immediately that the tract disgraced the government by implying that the policy of toleration was a mere pretense and that people in high places, within church and state, really preferred a policy of persecution. That constituted seditious libel. Thus, Defoe succeeded in provoking outrage against himself. The government advertised his capture as a seditious libeler, and the House of Commons declared that, "this book being full of false and scandalous reflections on this parliament, and tending to promote sedition," the public hangman must burn a copy. Tried at Old Bailey, Defoe was sentenced to pay a severe fine, to stand three times in the pillory, and to be imprisoned in Newgate "during the queen's pleasure," remaining there at least until he put up sureties for his good behavior for seven years. His real opinions and his excessive punishment earned him the sympathy of the crowds when he suffered the pillory. He served fourteen months in Newgate Prison. His case revealed that, only a few years after passage of the Blasphemy Act of 1698, religious persecution seemed intolerable. Public opinion, however, can be volatile.

A mere seven years later, a similar trial occurred with very different results. Another man stood in the prisoner's dock, charged with bigotry—technically speaking, charged with seditious libel—but, despite similarities, the cases were strikingly different. The accused tried in 1710 was a learned Anglican clergyman, the High Church Tory Dr. Henry Sacheverell. He was a fierce, fanatical demagogue, as well as a learned one. Patronized by orthodox Anglicans, Sacheverell had risen in importance since he published the 1702 tract that had triggered Defoe's hoax, which nakedly advocated what Sacheverell had implied. The implications became more and more explicit with Sacheverell's successive publications. In 1709, the lord mayor of London invited him to give the sermon in St. Paul's Cathedral. Sacheverell's sermon, which he quickly published, created a sensation.

The sermon bore the title *The Perils of False Brethren, both in Church and State*. With an epithetical viciousness, Sacheverell developed the theme that the latitudinarians within the church, in league with the dissenters and supported by Whigs in public office, were throttling Anglicanism. The Toleration Act, he contended, nursed the church's enemies. Although both houses of Parliament had joined in a resolution pronouncing that the church was "in a most safe and flourishing condition," and Queen Anne had issued a royal proclamation with the same message, Sacheverell argued that false brethren within and without the church, Whig Protestants all, plotted its schism and ruin. He identified the false brethren as those who supported the Toleration Act, liberty of conscience, and occasional conformity. Daringly, he used characterizations easily identifiable with particular Low Church bishops and ministers of state. He also traduced the memory of the late king, who had vigorously endorsed the Toleration Act and appointed the bishops whom Sacheverell depicted as traitors to church and state. Moreover, Sacheverell challenged the authority of Parliament, which had enacted the toleration policy.

By the standards of his time, he was guilty of seditious libel, but instead of treating his case by routinely prosecuting him in court, the government turned his prosecution into a political circus. The House of Commons impeached him for high crimes and misdemeanors, and the House of Lords tried the accusations that he had suggested that the late revolution had been accomplished by odious and unjustifiable means, that the Toleration Act was unreasonable, that it imperiled the established church, and that anyone who defended liberty of conscience was a false brother. For such reflections on the queen, Parliament, and the church itself, the government sought to convict Sacheverell in the most sensational way and by a means that sanctioned any punishment. No common-law court could have unfrocked Sacheverell or even suspended him from his performance as a clergyman. In a case of impeachment, however, the Lords had virtually unlimited powers of punishment.

The decision to prosecute by impeachment was essentially political and vengeful, and it boomeranged. The government staged the trial in Westminster Hall to accommodate the largest possible audience; each peer controlled seven tickets of admission. The trial lasted more than three weeks, and each day Sacheverell's carriage going to and from Westminster Hall was escorted by wildly enthusiastic supporters who packed the streets and yelled their good wishes. Sacheverell's inflammatory sermon rapidly sold at least forty thousand copies, a figure beyond compare. He became enormously popular with Anglican churchgoers and low-ranking clergymen. His sermon actually incited riots against dissenters and their churches, yet the arrogance and boldness with which he spoke so powerfully in his own behalf added to his public acclaim.

Sacheverell defended himself with shifty evasions and fine distinctions that were politically shrewd and probably true, if not the whole truth. For example, he argued that the false brethren of whom he spoke were only those who sought to subvert church or state, or who were occasional conformists, or who were "for a latitudinarian, heterogeneous mixture of all persons, of what different faith soever, uniting only in protestancy"—a group whom he regarded as unfaithful to the church, not submissive to its discipline, and not complying with its liturgy.[38] False brethren, in short, were those who upheld false doctrine. He had opposed only the enemies of the church, the schismatical, the blasphemous—anyone who was "a traitor to God."[39] Anyone who thought him guilty of seditious libel misunderstood him. Sacheverell's lawyers spent one entire day of his trial reading to the audience his proofs, speedily published, that the church was in danger and that a toleration policy which went beyond the Toleration Act, as he understood it, was promiscuously harmful; he proved that the government had allowed vice, irreligion, and blasphemy, by having allowed the writings of blasphemers to go unpunished. That is, he read into the record selections from the writings of freethinkers, rationalists, deists, and anti-Trinitarians—atheists all, to Sacheverell. Among his blasphemers were John Toland, Matthew Tindal, and Anthony Collins.[40]

The House of Lords convicted Sacheverell by a vote of sixty-nine to fifty-two, including a seven-to-six split among the bishops who participated. But the sentence revealed a Pyrrhic victory: no imprisonment, no fines, no deprivation. The Lords simply suspended Sacheverell from preaching for three years but did not otherwise prevent him from exercising his duties as a clergyman; he was not even prevented from enjoying preferments. The Lords also ordered that his offensive works be burned by the hangman, and that the hangman burn in addition the blasphemous book entitled *Collections of Passages referred to by Dr. Sacheverell, in his Answer to the Articles of his Impeachment*—the material that his lawyers had read aloud to the Lords and the audience. Thus, the majority party showed that it disapproved of blasphemy and atheism as much as Sacheverell did—thereby advancing his point that the government had permitted irreligion to flourish at the church's expense. His supporters moved the proclamation of a fast day to appease "divine vengeance, which there was just reason to fear, on account of the horrid blasphemies lately published in the kingdom." Whigs blamed Sacheverell for repeating and reprinting those blasphemies to the scandal of good Christians.

So Sacheverell went free, and on his way back to Oxford some fifty thousand people acclaimed him. His trial had become his triumph. Soon the government ministers who had supported his prosecution were dismissed from office. The political world stood upside down as the Tories won a huge victory in the parliamentary elections only five months after the trial had ended. No doubt the unpopular war with France, which was going badly, accounted for the defeat of the Whigs, but Sacheverell's case damaged their cause. The Tories did not win another general election for nearly a century.

The accession to power by Sacheverell's supporters did not incite a rash of prosecutions for blasphemy or any crimes against religion. The impulse to prosecute remained central to the extravagant High Church men who accepted the Toleration Act in the narrowest way; moreover, the flow of deist and anti-Trinitarian literature made the opportunities for prosecution quite plentiful. But the Blasphemy Act of 1698 remained unenforced, and even the common law, which was so flexible and comprehensive, remained hardly more than just a threat. The explanation for the scarcity of blasphemy prosecutions is that, despite the acrimony among writers of tracts, the policy of toleration had become so popular that resort to criminal law, whether statutory or judge-made, invited public disfavor. Learned men arguing fine points on incomprehensible matters of theology, such as the doctrine of the Trinity, engaged the attention of other disputatious scholars, but none of their views seemed to jeopardize the road to salvation for most people. Sacheverell had aroused the populace by his argument that the Church of England was in danger from false brethren, not by his defense of the Athanasian Creed. Attacks on it stirred yawns, except from intellectuals who cared deeply about religious theories. Sacheverell aroused sympathy because he was being victimized, not because his views on toleration converted readers.

Richard Burridge, by contrast, was a victim about whom no one cared. In 1712, a jury convicted him for his blasphemous utterances— hardly a Tory triumph. Burridge was a well-educated scoundrel of no account whatever in the torrid controversies among theological writers. He made his living as a hack journalist, one of Grub Street's many mercenaries. He had already served a year in Newgate Prison for having published some libel against church and state. In 1711, when he was in prison again—this time in the Gatehouse in Westminster, for nonpayment of a debt—he drank a blasphemous toast to "the Confusion of

Almighty God, a Health to the Devil our Minister, and Damnation to the Resurrection." According to Burridge, who wrote the only account of his paltry blasphemy case, he was the innocent victim of the keeper of the prison. Seeking to revenge himself for Burridge's accusations of cruelty and extortion, the keeper suborned other inmates to testify against him.[41]

Even if Burridge was guilty as charged, his case seems unusual. Not only had prosecutions for blasphemy become infrequent; the government did not ordinarily bother to prosecute a sleazy person who influenced no one and whose conviction would not serve as an example that would scare profane or cursing drinkers. "Damnation to the Resurrection" was certainly an offense to Christianity, but did not technically breach the terms of the Blasphemy Act of 1698. The statute reached only denials of a person of the Trinity, of Christianity, or of the divine authority of the Bible. Burridge had not made such a denial. Moreover, he had no prior conviction for blasphemy, whereas the statute provided for imprisonment only on a second offense. The prosecutor thus brought his case under the common law, which protected Christianity from aspersions. The keeper of the Gatehouse may have been a person of some influence with the authorities. Without doubt, high church officials, who had considerable influence with the Tories in power, would have found Burridge's curse shocking. So did the jury. Chief Justice Thomas Parker sentenced him to a year's imprisonment.

By contrast, William Whiston was a man of monumental importance. An ordained Anglican clergyman, he was a slightly dotty mathematical genius of great reputation, who employed the new science to prove the truths of Christianity, as he understood it. His understanding became increasingly heterodox along lines denoted Arian in his time. He thought of himself as Eusebian on the question of the Trinity, because he supported the view of Eusebius (260–340), the first great church historian, who fought against the Nicene Creed and its doctrine that the three persons of the Trinity shared the same essence. What Whiston thought on that esoteric question, which made Christianity fissiparous at its core, mattered, and mattered enormously, to state and church, for Whiston was the leading Newtonian of his time, Newton's protégé, Newton's successor as Lucasian Professor of Mathematics at Cambridge, an intimate of the great men of the time, and, together with his close friends Samuel Clarke and Bishop Benjamin Hoadly, among the foremost latitudinarians in the land. Whiston was big game for the blasphemy hunters.

By 1710, he had arrived at the definite conclusion that the early Christian church had embraced the views associated with Arius, or Eusebius, respecting the divine nature of Christ. In that year, he was summoned before the vice-chancellor of Cambridge and nine heads of colleges, who presented him with depositions proving that in a lecture he had asserted that only one God existed, that God the Father and He alone was that one God, and that the Son, although exalted above other human beings and worthy of worship for his divine mission, had himself not been of God's essence. When Whiston refused to comment, the vice-chancellor presented him with a paper containing statements he had made "against religion"—such as, "That the creed commonly called the Creed of St. Athanasius, is a gross and unchristian innovation and corruption of the primitive purity and simplicity of the Christian faith"—and his examiners ordered Whiston to retract the statements in the paper or be severed from the university.

Whiston refused to retract, refused to affirm the orthodox doctrine of the Trinity, and refused to answer what he called "ensnaring questions." They exhorted him to "leave his errors, and return to the Church of England," and when he again refused, they deprived him of his office and banished him from the university. Whiston then published a tract justifying his views on primitive Christianity and the Trinity; he dedicated the work to the prelates of the church and to the lower-ranking clergy, who had assembled in a convocation of the church. The dedication having exacerbated the provocation, the lower house of the convocation, presided over by a High Church reactionary, arraigned Whiston before the upper house, the bishops, for having advanced "several damnable and blasphemous assertions against the doctrine and worship of the ever-blessed Trinity . . . and defaming the whole Athanasian [Creed]." The lower house asked the upper house to condemn Whiston and suppress "the said blasphemy."

The upper house, unsure whether a convocation had jurisdiction over "heresy" and over the heretic, sought the government's opinion. The queen referred the whole matter to a special commission of her twelve highest-ranking common-law judges, her attorney general, and her solicitor general. Four of the judges decided that the convocation had jurisdiction over the heresies only, but not the heretics, while the other eight judges and the queen's two law officers sustained the convocation's jurisdiction in all respects, but they agreed too that the common-law courts might review a decision by the convocation of the church and even issue a writ prohibiting that decision. Both houses of convocation then censured Whiston's book and made the political mistake of asking for the queen's endorsement of their decision. She "lost" the documents, which the convocation eventually re-presented to her. Time passed, in which Whiston kept publishing his religious opinions—in four volumes, no less. In 1714, Queen Anne died, without having taken a position on Whiston.

The outstanding fact about the case, then, is that, although her ministers of state were Tories, in sympathy with High Church policies, they found it impolitic for the government to endorse the censure of Whiston, for censure would have led, logically, to a prosecution for blasphemy, and that could have led to trouble for the government. Bishop Gilbert Burnet, a latitudinarian, understood the politics of the matter when he observed that letting the issue die was best for state and church; as he said, "the true interest of the Christian religion was best considered when nice disputing about mysteries was set aside and forgotten."[42]

Government officials might agree with Burnet, but High Church men had a lower threshold of tolerance, and Samuel Clarke's defection from orthodoxy was more than they could take. Clarke, an intimate friend of Whiston, enjoyed the reputation of being England's pre-eminent philosopher-theologian after the death of John Locke. Unlike Locke, he developed his system of thought from axiomatic principles that lacked empirical warrant, which made his conversion to heterodoxy all the more insufferable. Deists and anti-Trinitarians were not likely to persuade those who knew their true colors, but when the pre-eminent metaphysician in the country openly doubted, even denied, the doctrine of the Trinity, the danger existed that other Anglican clergymen might follow him. Clarke had previously been in the forefront of the attack on oracles of reason who had rejected revealed religion. As recently as 1709, he had defended the proposition that no article of Christianity conflicted with right reason. But his 1712 book on *The Scripture Doctrine of the Trinity* preached muted deism or, at the least, undisguised Arianism. Clarke's admirers included Queen Anne and Archbishop Wake. His defection constituted a challenge that could not be ignored.

The lower house of convocation, always the most conservative force of the Church of England, not yet thwarted on the issue of Whiston, moved Clarke's censure for blasphemous assertions that the three persons of the Trinity did not share the same substance, power, and eternity, and for other heresies. Archbishop Wake interposed to protect Clarke, whom he regarded as a good man with a record of having written in behalf of the true faith and against "Deists and libertines." Wake and other prelates persuaded Clarke to mollify the lower clergy. Clarke then issued a five-point statement for the prelates in the upper house of the convocation to consider, beginning with an ambiguous proposition on the Trinity: "My opinion is, that the Son of God was eternally begotten by the eternal incomprehensible power and will of the Father, and that the Holy Spirit was likewise derived from the Father by or through the Son, according to the eternal incomprehensible power and will of the Father." The subordination of the second and third persons of the Trinity to the first, who alone could communicate divinity, was, at the least, Arian, but in the context of the remaining propositions conveyed the impression of a retraction. Clarke seemed to promise the inclusion of the Athanasian Creed in his church, and he surely apologized for any offense he had given to the convocation. Indeed, his tone suggested that he had caved in. Whiston and others like-minded scorched him for lacking the courage of his convictions. Clarke then sent to Archbishop Wake an additional statement disclaiming an intention to retract anything he had written. Wake, after consulting some friendly bishops, wrote Clarke that his good friends in the upper house had urged him to rest on his original statement in order to avoid censure by enemies, or, Wake cautioned, no one could know where the matter might end. Clarke then surrendered without conditions, and the upper house of the convocation resolved that no need existed to proceed further. Although the lower house demanded more explicit retractions, it could do nothing else on its own. Thus, Wake saved Clarke, who kept his word not to write further about the Trinity; nevertheless, Wake later prevented Clarke's promotion to the rank of bishop.[43]

Clarke's case, like Whiston's, showed that, when the Tories were in power, toleration had distinct limits; but no rational explanation exists for the seemingly haphazard targeting of victims. John Toland, Matthew Tindal, Anthony Collins, and other deists, whose criticism cut closer to the bone than that of the latitudinarian Low Church men, wholly escaped penalties, civil and criminal. Heretical views from two former Boyle lecturers, both clergymen in the established church, constituted greater dangers than the deists posed, but the criticism of the deists was far more radical, and more clearly violated both statutory and common-law principles against blasphemy. Moreover, the prosecution of Burridge, who was no danger to church or state, reduces to hash the notion that the proceedings against Whiston and Clarke stemmed from the dangers that they personally posed.

Toleration and the expiration of the licensing system merely diminished the danger of expressing anti-Trinitarian and deistic ideas. If the authorities disliked an opinion, they regarded it as an abuse of the freedom to print without prior censorship; the author risked prosecution for some form of criminal libel. Defoe paid the consequences of misusing freedom when he was convicted for seditious libel, and Emlyn for blasphemous libel. Given the risk of utterance, freethinkers on the subject of religion or government had a personal stake in expanding the bounds of permissible freedom.

The mere existence of the offense of blasphemy spurred potential victims to defend religious liberty and freedom of the press, although even radicals, at the time, could imagine only a stunted scope for either of those freedoms. John Toland sounded like a pluperfect liberal on the right to advance any opinions concerning religion so long as they were not "papist" or atheist. Moreover, he never confronted the question whether blasphemy should constitute a crime, and he drew limits on political criticism. Although professing to champion freedom of the press, he deplored the circulation of seditious innuendoes and licentious verbal abuse directed against government ministers. He even recommended that the government defend itself by extending a stamp tax on newspapers, and by altogether prohibiting certain papers.[44]

Matthew Tindal, one of the foremost deists of the early eighteenth century, had a keenly personal interest in the offenses of seditious and blasphemous libel. His works were burned as blasphemous, his printers suffered prosecution for publishing against the government, honing Tindal's appreciation of the freedoms of religion and of the press. He declared that "there is no freedom either in civil or ecclesiastical [affairs], but where the liberty of the press is maintain'd." Tindal claimed that everyone "has a natural Right in all matters of Learning and Knowledge" to discover what can be said by speech or press "on all sides of every subject, including civil and governmental matters, even if antiministerial." That surely constituted an enhanced view of the freedom. Tindal may have been the first to elevate freedom of speech and press to the status of a natural right—a rhetorical achievement, to be sure, but a crucial step in the creation of a theory of intellectual liberty. The process by which the phrase "freedom of speech" was transformed from a description of a privilege of parliamentarians, for whom it had originated, to a personal right of citizens turned, in part, on the assimilation of freedom of speech into a theory based on natural rights. Tindal was also the first person on either side of the Atlantic to imply that citizens should have the same right to freedom of speech that legislators had in the House of Commons. He made this vital point obliquely by asking, "If the Honourable House of Commons have upon a solemn debate thought fit to publishe their proceedings to prevent being misrepresented, why should they deny those that Represent the same Liberty?"[45] One might have expected numerous people to have extrapolated a civil liberty from the parliamentary privilege simply by arguing that, if the representatives of the people enjoyed a broad constitutional right to debate any issue concerning public policy and the conduct of the government, then the people—who possessed ultimate sovereignty, and to whom the representatives were responsible—should possess the same right of discussion. This advanced idea, at which Tindal hinted, did not receive full discussion until the close of the century.

Although Tindal, a former law-fellow at All Souls College, Oxford, was one of the earliest freethinkers with legal training, he did not evaluate the common law's restrictions on expression or offer a solution for the legal problems that latitudinarian or radical views might precipitate. Indeed, he never indicated disagreement with the notion that the press had become free when removed from prior restraints. His tracts defending himself, his printer, and his bookseller, upon their presentment by a grand jury for publishing a blasphemous attack on the established church, rested the argument on liberty of the press without questioning the doctrine of subsequent punishment for the abuse of liberty.[46]

John Asgill, whose blasphemous crimes consisted of his eccentric interpretation of the soul, was a religious mystic and a politician, whose books were condemned to the fires; he himself suffered the distinction of having been expelled from both the Irish and the English Houses of Commons. With this record behind him, in 1712 he wrote *An Essay for the Press*, in which he ignored the law of criminal libels that had been used to censure him. Although he hailed the communication of one's thoughts as a "natural Right of Mankind," as had Tindal, and he argued, cleverly, that the abuse of this right no more justified suppressing it than hypocrites crowded in with the true worshippers justified shutting church doors, he confessed the necessity of maintaining restraints upon the press. He drew the line against licensing and taxation of the press, and he took his stand on the superficial notion that "licentiousness" was caused by anonymous publications; he proposed to outlaw them and require all authors to identify themselves. But he followed the custom of the time in having published his own essay anonymously. And he gave consideration neither to the possibility that the danger to the press's freedom derived largely from the necessarily vague concept of licentiousness, nor to the possibility that many discussions of public value were advanced anonymously to protect their authors from subsequent punishment.

Asgill, like Toland and Tindal, was among the eminent defenders of civil liberty in his time. But all were *of* their time and could not escape its premises, one of which no thinking man attacked: the state had an incontestable right to proscribe both blasphemous and seditious libel. Without a frontal assault on these commodious crimes, libertarian thought was doomed, at bottom, to a narrowness that allowed the victims of prosecution only one escape: a denial that their expressions constituted the crime charged—a matter that the law reserved for courts to decide, leaving to juries little more than the function of determining whether the accused had in fact employed the words attributed to him.[47]

Anthony Collins did more than any other deist to argue for the rights of religious radicals. A prosperous country gentleman who was a prominent Whig, Collins served as a justice of the peace and as a county treasurer. He had met Locke and conducted a correspondence with him. Accordingly, the opinions of Collins were more likely to be influential than those of some rationalist crank or extremist like Toland, Tindal, or Asgill. In Collins's *Discourse of Free Thinking*, which rejected the doctrine of the Trinity as unscriptural and unintelligible, he insisted on the right of private judgment rather than obedience to ecclesiastical authority or divine revelation. The word "freethinking," by which Collins meant the sovereignty of unfettered private judgment, received "a universal notoriety" as a result of this 1713 book, which made it a controversial term connoting deism.[48] In the book, Collins argued two propositions at considerable length: first, that restraints on expression resulted in cultural stagnation and ignorance; second, that every man had a right to think and express himself freely for the purpose of determining the meaning and validity of any view in history, science, philosophy, religion, or other realms of knowledge. His *Philosophical Inquiry concerning Human Liberty* continued the thesis but did not advance it. In still another work, Collins defended the use of ridicule, jest, and raillery in all disputation; deploring restraints that prevented authors from speaking their minds, he pleaded for freedom of debate in any matter of "speculation."[49]

Clearly, however, Collins referred in context only to scholars and divines; he did not champion ordinary political reporting and criticism. He also had a way of tacking on to a libertarian thesis a concession to orthodoxy that, innocently perhaps, bulldozed the ground out from under him. For instance, his "Apology for Free Debate and Liberty in Writing" was dedicated to the following proposition: "As it is every man's natural right and duty to think, and judge for himself in matters of opinion; so he should be allow'd freely to profess his opinions, and to endeavour, when he judges proper, to convince others of their truth; provided those opinions do not tend to the disturbance of society."[50] Any crown prosecutor might warmly embrace that proposition, despite its natural-rights premise, because the qualifying provision accepted in principle the law of criminal libel. Mere opinions were punishable if they had the bad tendency, even if remote, to disturb society. Moreover, Collins acknowledged that "The greatest contenders for liberty of debate in matters of religion do contend for some restraints upon that liberty, and think, that there are certain propositions which ought not to be call'd in question, as being necessary to be profess'd for the support of peace and order in society, or at the least not deny'd."[51] He did not explain that, and, although he was a magistrate, he did not discuss the law of verbal crimes. Yet the book in which he made this argument was a sustained assault on the supposed inerrancy of the Bible. Collins had not provided an analytically worthwhile argument. He himself rejected Jesus as Messiah, repudiated the doctrine of the Trinity, and believed the Bible to be inaccurate and unreliable; he himself, that is, had advanced propositions that most people and the law thought should not be called into question. In 1713, when the Tories enjoyed political power, Collins's *Discourse of Free Thinking* had produced so vitriolic a reaction that, after his printer named him to the authorities as the author, Collins felt impelled to visit the continent for his safety.[52]

In a tract of 1727, in which he rejected divine revelation, Collins again made the argument for freedom, resting his case as much on natural right as on natural religion. He contended that the "Saviour's rule of doing to others what we would have others do to us" justified an avoidance of prosecuting heterodox religious opinions. He specifically included Socinians but not Roman Catholics in his list of religions and sects that the law, he wrongly claimed, allowed. In that tract he mentioned a powerful argument for freedom of religion—the overt-acts test later associated with Jefferson's Virginia Statute of Religious Freedom. As Collins made the argument, religion constituted an intensely personal matter. He distinguished such matters from those in which society had a stake. "The religions, for example, of the Jews [and] Socinians . . . are personal matters, as being not in the least immoral, or injurious to society, and in which no man has any concern but the several professors, who . . . are alone, or personally accountable to God for it." By contrast, society had a deep stake in impersonal matters such as peace, sobriety, honesty, and justice. Violations of these by the commission of crime were the business of magistrates. Collins's point was that the profession of opinions about religion did not lead to public disorder or overt acts that breached the law and therefore ought to be exempt from the jurisdiction of government.[53] It was not an argument that Collins invented or developed, but it was a rare and profound one that possessed the only effective libertarian defense in a system of law that punished verbal crimes. Collins implicitly agreed that certain words passed the bounds of toleration, but only when they provoked criminal conduct.

CHAPTER FOURTEEN

Blasphemy and Obscenity

T HE JAILS of Britain should have bulged with blasphemers. By the law of both Parliament and King's Bench, blasphemous libel was a heinous crime, and, to judge by the torrents of hysterical tracts bemoaning the prevalence of the crime, anti-Trinitarians and deists committed it daily. Imprisonment of blasphemers should have been as common as imprisonment of debtors and pickpockets. Yet the anti-Trinitarians and deists flourished, expressing themselves with near impunity. The frequency of prosecutions rivaled the appearance of leap years. Even when the Tories held power under Queen Anne, they managed to do little more than burn several books, deprive William Whiston of his professorship at Cambridge, humble Samuel Clarke into temporary submission, and jail a drunk who drank a toast to the devil's health. The Tories also passed an Occasional Conformity Act, limiting public offices to those who practiced religion according to the rites and ceremonies of the established church, and a Schism Act, intended to close dissenter academies and to allow only Anglicans to teach or keep schools. However, neither of these statutes was enforced, and in 1718 Parliament repealed both. Toleration is relative, a matter of degree: England was growing in its tolerance of Protestant nonconformists and had never been freer. Jews could worship freely but had no civil rights. Roman Catholics were also subjected to severe discrimination.[1]

In 1717, Benjamin Hoadly, the bishop of Bangor, probably the most latitudinarian bishop in Britain, delivered his famous sermon before the king on *The Nature or the Kingdom of Church of Christ*, inciting the Bangorian Controversy, to the utter dismay of conservatives. Even moderates expressed shock. Hoadly came near advocating disestablishment. He advanced the thesis that no ecclesiastical or civil authority could require subscription to any confession of religious belief, or even create a hierarchy in which anyone exercised authority over Christ's subjects in matters of religion. His views encouraged those who questioned the doctrine of the Trinity and opposed subscription to articles of faith.[2]

The archbishop of Canterbury, William Wake, who had been a Whig, felt driven to deplore Hoadly, dissenters, and every sort of anti-Trinitarian. He reminded the House of Lords that English law offered no freedom to "Socinians, Arians, [or] Deists" who were "not so much as tolerated."[3] The "Latitudinarian writers (who call themselves free-thinkers)," he wrote privately, opposed "all confessions of faith, all subscriptions of any articles of religion whatsoever, as contrary to that submission we owe to Christ our king." Wake would have none of that. "These men are some of them Deists," he asserted, "some Socinians; a better sort of Arians; all of them enemies to the [Anglican] Catholic Faith, in more or less of the most fundamental articles of it." He hoped the day would come when he could see "a sentence brought against these heretics."[4] After Hoadly's sermon, Wake lamented "the new species of libertines" who wanted "to reduce the whole creed of a Christian man to this sole proposition, that they believe the Scriptures of the New Testament to be divinely inspired; and therefrom each individual should collect for himself what he ought to believe." And to his Swiss correspondent he acknowledged that Arians and Socinians had publicly opposed the "mystery of the Trinity," the divine nature of Christ, and the deity of the Holy Spirit.[5] More than a decade later, he declared, "It is a reproach to us that so many advocates for Deism are suffered openly to appear in public on its behalf and to blaspheme our holy religion. . . . But, indeed, our ecclesiastical discipline is so weakened and even subjected to the civil authority, that we know not how to prevent it."[6] These were the views not of a High Church Tory but of a moderate Whig.

Whitlocke Bulstrode, a judge at the quarter sessions court in Middlesex County, shared Wake's concerns. Bulstrode developed special instructions to the grand juries he addressed as he toured his circuit. He focused in 1718 on the dangers of blasphemy and the need for grand juries to return accusations against all blasphemers. By blasphemy, Bulstrode explained, he meant speaking evil of God or religion, and sometimes profane cursing and swearing. He sketched the biblical history of the crime, reminding his listeners that it was so terrible that it deserved the death penalty. Anyone who had no awe of God had no check that would keep him within the bounds of truth. Religion was the binding force of society; nothing that reviled it should escape unpunished. "Take care of Religion, and suppress Vice," Bulstrode instructed, and "present [accuse] the Authors of Books writ against Religion," or books that revile the Scriptures or deny God. In a variant charge, he added that the crime also encompassed books or pamphlets against good morals, or tending to dishonor God, or criticism against revealed religion, or any words that represented Christ "as a mere Man." Present the authors, printers, and publishers of Socinian or deist works, such as the books of John Toland,

Bulstrode demanded. Bulstrode's first charge did so well as a pamphlet
that he had a second, similar one published a few months later.[7]

The case of the ejected ministers of Essex and the Salters' Hall controversy, which followed, showed how anti-Trinitarian views had penetrated even the pulpits of Presbyterianism by 1719. Thomas Emlyn,
once a Presbyterian, led the way to what he called "Unitarianism," and
preached freely in London. His works and similar ones, usually called
Arian, had a wide readership, but nothing like that of Samuel Clarke's
1712 volume, *The Scripture Doctrine of the Trinity*, which High Church
Anglicans had censured as blasphemous. Clarke had been stilled as a
controversialist, but his book achieved considerable popularity as the
years passed, and it had an increasing impact on the thinking of the
dissenters as well as Anglicans. Two Presbyterian ministers in Essex who
became Arians refused to subscribe to the doctrine of the Trinity; they
lost their pulpits. The spread of Arianism to Exeter in the far west
provoked concern. Orthodox Presbyterians in Exeter turned to their
brethren in London for support and advice, in the hope of averting the
spread of blasphemy within their church. The Exeter controversy
reached the ranks of most dissenters.

In London, well over a hundred dissenting ministers, Congregationalists and General Baptists as well as Presbyterians, assembled in Salters'
Hall in 1719 to discuss what should be done. The assembly soon split into
two camps, one that tended toward Arianism and believed that free principles, charity to all Christians—even to deists—and no subscription to
creeds should prevail. Many latitudinarians among Trinitarian Christians
endorsed that view, implicitly rejecting the conventional one that denial of
the Trinity or of Christ's divinity was blasphemous. The traditional side
demanded more than belief in the divine inspiration of the Bible and any
interpretation of it professed in good faith; they made a motion to express
faith in the doctrine of the Trinity. The latitudinarians—we would call
them "liberals"—immediately cried "persecution." The Salters' Hall assembly of the dissenting Protestant ministers of London then defeated the
motion by a vote of fifty-seven to fifty-three. That vote was a transforming
event in the history of English Protestantism—and in the history of the
offense of blasphemy. Anti-Trinitarianism had significantly penetrated
dissenter thought and produced schism in dissenter churches. Trinitarian
Presbyterians divided among themselves; some, perhaps a majority, remained Trinitarian but believed that religious liberty required a rejection
of creeds. At the least, the controversy showed that dissenters as well as
Anglicans were drifting toward Arianism, and what some saw as blasphemy constituted religious truth to others. George Berkeley, Britain's
foremost philosopher, himself an Anglican divine, could not understand
that. Believing that God would wreak vengeance on a nation that indulged

blasphemy, Berkeley argued that blasphemy should be inquired into and "punished with the same rigor as treason against the king." That had once been the dominant conventional view.[8]

One blasphemer grossly overstepped the bounds of freedom of religious expression when he lampooned the doctrine of the Trinity. Expressing disbelief, even denial, although illegal, could be regarded as the exercise of conscience. Relating dirty jokes about the Trinity and ridiculing it on a sustained basis in intemperate language could not be justified as the uncontrollable promptings of conscience or of intellect. The writer of the blasphemous pamphlet against "the Tritheistick Doctrine of the Trinity" was one Joseph Hall, described in the *Journals of the House of Lords* as "a gentleman and serjeant at arms to the king." He published his tract in London in 1720, provoking complaints to the Lords, who showed their alarm by appointing a committee of ninety-nine members to inquire into the matter. The archbishop of York reported for the committee after only three days, naming the publisher and recommending this resolution: "That the whole Book is a Mixture of the most scandalous Blasphemy, Profaneness, and Obscenity; and does, in a most daring, impious Manner ridicule the Doctrine of the Trinity, and all Revealed Religion." Soon the committee discovered the identity of the author, printer, bookseller, and everyone connected with the tract. Hall was arrested and examined before the House of Lords. He confessed his authorship except for some printing errors. The peers ordered the attorney general to prosecute Hall and his accomplices and commanded the destruction of all copies of the tract by public burning. Hall and the others were convicted of blasphemy. He appealed on the ground that certain evidence against him should have been inadmissible, but the chief justice ruled against him. Seven years later, in a wholly different case involving obscene blasphemy, the attorney general informed the King's Bench that Hall was still in custody. Nothing more is known about him or the case.[9]

Archbishop Wake informed a correspondent that "deism, if not atheism," continued as a "growing evil," and the House of Lords had done justice in the case of Hall's blasphemous book. "The judges," he added, "have declared that our law is very express both in the description and punishment of blasphemy; yet in despite of all this, men go on every day to oppose our Lord's divinity; and no prosecution is made of this crime, though confessed to within the law in force."[10] The House of Lords had concluded its inquiry into Hall's blasphemy by instructing its committee "to consider the Occasion of the Publication of blasphemous Books of late, the State of the Laws now in Force against Blasphemy and Profaneness, and the Means to prevent such Impieties for the Future." As a result, a bill was introduced in 1721 to extend the definition of blasphemy.

The introduction of the bill followed immediately after a royal proclamation against "blasphemous and scandalous clubs." George I had learned of the existence of a London group calling itself "The Hell-Fire Club," of which the duke of Wharton as well as "other persons of quality" were members. The king ordered their disbandment; he also took measures to ensure that no member of his royal household or court engaged in blasphemy. An earl who had criticized Whiston's views as blasphemous used the occasion to complain to the House of Lords that the growth of atheism demanded a new measure against blasphemy. No one explained the infirmities of the act of 1698, or why it was not enforced by the crown's prosecutors. Nor did anyone explain why a new act of Parliament was necessary when the common law spaciously accommodated itself to any sort of blasphemy against religion, Christianity, God, Christ, the Trinity, or the Bible.

The proposed bill to suppress blasphemy, which really was rampant by orthodox standards, seemed calculated to bulwark the creeds expressed in the Thirty-nine Articles, the foundation of the Church of England. The bill also sought to restrict the toleration of dissenting Protestants who did not believe in the doctrine of the Trinity. The bill provided that, if anyone spoke or wrote against God, the divinity of Christ or of the Holy Ghost, or the doctrine of the Trinity, or "the truth of the Christian religion," or the divine inspiration of the Bible, he should be imprisoned until he confessed his error. It provided too that any dissenting preacher who denied "any of the fundamental articles of the Christian religion" should not be protected by the Toleration Act. Finally, it authorized bishops to require any person in holy orders to subscribe to an orthodox confession of faith or lose ecclesiastical benefices, and it authorized his criminal prosecution.

Archbishop Wake presented the main speech for the bill. He could not imagine that a Christian legislature would be unwilling to enact a bill whose purpose was to prevent the reviling of the Christian religion. The bill did not diminish the toleration policy, he contended; the Toleration Act, he reminded, took care that no dissenters should be indulged "to the prejudice of these fundamental doctrines of the Trinity." Alleging that the bill did not inquire into men's private opinions, he thought it merely prevented the spread of opinions "never thought fit to be allowed in any state." Indeed, it aimed not at opinions, he inaccurately asserted, but at "open attempts and actions." After reviewing the history of Socinian and Arian opinions in England, from the time of John Biddle during the Interregnum, Wake read extracts from the works of Whiston and Clarke to illustrate the "monstrous attempts" against Christianity that the bill sought to prevent. He did not know whether it would succeed, but was certain that the laws against blasphemy that already existed had failed. "We need therefore some further provision," he concluded.[11]

Liberal views prevailed. Lord Onslow, in opposition, declared that he could not support a bill "that was for persecution." Several peers contended that, the doctrine of the Trinity being unscriptural, the bill was "repugnant to the holy Scripture." The earl of Peterborough declared himself in favor of a parliamentary king but not a parliamentary God or a parliamentary religion. Dr. White Kennet, the bishop of Peterborough, asserted that the bill "seemed to tend to the setting up of an inquisition."[12] The House of Lords defeated the blasphemy bill by a vote of sixty to thirty-one. Eight prelates voted against it, only five, including Wake, for it.[13] That the peers could reject the blasphemy bill by a two-to-one majority suggests that toleration extended in reality to freethought, notwithstanding the narrowness of the law on the books.

Prosecutions during the 1720s showed that no need existed for a new measure on blasphemy. In 1723, Wake elatedly reported to a correspondent that he had managed to suppress an English translation of the works of Michael Servetus. Servetus, the first systematic anti-Trinitarian theorist, had been roasted to death by John Calvin in 1553 for his "execrable blasphemies." His great book, *Christianity Restored*—"an infinity of blasphemies," Calvin called it—sought to restore Christianity to what it had been before becoming corrupted by pagan doctrines in the fourth century. Dr. Richard Mead, the king's physician and England's foremost bibliophile, sought to publish Servetus's works in 1723, but Wake got word of it somehow, procured a warrant to seize the whole printing, and burned all but a few copies. Mead and his printer were imprisoned.[14]

In 1724, a committee of the House of Lords censured everyone connected with particular issues of *The British Journal*, a weekly paper which contained "a scandalous Libel, highly reflecting upon the Christian Religion." Those issues carried essays signed "Cato," pseudonymously by John Trenchard and Thomas Gordon, radical Whigs who stood in the forefront of the struggle for expanding the rights of conscience and of political expression. Their pieces were collected in various editions, under the title of *Cato's Letters: Or, Essays on Liberty, Civil and Religious*. The four-volume collection went through six editions between 1733 and 1755; it was, wrote a historian of American political theory, "the most popular, quotable, esteemed source of political ideas in the colonial period."[15]

The essays did not warrant being charged with blasphemy or reflecting on Christianity. They savaged the episcopal hierarchy and priests generally, for their love of power, corruption, bigotry, and persecution, not for their religious beliefs, except as to the doctrine of the Trinity. "Cato" did not revile or even ridicule the doctrine. He simply argued that it was incomprehensible and had to be taken on faith, a criticism of those who contended that the doctrine did not transcend human reason. But his vehement anticlericalism and attacks on the establishment led a grand jury to charge that Cato had "openly blasphemed and denied the doctrine of the ever-blessed Trinity." The grand jury also charged that the obviously deistic principles advanced by Cato denied God's governance in human affairs; his aspersions on the clergy also brought Christianity into contempt. Trenchard and Gordon never faced trial, however, because they had the backing of powerful Whig leaders.[16]

At about this time, in 1723, the grand jury of Middlesex also accused Bernard Mandeville of blasphemy in his book, *The Fable of the Bees.* The jury charged that his blasphemy was so "diabolical" that it had "a direct Tendency to the Subversion of all Religion and Civil Government." Mandeville spread a "general Libertinism" and "exploded" Christianity by running down religion and virtue as prejudicial to society and to government, while he urged that all sorts of vices were necessary for the public welfare. Five years later, another Middlesex grand jury presented Mandeville, alleging that he had undermined the authority of the Bible and advocated "a Freedom of thinking and acting whatever Men please." His *Fable of the Bees* was "atheistical" and had "many blasphemous passages." The grand jury complained that in 1728 a fifth edition had appeared, despite the earlier grand jury's condemnation. In his latest revision, Mandeville had even incorporated the grand jury's charges of 1723 together with his "scandalous and infamous Reflections."[17]

Mandeville's book, one of the most controversial and widely read of the eighteenth century, did in fact advocate the view concisely put in the subtitle: *Private Vices, Publick Benefits.* He wrote with sardonic wit as he developed that wicked paradox, claiming that vice, crime, and luxury were beneficial to society and government. Mandeville even declared that "what we call Evil in this World, Moral as well as Natural," rather than virtue, was the "Foundation of Society." Religion taught virtues that could be acquired by reason and self-denial; those virtues were damaging. The "moment Evil ceases, the Society must be spoiled." He argued that a nation of atheists could be as moral as one of Christians, and would probably be healthier, more prosperous, and more powerful. The analogy to the beehive concerned the vicious conduct of each bee that resulted in a thriving hive. Mandeville's "evil" consisted of private vices—selfishness, materialism, and passion. In effect, he described a capitalist order in which vice or self-interest constituted the spring of human conduct. His work was a precursor of Adam Smith's and of laissez-faire. It made religion sound irrelevant or damaging to social welfare, and as a result it seemed to advocate atheism and immorality. Not surprisingly, *Fable of the Bees* also seemed blasphemous. Mandeville's case never came to trial, however, because he was befriended by the earl of Macclesfield, who had been lord chancellor. Mandeville's cause probably gained from a fact that he pointed out: he intended his book only for people of "knowledge and education," who could understand speculative theory and afford the price of 5 shillings.[18]

The next person to be attacked for blasphemy was the Unitarian Edward Elwell, a prosperous merchant of Wolverhampton in Staffordshire. An extraordinary man, whose tracts sold cheaply and were intended for all people, he turned his prosecution for blasphemy at the Stafford Assizes in 1726 into a personal triumph. His trial seems to have been unusual too, even after one makes allowances for the fact that we know about it only from his own account, written well after the event. A great crowd attended, he recalled, "for it was thought there was a thousand people at the trial." Sixty years later, an aged man still remembered the vivid impression Elwell had made on the court and the spectators.[19]

At the time of his prosecution, Elwell looked much older than his fifty years. Tall and white-haired, he wore a long beard and flowing garments. Although he lacked a university education, he wrote several Unitarian tracts and effectively defended himself at his trial, speaking with striking fluency, earnestness, and presence of mind. He may have been a religious eccentric, but his piety and integrity won the respect of his trial judge.

Always a strong individualist, Elwell, once a Presbyterian, had studied his Bible and formed his own religious opinions. He believed that Saturday, the seventh day, was the Sabbath; therefore, he did no business that day, yet opened his shop on Sunday. That practice earned him the sobriquet "Jew Elwell," by which he was known long after he left Wolverhampton for London, following his acquittal. His tracts promoted his religious beliefs and defended civil and religious liberties generally. He vigorously rejected the doctrine of the Trinity as illogical and unbiblical, but his words lacked hostility, vindictiveness, or meanness.

Archbishop Wake, with whom Elwell initiated a correspondence, must have seen something in his work that merited a reply, despite strong disagreements. In 1724, the archbishop, having read Elwell's *A True Testimony for God*, felt upset enough to ask for its suppression. The tract ridiculed the divinity of Christ "not in a scholastic manner to convince men of learning but in a popular way," the archbishop wrote. But he explicitly urged that Elwell "may not suffer at all for it," especially because he seemed eager to be martyred. The archbishop declared himself an enemy "to everything that looks like persecution on account of religion. But yet the book may be suppressed though the writer not be punished."[20]

Two years later, in 1726, when a prosecution was begun against Elwell, he attributed it to the malice of local clergymen. The priests raged, he wrote, until a grand jury indicted him for blasphemy. According to Elwell's strange account, he replied negatively to the question from his judge whether he had a copy of the indictment; the judge, Alexander

Denton, blamed the clergy rather than the government for having failed to provide it. Clearly, however, Elwell had read the indictment, which he said was as big as a book; it quoted generously from his own book to prove that he had blasphemed. On learning that Elwell did not have a copy of the indictment, Judge Denton declared that, if he would give bail, the trial would be postponed until the next Assizes. Elwell, who apparently had no counsel, replied that he refused to give bail and wished to plead to the indictment. When Judge Denton agreed, Elwell discoursed for over an hour about his belief in the "pure, uncorrupted Unitarian doctrine of one God," proving, presumably, that his rejection of the doctrine of the Trinity followed the Bible and therefore could not be blasphemous. He also condemned the "hell-born principle of persecution."[21]

Elwell apparently spoke without interruption, as if no prosecutor were present to object to the irregular procedure. According to Elwell's account, when he finished, a justice of the peace walked to the bench, put his hand on the judge's shoulder, and declared that he knew personally that Elwell, his neighbor, was an honest man. Judge Denton then commended Elwell for his biblical knowledge and inquired whether he had ever consulted with learned bishops of the established church. Elwell proudly replied that he and the primate of England had corresponded on the matter, and he had four letters from Dr. Wake to prove it. But Wake had not convinced him; Elwell would accept only biblical evidence, whereas the archbishop relied on postbiblical statements to prove the doctrine of the Trinity.

After consulting with the local clergy, Judge Denton told Elwell that he had given offense by writing against commonly received doctrines. Would Elwell promise not to write any more tracts on his religious beliefs? "God forbid," Elwell replied, "that I should make thee any such promise" contrary to God's "word and pleasure." According to Elwell, Denton then announced that the defendant was acquitted, and the clerk of the court informed him that he was free to go. Neither the king's attorney nor a jury figured in the proceedings, from which Elwell emerged to the crowd's acclaim. He ended his story by referring to the "stupidity" of the Trinitarians, who "feed upon ashes." Clearly, however, Elwell would have fed upon the ashes if Archbishop Wake had wanted him punished or if Judge Denton did not, in Elwell's words, have a "heart knit in love to me."[22] Elwell's case showed that, notwithstanding the Blasphemy Act of 1698, the common law punished anti-Trinitarianism only when it was accompanied by malice against Christianity.

Soon after this occurred one of the most important developments in the history of the law of blasphemy. The law of obscenity derived from the doctrine that religion, Christianity in particular, is part of the common law of the land. In effect, the King's Bench split obscene libel off from blasphemous libel, creating an entirely new branch of libel law. Obscenity, which resists a definition that will allow courts to know what falls within legal limits and what falls outside, deals mainly with bodily functions, sexual and excremental, but primarily sexual. Obscenity may be prurient, but sexual arousal is not necessarily its intent or its effect.

English law lacked a means of coping with printed obscenity before blasphemy became a common-law offense. The law of libel protected the reputation of particular individuals, of the government, and, after Taylor's case in 1676, of Christianity.[23] Obscene books and pamphlets existed in Elizabethan and Stuart England, of course; references to "lewd," "indecent," "bawdy," "naughty," or "obscene" works abound. Occasionally, complaints against them had triggered prosecutions, but for breach of peace or some other trumped-up crime. Obscenity itself simply was not criminal. Prerogative courts, such as the Star Chamber or High Commission, had taken rare notice of obscenity but made no clear law. After the abolition of those courts in 1640, the ecclesiastical courts supposedly took jurisdiction of moral offenses that prerogative courts once may have had in theory. But no ecclesiastical case law on obscenity developed; anyway, ecclesiastical courts could impose only ecclesiastical punishments that could have no preventive or retributory effect on dealers in obscene works. Not that England was impotent in the matter; it was indifferent.

When Parliament passed the Licensing Act of 1662, it aimed only at persons who presumed to print heretical, seditious, schismatic, or "offensive" books or pamphlets. But those works had to be "offensive" in the sense of conveying a doctrine or opinion contrary to the Christian faith or the Church of England, or in the sense of scandalizing religion, the church, the government, officers of church or state, corporations, or particular people.[24] Similarly, when a royally sponsored society pledged itself in 1694 to combat vice, its proposal for the reformation of public manners censured blasphemy, Sabbath-breaking, whoring, and drunkenness, not obscenity. And when Queen Anne in 1702 issued a proclamation against gambling, profanity, blasphemy, and other vices, she made no reference to obscenity. Nevertheless, it was becoming recognized as a crime. In the 1680s, some prosecutions in the quarter-sessions courts had resulted in convictions. The defendants in those cases did not seek a review.[25]

In 1707, however, the crown prosecuted some printers directly in the Court of Queen's Bench, as if obscenity were a crime that merited the attention of the highest criminal court in the land. One of the defendants, James Read, stood charged with having published a lascivious libel in the form of a slim book of poetry entitled *The Fifteen Plagues of a Maiden Head*. Lord Chief Justice John Holt, the great jurist himself, presided. After conviction, Read moved in arrest of judgment on the ground that the court had no jurisdiction over a matter that constituted no crime at common law. Holt sustained him, declaring that the ecclesiastical courts had exclusive jurisdiction. "If we have no precedent," he ruled, "we cannot punish. Shew me any precedent." The parties had disagreed about the meaning of the 1663 case of Sir Charles Sedley, whose outrageous, drunken behavior included "preaching Blasphemy to the People," publicly exposing himself, and "throwing down bottles (pist in) vi et armis [with force and violence] among the people."[26] In response to the crown's argument that Sedley's case provided the necessary precedent for the criminality of obscenity, Justice John Powell said that Read's case

> is for bawdy stuff, that reflects on no person; and a libel must be against some particular person or persons, or against the government. It is stuff not fit to be mentioned publicly. If there is no remedy in the Spiritual court, it does not follow there must be a remedy here. There is no law to punish it. I wish there were; but we cannot make law. It indeed tends to the corruption of good manners, but that is not sufficient for us to punish. As to the case of sir Charles Sedley, there was something more in that case than shewing his naked body in the balcony; for that case was quod vi et armis he pissed down upon the people's heads.[27]

Read's case demonstrated that obscenity constituted no crime at common law, and that Sedley's crime consisted in violent behavior rather than obscenity or, for that matter, rather than mere blasphemy. The case of Edmund Curll, decided by King's Bench in 1727, reversed Read's case, focusing English (and American) law on a new crime.

Edmund Curll was a publisher and bookseller of notorious reputation because of his shady business practices and his indecent books. In 1725, he was convicted in the King's Bench for publishing obscenities but was released on the ground that only the ecclesiastical courts had jurisdiction over the offense. In fact, those courts had never tried a case involving a printed or written obscenity. In 1728, Curll was again prosecuted for the same crime in the same court, was again convicted, and again moved to have his conviction set aside.[28]

The attorney general of England, Lord Hardwicke, personally argued the prosecution's case against the motion for arrest of judgment. He insisted that obscenity was a common-law offense, because it corrupted the morals of the people and constituted a breach of the peace. The peace might be broken without actual force, he contended, if a libel was against the government or religion or morality. Uttering blasphemous words tended to subvert both church and state. Christianity was part of the law of the land; therefore, morality was part of the law too. Read's case, he concluded, had been wrongly decided twenty years earlier.

Lord Chief Justice Robert Raymond declared that "this is a case of very great consequences," which might be easily decided but for the precedent in Read's case. Raymond agreed with the attorney general, saying that "libel" is not necessarily a technical word, "and if it reflects on religion, virtue, or morality; if it tends to disturb the civil order of society, I think it is a temporal offence." Justice Fortescue disagreed, although he acknowledged Curll's to be "a great offence." The law simply did not punish it. Another member of the court observed that particular immoral acts such as drunkenness and swearing were punishable; he thought that an obscene book should also be punishable, even if it targeted no one in particular. If it had "a general immoral tendency," it affected everyone. A fourth member of the court who expressed an opinion was also inclined to the view that obscenity should be regarded as a crime at common law. He reasoned that a breach of peace tended to weaken morality. The remaining members of the court were divided or indecisive. Because of the importance of the case, the uncertain court agreed to hold it over to the next term and hear rearguments.

The sudden retirement of Justice Fortescue resulted in the appointment of a man with the views of the attorney general on the subject of obscenity. At the same time, Curll somehow offended the court. As a result, it changed its mind about rearguments and unanimously held that an obscene libel constituted a temporal crime. The judges seem never to have considered that Parliament should enact a statute making it a crime. They reasoned, rather, that religion was part of the common law "and therefore whatever is an offence against that, is evidently an offence against the common law. Now morality is the fundamental part of religion, and therefore whatever strikes against that, must for the same reason be an offence against the common law." They offered as a case "to this very point" *Rex* v. *Taylor*, in which the court had ruled, in 1676, that blasphemy was a common-law crime because Christianity was part of the common law. In that case, never before associated with obscenity, Taylor had said "Christ is a bastard" and "a whore-master" and that religion was "a cheat."[29] Read's case, the court said, had been wrongly decided. Curll was fined and pilloried for his crime. When he was removed from the pillory, a crowd triumphantly carried him to a nearby tavern to celebrate.

The reliance of Curll's judges on Taylor's case as the governing precedent made sense from the standpoint of Christian moralism. Even from a legal standpoint, both cases involved libels that victimized religion; in Curll's case, the obscene book was entitled *Venus in Her Cloister, or the Nun in Her Smock*, purportedly an exposé of the sex life of nuns. It was more anti-Catholic and anticlerical than bawdy, but it did assault religious sensibilities.

The connection between obscene libel and blasphemous libel continued for a long while, which is why no rash of obscenity prosecutions followed Curll's case. It scarcely affected the expression of sexual frankness. Throughout the eighteenth century, the few cases involving obscene libel retained a religious aspect in some way; a merely indecent publication did not warrant a prosecution for obscene libel. Indeed, the most famous obscene book of the century, *Fanny Hill: Memoirs of a Woman of Pleasure* (1749), by John Cleland, faced only some threats, instigated by Thomas Sherlock, bishop of London, who accurately described it as the lewdest book ever; but it sold openly, and the author and his printers and booksellers were never prosecuted. *Fanny Hill* described explicit sex, without in any way involving religion.[30] Mere immorality did not constitute the essence of the literary crime of obscene libel.

Not even physical nudity was regarded as obscene until the next century. Two similar cases show the change in public, or legal, understanding of obscenity. In 1733, just a few years after the decision in Curll's case, a woman was prosecuted for running in public naked to the waist. Despite the government's reliance on the Sedley and Curll precedents, and the contention that the woman's nudity violated good morals, the indictment was quashed, "for nothing appears immodest or unlawful."[31] In 1809, however, a man was convicted for bathing nude in public, although the judges discharged him because "this is the first prosecution of this sort in modern times."[32] Obscene libel unconnected with blasphemy, or with religion in some way, took a long time to mature as a separate branch of libel.

Conventional blasphemy remained a potentially dangerous crime. The Reverend Thomas Woolston's case of 1729 was the most important blasphemy prosecution since the King's Bench had first laid down the rule in 1676 that blasphemy constituted a common-law crime because Christianity formed part of the law of the land. When Woolston died in 1733, an anonymous friend wrote of him that he "dyed under Persecution of Religion."[33] Nearly every reference to his case mentions that he died in prison. That was true, but under the Rules of the King's Bench, which he enjoyed as a crown favor, Woolston's home had been his prison. He might have regained his liberty if he had sworn never again to publish his opinions of religion. That would have violated the promptings of his conscience, and he refused to trade his intellectual freedom for his freedom of movement. Nor was he averse to the sense of martyrdom that his status as a prisoner had thrust upon him.[34]

Woolston was an Anglican priest and a patristic scholar of Cambridge

University. He had graduated from Sidney Sussex College, earned a master's degree, took religious orders, and became a resident fellow. From the early church fathers, Origen in particular, Woolston learned to interpret the Scriptures allegorically. In 1705, he published his first book, *The Old Apology for the Truth of the Christian Religion*, an orthodox account based on his lectures and sermons, in which he purported to demonstrate with much ancient learning that Moses forecast Jesus and that the Old Testament prophesied the events of the New.

In 1720, at the age of fifty-one, when Woolston was regarded as a master of the church fathers, he suddenly left the university for London and began a career as a productive writer of allegorical interpretations of the Bible. After several Latin publications, a flow of English tracts followed. One sympathetically depicted the Quakers, whose allegorical views Woolston used to browbeat the literalism of the Anglican clergy.[35] In a similar work of 1721, he defended the apostles and primitive church fathers for their allegorical interpretation against the literalists of his own time.[36] Allegory reinforced Woolston's personal views and enabled him to censure the "hireling priests" of the establishment as ignoramuses, even heretics.

The usual interpretation of Woolston's writings is that they proved him to have been a loony deist. Nothing else seems to account for a respectable Anglican priest and distinguished scholar's having suddenly turned against his church and religion. Leslie Stephen, in his influential *History of English Thought in the Eighteenth Century*, spoke of "poor mad Woolston, most scandalous of the deists," referred to his mental derangement nine times, and concluded that his "morbid delight in giving scandal . . . only leaves us in doubt whether his profanity was a symptom of lunacy or one of the methods of pandering to vicious popular tastes." Given that choice, Stephen declared that Woolston spoke "the language of an inhabitant of Bedlam."[37] Others have claimed that his writings "contain the most undisguised abuse which had been uttered against Christianity since the days of the early Christians," explicable only by insanity;[38] that he declared that "Christ was not even a good man;"[39] that he was "not sound in his intellect" and was "scarcely sane";[40] and that he was "rabid" and that "his madness was on the side of deism."[41] Some of these judgments come from sympathizers with free thought. All seem to parrot orthodox tract writers of Woolston's own time. The Reverend Thomas Stackhouse, for example, one of the most influential of the sixty or so controversialists who entered the lists against Woolston, wrote that his prejudice against Christianity and his shocking allegorical interpretations of the New Testament were the product of a "great Disorder of Mind." Stackhouse found no other explanation of why a sincere scholar and clergyman would be a "blasphemer of the holy name of Jesus."[42]

Woolston himself prayed that God would continue him "in that state of reason he had been graciously pleased to restore me to."[43] And almost every writer of his time and since has classified him as a deist. But Woolston regarded himself as a good Christian or, at least, insisted that he was a believing one.

Because of Woolston's prolonged absence from the university and his refusal to resume residence, he was deprived of his fellowship, though he attributed its loss to the hostility against his writings.[44] In 1725, a grand jury indicted him for blasphemy, because he had carried his allegorical interpretation so far that he seemed to question the truth of Mary's virginity and of the resurrection of Christ.[45] However, the prosecution dropped Woolston's case. William Whiston, Locke's successor, who had also lost his position at Cambridge because of unorthodoxy yet remained an esteemed scholar, interceded in Woolston's behalf with Sir Philip York, the king's attorney general. Woolston himself obtained an audience with the archbishop of Canterbury, and made a favorable impression. Wake declared his opposition to "all Prosecutions in Matters of Religion" and to this prosecution in particular. Woolston and the primate apparently enjoyed each other's company; they discussed the church fathers, and Woolston, who thought of himself as the pre-eminent patristic scholar, declared that he had never heard anyone talk with more judgment and learning than Archbishop Wake.[46]

The prosecution against him having been scotched, Woolston became bolder in his publications. Believing rationalists and unbelieving deists had both attacked the Bible; its defenders found security for their faith in Gospel stories of the miracles wrought by Jesus. Most of Woolston's previous assaults had been aimed against "the hireling clergy." His allegorical interpretations had derided his fellow priests and their hierarchical superiors, whom he seemed to despise, because they preached for money and believed in a literal interpretation of the Scriptures. To Woolston, only dimwits took the Bible literally; they killed rather than nourished the spirit, and they inculcated superstition as the foundation of Christianity. Although the corrupt, hireling clergy remained his bête noire, he decided to focus on the miracles to prove the errancy and foolishness of literally accepting the Gospel accounts, and he seems to have followed the strategic plan of exposing to his allegorical interpretations the lesser miracles first, gradually working up to the major one, the resurrection of Jesus.

In 1727, Woolston published the first of his six *Discourses on the Miracles of Our Saviour*.[47] Each discourse took up miracles of increasing marvelousness, and Woolston dedicated each book to a different bishop by name. The first, dedicated to Edmund Gibson, bishop of London, who finally brought the prosecution against Woolston, immediately raised the question whether Woolston used the allegorical interpretation in his discourses as a device to mask an attack on the fundamentals of Christianity as well as on the clergy who preached literal belief in the New Testament. Was he seeking to minimize the danger of prosecution? Or did he call himself an "Allegorical Christian" and employ allegorical interpretation because he genuinely believed in it, had consistently used it in most of his writings, and meant what he said—namely, that he sought to place Christianity upon a better footing by returning it to the primitive church as the early church fathers allegorically described it? Insistently he represented himself as a "true Believer of the Religion of Christ" and as "a real advocate for the Truth of Christianity." Every one of the discourses stressed his purpose to "prove Christ's Religion and Messiahship."[48]

Was allegory fiction, fable, and fraud, or was it inspired insight into the real meanings of the Gospel? Even if Woolston intended his allegories to be constructive, he gave most of his space to exposing the improbabilities of each miracle, little space to his reinterpretation of each, and still less to saying anything constructive. For example, when discussing the first miracle in the first discourse, Jesus driving the merchants out of the Temple precincts, Woolston embroidered the theme that one man without a whip could not have put so many to flight, would have opened himself to damage suits, would have been liable for inciting a riot, and achieved nothing, because everything returned to normal soon after. In keeping with his systematic rejection of a literal reading as passing bounds of belief, as "downright Antichristianism," and as "fraud" and "deceit," Woolston, borrowing from church fathers, construed the Temple as the Christian church and the merchants as those who sold Christ's message, the hireling clergy. The real meaning of the allegory, he declared, was that the church would one day be purified by the ejection of those who sought to make "merchandise of the Gospel."

Woolston interpreted almost every miracle in a way that allowed him to lambaste the clergy of the Church of England. Thus, the barren fig tree showed how barren was the clergy; the blind and halt and paralyzed were those who accepted a literal interpretation of the Bible; and the turning of water into wine was the turning of the letter into a spiritual interpretation. To Woolston, the resurrection was an absurd lie; the disciples had stolen the body.[49] But the resurrection possessed significance because the sepulcher is the letter of the Scriptures and those who crucified Jesus are the ministers of the letter. Woolston did little to restore the true Gospel, after having exposed the miracles to his logic and lampoonery, as well as his billingsgate.

If Woolston had written in Latin for an audience of fellow scholars, or had addressed himself to them in English in the usual forbidding style of a pedant, he might have angered some bishops without provoking the government to intervene with a prosecution. But Woolston possessed a robust, clear style embellished with some wit and vulgarity. He had the literary gift of knowing how to make a pedant's point in crisp, vivid English, laced with ridicule and ribaldry. As a result, his prose was readable, and his discourses on the miracles sold enough copies to make him popular to many, notorious to others, and prosperous if he had not insisted on paying all publication costs. Voltaire and Dean Swift both testified from firsthand knowledge that Woolston's books were huge successes. The discourses quickly ran to six editions and sold at least thirty thousand copies. Thus, even if Woolston meant to buttress Christianity by showing new allegorical meanings that were more sensible than the literal ones, he seemed to constitute a danger to the established church. What he said offended many people and made others laugh at the miracles stories when taken literally. Those who had relied on the miracles as proofs of Christianity, with which they could refute skeptics, concluded, as did the Reverend Stackhouse, that the Reverend Woolston was not just a turncoat but had become "an Enemy of Christianity, a Blasphemer of the holy name of Jesus."[50]

Early in 1727, even before the appearance of the last two discourses on miracles—the fifth on the resurrection of Lazarus and the sixth on Jesus' own resurrection—the government filed four "informations" or accusations against Woolston, one for each discourse. Charged with having blasphemed in each one, he was tried by jury in the great Guildhall of London, before the King's Bench presided over by Lord Chief Justice Robert Raymond. Although he praised Raymond for his impartiality, Woolston objected to being tried by persons, however learned and worthy, who were as unqualified to judge him in religious matters as he was to judge them on points of law. He mentioned too, at his 1729 trial, that he had talked to Archbishop Wake about the prosecution and his books. Wake had remarked that he wished Woolston had not dwelt so much on hireling priests. Woolston had replied, he told Chief Justice Raymond, that "the Shoe pinches."[51] Whether the primate felt the insult and abandoned Woolston to his fate, or was unable to call off his outraged clergy, remains uncertain.

In any case, Woolston wholly misunderstood Wake's true feelings about him. In a private letter, Wake stated that "the enemies of Christianity," in order to ridicule Christ's miracles, had set up a man who was once made mad "and whose friends would persuade us he is so still, to cover him from the punishment his blasphemies deserve." Woolston's writings, Wake continued, pleased "the younger sort of Atheists," who relished seeing sacred matters lampooned, but "this man (under the shelter of madness) goes unpunished and even unrestrained, to the scandal of our country." Wake added, however, that "we have the government with us against these bold men. . . ."[52] As a matter of fact, the attorney general, who behaved relentlessly, took personal charge of the prosecution.

In his opening statement, the attorney general depicted Woolston's discourses on miracles as "the most Blasphemous Book that was ever publish'd in any Age whatsoever, in which our Saviour is compared to a Conjurer, Magician and Imposter, and the Holy Gospel, as wrote by the Blessed Evangelists, turn'd into Ridicule and Ludicrous Banter, the Literal Scope and Meaning wrested, and the whole presented as idle Romance and Fiction."[53] Although Woolston's counsel—a Mr. Birch, who volunteered his services—repeatedly insisted that Woolston had given metaphorical meanings to the miracles in order to strengthen Christianity, the attorney general demanded to know why Woolston had not engaged in serious discourse instead of ridicule and burlesque. When Birch denied Woolston's criminal intent to bring disgrace on Christianity and reiterated that the defendant meant to assist it, the prosecutor retorted that the author of a treasonous libel would not be excused merely because he also said, "God save the King."

The evidence against Woolston consisted in his discourses. The prosecution read choice extracts from each of the four discourses, miracle by miracle, giving the jury to understand that the extracts brought Jesus and his doctrines into contempt and scorned the New Testament. Woolston argued that in each discourse he had reconstrued the miracles in a mystical sense to suggest wonders that the spiritual Christ would do in the future. However, Lord Chief Justice Raymond instructed the jury that in the opinion of the court the defendant's allegation that he had sought to affirm the true basis of Christianity could not be credited. That Woolston had not denied the Scriptures did not exempt him from the law's retribution if he ridiculed or vilified them. Raymond repudiated the argument that the crime, if it existed, merited only ecclesiastical jurisdiction, and that its prosecution had the dangerous tendency of encouraging prosecutions for mere differences of opinion, which the law tolerated. Raymond declared that the divine laws, being part of the law of the kingdom, were protected by it. In Taylor's case, Hale had said, as if it were self-evident, that Christianity was part and parcel of the laws of the land; Raymond accepted and repeated that crucial dictum. Blasphemy was therefore punishable because it constituted "an attempt to subvert the established religion." No one could blaspheme or deride Christianity without striking at its root and breaching the common law. In response to the technical argument that the indictment should have been dismissed because the crown had not prosecuted under the Blasphemy Act of 1698, Raymond also ruled that a crime at common law remained a crime despite the lesser punishment fixed by Parliament for a first offense.

The jury returned a verdict of guilty on all four informations without leaving the room to deliberate. Raymond sentenced Woolston to a fine of £100, one year in prison, and payment of sureties in the amount of £2,000 to ensure that he would never again publish his religious opinions.[54] In confinement, Woolston finished his final two discourses, one on the resurrection of the dead by Jesus and the other on Jesus' own resurrection, which Woolston described as "the most . . . barefaced Imposture ever put upon the world," one that was "most monstrous and notorious" when understood literally.[55] The government ignored both books, but the bishops published replies calculated to maintain the faith and to denigrate Woolston's scholarship.[56]

Leslie Stephen, the historian, endorsed the views of the bishops and Chief Justice Raymond. Stephen not only felt "disgust" on reading Woolston but discerned "no particular conviction or intelligible purpose."[57] Stephen could not find any redeeming merit in Woolston's argument in favor of freedom of thought even for the expression of opinion regarded as blasphemous by society.

Although Woolston placed himself somewhere between an "infidel" or "freethinking" deist at the one extreme and a literalist on the other, he championed liberty of utterance even for freethinkers. He acknowledged that "to write any Thing that tends to the Subversion or Prejudice of the Civil Society" was "an heinous Crime," thus seeming to invalidate his pleas for intellectual liberty for himself. But he denied having committed that crime and did not regard blasphemy as subversive. "Blasphemy," he contended, was merely a "Bugbear Word" used to frighten the people and make them abhor its supposed advocates. But even blasphemers, he contended, were entitled to the revenge of God rather than of the civil magistrate. God, being omnipotent, knew how and when "to reckon with such Blasphemers, without calling upon the Civil Magistrate to do it for him." Woolston would limit punishment to repudiation by those who would reprimand the blasphemer for his ideas and lack of manners. He would allow "universal and unbounded Toleration of Religion, without any Restrictions or Impositions on Men's Consciences." Such a freedom would multiply the number of sects, but Woolston regarded that prospect in the most favorable light. He believed that ten thousand different notions of religion would no more harm society than as "many different Noses do." Different sects served as "a Check upon each other," promoted virtue both public and private, and led to a "Downfall of the Ecclesiastical Power" and of "an hired and establish'd Priesthood."[58] Such remarks skirted close to seditious libel, because Woolston assaulted the state church, at whose head stood the monarch.

Woolston, after being convicted, accepted Raymond's ruling that he had transgressed the law of the land by writing "against Christianity, establish'd in it," but he criticized the law; he also continued to advocate that Christianity benefited by an extension of liberty even to infidels and deists. "Whatever our zealous Clergy may think, one Persecution of an Infidel does more harm to Religion, than the Publication of the worst Book against it." He trusted that truth and disputation could not harm Christianity. He supported the liberty of the press, he wrote, not for his own security but for the betterment of the religion of Jesus Christ. Even if one assumed the very worst about his theological ideas and intention, "what Harm can my Arguings for them do to the Community? None at all. If they are not of God, they will come to nought sooner and better than by a Persecution of me for them. But if they are of God, they will stand and prevail against all Opposition of the Clergy" if they take any measures beyond "what Reason and Religion" allowed. Neither atheists nor deists presented more dangerous consequences to the modern priesthood than prosecutions of Christian allegories. Woolston's argument for freedom of expression in religious matters and for liberty of the press had no support whatever from state or church, but that argument was well wrought for its time, and time would validate it, on the whole.[59]

His prosecution had come at the peak of the deist movement in England. Matthew Tindal's book escaped prosecution, probably because Tindal, who called himself a "Christian Deist," sought to reconcile rationalism and supernaturalism rather than reject or scoff at the supernatural.

Woolston's case stirred an astonishing number of publications, mostly in opposition to his religious views. One writer, Edward Waddington, bishop of Chichester, struck a small blow for freedom of expression when he professed that no one should be punished for declaring his atheism or for writing against the Christian religion; Waddington believed, however, that Woolston's offensive style was blasphemous. Still, when the law made criminal the mere denial of Christianity, the bishop's view had a latitudinarian character. Dr. Nathaniel Lardner, who became a great nonconformist leader, had the truly libertarian view. He would, like Waddington, have preferred a discussion that was conducted in tones of gravity, and he deplored Woolston's style as much as the bishop did. But Lardner understood that if people had an allowance to write against Christianity, as Waddington proposed, "there must also be considerable indulgence as to the manner likewise." Christian forbearance obligated Christians to suffer the offensiveness of Woolston's writings. "The proper punishment of a low, mean, indecent, scurrilous way of writing," declared Lardner, should be scorn and indignation, leaving "all further punishment to HIM, to whom vengeance belongs." Legal coercion dishonored Christianity, thought Lardner, and invited a sense of abuse. Thus, Lardner accepted Woolston's theory of freedom for any opinions on the subject of religion, even if blasphemous.[60]

Two legal works of 1729, the year of the trial, deserve attention. One was by John Disney, an Anglican clergyman who had been a lawyer and a magistrate. His book, *A View of Ancient Laws against Immorality and Profaneness*, included a learned, orthodox discourse on the law of blasphemy. Disney troubled to learn his subject and presented a comparative view of it that covered ancient Jewish law, Greek writers, the laws of Justinian, and subsequent civil-law developments. All of it showed that blasphemy was a severe crime in any civilized society. Accurately, Disney defined blasphemy as denial, reproach, or insult to "the Being and Attributes of God, the Person or Character of Christ, the Operations of the Holy Spirit, or the Truth and Authority of the Scriptures; to ascribe to any of these, what is unworthy of them, and degrading; or to any Creature, an Excellence which only can belong to God." Disney urged that the honor of God be avenged by the magistrate whenever affronted. Magistrates, he insisted, must exert their authority against blasphemers.[61]

The contrary view appeared in the second legal work of 1729, a tract by a pseudonymous author who signed himself "John Wickliffe" after the great Protestant reformer. He offered *Remarks Upon two late Presentments of the Grand-Jury of the County of Middlesex*, referring to the accusations of blasphemy that had been leveled against Mandeville's *Fable of the Bees*, some essays by the authors of *Cato's Letters*, and Woolston's tracts. "Wickliffe" was not a deist. He identified himself as a member of the Church of England, indicated that he believed in Christ, and referred to "that ridiculous creature Woolston" and to his "absurd Books." Wickliffe was more than a latitudinarian; he was the only writer who rejected the idea that denial of God, Christianity, Christ, the Trinity, or religion should be taken as a crime. He made no distinction between belief and conduct, the usual latitudinarian tactic of supporting freedom of thought on condition that the thoughts did not lead to some action deemed criminal by society. "Civil Liberty," Wickliffe wrote, "is a Liberty to do what we judge proper," conditioned only by the restriction "that we don't hurt any body else by it." He also believed in what we think of as separation of church and state. Not until the close of the eighteenth century would any other writer match Wickliffe's liberalism.[62]

He divided his tract into three sections. In the anticlerical preface, he explained that he wrote in favor not of infidelity but of "the Liberty for other Men to write in behalf of it," if they thought fit. By "infidelity" or infidelism he meant repudiation or denial of religion, God, or the Bible. He believed that the grand juries that had accused Mandeville and Woolston of blasphemy had acted out of a misguided zeal that harmed the public. He meant to prove that the only way, not just the best way, of coping with people called blasphemers was to proceed as two bishops had in Woolston's case, the "mild way, by Dint of Pen and only." In the second section, he reprinted verbatim the two grand-jury presentments, of 1723 and 1728. In the third section, he mercilessly analyzed every allegation made in those accusations in order to support the contention in his subtitle: *The Folly and Injustice of Mens persecuting one another for Difference of Opinion in Matters of Religion: And the ill Consequences wherewith that Practice must affect any State in which it is encouraged.* He consistently treated ridicule and offensiveness as expressions of differences of opinion.

Wickliffe agreed with the grand juries that publication "against our most Holy Religion" had a direct tendency to propagate infidelity but disagreed that infidelity meant a corruption of moral values. Morality, he contended, did not depend on the Christian religion. He saw no crime or blasphemy in expressing disbelief in Christianity or religion. Disdaining the assertion that blasphemy undermined the foundation of government or religion, he declared that the way to deal with it was not by force or punishment but by promoting Christian practices and propagating the faith. He knew of nothing more subversive to Christianity or good government than the suppression of blasphemy by law or force. He believed that the right to worship God as one pleased "or not at all" belonged to everyone, without exception. Despite his association of Roman Catholicism with bigotry and persecution, he believed that Catholics were entitled to equal rights. He defined religious liberty as the liberty of anyone to say and do as he pleased with regard to religion, "provided that in so doing he hurt no Man." Contrary to the grand juries, he declared: "For the Life of me, I cannot find how any Man's believing or not believing the Christian religion, makes the Foundation of his Majesty's Government . . . a bit the better or worse." Disbelief did not alter the king's title to the crown, or his status as the head of the established religion.[63]

As for the doctrine of the Trinity, he saw nothing wrong or criminal in "exploding" it or the Scriptures, nor anything wrong in what one grand jury had called "the Freedom of thinking and acting whatever Men please." The grand jury had also condemned, as "diabolical attempts against religion," the blasphemy or denial of the Trinity or the advocacy of the Arian heresy. Wickliffe asserted that, in all probability, no one connected with the accusations had any idea what the Arian heresy was; rather, they took the position that if the blasphemers "don't believe as we do, they had as good not believe at all." Arians, Wickliffe observed, believed in Christ. In any case, real "zealots for Infidelity" should be left alone. To think that God's honor must be avenged for fear of His divine wrath was absurd and presumptuous. No one could know that a famine or some other catastrophe was a visitation of God to punish the existence of blasphemy or punish the failure to revenge it. God could take care of Himself and needed no "privy counsellors" to act in his name.[64]

Blasphemy did not bring contempt on religion, Wickliffe continued. No matter how "vile and unjust the accusations," religion survived and thrived. Reflections on the clergy, deserved or not, might hurt the clergy but could not damage religion, which had survived centuries of assaults by infidels. In response to the assumption by the grand juries that the welfare of religion and government is the same and that an encroachment on one subverted the other, Wickliffe argued that the state could subsist quite prosperously without religion. "King, Lords and Commons may still go on. The Exchange and Westminster-Hall be as much frequented. Trade may flourish, and Justice be duly administered," even if the establishment became Arian, Jewish, or infidel. Jurisdiction over religion, Wickliffe believed, did not belong to the state. The state had no governance over conscience, which involved matters not of this world. Religion rested on "the Minds and Consciences of Men, the other [the state] on the outward Peace and Affluence of the Publick." Wickliffe attested that no nation had "so pure a Religion" or good a government as Great Britain. He wanted no change in either but thought that prosecutions for blasphemy, even if state and church were in ten times the danger that existed, were "the worst way in the World, except Dragoons," of defending either. If infidels attacked with force, they had to be met with force, but if they attacked by publications, they should be met the same way.[65]

Wickliffe grounded his argument on the proposition that church and state should be separate from each other: "the Welfare of Religion (meaning the Christian Religion) and the State (meaning the present, or any other Form of Government) are not the same, but separate and distinct one from the other, as much as the Interests of this World differ from those of the next." He called that "the Independency of the Church on the State." One chose a religion as a means of salvation, a government as a means of securing the good of society, "which are very different Considerations, and quite independent of each other." Embroiling the state in a matter of "Argument" or "a Question in which it ought to be no way concern'd" showed a belief that Christianity could not survive criticism, and that exposed the state to the machinations of those who sought to use its force for their own protection. Blasphemers and infidels could produce as many volumes as they wanted, Wickliffe claimed, without harming the government or Christianity. Prosecutions, he said, revealed a distrust of Christianity to triumph over error and a need for "calling in a foreign Aid, for such I call Force, civil or military." "The growth of Heresy and Infidelity," he concluded, "can bring no dishonour in the World on those who continue in the Orthodox Faith." No one should be reproached for not punishing the views condemned by the grand juries "but such as love to copy after Popery." He was comforted by his belief that he lived under a God who would not wreak His vengeance on the nation whenever a grand jury thought He might because of something someone said.[66] In Wickliffe free thought found its best champion against those who believed that blasphemy should be punished by the state. In him the policy of toleration reached its logical conclusions.

In the following year, 1730, Sollom Emlyn, the son of a convicted blasphemer, wrote a marvelous essay on English criminal law as the preface to a collection of state trials. He stressed a couple of points about indictments for blasphemy that prosecutors, juries, and judges neglected; had those points been observed, Thomas Emlyn, Thomas Woolston, and other religious-minded men should have been acquitted of the charges against them. Sollom Emlyn, who published his father's collected works with a biography of him, observed that juries tended to overlook essential words of an indictment for blasphemous libel: that the words used must be false and malicious. That, he thought, constituted the "very gist of the indictment, and absolutely necessary to constitute the offence." No words could be a reproach to God or religion if true, and no opinion, however wrong, could be a blasphemous one unless expressed with a wicked or criminal intent to revile God or religion. "And yet how often have persons been found guilty upon these Indictments, without any proof either of the falsehood of the positions, or of the malice of him who wrote them?"[67]

Criminal intent, of course, was rarely demonstrated or demonstrable; that is why it was almost invariably inferred from the scandalous words. English law assumed, for example, that, if a man denied the doctrine of the Trinity or joked about tritheism, he must have had a criminal intent, whereas in fact Emlyn and Woolston, in contrast with Taylor or Hall, believed themselves to be faithful Christians without the least intent to revile, reproach, or ridicule religion. Emlyn's test of truth conflicted with the prevailing law of libel at the time—namely, that the greater the truth of an accusation, the greater the offense. Truth may not have been a helpful test of the lawfulness of words involving a belief based on faith; moreover, truth had not yet become a defense against a charge of libel. Neither Emlyn nor Wickliffe confronted the question of bruised sensibilities that arose from remarks that some religious-minded people took as insulting to their deepest beliefs. Wickliffe's reply—answer back and the truth shall win out—ignored the shock and affront that caused blasphemous libel to be regarded as criminal. Telling someone whose deepest convictions are involved that he ought not feel outraged does not soothe him. Nevertheless, Wickliffe was right when he said that words cannot damage religion or God. Emlyn was ahead of his time, as was Wickliffe. Blasphemy prosecutions had prompted them to produce significant contributions to the theory of intellectual freedom.

CHAPTER FIFTEEN

The "Age of Reason"?

"THE SOCIETIE for Free and Candyd Enquirie," better known as the Robin Hood Society, flourished in eighteenth-century London. The name Robin Hood Society derived from the sign over a public house, long its meeting place, although the society met at various locations over the decades. It was a major forum for discussion and debate that attracted all sorts of people from different stations in life. It was more than just "an association of Deists who met for the purpose of theological questions."[1] As a matter of fact, the long-standing president of the society, a baker, defended the established church, of which he was a member. People of all denominations were members, including a Roman Catholic priest, Quakers and other dissenters, and communicants of the Church of England. A 1752 account gave the membership as "about 300" and described the members as consisting of shoemakers, apothecaries, lamplighters, and parish schoolmasters, who met to debate "the most important subjects of Religion, Politics and the Moral Fitness of things." Although petty tradesmen and artisans regularly attended, so did lawyers, politicians, doctors, poets, and actors. A writer in *The Gentleman's Magazine* in 1754 expressed surprise to find "such amazing erudition" among the "clerks, petty tradesmen and the lower mechanics" who spoke up. "Tindal, Collins, Chubb, and Mandeville, they seemed to have got by heart. . . . A shoemaker harangued his five minutes upon the excellency of the tenets maintained by Lord Bolingbroke."[2]

Although sectarians of different beliefs and members of the establishment attended and participated, the society had a reputation for radicalism and free thought. Deists spoke regularly, including Thomas Chubb, a chandler of slight education but formidable intellect, and Peter Annet, who invented two systems of shorthand and was a minor public functionary. Chubb and Annet gained notoriety for their deist publications. Annet, whom an enemy described as "President of an Infidel Society," was remembered long after as a "Satyrist" who expressed himself "with a strength rather dangerous."[3]

A kindred spirit was Jacob Ilive, who preceded Annet to the prisoner's dock. Ilive, a printer and pamphleteer, possessed oratorical talents but little sense of restraint. In 1755, he anonymously published his slashing *Remarks* on the opinions of Thomas Sherlock, the bishop of London. Within a year, Ilive was caught and convicted for "a most blasphemous book . . . denying in a ludicrous manner the divinity of Jesus Christ" and "all revealed religion." He received a severe sentence—imprisonment at hard labor for three years; he served two years before his release. His case is obscure, having left only slight traces in secondary accounts.[4]

Annet's case seems to have made a more considerable impression, perhaps because of his prominence at the time and his previous record. He had been a schoolteacher until obligated to resign his position as a result of his "great Indecency and Blasphemy" in a published reply to the same Bishop Sherlock ten years before Ilive's reply.[5] Sherlock had been one of Woolston's many critics, having written a tract to reply to Woolston's rejection of the resurrection of Christ. In 1744 and 1745, Annet assailed Sherlock's views in two tracts on the resurrection in which he defamed the Gospels as unworthy of belief and compared the resurrection to fables, frauds, and forgeries. That he merely lost his employment suggests that freedom of expression thrived in England even on matters that cut to the Christian bone. Annet prospered and continued to publish, fearlessly. And he was let alone after he published a tract depicting St. Paul as a liar, a hypocrite, and a power-hungry impostor.[6]

In 1761, Annet began publication of a weekly named *Free Enquirer*. The government shut him down after the ninth installment, although he wrote nothing more savage or contemptuous than he had in earlier works. *Free Enquirer* assaulted the Old Testament, chiefly Moses and the Pentateuch. His professed objective was to emancipate Christianity from Judaism and to show it to be a "natural" religion as old as creation. Some of Annet's remarks were amusing, such as his comparison of miracles by Moses to stories in *Don Quixote* and *Gulliver's Travels*. But he was also vicious and vulgar, though no more so than previously. His ridicule finally passed the point of toleration. An indulgent *Gentleman's Magazine* theorized that in any form of government, whether or not influenced by religion, some compositions are venerated as so sacred that to write or speak contemptuously or indecently of them will be treated as blasphemy, a fit subject for legal censure. Annet, "withered with age" and prejudice, had engaged in "rough and opprobrious expressions," earning retribution. But that did not explain why his previous work had escaped legal censure. Indeed, the writer himself observed that, however "rude and barbarous" the indictment of the Pentateuch, it did not merit from Christians as severe a punishment as an audacious attack on the Gospels.[7]

Some bishop's patience had become exhausted, perhaps, or the attorney general needed to still dissent early in the reign of a new king. Annet claimed that the attorney general gave his judges to understand that the king himself directed the prosecution and sought exemplary punishment.[8] The crown prosecuted him before the King's Bench, the highest criminal court. The indictment for blasphemy accused Annet of having sought to "propagate irreligious and diabolical opinions in the minds of his majesty's subjects and to shake the foundations of the Christian religion and of the civil and ecclesiastical government established in this kingdom."[9] According to Blackstone's *Reports*, Annet pleaded guilty and threw himself on the mercy of the court, which considered his poverty, his age (seventy), and "symptoms of wildness," with the result that the court "mitigated their intended sentence" by declaring that he should be imprisoned for only a month (time already served in Newgate in leg irons), should stand twice in the pillory with a paper on his forehead inscribed "Blasphemy," and should then be sent to a house of correction at Bridewell to work at hard labor for one year, to pay a fine, and to pay heavy sureties for his subsequent good behavior.[10]

A year later, in 1763, the celebrated Wilkes case began, a trigger to what became a long debate on freedom of the press. The English press having rapidly expanded, the political parties capitalized on the print industry—journalists, typesetters, publishers, and booksellers—to publicize their views and excoriate their opponents. London alone, at the beginning of the reign of King George III, had almost ninety newspapers and innumerable presses cranking out tracts and books. Every faction had its literary hatchet men who practiced their invective and scorn on those in power and those who aspired to it. The press had become a force in English politics. Horace Walpole called it "a third House of Parliament." The press placed the government under censureship even as it felt itself to be manipulated and subsidized by it. Writers and publishers sought profits by selling information and partisanship to serve factions. Ministries deemed a kept writer to be about as valuable as a reliable vote among the placemen in the House of Commons. The press, bold and robust, discovered that scum and scandal sold well, making the risk of prosecution worth taking.

John Wilkes, one of the heroes of English liberty and a member of the Commons, fancied himself a literary fellow as well as a rather bold polemicist. Wilkes's studied insult to a royal speech of 1763, published in the forty-fifth issue of Wilkes's *North Briton*, provoked George III. The attorney general filed criminal charges, and a secretary of state issued general search warrants leading to the arrest of forty-nine persons, including Wilkes, his printer, and his publisher. The House of Commons voted his *North Briton* No. 45 to be a seditious libel and ordered that it be burned.[11]

Simultaneously the government nailed Wilkes on a blasphemy charge, surely the most contrived, even preposterous, blasphemy charge in English history. A ribald fellow, Wilkes composed a clever, obscene parody on Pope's *Essay on Man*, which he called *Essay on Woman*. It was also a savage satire on the pedantry of William Warburton, the bishop of Gloucester, who in 1751 had published a terrible edition of Pope. In the privacy of his own home, Wilkes secretly had a printing press and a live-in printer, whom he had ordered to run off a dozen copies of his *Essay on Woman*. The printer, in whom Wilkes had misplaced his trust, did a thirteenth copy for his own amusement. He also dropped a proof sheet, which in opéra-bouffe style became the wrapping for someone's lunch. Because the wrapper had a couple of lines calculated to amuse and stir a lustful curiosity, one thing led to another, engaging the attention of a parson of dubious reputation, who was a chaplain to a member of the House of Lords. The parson did some detective work, which touched off a little inquisition on the part of the government. Its objective was to crush Wilkes in any and every way possible, as well as discredit him among the prosperous Protestant dissenters who supported him. Threats plus a huge bribe led Wilkes's printer to reveal everything.

The government seized copies of *Essay on Woman*, and discovered that it was not only obscene: with the right inferences, it was also blasphemous. The title page depicted an enormous phallus, which a verse in the book described as thirteen inches long and a preface described as belonging to a famous archbishop. Under the phallus was a Greek inscription that meant "Saviour of the World." The title page credited Bishop Warburton for the arcane and dirty commentary that accompanied the verses, which were as explicit as four-letter words could make them. The Greek inscription, as a defender of Wilkes would point out, could be found on an ancient depiction of a phallus that preceded the birth of Jesus by centuries, yet Wilkes's enemies affected to believe that "Saviour of the World" insulted Christ. Bishop Warburton, in a speech to the House of Lords, before whom the *Essay on Woman* was read, claimed that he prosecuted Wilkes at the request of King George himself—and for the reputation of religion. Wilkes's disgusting work, he contended, disgorged "horrid insults on religion" and "shocking blasphemies against the Almighty." The Lords voted the work to be both obscene and blasphemous. They inferred the blasphemy in farfetched ways. They saw it in a footnote saying that the jackass was once held in esteem because of the size of its penis but, ever since the animal "was the vehicle of the Godhead into Jerusalem, he has been ridiculous." An accompanying poem that mentioned God as Creator and referred to His grace was in the form of a prayer that celebrated sexual intercourse. "The Dying Lover to His Prick" supposedly made fun of St. Paul's cry, "Oh death, where is thy sting," and a maiden's prayer praised the phallus and declared that "equal adoration be paid to the neighbouring pair with Thee, Thrice blessed Glorious Trinity," a reference to penis and testicles that the supposedly reverent folk took as a lampoon on the doctrine of the Trinity. Perhaps it was, for Wilkes himself admitted that he had "laughed" at that doctrine. He agreed that the government had a right to punish "outrageous and indecent attacks" on whatever was deemed sacred, but added, "In my own closet I had a right to expose and ever try, by the keen edge of ridicule, any opinions I pleased." If he had laughed at the Trinity, "it was in private." He protested that the government had ransacked his study "to convert private amusements into state crimes."[12] The view that prevailed, however, was that Wilkes had lubriciously insulted God and Christ by carnal obscenities in the form of prayers and poems.[13]

The House of Lords resolved that *Essay on Woman* constituted an obscene and impious libel as well as a "most wicked and blasphemous attempt to ridicule and vilify the person of our most blessed Saviour." Facing severe penalties, Wilkes skipped the country. In 1764, the government tried him *in absentia* before the King's Bench and convicted him of all charges. Because of his absence, he was not given a prison term or fines. He was sentenced, rather, to outlawry—subject to being killed on sight by anyone, with impunity, because he was outside the protection of the law.[14]

In 1768, however, a change in the political climate in England made it possible for Wilkes to return, surrender himself, and sue for the reversal of the sentence of outlawry. Lord Mansfield, after a great argument between counsel, found technical grounds for overturning that cruel sentence, but committed Wilkes until determination of the sentence he should have received if he had not fled the country in 1764. Although Wilkes was speedily on the way to becoming England's most popular politician, the King's Bench belatedly imposed a sentence of imprisonment for ten months and a fine of £500 for the seditious libel in *North Briton* No. 45, and a similar fine plus an additional term of one year for the blasphemy in *Essay on Woman*. From his prison cell, the political firebrand seemed to set both England and America ablaze. The motto "Wilkes and Liberty" remained inciting even when he was later resplendent in the furs of the lord mayor of London.[15]

Following the conviction of Wilkes for blasphemy, enforcement of the law against that offense simply lapsed until the French Revolution. Then Tom Paine made the denial of Christian beliefs seem too dangerous to tolerate. Until that time, however, the government and its established church acted as if they were so secure and complaisant that they indulgently accepted almost as natural a riptide of Unitarian beliefs. Arianism, with its strange notion of Christ as a very subordinate deity, had infected the Church of England from the time of Samuel Clarke and William

Whiston, and it had even spread its contagion to Presbyterianism and other dissenter sects, since the time of the Salters' Hall controversy in 1719. As the decades of the eighteenth century passed, reason and its twin accompaniments, nature and science, radicalized Arianism so that its anti-Trinitarianism became a complete rejection of Christ as a divinity; the prevailing view regarded Jesus as having been only a man, one who had a divinely inspired mission perhaps, but who had not in any sense been God.

As the historian of Unitarianism wrote, Arianism—and, he should have added, Socinianism—steadily expanded "and then at the end of the century insensibly slipped over into Unitarianism. . . . The names Presbyterian and Independent gradually lost their original meanings. . . . The old Presbyterian denomination silently disappeared when at the end of the century the Unitarians began to be organized."[16] In 1764, just a year after the Wilkes prosecution, the Reverend William Robertson, who had already rejected the Athanasian Creed, resigned his position in the Church of England. Within a decade, Theophilus Lindsey, who would describe Robertson as the "father of Unitarian nonconformity," also renounced the established church and established London's first church with a "pure Unitarian form of worship."[17] Most of the original two hundred congregants were members of the Church of England. Unitarianism shortly multiplied with astonishing speed, counting among its distinguished leaders John Jebb, John Disney, Richard Price, and Joseph Priestley. Dissenters and establishmentarians felt its impact.

What is remarkable about all this is that it constituted criminal activity yet openly flourished. England's laws remained reactionary, its actual practice a sort of blind-eyed libertarianism. Parliament refused to liberalize the laws. It refused persistently, for example, to revoke the Corporation and Test Acts, against which the dissenters had remonstrated for decades. In a literal sense, these rarely enforced statutes prohibited anyone from holding public office without taking communion according to the rites and doctrines of the Church of England. Violation was widespread, with the connivance of church and state, but repeal seemed un-English, notwithstanding dissenter protests, which were grounded on both natural-rights theory and a demand for equality of civil rights. The policy of status quo meant no principled modification of the law but not even lackadaisical enforcement of it. Bishops would not upset the comprehensiveness and peace of the church by holding offenders to even the spirit of the law. The government acted as if toleration meant freedom for any opinions and practices on religion, so long as the king's peace was preserved and the government did not have to concede its law-enforcement failures any more than nonconformists in and out of the church had to obey the law other than perfunctorily.[18]

England ignored blasphemy as an offense to such an extent that confronting the letter of its laws seems startling. Sir William Blackstone published the fourth volume of his *Commentaries on the Laws of England* in 1769, including a chapter entitled "Of Offences Against God and Religion."[19] For the most part, that chapter was not only black-letter law; in many respects it was also dead-letter law. He analyzed eleven different categories against "the revealed law of God" punishable by the "law of man." He managed to discuss features of the law of blasphemy in most of those categories. The first was apostasy, which he regarded as "immediately injurious to God and his holy religion." From the belief that judicial oaths were founded on the precepts of Christ and an acceptance of a future state of rewards and punishments, he concluded that apostasy was criminal and, therefore, "all affronts to christianity, or endeavours to depreciate its efficacy, in those who have once professed it," deserved punishment. He warned against "civil liberties . . . being used as a cloke of maliciousness, and [against] the most horrid doctrines subversive of all religion" being publicly avowed. As a result, the law did not admit unbelievers to the privileges of society, and by way of proof he offered provisions of the Blasphemy Act of 1698 punishing denial of the truths of Christianity or of the divine authority of the Bible.

Blackstone then discoursed on heresy as a second category of offenses against religion. Enlightened measures had ended heresy as a "badge of persecution" in English law. "In what I have now said," he added, "I would not be understood to derogate from the just rights of the national church, or to favour a loose latitude of propagating any crude undigested sentiments in religious matters." Again he invoked the Blasphemy Act of 1698, referring to its punishment for those who denied the doctrine of the Trinity. Analogously, he discussed reviling the church and "setting up private judgement in virulent and factious opposition to public authority," concluding that "contumely and contempt are what no establishment can tolerate."

Blackstone next explained that the Toleration Act had removed criminal penalties for Protestant nonconformists who were not "oppugners of the Trinity." His discussion of blasphemy as a separate category of offenses added nothing new to what he had already said. After referring to denials of God, reproaches against Christ, and exposing the Bible to ridicule or contempt, he also explained the law's censure of profanity or common swearing and cursing. In still another category of offenses, he discussed witchcraft, the denial of which, he asserted, "flatly contradicted the revealed word of God." Witchcraft had long been regarded as a form of blasphemy or something akin to it as treason against God. Among the remaining categories of offenses against religion was another variant of blasphemy—religious imposture, the claiming of a special commission from God or of His attributes. Sabbath-breaking and public lewdness ended his list. He failed to discuss obscenity, a crime that, as we have seen, originated as another form of blasphemy. Yet many of his categories of offenses against religion directly implicated the offense of blasphemy.

A spirit wholly different from that of Blackstone infused the law in life—as practiced. To some extent, he even misrepresented the letter of the law. For example, he left an impression that the Toleration Act merely freed dissenters from the penalties of the law but not from the crime of nonconformity. Indeed, in 1769 Blackstone declared that "nonconformity is still a crime by the laws of England, and has heavy penalties attached to it, notwithstanding the act of toleration."[20] Yet, prior to the publication of Blackstone's *Commentaries*, a court consisting of England's highest common-law judges said otherwise. In "the sheriff's case," between the city of London and the dissenting Protestants, the judges reversed fines imposed by the city on dissenters who had refused nomination as sheriff, an office whose holders must have received the Lord's Supper according to the rites of the established church. The city appealed to the House of Lords, where the judges reaffirmed their opinions on the ground that the Toleration Act "renders nonconformity no longer a crime" but a form of worship "warranted by law, and intitled to the public Protection." William Murray, Baron Mansfield, the foremost lawyer in the House of Lords, delivered a stirring speech to the same effect. Mansfield made certain, however, to except from the ambit of freedom the expression of atheism, infidelity, and blasphemy, or the reviling of Christianity. The significance of the sheriff's case consists in its revelation of the profound growth of English toleration. Blackstone correctly described what the law had been, not what it had become.[21]

A broader reply to Blackstone came from a leading nonconformist minister, Philip Furneaux, who had masterminded the dissenters' battle in the sheriff's case and whose prodigious memory had allowed him to report accurately the whole of Mansfield's speech. Furneaux's slim volume criticizing Blackstone's chapter on offenses against religion constituted the first sustained analysis of the problem of blasphemy. Furneaux challenged the law's imposition of any restraints or punishments on the expression of religious opinions and opinions about religion. Apostasy, deism, and infidelity did not offend Furneaux, because his faith in Christianity was unshakable. He thought that penal laws that sought to support Christianity hurt and dishonored it; it flourished with only voluntary support based on private judgment. The very concept of blasphemous libel struck him as repugnant, because it damaged liberty of conscience. He believed that the law should ignore the propagation of atheism, the denial of God, ridicule of the doctrine of the Trinity, railing against the ordinances of any churches, exposing the Bible to contempt, and any other views that had the tendency of producing in the minds of the people a bad opinion of religion or of Christianity. The advocacy of beliefs about religion, according to Furneaux, should be free. He flatly rejected the bad-tendency test of the lawfulness of an opinion, proposing in its place the punishment of only overt acts that adversely affected the public peace. He thought that the good reputation of God or of Christianity did not depend on suppression or criminal sanctions.

Furneaux was not the first to advocate freedom of expression or the restriction of the civil authority to the punishment of overt acts. Roger Williams, William Walwyn the Leveller, Spinoza, Montesquieu, Wickliffe, and an anonymous contemporary of Furneaux who called himself "Father of Candor" had all suggested the overt-acts test.[22] That was to their vast credit, but they had only suggested it. Furneaux built his theory of free inquiry around it. He did not even take up much space with a problem that other libertarians thought worthy of serious consideration: the bounds of licentiousness, or the rightfulness of punishing supposed abuses of free expression. To Furneaux, such analysis was worthless, because he understood licentiousness to be entirely subjective, except as to public profanity—swearing and cursing, which were devoid of ideas.

"Are we," he asked, "to leave every man at liberty to propagate what sentiments he pleases?" His affirmative answer was unqualified. To those who objected that such a policy would give free rein even to views that tended to introduce "immorality and licentiousness," which government should check, Furneaux replied that, if the government could punish views on religion because of their supposed bad tendency, the government would be the judge of that tendency, thus allowing it to measure out religious liberty. Blackstone had placed religious liberty under the magistrate's control, allowing him to decide whether morality or religion had been damaged by some opinions. That allowed the magistrate to draw a line between religious opinion and its tendency on the one hand, said Furneaux, and criminal conduct on the other hand. The magistrate had jurisdiction over only the latter; the former belonged to "a future world," to conscience, and to God, "the only sovereign Lord of conscience." However unfavorable the tendency of an opinion on religion, the government's rightful power reached only overt acts, not merely the bad tendency of opinions. "Punishing a man for the tendency of his principles, is punishing him before he is guilty, for fear he should be guilty."[23]

Furneaux did not ignore the reasons conventionally offered for the suppression of atheism and affronts to Christianity. Blackstone had relied, for example, on the need to preserve the sanctity of oaths. Furneaux retorted that oaths did not depend on Christianity, and that principles of morality did not depend on Christianity or even on religion. Moreover, wrong and bad principles were "beyond the province and jurisdiction of the magistrate." Furneaux acknowledged that blasphemous opinions affronted Christianity and were offensive to every Christian. He argued, however, that opinions should not be punishable simply for being offensive. The style of expression and the substance of what is said ought to be met with refutation. The manner or style of expression, Furneaux asserted, was "a thing, comparatively, of little consequence." Calumny might be punishable by law when an injury was done to a fellow being, but that was not the case in the matter of religion. Neither God nor Christ could be damaged by a blasphemer, regardless of his malice or his scurrilous words. Nor would criminal penalties bring about repentance in the offender or a change of his convictions. God cannot be insulted by man, and His reputation and that of Christ required no vengeance from man. Blasphemy implied an offense against God or Christ; it should not, therefore, come within the government's cognizance. Furneaux believed that society had the legitimate authority to curb and punish blasphemy in the form of "profane swearing," out of a regard for common decency and good order. But he would not approve the extension of the concept of blasphemous libel beyond "something like common swearing," because that would encroach on religious liberty, "for what is blasphemy, in the general sense of the term, but uttering something dishonourable or injurious to the Divine Being? And what controverted religious sentiment is there, which under this general notion, by a court and a jury of bigots, may not be condemned as blasphemy?" The Athanasian called the Arian a blasphemer, the Calvinist the Arminian, and so it went, with the result that the same law would be applied differently as different parties prevailed and "would prove fatal to the religious liberty of all of them in their turn." Insults to religion should, like transgressions of divine law, be offensive to good people, but ought not on that account to be criminally punishable, however shocking. Furneaux would not even make an exception for infidels who, with "offensive indecency, vent their impotent rancour against the religion of Jesus."

To those, like Blackstone, who believed that allowing such licentiousness would have a bad effect upon the common people, Furneaux counseled patience and faith; he believed that Christians could expose and answer blasphemers, whose resort to contempt and abuse would merely bring infamy upon themselves. Such conduct on their part, he thought, rendered their arguments less formidable. He believed too that punishing their opinions gave them the wrong sort of publicity by exciting people's curiosity about their scurrilousness. Good Christian that he was, Furneaux ended his chapter on blasphemy by declaring that whoever sought to support Christianity by inflicting pains and penalties on blasphemers "forgot the character and conduct of its divine author."

Furneaux had proposed the ultimate freedom for words about religion. He advanced the theory of free thought some light-years by rejecting outright the concept of blasphemy as a crime. He did not address himself to political speech or to any sort of speech other than about religion, although he believed that "religious and civil liberty have a reciprocal influence in producing and supporting one another."[24] Whether Furneaux went too far is a question that still crops out in the form of the permissible latitude for public obscenities. His overt-acts test would not be effective against verbal solicitations to crime or to incitements to crime, only to the crimes themselves. A test of criminality that weighs the danger of a criminal deed's being immediately provoked is particularly relevant in the case of a publication, where the writer, unlike a speaker, cannot be interrupted. To his credit, however, Furneaux erred, if at all, on the side of freedom. His argument against punishment of blasphemy can be refuted on emotional but not on intellectual grounds. Those who favor permitting the law to avenge bruised sensibilities do not consider Furneaux's Christian argument that God can protect his own reputation. One might add that the odor of blasphemy rises from the thought that God requires man's assistance.

For over a quarter of a century following the publication of Furneaux's critique of Blackstone, the government failed to prosecute anyone for blasphemy. The crime was committed daily in every Unitarian or deist utterance, yet the law remained as if moribund. Thomas Paine's *Age of Reason* revived and revitalized the law and touched off a series of prosecutions that mounted and peaked during the period 1821–34, when the number of convictions rose to seventy-three, or about five a year. A majority of them related in one way or another to Paine's *Age of Reason*.[25] This book transformed England's policy on toleration of deists, made deism an unendurable threat to Christianity, and radicalized religious thinking on the political left.

By itself, the book might have been little more than a squib. But Tom Paine was the greatest pamphleteer in the English language; the book was the religious counterpart to its seditious predecessor, *The Rights of Man*; and both books appeared to be genuinely dangerous, because they appeared in the context of mass unrest stirred by the French Revolution— and Paine himself was a certifiable, professional revolutionary. He had, from the British standpoint, treasonably aided the Americans by publishing the wildly successful incitement to independence, *Common Sense*. And he published *The Age of Reason* while in France, where he participated in its revolution as a member of the French Convention.

To be sure, Robespierre and the Jacobins imprisoned Paine when they gained power, and for ten months he lived in prison, fearing for his life. Although he was a revolutionary in British eyes, the Jacobins knew

him as merely a liberal reformer, a petit bourgeois who opposed the
execution of Louis XVI and condemned the Terror, of which he nearly
became a victim. So long as Gouverneur Morris remained the United
States ambassador to France, Paine expected the guillotine. James Mon-
roe, on becoming Morris's successor, saved Paine by demanding that he
be accorded his rights as a distinguished American citizen. None of this
mattered to England. Those who held political power and economic
privileges had strong reason to think of Paine as a formidable revolutionary whom they had to silence. Although they could not reach him, and
could only convict him *in absentia* for seditious and blasphemous libel,
they could reach and imprison his publishers and booksellers in order to
suppress his work.

Paine was really different from his deist precursors. They had had no
social program, and their religious ideas had no connection with democratic policies. Indeed, some religious liberals had been political conservatives, including Lord Bolingbroke, David Hume, and Conyers
Middleton. Deists, no matter how maligned as infidels and subversives,
had included members of the aristocracy and of the established church,
and for the most part they considered themselves Christian. Tindal had
even called himself a Christian deist. None of the deists before Paine had
concerned themselves with the condition of the working classes. Quakers
had an antislavery program but were otherwise sleek and prosperous.
The merchant princes may have been Protestant dissenters, but they
were Trinitarian for the most part. The dissenters had no alliance with
the poor.[26] The Methodists, a religiously conservative spin-off from the
Church of England, evangelized the poor; the deists did not, nor did the
dissenters. Woolston, Chubb, Ilive, and Annet could write English well
enough to be understood by miners or maids, but had slight impact or
concern. Woolston was a pedant, and Chubb, though an artisan, was an
arrogant intellectual who believed that he wrote for and could be rightly
understood by only "the more intelligent part of our species, who are not
interested in popular opinion."[27] Ilive and Annet may have had different
interests. But by the end of the century, they were forgotten and left
hardly a trace. As Edmund Burke asked, in 1790, "Who, born within the
last forty years, has read one word of Collins, and Toland, and Tindal,
and Chubb, and Morgan, and that whole race who called themselves
Freethinkers? Who now reads Bolingbroke?"[28]

No one could ask, "Who reads Tom Paine?" Almost everyone did. If
the hod carrier, prostitute, and common soldier could read, Paine was
their favorite, and if they could not read, they could understand what
Paine meant if someone read him aloud. *Common Sense* had been the most
widely read tract in America. *The Rights of Man* and *The Age of Reason* set
records as best-sellers in the hundreds of thousands of copies. Paine

poured his profits from first editions into subsidies for extremely inexpensive editions. Almost anyone who could understand English became familiar with Paine, and he energized his readers. They formed debating societies and political clubs and preached his doctrines. As in America, wrote Eric Foner, so too in England, "Paine articulated and intensified existing popular discontents and longings, particularly resentments among artisans and laborers against their political powerlessness and often desperate economic conditions." The political societies formed at the inspiration of Paine's work signaled the emergence of the lower classes "into organized radical politics." *The Rights of Man*, as E. P. Thompson stated, "is a foundation-text of the English working-class movement."[29]

Apart from the radical political and constitutional theories of *The Rights of Man*, Paine advocated something like the welfare state—government responsibility for disadvantaged citizens. He proposed wholesale reformation of the tax system, replacing iniquitous taxes and the reduction of excises that burdened consumers, while introducing steeply graduated income taxes and inheritance taxes—and the abolition of primogeniture—to break up large estates and alter the class system. He proposed baby bonuses for poor women, free public education for all children, unemployment compensation, old-age pensions, veterans' pensions, public shelters for the homeless, and free meals for the hungry—and all of this not as a matter of charity but as of right.

The enormous popularity and radicalism of *The Rights of Man* made the book intolerable to the English authorities whom Paine savaged. As noted, he was beyond their revenge, but they prosecuted and convicted him anyway, *in absentia*, for the crime of seditious libel, and then went after his publisher, booksellers, and those who organized political societies that championed his opinions.[30] Howell's *State Trials* reports more prosecutions for seditious utterances in the two years following Paine's *Rights of Man* than the total number reported for the entire eighteenth century up to that time.[31] As a matter of fact, in late 1792 the attorney general reported that he had on file two hundred accusations for seditious libel.[32] Thomas Erskine, who defended Paine against that accusation, advocated a liberty of the press that so broadly protected political expression that it would have exempted political opinions that fell short of the successful incitement of some criminal act. "I maintain," Erskine asserted, "that OPINION is free, and that CONDUCT alone is amenable to the law."[33] Significantly, Erskine's tolerance for political expression did not extend to religious expression. In 1797, he abandoned Furneaux's overt-acts test and restricted his own libertarian principles when he prosecuted the publisher of Paine's *Age of Reason* for the crime of blasphemy.[34] He was not inconsistent; he simply believed that freedom of expression on religious matters should not have the same scope as on politics. Unlike

Furneaux, Erskine would not apply the overt-acts test to opinions that assaulted the Christian religion. It was sacred; the government was not.

Neither was sacred to Paine. But he was no infidel. From his old friend Sam Adams, who wrote angrily in the mistaken belief that Paine had published "a defense of infidelity," to Theodore Roosevelt, who denounced Paine as a "filthy little atheist," *The Age of Reason* has been maligned for the wrong reasons. Atheism, even if presented with Paine's power and clarity, could be treated with contempt, but he repudiated atheism, and his *Rights of Man* made him a dangerous antagonist. As Paine explained to Adams, he wrote *Age of Reason* partly because he believed that "the people of France were running headlong into atheism, and I had the work translated and published in their own language to stop them in that career, and to fix them to the first article . . . of every man's creed who has any creed at all, I believe in God." Paine believed in God; he did not believe in Christ or Christianity.[35]

After Paine, deists could not make believe that they were also Christians; members of the Church of England who professed deism had to make a choice. Paine made Christianity and deism incompatible, and he made deism far more attractive except to those who took their religion on faith or emotion rather than on reason, as they had alleged. Christianity, Paine argued, was the enemy of reason. He went much further in *The Age of Reason* by arguing, as no one ever had before, that the Bible and Christianity blasphemed God. Little wonder that *The Age of Reason* became the book most frequently prosecuted for blasphemy.

"Of all the systems of religion that were ever invented," Paine asserted, "there is none more derogatory to the Almighty, more unedifying to man, more repugnant to reason, and more contradictory in itself, than this thing called Christianity." It was too absurd and inconsistent to believe in or to practice, and it produced "only atheists and fanatics."[36] He elaborated on every aspect of that accusation. Paine believed that Christians were "infidels" and that Christianity derived from pagan myths as well as the Old Testament, which he abhorred. He attributed the story of Jesus Christ as Son of God to the fact that Jesus was born when "heathen mythology" was still influential and when extraordinary men were commonly reputed, in myths, to have been sons of their gods. "It was not a new thing, at that time, to believe a man to have been celestially begotten; the intercourse of gods with women was then a matter of familiar opinion."[37]

Paine respectfully described Jesus as "a virtuous and an honourable man," who had preached and practiced a most benevolent morality. But Paine found the supernatural stories of the conception and resurrection of Jesus to have "every mark of fraud and imposition."[38] The story of the conception, according to Paine, was "blasphemously obscene." A young virgin engaged to be married got "debauched" by a ghost at the behest of God. "Were any girl that is now with child to say, and even swear it, that she was gotten with child by a ghost, and that an angel told her so," she would not be believed. But because "the Christian faith is built upon the heathen mythology," the "ludicrous imposture" received acceptance.[39]

The story of the resurrection was, for Paine, a "fraud," but not without amusing aspects. He even found something to ridicule in the story of the crucifixion, which he accepted as historically probable. But the miraculous circumstances received his careful scrutiny. Matthew reported an earthquake, "and the graves were opened; and many bodies of the saints which slept arose, and came out of the graves after his resurrection, and went into the holy city and appeared to many." Paine tested the verse to determine whether it was consistent with the other Gospels, and whether their authors had been eyewitnesses. He found numerous contradictions and evidence enough to conclude that the evangelists were liars, inventors, and mythologists, but neither eyewitnesses nor historians.[40] As for Matthew's account, Paine wrote:

> It is an easy thing to tell a lie, but it is difficult to support the lie after it is told. The writer of the book of Matthew should have told us who the saints were that came to life again and went into the city, and what became of them afterward, and who it was that saw them—for he is not hardy enough to say he saw them himself; whether they came out naked, and all in natural buff, he-saints and she-saints; or whether they came full dressed, and where they got their dresses; whether they went to their former habitations, and reclaimed their wives, their husbands, and their property, and how they were received; whether they entered ejectments for the recovery of their possessions, or brought actions crim. con. against the rival interlopers; whether they remained on earth and followed their former occupation of preaching or working, or whether they died again, or went back to their graves alive and buried themselves.[41]

That was an example of how Paine analyzed miracles. (He got off a fair one-liner when he demanded to know, if it was a miracle that was wanted, why Jonah hadn't swallowed the whale.) He deplored the depiction of other miracles for "degrading the Almighty into the character of a showman, playing tricks to amuse and make people stare and wonder."[42] Paine relished describing contradictions in the New Testament, from the miraculous conception to the ascension. He observed, for example, that only Matthew and Luke offered genealogies. Matthew traced twenty-eight generations from David to Joseph, whereas Luke provided forty-three generations between the same two men, and only the names of the same two appeared in common on both lists. The four evangelists could not even agree about the inscription on the cross.[43]

Again and again, Paine presented evidence that convinced him that "it is impossible to conceive a story more derogatory to the Almighty, more inconsistent with His wisdom, more contradictory to His power, than this story" of Christianity in the New Testament.[44] The doctrine of the Trinity also constituted blasphemy to Paine, because it "enfeebled belief of one God." According to "the Christian Trinitarian scheme," one part of God is represented by a dying man and another by a flying pigeon or dove. The Bible offended him because it set up "an invented thing called revealed religion" that presented "wild and blasphemous conceits" about God.[45]

The Old Testament fared no better in Paine's analysis. Its authors were not those to whom its books were attributed, and few presented an elevated morality, none divine revelations. Much of the Bible said to be done at God's command shocked humane beliefs. Ferocious mass murders were supposedly commissioned by God Himself. To believe that, Paine declared, required disbelief in God's moral justice and meant that God has been guilty of heinous crimes. Paine regarded such a depiction of God as blasphemy, dishonoring the Creator.[46] He concluded that the Bible could not be God's work, because of the inhumane cruelty and injustice ascribed to His commands. Contemplating both books of the Bible, Paine concluded:

> The most detestable wickedness, the most horrid cruelties, and the greatest miseries that have afflicted the human race have had their origin in this thing called revelation, or revealed religion. It has been the most dishonorable belief against the character of the Divinity. . . . Whence arose all the horrid assassinations of whole nations of men, women, and infants, with which the Bible is filled, and the bloody persecutions and tortures unto death, and religious wars, that since that time have laid Europe in blood and ashes— whence rose they but from this impious thing called revealed religion, and this monstrous belief that God has spoken to man? The lies of the Bible have been the cause of the one, and the lies of the [New] Testament of the other.[47]

Throughout this unrelenting assault on the Bible and on Christianity Paine interspersed his deist creed, oozing with benevolence, humanity, and simplicity. "I believe in one God, and no more," he declared, "and I hope for happiness beyond this life. I believe in the equality of men; and I believe that religious duties consist in doing justice, loving mercy, and endeavouring to make our fellow creatures happy." God was "the great mechanic of the creation." Through His creation, God spoke to all people in a universal language, not just in Hebrew or Aramaic. His creation was the deist's only bible. God's unfathomable power might be imagined from the immensity of the universe, His wisdom from the incomprehensibility of the order that He governed. "The only idea man can affix to the name of God," said Paine, "is that of a first cause, the cause of all things." Only by the exercise of reason can man contemplate God. The religion of the deist, Paine asserted, consists in contemplating His works and in trying to imitate Him in everything. God created not merely this earth but the entire universe. "From whence, then," Paine asked, "could arise the solitary and strange conceit that the Almighty, who had millions of worlds equally dependent on His protection, should quit the care of all the rest, and come to die in our world, because, they say, one man and one woman had eaten an apple."[48] Cracks like the last, and his opinions about Christianity—not his opinions about deism—made Paine a blasphemer, not just an iconoclast. His deism was toothless and unoriginal. His blasphemy was unprecedented in its sneering polemics, and it was altogether unprecedented in its insistent depiction of Christianity and the Bible as blaspheming God.

For having published a blasphemous book, *The Age of Reason*, Thomas Williams of London was tried by a special jury before the King's Bench, presided over by Lloyd Kenyon, Mansfield's successor as lord chief justice of England. According to Erskine, the prosecutor, a special jury consisted of handpicked men pre-eminently qualified by their education to pass on "a cause so very momentous to the public." Erskine refused to proceed to trial when at first the twelfth special juror did not appear; he would not risk a verdict by a jury that had even one person chosen from the ordinary jury lists. He got his twelfth special juror. The fact that Williams published Paine was uncontested. The jury's task was to decide whether he had published a blasphemous book.[49]

The case wore a distinct class character. John Bayley, who became one of the justices of the Court of King's Bench, observed, in his introduction to the report of the trial, that publication "excited a general avidity to read the book, particularly amongst the middling and lower classes of life." Erskine himself observed that the book robbed the "poor and humble" people of the consolations of Christianity. He described the penniless man surrounded by his children, "looking up to him for bread when he has none to give them," the poor fellow "sinking under the last day's labour," losing the hope that a time would come in the afterlife "when all tears shall be wiped from the eyes of affliction"—his confidence in that day having been mercilessly destroyed by *The Age of Reason*.[50]

The trial consisted of an introductory speech by Erskine, the argument by the defense counsel, and Erskine's reply. Lord Kenyon instructed the jury that the "nefarious" book had been published for "malignant purposes." The jury, without leaving their box, "instantly found the defendant GUILTY."[51]

Erskine, one should not forget, was England's leading champion of freedom of the press. He insisted that he had not altered his opinions a jot or a tittle on that subject. Williams had abused his liberty by publishing blasphemy. The English constitution protected freedom of controversy on religious subjects, as well as political ones, and also protected freedom of worship. Erskine found that "sufficient"; the law did not need to offer impunity to those who "wholly abjure and revile the government of their country, or the religion on which it rests for its foundation." No man, he declared, had a right to deny the very existence of Christianity and pour on it "such shocking and insulting invectives." Such unlimited freedom invited "the lowest" classes to display "insolence and disobedience."[52] To his credit, Erskine told the jury that he believed people should be free to deny Christianity "though the law of England does not permit it." He did not dread the reasonings of deists against Christianity, because "if it be of God it will stand." But this book went too far; it was indecent and licentious. And its author was a very special person. He had written on government and public liberty in *The Rights of Man*, which Erskine had defended in court; that the author of *The Rights of Man* was the author of *The Age of Reason* made the blasphemous book more attractive to those who had endorsed the principles of the earlier book. "This circumstance renders a public attack upon all revealed religion from such a writer infinitely more dangerous."[53] *The Age of Reason* subverted the truths of Christianity in the nastiest ways, and thereby undermined the government and the constitution, both of which rested on Christianity. Erskine's argument was hardly consistent, but it justified making blasphemy the exception to liberty of conscience and to liberty of the press.

Counsel for Williams was Steward Kyd, a follower of Paine, also a deist and a radical. In 1794, Kyd was one of several persons, including Thomas Hardy and John Horne Tooke, whom Erskine had successfully defended against charges of treason.[54] Kyd insisted that *The Age of Reason* was not a blasphemous book, because its author had not written it with a malicious intention—scarcely an effective argument to the devout Christians of the special jury. Kyd sought also to prove that Paine had respectfully treated Jesus and most reverently treated the Almighty, in whom Paine professed belief. Paine had written to protect the honor of God from the blasphemous belief, Kyd asserted, that the Bible was the revealed word of God. In response to Erskine, Kyd argued that, if men have a right to contest Christian truths, they must be allowed a latitude in the manner of their expression of the matter. Indignation and reply, not prosecution, should be England's policy, leaving God to avenge His reputation against defamers. For the most part, Kyd sought to prove that Paine's arguments were reasoned and truthful, not scurrilous or malicious.[55] The jury believed Erskine and Lord Kenyon. Without leaving the box, the jury "instantly" found Williams guilty. Kenyon sentenced him to a year at hard labor and the sum of £1,000 to ensure his good behavior for the remainder of his life.[56]

The eighteenth century—"the Age of Reason," Paine had called it—had been a century of unprecedented toleration. Never had England been nearly as free for the expression of religious diversity, whether at worship or in disdain of it, whether expressing religious sentiments or repudiating them. Ironically, that long era of toleration closed with the prosecution of the publisher of *The Age of Reason*. His case capped a burst of intolerace during the 1790s, born from the panic inspired by fears of the French Revolution. The imprisonment of Williams beckoned the coming of a new century, when the victims of blasphemy laws no longer were Christian anti-Trinitarians, as for centuries past, but deists and, later, atheists, no longer merely religious dissenters but political radicals too.

CHAPTER SIXTEEN

Eaton to Carlile:
Deism for the People

I N 1808, Sir Samuel Romilly complained: "If any person be desirous of having an adequate idea of the mischievous effects which have been produced in this country by the French Revolution and all its attendant horrors, he should attempt some reform on humane and liberal principles. He will then find not only what a stupid spirit of conservatism, but what a savage spirit, it has infused into the minds of his countrymen."[1]

In the early nineteenth century, almost any reform measure could be defeated by being associated with Jacobinism. Parliament still refused to repeal the Test and Corporation Acts, despite dissenter opposition for over a century. Parliament did nothing to alleviate the civil disabilities of Catholics and Jews. It refused to abolish the death penalty for pickpocketing, even for a few pence. It defeated proposals to make trade unionism lawful. It retained the rotten-borough system of representation, despite attacks. And yet no European nation was as free as England, and none offered a broader toleration in matters of religious opinion, as a matter of practice. England had reactionary laws in such matters, statutory and common law, but enforced them infrequently, and only when radicalism in religion intersected radicalism in politics, as in the case of Tom Paine's promoters. A mere atheist who denied the existence of God by alleging the absence of proofs would not be—indeed, was not—a victim of the law, nor were the numerous Unitarians and other varieties of anti-Trinitarians. The last such people to be prosecuted for a temperate expression of their opinions were Emlyn and Elwell, in the early eighteenth century. Deists had occasionally been in trouble with the criminal law, but not when, like Conyers Middleton or Thomas Chubb, they avoided the ridicule and reproach of Christianity in their disagreements with it. In the early nineteenth century, only anti-Christian deists who propagated the religious opinions of Paine had reason to fear the criminal law, but not merely because of their opinions on religion. Their disagreements went beyond theology to politics: they loomed as dangerous subversives, not merely irreligious freaks.

The Reverend Francis Stone was not prosecuted; he was defrocked. A clergyman of the Church of England for over a half-century, Stone gradually accepted Unitarianism and could have been ignored as an eccentric, as were other anti-Trinitarians within the church. But in 1807 Stone, in canonicals, preached before an audience composed mainly of other clergymen, voicing his mature beliefs. On that occasion, he imprudently and conspicuously rejected the supernatural birth of Jesus, claimed that Jesus had been merely a man, and rejected the doctrine of the Trinity. The church felt obligated to prosecute Stone. A criminal prosecution by the state against an aged clergyman would have risked the opposition even of clergymen who deplored Stone's views. Stone's persistent proclamations forced the church to take charge. An ecclesiastical court in London, on which sat the bishop of London, summoned Stone to determine whether he could, consistent with his Anglican vows, continue to hold his benefice. Unitarians claimed that the accusations against him were heresy and blasphemy. The court found him guilty and deprived him of his office—in effect, defrocking him. The case inspired a public controversy, in which religious liberals lathered themselves into denouncing the church's intolerance. But the church rightly believed that Unitarianism and the Thirty-nine Articles were incompatible. Obeying the letter of the law, the ecclesiastical court deprived this cleric who no longer subscribed to the articles. Under the Blasphemy Act of 1698, Stone could have suffered a criminal punishment, like that which shortly befell Daniel Isaac Eaton.[2]

Eaton, once a shoemaker, was also a Unitarian. In addition, he was a political radical, a publisher, and a bookseller. In 1793, he had been prosecuted for selling *The Rights of Man*, but the jury found him guilty only of selling, implying that he was not guilty of seditious libel. He had been acquitted of the same charge in 1794, but convicted in 1795. He fled to America to escape punishment, and as a result had been outlawed. When he returned to England four years later, he was imprisoned and all his property confiscated; his books, valued at nearly £3,000, were burned. He spent fifteen months in prison, yet failed to learn his lesson. In 1811, he published a new edition of *The Age of Reason*, and, in 1812, a supplement to that volume, which Paine had written as "Part III" while he lived out his years in America.

In 1812, the crown prosecuted Eaton in the King's Bench, and he was tried by a special (packed) jury of merchants who professed orthodox Christian views. The attorney general conducted the prosecution before Lord Chief Justice Ellenborough, a harsh and autocratic judge. Eaton, without counsel, defended himself against the charge of blasphemy; he did not have a chance. When he sought to show that the Bible contained contradictions, Ellenborough stopped him for "reviling" Christianity. Alleging himself to be a Christian, Eaton finally won approval for reading a speech whose objective was to prove that God was merciful, unlike the vengeful God of the Old Testament. But the attorney general ranked Eaton's blasphemy (Paine's, really) among the greatest crimes a person could commit, and Ellenborough, having reminded the jury of the precedents and of the fact that the law made criminal any denial of Christianity, told the jury he left it to them, "as twelve christian men, to decide whether this is not a most blasphemous and impious libel." The jury immediately returned a verdict of guilty. Ellenborough sentenced Eaton, then over sixty, to stand in the pillory and serve eighteen months in Newgate Prison. Somehow Eaton again published *The Age of Reason* and Baron d'Holbach's *Ecce Homo*, an atheistic account of Jesus. Eaton was again convicted, but he was not sentenced because of his age and poor health. He died in 1814.[3]

Eaton's case inspired Percy Bysshe Shelley, then only twenty years old, to publish a passionate essay accusing Ellenborough of "persecution." Notwithstanding the romantic gush about people of all religions and no religions living together in "brotherly love," Shelley represented the cause of freedom by advocating the right of anyone to publish whatever he pleased on the subject of religion.[4] One scholar has praised Shelley's overheated effusion as a "work of power and insight" worthy of being ranked "among the classics of the struggle for freedom of speech." That is hyperbolic nonsense, but Shelley deserves credit for angrily denouncing prosecutions for blasphemy. Five years later, when Shelley lost custody of his children by his first wife, one of the accusations against him was that he was an atheist who had published a poem, *Queen Mab*, "which blasphemously derided the truth of Christian Revelation and denied the existence of God."[5] Shelley himself never suffered a prosecution for blasphemy, but in the 1820s and the 1840s his publishers would be victimized by the laws against it, because some of his poetry was both anti-Christian and atheistic.

Eaton's Unitarianism had nothing to do with his prosecution for blasphemy. He was convicted for publishing and selling Paine's deistic work on religion. By the time of his trial in 1812, Unitarians had achieved respectability, notwithstanding the anomalous fact that every Unitarian sermon that embodied the fundamental doctrine of the religion criminally violated the Blasphemy Act of 1698. Unitarians had attained positions of leadership in the professions as well as in commerce, and they were accepted as equals in London's high society—not just Unitarians who remained within the Church of England yet disbelieved the doctrine of the Trinity, but even those who belonged to independent Unitarian churches. Some were even members of Parliament, including a leading reformer, William Smith. He was enormously wealthy from his merchant enterprises, and an envied collector of paintings. Since 1784, he had been a member of the House of Commons, where he distinguished himself as a supporter of radical programs such as the abolition of the slave trade, religious liberty, extension of the suffrage, better apportionment of representation, and more frequently elected parliaments. For decades, Smith led the fight for repeal of the Test and Corporation Acts, which discriminated against dissenters. In the 1820s, he championed Roman Catholic emancipation. His importance in respect to blasphemy derives from his leadership in legitimating Unitarianism. He secured the enactment of the parliamentary measure that ended criminal penalties on Unitarian beliefs about the doctrine of the Trinity.[6]

Smith's original draft of the bill, if adopted, would have constituted one of England's foremost libertarian documents. He proposed that every person should have freedom to express his opinions about God. That, in effect, would have adopted Furneaux's overt-acts test as to opinions about the divinity of Christ and the Holy Spirit, as well as opinions about them as objects of worship or prayer. Without doubt, Smith's object was to abrogate the offense of blasphemy respecting the Trinity. His original draft would have also given lawful expression not just to Unitarianism, which was at least Christian, but also to Paine's anti-Christian deism, which at least was theistic, and even to atheism, which was anti-Christian and antitheistic. The House of Commons approved his bill, but in a conference with the archbishop of Canterbury, Smith learned that he would not have the support of the established church in the House of Lords unless he restricted the bill.

The archbishop agreed to the repeal of all statutes that inflicted penalties for impugning or denying the doctrine of the Trinity, but he did not want "to open a door for admission of all manner of profaneness and impiety in the mode of treating subjects of so solemn a description; and therefore that the crime of blasphemy should still be left open to the animadversion of the common law." Smith agreed to a revision, because he too believed, he said, that blasphemy consisted of "the use of language and epithets in themselves reproachful, reviling, and abusive" leveled at God. In effect, Smith and the archbishop agreed that the law should continue to punish blasphemy against God but not against Christ or the Holy Spirit. The archbishop believed that Christianity and the Bible could also be blasphemed, and Smith did not disagree. Although he did not believe that Christianity or the Bible had to be protected against blasphemy by the criminal law, he compromised in order to obtain his prime objective, the legalization of Unitarianism.[7] Accordingly, Smith agreed that his original version of the bill was overbroad; it permitted a latitude of expression not needed to achieve its purpose.

He had no desire to antagonize anyone who believed that religion, God, Christ, and the Holy Spirit should be defended from "indecent" or "mischievous opinions."

But Smith next learned that, even with the church's support, he would not win government votes unless he compromised still further. Lord Chancellor Eldon and the Lord Chief Justice Ellenborough insisted that the bill be recast merely as a repeal of specific sections of statutes that had subjected Unitarianism to criminal penalties, but they promised swift passage of a bill revised along their lines. Smith complied. He had no other choice. Jeremy Bentham subsequently criticized him for having capitulated to church and state in his negotiations for the enactment of the measure. He objected to the absence of a "sweeping" clause in the final version. It left the common law of blasphemy intact except as to the doctrine of the Trinity, and it did nothing to alter the "obnoxious" legal principle that Christianity was part and parcel of the law of the land. Any opinion deemed by a court to be an offense to Christianity, as the court understood Christianity, remained criminally punishable, Bentham complained. He was right. As revised, the statute even kept the door open to convictions for blasphemy based largely on the emotional reactions of prosecutors, juries, and judges to language they found reprehensible.[8]

The Trinity Act was actually entitled "An Act to Relieve Persons Who Impugn the Doctrine of the Holy Trinity from Certain Penalties." Its first paragraph repealed the clause of the Toleration Act of 1689 that had explicitly withheld the benefits of that measure from persons denying the doctrine of the Trinity. The second paragraph repealed the clause of the Blasphemy Act of 1698 that punished the denial "of any one of the persons in the Holy Trinity to be God." The final paragraph repealed the blasphemy acts of Scotland, which had ordained the death penalty.[9] The Trinity Act was intended as a toleration act for Unitarians, and in fact it had the effect of extending to them the Toleration Act of 1689. That great statute was an act of "indulgence," this one an act of "relief." But it was also an act of indulgence or sufferance. It suffered the existence of Unitarians. It offered them the privilege, always revocable, of being exempt from criminal penalties. Toleration in Britain was like that—always an allowance or sufferance, never a right, whether natural or positive or vested. It had a begrudging character. Toleration was a point of mid-passage between persecution and liberty, a designation for second-class subjects. In his speech introducing the bill that became the act, Smith declared that it "was not connected with any civil privileges, but was solely to remove certain penalties on deniers of the Trinity."[10] When the "Trinity Bill" reached the House of Lords for its final consideration, the archbishop of Canterbury, who supported it, said that its objective was to remove penalties and impediments from the worship of Unitarians, thereby granting them "liberty of conscience, in their peculiar interpretation of the Scriptures," so that they could have the same liberty that "was extended as amply as to other dissenters, in that tolerant spirit which characterized the church of England." Thus, the act was a gift of the benevolent establishment.[11]

Despite its faults, and they were many, the Trinity Act constituted a great triumph, because anti-Trinitarianism, which in effect became lawful, had been the basic blasphemy throughout the preceding history of the offense. The numbers who died for it in Roman Catholic England must be counted by the dozens. In Protestant England, Queen Elizabeth, who professed not to make windows into men's souls, nevertheless burned at the stake four radical Protestants whose crimes included denial of Christ as God. The last men to die in England for their religion, Bartholomew Legate and Edward Wightman, in 1612, also shared beliefs later described as Unitarian. John Biddle and the other mid-seventeenth-century Socinians who had been jailed or exiled were anti-Trinitarians. In Scotland, the last person to die for religion, executed in 1698, was a Unitarian. Subsequent prosecutions in England and Scotland ended in imprisonment for denial of the doctrine of the Trinity. Consequently, the lawful acceptance of Unitarianism as a Christian sect entitled to the same status as other dissenting Protestants must be regarded as a major victory for toleration. Since Unitarianism was not named, the act actually could be applied to any persons who "impugned" the fundamental doctrine of Christianity. Its terms could be applied to Jews, Muslims, deists, agnostics, and even atheists, or to any member of an Asian religion other than Christianity. But the extensiveness of the act depended on judicial interpretation, and judges would construe it as narrowly as possible. Indeed, Lord Chancellor Eldon ruled in 1817 that, because the act merely repealed certain criminal penalties, it left the common law untouched; consequently, "it is impossible to contend," said Eldon, "that there could no longer exist a punishment for Blasphemy at Common Law, independent of the statute. On the contrary, the Common Law is left by the statute exactly as it was before the statute passed." Thus, a trust created in the eighteenth century for the propagation of dissenter Protestantism could not benefit Unitarians, despite the Trinity Act of 1813, because "it left the common law exactly where it was."[12] Similarly, two years later, in 1819, Eldon held that a school endowed in perpetuity for the free instruction of local youth could not benefit Jewish children, because "Christianity is part of the law of England."[13] In the same year, in the prosecution of Richard Carlile, the deist, for the crime of blasphemy (discussed below), the lord chief justice of the King's Bench refused to permit the Trinity Act to be construed to protect deists.

Such rulings were not inconsistent with the constipated character of the Trinity Act. It was typically British. It was passed without éclat at the time and has rarely been noticed since. It took a step forward by facing backward—to an extension of the Toleration Act of 1689. It was a victory for the constitutional liberty of the subject, celebrated as if someone had muttered something about "Magna Carta and all that rot." The Toleration Act itself had the identical character. Censorship of the press had been abolished in England simply by allowing the licensing acts to expire. Similarly, in the words of Sir William Holdsworth, the great historian of English law, "We look in vain for any statement of constitutional principle in the Bill of Rights" of 1689.[14] Nor was there one in the Trinity Act.

Four years later, in 1817, the government systematically sought to intimidate the press, mainly by the enforcement of the common law against blasphemous libel. Late in 1816, William Cobbett had "invented" the cheap or twopenny press. Eighteen sixteen was a very special year, because the government had its first chance to respond. Until late 1816, newspapers cost about a shilling, well beyond the pocket of a workingman. An act of 1815 had increased the price of stamped paper, on which the papers were printed, to 4 pence a sheet and 3s. 6d. for a periodical. Circulation of papers and magazines rarely passed three thousand copies. Cobbett got the idea of publishing a journal of opinion in a single open or unfolded sheet, thereby circumventing the stamp tax and allowing him to reduce drastically the price of his weekly. His circulation swiftly increased to over forty thousand per copy, and for the first time England had a paper most of whose readers felt victimized by the political and economic system. Wooler's *Black Dwarf* and other radical weeklies imitated Cobbett and made life intolerable for the ministers of state. Skittish conservatives imagined the possibility of an overthrow of the government. Public riots by workingmen, an assault on the prince regent, reports of treasonous conspiracies, and the torrent of abuse from the radical press, which no doubt aggravated resentments and spread discontent, demanded harsh measures in the opinions of members of the Tory government.[15]

Prosecution for blasphemous libel appeared to government strategists to be the most efficacious way of silencing radical publications that promoted the ideas of Tom Paine. Prosecutions for seditious libel seemed less likely to win verdicts of guilty, because people might tolerate the ridicule and vilification of government measures but not of religious opinions. From the standpoint of the Tory government, which was in power when the Napoleonic Wars ended, suppressive measures promised relief from a new menace, the "cheap press." It relentlessly assaulted the monarchy, the establishment of religion, the House of Lords, and the inequities in the political system resulting in malapportionment of rep-

resentation, limited suffrage, and infrequent elections. Political radicalism, in the tradition of Paine, frequently intersected religious radicalism.
A weekly newspaper demanding revocation of the stamp taxes, freedom
of the press, and equal voting rights most likely also preached deist
doctrine, or satirized the Bible, or flirted with atheism.

Lord Sidmouth, the home secretary, had the responsibility of enforcing the laws against criminal or public libels—seditious, obscene, and
blasphemous. Sidmouth was a short-tempered reactionary who hated
radicals of all kinds. He was empowered to issue warrants for search,
seizure, and arrest, and he had troops to back him if necessary. He could
decide what was libelous, what should be prosecuted, and how it should
be prosecuted. He could determine whether a charge of seditious or
blasphemous libel would most likely stick, and whether a crown lawyer
should file a criminal accusation by an *ex officio* information, which required no grand-jury action, or seek an indictment. In March 1817,
Sidmouth issued an order for magistrates to suppress all suspected libelers, to hold them for steep bail, and to imprison them if they could not
pay. On behalf of the government, Sidmouth meant to silence the radical
press. He decided that, if the offender had addressed himself to religious
matters, exposing him to a charge of blasphemy, he should be charged
with that crime; if he expressed himself on political subjects, the charge
would be seditious libel.[16]

Cobbett escaped to America. In his absence, Thomas Wooler, a political agitator who began publication of his *Black Dwarf* in January 1817,
became the first and major target of the government. Working-class readers loved his grim wit and savage ridicule of people in power. Wooler was
prosecuted for seditious libel, because his weekly scarcely vented on
religious subjects. His acquittal at two successive trials confirmed the
government's notion that juries might more likely vote guilty verdicts if
the defendant stood charged with blasphemy. The attorney general filed
eighteen *ex officio* informations for blasphemous libel in 1817.[17]

In the midst of all these prosecutorial plans, a liberal voice was heard
when a leading Unitarian, the Reverend Robert Aspland, published his
sermons on blasphemy. He knew his Furneaux and disseminated the
same views of the subject. He found in Christ's principles Christian
reasons for not prosecuting blasphemy, but he even produced a "heathen"
historian, Tacitus, for the principle "Leave to the Gods the revenge of
their own wrongs."

Aspland construed blasphemy in the narrow sense of reviling God, a
sin for which the punishment should be left to the Almighty. As a
Unitarian, Aspland decried describing as a criminal offense, punishable
by the state, any opinion on religion. Most persons punished as blasphemers abhorred blasphemy and never thought of themselves as blas-

phemers. They simply differed in opinion from those who enforced the law. "There is no supposed error," asserted Aspland, "which an uncharitable mind may not by some fanciful train of reasoning trace up to a direct hostility to Almighty God."

The term "blasphemy" was commonly used to make odious the holders of opinions that a community rejected as offensive, making the propriety of punishing blasphemy "the same as whether persecution be morally right; for to punish error, under whatever name, is persecution." Aspland insisted that "freedom applies to all opinion or to none." On the question whether a majority could rightfully exclude opinions that they felt to be offensive, he believed that the rights of the dissident must be protected for the good of society. Punishing so-called blasphemers injured society by repressing opinions that time might vindicate, however wrong or offensive they seemed to be. In support of that proposition, Aspland instanced various heresies that had become orthodoxies. He understood the difference between ridicule and argument, but knew of no way to distinguish fair and reasonable criticism of religious views from malignant deriding. In short, Aspland recognized the risks of freedom but believed that they constituted a price that had to be paid to maintain that freedom. He would leave the punishment of real blasphemy to God and never allow the government to punish any opinion on the subject of religion.[18]

The Tory government in power in 1817 operated on a different wavelength. It regarded blasphemy as an offense that a jury could be persuaded to punish, and thus as a means of silencing critics. But the government fared badly in 1817. Nothing seemed to go right. Dozens of people arrested and jailed for treason had to be released when the act suspending the right to the writ of habeas corpus expired at year's end, because of inadequate evidence to try them.[19] Publishers and journalists accused of criminal libel could not be found, or for some other reason could not be put to trial. The case of John Wright of Liverpool, for instance, came to the attention of some liberal members of the House of Lords, who protested against Wright's prosecution for blasphemy on account of his Unitarian beliefs. Earl Grey objected that Wright had committed "no crime" simply because he denied the divinity of Jesus, the doctrine of the Trinity, the immortality of the soul, and the belief in rewards and punishments. Grey had read Wright's sermon and, said he, even some members of the Church of England agreed with Wright's views. Moreover, Grey denounced Sidmouth's instructions to magistrates, and also the tremendous powers of the crown officers in being able to file *ex officio* informations against alleged blasphemers and throw them in jail for inability to pay bail. Wright, a clergyman, managed to raise bail and, thanks to the efforts of supporters in the Lords, remained free, because the government discreetly dropped the charges against him.[20] As

1817 drew to a close, not one of the eighteen cases of blasphemy for which the government had begun prosecution had gone to the jury.[21] A few of the eighteen blasphemy defendants were also charged with seditious libel, as in the case of William Hone's second prosecution.

The government's policy of suppression did not fail, although it secured no convictions. Some of the accused libelers were arrested to harass, intimidate, and impoverish them; they remained in jail if they could not afford bail, and had to pay court costs. The right to a speedy trial did not then exist in England, and the right against excessive bail meant little to judges who sided with the prosecution. Richard Carlile, who would become the government's bête noire and England's foremost blasphemer, spent four months in jail in 1817 because he could not raise the steep bail that a court imposed. For the same reason, William Hone served two months. Although few cases were brought to trial in 1817 and none resulted in conviction, persons accused of libel, seditious or blasphemous, were jailed anyway.[22]

The fact that Cobbett was abroad and Wooler was acquitted left William Hone looking like the most fearsome libeler among those available for trial. The government could not know that Hone was the wrong man to pick. He had formidable inner resources. Scarcely known at the time, a mere bookseller and author of irreligious satires, Hone had an incandescent sense of injustice on behalf of the working classes and victims of society, and he was fearless. He himself was the son of a poor man, a strict nonconformist Protestant who had taught him the Bible and saw to it that he clerked in a solicitor's office for a couple of years. Hone was industrious, indefatigable, and indomitable. He was also exceptionally articulate and well read. He had a gift for expression, and he preferred the parody as a literary form. Nothing in his past, however, gave the attorney general of England or its chief justice reason to believe that in William Hone they had a pugnacious and determined antagonist in the tradition of John Lilburne and John Wilkes.[23]

On December 17, 1817, the day before his first trial, Hone was a nobody. Within three days, he three times defeated the government, walked freely among twenty thousand wildly cheering Londoners, and then was guest of honor at a great public meeting jammed with prominent reformers and radicals, who raised a sum of £3,000 to reward him for having "so nobly and successfully struggled against Ministerial persecution" and for having valiantly defended trial by jury and the freedom of the press. Sir Francis Burdett, a member of Parliament and a tribune of the people, acclaimed Hone at that meeting, declaring that the government "seemingly intended only to crush a humble individual; but they meant, in reality, through his person, to destroy the free press of the country."[24]

Hone was the government's enemy because of his merciless parodies. He made readers laugh at the ministers and their policies. He seemed also to make them laugh at Christianity, and that gave the government its means of jailing him. Three of his parodies attacked the catechism of the established church, its litany, and its creed; and for each of the three parodies he was accused of blasphemy, then separately tried on successive days, prosecuted by Sir Samuel Shepherd, the attorney general, before the King's Bench. At the first trial, Hone's judge was Charles Abbott, soon to become Ellenborough's successor as chief justice. Abbott discovered that, when he interrupted Hone for remarks that had no bearing on the matter before the court, Hone testily lectured him. Ellenborough himself, old and ill, with a nasty disposition, presided over the second and third trials.

The blasphemy charge in the first trial was based on parodies of the church's catechism, the Lord's Prayer, and the Ten Commandments, "three sacred parts of Christian belief," declared the attorney general, "brought into contempt" by Hone. Hone's defense against all the alleged blasphemies was that he intended no contempt against religion and had merely used a religious form as the basis for a political attack. The prosecutor claimed, however, that the parody "had nothing of a political tendency about it" but lampooned the religion and worship of the established church. He seemed upset that Hone's work circulated so cheaply, placing into the hands "of the lower classes of society" materials with which they were "not fit to cope" and which, by their very nature, were calculated to weaken the awe and reverence felt for Christianity. The "ignorant and uninformed" could not be expected to obey the law if they lost that awe and reverence.[25]

Hone's catechism did, in fact, follow the church's catechism but, contrary to the attorney general, its content was wholly political, as were Hone's version of the Ten Commandments ("Thou shalt not call starving to death murder. . . . Thou shalt not say, that to rob the Public is to steal"), and as was his version of the Lord's Prayer: "Our Lord, who art in the Treasury, whatsoever be thy name, thy power be prolonged, thy will be done throughout the empire, as it is in each session," etc. Hone's litany was entitled "The Political Litany," yet the attorney general found it appalling, even if only in form, because the litany of the church, which it mocked, was a solemn prayer addressed to the Almighty, to Christ, and to the Holy Ghost, and was considered a sublime part of the public service of the church. Hone had "turned it to ridicule." He had done the same with the Athanasian Creed, which was part of the same service and was established by the law of England. Hone damaged the sacred character of the creed by scoffing at a trinity of his own devising, the ministries of Old Bags, Derry Down Triangle, and the Doctor. Each was incomprehensible, but they were not three incomprehensibles, only one. Each was Humbug, yet they were not three Humbugs, only one. Each was also a quack, an "All-twattle," and a fool, yet not three but one. None was greater or less than another, but they were co-charlatans together, to be worshipped together.[26]

Hone's trinity seemed the most shocking of his parodies. He failed to explain the names of the three or to identify them. Even though he intended certain members of the government, whom he named at the third trial, his parody aped the sacred creed just enough to allow it to be taken as irreligious or blasphemous, not political.

Hone's defense of himself was heroic. His torrential energies and quick thinking enabled him to talk almost nonstop—for over five hours at the first trial, over six hours at the second, and over eight hours at the last one. He depicted himself as a victim of injustice and censured all the proceedings against him as "unconstitutional." He was wholly at the mercy of the attorney general, he complained. That officer had filed an accusation against him by an *ex officio* information, a means of evading the accused's right to grand-jury proceedings; he had been summarily arrested, was denied a copy of the charges against him, and could not afford the ruinous cost of £100 for legal counsel. Hone also criticized the way his special jury had been formed, from a list of people chosen by the prosecution. He feared that the jury would be timid, and he challenged them to act independently. He made the prosecution look like a continuation of the Star Chamber, whose spirit, he bristled, lived again in the court that tried him.

When Judge Abbott sought to silence him for not speaking to the issue, Hone was outraged. Ellenborough's distempered conduct of the second trial provoked clever self-serving outbursts from Hone. Ellenborough, for example, declared that he refused to receive in evidence illustrations of the religious parodies of others, to which Hone retorted, "I would ask your lordship, if you really mean to send me to prison without a fair trial? If your lordship does not mean to do that, you will let me make my defense to the jury." When Ellenborough asserted that he would hear "what relates to your defense, but I will not let you be wasting time," Hone exploded that it was he who was on trial, he who was the "injured man," and, "When I shall have been consigned to a dungeon, your lordship will sit as cooly on that seat as ever; you will not feel the punishment. I feel the grievance, and I remonstrate against it." Eventually, Ellenborough, like Abbott before him, let Hone alone. Hone even insulted Ellenborough's opinion as to what constituted a libel, on the ground that only his jurors could decide whether his words were criminal. He would withstand the "browbeating" of Ellenborough, he told his jurors.[27]

Hone professed to be ignorant of Ellenborough's "technical rules of evidence" and simply would not be stopped from showing, in a learned manner, that Martin Luther had parodied the Psalms, that Dr. Boys, the dean of Canterbury, had parodied the Lord's Prayer, that George Canning, one of the ministers of state, had parodied the Scriptures, and that others, including Milton, had done the same—and none had blasphemed. His point was that one might use a sacred form to produce laughter and the scorn of secular subjects, as he had done. He was a Christian, he contended, not a blasphemer, and he had not intended to expose religion to contempt. As soon as he learned the character of the charge against him, he had withdrawn the questionable parodies from the market, even though he stood to make a considerable profit from the publicity. If blasphemy had been his objective, he would have continued sales.

Hone had a strong argument. As he said of his caricature based on the doctrine of the Trinity, "It was not written for a religious purpose, but for a political purpose—to produce a laugh against the Ministers." He meant to "laugh his Majesty's Ministers to scorn . . . and ha! ha! ha! he laughed at them now, and he would laugh at them, as long as they were laughing stocks!" And he repeatedly reminded the men in the jury box: "His lordship presides in this Court, but not to try me. You are my judges; you are to try me."[28]

Hone overawed his juries; he stiffened their spines; he demonstrated a courageous political purpose. Accordingly, the conventional summations by the attorney general on the dangerous tendencies of Hone's parodies and the charges delivered by the judges, always finding Hone's parodies to be criminal, fell on deaf ears. The first jury returned a verdict of not guilty after deliberating only fifteen minutes. The verdict produced loud acclamations in the court and "the language of joy" in the streets. Hone swiftly attained popularity. The next morning, all avenues to the courthouse were blocked by enormous crowds; "not one-twentieth of the multitude could find standing accommodation" when the courtroom doors opened for the second trial. More significantly, only six of the twelve special jurors turned up, forcing the prosecution to choose between a postponement, which would have prejudiced the crown's case, and consent to the selection of "six common Jurymen." Hone made the most of the choice of the six. When the jury returned a verdict of not guilty, pandemonium broke out in the court, with loud and reiterated shouts of applause triggering even louder acclamations from the crowds in the streets. At the third trial, common jurors again joined special jurors. Hone's acquittal after the jury's twenty minutes of deliberation produced roars of approval from approximately twenty thousand people jamming the neighborhood.[29]

At the victory celebration a week later, when supporters subscribed a fund of £3,000 for Hone's support, resolutions were adopted in favor of freedom of the press, trial by jury, the right to parody religion, and the debt every friend of constitutional liberty owed to Hone. Two of the many resolutions deserve repetition. One declared: "That a hypocritical prostitution of Religion, and a pretended zeal for its defense, when used by corrupt Statesmen as a mask for political persecution, must ever be held by sincere Christians as the worst profanation of its sacred name." That and the verdicts, of course, paralyzed the government's thought of prosecuting for blasphemy for a while. The other resolution neatly summarized the significance of the Hone cases: "That it is evident . . . that the real object of Ministers was not to protect Religion; but to crush an apparently defenseless individual, who had exposed their political delinquencies, to stifle public discussion, to destroy the Liberty of the Press, and to uphold existing abuse."[30]

That freedom of conscience received no mention from Hone or his supporters indicated that radicalism relied mainly on freedom of the press, because the parody was political. Hone's acquittals won genuine freedom for religious and political parodies, which were not thereafter prosecuted. Hone's own parodies sold almost a hundred thousand copies, thanks to Richard Carlile's reprinting of them without Hone's approval. Their immense sale showed that prosecution of a "libel" had the effect of advertising it, but the government did not learn this lesson until it sought to muzzle Carlile. In a land as free as England, muzzling Carlile was as likely as filling in the Thames.

Richard Carlile, England's most notorious blasphemer, achieved more for the freedom of the press than any other person in the country's history. Freedom of the press was, in a sense, Carlile's religion. He spent almost ten years in prison for the uncompromising espousal of his radical beliefs, a willing and self-proclaimed martyr to the cause of a free press. He dominated that cause overwhelmingly. Six of his ten years in prison paid for crimes of blasphemy, which he committed primarily by reprinting and selling Paine's *Age of Reason*. Carlile, who suffered cruelly, fought the government to a standstill, directing his cause from his prison cell. His wife took over his shop, and she too was convicted of blasphemy, then his sister, then his employees one by one, and finally strangers who volunteered to share Carlile's cause of a free press and his fate as well. The Carlile blasphemy trials dragged on for several years. Slowly the government learned that it could neither still Carlile's voice nor make him yield. Slowly the government learned that it had created a martyr, a nationally renowned person, giving the utmost publicity to his blasphemies, which it had intended to suppress. Slowly the government learned that it had to find some way to tolerate a free press. When Carlile was released in 1826 from the blasphemy charge (there were others), he pardonably declared that he had freed the press. Indeed, he had, at least for a few years. Blasphemy prosecutions would still occur, but the government carried the scars of the Carlile trials.

Eighteen seventeen, when economic conditions were terrible, had been the crucial year of transition in Carlile's life. "In the manufactories where I was employed," he remembered, "nothing was talked of except revolution. . . ." After he lost his job as a tinsmith, he determined to do something to further the workingman's cause. He was twenty-seven, unemployed, and had the best education that the village free school in his native Aldington in Devonshire could offer until he had reached the age of twelve, when he was forced to go to work.[31] In London in the spring of 1817, "fired with ardour by the political publications of the day," he decided to try making a living as a vendor of radical weeklies. With a borrowed £1 note, he bought copies of Wooler's *Black Dwarf* and peddled them throughout London, sometimes walking thirty miles a day to earn 18 pence. "When I first started as a hawker of pamphlets," he said in one of the articles he wrote from prison, "I knew nothing of political principles; I had never read a page of Paine's writings; but I had a complete conviction that there was something wrong somewhere, and that the right application of the Printing Press was the remedy."[32]

He entered the publishing business at a time when others, as he put it, "were shrinking" from the sale of radical journals; "it was just as the Habeas Corpus Act was suspended; just as Lord Sidmouth put forth his circular [ordering the arrest of all suspected libelers], a fortnight before Mr. Cobbett fled to America." He resolved, nevertheless, to "get into the front of the battle and set the best possible example."[33] William T. Sherwin, the publisher of *Sherwin's Weekly Political Register*, employed him, and Sherwin shortly thereafter decided that publishing was too risky. As a result, Carlile became the publisher, taking liability under the law, while Sherwin retained his printing shop. Carlile's "ardour" would not be "dampened by difficulties or danger." He began reading omnivorously while learning his business as a bookseller, an editor, and a publisher. He pirated Hone's parodies, which could not be protected by copyright because of the formal accusation of blasphemy—suspected libels had no benefits from the law. Capitalizing on Hone's wit got Carlile arrested for blasphemy and jailed for failure to pay bail. When Hone was acquitted at the end of the year, to the government's enormous embarrassment, Carlile was released. He had been in the King's Bench Prison for eighteen weeks, and emerged penniless, but, he wrote, he "had got a name."[34] He had also gotten additional accusations of criminal libel, seditious and blasphemous. However, the government, shocked by Hone's acquittals, did nothing to further prosecutions.

"1818. Began this year," Carlile reminisced in prison, "with publication of new Parodies and new editions of old ones. Government evidently sick with the prosecutions of 1817. Not one successful verdict in London!" In London that year, he added, "the Press was free. The Political Works of Thomas Paine were publicly published and unopposed by the Government."[35] In fact, Carlile published *Common Sense* as well as *The Rights of Man*, in editions for every pocketbook. And in 1818 he read, for the first time, *The Age of Reason* and became a deist. He had been a nothingarian, but found Paine's opinions on religion captivating. He published the book, even though Eaton and Williams, its previous publishers, had been imprisoned for blasphemy. He went still further by editing a new journal, a sixpenny weekly of radical religious works, called *Deist or Moral Philosopher*. At the same time, he opened a larger shop on Fleet Street.

Carlile now committed himself to propagating the views of Tom Paine. Never an intellectual or a theorist, Carlile was too practical to devote himself to justifications of a free press. He could not have written Milton's *Areopagitica*, but could never have served as a censor for Cromwell; he could not have written Locke's *Letter concerning Toleration*, but could never have endorsed the idea that atheist opinions or any others should be suppressed.[36] Carlile was an absolutist: all opinions without exception should be lawfully protected. He spun no theories about the freedom of the press. He practiced that freedom with a robustness unexampled, and he devoted himself to Paine. Despite his incapacity to expound on the meaning and scope of a free press, he realized that he had an obligation to publish Paine. To say that Carlile could not be intimidated is, first, as flat a statement as saying that he was a true believer, and, second, is irrelevant: he merely did his duty in exercising the freedom of the press. "My whole and sole object, from first to last, from the time of putting off my leather apron to this day [1823], has been a Free Press and Free Discussion." As for Paine, Carlile understood that man could not rise from degradation until his mind was elevated "with useful knowledge and sound political principles. This Paine saw, and no human being before or since has ever elevated the minds of mankind to so great an extent." Paine taught disobedience to existing powers that were not constituted for the welfare of society and sought to reconstitute society "not by violence, but by temperate discussion and a dissemination of correct principles."[37]

Paine had hardly been temperate, nor was Carlile. Emerging from six years of imprisonment, he acknowledged that he had been an extremist. He had seen that England tolerated public discussion but punished the "foremost," those on the outer fringes of opinion.

I also saw that by my going to extremes with discussion and speech, I should remove all fears as I removed all danger of prosecution from those who had been foremost, or who might be disposed to follow me at a safe distance. On this ground every free-minded literary man ought to have given me his support, for my long imprisonment was in fact a sort of penal representation for the whole. I confess that I have touched extremes which many thought imprudent, but which I saw to be useful with the view of habiting [habituating] the Government and the people themselves to all extremes of discussion, so as to remove all idea of impropriety from the media which were most useful.

That was as close as Carlile got to theorizing.[38]

Several of Carlile's publications earned him accusations of criminal libel, but *The Age of Reason* was his greatest offense. Soon after its publication, a grand jury at Old Bailey, instigated by the Society for the Suppression of Vice, indicted Carlile for blasphemy. By then, in early 1819, he had prosperous supporters and made bail. When he continued to sell copies of *The Age of Reason*, the attorney general filed an *ex officio* information against him for the same crime. The government's irresolution of 1818 was dead; 1819 would be a siege year against the radical press. As E. P. Thompson said, the government "launched upon the most sustained campaign of prosecutions in the courts in British history" in that year.[39] One study based on reports to Parliament showed a total of thirty-three informations and sixty-three indictments, making a total of ninety-six accusations for the year, against seditious and blasphemous libelers.[40] The same study shows a decline in 1820 to merely thirty prosecutions. A report to the House of Commons shows ninety-nine prosecutions in 1819, fifty in 1820, and a total of 245 between 1817 and 1822.[41] Another report to the House of Commons, in 1821, giving only totals of convictions obtained in 1820, shows three convictions on charges that included both seditious and blasphemous libel, fifty for seditious libel, and twelve for blasphemy alone—a total of sixty-five convictions in just one year.[42] That seems inconsistent with the data in another report, which alleges that the total number of convictions from 1821 to 1834 was seventy-three for blasphemy and twenty-seven for seditious libel.[43] Whatever the true numbers of prosecutions and convictions for blasphemy, they were unprecedentedly huge. Carlile's was the first and, by far, the most important case. If he had been acquitted, the other cases would have been aborted.

He was arrested for a third time in 1819, on blasphemy charges, and remained four days in Newgate until he could be bailed. Defiantly he kept selling *The Age of Reason*. By the summer of 1819, he had pleaded not guilty to nine separate accusations. One, by another indictment, was for blasphemy committed by the publication of an American work, *Principles of Nature* by Elihu Palmer, a deist from Connecticut. Another accusation was for a seditious libel that he had written for *Sherwin's Weekly Political Register*. Despite all the charges, the government did not bring Carlile to trial. His report on the "Peterloo Massacre" changed that situation.

Carlile was an eyewitness to the massacre in St. Peter's Field outside of Manchester on August 16, 1819. Cavalrymen, their sabers slashing, rode down unarmed workingmen and their families, gathered for a peaceable protest meeting. The official intention had been to arrest the speakers, but the troops were panicked by the enormous crowd, which Carlile exaggerated at three hundred thousand. Over three hundred people were wounded or injured from trampling, and at least eleven were killed. "Peterloo" was a word play on St. Peter's Field and Waterloo, in disrespect for the arch-Tory, Wellington, who had just joined the government. The government approved of the cavalry's conduct, but national sentiment was outraged. Carlile's account was seditious. The government intensified its suppressive policies in an effort to intimidate critics. It frightened William Sherwin out of business, which he turned over to Carlile.[44]

Carlile by now had become a major radical spokesman. He was not only flinty, principled, and iron-willed, but overcocky and militant. His first action on taking over Sherwin's twopenny weekly magazine was to change its name to *The Republican*. He did in fact stand hard against the monarchy, the aristocracy, and the House of Lords. He wanted a democratic government of the people, equitably apportioned, with every man entitled to vote. He was becoming unendurable.

Lord Sidmouth ordered another *ex officio* information to be filed against Carlile for seditious libel, the tenth criminal accusation against him. Sidmouth favored a prosecution for treason, but the Cabinet overruled him and shrewdly resolved to proceed with the blasphemy charges. Carlile understood; trying him for blasphemy had "the double purpose of getting rid of me as evidence and drawing the public attention from the Manchester affair."[45] The political charges had the least chance of convincing a jury, the offenses against religion the greatest chance. As Carlile understood the significance of the pending trial, a guilty verdict would sanction the ministry's policies. "A verdict of *Not Guilty*," he wrote, "will stagger and shake them from their holds, will destroy the remains of ignorance and superstition and establish the Liberty of the Press and Free Discussion. . . ."[46]

Unlike Hone, Carlile was hardly a nobody at the time of his trial. He had been invited by the radicals in Manchester to be present at their protest meeting as a nationally known journalist who supported workingmen's causes. His natural talent for calling attention to himself promoted his name, and he was egomaniacal. He frequently dared the government to prosecute him, if for no other reason than to stimulate sales of his publications. He taunted the attorney general in letters, which he published; every legal step taken against him became news in his magazine; he assaulted the Society for the Suppression of Vice in an open letter, decrying its "malignant efforts to prevent a free enquiry after truth and reason." In London, the British Forum debated, over a period of several weeks, whether the prosecution against Carlile should be applauded as a vindication of Christianity and reproof of infidelism, or censured as a violation of the freedom of the press. As the autumn approached, bringing Carlile's inevitable trial closer, he flamboyantly served public notice that he meant to subpoena the archbishop of Canterbury, the chief rabbi, and the heads of all Christian denominations and sects. His intention was to show that the religion of Jesus had innumerable interpretations and that Christianity could not be blasphemed if its meaning was unclear. *The Republican* also sought to distinguish deism from atheism. It reprinted Paine's credo, stressing belief in God as the Creator. Carlile, for all his obnoxiousness, had friends and supporters of influence, including members of Parliament, who attended his trial. Thousands mobbed the streets near the courthouse each day.[47]

The nationally reported trial before the King's Bench lasted four days in October 1819. Four common jurors, including three artisans, joined the special jurors, who were merchants. The attorney general, Sir Robert Gifford, opened the case for the crown by assuring the jury that the prosecution of blasphemy in no way violated the great latitude for free discussion. Christianity was the religion of the state and therefore part of the law of the land. To revile it was criminal. The jurors, by their oaths, he asserted, had pledged themselves to believe in the sanctity of Christianity as the revealed word of God. He would leave it to them to decide whether their holy religion, on which all their civil and religious institutions had been founded, was merely a fable and an imposture. The prosecutor then reviewed the major precedents, the cases of Taylor and Woolston and of the previously convicted publishers of *The Age of Reason*, Williams and Eaton. In the usual legal hyperbole, he asserted that Carlile, by publishing the same book, had published "one of the most abominable, disgusting, and wicked attacks on religion and its author, that has appeared in the world."[48] He quoted generously from Paine to prove the point. Significantly, those quotations included Paine's statements that the Bible was a blasphemous book. Although Paine made astonishingly strong statements, such as "he that believes in the story of Christ is an infidel to God," his language had been no more coarse than that of the Bible, but the attorney general condemned not only the opinions that Paine had expressed but the coarseness of his manner of expressing them. The case for the prosecution closed with a complete reading of all counts in the accusation of blasphemy—to Carlile's satisfaction. He wanted the words of Paine to be quoted repeatedly, for he heard in them the voice of reason; the attorney general heard blasphemy in the same words.

The crown's most powerful argument revealed the fact that blasphemy, although an offense against religion, had come to be regarded as a class crime. Blasphemy threatened religious belief, without which poor Christians might no longer accept their lot. Blasphemy remained an offense against religion only in name or in form. It had actually become an offense against privilege; its punishment hedged against insurrection. The time had passed when the government claimed to prosecute because of the affront of blasphemy to God, religion, or Christianity; they had no need for revenge by mortals. The reason for prosecuting blasphemy, rather, derived from its dangers to the "public good"—that is, to the status quo:

> Prosecutions for such calumnies against religion are necessary for the public good, although the religion itself has no need of support from the arm of man, for in my conscience I believe that persecution alone can injure it. But this prosecution has not been instituted for the purpose of oppressing any individual. No, it has been only instituted for the purpose of protecting the lower and illiterate classes from having their faith sapped and their minds divested from those principles of morality, which are so powerfully inculcated by the Christian religion. The gospel is preached particularly for the poor. It is calculated to show them the vanity of all earthly things: it enables them to bear up against the pressure of misery and misfortune, and teaches them to rely upon those rewards which they shall earn by leading a life of honesty, sobriety, and deference to the laws of God, and of their country. But when such terrible productions as those now under consideration are put into their hands, into the hands of those who unlike the rich, the informed, and the powerful, are unable to draw distinctions between ingenious though mischievous arguments, and divine truth—the consequences are too frightful to be contemplated.[49]

Thus, blasphemy had to be suppressed in order to prevent the poor from being robbed of the consolations of religion. Without that, they might no longer docilely accept the status quo in return for promised rewards in an afterlife. The real concern, however, was not for the poor but for the rewards that the privileged enjoyed in this life. In a fundamental sense, then, blasphemy had come to be understood as a political crime, one that dealt with the distribution of power and privilege in society. The crime of seditious libel dealt directly with the criminality of opinions that undermined the respect that the people had for their government, whose policies reinforced gross maldistributions of wealth, power, and comforts. But middle-class jurors could easily understand that the accident of birth enriched the few and impoverished the many. Thus, an overt political prosecution for seditious libel offered less of a chance to secure their votes than a religious approach, which gave them a different appreciation of their duty: "It is to be decided by you, Gentlemen of the jury, whether Christianity is a fabulous imposture," and whether that religion, which supported the constitutional system, should continue to be regarded "with confidence and veneration."[50]

Clearly, the government and the classes that it represented believed that the crime in *The Age of Reason* consisted in the fact that it sold so cheaply. Had Carlile published it exclusively in the half-guinea edition, it would have reached only the educated classes—"the rich, the informed, and the powerful"—who could cope with it. But "the lower and illiterate classes" whom Paine reached, and whose opinions he cared about, must not be exposed to opinions that brought Christianity into contempt; they were expected to accept the religion that taught them submission. A book that prodded them to question it constituted blasphemy. As the attorney general declared, "I should give up in effect the Christian religion altogether, and give it up as not forming a part of the constitution of the country, if I allowed its merits to be discussed."[51]

Carlile defended himself. He had unwisely rejected an opportunity to be represented by a member of the bar, a friend of Jeremy Bentham, who volunteered to defend him out of conviction of the merits of *The Age of Reason*.[52] Later, in prison, Carlile claimed that he had been overconfident and had made mistakes. "I was then," he said, "not precisely prepared with the necessary written argument. I went into Court careless about everything beyond a determination to read Paine's book to the Jury."[53] Even if he had done better, the jury would have convicted him. He conducted his defense brilliantly despite incessant interruptions by Chief Justice Charles Abbott, who presided, as well as by the attorney general. He had a good strategy and reasonable arguments, and he demonstrated an effective ability to think quickly on his feet.

He meant to rely on freedom of religious opinion and on liberty of the press. In response to the principle that licentiousness could not pass for liberty and that liberty did not include a right to blaspheme, he argued that deist opinions came within the law's protection as a result of the Trinity Act of 1813. He read the act to the jury. It explicitly repealed the provision of the Blasphemy Act of 1698 that had made criminal the denial of the doctrine of the Trinity and the still earlier provision of the Toleration Act that had exempted from that act's protection those who made a similar denial. The purpose of the Trinity Act had been to offer to

Unitarians the same protections enjoyed by other Protestants who did not conform to the Thirty-nine Articles of the Church of England. The first of those articles, established by law, provided for the doctrine of the Trinity. In effect, the act of 1813 gave deists the same relief as Unitarians and tolerated the impugning of the Trinity. That, Carlile reasoned, had the effect of repealing all laws against blasphemy. Speaking ill of God had become merely a matter between the offending person and God, not a matter of law. "But this act [of 1813] which I have read, allows persons who disbelieve the Trinity, and so far to blaspheme or impugn that doctrine, on which Christianity rests for its support."[54] Therefore, no law existed to warrant his being tried for a difference of opinion on religious matters. Disbelief, he offered, did not constitute reviling. Carlile repeatedly offered that argument.[55]

The difficulty with that argument was that the act of 1813 did not repeal the Blasphemy Act of 1698 in its entirety; it repealed only the clause on persons denying the Trinity, leaving unimpaired the clauses against denying Christianity to be true and denying that the Bible possessed divine authority. At least a dozen times, Chief Justice Abbott broke in on Carlile's argument to correct him, but Carlile, hoping for support from the jury, rejected his judge's opinion as mere opinion. Even if Carlile had been right, the act of 1813 did not repeal the common law which made Christianity part of the law of the land and punished blasphemy, defined as speaking ill of religion, of Christianity, or of the Bible.

Carlile believed that his only chance for an acquittal consisted in his proving to the jury's satisfaction that Paine's criticism of the Bible had been correct. Abbott absolutely refused to allow him to do that, but allowed him to distribute copies of *The Age of Reason* to members of the jury, and even allowed him to read that whole book to the jury. This took most of the twelve hours of the first day of the trial. Carlile felt triumphant, because by reading the book into the court proceedings he was able to republish it as part of the public record. In one form or another, the book sold many thousands of copies thanks to the publicity given to it by the trial, and Carlile earned a profit of at least £900. He estimated his profit in 1819 from deist publications to have been £4,000. The home secretary, Robert Peel, informed the Commons in 1823 that Carlile's 10s. 6d. edition of *The Age of Reason* had sold fifteen thousand copies.[56]

Carlile sought repeatedly to show that the book contained nothing immoral, that it advocated a belief in God, and that he had no malicious intent in publishing it. The second day, when he sought to develop these points, he found himself constantly thwarted by the court. Abbott, understandably, would permit no calumny, reproachfulness, reviling, offensiveness, or irreverent discussion of the Bible or of Christianity. But Carlile denied treating the subjects in that manner, and denied too that

Paine's manner of expression breached the law. Two problems complicated the situation.

In the first place, Paine had been irreverent and offensive. He had declared with some frequency that the Bible itself blasphemed God, and those passages, repeated in the counts in the indictment, seemed shocking. The whole of *The Age of Reason* struck Christians as offensive. And Carlile repeated as his own belief the opinion that "the book which is called the revealed word of God is a blasphemy of that God"—and when he said it, "A murmor of indignation pervaded the Court." Similarly, "Considerable agitation was created in Court" when Carlile said, "I do not think the Bible is true, as history."[57] Carlile claimed to be shocked by the blasphemy in the indictment against him. Every one of the eleven counts stated that he had excited "the great displeasure of Almighty God." "Is this not gross assumption?" he queried. "Is it not blasphemy? We ought to venerate the Deity; and not speak of him as if he were subject to human passions and frailties." Paine, he alleged, had a higher or more sublime notion of the Deity than was found in the Bible.[58]

In the second place, Abbott regarded mere denials as criminal. That is, he treated a simple expression of opinion, not uttered in any coarse way, as the very reviling that the common law punished. In a refrain that ran through the trial, the chief justice incessantly repeated that the defendant could not defend himself by offending Christianity and the Bible as a result of denying their truths. Carlile had no chance, because the court regarded his mere expressions of belief as blasphemy. *What* he or Paine said, not just *how* either said it, was criminal. How an opinion was said was criminal if that opinion was stated with calumny or reviling, but Carlile's crime, multiplied almost every time he opened his mouth in court, consisted of matter, not manner.

For example, when Carlile declared that the Bible contained important inconsistencies and contradictions, thus raising the questions about its inerrancy, Abbott interjected: "You cannot go into the truth of the Christian religion." Carlile insisted that he could not defend himself unless allowed to prove that Paine was right in his criticisms, but Abbott found him to be offensive by questioning the divinity of the Bible. "You have not pointed out the divine origin of the Scriptures," Carlile retorted. "I am not of [the] opinion that it is divine; and I wish to state my reasons for holding that opinion." Abbott refused to let him offer his reasons. Carlile objected to the "continual interruptions," which made it "impossible that I can proceed." He wished to read and comment on the book he was accused of having blasphemed, in order to show that he was not guilty. "If the book I wish to read be the work of the Deity," he asserted, "it cannot be injured or shaken by the observations of any man. It is, in my opinion, not the work of the Deity." To that, Abbott rejoined that

Carlile was again "offending." When Carlile sought to read conflicting and inconsistent parts of the Bible in order to question its divine origins, the chief justice repeated that, "as an English judge, I cannot allow any man to deny that the Holy bible is of divine authority." Carlile wanted to know if he had been prohibited from reading from the Bible because it was "not fit to be read," to which Abbott replied, "Not to be read irreverently." The foreman of the jury intervened to say that the jury did not need to hear the Bible read, and the judge, in agreement, repeated that "he would not suffer the defendant to question the Scriptures" and a few minutes later added, "you are not at liberty to do anything to question the divine origin of Christianity." Again: "I cannot let men be acquitted of a charge of violating the law because they are unbelievers."[59] Thus, unbelief became reviling.

Carlile complained that he had intended to examine "thirty or forty witnesses" as to their beliefs, to show that all were tolerated and yet differed as to what the Bible meant—differed as to its truths. He wanted to prove that there were reasons for doubting its truths. Abbott simply refused: "You must not deny the truth of the Christian religion." Carlile declared that he would not take the law from the court, for "the jury are my judges." That had worked for Hone, because he had the jury laughing at the government. Carlile could not poke fun at the Bible, as Paine had. The jury's evident opposition disheartened him. "My lord," he declared, "I have no hope of bringing the jury round to my opinion; but I had a strong hope that if I was allowed to proceed I should show that I had some reasons to doubt, and that I might have doubted without a malicious intention."[60]

Abbott replied that *The Age of Reason* had not expressed doubts; it reviled Christianity and denied its truths. Carlile, who thought that the act of 1813 had given him the right to doubt, believed that Abbott's decision had "set aside the statute." "I stand in an Inquisition," Carlile replied, to which Abbott rejoined: "You stand in a court where the Christian religion must be observed as the law of the land, and where no man is allowed to revile it." Carlile then fell apart. He had been on his feet, he said, for over nine hours without any refreshment but water. He was exhausted. In consequence of having been interrupted in his defense, he complained, he felt "confusion and derangement." He had wanted to produce extracts from church fathers to show that the books of the New Testament had not been written by those whose names they bore. He had wanted to read Bolingbroke, Gibbon, and Hume to show that Paine expressed moderate opinions. He had wanted to quote eminent divines in support of the full freedom of opinion in religious matters, to show that his and Paine's views should be tolerated. Deism should be tolerated, he added. It had been greatly abused and confused with atheism. He believed in God, he rambled, but now could not continue.

Despite the lateness of the hour and Carlile's pitiful condition, Abbott declined to grant his request to postpone the proceedings until the next day. Apparently, Abbott hoped to wind up the first trial on the second day. He refused to "waste time," he said. He would not allow Carlile to read any author who denied the Christian religion, nor would he permit irrelevant evidence from witnesses testifying about the differences among Christians. Carlile thought his case might be helped by putting some Unitarians in the witness box, so that he could question them on the Trinity, to show that they shared Paine's opinion. "If so," observed Abbott, "I would not hear them." Carlile was perhaps not wholly wrong in saying that Abbott had set aside the act of 1813. Nor would Abbott receive witnesses who might question "the correctness of our authorised version of the Scriptures."

Carlile had no alternative but to fall back entirely on a plea for toleration. He wanted to read Locke and others on toleration. Abbott insisted that he lost nothing by not having them read, because everyone agreed "on the reasonableness of permitting a freedom of thinking on, and discussion of religious subjects, as long as the discussion is conducted in a calm, temperate manner," but he would not suffer tolerationists to be read if Carlile meant "to quote them to disprove Christianity." Abbott wished to continue, but the defendant was not the only one who was tired and hungry. The foreman of the jury, who had spoken up several times to object to Carlile's defense or to support the prosecution, now declared that the jury agreed to adjourn until morning, if the defendant would pledge to "limit" his defense. Abbott relented. The court arose at 7:30 P.M.[61]

William Hone and two unnamed "friends to the liberty of the press," who had been present in court, assisted Carlile in preparation for the third day of the trial. They copied in longhand, for Carlile's use, from authors who had most ably written in defense of "toleration and unrestricted freedom of opinion on religious subjects." The authors included John Locke, Archbishop John Tillotson, Philip Furneaux, Bishop Richard Watson, Robert Hall, and Robert Aspland. In addition, they heaped on Carlile a load of books.[62] On the third and final day of the trial, Carlile introduced his authorities, in the hope of obtaining an acquittal based on the jury's extension of toleration to deist works. He had nearly as bad a time as previously. The jury, on hearing the chief justice's summation of the law against the defendant, took half an hour before returning with its verdict of guilty.

On the next day, a new jury was sworn in to try Carlile on a second indictment for blasphemy, committed when he had published Elihu Palmer's deist book, *The Principles of Nature*. Most of it, like *The Age of Reason*, presented strong arguments that were well reasoned but sometimes scoffed, as this count in the indictment suggests:

This story of the Virgin and the Ghost, to say no more of it, does not wear the appearance of much religion, and it would not, it is presumed, be difficult in any age or country to find a sufficient number of men who would pretend to be Ghosts, if by such pretensions they would obtain similar favours, especially with the consoling reflection superadded of becoming the progenitors of the pretended Saviour of a wicked and apostate world. How absurd and contradictory are the principles and doctrines of this religion. In vain do its advocates attempt to cover this transaction with the machinery of Ghosts and supernatural agents. The simple truth is, that their pretended Saviour is nothing more than an illegitimate Jew, and their hopes of salvation through him rest on no better foundation than that of fornication or adultery.[63]

The second trial was much the same as the first. Everyone, more briefly, repeated the same arguments. Carlile sought to read the book to the jury, but the foreman interrupted to say that he was pursuing an improper line of defense. Utterly defeated, Carlile shortly declared that he had nothing more to say. Abbott summed up, and, without leaving the box, the jury pronounced a verdict of guilty. On the next day, when a third trial was scheduled to commence for the crime of seditious libel, committed in his report on the Peterloo Massacre, the government decided not to overplay its hand. It moved to let the seditious-libel charge stand over to a future term. Carlile was taken prisoner. He appealed for new trials on his blasphemy convictions, but the King's Bench held against him by ruling that he had no grounds for retrials, and they sustained the validity of the indictment, which Carlile had challenged, on the basis of the common law. The court then sentenced him to a fine of £1,000 and two years in prison for publishing *The Age of Reason*, and a fine of £500 and a year in prison for publishing Palmer's book. Moreover, as a condition of release at the end of his sentences, he had to post a £1,000 bond as insurance that he would keep the peace for the remainder of his life.[64] Within an hour of his conviction, government officers conducted a warrantless raid on Carlile's shop and seized everything of value—money, publications, and printing stock; in effect, the government robbed Carlile, ostensibly to pay his fines, and closed him down for a month. He himself had been rushed off to Dorchester Prison in the middle of the night, where he was kept in solitary confinement, over a hundred miles from London. He bitterly complained that the confiscation of his property was comparable to a fine of £5,000. He was bankrupt, despite the amazingly successful sales of *The Age of Reason*. Within a month of the trial, his wife, who managed his shop, sold ten thousand copies in twopenny sheets describing the proceedings of the first day of his trial, when he had read the book into the record.[65]

The conviction of Carlile showed, once again, that a politically unsafe book concerning religion could be punished as a blasphemous libel. The convictions of Williams and Eaton had shown that too. At the trial of Williams, Erskine, as the prosecutor, had vividly sketched a bathetic picture of how *The Age of Reason* robbed the penniless laborer, unable to feed his hungry children, by depriving him of a belief in a happier afterlife. Erskine, a political liberal, cared not a fig for the laborer or his children or their loss of religious consolation. His concern was for the security of the constitutional system if Paine's views on religion prevailed. Similarly, the attorney general who prosecuted Eaton worried lest people lose respect and veneration for Christianity, and lose also the "happiness hereafter" that it promised. The "evil consequences" would be a loss of morality, endangering the state. "Our civil and religious constitutions are so closely interwoven together," he had reminded the jury, "that they cannot be separated—the attempt to destroy either is fraught with ruin to the state."[66] In Hone's case, the same concern appeared, when the attorney general took alarm at the possibility that "the lower classes" would lose their awe and reverence for the law if they lost it for Christianity. The class character of blasphemy prosecutions and their fundamentally political nature seemed confirmed by the prosecution of Carlile.

Although *The Age of Reason* dealt with religious belief, it was politically unsafe. It was too well argued, too cheap, too readable. If it had cost more than working people could afford, the law would have ignored it as a book intended for a prosperous, respectable, middle-class audience, or for scholars, whose quibbles with one another mattered not at all. If temperately written, such a work could question, criticize, and even deny Christian tenets and the divine authority of the Bible. Such a work risked prosecution only if it reflected a nasty or malicious attitude, in which case the law would denounce it for reviling religion. Style, not substance, mattered if a work was intended for educated readers. However, substance counted, regardless of how temperate the style, if the work was directed to the audience of the twopenny press. Then religious radicalism became the equivalent of political radicalism, with the result that the publication became criminal if it offended, questioned, criticized, or denied. The reason was simply that by so doing it prompted the lower classes to feel an unease with the religion that helped keep them in their places, teaching them obedience in this life in exchange for rewards in some afterlife. Denial, even questioning, burst the bounds of acceptable discourse and became the equivalent of calumny or reviling.

A political interpretation of blasphemy prosecutions at this time in English history makes sense in light of the extraordinary toleration shown to religious diversity—on condition that it was religious rather than irreligious—and also in light of the fact that prosecutors and judges no longer fit an old pattern of membership in the Church of England. Erskine was a latitudinarian and a political liberal. One of Carlile's prosecutors had defended Eaton and become a Unitarian. The attorney general who prosecuted Carlile was a Unitarian, a fact of which Carlile took note several times in the hope of showing that deists were entitled to the same latitude of toleration. A dotty old Anglican clergyman who had taught Charles Abbott in college had been at hand, ready to testify that the chief justice himself had been a deist.[67] Carlile and the other publishers of *The Age of Reason* had not been victimized by religious bigots. Their prosecutors were not engaged in a religious mission, did not guard the gates of salvation from heretics, and did not profess to avenge God's reputation against a libeler out of fear that doing nothing might invite divine wrath.

Frightened by deism as a harbinger of Jacobinism, the government did what it knew best: it resorted to force. The "Six Acts" of late 1819 included provisions that sought to eliminate the twopenny press. By closing all loopholes in the stamp duties, the new measure put the cheap weeklies and all inexpensive papers into the same taxable categories as regular newspapers, forcing up the price of the cheapest to at least sixpence. Failure to pay the taxes exposed a publisher to ruinous fines. The same measure required every periodical publisher to post at least a £200 bond as surety for the payment of any fines that might be imposed in the future, for failure to observe the printing laws or for publication of some criminal libel.[68]

The government enjoyed easier victories against the libelers outside of London, where juries might be less sophisticated. In 1819 in Warwick, a packed jury convicted Joseph Russell, a Birmingham radical printer, for publishing and selling Hone's parodies. The prosecutor told the jury that, by depriving his readers of their religious feelings, Russell led them "to anything." "How was it in France, where the Revolution had destroyed so many millions? That change could not be brought about till the people had first been deprived of their religion." He explained in the usual way: one whose reverence for religion had been destroyed would no longer bear with patience the misfortunes of this life in the hope that he "shall be called to receive his reward in everlasting happiness." Russell defended himself ably, but he lacked Hone's wit. Lord Chief Justice Abbott, presiding at the Warwick Assizes, informed the jury that Russell was guilty of a most malicious blasphemy and added, "you must be aware the price of it is calculated to increase the evil by insuring extensive circulation." Without leaving the box, the jury convicted.[69]

In Chester, a hatter named Joseph Swann sold *The Comet*, a deist weekly, and was imprisoned for blasphemy. In a letter to Carlile, he aggravated the crime by saying that England would not have just laws until people read *The Age of Reason* and other deist publications instead of the Scriptures. His penalty was imprisonment for two years, plus two more for a related crime of seditious libel. The sale of Hone's parodies resulted in blasphemy convictions against Thomas Hynes in Plymouth and James Tucker in Exeter.[70] Tucker, who was Carlile's agent, received a prison term of fifteen months.

When religion is strongly valued for its secular rather than its spiritual virtues, an attack on it is feared as an erosion of the cement that binds society. Thus, the bishop of Llandaff could tell the House of Lords that the terrors of the law must suppress anti-Christian writings not addressed to the educated classes. Similarly, Lord Sidmouth, like William Wilber-force, who founded the Society for the Suppression of Vice, regarded the press as part of some conspiracy that threatened to subvert religion, property, and the constitution. Wilberforce himself believed that "the enemies of our political constitution were also enemies of our reli-gion. . . . Heretofore they inveighed against the inequality of property, and used every artifice to alienate the people from the constitution of their country. But now [1819] they are sapping the foundations of the social edifice more effectually by attacking Christianity." Wilberforce added that only religion restrained "the multitude," who would be lawless with-out it.[71]

CHAPTER SEVENTEEN

Carlile's Shopmen and Free Expression

I N LONDON, Carlile's prosecution and the accompanying effort of the government to suppress blasphemous and seditious libels ignited a firestorm of public controversy on the meaning of freedom of the press. Not one supporter of the government added a single idea to the conventional ones employed by the attorney general or by the judges, nor did one make an old point in a robust or intriguing way. By contrast, several critics of the government expressed themselves memorably. One was John Gale Jones, himself a notable stalwart of a free press, who preceded Carlile as the personification of open discussion. Three times he had faced serious legal difficulties for provocative remarks. As the founder of the British Forum, Jones sponsored several debates on the prosecution of Carlile. At one of these, before a capacity audience, Jones himself answered a speaker who had vindicated the prosecution as a necessary means to limit the spread of infidelity.[1]

Jones, who defended deist ideas, argued the case for unfettered opinion on the subject of religion. Tyranny, superstition, and injustice had to be exposed in forcible language, he contended. He drew the line at obscenity, but would not describe intemperateness as licentiousness. As for the evil tendency of broadcasting Paine's opinions and the insults they conveyed, Jones replied, "still they are but opinions; and is not the press equally free and open" to those who rejected them? Christians overwhelmingly outnumbered deists and supported clergymen of zeal and ability. Or were they "so incapable of controversy, or so indifferent to the welfare and security of that faith, whose tenets they profess . . . that they cannot overpower the feeble efforts of a few infidel writers, but must seek the aid of the secular power to demonstrate the truth and efficacy of that holy religion?" Coercion could not thwart free inquiry and, as a matter of fact, spread the very opinions it sought to silence. The prosecution of Carlile excited interest in Paine. Thousands who had neither read nor

even heard of Paine until the prosecution of Carlile had their curiosity
strongly aroused. Every town and hamlet throughout the kingdom would
hear the alleged blasphemies broadcast by the indictment and trial, and
people would ask why a religion that had the support of church and state
should be compelled to resort to force to protect itself from free examination. The prosecution, according to Jones, constituted "a libel on the
civil and ecclesiastical authorities" by giving the impression that they
could not cope with unpopular opinions. The question was not whether
Paine's opinions were right or wrong, but whether Carlile could be justified in publishing them. Christianity itself, according to Jones, protected Carlile's right, although, if its benevolent founder lived in London
in 1819, said Jones, the oppressive Society for the Suppression of Vice
would instigate his prosecution. He too had denounced false systems and
pernicious doctrines of both church and state, and he too had preached
equality as well as "community of goods."[2]

In a letter to his publisher written soon after Carlile's conviction,
Percy Bysshe Shelley erupted in one of his volcanic distempers. In the
course of an interminable rant about injustice and the virtues of freedom,
Shelley observed that Christians, who claimed to resent blasphemy because of its intemperateness, had not been known for mild or philosophical expression. Religious leaders had frequently resorted to impugning
the beliefs of others. What made Shelley's letter worthy of notice was the
paradox he discerned between Peterloo and the prosecution of Paine's
publisher. First, he wrote, employers released a cavalry troop "with
sharpened swords upon a multitude of their starving dependents," and
then came news of the conviction of Carlile for blasphemy, one of whose
features was Paine's "denying that the massacring of children and the
ravishing of women, was done by the immediate command of the author
and preserver of all things. And thus at the same time we see on one hand
men professing to act by public authority who put in practise the trampling down and murdering an unarmed multitude without distinction of
sex or age, and on the other a tribunal which punishes men for asserting
that deeds of the same character, transacted in a distant age and country,
were not done by the command of God."[3]

Although Shelley and Jones shared at the least an inclination toward
deism, W. J. Fox, the diminutive but eloquent Unitarian preacher of
London, presented a Christian view in opposition to blasphemy prosecutions. He regarded them as "a libel on Christianity." When Jones made
the same point, he was exposing Christian hypocrisy, whereas Fox was
preaching Christianity, which for him consisted primarily in the golden
rule. If deists would listen, he declared in his sermon the week after
Carlile's conviction, persuade them. If they would reason, argue with
them. If they wrote or published, reply; if they misrepresented, expose

them, "but in the name of Christ, do not persecute them, do not abet or sanction their persecution," which Fox regarded as a way to disgrace religion and obscure its truth.[4]

Unitarians had an interest in freedom of opinion on religious subjects. The conviction of Carlile, Fox argued, had the effect of abrogating the protection granted by the Trinity Act of 1813. Its purpose had been to protect Unitarians, not unbelievers, but the legal doctrines that maintained the prosecution exposed Unitarianism to prosecution also. The attorney general, supported by the court, had contended that a "contumelious" attack on the Trinity would be criminal. "Contumelious" was merely a word of surplusage by a court that regarded the denial of the truth of a religious doctrine as reviling. Christianity was part of the law of England only because of the unwritten or judge-made law. If it was part of the law of England, it had become so by disproving the former religion; its very success vested "the right to attack the religion of the country." To vitiate that right, as the conviction of Carlile did, vitiated the title of Christianity as part of the law of the land. Moreover, the term "Christianity" was itself vague, or was rendered vague by the diversity of opinions held by those who claimed the name in common. "What is the Christianity, to impugn which is a legal offense?" Roman Catholicism? Quakerism? Unitarianism? Whatever Christianity was, if it was the law of the land, it fixed the penalty for those who denied and reviled it: the law of Christianity was "the law of charity, kindness, forbearance, forgiveness, rendering good for evil, blessing for cursing," which made the prosecutions of blasphemy "illegal, because they are Antichristian."[5]

Many of the "lower classes," Fox asserted, were not Christian; they were "unbelievers." Moreover, a large proportion of the "higher classes," he thought, also consisted of unbelievers "who, while they discard Christianity themselves, think it an useful superstition to keep their inferiors in order." Deists, at least, had the virtue of being open about their opinions. Without doubt they were intemperate, but they had good cause. Christianity had been corrupted and had been guilty of enormities. The Bible, which deists attacked, was not inerrant. Christianity preceded the books of the New Testament. Some deist criticisms of the Gospels were valid, but what mattered was that Christ, God's messenger, had taught the resurrection of the dead and had risen himself in confirmation of his doctrine.[6]

Allegations by some Christians that deists undermined morality had no foundation. Deists should not be confused with atheists, for an immense difference existed between their creed of one God and the atheist's of no God, a difference as important as that between revelation and no revelation. To allege that deist opinions dissolved the bonds of society was "mere declamation" based on ignorance or bigotry.[7]

Focusing on the question of reviling and insult, Fox recalled that these were matters of taste. Deists spoke foully and revoltingly sometimes, but so did Christians. "For every abuse and misrepresentation a parallel may be easily found in theological controversy." The defenders of Christianity were not entitled to a greater license than those who impugned its tenets. In any case, "every epithet of reproach, contempt, or abhorrence, applied [by Paine] to the Scriptures themselves, has also been applied by professed Christians to those who differed from them in the interpretation of that volume, while they equally maintained its authority." Christians had been accusing one another of blasphemy for centuries. They were themselves guilty of the abuse and reviling that disgraced deist arguments. Self-disgrace constituted enough discredit for Fox, without the aid of prosecution. Prosecution had the effect of making its dissident victim a hypocrite, if he was silenced, or a martyr. Fox advised against confirming the "worst prejudices" of deists by making them hate Christianity all the more. Moreover, prosecution breached the principles of "impartial justice and equal justice and equal right," because Christians no more had a "natural right" to punish deists than deists to punish Christians. Prosecution could be justified only as "an usurpation of the majority over the minority, only to be vindicated on the assumption that power is right."[8]

Some conceded that, although the Gospel needed no legal buttresses, the poor and ignorant should be protected from "sophistical and demoralizing works." Fox replied that the only protection consisted in education. The best defense was refutation. "Danger from books implies ability to read those books, and he who can read one book can read another; he who can read Paine can read the Bible. The New Testament, originally addressed to the poor, is a continued appeal to the understanding." England's policy of toleration meant that the poor and ignorant had become "legally recognized as judges of the Trinitarian controversy, the Arian controversy, the Arminian controversy, the Episcopalian controversy; and surely not more ability is required for deciding the merits of the Deistical controversy. Our Lord appealed to the poor on the divinity of his mission," Fox added, and England was as enlightened as ancient Judea. "The feelings of pious Christians," he acknowledged, "are doubtless wounded by insulting language offered to all they revere. Let them meet it by a Christian spirit," and he quoted Luke 6:27–37, from the Sermon on the Mount. "Surely if there be any direction in the New Testament for our behaviour towards open oppugners, revilers, of our religion, we have it here." Fox would allow the unfettered expression even of atheism. "Look back on your own founders," he reminded Unitarians, and, indeed, Christians. "Look back on your own martyrs, your reformers; what you say of Deists was said of them; what you do to

Deists was done to them; they outraged the feelings of the society in which they lived; they were condemned for the defense of the ignorant; they were held blasphemers; they were dragged as criminals at the bar."[9]

Christian interpretations were numerous and varied. One Frederick Fox strongly approved of blasphemy prosecutions, and of Carlile's in particular. Fox found no meaningful distinction between deism and atheism, since both denied revelation and the one led to the other. In a civilized community, Fox declared, no man had the right to disseminate opinions that brought into contempt its most sacred institution.[10]

Such views were by no means the property of reactionaries only. The great Baptist clergyman Robert Hall, who had a libertarian record for courage and boldness that no one outshined, shared the opinion of Frederick Fox, not of W. J. Fox. In 1821, Hall republished his justly celebrated *Apology for the Freedom of the Press, and for General Liberty*. He advocated that everyone should have an absolute liberty to discuss "every subject which can fall within the compass of the human mind," and he seemed to mean what he said. Like Furneaux, he denied that the magistrate should have a power to punish the mere expression of opinions. Hall also adopted the overt-acts test, distinguishing between words, sentiments, and opinions on the one hand and "conduct" or "behaviour" on the other. He made an otherwise commonplace point, that freedom of expression should be cherished as a step to the truth, by observing that opinions of social value were frequently mixed with error. Publications, he stated, "like every thing else that is human, are of a mixed nature, where truth is often blended with falsehood, and important hints suggested in the midst of much impertinent or pernicious matter; nor is there any way of separating the precious from the vile, but by tolerating the whole."[11]

Yet Hall was primarily interested in freedom of political opinion; like Erskine, who expressed similar views, Hall felt provoked to speak out against the numerous prosecutions for seditious libel, but, also like Erskine, he believed that freedom of opinion on religious matters should not enjoy the same scope. Government derived from the people, they believed, and therefore was subject to utterly unfettered political expression, but religion derived from God. However, Hall had not incorporated any distinctions in his *Apology*. Accordingly, a reviewer assumed that Hall had in effect endorsed the right of Paine, Hone, and Carlile to publish as they pleased. He pleaded, said the reviewer, "for annual parliaments, for universal suffrage, for the unfettered publication of every kind of blasphemy." To that Hall replied in the same journal, "But when did I plead for the publication of blasphemy, fettered or unfettered? To plead for the liberty of divulging speculative opinions is one thing," he stated, "and to assert the right of uttering blasphemy is another. For blasphemy, which is the speaking contumeliously of God, is not a speculative error; it is an overt act; a crime which no state should tolerate."[12]

By describing the expression of an opinion on a religious matter as "an overt act," Hall retained consistency. But a blasphemous libel was no more an overt act than a seditious libel, whose expression Hall mightily defended. However, he had always sided with the common evangelical position on the blasphemy issue. In 1799, in an essay on "Modern Infidelity Considered," he refused the protection of a free press to atheism. He reasoned that the *philosophes*, as avowed enemies of revelation, had paved the way for the Reign of Terror. Like Wilberforce, he really believed "that the principles of infidelity facilitate the commission of crimes, by removing the restraints of fear," and that "atheism is an inhuman, bloody, ferocious system." He made no exceptions for "infidels" such as Hume, Bolingbroke, and Gibbon, who had addressed themselves "to the more polished classes of the community." Infidelity, which he did not trouble to distinguish from atheism or deism, had become much more dangerous, though, because it "solicits the acquaintance of peasants and mechanics, and seeks to draw whole nations to its standard." What once was a literary vanity had become "the organ of political convulsion." Thus, Hall, a libertarian stalwart, countenanced blasphemy prosecutions.[13]

Hall's views make all the more daring those expressed pseudonymously by "Christophilus" in his book, *A Vindication of the People from the Charge of Blasphemy, and a Defence of the Freedom of the Press*, published in 1821, the same year that Hall reprinted his work. Christophilus seemed at first to be taking the same view. He censured Carlile for having reprinted *The Rights of Man*, "a work which the most extravagant opinion for the liberty of the Press could not justify," and applied the same language to the reprinting of *The Age of Reason*. He even criticized the government for having let Carlile alone for "a two years' impunity of blasphemy," during which time not a week had passed when he had not merited conviction for both blasphemy and sedition.[14] Yet Christophilus reversed Hall. Hall had argued for absolute liberty of opinion and then exempted blasphemy. Christophilus argued for the prosecution of Carlile and then included blasphemous libels among the opinions he believed should be free.

Christophilus contended that the common cry of blasphemy was a diversionary attack by political factions that sought scapegoats. Although he would face the problem of reviling Christianity, he first extensively assaulted as "*real* blasphemy" a variety of words and conduct never regarded as blasphemy. He would not allow it to be defined by those who relied on judicial opinions to suit their own cause. To Christophilus, bigotry was a blasphemy against Christianity, and arguments for religious liberty were denounced by religious bigots as blasphemy. "Real blasphemy," he said, consisted in a Christianity that divided the country into the unequal divisions of rich and poor, contrary to Christ's commandment "that ye love one another as I have loved you." Christophilus found blasphemy in a profusion of oaths sanctioned by Parliament in matters involving excises, customs, and the law—what Blackstone had called "pious perjuries." Real blasphemy consisted also in the oath taken by those who represented rotten boroughs; they sold themselves to the highest bidder, yet swore that they had received no personal rewards. He discovered blasphemy even in the infliction of the death penalty, in the clergy's meddling in secular affairs contrary to their vows to give themselves wholly to their vocations, in the exclusion of Catholics and Protestant dissenters from the universalities (he didn't mention civil disabilities imposed on Jews), and in the "prostitution of the Lord's supper" by requiring the sacrament as a test of eligibility for civil office. These, he thundered, "are a few of the real blasphemies of the times."[15]

When he turned to the subject of liberty of the press in matters of religion, Christophilus confronted the more conventional issues of blasphemy. His position, he said, was a Christian one: religion denied the aid and protection of any penalty or restraint of any kind or degree. Despite the allegation that he excepted infidelity, he challenged the King's Bench and the attorney general on the doctrine that Christianity formed part of the law of the land and therefore should be protected by criminal penalties against insult. "*Christianity*," he argued, "disowns the principle of their prosecutions, and teaches the very opposite doctrine." He acknowledged that Christians had engaged in warfare, carnage, massacres, and persecutions in the name of God, but he reasoned that they acted not as Christians. Experience, paid for in blood over the centuries, taught the "utter incompetency of human tribunals, of judges, juries, and gaolers, in matters of religion." He could find no exception to the liberty of mankind on subjects of inquiry and belief, least of all in the area of religious belief. "The most extended liberty, even to unbelievers," he sought to show, was the "only cure" for un-Christian behavior in God's name.[16]

He conceded that irreligious publications were harmful, "but allowing them to do a certain quantity of mischief, our argument is, that on a balance of the evils resulting from the permission and forcible repression of the works of unbelievers, the preponderance is greatly against their repression." Christophilus contrasted the words and conduct of Christ with those of Christians. Like W. J. Fox, he emphasized the golden rule as the Christian answer to blasphemy. He observed too that blasphemy and infidelity were often found "where genius and talent reside." The price for tolerating blasphemy seemed to be worth its insults. A religion too good to be examined, he said in a paraphrase of Archbishop Tillotson, is too bad to be believed. He also relied on Dr. Nathaniel Lardner's view that the proper punishment of scurrility in religious matters is contempt and argumentation. Christophilus also knew his Furneaux, whom he quoted generously on the subject of blasphemy. In response to the view that the common people, not being philosophers, could not be trusted with a book by Tom Paine, he observed that they had been the best friends to Christian revelation. Christian liberty, he concluded, required "the most unrestricted Liberty of the Press," and, unlike Hall, he did not except blasphemous opinions from protection.[17]

Another writer who espoused a radical viewpoint but from a secularist's position was James Mill, the great historian of British India and scholar of political economy. His essay, "Liberty of the Press," written for the *Encyclopaedia Britannica*, was widely circulated and influential as a tract. He dealt almost wholly with the freedom to publish political opinions. However, unlike Thomas Erskine and Robert Hall, who had also lambasted the government's punishment of opinions, Mill made no exception for religious opinions. Indeed, he concluded his essay by asserting that the freedom of the press should be as complete with respect to opinions on religion as on political opinions. Mill repudiated the distinction that Erskine and Hall had made between government and religion, the one deriving from the people and the other from God. He emphasized that, whatever the derivation of religion, the people were as unsafe in allowing others to choose it for them as they were in allowing others to choose their opinions on government.

Freedom of discussion, Mill contended, meant the power of presenting all opinions "equally," as well as "recommending them by any medium of persuasion which the author may think proper to employ." He repudiated distinctions between "decent" and "indecent" discussions in religion or politics. Such distinctions had no basis other than judicial taste: to Mill, the "indecent" was undefinable other than as something that a judge disliked. All opinions, true and false, had to be accorded equality of expression, Mill contended, regardless of whether the writer restricted himself to "calm and gentle" language or employed vehement expressions that were "calculated to inflame" and might be "indecent." He believed that, unless all opinions were entitled to the same freedom, the only opinions that would enjoy freedom were those that were sanctioned, popular, or inoffensive. Censorial language, to Mill, so frequently implied truths that truth could not be reached, if at all, without such language or passionate expression. Different people, he observed, made different associations with the same words, with the result that words exciting the emotions of one left another unmoved. Judges who had authority to punish expressions supposedly false, indecent, or passionate exercised an illegitimate power because such punishment was injurious to the best interests of society: they could abridge the statement of opinions in which society might have a stake.[18]

A writer who, like Christophilus and Lardner, believed that the common people could be trusted to choose Christianity over deism or atheism was young John Stuart Mill, the son of James Mill. In an essay "On Religious Persecution," published when he was only eighteen, John Stuart Mill exhibited a marvelous sense of irony. After his first paragraph, which follows, he challenged readers to decide whether it described the first Christians, the authors of the Protestant Reformation, or Carlile and his deist associates:

> About this time there arose a set of men who denounced the prevalent system of religion as superstitious and idolatrous; who believed themselves destined to be its reformers, and aimed at reducing it to certain simple principles; who pursued this object with fearlessness and perseverance, although they had to encounter the opposition both of public opinion and of the constituted authorities; and many of whom, when tried for blasphemy, scrupled not to repeat, in the face of their judges, the obnoxious repressions for which they had been arraigned, and were about to suffer. They gloried in addressing themselves to the multitude; and the sympathy, which was excited by the proceedings against them, induced many to listen with a favourable ear to their opinions.

Mill did not think that the recent prosecutions of unbelievers in Christianity possessed any merit.[19]

He asked whether the nation's welfare demanded that attacks on its prevalent religion be deemed a crime. By "attacks," he said, he meant speaking or writing against the religion, not physically assaulting its worshippers or interrupting them at service. Mill believed that no Christian could answer affirmatively and remain true to his religious history. Yet missionaries propagated Christianity around the globe by attacking and reviling the religions of others. Mill knew no reason why Christianity should not be exposed to the same attack. Experience showed, he asserted, how unreliable was the assertion, made by judges and clergymen, that truth and morality depended upon a belief in Christianity or in God. He thought too that keeping deists in the open was safer than driving them underground. In the open, they were candid in asserting their opinions. Consequently, a person who bought a deist book, which carried hostility to Christianity on its title page, knew what he was about; he could read it alertly. But the case was quite different, Mill maliciously added, when the reader turned to history, a novel, a poem, a metaphysical essay, or a scientific treatise, any of which might be employed as vehicles of skepticism to undermine belief. Mill alleged that, when the foundations of faith were sapped without noise, the dangers were greatly magnified; better to leave the deists alone to profess their opinions directly.

Deist opinions also had the salutary effect of helping to keep the clergy intellectually honest. "A zealous writing and publishing unbeliever is as formidable to a bishop as an attorney general to a political libeller." Early Christianity had the same salutary effect on heathen Rome as did Protestantism on "Popery." An old church reformed "as soon as a new church sprung up to watch and accuse it." Tolerating all sects served a similar interest, but not as effectively as tolerating disbelievers. Although the hostility of the sects toward one another made them "censors on each other," their common faults produced "mutual indulgences, which the unbeliever would not feel, and out of which they may be shamed by his exposure." Mill genuinely believed that Christianity benefited from the criticisms leveled at it by its deist critics.[20]

Besides, he argued, prohibition of the truths of Christianity could be supported only by principles that justified intolerance of particular sects. History showed that heresy as well as infidelity had been censured as blasphemous. "All the reasoning against the denier of Christianity applies equally to the denier of its essential doctrines," and majorities had determined which of those doctrines were essential. When faith had sunk to those who believed in "the creed of the Homoiousians [similar essence], the Homoousians [same essence] persecuted them to death as blasphemers." The term "blasphemer," Mill contended, always designated a different faith. Where unbelievers existed, "blasphemer" meant one of them, but in their absence it meant Unitarians. "Wanting them, it means Arians; wanting them, it means Arminians; and wanting them, it means Protestants. It always catches those who are hindmost in the race of faith. Till Christians lose the knack of using it, there can be no toleration unless some who are called blasphemers are tolerated."[21] Mill concluded from this experience that toleration looked attractive "when, from an extreme party, it became an intermediate one, and the *odium theologicum* was transferred to the new-comers."[22]

Deism was the newest faith. Only recently, Mill observed, had it been "addressed to the multitude, because it is only of late years that the multitude has begun to read." Before the French Revolution, skepticism was "one of the privileges of high life," religion a "vulgar prejudice." But the revolution had changed all that, making Christianity popular again "in the hope that it would help to keep the people quiet, teach them to pay their taxes without grumbling, and restrain them from subverting the established order of things." That accounted for the prosecution of Carlile and his followers. The experiment of prosecution had been tried, the severity of sentences had been increased, and the number of indictments had multiplied, "and what are now the results?" Circulation of the obnoxious publications had increased "an hundred-fold." Before the prosecutions, a copy of *The Age of Reason* could be obtained "surreptitiously" by one who wanted it. Then Carlile published it openly and was prosecuted for it. Four years had passed. Mill figured that "we then owe to the prosecutions the circulation of upwards of twenty thousand copies of the *Age of Reason*; and as among the poor classes it is notorious that there are several readers to one purchaser, it may be estimated that at least one hundred thousand persons have been led to the perusal of that work under circumstances highly favourable to its making an impression on their minds." Mill noted that there was no such demand for Paine's political works, which had not been prosecuted, only for the theological ones, which had been prosecuted.[23]

Prosecution created a *prima facie* case against Christianity, according to Mill. Christianity deserved to fall if it could not stand its ground against deism without relying on prosecution. Learned and eloquent supporters defended Christianity. The established clergy numbered about eighteen thousand educated men, and the dissenting ministry another eight thousand. All seminaries were Christian, and religious periodicals were published in immense numbers. In 1819 alone, the year of Carlile's trial for blasphemy, the Religious Tract Society "added a million and a half of tracts to its issue," making its revenue about £9,000; the revenue of the Christian Knowledge Society exceeded £50,000; that of the Bible Society, £100,000. With such forces behind it, Christianity needed no criminal penalties to make it prevail. To argue the necessity of prosecutions libeled Christianity.[24]

Did blasphemy have to be prosecuted because it consisted of reviling and contumely? Judges repeatedly said that moderate and temperate denial of the Bible or Christianity was not punishable, although, in fact, it was punishable under the Blasphemy Act of 1698. Moreover, the very judges who alleged that Christianity could be attacked decently also refused defendants the opportunity of making decent denials. Almost invariably, judges regarded denial as calumny. Mill concluded that the line between argument and reviling was "too difficult even for legal acuteness to draw," with the result that "he who disbelieves and attempts to disprove Christianity can put his arguments into no form which may not be pronounced calumnious and illegal." The "only" protection for free inquiry, then, was to tolerate the intemperate as well as the "decorous" denial. Substance or matter had to be exempted from the criminal penalty, not just the manner of its expression. "Where the feelings are so deeply interested as they always must be on theological subjects," Mill observed, "it will necessarily happen that the party attacked will call that reviling which the party attacking deems fair discussion." A compensating factor was that the unbeliever lost his effectiveness in proportion to his becoming abusive. Anyway, no one was compelled to read his abuse. Blasphemy could not and should not be a crime, Mill added, because it did not breach the peace. Indeed, despite the increased circulation of deist publications in the past several years, the country had been no more disturbed by breaches of the peace than formerly.[25]

Mill insisted that he had defeated the primary argument for the prosecutions. No need existed to protect the poor and ignorant who bought so many more Christian publications than deistical ones. The prosecutions spread deist opinions. The best response to them was education. Educate the lower classes "as extensively and rapidly as possible. Everybody allows that there is no danger now [from deism] to the educated class. Let there be no other class."[26]

Mill closed with strictures on the vagueness of the law itself. Arguments for the excellence of Christianity do not read well in a trial "during which the accused is authoritatively silenced, should he attempt their refutation." Nor did the law permit equal privilege of speech; it allowed both prosecution and bench to interrupt and defeat the defendant. Nowhere was the law on such matters clear. Blasphemy itself was undefinable. Mill instanced the case of a deist society in Edinburgh composed of persons too free in their opinions for the church and too orderly in their habits for the tavern. The members came together periodically to read and argue speculative matters. They could scarcely have been more peaceable in their behavior. In late 1822, after about two and a half years, the police, without provocation or warrant, burst in, searched everyone for books and papers, seized the library, and arrested the officers on charges of blasphemy, which were dismissed some six months later—and all against the provisions of the Trinity Act of 1813, which had repealed the Blasphemy Act of 1698 with respect to Scotland. The case could not have happened except that the judges claimed Christianity to be part of the law of the land. If it was, what did Christianity hold as to blasphemy? The New Testament contained nothing to authorize its adherents to inflict punishments on its opposers. The Old Testament restricted blasphemy to cursing God. Mill, in closing, finally lost his detachment. Recalling that the charge against Jesus was blasphemy, he exclaimed that for Christians to use the crime against others was "most monstrous."[27]

Mill's article of 1824, however precocious, profited from the experience that had accrued since Carlile's prosecution. On the other hand, John Gale Jones and W. J. Fox had published their lectures in the year of his trial. They provided wisdom enough to warrant a complete reversal of government policy, but the government had its own wisdom. Jones and Fox preached nonsense, in the opinion of the government's ministers and agents. Crushing Carlile was the initial step of a systematic program to rid England of blasphemers, especially among the radicals who espoused Paine's views. Carlile's imprisonment was meant to be exemplary, a warning to any who might emulate him. But the government did not have the slightest understanding of the immensity of the problem that it confronted.

London's first blasphemy trial after Carlile's occurred in early 1820, in the King's Bench before Chief Justice Abbott. The defendant, Robert Wedderburn, represented himself as a Unitarian minister who was the grandson of a Jamaican slave and a wealthy planter. His case was all the more unusual because the words for which he was accused of blasphemy were uttered in a sermon in his chapel, a place described by his prosecutor, the solicitor general of England, as notorious for its debates "on political and religious subjects; and, from the extraordinary freedom with which every topic was handled," it had attracted the attention of the authorities. The subject for discussion was Carlile's case, particularly the question whether the lord chief justice of England had refused to allow Carlile to read the Bible for fear that "the absurdities it contained should be exposed."[28]

Two police officers who had been present testified to Wedderburn's words, which he did not deny. Abbott allowed him to read a statement in his defense. Wedderburn denied that he had blasphemed God, but he did repeat the view of Paine that the Bible blasphemed God. When Abbott allowed him to speak without interruption, he pleaded at length for the right to disbelief. He thought he had spoken coolly and seriously, without reviling. Tens of thousands of ministers of the established church and of dissenter sects could answer his arguments against Christianity, he asserted; he did not understand why Christianity had to resort to the "arm of power" to suppress him. In his opinion, the belief that Christianity rested on force was a far greater libel on it than anything he had said or believed. If he had used strong language, it was no stronger than that used by Christians against other Christians.[29]

In reply, the solicitor general emphasized that Wedderburn had not refuted the evidence of his guilt and had even admitted that he had spoken plainly in his chapel because "his audience were of the lower order," obligating him to address them in a language they understood. "This," said the prosecutor, "was the very reason" why the defendant ought to be prosecuted. A person professing the sentiments and possessing the popular talents of the defendant was "particularly dangerous among the classes of people to whom he alluded."[30] Judge Abbott seemed to agree. He complimented the defendant for his able defense but instructed the jury that the charge had been clearly proved, and that Wedderburn had not been accused of holding the wrong opinions but, rather, of "openly reviling" the religion on which the administration of justice was based. The jury returned a verdict of guilty but recommended mercy because he had been brought up as a street urchin without parental guidance. Abbott committed him to Newgate, for want of bail, while the King's Bench deliberated the jury's recommendation.

At the next term of court, before sentence was passed, Wedderburn delivered a moving plea for religious liberty and freedom of speech. The solicitor general reminded the court that he had done much mischief by reviling Christianity before the lower classes, a crime that "can never be tolerated." The court prefaced sentence with the same conventional remarks. The educated classes could withstand Wedderburn's sort of attack on Christianity but not those on whose behalf the prosecution had been instituted—Wedderburn's own parishioners. He was sentenced to imprisonment for two years plus payment of sureties for good behavior thereafter.[31] Wedderburn served his time in Dorchester Prison, whose most notorious inmate was Richard Carlile.

In Dorchester Prison, Carlile confronted economic ruin and the prospect of confinement for three years. The government had seized his stock in trade, somewhere between fifty and seventy thousand pamphlets and books, as well as the furniture and fixtures in both his home and his shop on Fleet Street. He called it "legalized robbery," because nothing was sold at auction in payment of his fines; having been bankrupted, he could not pay his fines. Precisely for that reason, he was kept in prison even after he had served the three-year term. He was not to be released for over six years. Eventually, the contagious diseases and winters in the badly heated prison broke his health and shortened his life, but they could not break his spirit. He resolved to continue his business and the struggle for radicalism and a free press while imprisoned, and he did. When the weather was warmer, prison proved to be endurable. He lived alone, isolated from other prisoners even during exercise time; the government did not trust him to talk politics or religion to anyone. Nevertheless, his room was "large, light, and airy," he had hot water, and he could get plenty of wholesome food as long as he was able to pay the prices of the keeper of Dorchester Prison. Contributions from supporters made that possible. Carlile, incidentally, estimated, at the end of five years in prison, that he had received gifts of £1,356. He had adequate furnishings, all the books he wanted, and writing materials. He actually called the prison "comfortable . . . altogether a neat and clean place." The government wanted to suppress his publications, but inexplicably allowed him to write and use Her Majesty's mails as safely as anyone. Nothing that he wrote was censored, seized, or lost. And so from prison he continued to edit his weekly, *The Republican*.[32]

During 1820, his first year in prison, Jane Carlile, his wife, out of economic necessity, took charge of Carlile's shop. She did not scare, and she was plucky and loyal. The sheriff and the Society for the Suppression of Vice threatened her with prosecution if she followed her husband's instructions. She ignored them and did as she pleased, ignoring her husband too only when he advised the publication of matter already found to be criminally libelous by a jury. Otherwise, she was as radical as he in politics and religion. As a result, she was, Carlile reported, "repeatedly arrested and held to bail, persevered and obtained a good business." By the spring of 1820, she was turning a profit. She had plenty of help from well-wishers. Some people paid her double and triple the sale price of her publications, and prosperous gentlemen—on one occasion as many as twenty—were at hand to provide bail when needed; they bailed her out at least four times. The charges against her mounted, as the government began to realize that it faced another Carlile who was irrepressible. The authorities began to consider taking the final step of bringing her to trial, even though she nursed a three-month-old baby. In October, Jane Carlile was summoned to the Guildhall for trial before the King's Bench for the crime of blasphemy.[33]

On that same October day in 1820, Thomas Davison, a radical publisher who was a protégé and competitor of Richard Carlile, also faced a jury in the Guildhall on a charge of blasphemy before the King's Bench. The courtroom was packed, because Jane Carlile was to be tried, but Davison's case was called first. Judge William Draper Best presided that day. Carlile called him "the gouty, corrupt, and vindictive Best."[34] Davison's crime consisted in the sale of an issue of Carlile's *Republican* and of an issue of *The Deist's Magazine*, both of which carried a letter against which the Society for the Suppression of Vice preferred charges of blasphemy, and a grand jury indicted. The offensive remark was: "Before the people can be blest with, and cordially receive, a perfect Government and a pure and equitable code of law, they must reject the Bible as being the word of the true God, and also totally disbelieve the divinity of Christ." The prosecutor described these words as not fair or reasoned but a "rather vulgar scoffing and scurrilous abuse." The judge agreed, informing the jury that "to vilify all that was sacred" was not liberty of the press.[35]

Davison relied, nevertheless, on both truth and the liberty of the press as his justifications. A poor man, unable to afford a lawyer, he defended himself by reading a prepared statement which Best persistently interrupted. Worse still, Best characterized Davison's remarks as scandalous libel. Davison had earned that from the court by declaring that a lawyer would have given him no more than a sham defense. When Best stopped him, he retorted, "You must not interrupt me in my defence." Best warned him that he could not trespass on the decorum of the court, to which Davison said that the judge might as well throw him in the dungeon. Because of that, Best fined him £20 for contempt. Objecting that he would not be restrained in his defense, Davison inveighed against the injustice of his having to answer criminally for "a mere matter of opinion." He was right in his characterization of the publications for which he was being tried, but he aggravated the situation in court by describing the Christian religion as "a fraud and imposition on mankind." Best fined him £40 more for his "indecency." Davison wished the jury to be his judges, but Best refused to allow Christianity to be scoffed. Davison remarked, "Then I must leave off my defence if I cannot conduct it in the manner I wish." Davison tried to continue, but when he said that members of the upper classes were "infidels and skeptics" in religion, Best fined him still another £40. Davison resumed his defense, but he abandoned trying to justify the remarks that had gotten him charged with blasphemy. He switched to arguing that he had a right to free inquiry on religious subjects, and he read from eminent authors to prove that deists were entitled to the same toleration as Unitarians.

In his instructions to the jury, Best declared that his objective in repeatedly interrupting the defense and fining him for contempt had been to prevent a "deluge of blasphemy," but out of mercy he remitted the fines. He informed the jury, nevertheless, that, as a matter of law, the remarks of the accused constituted "blasphemous attacks upon the Bible and Christianity." The jury "deliberated a few moments and returned a verdict of guilty."

The unfairness of the trial prompted several lawyers to protest. One, Henry Cooper, a close friend of Lord Erskine, moved for a new trial before the King's Bench. Cooper criticized Best's unprecedented conduct and challenged the legality of his having imposed on the defendant ruinous fines for contempt during the course of his statement. The defendant, as a result, "wholly abstained from urging what he conceived to be material and necessary matter to his defence." Even Lord Ellenborough had allowed Daniel Isaac Eaton to make his defense.[36] Best defended himself, and his brethren supported him, denying that there was any cause for a new trial. Chief Justice Abbott alleged that, if he had thought that his supporting Judge Best could have the effect of restraining anyone from making a bold and legitimate defense, he would decide otherwise. But if the utterance of blasphemy could not otherwise be stopped, a judge betrayed his trust if he did not impose fines for contempt. The other judges agreed. Best himself had the last word, by remarking that, since the trial of Carlile, people tried for blasphemy thought they could defend themselves by insulting the authorities and uttering horrid blasphemies. They were wrong, and therefore no basis for a retrial existed. Davison served his sentence of two years' imprisonment. He died young, in 1826.[37]

Jane Carlile's case was called late in the afternoon of October 23, after the jury had convicted Davison. A different packed jury was sworn, but Best still presided. Mrs. Carlile was charged with blasphemy for having sold William T. Sherwin's *Life of Thomas Paine* and a copy of *The Republican*. Richard Carlile was nearly dumbstruck. Although Sherwin's book was completely sympathetic to Paine, it had been sold for many months without protest, and its price was steep—7s. 6d. The second count in the indictment was identical to the one in Davison's, an issue of *The Republican* carrying the letter from a correspondent claiming that England would not have an equitable government until people understood that the Bible was not the revealed word of God. To a deist that was a mild remark, surely not a contumelious one. In any event, Richard Carlile had printed and sold both publications long before his wife took over his shop. He took satisfaction in hearing that sales in the shop had "quadrupled" because of her prosecution, but lamented that, because her case had been called late in the day, after Davison's trial, the London papers had been able to give "but a very brief report of it." For all his criticisms of judge and jury, Carlile did not complain that she had been unable to make her defense. Lawyers sympathetic to the Carliles belatedly volunteered assistance. One found a technical deficiency in the indictment for blasphemy, just as she came up for trial for the seditious libel, in mid-January 1821. Her crime in that instance consisted in selling a copy of *The Republican* that included a politically offensive essay by her husband. The jury convicted. She received a sentence of two years in Dorchester Prison, where she shared her husband's room.[38]

From the time of her first conviction, for blasphemy, Jane Carlile could not continue to manage the shop, the "Temple of Reason," in Fleet Street. She was free on bail until sentenced three months later, but she dared not risk a second conviction on the same charge, for fear of being punished by banishment. Carlile stopped editing *The Republican* at the end of 1820. He explained that sales had diminished because his vendors were being arrested, and too few were willing to take the risk of selling his weekly. Moreover, the attorney general threatened to arrest every person who served in his shop, bind them all to their recognizances for good behavior, and then confiscate the bail if they continued to sell his weekly. "This is a persecution that no tradesman can stand against." Besides, editing a thirty-six-page weekly in prison, 120 miles from London, was becoming difficult, and too many mistakes crept in. Finally, he was convinced that his sister, Mary Ann, who had taken over the management of the shop, "bid fair to be in gaol in the spring of the year."[39] He was wrong. She remained free until the summer of 1821.

On July 24, 1821, Mary Ann Carlile, who shared the family pluckiness, stood trial at the Guildhall twice, that same day. In one case, on a charge of seditious libel, Henry Cooper represented her. Cooper was the lawyer who had sought to gain Davison a new trial on the ground that Judge Best had prejudicially conducted the case and prevented a defense. The jury could not reach a verdict in Mary Ann Carlile's seditious-libel trial—in effect, a triumph for her.[40] However, the second trial went badly. The government had a packed special jury to try her on an indictment for blasphemy that was based on her publication and sale of Paine's supplement to his *Age of Reason*. The supposedly offensive remarks, itemized in the indictment, occurred in a passage in which Paine scoffed at the Christian allegation that the Old Testament prophesied Christ. Paine called the prophecy "absurd" and "false," concluding that Christianity "fell," because, by its own reasoning, it was based on the Old Testament, which proved to be without foundation. Another offensive passage alleged that the Old Testament was "so full of contradictions and wickedness" that it "could not be the word of God and that we dishonour God by ascribing it to him."[41]

The defendant received permission to read her written defense. Whoever wrote it mounted a shrewd, learned, and temperate argument. Mary Ann noted that Paine's pamphlet had sold in America without giving offense or provoking prosecutions. Her prosecutor suggested that the government did not think that Christianity could withstand Paine's criticism. She asked the jury to consider that the law did not protect Christianity from all examination but "merely from being reviled by those who might doubt or disbelieve its truths." Paine's paragraphs in the indictment were "written in as respectful a manner as it is possible when the object is to bring falsehood to the test of truth." The language in question could not justly be described as reviling. Indeed, Paine had written in a "mild and becoming manner." Even if he had not reviled, no act of Parliament prevented it, only the common law, which formed the basis of the indictment. The common law, she said, "is nothing but common abuse."[42]

At that point, Judge Best interrupted to say that he would not let the laws of the country be reviled. He advised her to expunge from her defense "such objectionable matter." She refused and sought to continue her reading. Stopping her, he advised that there were friendly lawyers in court who would review her defense and help her expunge it of offensiveness. A juror urged her to respect the judge's advice. She left the court for a few moments, then returned to say: "If the Court means to decide that an Englishwoman is not to state that which she thinks necessary for defence, she must abide the consequences of such a decision." Best then took the case from the prosecutor and summed up the evidence against Miss Carlile. He informed the jury that, as a matter of law, the remarks in the indictment constituted blasphemous libel, because anything that tended to vilify the Christian religion or the books of the Bible was a crime. He praised the virtues of religion, but allowed that religion might be questioned "with respect." When "shaken," as by Paine's language, the Christian religion, "from Heaven," could lose its hold on "the minds of the lower orders." The jury "immediately pronounced the defendant guilty."[43] The *Suppressed Defence* of Mary Ann Carlile, which Carlile's press soon hawked on the streets for a shilling, ran about thirty-five pages and purported to demonstrate that Christianity was not part of the law of the land, that blasphemy was not a crime that could be committed against religion, only against God, and that Paine had not committed it—rather, the Bible had.[44]

Five months passed, during which Mary Ann Carlile, out on bail, awaited a hearing on a motion for a new trial. Henry Cooper represented her in an argument before the King's Bench to set aside the verdict and grant a retrial. Once again, the judges of England's highest criminal court closed ranks against criticism of their conduct of public libel cases. Best justified his conduct on the ground that Mary Ann Carlile had meant to defend herself "against one blasphemy by uttering a hundred." He had done his duty to stop that. The others agreed. Chief Justice Abbott asserted, "The attempt is, in other words, to make a public court of law a public theatre for the promulgation of blasphemy." Best had conducted the case rightly. Unanimously the judges agreed that no basis existed for setting the verdict aside or for granting a new trial. The court then made its reflexive speech about its duty "to the poor . . . whose greatest enemy you [Mary Ann Carlile] are." They sentenced her to a fine of £500, a year in Dorchester Prison, and the posting of sureties for good behavior in the amount of £1,200.[45]

When Mary Ann Carlile joined her brother and sister-in-law in Dorchester Prison near the close of 1821, any reasonable assessment of the situation should have led to the conclusion that the government had at last silenced Carlile. But Carlile was not a reasonable man. Facing defeat and seemingly without resources, he decided to attack. He could do so only because reinforcements unexpectedly arrived. People whom he did not know turned up at his shop, wanting to devote themselves to his cause. Carlile had become something of a heresiarch as he masterminded the struggle, but his womenfolk also inspired zealous republicans to do their bit for the cause, doomed though it seemed. "Had Mrs. Carlile flinched," he wrote, "my business would have gone to wreck, for I verily think that there would have been no volunteers but for Mrs. C. and my sister going one after the other. It gave a sort of zest to the thing, and everything has gone well since."[46] In December 1821, Humphrey Boyle of Leeds arrived at Carlile's shop to "battle" the government and the Society for the Suppression of Vice. Then Joseph Rhodes arrived from Manchester, and soon people converged on the Temple of Reason from many parts of England. One who was indomitable was Susannah Wright, a Nottingham lacemaker and the wife of a bookseller, who became the head of the shop and housekeeper. "I will stand my ground," Carlile wrote from Dorchester, "as long as there is another man, woman, or child to stand by me."[47] Notwithstanding all the difficulties, at the outset of 1822 he resumed publication of *The Republican*. He continued editing the weekly until released from prison in late 1825.

The government responded angrily with force. It arrested his shopmen, including the fresh volunteers, and in February 1822 conducted a major raid on the shop, seizing everything except the presses. Inexplicably, the government did not deny Carlile access to pen and ink in his prison; it did not seize his mail; it did not damage his press. It seized his property, on the pretext that the proceeds would pay his fines, yet never sold the confiscated property to pay those fines. In 1822, as in 1819, the government made Carlile destitute and closed his business. In a petition to Parliament protesting the seizure, Carlile listed the confiscated materials, including the titles of tracts and books. Bailiffs kept the shop closed "for several months," he said in his petition. "He was detained in prison, because he does not pay the very money which has been taken from him." If the government did not remit his fines, he complained, he would be held in "perpetual imprisonment."[48] The harshness of the government's measures intensified the martyrdom of the Carliles, who reopened the Temple of Reason at a new address. They had not only zealous volunteers but financial supporters.

In the House of Commons, the solicitor general defensively justified the seizures but disclaimed responsibility for any irregularities, adding that Carlile might go to the courts for redress. Opposition members of the Commons protested against the "very unconstitutional severity" of his punishment and the policy of holding him in "perpetual imprisonment." Thomas Denman, one of England's great lawyers, who would become lord chief justice, criticized the heavy fines against Carlile and observed that his case "proved that irreligion could also produce its Martyrs." The *Morning Chronicle* noted that the publication of the list of Carlile's confiscated publications gave "the most extensive publicity to catalogues of sceptical works." Then, in a criticism of the conduct of blasphemy trials, the same paper noted the injustice whereby the prosecutor had the exclusive privilege of carefully culling and reciting the most blasphemous passages, while the defendant was prohibited from referring to the same passages lest he repeat his blasphemy.[49]

In the spring of 1822, while Carlile tried to recover from the latest seizures, the government prosecuted four of his volunteer shopmen, including Humphrey Boyle and Joseph Rhodes. They were charged with the sale of Paine's blasphemous works. Boyle claimed to be "but a humble mechanic" of "limited" education, yet he conducted his defense with astonishing skill and articulateness. His judge was Thomas Denman, presiding before a common jury at Old Bailey. Boyle perceptively opened his defense with the remark that all the blasphemy prosecutions of late "are part of a conspiracy among a privileged and interested few to controul the opinions of the multitude." Relying on his right to freedom of discussion on any subject, he spoke passionately about the inequities of the government's policies and prosecutions. Denman let him say whatever he pleased, but when Boyle indicated that he wished to read portions of the Scriptures to show that the Bible is an obscene book, thus proving the truth of Paine's charges, Denman cleared the court of women and children. Boyle next sought to prove that the Bible depicted God blasphemously. Finally, he contended for an equal toleration of deist opinions. The question in his trial, Boyle stated, was whether a free press would triumph or whether the government would be permitted to annihilate it. After an objective summation by Denman, the jury "without hesitation" returned a verdict of guilty. Boyle's sentence was imprisonment for eighteen months plus sureties for good behavior for five years. Rhodes's trial ended in a conviction too; he got two years.[50]

William Vamplew Holmes, another of Carlile's shopmen, who had come from "the West," was also sent to trial at this time, on a charge of selling one of Carlile's tracts, described in the indictment as both blasphemous and seditious. Holmes too was tried before Judge Denman, who allowed him the utmost latitude. Addressing the jury for several hours, sometimes rambling, sometimes powerful, Holmes argued that deists should be entitled to the same right of free discussion and toleration as other Englishmen. His trial, he declared, was less an investigation of a crime than a theological and political disputation. At stake was the "inalienable right" of every Englishman to exercise his own reflective power as he chose, "without let, controul, or hindrance," on any matter concerning the existence of a supreme being and the creation. He had an obligation to express opinions "polemical and controversial." "My defence this day is no more than a discussion of a natural right to exercise and to publish opinions upon abstract principles of religion and politics." He was accountable only to God for his religious opinions. In the course of defending deism from charges of atheism, he asserted that Christians who persecuted freethinkers were "the real Atheists," because they disbelieved God's power to vindicate Himself. If Christians really believed in an omnipotent God, as he did, they would not rely on the government to prop up their religion or punish its critics. Judges alleged that no one could impugn the Bible because it was part and parcel of the law of the land, revealing again that Christians did not trust the will of God to prevail. "Free toleration" had been extended to all Englishmen, even to Jews, Turks, and pagans. Deists claimed a right to express their opinions even as to the absurdities, inconsistencies, and "mischievous doctrines" of other religions. English law boasted of its impartiality; liberty of the press and religious toleration both demanded that that impartiality should extend its protections to deists. Holmes expressed confidence that a jury of his peers would vindicate his views. The jury took twenty minutes to convict him. Denman sentenced him to two years in prison and £500 to ensure his good behavior for the remainder of his life.[51] None of the Carlile shopmen made a better defense based on the principles of toleration and equality.

In the summer of 1823, Susannah Wright was convicted by a special jury which tried her case before Chief Justice Abbott. Several times he halfheartedly sought to stop her, but she continued reading her defense as if he did not exist. She was not a Christian, she declared, but, like Carlile, demanded the same freedom as Unitarians. She denied having blasphemed, and read to the jury the 1819 sermon of W. J. Fox, the great Unitarian minister, who had advocated toleration for deists, even for atheists. She addressed the jury for several hours, taking time out, with the court's permission, to suckle the infant child she held in her arms. "Assembled thousands" cheered her, but the jury took two minutes to return a verdict of guilty. She was fined £100 and sentenced to eighteen months in Newgate.[52]

At the trial of Samuel Waddington, another of Carlile's shopmen, who was convicted for the blasphemy of selling Paine, the evidence showed that the shopmen had devised a complicated apparatus whose purpose was to prevent the purchaser from being able to identify the seller. The seller remained hidden in another room while feeding publications through one chute and collecting money through another; speaking tubes permitted voice communication from one room to another or one floor to another. However, the sale of a blasphemous work justified the government's obtaining a warrant to search the entire establishment, arresting everyone in it. Waddington was caught in a dragnet arrest. His case stands out only because he brought an appeal before the entire King's Bench, on the ground that the Trinity Act of 1813 extended toleration to deists. Carlile himself had made that argument at his trial, and Chief Justice Abbott had rejected it. Abbott did so again in Waddington's case, reasoning that to call Jesus an impostor did not merely deny the doctrine of the Trinity; it libeled the founder of the religion that was part of the law of the land. Abbott's brethren on the King's Bench agreed. Judge Best, in a reactionary opinion, explained. The 1813 act of Parliament had altered preceding acts but had not changed the common law, of which Christianity was part and parcel, and therefore did not alter the common law relative to blasphemous libels. Waddington had not just denied Christ; he had denied him by denying the truth of the Bible.[53] William Tunbridge, another Carlile shopman, was convicted and harshly sentenced for the crime of selling a copy of Palmer's deist book, *The Principles of Nature*, for which Carlile had also been convicted.[54]

Public opinion by no means supported the Carliles, but the sacrifices of the family and of his volunteer shopmen stirred a sense of admiration for their courage. The government found itself on the defensive. John Stuart Mill wrote that the suppression enlisted "that sympathy which human nature will generally feel with those who are, or seem to be, persecuted." In the case of Carlile and the many supporters who followed him to prison, the "severity of the punishment" seemed "striking." The books that they suffered for found readers where none before had existed, and:

> An obvious attempt to put a man down on account of his opinions, raises up for him coadjutors who would else never have thought or cared about those opinions. A little army of volunteer shopmen has kept up the sale of Carlile's publications, and still keeps it up. Every one enters the house well knowing that his next removal will be to gaol; but knowing also that he shall have a successor. The Vice and Constitutional Societies, and the Attorney General, have co-operated for a most portentious creation; they have generated the fanaticism of Infidelity. Its spirit has wholly changed, and now exhibits all the proselyting enthusiasm of a Sect. The means which have formed this power cannot be the best to look for its destruction.[55]

In the House of Commons, Joseph Hume, the leader of the radical faction, presented a petition from Mary Ann Carlile in March 1823. Jane Carlile had recently been released from Dorchester Prison, but Mary Ann, like her brother, owed fines and sureties that she could not pay. Hume pleaded for her release. She had been prosecuted at the instigation of private societies, the Constitutional Association, which hunted down seditious libelers, and the Society for the Suppression of Vice, which targeted blasphemers. Hume censured both societies as "conspiracies against the liberties of the subject." Mary Ann was one of their victims, and so was the right of free discussion. Hume criticized the courts for their doctrine of silencing individuals who expressed opinions contrary to Christianity. She was no reviler; she had published and sold books more temperate than Christian works, in his opinion. Her crime was a nebulous one. Parliament could not define blasphemy, he asserted, any more than the courts could. Hume read to the Commons what he thought should be the prevailing law: Virginia's Statute for Establishing Religious Freedom, which adopted the overt-acts test for opinions on the subject of religion. Mary Ann had suffered enough for her opinions. Her term of imprisonment had expired four months earlier, yet the government kept her imprisoned because of her inability to pay an excessive fine. Having made that speech on her behalf, Hume presented her petition, detailing Judge Best's refusal to allow her to make her defense.[56]

David Ricardo, the eminent economist and liberal, eloquently argued that prosecutions should never be instituted for opinions about religion. The attorney general explained why the government did not wish to mitigate the sentence against Mary Ann. Her blasphemy "called for unusual severity of punishment," he said. It was part of a conspiracy on the "part of the family of the Carliles to triumph over the laws and religion established for the general benefit," declared the home secretary, Sir Robert Peel. He intended to do his duty. "The law of the country made it a crime to make any attempt to deprive the lower classes of their belief in the consolations of religion," he stated, "and while this law remained unrepealed he should think himself wanting in his duty if he shrank from applying and enforcing it." Unfortunately, no one asked Peel to identify that law. However, Sir Francis Burdett, who himself had been a victim of the laws against criminal libel, spoke in behalf of justice for Mary Ann, vehemently associating the government with the Spanish Inquisition. Like Hume and Ricardo, he flatly opposed the existence of the law against blasphemy; no opinion on religion should ever be deemed criminal, he argued. Wilberforce, the head of the Society for the Suppression of Vice, defended his society and the government. In the end, the Commons voted not to act in the matter, but Hume won his motion to have Mary Ann Carlile's petition published, and he managed to get into the record quotations from Dr. Nathaniel Lardner against the prosecutions of blasphemy.[57] The morning papers featured a summary of the debates, bringing respectable liberal opinion before a broader public. Mary Ann Carlile was not released from prison until November 1823, a year after her term had expired.

Periodically, the government continued its prosecutions of Carlile's shopmen, who continued arriving from different parts of England. One of the volunteers was young James Watson, who would become one of Britain's major freethought publishers. He was prosecuted for publishing or selling Palmer's deist book. In his defense, while rebutting the charge that he had maliciously sold a blasphemous work, he responded that the book had been "maliciously bought." How, he asked, could he have maliciously sold a volume to a stranger who had requested him to sell "that he might institute this prosecution against me?" The book itself had no criminal character, he argued, and the law should protect only against private injury. Religion could not be injured. Sir Matthew Hale, who had first laid down the doctrine that Christianity was part of the law of the land, had also believed in witchcraft and condemned women to be burned as witches. Blasphemy and witchcraft were of a piece, undeserving of condemnation as crimes. An opinion on religion could not be a crime, he argued. Watson spent an educational year in prison, reading Hume and Gibbon.[58]

Another shopman of Carlile's who was prosecuted and had something fresh to say was Joseph W. Trust. He had posted placards in the window of the shop advertising it as a mart for sedition and blasphemy, but before a jury he took a different tack. His crime, like Watson's, consisted of selling Palmer's book. He focused on the right to read and on the proposition that the book vindicated God. Elaborating on a point Carlile had once made, Trust lambasted the indictment's charge that the book had blasphemed "to the high displeasure of Almighty God." The attorney general had introduced God into the record as if He were a patron or an intimate acquaintance. "I shudder at the very thought of such a blasphemy as this!" exclaimed Trust. "What an indecent affection of familiarity! What a shocking attribute is this man's, who attaches to the name of Almighty Power the words he has put into the information." Trust confidently asserted that God could "not be alarmed nor offended by pen, ink, and paper, nor even by that mighty machine the Printing Press." Moreover, Palmer's book vindicated God's reputation.

Books, he admitted, could be provocative. "But though the book can provoke passions," he asserted, "it is a poor harmless thing; it cannot resist tyranny, it cannot defend itself. . . . It is the human compass: distort it as you will, its sensible needle always returns and points the human mind to the pole of truth, unless it be injured in its operations by the iron influence of priestcraft and tyranny." Why, then, fear books? "The man who is afraid to read any kind of book, or allow other men to do the same," he declared, "must be very wicked, very weak, or very ignorant." And he defended the right of every man to read what he pleased. He himself had done nothing but publish a good book that commented on another book, the Bible. No one got hurt by it; no one had to buy or read what he sold. He too, however, was convicted.[59]

Despite the 1823 convictions of the shopmen, Carlile sensed triumph in the fact that both the Constitutional Society and the Society for the Suppression of Vice went out of business. He even thought that both the attorney general and the judges of the King's Bench were "growing heartily sick of such prosecutions." In fact, the King's Bench did not thereafter try any of Carlile's shopmen for blasphemy: the government had to rely on lesser judges sitting in Old Bailey. Confident of eventual victory, Carlile, who was becoming atheist, exulted: "I tell Jehovah to his face that I will worship no other God but the Printing-press!" The slackening of prosecutions encouraged Carlile's shopmen to open a new and bigger Temple of Reason on Fleet Street, and his business flourished. The government then made a final crackdown, the most systematic and relentless of all. In May 1824, day after day, any person selling Carlile's publications was arrested. Within a short time, eleven shopmen were in custody, and none was left to print or sell.[60]

As they awaited trial in June, Carlile, in the highest spirits—prosecutions always invigorated sales—recruited more volunteers for what he called "General Carlile's Corps." After the mass arrests of May 1824, he published notice "that all persons will present themselves, to sell books in the said shop, free of cost in getting there, are desired immediately to forward their names that they may be regularly called upon, so as to prevent the stoppage of sale in the said shop." He insisted that the only motive of the volunteers must be "a love of propagating the principles, and a sacrifice of liberty to that end." The government had launched an experiment to see how far the opposition could be carried, and Carlile determined that he would show "Peel & Co." that he and his followers could not be exhausted.[61] "Your strength," he told Peel & Co., "lies in the ignorance of the people, mine in removing that ignorance, and that ignorance is not to be removed without agitation. By your prosecutions it is heard wherever a newspaper goes that the Bible and Christian religion are disputable things. . . ." The government's strong point, he told Eldon, the lord high chancellor, consisted in prosecutions of his shopmen, "and that is very dirty, paltry work; mine, in their speeches before the Courts, in their bravery, in their triumphant arguments. . . ." He would persevere, he warned, until the government would have to build more prisons to hold his followers. "I am a hundred times more formidable," he boasted, "than in 1819."[62]

In June 1824, the shopmen under arrest were tried, one after another, at the Old Bailey on familiar blasphemy charges. The public crowded the courtroom day after day, even though the arguments were also familiar: all the previous trials had been extensively publicized. There was nothing new to be seen or heard, although the defendants put on a good show. They alone did not seem jaded; they exhibited the enthusiasm of new converts to a cause that had seized them to their innermost depths. Each energetically fought for a free press, for toleration for all beliefs on the subject of religion, and for impartial justice. For each, his trial occurred in the springtime of newfound truths that demanded expression. Predictably, each was convicted and subjected to a harsh sentence. So many of Carlile's shopmen ended up in Newgate Prison that they launched *The*

Newgate Monthly Magazine, which was published for two years in Carlile's shop.[63]

Those were the last of the Carlile convictions for blasphemy. Fresh zealots arrived in Fleet Street to take their battle posts at Carlile's sales counters, but the government simply stopped the arrests and the trials. Every book and pamphlet, for which so many people had been imprisoned as sellers of blasphemy, now sold without restraint, not only in London but throughout England. The government had won a classic Pyrrhic victory: it won every battle, but at such a cost that it lost the war. *The Newgate Monthly Magazine* trumpeted in its last issue that readers should imagine the feelings of the patriot soldier crowned with honors and victory, and "then you may judge of our feelings at the close of this work . . . and the triumph of FREE DISCUSSION." T. H. Wooler, the publisher of the radical *Black Dwarf*, which Carlile had hawked as a vendor when he had first entered publishing in 1817, summarized as follows:

On the great question he has conquered. He has defeated the Attorney-General, the Vice Society, and the Bridgestreet Gang [the Constitutional Association]. The Judges are tired of hearing the prosecutions of his agents. A new shop has opened in Fleet Street. Every publication which has been prosecuted is sold openly in the shop, without any contrivance or evasion. . . . The battle is won, though he has been taken prisoner. To torture him is not to regain the field.[64]

The government could not regain the field or even save face. Peel, since 1822 Sidmouth's successor as home secretary, had been a slow learner. In a public letter, Carlile contemptuously scorned him as one who learned nothing, but he did learn. He learned that young Mill had accurately analyzed the situation. Prosecutions prodigiously increased the sales of blasphemous works, created sympathy for the defendants, and bought the government no popularity; they also cost the treasury a considerable sum. Peel slowly relented in his hard attitude toward Carlile. Moreover, in 1824, Sir John Copley succeeded Sir William Gifford as attorney general. Copley was not necessarily more liberal, but he was considerable wiser; he simply refused to permit new prosecutions for blasphemy in any court whose docket he could influence. Nor did Copley scruple to hold in prison any of Carlile's shopmen who had served their terms but were unable to post sureties or pay fines. The Cabinet resolved in 1825 not to countenance any further prosecutions. Carlile remained in Dorchester, however.[65]

In March 1825, Henry Brougham, a leading Whig, presented to the

House of Commons a petition from Carlile, requesting the enactment of a law that would extend to them "Freedom of Discussion" and a release from all penalties. Brougham deplored the government's policy of creating martyrs out of fanatics. He supported the petition not on the basis of freedom of the press but on the principle of toleration for religious dissenters, without exception. Fairness demanded an end to the contradiction of allowing the rich to read Gibbon and Voltaire but disallowing Paine and Palmer to the poor.[66]

In prison, Carlile served notice that he would not accept any offer of liberation conditioned on his payment of sureties or fines. He seemed to hint that he was considering new tribulations for the government by extending his struggle for a free press to include obscene libels as well as seditious and blasphemous ones. Carlile deplored obscenity, either in the sense of explicit sex or of filthy language about it. But convention considered as obscene the open discussion of matters of sexual freedom and contraception, which Carlile deemed of overwhelming importance to workingmen and women. In 1825, he published a twenty-page essay, "What is Love?," in *The Republican*, in which he blamed religion for turning love into sin and burdening people with poverty, misery, and unwanted children. The remedy was an "equality" for women and the use of birth control without stifling sexual expression. He reprinted a handbill addressed to working folk, advocating a French contraceptive device in the form of a moist, soft sponge. He provided all the details for its best use. His objective, he said, was to remove "all dread from the necessary practice of intercourse between the sexes," a matter that he did not think indecent. Couples should not have more children than they wished or could afford; unhealthy women ought not bear children; illegitimate children were undesirable; and sexual freedom should be made "a pleasure independent of the dread of conception that blasts the prospects and happiness of unmarried females."[67] The government hardly relished the prospect of a rash of publications that would test the laws on obscenity. It preferred peace and quiet. In November 1825, the keeper of Dorchester Prison, on receiving formal notice that the government had remitted all Carlile's fines and sureties, suddenly released him.

As might be expected, Carlile celebrated his freedom in the most provocative way: he published an avalanche of works that had been condemned as blasphemous. Wisely, the government ignored him, and public interest declined. An enthusiast and a sensationalist, Carlile searched for something new. In prison he had abandoned deism for agnosticism and then became an atheist or, at least, a "Christian atheist."[68] Atheism possessed slight shock value to those who had never distinguished deists from atheists and had always believed Carlile to be an infidel. He experimented with the editing of different newspapers and magazines, but lacked a focus until he came under the influence of the bizarre Reverend Robert Taylor.

Taylor seems to have been a brilliant, flamboyant eccentric. He became a physician but then decided to enter the ministry of the established church. After winning the highest honors at Cambridge, he was ordained in 1813. His readings in Gibbon and Paine had produced doubts, and his sermons began to reveal deist principles. Loss of his position led him to attack the church and embrace "natural religion." He established his own church in London, the Society of Universal Benevolence, where his preaching, sponsored by Richard Carlile, won notoriety and considerable business. He had a theatrical presence, a voice like an organ, a rich command of language. Preaching in full Anglican canonicals and immaculately groomed, he proved attractive to well-dressed young women. His deism was not Paine's; it was heavily mystical and allegorical, and, if government witnesses were believable (Taylor denied it), he was also ribald and railing. In any case, he was either immensely impolitic or a bit of a religious zany. He publicly advertised a lecture on "The Character of Christ" as a "philippic in exposure of the most atrocious villainies that characterise the Jewish Vampire." Although Carlile disagreed on many religious matters, he relished Taylor's showmanship, which he thought he could exploit as good business. The two became close. Having created a new magazine to disseminate Taylor's views and lectures, Carlile was not averse to a prosecution for blasphemy that would stimulate sales. The government obliged by bringing Taylor to trial before Lord Tenterden (Charles Abbott), the head of the King's Bench, in October 1827.[69]

The blasphemy charge was based on a discourse delivered in Salters' Hall. Government informants who had been present testified that the defendant had claimed that the New Testament described fictitious persons and events, that Jesus never existed, and that Christianity was based on myths. They testified too that he had presented these views by scoffing and lampooning sacred matters. Taylor denied everything. Fashionably coiffed and wearing his priestly robes, sumptuous rings, and long kid gloves, he demonstrated a capacity for nitpicking distinctions in theological matters. He claimed that he had not blasphemed, because he had engaged in a scholarly disputation, but he waffled. He claimed to be both a Christian and a deist, who abhorred coarseness and attacks on the doctrine of the Trinity. In a three-and-a-half-hour speech, he gave the impression that he was arrogant and deceitful—"I was maintaining the . . . divinity of Christ in opposition to the Unitarian heresy." He did not refer to freedom of speech or of religious opinion, although he inconsistently relied on the Trinity Act of 1813, which had extended toleration to Unitarianism. The chief justice instructed the jury that the defendant's opinions, offered "in a tone of sarcasm and coarseness," constituted blasphemy, and the jury obediently convicted. Taylor received a sentence of one year in prison and sureties for good behavior in the amount of £1,000. It was the dullest blasphemy trial on record.

The London Magazine, indifferent to Taylor, roasted Lord Tenterden for his poorly reasoned explanation of why blasphemy was criminal. Christianity, he had said, was part of the law of the land, "as perfectly inviolable in that substance, and as fully entitled to the protection in every manner and degree, as our civil constitution itself." "If we were informed that Christianity was part and parcel of an old woman's frowzy flannel petticoat," responded *The London Magazine*, "we would not presume to doubt it; but, having acceded to the truth of the fact, we must yet ask what connexion there is between it and the desired consequence." One sort of "galimathias" or gibberish was as good as another.

> Let us say that "The Christian religion in its substance is a part of the sirloin of beef, as perfectly inviolable in that substance, and as fully entitled to protection in every manner and degree as our plum-pudding itself." Nonsense; if the Christian religion were in its substance a part of the sirloin of beef, a sirloin of beef is not inviolable in its substance; and so the proposition comes to nothing. True, and if the Christian religion be part and parcel of the law of the land, the law of the land is not inviolable in its substance. Its substance and form are, under the blessing of heaven, undergoing change in every session of Parliament. The Christian religion is neither a part nor parcel of any thing in the world, it is no more a part or parcel of the law of the land, than it is a part or parcel of Lord Tenterden's wig; it is simply and solely a belief in the truth. It were a great evil to shake men's belief in the truth; but in all things except religion we have such reliance on the power of truth, that we think it unnecessary to defend it with pains and penalties.

The magazine added that religion should not constitute an exception.[70]

When Taylor got out of prison, he and Carlile, the Cambridge fancy man and the Devonshire tinsmith, conducted "Infidel Tours" of the Midlands, lecturing on religion; then they returned to London, where they kept their show going at the Rotunda, a major center for radicalism in religion and politics. Their discussions prompted this comment in the conservative *Quarterly Review*: "Blasphemy was soon found to be a more attractive commodity than treason, as well as an approved preparation for it. . . . The reader would be not more greatly astonished than shocked were we to relate what passes at these meetings; the revolting ribaldry, the nefarious impiety, the daring and rabid blasphemies. . . . Large as the theatre is, it is crowded."[71] On Good Friday and on Easter Sunday of 1831, Taylor preached sermons that deserved *The Quarterly Review*'s fervid descriptions. Not content with derisive disparagement of the Gospels' account of the Passion of Jesus, which Taylor regarded as forgeries and lies, he grotesquely lampooned Jesus, the crucifixion, and the resurrection. If ever a prosecution for blasphemy was justifiable, it was this case, all the more galling because Taylor was dressed in full canonicals. The government cleverly denied him a theatre when it tried him, as quietly as possible, before the Surrey Court of Sessions, presided over by an obscure judge who, on the inevitable verdict of guilty by a hostile jury, sentenced Taylor to two years' hard labor in a mean prison. On his release, he broke with Carlile, married a wealthy elderly lady, and left for France, never to return.[72]

Carlile, who had left prison an atheist in 1825, continued his religious metamorphosis, but did not abandon his political radicalism. Borrowing Taylor's allegorical mode of interpreting religious matters as a way of explaining nature, he could be murky. But his understanding of workingmen's causes remained sharp. In one of his magazines, *The Prompter*, he defended riotous agricultural laborers as having no recourse left but violence and the expression of vehement ridicule of the government. That got him into serious trouble. The charge was seditious libel. He defended himself with gusto for five and a half hours, justifying the right of rebellion under certain circumstances and relying, of course, on the freedom of the press. The jury convicted him, as usual, and the sentence was two years in prison plus fines and sureties, which he refused to pay; that defiance kept him in prison for another eight months.[73]

In prison, Carlile embraced a sort of Swedenborgian mysticism, and astoundingly announced his conversion "to the truth as it is in the Gospel of Jesus Christ. I declare myself a believer in the truth of the Christian religion," declared England's foremost blasphemer. But, like Taylor, he had his own version of the truth and of Christianity, and as if nothing had changed, he challenged orthodox Christians, "the idolatrous pretenders to Christianity," to debate.[74] In prison he also published *Isis*, edited by the woman who would become his common-law wife. *Isis* has been called "the first journal produced by a woman in support of sex equality and political and religious freedom."[75]

Carlile's final term in prison resulted from what began as a refusal to pay taxes for the benefit of the established religion. The threat of prosecution aggravated his defiance. In his shop window he displayed the figure of a bishop linked arm in arm with the devil. Because of that he was prosecuted for maintaining a public nuisance. He refused on principle to post a modest sum as surety for his good behavior. That got him a three-year sentence, though he was released after four months. In his last years, he was a licensed preacher, the Reverend Richard Carlile. In 1842, the year before his death, he attended the trial of George Jacob Holyoake for blasphemy, staying with the defendant and advising him for ten days. Carlile's final periodical was entitled *The Christian Warrior*.[76]

CHAPTER EIGHTEEN

Early American State Cases

THE LAW of blasphemy had vegetated in eighteenth-century America. It was a vestigial relic of a dead age, and should have disappeared altogether after the American states became independent of Great Britain. Like preferential treatment for the Church of England, blasphemy law should have encountered insuperable constitutional objections because of state guarantees of the free exercise of religion and provisions against the preferential treatment of one religion above others. Additionally, the freedoms of speech and the press flourished in America. Of course, the enormous diversity of the states made the prosecution of blasphemy possible somewhere in the country; logically, that most likely should have been in New England, where Massachusetts, Connecticut, New Hampshire, and Vermont continued constitutional policies that allowed establishments of religion that, as a matter of law if not of fact, showed no preference to one denomination over another.[1] The reality of the situation, however, was that isolated blasphemy prosecutions broke out in the mid-Atlantic states, which had enjoyed the fullest religious diversity and freedom.

There is no knowing what triggered a prosecution, especially in such an unlikely place. The number of prosecutions in the states was so few and the records so sparse that the prosecutions seem unlikely, inexplicable. An outraged citizen might complain to the authorities about someone's religiously offensive remarks. A peace officer might on his own initiative make an arrest on hearing such remarks. A prosecutor, acting zealously on behalf of religion, might file charges or ask a grand jury for an indictment. A judge might convince a grand jury to present some notorious blasphemer. We simply do not know how the few extant cases were instigated; we know even less about the possibly large number of cases in which circumspect prosecutors decided not to proceed with a complaint, perhaps because it might give undue publicity to offensive remarks or might be suppressive. The American temperament looked askance at prosecutions for bad opinions. The prosecutions for seditious libel under the Sedition Act of 1798 were so infamous precisely because they were so aberrant. American law might be narrow on the freedom of the press, reiterating one's criminal responsibility for his abuse of freedom of expression, but American practice strongly inclined to countenance aspersive, sleazy, muckraking criticism in the speech of citizens, in tracts, and in newspapers. Indulgence and counterargument seemed the norm, whereas prosecution for opinion seemed un-American.

Yet the aberrant cases included several of importance at the appellate level. Unlike in Britain, where trial records are plentiful, they are rare in America. Appellate records exist, though appellate decisions on blasphemy occur infrequently. In every state that prosecuted blasphemy, the state appellate court had to decide for itself whether the offense existed in its common law or, if a statute punished the crime, whether a constitutional guarantee of free speech or of religious liberty invalidated the prosecution. A decision in one state might influence another but was not binding beyond the jurisdiction of the court that had made the decision.

People v. *Ruggles*, decided by the New York Supreme Court of Judicature in 1811, remains to this day one of the most important blasphemy cases in our history.[2] Its distinction arises for two reasons: it was the first reported state case on blasphemy, and the exceptionally prestigious and learned chief justice of the court, James Kent, delivered the opinion. Kent's *Commentaries on American Law*, written after his retirement from the bench, justifiably entitled him to recognition as the American Blackstone, and enhanced the influence of his judicial opinions.[3]

As a case of first impression, *People* v. *Ruggles* deserves treatment in a fullness that the sources do not permit. All that is known of the case is the short account in the official reports of the state supreme court. No trial record survived, and no newspaper stories exist. Not even Ruggles's first name is known. In Salem, New York, he loudly declared in the presence of many people, "Jesus Christ was a bastard, and his mother must be a whore." That conventionally scurrilous utterance earned Ruggles an indictment for blasphemy. He was tried and convicted before Judge Ambrose Spencer, a member of the Supreme Court of Judicature. Spencer sentenced him to imprisonment for three months and a fine of $500, then an enormous sum.

On appeal to New York's court of last resort, an attorney named John L. Wendell, representing Ruggles, made a skillful argument on his behalf. He contended that the offense of blasphemy was not punishable in New York, because no statute had been passed against it. In Britain, blasphemy became a common-law offense, because the establishment of the Church of England made Christianity part of the law of the land. But

Christianity was not part of the common law of New York. No statutes
on religion existed excepting Sunday laws. The state constitution guaranteed the free exercise of religion for everyone. Its exception as to licentiousness referred to conduct, not opinions. Any religion might
lawfully be preached in New York. "For aught that appears," Wendell
said, "the prisoner may have been a Jew, a Mahometan, or a Socinian;
and if so, he had a right, by the constitution, to declare his opinions." He
did not attack religion generally, offend against morality, or destroy confidence in oaths. Wendell apparently argued also that, even if the court
were to regard blasphemy as an offense at common law, Ruggles had not
been guilty of it. Wendell did not cope with the provision of the New
York constitution of 1777 that adopted the English common law excepting such alterations as the legislature might make, and excluding all parts
of the common law "as may be construed to establish or maintain any
particular denomination of Christians."[4]

Chief Justice Kent, writing for a unanimous court, rejected Wendell's
arguments. Although the court consisted of three Democrats and two
Federalists, the opinion was nonpartisan. Unbound by English precedents, and in the absence of any reported American cases on blasphemy,
the court could have adapted the common law to the constitutional guarantee of religious liberty; it could have rejected the English law of blasphemy. Kent was a great judge, and great judges can find ways to improve
the standing law. But Kent and his court were far too conservative for
that. He himself, though not a religious person, regarded religion as a
bulwark of good social order. And whenever a statute did not provide
guidance, his biographer wrote, he was "free to indulge to the utmost his
inclination to make the common law of England the law of the state of
New York."[5] As an ultra-Federalist, Kent possessed a profound reverence for English authority.

The sole question before the court, he declared, was whether blasphemy constituted an offense, absent a statute criminalizing it. Defining the offense, he said that it consisted of words "maliciously reviling
God, or religion," and not in a "serious discussion upon any controverted point in religion." Ruggles's language was blasphemous because
he reviled Christianity "through its author." But did blasphemy violate
New York law?

It violated common law, Kent reasoned, and he cited the English
authorities, including Taylor's case of 1676, when Lord Hale had ruled
that, because Christianity was part of the law of the land, to reproach it
in a contumelious manner tended to weaken the foundation of moral
obligations and the sanctity of oaths. Kent also relied on Woolston's case
of 1738, when Lord Raymond declared that he would not allow a discussion whether defaming Christianity was an offense, because whatever

struck at its roots tended to the dissolution of civil government. Kent also knew Lord Kenyon's opinion of 1797 sustaining the conviction of Williams for publishing *The Age of Reason*. Reviling Christ, Kent held, constituted a crime, because it "tends to corrupt the morals of the people, and to destroy good order." That England had an establishment of religion made no difference; the offense existed in England independently of the establishment.

Kent then asked why blasphemy should not be "an offense with us?" Nothing prevented application of the common law; moreover, New York needed "moral discipline" and "those principles of virtue, which help to bind society together." The people of the state professed the general doctrines of Christianity. Thus, "to scandalize the author of these doctrines . . . is a gross violation of decency and good order." No government, Kent claimed, allowed the religion of the community "to be openly insulted and defamed."

Did the constitutional guarantee of free religious opinion alter the situation? Kent insisted that the state constitution did not protect the reviling of Christianity. The situation differed as to the religion of Mohammed or of the grand lama, because "we are a christian people, and the morality of the country is deeply ingrafted upon christianity, and not upon the doctrines or worship of those imposters." Having ruled that only Christianity could be blasphemed, Kent reviled other religions by claiming that invectives against them showed no malice, because they were "superstitions equally false and unknown." Thus, prejudice underlay the criminality of blasphemy as well as Kent's talk about the need for virtue, decency, and good order.

Kent added that blasphemies against Christianity struck "at the root of moral obligation, and weaken the security of the social ties." He found support for this view in the language of the constitutional guarantee of "free exercise and enjoyment of religious profession." That guarantee carried an exception for "acts of licentiousness" or "practices inconsistent with the peace and safety of this state." Blasphemy, he concluded, was inconsistent with the "reverence" due to oaths and lessened their "religious sanction."[6]

That the court could have decided otherwise is a fact. In a later Ohio case, the state high court quoted a state constitutional guarantee of religious liberty that scarcely differed from New York's, and remarked: "it follows that neither Christianity, nor any other system of religion is part of the law of this state."[7] That the New York court should have found blasphemy to be an offense at common law despite the constitutional guarantee was not unreasonable. That it should have found that only Christianity could be blasphemed is surprising, given the breadth of the constitutional guarantee and the existence of a small but noticeable Jewish

population in New York. In 1838, an English court would also hold that
only Christianity could be blasphemed, but England had an established
church, whereas New York's constitution outlawed any establishment.[8]
That the court should have gratuitously aspersed the religions of any
people, Muslims and Buddhists in particular, was offensive. That the
court should have linked religion to morality as a bulwark of social order
was probably a way of expressing the belief that without religion the poor
might menace Kent's class or, at least, not be held in check as easily. That
the court should have supported religion as the basis for the sanctity of
oaths ignored the fact that an unsworn affirmation to tell the truth was the
righteous way of Quakers and of Jesus himself. That the court should
have found a crucial exception to the constitutional guarantee of liberty
for opinions on religion unfairly ignored the fact, stated in the argument
of counsel, that blasphemy was a verbal crime, not an "act" or a "practice." Blasphemy might be licentious, as Kent believed, but it was licentious utterance, not conduct. Not the slightest evidence existed to show
that Ruggles's blasphemy, in the words of the constitution, threatened
"the peace and safety of this state." Punishing blasphemy, moreover,
neither promoted reverence and morality, nor strengthened the security
of social ties. In effect, the court merely announced its opinion that,
because Christianity was a Good Thing, profane public disrespect for it
should be punished.

People v. Ruggles did not inaugurate an era of intolerance in New York,
or even a wave of prosecutions for blasphemy. On the contrary, there
were no further convictions. Kent's opinion did not put the fear of God
or of imprisonment in deists, freethinkers, and atheists. The court's opinion, carrying Kent's influential name, did fashion the law, but it was
controversial.

In 1821, at a New York constitutional convention that framed a new
constitution for the state, Kent's views weathered a sustained attack.
Erastus Root, who led the attempt to democratize the government and
especially to broaden the suffrage, moved that the article on religious
freedom should be amended by a statement that the "judiciary shall not
declare any particular religion to be the law of the land." Root censured
the court for its opinion in the Ruggles case, which, he asserted, made
Christianity part of the law of the land. The sheriff of New York City,
he observed, was a Jew who, because of Ruggles, "is guilty of blasphemy
every time he enters the synagogue," as would be a "Musselman" for
reading the Koran. Root demanded freedom of conscience, as if it did not
exist, and insisted that religion should not be supported by law.[9]

As a member of the convention, James Kent, then chancellor of the
state, responded. Root, he declared, has misunderstood the case. The
court had not adjudged Christianity to be established by law. Rather, it

had held that to revile the author of Christianity in a blasphemous manner with malicious intent was an indictable offense against public morals and decency. Although Christianity was not established, it was the religion of the people of the state and the basis of morality. Kent also emphasized a point barely made in his opinion, that blasphemy outraged public decorum and offended public taste.[10]

Root replied by reading the entire report of *People* v. *Ruggles*, and then amended his motion to delete the reference to the judiciary: "It shall not be declared or adjudged that any particular religion is the law of the land." Kent voted for the motion, which easily passed, sixty-two to twenty-six. The chancellor explained his vote by saying that the motion could do no harm and might be a security. For the time being, however, the convention clearly repudiated his *Ruggles* opinion.[11]

Twelve days later, however, the issue arose again, when the convention debated the language of the proposed new constitution. Ambrose Spencer, who had become chief justice, moved deletion of Root's clause against an establishment of religion. Its final adoption, he warned, would "prevent punishment for blasphemy, and thereby endanger the morals of the community." Spencer understood the reference to "particular religion" to mean Christianity, not a particular Christian sect. "Are we prepared to send forth to the people a provision in our constitution, that shall suffer any man to blaspheme, in the most malicious manner, his God, and the religion of the Redeemer of the world?" If that provision were adopted, no court could punish even the most infamous blasphemy. Martin Van Buren, the future president, disagreed, but Rufus King, a framer of the Constitution of the United States, upheld Spencer. King even agreed that only Christianity could be blasphemed, and he wanted all such blasphemy to be punishable. Kent himself replied to Van Buren by contending, again, that his court had not declared Christianity to be the legal religion of the state. Yet, because it was in fact the religion of the people of the state, to blaspheme it was a crime. He then contradicted himself by saying: "In a sense, we may consider the duties and injunction of the Christian religion as interwoven with the law of the land, and as part and parcel of the common law." Blasphemy, he declared more accurately, was a crime only if an attack on Christianity offended public morals.[12]

When Spencer disputed Kent's argument by maintaining that Christianity was the established religion, Kent repudiated his views and those of Rufus King. Anyone might attack Christianity, Kent argued, without blaspheming, if he did so in a decent manner. This view of the matter would become law in Britain later in the nineteenth century. New York, however, left its law on blasphemy shrouded in a disagreement between its former and subsequent chief justices as to the meaning of *Ruggles*.

Whatever their disagreement about whether Christianity was part of the law of the land and whether any attack on it, or just an indecent or reviling attack, constituted blasphemy, Kent and Spencer united in the final vote on Spencer's motion. Inexplicably, the convention, which had overwhelmingly adopted Root's motion, reversed itself and by a vote of seventy-four to forty-one finally adopted Spencer's to kill Root's.[13] Thus, *People* v. *Ruggles* prevailed. Blasphemy remained a crime in New York, and it meant, at the least, an indecent or reviling attack on Christianity. Attacks that did not outrage or shock believers seemed lawful.

In 1821, the year of the convention, Judge William Jay of the West-chester County court expounded the meaning of the free-speech clause of the state constitution to a grand jury. The guarantee, he declared, extended equally to religious and political topics. Accordingly, "infidels" as well as Christians had an "equal and undoubted right to publish the sentiments, and to endeavor to make converts to them." Jay did not mention the Ruggles case, which he obviously opposed.[14] In the same year, one Jared W. Bell was prosecuted for blasphemy in New York City. The criminal words allegedly used by him described God as a "damned fool," and Christ too. The conventionally orotund language of the indictment declared that Bell had been "seduced by the instigation of the Devil" to vilify the Christian religion, "to the great dishonor of Almighty God." The evidence, however, showed that the witnesses against the defendant might be prejudiced, and that he attended church regularly. The judge informed the jury that "it was hardly possible that he [Bell] could have uttered the words" attributed to him, and the jury voted to acquit.[15]

The same verdict was rendered by a jury in a New York case of 1823 in which the words attributed to the defendant reviled Christianity: "God almighty is a whoremaster, the Virgin Mary a damned whore, and Jesus Christ is a bastard." But the only proof that the defendant used that language derived from a person who said the defendant had told him so. The defendant himself offered to prove that he was "so beastly drunk that he did not know what he said." The judge ruled that, although drunkenness furnished no excuse, no lawful evidence existed against the defendant, since no one testified to having heard him say the words.[16] So ended an inglorious history of blasphemy prosecutions in New York.

Old John Adams lamented that blasphemy prosecutions existed in America, and that even his own state had a law against the offense of blasphemy. "Now, what free inquiry" could exist, he declared in a letter to Jefferson, "when the writer must surely encounter the risk of fine or imprisonment for adducing any argument for investigation in the divine authority" of the Bible? "I think such laws a great embarrassment," he added, "great obstructions to the improvement of the human mind. Books that cannot bear examination, certainly ought not to be established as divine inspiration by penal laws." He wished that all such laws would be repealed.[17]

Pennsylvania's high court did not confront such a law until 1824, when it decided *Updegraph* v. *the Commonwealth*.[18] No evidence indicates that the state supreme court had any knowledge of the 1799 precedent in Dauphin County involving a conviction for remarks made in "High German." Pennsylvania had been one of the most enlightened places in America. Only Rhode Island had been freer in matters that concerned differences about religion, and only Pennsylvania, among the original states, guaranteed freedom of speech, as well as of the press, in its first constitution. A decision against the constitutionality of blasphemy laws was possible.

The Pennsylvania Supreme Court that decided *Updegraph* was uncommonly distinguished. Its five members included William Tilghman, the chief justice, and John Bannister Gibson, his successor, both of outstanding talent. Thomas Duncan, who wrote the Updegraph opinion, was also an able judge. The crime of blasphemy, however, was apparently so abhorrent to these men that it subverted their judicial craftsmanship and detachment.

Updegraph's crime, for which he was convicted at a trial in Pittsburgh, consisted in declaring that the Bible was "a mere fable," containing many contradictions and "lies." He made that remark as a member of a debating association in the course of a debate about religion, and he had not reviled the Bible. Nevertheless, a grand jury indicted him for blasphemy, and a trial jury convicted him. Although he received only a token sentence, a fine of 5 shillings plus costs, the principle of free speech mattered so much to him that he appealed. He won a Pyrrhic victory. The high court reversed his conviction on a technicality, but decided against him on the free-speech issue. The technicality was the omission of the word "profanely" from the indictment. That mattered because the colonial statute under which Updegraph was prosecuted required, redundantly, that the individual both "blaspheme" and speak "profanely" of God, Christ, the Trinity, or the Bible.

Updegraph had argued that the statute had been superseded by the state constitution, which protected the right to express opinions on any subject as long as this did not tend to breach the peace. He also claimed that the English common law respecting religion had no existence in Pennsylvania. Judge Duncan, for the court, contemptuously dismissed such views, revealing an astoundingly close-minded attitude toward criticism of Christianity. Duncan should not have even addressed these matters, given that the court decided to reverse the conviction because the indictment was bad. Everything he said beyond that fact constituted *obiter dicta*.

Duncan claimed he was sorry to learn that the debating society was "a nursery of vice, a school of preparation to qualify young men for the gallows, and young women for the brothel." Any supporter of good morals, he declared, considered such debating societies as a civic disgrace. From the words spoken by Updegraph, Duncan could not believe that the debate had been "serious"; rather, Updegraph's language "was the outpouring of an invective so vulgarly shocking and insulting, that the lowest grade of civil authority ought not to be subject to it, but when spoken in a Christian land, and to a Christian audience," it violated public morals and so was criminal. Even if Christianity was not part of the law of the land, it was the "popular religion of the country, an insult on which would be indictable, as directly tending to disturb the peace." Duncan gratuitously declared that Christianity was part of Pennsylvania's common law. If it were not, he reasoned, cursing, blasphemy, incestuous marriage, perjury, and adultery—all banned by Christianity—would be lawful, and the measures against them would be restraints upon civil liberty. Duncan's reasoning was as farfetched as it was biased. He intemperately defended "the constitutionality of Christianity," which he misdefined as the issue presented by the case.[19]

Invoking the English precedents and Kent's opinion in *Ruggles*, Duncan insisted that, if Updegraph's view of the scope of free speech prevailed, blasphemy and profanity "must reach their acme with impunity, and every debating club might dedicate the club room to the worship of the Goddess of Reason, and adore the deity in the person of a naked prostitute." To hold otherwise meant "the removal of religious and moral restraints."

Duncan believed that his opinion protected anyone who "fairly and conscientiously" promulgated opinions on religion without malice. Yet he inconsistently took the view that, because the law could not test the degree of danger from an opinion, any danger to the public peace, no matter how remote or slight, "is a public wrong." Moreover, he made the law of Pennsylvania as reactionary as that of England when he held that the offense of blasphemy included not only contumelious reproaches and scoffing, but also "denying the Being and Providence of God." In England, that was a statutory crime, but Duncan made mere denial a common-law crime, regardless of scoffing or reproaching. "Christianity is part of the common law of this state," he insistently repeated. Yet he also, inconsistently, declared that "only the malicious reviler of Christianity" would be punished as a blasphemer. Jews and Unitarians had the law's protection. Only the revilers, who corrupted morals and society, stood in jeopardy.[20]

The opinion disgraced Pennsylvania law, not because it upheld the criminality of blasphemy against a claim of free speech, but because of its distempered exaggerations and *obiter dicta*. They revealed how injudiciously the court treated Updegraph's claim to free speech, and how prejudicially it regarded his moderately expressed opinions.

In 1824, the year of Updegraph's case, Thomas Jefferson wrote a letter to the English radical Major John Cartwright. The letter became celebrated because of its attack on the doctrine that Christianity was part and parcel of the law of the land. Separationists used the letter, which had been widely republished, to help support Jefferson's doctrine that "a wall of separation" should exist between church and state. Cartwright had reached the conclusion that no foundation existed for the doctrine of the common law's incorporation of Christianity, because he had a theory that the common law had existed before the Anglo-Saxons knew about Christianity. Jefferson sought to extend his argument. In the year 1458, he stated, a question had arisen as to how far the ecclesiastical law was to be respected in a common-law court. Chief Justice Prisot of the Court of Common Pleas, expressing his opinion in law French, referred to "*ancien scripture*." In 1613, Sir Henry Finch, in a book on the common law, had quoted Prisot and rendered the crucial line as: "To such laws of our church as have warrant in *holy scripture*, our law gives credence." That gave the impression that the common law sustained Christianity. According to Jefferson, however, Finch mistranslated "*ancien scripture*" as "*holy scripture*" instead of "ancient scripture." Then, Jefferson continued, Edmund Wingate, in his 1658 book on legal maxims, turned the mistranslation into a maxim of common law, a mistake repeated by William Sheppard in his work on the common law. Finally, Lord Hale, in Taylor's case, expressed it in the famous words: "Christianity is parcel of the laws of England." As Jefferson noted, Hale cited no authority, but, by various "echoings," the doctrine had become so entrenched that in Woolston's case in 1728 Lord Raymond refused to allow a discussion of whether writing against Christianity was a common-law offense. Blackstone next repeated the doctrine, and it survived unquestioned—all, according to Jefferson, because of a mistranslation in 1613 of a line in a 1458 opinion by Prisot. Jefferson thought the doctrine was a sort of judicial "forgery"; the judges had "stole this law upon us," he said, describing the doctrine as "the most remarkable instance of Judicial legislation, that has ever occurred in English jurisprudence, or perhaps in any other."[21]

Jefferson got his legal history right, but in his eagerness to sever church and state he drew from it a completely wrong conclusion. Not that "*ancien scripture*" does mean "holy scripture" or the Bible. Rather, as Jefferson himself observed, in Taylor's case Lord Hale did not rely on Prisot or Finch; nor did Lord Raymond in Woolston's case. And those were the two great cases that established the doctrine that Christianity was part and parcel of the common law. Moreover, when Blackstone expounded the law of blasphemy, he relied on Hale and Raymond, not on Prisot and Finch. The doctrine had not been founded on Finch's mistranslation.

Justice Joseph Story of the United States Supreme Court, a devout Unitarian who believed that Christianity bulwarked the social order, deplored Jefferson's view that Christianity was not part of the common law. Parliamentary law had fixed the death penalty for heresy, and many statutes had been enacted to enforce Christian rites and doctrines, Story observed.[22] He was right, but proved nothing as to the question whether the common law, as distinguished from statutory and ecclesiastical law, embodied Christianity.

In a short piece in *American Jurist*, published in 1833, Story expanded his argument against Jefferson. In an effort to disprove Jefferson, Story contended first that *"ancien scripture"* had in fact referred to the Bible, not just old church law. But that was a silly conclusion, because the case in which Prisot had made the statement translated by Finch involved an advowson or ecclesiastical office, about which the Bible says nothing but the church law says a great deal. Story stood on firmer ground when observing that the formative common-law cases did not rely on Prisot or Finch, but Jefferson never said that they did. Story stood on the firmest ground when adding that Christianity had the support of the common law in the enforcement of laws establishing the Church of England, and that the common law regarded reviling the establishment as a criminal libel.[23] Nevertheless, that fact took for granted the point to be proved: whether reviling was criminal because Christianity was part of the common law.

The doctrine did not mean that anyone was lawfully obligated to believe Christianity. Story claimed that he took its "true sense . . . to be no more than that Christianity is recognized as true, and as the established religion of England."[24] But if it meant only that, it would have slight foundation in the United States, given the First Amendment and the fact that the last state religious establishment died in 1833. If the doctrine meant only that the moral teachings of Christianity underlay the common law, no justification existed for not sustaining the moral teachings of other religions, let alone of Christian sects that repudiated Church of England doctrines and rites. What the doctrine meant was by no means clear, and Story's assault on Jefferson's criticism hardly justified the opinion of an American state court in reading the English doctrine into its common law.

In an 1844 opinion for the court, Story mentioned that that doctrine was part of Pennsylvania's common law. But its truth, he added, must be qualified, because the state constitution completely protected every variety of opinion on religion, including infidelity. "So that we are compelled to admit, that although Christianity be a part of the common law of the State, yet it is so in this qualified sense,—that its divine origin and truth are admitted, and therefore it is not to be maliciously and openly reviled and blasphemed against, to the annoyance of believers or the injury of the public." That, he added, was the holding in *Updegraph*.[25] Thus, in the end, Story's support of the doctrine boiled down to its being the basis for prosecuting blasphemy, a subject on which anything he said was *obiter dictum*.

Because Jefferson opposed prosecutions for blasphemy, he attacked the doctrine, as Story supported it to justify them. Jefferson would have had a stronger case if he had explained why freedom of expression required abandonment of the doctrine instead of nitpicking its origin. His nitpicking ignored the strongest links in the chain of argument that perpetuated the doctrine that Christianity was part of the common law. The links consisted of the entire body of common-law precedent from 1676, the year of *Rex* v. *Taylor*. Prisot and Finch counted for nothing in the creation and development of that body of law. Jefferson's views took a pounding in the next blasphemy case, which was decided in Delaware.

Delaware, like Pennyslvania, had a tradition of religious and political freedom; neither had ever experienced an establishment of religion. Delaware's constitution safeguarded citizens in the expression of their opinions on any subject, though it held them responsible for "the abuse of that liberty." Thomas Jefferson Chandler abused that liberty in 1836 when he declaimed that "the virgin Mary was a whore and Jesus Christ was a bastard"—a conventional blasphemy ever since Lord Chief Justice Hale had decided *Rex* v. *Taylor* in 1676. Chandler repeated the same words on another occasion and was again prosecuted, this time for blaspheming God as well as Christ. The jury acquitted him of the charge of blasphemy against God but convicted him of blaspheming Christ.[26]

Delaware's statute of 1826 made blasphemy a crime without defining it, leaving its meaning to be determined by the common law. Chandler's counsel, appealing his conviction, contended that the statute unconstitutionally preferred Christianity over other religions, and that Christianity was no part of the law of Delaware, a contention supported by reliance on Jefferson's famous letter to Major Cartwright.

Chief Justice John M. Clayton delivered the court's opinion. A great lawyer who distinguished himself as a United States senator, he probably would have become an influential jurist had he not resigned after less than three years to become senator again and then secretary of state in President Zachary Taylor's Cabinet. As Delaware's chief justice, Clayton brought to the court a judicious temperament and the sort of learning that graced a Kent or a Story. His 1837 opinion in Chandler's case is as erudite and cool as that of any judge in a blasphemy case.

Clayton discoursed on the English precedents as well as *Ruggles* and *Updegraph*. Blasphemy, he found, was a common-law offense, because it endangered the peace and safety of society. Jefferson's views on the subject came under his withering scrutiny. Clayton did not refer to Story's rejection of Jefferson. On his own, Clayton assailed Jefferson, who had proved that church law rather than the Bible was meant by *"ancien scripture."* Clayton observed that church law had "usurped the consciences of men" and "burnt the body under the pretext of saving the soul." Friends of religious liberty, he said, should prefer the Bible to church law. Clayton continued his rejection of Jefferson for several pages. He finally concluded that in Delaware, as in England, because the prevailing religion of the people was Christianity, malicious reviling of it was criminal.[27]

But Clayton lacked consistency. When confronting the question whether the statute criminalizing blasphemy conformed to the state constitution, he noted that it outlawed "a preference given by law" to any religion. He proved, correctly, that Delaware from its founding had given preference to Christianity in its laws. Only those who professed a belief in Jesus, for instance, could hold office. Clayton insisted that there was a difference between a "religion preferred by law, and a religion preferred by the people." Delaware, however, reflected both preferences, and Clayton himself proved that the state law preferred Christianity. He should therefore have held that the blasphemy act violated the constitution, but he decided to the contrary. Observing that the constitution itself continued the common law unless repealed by the legislature or unless the common law was found to be inconsistent with the constitution, Clayton failed to examine the scope of religious liberty or of free speech to determine whether either protected shocking or insulting language.

Unlike Kent in *Ruggles*, Clayton sounded tolerant. He even said that, if a majority of the people decided to adopt Judaism or the religion of Mohammed, malicious reviling of it would be criminal. His argument that blasphemy constituted a crime depended on the assumption that to revile the dominant religion necessarily tended to breach the peace. No evidence existed to indicate that Chandler's remarks had led to violence. Judges, in America as well as Britain, merely asserted that a bad tendency was equivalent to a breach of peace. Clayton asserted that a Christian, on hearing Chandler's words, would believe that they had referred to his God. If the law did not criminalize such language, he ruled, the Christian would likely take to violence, even "Lynch law."[28] That supposition had no support from the evidence in the case.

Clayton had read Philip Furneaux, whom he quoted at length. Furneaux had advocated a distinction between mere words and overt acts that were criminal, and had elaborately argued that to entrust a court to determine the bad tendency of words violated the free expression of opinion on religion. Nevertheless, Clayton distinguished between words that blasphemed and words that related to religious principles. He sounded as if he agreed completely with Furneaux, yet decided in a manner explicitly repudiated by Furneaux. "It will be seen then," Clayton declared, "that in our judgment by the constitution and laws of Delaware, the christian religion is part of those laws, so far that blasphemy is punishable." For each of the two convictions Clayton upheld a sentence of $10 fine, ten days in solitary confinement, and steep sureties that Chandler would not again blaspheme.[29]

The courts of New York, Pennsylvania, and Delaware all agreed that blasphemy was a criminal offense, that it existed as an offense in the common law of each state, and that no state constitutional provision bearing on freedom of expression could be regarded as conflicting with the punishment of blasphemous words. They also agreed that the essential reason for punishing blasphemy was that it tended to breach the public peace, because it offended the beliefs of the people. Yet the conclusion must follow that, whatever the courts of those three states held, the really significant fact is that so few prosecutions for blasphemy occurred in the United States during a period when the number of blasphemy prosecutions in England peaked. Even in these three states, the cases that were adjudicated seemed aberrational, because prosecutions were so rare. For all the judicial talk about breach of the peace, Americans seemed to ignore blasphemy. Not a single instance in all our history exists in which members of an audience were so outraged by a speaker's remarks about religion that they virtually assaulted him. Yet, although Americans did not get into fistfights or engage in riots because of blasphemous remarks, sometimes no way to avoid "blasphemy" seemed possible, as the Kneeland case showed.

The most important and colorful of all American blasphemy cases was *Commonwealth* v. *Kneeland*, decided by the highest court of Massachusetts in 1838 in an opinion by its chief justice, Lemuel Shaw.[30] The defendant, Abner Kneeland, was a cantankerous, inflexible heretic, regarded as an immoral being who had crawled forth from some Stygian cave to menace Massachusetts. Not the least of his infamy is that his career provoked one of the worst opinions, among twenty-two hundred of them, written by Chief Justice Shaw, whom Oliver Wendell Holmes regarded as "the greatest magistrate" in American history. Respectable men may have been right in believing that Kneeland polluted everything that he touched.

If one believed Kneeland, however, he was merely a harbinger of free thought and a noble exponent of liberty of conscience. His name might now be shrouded in oblivion but that an outraged community, upon which he had inflicted his opinions, retaliated by making him a martyr.

He was the only man to be jailed in Massachusetts for the crime of blasphemy during the nineteenth century.

In the *Bible of Reason* that Kneeland preached to his audiences, Samuel Gridley Howe, the Unitarian humanitarian, read with alarm "that infidelity is spreading like wild-fire, and that in fifty years Christianity will be professed only by a miserable minority of male bigots and female fools." With a reformer's urgency, Dr. Howe reached for his pen "to make the public aware of the leprosy that is creeping over the body politic." He demonstrated that Kneeland, "the hoary-headed apostle of Satan," had characterized the rich as tyrants, the clergy as hypocrites, the Holy Bible as a string of lies, and judges and lawyers as knaves. Kneeland also incited class hatreds, counseled a union of farmers and workingmen, railed against property, complained of high prices, derided the sacredness of marriage, and taught sex education.[31]

What made Kneeland a danger was not only his opinions but that his lectures at Boston's Federal Street Theatre attracted throngs of two thousand, and a like number subscribed to his *Investigator*. This periodical, according to a political enemy, was "a lava stream of blasphemy and obscenity which blasts the vision and gangrenes the very soul of the uncorrupted reader."[32] Samuel D. Parker, who prosecuted Kneeland for the Commonwealth, pointed out that the *Investigator* sold cheaply and was favored with a large circulation among the poor. Judge Peter Thacher in Municipal Court, when charging the jury that first convicted Kneeland, warned of fatal consequences should religious restraints disintegrate: no longer would the laboring classes be consoled to their humble position or be respectful of authority.[33]

It was the *Investigator* that got Kneeland into the legal controversy that would agitate Massachusetts for four years. Orthodox descendants of the Puritans, erecting their government during the revolution, had thought it necessary to appease the vanity of God by implementing a constitutional recognition of His existence with an act against blasphemy passed in 1782. Under this statute, an indictment was brought against the editor of the *Investigator* for having "unlawfully and wickedly" published, on December 20, 1833, a "scandalous, impious, obscene, blasphemous and profane libel" of and concerning God.[34]

The penalties admissible under the blasphemy act, Kneeland claimed, recalled witch-hunting days.[35] Any person willfully blaspheming the name of God by denying Him, or by cursing or contumeliously reproaching Him or any part of the Trinity or the Bible, could be punished by imprisonment of up to one year, by the pillory, by whipping, or by being made to sit on the gallows with a rope around his neck.[36]

The indictment contained three counts based on articles in the *Investigator*. The first count alleged a gutter obscenity relating to the miraculous conception of Christ; and the second, an irreverent ridicule of prayer; the third was based on part of a published letter to the editor of the *Universalist Trumpet*—the only article written by Kneeland himself—in which the variations of blasphemy had been contemptuously exhausted. He had written, "Universalists believe in a God which I do not; but believe that their god is . . . nothing more than a chimera of their imagination." Universalists also believed in Christ, but Kneeland declared that "the whole story concerning him" was "as much a fable and fiction as that of the god Prometheus." Kneeland added that he attributed the miracles, which Universalists believed, to "trick and imposture." Finally, he rejected their belief in resurrection of the dead, claiming that he believed death to be "an eternal extinction of life."[37] This was enough evidence for the state to conclude that the flag of atheism had been planted in its midst in preparation for an "exterminating warfare" against Christianity.[38]

The case against Satan's apostle also had a political character. In 1835, John Barton Derby, who had once been a Jacksonian, revealed that Abner Kneeland was a leader of the Democratic radicals. "Nineteen-twentieths" of those who attended his "infidel orgies" were Jacksonians, including some who were among the party's most active and influential members. Appropriately, Kneeland was represented by Andrew Dunlap, a high-ranking member of the Massachusetts Democratic Party and formerly state attorney general.[39]

Whiggery had small occasion for regret at the conviction of the *Investigator*'s editor by the God-fearing men who sat as the jury in Judge Thacher's court. But only the first of five trials had been completed. Kneeland appealed his cause, and in the spring of 1834 the second trial began before Judge Samuel Putnam of the Supreme Judicial Court. Putnam, like Thacher, was a Whig.

Parker, the Commonwealth's prosecutor, who was the son of an Episcopal bishop, repeated at the second trial the arguments he had used at the first.[40] He supported the constitutionality of the act against blasphemy by defending Christianity from "every . . . enemy who had attacked it"—Hobbes, Hume, Gibbon, Voltaire, Rousseau, and Paine included. Christianity, Parker declared, was part and parcel of the state constitution and of the common law. If Jefferson, that "Virginian Voltaire," had believed otherwise, his remarks were an "imbecile dart" at Christianity, proof of his notorious hostility toward it. The trial was not an inquisition, nor were those "hackneyed topics, the liberty of the press, the liberty of conscience, and freedom of inquiry," at stake. If there was persecution, it came from the defendant against religion "and the very foundations of civil society." Blasphemy was no lawful exercise of freedom; its repression signified no intolerance. The guarantee of a free press simply referred to political topics.

The article in the *Investigator* relating to virgin birth Parker thought "too obscene . . . too revolting" to bear discussion. As for the article on prayers, God had been called an "Old Gentleman," indecently and with unbecoming levity, and, most irreverently, had been compared to President Jackson. Any person "one grade above an idiot" could see that God had been exposed to blasphemous derision.

Although Parker argued that Kneeland, as editor, was liable for the first two articles, they had been reprints from the New York *Free Inquiry*. Parker made his strongest case on Kneeland's public letter to Universalists, arguing that Kneeland had blasphemed by his willful denial of God, his remarks on the history of the Saviour as a fable, and his reference to miracles as a trick. The social reformers Fanny Wright and Robert Dale Owen would reproach Kneeland as a renegade if he disavowed his atheism.

Blasphemy, Parker asserted, was but one part of the system introduced by the disciples of Owen and Wright. Not only was atheism to be enthroned, but moral restraints were to be removed, illicit sexual relations encouraged, the laws of property repealed, and the horrible utopian experiments of New Harmony and Nashoba introduced in Boston itself. Kneeland, as lieutenant general of this system, sought converts for it among the young and the poor, "with a view first to demoralize them, and then to make them apt instruments to root up the foundations of society, and make all property common, and all women as common as brutes." This peddler of obscenity spread "revolutionary and ruinous" principles, among which Parker counted a knowledge of contraceptive methods and the "Physiology of the Female Genital System," all of which amounted to a "complete recipe" for teaching the young "how they could have intercourse with safety and without discovery." Parker also insinuated that the meetinghouse of the infidels was little more than a brothel. "I have been informed," he lecherously advised the court, that "there are beds in the Dressing Rooms at the Federal Street Theatre." Plainly, he considered Kneeland guilty not merely of blasphemy but also of lasciviousness, atheism, adultery, communism, and other varieties of "moral and political poison." The prosecutor had paraded his imagination before the court and found the defendant guilty by association.

The most conspicuous feature of Judge Putnam's charge, like Judge Thacher's before it and Judge Wilde's yet to come, was the haze of partiality enveloping it. The jurors, hastily doing their duty as requested, voted for a guilty verdict within ten minutes, except for one dissentient who hung the jury. The dissentient juror was Charles Gordon Greene, Jacksonian editor of the *Morning Post*.[41]

A third trial, in November 1834, before Judge Samuel Wilde of the Supreme Judicial Court, also ended in a hung jury.[42] David Henshaw, boss of the Democratic Party of Massachusetts, now wrote a pamphlet that exhibited the biased charges in each trial. Of all the incidents that had excited public opinion during the past year, he wrote, none more vitally affected "the civil liberties of the country" than Kneeland's trial for blasphemy, because it "strikes at the root of the liberty of conscience, and the freedom of the Press," and involved "the preservation or the destruction of the free institutions of this country."[43] But a fourth trial, in November 1835, again before Judge Wilde, ended in a conviction.[44]

A sentence of sixty days hung over Kneeland. He had preached God's word for over thirty years, first as a Baptist and long as a Universalist, but he had passed to skepticism and then to free thought.[45] He had been called an atheist—what had he not been called!—but he was determined to show the justice of his cause. He would make a final appeal to the full bench of the Supreme Judicial Court.

The case of *Commonwealth* v. *Kneeland* was heard in March 1836. Dunlap was dead. Only one man could act as Kneeland's counsel: himself. He was a scriptural scholar, a carpenter, a minister, a phonetics expert, a legislator, a philosopher, author of common school spellers, and something of an obstetrician. Why not serve as the advocate of his own cause? He had represented himself creditably at his last trial, and he could do so again before Chief Justice Shaw and the high court.

The state was represented by its attorney general, James T. Austin, who had won lasting fame for belittling the murder of the abolitionist Elijah Lovejoy, and for having accused the seraphic William Ellery Channing of inciting insurrection.[46] Austin emulated Parker's argument, forcing Kneeland to complain to the court that "every species of personal abuse . . . which our language could furnish" was heaped upon him.[47]

Kneeland, who was sixty at the time, made a strong argument. He repeated all of Dunlap's points and more, first contending that the charges as recorded in the indictment constituted no offense. Judge Putnam had admitted that even an atheist might propagate his opinions, and Judge Wilde had admitted that the truth of the Bible might be denied, although both annexed the condition of speaking decently. Were his crimes, then, merely an offense against decency? Yet he had by no means transcended the usual ferocity and extremism of theological argument—a fact for which he offered proof.

There was no blasphemy in the article on the miraculous conception. The Virgin was not even named in the statute. Moreover, there was no obscenity that should make strong men blench. The article, Kneeland observed, quoted Voltaire's *Philosophical Dictionary*, a book that circulated in the respectable Athenaeum and in the Harvard library. The author of the article also derided the idea of virgin birth by suggesting the improbability of conception without the intervention of the male genitals. The indelicate word "testicle," which had been employed, derived from a classical language and could be found in any dictionary. If that was obscene, Kneeland shrugged, "Evil to him who evil thinks."

There was no blasphemy in that article on prayers. Certain modes of prayers had been satirized, yes, but the Puritans had disparaged prayers too. Charles Chauncy, the second president of Harvard, had attacked prayers as a "hell-bred superstition," an ebullition of bitterness not poured forth in the *Investigator*. Why had Christians taken offense at the *Investigator*'s satire? "Birds do not generally flutter much till they are hit."

Nor was there blasphemy in the public letter he had addressed to the Universalist editor, the count in the indictment mainly relied upon by the attorney general. That letter had been written in the mildest of language, without cursing or contumely. The statute did not prohibit a disbelief in the doctrines of Christianity. Anyway, Kneeland continued, he had simply expressed a disbelief in the creed of the Universalists, a fact that he sought to prove by an elaborate grammatical analysis of his words: "Universalists believe in a God which I do not. . . ." Yet, even if his words should be construed to express a general disbelief in the existence of God, it would not be a denial of God within the meaning of the statute. A disbelief is an expression of doubt; a denial is a positive assertion without any doubt; and the statute referred only to willful denial. "I do say," Kneeland declared, "and shall until my dying breath, I never intended to express even a disbelief in, much less a denial of, God."

Was this Boston's Robespierre speaking, Satan's apostle? In that same letter to the Universalist editor, he had written, "I am not an Atheist but a Pantheist." He did believe in God. God was everything, nature, the universe; He embraced all intelligence and all existence. "I believe," Kneeland had said, "that it is in God we live, move, and have our being; and that the whole duty of man consists . . . in promoting as much happiness as he can while he lives."[48] Kneeland's creed was as spiritual as that of the Transcendentalists.

Having argued that he had not blasphemed even under that law "as cruel as the laws against witchcraft," Kneeland proceeded to argue its unconstitutionality. He proposed that it violated article II of the Massachusetts Declaration of Rights, which declared that no subject would be restrained "for worshipping God in the manner and season most agreeable to the dictates of his own conscience; or for his religious professions and sentiments." Judge Wilde's instructions in the former trial had stripped Kneeland of this protection by holding that his atheistic denial of God's existence was an irreligious profession. Kneeland had appealed because of this erroneous charge.

To Kneeland, article II should be interpreted broadly, under the maxim of Jefferson that "error of opinion may be safely tolerated, when reason is left free to combat it." Universal toleration was the constitutional standard. His own sentiments, he urged, were religious, not irreligious, but the article protected all sentiments respecting religion. If the court could brand his sentiments as irreligious, a "discreditable quibble would destroy the whole object of the provision in the Bill of Rights," permitting the legislature to harass by penal measures anyone who might maintain a view respecting religion that the government might choose to regard as irreligious. Conformists face no danger of being persecuted. Article II, Kneeland argued, was intended for those who needed its protection, those who professed unpopular opinions respecting religion. Concluding, he said he stood "as firm as the rock of ages" on the rights of conscience together with the freedoms of speech and press.

More than two years passed before the court gave its opinion. But the case was not forgotten. Massachusetts had people who valued the rights of conscience and dissent. William Lloyd Garrison could recall that, when every Christian church in Boston had turned him down, Kneeland had offered him the use of his meetinghouse. Emerson, working on his "Divinity School Address," might have remembered that George Ripley had been censured by the orthodox for teaching Transcendentalism. Theodore Parker knew that George Noyes, the biblical scholar, had been threatened by Attorney General Austin with prosecution for heresy. Almost all who were given to heterodox ideas—utopians, abolitionists, Transcendentalists—balked at using the strong arm of the state to silence Kneeland. In March 1838, Dr. Channing wrote to the abolitionist lawyer Ellis Gray Loring: "My intention is to see and converse with Judge Shaw on the subject. That a man should be punished for his opinion would be shocking,—an offense at once to the principles and feelings of the community."[49]

All was in vain. In April 1838, Chief Justice Shaw delivered the opinion of his court sustaining Kneeland's conviction.[50] His opinion revealed not his greatness but the truth of Richard Henry Dana's observation that Shaw, a conservative Whig and a Unitarian, was "a man of intense and doting biases."[51] By no coincidence, the one judge who dissented from Shaw's opinion was Marcus Morton—the only Jacksonian on the bench.

Shaw explained that the delay in handing down the decision was occasioned by the difficulty of the questions raised by the case, and by a difference of opinion among the judges. He thought the first question for decision was whether the language of the defendant as set forth in the indictment constituted blasphemy within the meaning of the statute. Blasphemy, Shaw wrote, may be described as "speaking evil of the Deity with an impious purpose to derogate from the divine majesty, and to alienate the minds of others from the love and reverence of God." He defined it further as "purposely using words concerning God, calculated and designed to impair and destroy the reverence, respect, and confidence due to him. . . . It is a willful and malicious attempt to lessen men's reverence of God." And the statute prohibited a "willful denial of God." Shaw had "no doubt" that Kneeland's public letter to the Universalists amounted to the offense. Although Kneeland had couched his language in the form of a disbelief, "if" he had intended a willful denial of God's existence, his disbelief constituted a denial. Whether his language was in fact used with unlawful intent "was a question upon the whole indictment and all the circumstances," Shaw declared, "and after verdict, if no evidence was erroneously admitted, or rejected, and no incorrect directions in matter of law were given, *it is to be taken as proved*, that the language was used in the sense, and under the circumstances, and with the intent and purpose, laid in the indictment, so as to bring the act within the statute."[52]

For more than two years, this decision had been in the making, and in the end, the fundamental question—had Kneeland blasphemed?—was settled without reasoned consideration. It was "taken as proved" simply by accepting the verdict of guilty. Furthermore, Shaw neglected to determine whether Kneeland was liable for the articles that he had not written. What, then, had been the purpose of hearing the case on the "whole indictment and all the circumstances," as the court itself had ordered at the very beginning? All that Shaw had offered was a definition of blasphemy that could meet with no disagreement. Kneeland himself had proposed the same definition to prove that he had not committed blasphemy.[53] Shaw's opinion was and remained a neatly orchestrated abstraction at no point touching the realities of the case.

Shaw next addressed the argument that the statute was repugnant to the state constitution. He cited with approval the decision by Chancellor Kent in Ruggles's case that blasphemy was a common-law crime not to be abrogated by a constitution carrying the doctrine of unlimited tolerance.[54] That point intolerably implied that the common law, which was judge-made law, overrode the fundamental law of the constitution. The same point also implied that, in spite of the state constitution and whether or not the statute was valid, Kneeland was guilty at common law, because Christianity was part and parcel of the common law. Shaw proceeded, nevertheless, to examine the provisions of the Massachusetts Declaration of Rights supposedly violated by the statute.

Article XVI provided that "the liberty of the press is essential to the security of freedom in a state; it ought not therefore to be restrained in the Commonwealth." Shaw construed this to mean only that individuals would be at liberty to print, without previous permission of any officer of the government, although they would be responsible for the material printed. That interpretation fixed the meaning of the constitutional guarantee of freedom of the press as no more than the common-law guarantee as expounded by the royal judge, Chief Justice James De Lancey, in the Zenger case of 1735, or as expounded by the Tory oracle of the common law, Sir William Blackstone, in his book on the laws of England.[55] Kneeland's argument relative to the liberty of the press, Shaw said, was best refuted by reformulating it: "every act, however injurious or criminal, which may be committed by the use of language, may be committed with impunity if such language is printed." Kneeland, of course, said nothing warranting Shaw's distortion, but, having set up his straw man, Shaw then demolished it. "Not only would the article in question become a general license for scandal, calumny, and falsehood against individuals, institutions and governments . . . but all incitation to treason, assassination, and all other crimes however atrocious, if conveyed in printed language, would be dispunishable."[56]

Shaw's proposition was intellectually reprehensible. Not the least basis existed for his characterization of Kneeland's argument. On the contrary, Kneeland is officially reported to have said, "I do not contend, however, that a man who slanders his neighbor in print, shall not be answerable for the injury he inflicts." And he had said nothing about freedom for criminal incitement. He had only contended that article XVI guaranteed him the right to propagate his opinions on religion or any other subject. Nonetheless, Shaw ruled that article XVI constituted no ground for excusing publication of the articles specified in the indictment, or for invalidating the statute. Shaw's construction of the article as a mere prohibition of prior restraints upon publication emasculated its constitutional basis by reading it to mean what it had previously meant at common law. He made article XVI superfluous.

Nor could Shaw find any violation of article II, which safeguarded religious liberty. The statute merely made punishable the willful blaspheming of the name of God. "Willfully," said Shaw, meant "with a bad purpose"; in this statute, an intent "to calumniate and disparage the Supreme Being." But, Shaw added, the statute did not prohibit the fullest inquiry and freest discussion for "honest" purposes; it did not even prohibit a "simple and sincere avowal of a disbelief in the existence and attributes of God." So construed, the statute did not restrain the profession of any religious sentiments; it was intended merely to punish "acts" that would have a "tendency to disturb the public peace."[57]

This section of the opinion possessed the dubious distinction of ignoring the case at bar of a man who had at worst disbelieved virgin birth, quoted Voltaire, satirized prayer, and denied God in temperate language. If the statute did not prohibit free discussion and avowals of disbelief, Kneeland should have been tending his presses instead of anticipating prison. If his purposes were not honest, and if he had disturbed the peace in a manner not protected by the guarantees of civil liberties, then Shaw evaded reasoned judgment on the particulars. No one had accused Kneeland of dishonest expression or breach of peace. Because Shaw construed the statute to prohibit only "acts" that have a "tendency to disturb the peace," Kneeland faced prison for crimes he had not committed. His opinions, which were not "acts," fell far short of immediate criminal incitement, attempt, or solicitation.

The dangers to freedom inherent in Shaw's remote bad-tendency test of the criminality of speech were familiar to civil libertarians in America and England. Virginia's Statute for Establishing Religious Freedom, drafted by Jefferson and enacted in 1786, asserted that to permit a magistrate to intrude his powers "into the field of opinion and to restrain the profession or propagation of principles, on supposition of their ill tendency is a dangerous fallacy, which at once destroys all religious liberty," because the judge determines the tendency, making his opinion "approve or condemn the sentiments of others only as they shall square with or differ from his own." For that reason, and to protect freedom of expression, Jefferson concluded, "it is time enough for the rightful purposes of civil government for its officers to interfere when principles break out into overt acts against peace and good order. . . ."[58] Dr. Philip Furneaux had also advocated an overt-acts test. "Punishing a man for the tendency of his principles," he wrote, "is punishing him before he is guilty, for fear he should be guilty."[59] Shaw's opinion in Kneeland's case was wholly at variance with freedom of opinion on religion.

That opinion grieved Judge Marcus Morton, the sole dissenter. Morton, a Jacksonian who championed the laboring classes and civil liberties, considered as illiberal the view that article II embraced only religious, as contrasted with irreligious, professions. To Morton, the article was a "general proposition" enacted "for the protection of the rights of the people." It merited "a liberal construction, unrestrained by the prevailing tenets of any particular time or place." Thus, all beliefs and disbeliefs concerning religion were protected to the extent that no individual was responsible to any human tribunal for his opinions on the existence of God; "operations of the human mind especially in the adoption of its religious faith" are "entirely above all civil authority," Morton added. Religious truths did not need the "dangerous aid" of legislation.[60]

The act against blasphemy, Morton believed, could be regarded as constitutional only if construed not to penalize a mere denial of God. "No one may advocate an opinion which another may not controvert." Criminality depended on motive, a fact that provided a broad boundary between liberty and license. The denial "must be blasphemously done," inspired by malice for the purpose of injuring others. A willful denial imparted no crime, because "willful" meant, at most, "obstinate." Every person, Morton declared, "has a constitutional right to discuss the subject of God, to affirm or deny his existence. I cannot agree that a man may be punished for wilfully doing what he has a legal right to do." Morton concluded, "This conviction rests very heavily upon my mind."

The case had closed with a lone opinion that Abner Kneeland had not received justice from the Commonwealth. Shaw may have figured that he was doing his best to save civilization and religion, but he had converted Kneeland into an embittered martyr.[61]

Shaw had the authority to suspend sentence and bind Kneeland to good behavior, but Kneeland's attitude scarcely stimulated magnanimity. On August 8, Theodore Parker wrote: "Abner was jugged for sixty days; but he will come out as beer from a bottle, all foaming, and will make others foam. . . . The charm of all is that Abner got Emerson's [Divinity School] address to the students, and read it to his followers, as better infidelity than he could write himself."[62] Abner was not jugged, though, without a remonstrance by some people who felt strongly about civil liberties.

George Bancroft, the historian, received from Ellis Gray Loring a copy of a petition in circulation in Boston, which Loring advised that he had drawn and Dr. Channing had revised. "Many of the Unitarians and Baptists sign—none of the Orthodox Congregationalists. Garrison and the leading abolitionists sign." The petition requested the governor to grant Kneeland an unconditional pardon because "opinion should not be subjected to penalties. . . . The assumption by government of a right to prescribe or repress opinions has been the ground of the grossest depravation of religion, and of the most grinding despotisms." Channing's name headed the list, followed by 167 others, including Parker, Emerson, Ripley, Garrison, and Alcott. The names read like a "Who's Who" among the reformers and intellectuals. They likely had no impress whatever on Chief Justice Shaw's friend the Whig governor, Edward Everett, whose Democratic rival in the past four elections had been the Jacksonian dissenter Marcus Morton. The petition for a pardon, which competed with a counterpetition from the conservative clergy, was rejected.

Shaw, a minister's son, was too quick to see a "bad purpose" in a man who held repugnant views on religion. Kneeland, having served his time, emigrated with members of his First Society of Free Enquirers, to the freer air of frontier Iowa. There he established an unsuccessful utopian community, Salubria, and became active in Democratic politics. He died unreconstructed at seventy in 1844, surrounded by portraits of great rationalists and mourned by the child whose name he had suggested, Voltaire Paine Twombly.[63] *Commonwealth* v. *Kneeland* succeeded Kent's brief opinion in Ruggles's case as the definitive and most frequently cited American authority on the law of blasphemy.

CHAPTER NINETEEN

England Reconsiders
the Law of Blasphemy

ICHARD CARLILE could wear out the government and win real
freedom to publish and sell blasphemous works by the ton, but
he could not alter the law of blasphemy or contribute a tittle either to the
theory of a free press or to that of freedom of discussion on religion. No
one ever practiced so pluperfect a liberty of the press and of intellectual
freedom as he, yet thought so little about either philosophically. By
contrast, a man signing himself "John Search," a pen name, wrote a slim
volume in 1833, *Considerations on the Law of Libel, As Relating to Publications
on the Subject of Religion*, that reflected fresh thinking. He exasperated
people who regarded his work as a defense of the rights of infidels and a
scandal to religion. In 1834, the Reverend Joseph Blanco White also
entered the lists; he wrote a little book on the subject from the standpoint
of one who professed belief in the Bible as the revelation of God and in
Jesus Christ as his Saviour, and yet who endorsed Search's argument
against blasphemy laws.[1]

John Search may have been Archbishop Richard Whatley of Dublin, the patron of Blanco White, an Anglican priest who had defected
from Roman Catholicism. Whatley was sufficiently heterodox on the
Trinity, latitudinarian in his principles, sympathetic to equality of civil
rights for all, and secular to have written John Search's book. Whatley,
as vehemently opposed to Erastianism as was Search, hated state control of religion, which he believed to be too personal and sacred to warrant government supremacy over religious interests. Whatley had been
a professor of political economy at Oxford before becoming archbishop.
There is no proof that he was John Search, and White wrote that he
did not know the author. But there are no indications, either, that
Whatley's views differed from those of Search. In any case, Search was
probably a liberal cleric, as was Blanco White, who lived in Whatley's
residence. No deist, not even Paine, and surely no atheist had done as

much for the theory of freedom of discourse as those two Christians.[2]

The history of the development of freedom of thought in relation to the expression of opinions on religion reveals that believing Christians consistently had constituted the avant-garde of those who had advanced the most libertarian ideas. The same people were often persecuted by others who as fervently professed loyalty to true Christianity. The early English Baptists, prompted by the need to defend themselves from persecution, took positions based on religious principle that were still extremely radical in England well over two centuries later. Early in the seventeenth century, Thomas Helwys, Leonard Busher, and, above all, John Murton had argued that, because Christ's kingdom is not of this world, the government had no jurisdiction whatever over religion, with the result that even "heretikes, Turcks, Jewes or whatever," in Helwys's phrase, should be free to worship as they pleased and say whatever they pleased about religion without confronting a profane or earthly power. Murton, writing in 1615, even dealt explicitly with the problem of blasphemy, and concluded not only that the temporal authority had no right to harm anyone for his beliefs, even if shocking and irreligious, but that Christ's law had abrogated the Mosaic law, by which blasphemy was punished. Murton also believed that not even church authorities could punish blasphemers, first because death or excommunication sent souls to hell, and second because Christ taught gentleness and kindness. Later libertarians of the seventeenth century, such as Roger Williams and Henry Robinson, supported the overt-acts test, because they favored freedom of expression for any peaceable opinions on religion, even if hateful or contumelious, yet they sound almost derivative when compared with their Baptist predecessors from earlier in the century.[3]

No deist, Socinian, or Unitarian did as much for the theory of freedom as the Reverend Philip Furneaux, a Presbyterian, who made a Christian argument against the punishment of blasphemers. Unitarians had argued defensively that they were really Christians who had not blasphemed; few argued, as did the Unitarian leader W. J. Fox, who defended Carlile's right to free expression, that deists were also believers in God, but that in any case even atheists, who rejected God as well as Christianity, should not be molested for uttering their opinions about religion. Furneaux and Fox, like the early Baptists, supported a freedom of expression that transcended their own sectarian interests. John Search and Joseph Blanco White belonged to the same intellectual tradition of Christian libertarianism. In effect, they argued that Christians who upheld blasphemy prosecutions acted against the principles of Christianity. A few secularists also argued against blasphemy laws, but England scarcely had an equivalent to Thomas Jefferson or James Madison. It had a great tradition of sectarianism, and its comprehensive establishment included a latitudinarian wing of influence, with the result that liberalism in religion and liberalism in the theory of religious freedom had a Christian resonance there.

John Search had a talent for candor. He began his book with an accurate statement of the law on blasphemy, without the usual obscurantism, verbal stunts, and legal smog that complicated lawyers' statements:

> By the existing law of the land, so far as relates to the publication of religious opinions, any writing whatever, which shall tend to impeach the evidences of the Christian faith, or in any manner to impugn Christianity as a whole, is, I believe, indictable as a blasphemous libel, and punishable as such by fine and imprisonment, "or other infamous corporal punishment." Be the work, in all other qualities, what it may—be its tone and language temperate or insolent, serious or flippant—or its object pursued by sober argumentation, or gratuitous invective and contumely;—all this makes no other difference, I apprehend, in the eye of the law, than simply in the way of aggravation. The advised attempt to dispute the truth of Scripture is itself the legal crime: statute law and common law unite in declaring it such: and the writer is liable in every such case to the penalties forementioned.

Search refused to obscure the issue, as judges did, by considering the manner of what was said rather than the matter, or by giving importance to the fact that temperate denials often escaped prosecution, whether because of a forbearance on the part of the government or as a result of the "silent check of public opinion." Failure to prosecute had no more to do with the state of the law than judicial proclamations of toleration for all fair discussions. The same judges neutralized such proclamations by their reliance on precedent that inflicted intolerance, and on the language of the Blasphemy Act of 1698, which punished denial, whether or not temperately made. Search refused to believe that reviling or ridicule constituted the crime. No mode of expression, no sobriety of tone, no integrity of purpose could "legally" shield from the liabilities of the law a person who impugned or denied God, Christianity, or the divine inspiration of the Bible. Although a jury might acquit an impugner, juries almost always followed the instructions of a judge, thereby surrendering the accused to him for sentence.[4]

On the other hand, as Search acknowledged, lawyers and judges rarely stated the law of blasphemy "frankly and simply." They liked to present the offense mixed with "contingent aggravations," such as reviling, scoffing, or contumelious reproaching, to give the impression that the crime was impugning religion with "gratuitous insult." To do otherwise might alienate public support and give the impression that the vengeance of the law operated against "the simple crime of arguing on the wrong side" respecting events alleged in the Bible to have taken place in a distant country long ago.

Why, Search asked, should the law protect Christianity against blasphemy? Why protect Christianity at all? One reason might be that "our legislators and rulers," having convinced themselves of the truth of Christianity, assumed that their decision sufficed for the entire nation, and therefore a contrary view, being erroneous, had to be punished. This reasoning, however, had justified the establishment of Roman Catholicism as well as the Church of England, together with policies of persecution. The rulers determined all, and the people were supposed to take their word for it, without personal investigation of the subject. Search concluded that such reasoning had long ago become unacceptable. Even if the authorities had been infallible in their theology, they burst beyond their province by enacting laws protecting Christianity and punishing its defamers. People formed a society, Search declared, "not for the salvation of their souls, but for the protection of their persons and property." Parliament no longer claimed to be charged with the responsibility of caring for the spiritual interests of the people. The appropriate course had become to acknowledge the right of the people to think for themselves—provided, Search added, that they kept their thoughts to themselves. Search took note of the remarks of several judges to that effect, most recently the remarks of Lord Tenterden, the chief justice of the King's Bench, in Taylor's case. Tenterden had said that no man was answerable to the law for his private opinions, however erroneous or injurious, as long as he "kept them within his own breast."[5]

Looking for a better explanation of the reason criminal penalties should immunize Christianity, Search tested the notion that the state religion had been adopted not because it was true but because it was politically useful. All government rested on popular consent, he reasoned, and nothing could be more helpful to the government than to have the cooperation of the clergy, who could sway the religious feelings of the people and thus dispose them to favor the government. As the established religion, Christianity had become so vitally united with the constitution "as to involve its own stability with that of the civil Government also." It must therefore be protected, not just from invasion of its established rights, but from censure, "because censure might make it disesteemed, and disesteem might impair its stability, and thereby that of the Government with it." That was "a State plea," having nothing to do with the truth or falsity of Christianity. Moreover, it was not an argument derived from any quality attributable to the establishment itself but from its utility to the government.[6]

Yet judges who made and enforced the law of blasphemy failed to explain the reason for the establishment. For example, Lord Raymond, in Woolston's trial, had merely observed, "The Christian religion is established in this kingdom; and therefore they [the Court] would not allow any books to be written which should tend to alter that establishment." Search found the proposition wanting. In fact, he reasoned, one could criticize any law; the policy of a law or its wisdom was always subject to disapproval, providing one did not resist its authority. To say, "so and so is established; ergo, nothing must be written which might tend to alter it," proved nothing. Why was religion so vital to the state? "Is it from its great moral tie on human actions," he asked, "derived from the fear of God, and of a future judgement?" But, he responded, "this belongs to religion simply; to religion established or unestablished by State authority," even to religion overlaid with fables.[7] Why does religion become more vital to government when it is established, making necessary its protection from criticism? The reason could only be political—namely, that criticism tended to impair the strength of the government.

That was the reason judges formulated the "great and mystic" doctrine that Christianity is part and parcel of the law. The doctrine was simply a way of saying the religion is established by law, but "part and parcel" had no real meaning, despite its reiteration by the highest judges. Christianity, Search explained, had been the subject of legislation, and the existing laws on that subject formed a part or parcel of the general body of law. In like manner, game animals had been the subject of legislation, and the laws on that subject were also part or parcel of the law of England. Search continued:

Whether, or under what restrictions, the evidences of Christianity may be discussed, or a hare or pheasant shot, are questions which can be solved by one test only, viz. by reference specifically to the said laws so existing on either subject: but to say summarily of the Christian religion, that its truth must not be questioned, because it [the Christian religion] is part of the law of the land,—is, I allege, an abuse of terms precisely similar to that of saying that hares and pheasants must not, in such and such cases, be shot at, because they [hares and pheasants] are part of the law of England.[8]

Despite the illogic of the legal maxim, the law prohibited unfavorable discussion of Christianity.

The question, Search said, was whether the establishment of the religion necessarily included the prohibition against criticism of it. Search believed that the provisions for Christianity as the established religion did not include such prohibitions. A legislator or judge would reply, however, that "all our civil institutions are founded on Christianity." In fact, said Search, they were formed on a faith and doctrines that had been denounced and rejected since the Reformation. In any case, the institutions of government as well as government policies enjoyed no immunity from being impugned; thus, the religion established by law was entitled to no special consideration. Search found logically absurd the seminal statement by Lord Chief Justice Hale that "Christianity is part of the laws of England and therefore to reproach the Christian religion is to speak in subversion of the law." Hale, Raymond, Kenyon, Ellenborough, Tenterden, and other authorities, including legal commentators such as Sergeant William Hawkins and Thomas Starkie, had all taken the fact of the establishment of the religion—"part or parcel of the law"—as proof that it could not be impugned.[9]

Search reached a major conclusion. The only argument that advocates of coercion against blasphemy would acknowledge and defend, he asserted, was "the plea that, if free discussion were permitted—if Christianity might be impeached at all—the poor and ignorant would of necessity be misled: Christianity would be impeached, not only falsely,— but sophistically, licentiously, contumeliously, abusively; with calumny and fraud, with scoffing and insult, with ribaldry and coarse invective; and so be wrongfully degraded in the minds of the simple and ignorant.—So far as any plea is adhered to at all, I believe it is this."[10] Search thought this plea or justification for penalties had no foundation other than the rulers' old demand, "You must take our word for the truth of the State religion." As a Christian, Search found that repellent. He refused to assume the truth of Christianity, because he believed it could stand the test of critical analysis and should not rest on authority. He criticized the established church and Christians who wanted to rely on criminal punishments to insulate Christianity from its opponents. As long as their freedom was hampered, he contended, Christianity remained untested, its truths not vindicated. Search believed that Christianity had nothing to fear if the law did not muzzle even the harshest critics. He examined the advantages that Christianity had in any unfettered debate with its detractors, concluding that the truth of Christianity could be proved, but that every generation required those proofs in an unending open discussion.

Search might have strengthened his closing argument against blasphemy laws by facing a worst-case scenario, involving an atheist who was obviously distempered and who resorted to abusive language and severe ridicule. Instead of dealing with such a hypothetical problem, however, he considered in detail the question of the "sceptical writer" whom he believed was involved in all the recent cases. Although he did not mention Paine by name, his description of the skeptic fit Paine and his followers. Moreover, Search explicitly criticized the arguments of crown attorneys and judges in the cases involving Carlile, his womenfolk, and his shopmen. He spoke of the writer who did not think himself to be using invective or insult. People rarely agreed, he observed, on what is fair or unfair, temperate or intemperate. Popular feeling for the most part opposed the skeptic, a fact that Search took as "truly honourable to Christianity, were only enquiry free!" The skeptic, Search believed, "must needs be offensive in various ways to the devout believer." Questioning the divine origins of the Bible and the divine nature of Christ himself involved the skeptic in assertions that the believer would abhor as blasphemy, even if those assertions were not insultingly intended. Search found fault with Christians who received the skeptic's message as necessarily founded in contumely, base motives, and offensiveness. He also criticized bench and bar for their "deceitful" allegations that "decent" denials did not constitute blasphemy. Judicial opinions, he proved, showed otherwise. The judge had a disposition "in all cases" to press the law to its utmost letter, because of his bias in favor of the government and "the system from which he derives his own rank, power, and income."[11]

Some skeptics escaped prosecution, but that did not alter their liability to prosecution under the law. Search deplored the fact that such people were dependent upon the "sufferance" of state authorities or "the state of public feeling for the time being." Fluctuations in public mood and government policy allowed the indulgence of some skeptics some of the time. Search required freedom of inquiry at all times on religious matters, regardless of the bad manners or shocking language of anti-Christian critics. Search found offense in the thought that any person's freedom should be left dependent on the "contingencies of caprice," the nature of popular feeling, or the vengefulness of state authorities. His emphasis remained on the point that the honor of revealed religion required "an unlimited discussion of the grounds whereon we receive it: to lay its evidences freely open to the investigation of friends or adversaries, without reservation as to style or manner. . . ."[12]

When Search attracted critical fire from conservatives, Joseph Blanco White, then an Anglican priest but soon to become a Unitarian, answered them in his own little book. He reinforced Search's conclusions. Blasphemy prosecutions produced "a feeling of despondency" in White, because they violated "the true Spirit of Christ." On religious matters, he believed, "every man has an unlimited right to oppose, in argument, whatever any other man has a right to prove by argument. . . . I make no exception whatever." In principle, he claimed, a prosecution for blasphemy differed only in degree from the persecutions of the Inquisition. The moment we granted that the government might rightfully punish opinions because they were untrue, disruptive of the peace, or too offensive, we had also to acknowledge that government had a right to decide which were the opinions that had the undesired effect. That violated freedom of discussion and of religious belief.[13]

Developing that point, White noted that the government or the magistrate might punish opinions on one of two grounds: the magistrate possessed a superior knowledge on religious subjects, or he knew best how to preserve the peace of a society and the government itself. The first ground, according to White, was so absurd as to merit no discussion. After all, governments had supported the grossest errors over the face of the earth. They were the last to be trusted on matters involving religious truth. Magistrates might, however, be good judges of the need to check certain opinions that might disturb society or government. But the supreme authority in that regard lay in Parliament. Parliament had not demonstrated anything approaching infallibility in matters of religion. If it possessed supreme authority, the reason must be that it was the best judge of what was needed to maintain civil order. And Parliament had in fact decided to punish anti-Christian views for secular reasons. Religious reasons as the basis for parliamentary or judicial decisions merited no respect whatever; history proved that. Truth in religion was a matter that secular authority had no competence to judge, but it might offer secular reasons that deserved serious consideration.[14]

Nevertheless, the prosecution of blasphemy depended on the legal maxim that Christianity was part and parcel of the law of the land. White asked what was meant by Christianity in that legal maxim. It did not mean all the doctrines that all sorts of Christians had proclaimed to be Christianity. It did not even mean the doctrines of the Church of England, given that Baptists did not believe in infant baptism, Unitarians did not believe in the doctrine of the Trinity, and many sects rejected the establishment's view of communion. The maxim did not even mean the Christian virtues, because English law did not regard adultery as a crime, nor was fornication, want of parental or filial love, covetousness, envy, or malice the subject of criminal law. White could imagine no way in which it could validly be said that Christianity was the foundation of English law or part and parcel of it. Christianity was not even the foundation of morality, given that people behaved morally in non-Christian and indeed in pagan nations.[15]

White opposed any sort of punishment for opinions on religious matters. To him, fines and imprisonment for blasphemy or irreligious opinions constituted "the monster persecution," which he held to be the opposite of "the Spirit of Christ." The divinely inspired Bible, White believed, taught love, not punishments, even for unbelief and for blasphemy. Paul had confessed to blasphemy and persecution but added, "I obtained mercy because I did it ignorantly in unbelief."[16] Genuine blasphemy, which derived from malice rather than unbelief or ignorance, was a matter for God, not the state. "Human laws," White declared, "the laws by which the peace of society is maintained, have no concern with truth as truth." The maxim that Christianity was part and parcel of the law of the land was a "legal fiction," particularly if the point of the maxim was that certain opinions on religion ought to be punished. "Truth," which is what White believed to be the subject of religion, was none of the state's business. Its business was to punish "some overt act," not beliefs about religion. The Almighty needed no assistance from man or government to avenge Himself, if He was so minded. Even the Greek pagans understood that: "Deorum injuriae Diis curae"—(The gods take care of injuries to themselves).[17]

One could understand that the government wished to prevent the open denial and contempt of the religion of the country. Rome had believed the same when it punished the Christians. To White, the law of blasphemous libel simply violated "belief in the existence of one true revelation from God." The revelation taught the golden rule; it offered no example of penalties in defense of Christianity. The only provision of the New Testament that could provide a basis for criminal penalties in religious matters derived from a misunderstanding of the Greek Scriptures. St. Augustine, knowing no Greek, had relied on the Latin Vulgate, which mistranslated Luke 14:23 by using a word rendered in English as "compel." No other basis existed in the New Testament for imposing penalties for the wrong religious opinions, nor did the Greek version provide even that basis. The letter and spirit of all the rest of the New Testament conflicted with that passage when rendered as a justification of punishment.[18]

Declaring himself "in favour of perfect freedom of speech and writing," White, like Furneaux and other advocates of the overt-acts test, held that only "an evil known by experience, and not conjectural," should be the subject of criminal penalties. To punish people for the supposed bad tendencies of their opinions condemned them for the "conjectural consequences of their opinions." To White that was "tyranny," because it made "the apprehensions of those who punish" the only basis of the punishment. Blasphemy was punished because the government believed that it was a crime "in potentia," or an opinion that "may" produce dreadful consequences.[19]

White understood the risks of allowing "perfect freedom of speaking and writing." Arguments against Christianity might sway an uneducated person, and educated ones might "revolt at the first contact with gross and bold impiety." But gagging infidels and blasphemers deprived society of their arguments, thereby leaving them unanswered. Nothing that came from Carlile's shop, he alleged, was as effectual in bringing about the very thing that the existing law was supposed to prevent. White believed that Christianity could answer every argument against it, and under a perfect liberty of the press both educated and uneducated could rest assured that any argument that could be brought against Christianity had been made and would be effectively countered. Restraining the press in effect undermined Christianity, by leaving open the question whether it was true.[20]

In a postscript, White took note that John Search's opponents had made much of a quotation from Bolingbroke, the "well-known unbeliever," who had asserted the right of the government to restrain or punish the publication of opinions "against the religion of the state." White answered that only unbelievers could consistently uphold that power of the state: "A man who thinks that all religions are equally true and equally false—who sees in them only a better or worse instrument to assist the supreme magistrate in the business of civil government—such a man may consistently, and (according to his views) justly, demand a tacit approbation of any established religion." Not only Bolingbroke but Hume, Gibbons, and Hobbes had shared that view, and, White added, "I do not well see how any Tory (i.e. one who thinks that the people cannot be governed too much) if he happens to be also an unbeliever, could permit any one to oppose that form of religion which is established in any country whatsoever." The real difficulty, White thought, was explaining how a Christian could support criminal penalties on opinions that he found obnoxious. The difficulty derived from the fact that Christians believed that only one religion was true, that all others were false, that the government should prefer their choice, yet also wished "to exclude all possibility of their choice being proved to be wrong." "Popery," wrote the former Roman Catholic, took that position; he hoped that the Reformation had revealed the infirmities of that position, against which he had constructed the entire argument of his book. During his residence in England (he came from Spain), Parliament had abrogated the law's protection of the doctrine of the Trinity. Parliament should go all the way, White asserted, and abolish laws against blasphemy.[21]

In 1841, a Royal Commission on the Criminal Law reviewed the law of blasphemous libel. The commission consisted of distinguished academic lawyers who had labored since 1834 to produce seven reports on criminal law and procedure.[22] The section in the sixth report on offenses against religion devoted a sentence to a consideration of the protests against prosecutions for blasphemy. The commissioners acknowledged that a controversy existed between those who championed liberty of speech and action on religious subjects and those who believed that licentiousness should be punished. On the one hand, stated the report tersely, "it has been urged that an undue pressure placed upon the freedom of writing, speaking, and acting on such subject would not only impede discussion, and consequently the acquisition of knowledge respecting them, but would violate the principles of religious toleration." The commission made no reference to any of the "controversialists." Murton, Wickliffe, Furneaux, W. J. Fox, Christophilus, J. S. Mill, Carlile, John Search, and Joseph Blanco White might as well have never published on the subject of blasphemy. The commission should have systematically summarized their arguments and, if disagreeing, should have explained the reasons for refusing to accept them. Instead, the report pointed to supposed dangers. The influence of religion on behavior and the efficacy of religion as "an auxiliary to municipal law" would be diminished, and "the feelings of mankind upon a subject of great moment would be frequently outraged, if an unrestricted licence were permitted to all men to speak and write and act as they pleased" respecting religion. The commissioners did not note that the distinction between liberty and licentiousness, resting on outraged emotions, lacked a rational basis.[23]

Secularist expediency prevailed with the commission. Laws for the punishment of offenses against religion, it asserted, were "justifiable on mere temporal grounds upon two principles." The first was that religion served Caesar: it prompted obedience to the law, particularly among the "ignorant and unthinking," because it inspired moral conduct. To weaken its influence on "the great mass of inhabitants" risked further violations of penal enactments. Second, most people in civilized countries regarded religion as worthy of respect; therefore, "the criminal law may properly be employed to protect the feelings and opinions of the community on this subject from wanton insult."

The commissioners saw no danger to freedom of discussion from the prosecution of blasphemy. They failed to explain their summary judgment, but concluded that "there can be no doubt that open blasphemies against God and the wanton utterances of reviling and contumelious language respecting Christianity, ought to be prevented by the criminal law of every Christian country." As a civilized group of academics, the commissioners expressed contempt for the superstitious times of the past, when blasphemy was punished to avert calamitous visitations by God to avenge insults; the civilized commission did not explain why it believed that every Christian nation should punish blasphemy when in fact it found that "most of the penal systems of modern Europe contain no provisions against the crime of blasphemy." Only Prussia, Austria, and Bavaria, according to the commissioners, and the states of the United States that had adopted the English common law, provided criminal penalties to punish blasphemy. Nevertheless, the commissioners believed that blasphemy unquestionably deserved punishment, because it reflected malice and a "wanton disregard of the religious feelings of others," and it was "injurious to the community" by diminishing the efficacy of religion as a basis for moral conduct.[24]

The report of the commissioners could have been written by Hobbes, Bolingbroke, and Hume, or any bunch of Tory agnostics or skeptics who believed that religion—any religion—was "a good thing" for society and for government if that religion taught obedience to authority. The commissioners produced an Erastian or secular rationale for prosecuting opinions hostile to religion. Fundamentally, it was an orthodox report—not in the religious sense, but in the sense of deferring to conventional opinions. Christians who practiced their religion by living its principles could not have produced the report, nor could anyone who cared for proofs. In reality, libels on religion did not injure religion and did not increase the crime rate or political subversion. No one had ever demonstrated the existence of such injury or had even tried to; it was merely an allegation without foundation, making the apprehensions, however wrong, of state authorities the basis of guilt.

Religion had every advantage against the puny onslaughts of disbelievers; the overwhelming mass of people, organized society, the establishment of the Church of England, its clergy and the clergy of other Christian sects and denominations, the prodigious publishing efforts of Bible societies, the educational system, and the government itself—all were allied against the disbelievers. As Joseph Blanco White had written, "Let us not betray a fear that we distrust the powers of that TRUTH [Christianity], even among ourselves, where it has every external advantage of honour, education, wealth, conferred on its professors," rendering unnecessary the stopping of the mouths or the presses of its opponents.[25] The report of the commissioners must have been acutely disheartening to people like White who believed in the truths of Christianity and its capacity to prevail against its critics, however abusive. Indeed, the more abusive they were, the less likely their chances of persuading anyone except among the infinitesimal minority of those who already agreed. The report of the commissioners showed the futility of reasonable argument such as that offered by White or Mill. It showed the ineffectiveness of the principle championed by Milton that truth would prevail in an open contest. It showed the capability of the majority to tyrannize a despised and vulnerable, if obnoxious, minority.

It was indeed an obnoxious minority. It did insult the feelings of the majority, but that scarcely legitimated deference to the feelings of the majority; the commissioners should have spoken for the need for good judgment to triumph over emotion. Insult, offensiveness, and outrage are, of course, subjective; in a manner of speaking, those reactions reflect mere taste. The importance of religion in human affairs is beyond question; it is a subject that can shake a person to his innermost being. Yet the royal commission should have considered the utter subjectivity of reactions to hateful opinions on religion, and of reactions to attacks on the religion of most of the people. As fundamental as religion is, no opinion concerning it is as offensive as child labor, war, racism, inequality, superstition, poverty, or many other crimes against humanity.

Moreover, offensiveness in matters of religious opinion, one must sadly acknowledge, was a profoundly Christian practice. One need not go all the way back to the Reformation to recognize that. It screams out from reading Roman Catholics on Protestant heretics, or Protestants on "the whore of Rome." Luther was probably the most foul-mouthed of Christian leaders, but most of them tended to be nasty, vile, and contumelious when writing of other denominations and sects. Exceeding the malignity of established Protestant churches on the subject of "Anabaptism" strains the imagination. Reading Anglicans on Puritans and Puritans on Anglicans taxes the mind for comparable vituperation in other fields of civilized discourse. The founding generation of Quakers, when speaking about all other Protestants, took second place to no one in displaying the arts of offensiveness. Eighteenth-century England punished Emlyn, Woolston, Annet, Ilive, and other blasphemers, but the palm for insult was richly deserved by the Christian clergymen who retorted to them; nineteenth-century Protestants continued the scurrility and abuse when characterizing the publishers and sellers of Tom Paine. Unitarians, who were Christians, and deists, who believed in God, felt the lash of Christian verbal abuse heaped upon them in a tonnage that made their own remarks pitifully puny.

For the royal commission to justify the punishment of blasphemy as criminal on the ground that it insulted the feelings of others ignored Christian practice and the Christian treatment of skeptics. Indeed, who had the greater claim to feeling insult: the Christian, who did not have to read Carlile, or Carlile, who spent over six years in prison for his opinions? The prosecution by Christians of blasphemers because of their offensiveness was not only unjustified by the New Testament but contrary to its teachings. That was the point of several important writers who opposed all prosecutions for blasphemy—a point wholly ignored by the commission. Its justification of prosecutions on the ground that they encouraged moral behavior or obedience to the law had no merit in fact, and the argument from insult and injured feelings was unconscious hypocrisy carried to its zenith.

The prosecution of blasphemy probably did far greater harm to society than indulging the offensiveness of the blasphemers. Prosecution taught society not to learn self-restraint when confronted by differences, however insultingly expressed, by a zealous minority. Prosecution also taught society not to respect the right of that minority to express opinions on religion. Anti-Trinitarians and deists did not in fact injure society; not even atheists did. No empirical warrant existed for believing that the injury existed. Mill had pointed out that the government was secure despite the prosecutions that put Paine in the hands of thousands who would never otherwise have seen a copy of *The Age of Reason*. Carlile headed no fifth column; he did not send the poor out to pick pockets or murder. London was as safe during and after Carlile as before.[26]

Tolerating Carlile would not only have had the social advantage, from the standpoint of the government, of keeping public attention away from Paine's religious works—an advantage when compared with the costs of prosecution and imprisonment, as well as with the free advertising for deist works and the prompting of their sales. Toleration would have held aloft a torch that reaffirmed the values attacked by the blasphemers. They believed that Christianity was indefensible by argument, and that Christians were bigots. Toleration could have shown otherwise. Toleration signals that religion triumphs over its adversaries in a moral sense; staying the hand serves Christian values, whereas criminal punishment of opinions on religion undermines those values. Toleration is a sign of strength, as is counterargument and a recognition of the right of vile detractors to compete for the affections and beliefs of the public; toleration, by suffering the unfettered existence of those detractors, is a way of revealing contempt for them as harmless if disgusting purveyors of abuse. In fact, prosecution intensifies their abuse; toleration softens and confounds them. Toleration is a renewal of the majority's principles, whereas prosecution suggests that force alone is the primary justification for opinions advanced as truth.

Not acting meanly toward those whose opinions are insulting has an ennobling and emancipating effect on society. As Justice Louis D. Brandeis would say nearly a century later, in words that could have been said by the royal commission in 1841, the fear of injury should not by itself justify the suppression of opinion. "Men feared witches and burnt women," he said. "It is the function of free speech to free men from the bondage of irrational fears."[27] The deists from Paine to Carlile made Christians betray their principles (turn the other cheek, love their enemies, do unto others . . .) when they embraced force and tyrannized the spewers of anti-Christian thought. An argument can be made for the punishment of the incitement of hatred against persons who belong to religious, racial, or other minority groups; but that argument loses all efficacy when the vast majority is the butt of verbal insults. In the case of blasphemers, invariably some vulnerable minority or individual has gallingly assaulted the sensibilities of the powerful majority.

Another problem with penalties for irreligious opinions is that those opinions survive, even flourish, despite the penalties. Nor do penalties ever produce conversions. Persecution for religious reasons fails, even in authoritarian societies. In a society as free as England's, persecution had become impossible, and suppression had become an inevitable failure. It surely did not benefit Christianity in any way. The gain from prosecution that accrues from appeasing the wrath and vindictiveness of those who felt the insult of the blasphemy is probably more than offset by the doubts prompted by a resort to force. There surely is no proof that Christianity has been fortified by the imprisonment of someone as offensive, ridiculous, and basically harmless as Robert Taylor, the coiffed and bejeweled mythologist. If the state had ignored blasphemers, and if the churches had answered any points worthy of response, society stood to gain from the example of toleration and restraint. Prosecution is a recipe for making blasphemers thrive on the publicity that they seek. The royal commission of eminent academicians failed miserably when it concluded that insult to the feelings of believers, and diminishing respect for religion, invested temporal principles with such positive force in the prosecution of blasphemy that "no doubt" about the matter existed.[28]

The commissioners' reliance on the two temporal principles did not conclude their judgment, despite their lack of doubt. They discussed "the doctrines and leading provisions" of the law on blasphemy, beginning with a definition of the crime that they found acceptable. It was the statement in Hawkins's book on criminal law, *A Treatise on Pleas of the Crown*, in which he declared that blasphemy was the denial of God and the "contumelious reproaches" of Christ or of the Bible, exposing any part of the Bible to contempt or ridicule. The commissioners sought to exhibit a liberality of view by insisting on the need for contumelious reproach or malicious manner of expression as an essential ingredient of the crime, except as to the existence or providence of God. Content or matter alone counted in that regard: any denial of God, even if not scoffing or reproachful or contemptuous, constituted the crime. The commission also minimized the importance of the doctrine that Christianity was part and parcel of the law of the land. Lord Hale had so alleged in the seminal case of 1676 involving Taylor, who had aspersed Jesus and his mother, and had denounced religion as a cheat. Having stressed the contumely in that case, the commissioners conceded that Hale was not clear on the part-and-parcel passage, or, at the least, had been misunderstood. He meant only that oaths, on which the judicial system depended, were founded in religious belief, or that English laws were "subservient to the positive rules of Christianity."

If the commission had been right about the subservience of the law to Christianity, blasphemy would not be a crime, for Christianity does not make it a crime or require its punishment, except perhaps for reviling God. But the commission did not trouble to think through any of its points. In the sense that English law was founded on "the positive rules of Christianity," Christianity could be said to be incorporated within the law of England. Such was the commission's reading of Hale. It did not regard the part-and-parcel point as important, however, because anyone might criticize the law of England without criminal peril. What mattered was the definition of the crime: denial or reproach, as stated by Hawkins and reaffirmed by Blackstone. In the same spirit of liberality, the commission professed that Lord Raymond had traveled out of his case when declaring in an *obiter dictum* that any general denial of Christianity constituted blasphemy. What mattered in Woolston's case, said the commission, was that the defendant had used "indecent and opprobrious language." According to the commission, in every case of blasphemy, without exception, the judges had founded the offense "entirely upon the offensive manner of writing in the particular instances."[29] Even if that were true, decency or civility cannot be enforced, and room must be allowed for provocation that extenuates the unseemly manner. From Jesus, Paul, and Athanasius to Luther, Calvin, and Fox, great Christian religious leaders contending against apathy and error had freely employed offensive expression.

In a footnote, the commissioners respectfully quoted in full the remarks of the great dissenting clergyman and scholar Dr. Nathaniel Lardner, who had argued that, if men have an allowance to write against Christianity, they must have "considerable indulgence as to the manner likewise." Lardner had also emphasized the Christian need to show "meekness and forbearance" in the face of attack. He believed that neglect, scorn, and indignation were the only Christian means of coping with scurrility, though he believed too that decently stated arguments should be answered. Lardner would have left the punishment of blasphemers exclusively to God. All this the commissioners reprinted without meeting any of Lardner's points. They simply concluded that, although judicious and pious persons had argued that "great latitude" should be allowed to manner of expression, "public opinion" approved of the application of the penal law to blasphemy cases.[30]

The commission confronted the conflict between its view of the crime and the definition of the crime in the Blasphemy Act of 1698. Parliament had undeniably defined the crime as denial—mere denial, without regard to its manner—of any of the persons of the Holy Trinity, the truth of the Christian religion, or the divine inspiration of the Bible. The commission responded: "It may justly be questioned whether the penalties of this statute be not more severe than was necessary, or even politic." The statute, however, had "rarely if ever" been enforced. Indeed, prosecutions for blasphemy were invariably based on the judge-made common law. Moreover, Parliament in 1813 had rescinded the provision of the act of 1698 on the denial of any of the persons of the Holy Trinity. That meant that one could deny God the Father, the first person of the Holy Trinity, but the commission took no notice of the conflict between the act of 1813 and its view that the mere denial of God, without regard to manner, constituted blasphemy.

According to the commission, which made no effort to reconcile the different passages of its report, "insult" (manner) was the indispensable element of the crime, even as to God. Thus, at one point, the commission endorsed the Hawkins-Blackstone view that mere denial of God was a crime; at the next point, it acknowledged that the act of 1698 made criminal all denials of God, the truth of Christianity, or the divinity of the Bible. And then the commissioners asserted that "it is only where irreligion has assumed the form of blasphemy . . . and has constituted an insult both to God and man, that the interference of the criminal law has taken place." That re-endorsed the manner of denial, even as to God. Finally, in summing up with a presentation of a digest of the law as it should be, beginning with the definition of the crime as stated by Hawkins and Blackstone, the commission returned to mere denial, without regard to manner, concerning the truth of the Christian religion and the divine authority of the Bible.[31]

Besides its contradictions and inconsistencies, the commission misleadingly defined blasphemy of Christianity. The proposition that denial of the truth of the Christian religion constituted blasphemy really meant that blasphemy consisted in a denial of those doctrines and beliefs that the Church of England shared with other Christian denominations and faiths. "Christianity," as used by the commission and the courts of Great Britain, referred to Protestantism, at the most; English law certainly did not protect the doctrines and beliefs of the Roman Catholic church. For that matter, distinctive Baptist, Unitarian, Presbyterian, Quaker, or Methodist doctrines and beliefs were not protected either. Protestant sects and denominations outside the established church had no legal cover against blasphemous assaults, except insofar as they shared doctrines and beliefs with the Church of England.

The law on this matter was settled in Gathercole's Case, decided in 1838. Gathercole, having described the "popish nunneries" of Great Britain as brothels for the priests, urged that "all such popish stews ought to be burnt to the ground" as "disgraces" to Christianity. Because he targeted one particular nunnery for his scurrilous remarks, he was prosecuted for criminal libel: Baron Charles Alderson, speaking for the court, held that the defendant was entitled to an acquittal if he had merely libeled the Roman Catholic church, but that he must be found guilty if he had named and libeled a particular nunnery. "A person may, without being liable to prosecution for it," Alderson declared, "attack Judaism, or

Mahomedanism, or even any sect of the Christian Religion (save the established religion of the country)," because Anglicanism, having been established by law, was part of the constitution of the country, and, in like manner, Christianity in general was established—meaning the Christian beliefs and doctrines of the established church.[32] The commission on blasphemy did not criticize the opinion in Gathercole's Case.

The commission's report on blasphemy was an intellectually reprehensible performance, lacking rectitude, consistency, or even a scintilla of argument against the Lardners, Furneaux, Foxes, or Millses. Five of England's most distinguished academic legal minds, including the great John Austin, another noted legal writer, a reigning Downing Professor of the Laws of England, his successor as Downing Professor, and a future member of the highest criminal court, had labored to produce a muddled, chaotic, reactionary report and digest of the law of blasphemous libel. By way of extenuation, one must acknowledge that they could not escape the influence of over a century and a half of shabby reasoning, from Lord Chief Justice Hale to Lord Chief Justice Tenterden.

CHAPTER TWENTY

English Prosecutions
of the 1840s

W HILE the Royal Commission on the Criminal Law had been
deliberating, and a year before the publication of its report, the
government cracked down on a socialist book entitled *Letters to the Clergy
of All Denominations*, by Charles Junius Haslam. The government having
been unable to find Haslam, the attorney general mentioned his name and
added, "if there be such a man in existence."[1] In nine separate essays,
each available at just a penny, Haslam attacked the Old Testament,
always a target for "freethinkers." In one letter, he wrote:

> What wretched stuff the Bible [Old Testament] is, to be sure!
> What a random idiot its author must have been! I would advise the
> human race to burn every Bible they have got. Such a book is
> actually a disgrace to ourang outang, much less to men. I would
> advise them to burn it, in order that posterity may never know we
> believed in such abominable trash. . . . We actually look upon the
> book as the sacred word of God, as a production of infinite wis-
> dom. Was insanity ever more complete? I for one, however, re-
> nounce the book; I renounce it as a vile compound of filth,
> blasphemy, and nonsense, as a fraud and a cheat, and as an insult
> to God.[2]

That was like the deist argument made by Paine and his followers who,
believing in God, detested the Old Testament because it depicted God as
instigating murder, war, and immorality. Haslam was no atheist.

In 1840, Bishop Henry Philpotts of Exeter demanded that everyone
connected with Haslam's *Letters* be prosecuted for blasphemy. The *Quarterly Review* sided with the bishop and scorched the attorney general, Sir
John Campbell, for his failure to commence such prosecutions. Because
Haslam's publishers were radicals whose names were associated with

seditious libel and refusal to pay taxes on the press, the government readily saw merit in the bishop's demand. Haslam's letters, bound together as a book, had been published in Manchester by Abel Heywood and in London by John Cleave and Henry Hetherington. Grand juries indicted each for the crime of blasphemy. Heywood, who had already suffered fines and imprisonment for his crimes as a publisher, changed his plea of not guilty to guilty of blasphemy, in return for a suspended sentence. Cleave, another veteran of the radical movement, had also paid for espousing the cause of an untaxed press for workingmen; he had five previous convictions, had done time twice, and had seen his press smashed to bits. He stood his ground on the blasphemy charge but was convicted and sentenced to four months' imprisonment, fines, and sureties. After a month in prison, he recanted, promised not to sell any more blasphemous works, and won his release on posting £100 as surety that he would keep the peace or forfeit the money and return to prison.[3]

The most notorious of Haslam's three publishers was Henry Hetherington. The nation's foremost champion of a free press in the 1830s, he was in a sense Carlile's successor. Although Carlile had advocated the rights of labor, religion had been his principal focus. Hetherington was as radical in religion as Carlile but believed that religion was a trivial issue compared with socialism and the rights of labor. Above all, Hetherington fought for the abolition of the stamp taxes on the press.[4] After 1815, a fourpenny stamp tax on newspapers deliberately made the cost of newspapers more than the poor could pay. Carlile had refused to pay the tax. Beginning in 1830, all radical printers began a systematic campaign to avoid it. They began selling unstamped papers at a penny, and for six years unremittingly defied the law by publishing several hundred different penny papers. Hetherington began the most influential of these in 1831, *The Poor Man's Guardian*, a weekly. "Defiance," he claimed, "is our only remedy," and freedom of the press, the bulwark of the liberties of the poor, was the hope for improvement. He would publish on church and state, "to excite hatred and contempt of the Government and the Constitution" and "to vilify the ABUSES of religion." Three times he was imprisoned for six months. He triumphed in 1834, when the Court of Exchequer decided that his *Guardian* was too insignificant to qualify technically as a newspaper. Between 1830 and 1836, 740 men, women, and children who hawked the unstamped press went to prison.[5] The radical penny press wore out the government, which reduced the tax in 1836 to a penny, with the result that the agitation subsided.[6] In 1840, the government sought to punish its old enemy Hetherington for blasphemy.

Attorney General Campbell prosecuted Hetherington in the Court of the Queen's Bench before Lord Chief Justice Denman. Campbell quoted extracts from Haslam's *Letters* to prove that Hetherington had published an attack on Christianity "characterised by mere invective, ribaldry, and abuse, addressed to the vulgar, the ignorant, and unthinking." Such a publication shocked the feelings of believing Christians and had a tendency "to dissolve the foundation of the moral obligations on which society rests"—a baseless charge. Campbell claimed that anyone who doubted that God gave Moses the Ten Commandments might believe himself free to steal, and women "would consider themselves absolved from the restraint of chastity." A moment later, Campbell's feverish imagination led him to state that Hetherington's blasphemous publication "directly leads to crime." What most inflamed the prosecutor was that the blasphemy sold extensively to the poor for a penny.[7]

Hetherington, who conducted his own defense, cross-examined the policeman who testified that he had bought copies of Haslam's book at Hetherington's shop for a penny each. The officer, after acknowledging that he had read Haslam, conceded, "It did not shake my opinion—it did not make me burn my Bible; quite the opposite." That should have destroyed the prosecutor's argument about criminal incitement and subversion of public morals, but did not make the publication any less blasphemous as a matter of law. Hetherington made much of the fact that the blasphemous passages constituted a flimsy part of a book of almost five hundred pages, which, he alleged, was not in the least disrespectful of Christianity. Haslam had aimed at the Old Testament, not the New.

In any case, he argued, he could not read every book he sold or be held responsible for its contents. He relied on the free expression of opinion to sustain him. But he sought, also, to defend the offensive views by contending that the Old Testament contained passages insulting to God. He did not think that a bookseller should be imprisoned for selling "a book written in bad taste." He argued too that his prosecution would not suppress the book. Over five hundred people had been imprisoned for selling his *Poor Man's Guardian*, and he had been twice imprisoned; yet circulation had profited from the publicity, enabling him to pay his fines. "It has been just the same with these letters; they have remained unsold till this prosecution, but as soon as it was known that they were prosecuted, the man who published them [he meant Abel Heywood] could not print them fast enough." As for the law against blasphemy, Hetherington relied on Thomas Jefferson in an attempt to prove that the law had been founded on a misreading of an opinion of 1458 published in law French. The point was not a good one: even if Jefferson had been correct about that opinion, Chief Justice Hale, when writing in *Rex* v. *Taylor* in 1676, had not rested on the Yearbooks, and subsequent opinions holding blasphemy as a crime, on the ground that Christianity was part of the law of the land, had not referred to the 1458 opinion either. Still, Hetherington defended himself ably, and Chief Justice Denman complimented him for it.[8] But Attorney General Campbell, in reply, scored heavily when he proved that Hetherington had not just sold Haslam's book; Hetherington's name was on the title page as one of Haslam's three publishers.

Denman, a liberal Whig, conducted a fair trial. He accused Campbell, the prosecutor, of having misled the jury into thinking that Hetherington was the original publisher, who had contracted with Haslam for the book, rather than just its London agent. Nevertheless, in his instructions to the jury, Denman held Hetherington responsible for having knowingly distributed ("published") Haslam's book, whose character was immediately evident. Hetherington himself soon printed and sold a commentary on his trial addressed to Denman, praising the chief justice for having done "all in your power to induce the jury to acquit the accused."[9] Nevertheless, the chief justice informed the jury that "the impolicy of prosecutions of this sort" was none of their business; they had only to decide whether the defendant had sold a blasphemous book. The law made blasphemy a crime, and Haslam's book, Denman stated, had spoken "in the most disparaging terms of the Old Testament." The jury had to find whether "the tone, and style, and spirit" of the book were "temperate and decent" or reflected "insult, and ridicule." The jury returned a verdict of guilty without leaving the jury box.[10]

Hetherington engaged counsel and appealed to the Queen's Bench sitting en banc. He made the novel argument that the indictment had not charged a crime punishable at common law, because it described a libel against the Old Testament only. Although Christianity was part of the law of the land, Haslam's book had libeled only the Old Testament. Denman rejected that argument, on the ground that the Old Testament is so intimately connected with the New Testament that an attack on the former constituted an attack on the latter. Seriatim opinions by the other members of the court made that ruling unanimous. The court then sentenced Hetherington to four months in the Marshalsea, a debtors' prison. According to a friend, he was released after only six weeks.[11]

Hetherington did not repay leniency in kind. He seethed with anger, believing that the government discriminated against publishers who sold to the poor. At his trial, he had argued:

The true crime is that Haslam's "Letters" are sold at a penny. Why should two-guinea blasphemers be tolerated and penny ones prosecuted? How can the learned Attorney General, whose shelves are, doubtless, adorned with Drummond's Academical Questions, Voltaire, Gibbon, Volney, and Shelley, that beautiful and splendid emanation of human intellect, that saw through and exposed in that poem "Queen Mab" all the corruption and mysteries in soci-

ety, and all the impediments put in the way of human improvement, uphold this prosecution; and what must that law be which
can find the crime, not in the contents of the book, but in the fact
of its being sold for a penny? For two guineas you may buy a
magnificent book full of blasphemy. The Attorney General . . .
told the jury that such works were "dangerous to society if addressed to the vulgar, the uneducated, and the unthinking" . . .[12]

The double standard, one law for the radical penny press and another for
the swanky book-dealers, galled Hetherington. That double standard
might victimize him in still another way: he might undergo another
blasphemy prosecution for his publication of a pirated edition of Shelley's
Queen Mab.

When Shelley was twenty-nine, he recalled that he had written Queen
Mab in 1813, as he put it, "when very young, in the most furious style,
with long notes against Jesus Christ and God the Father, and the king,
and bishops, and marriage, and the devils know what."[13] In 1811, he had
published The Necessity of Atheism, for which Oxford expelled him. His
youthful effusions, filled with supercharged bombast and emotion,
thrilled radicals, who turned his work to their purposes. Because no
publication injurious to the public interest could be copyrighted or protected in any way by the law, anyone might reprint it. Queen Mab, like
Byron's equally irreverent Cain, was a favorite with radicals. Richard
Carlile had profited from it; so had Hetherington, who may have feared
prosecution for it—not for literary piracy but for blasphemy. Accordingly, to avenge himself for the law's double standard and perhaps to
ward off a prosecution for Queen Mab, Hetherington preferred charges of
blasphemy against several prosperous publishers and vendors who sold
expensive books to the respectable members of society. Among those
whom he accused was Edward Moxon, London's most aristocratic bookman, who published the complete works of the literary greats. In 1840,
when Hetherington issued his cheap, stolen edition of Queen Mab, Moxon,
at the behest of Mrs. Shelley, published the official collected works of
Shelley, including this raging, radical poem.[14]

Obligated to prosecute because of Hetherington's charge against
Moxon, the government halfheartedly brought Moxon to trial for blasphemy. Once again, Lord Denman presided over the Queen's Bench at
Westminster. Moxon retained the best possible counsel, T. N. Talfourd,
soon to become a judge. The prosecution perfunctorily showed that blasphemy was a crime, read passages from the indictment to indicate that
Moxon had blasphemed by the publication of Queen Mab, eulogized Shelley's genius, acknowledged Moxon's respectability, and concluded, amazingly, by expressing satisfaction in a verdict that would "establish that

publications on religion should not be a subject for prosecution in the future."[15]

For the defense, Talfourd acknowledged the publication but argued that the poem, rightly understood, was not blasphemous, that if it offended it was merely a juvenile outburst in the collected works of a literary giant, and that the buyers of Moxon's edition of Shelley constituted a class of readers who could absorb *Queen Mab* without being corrupted by it. His strongest argument elaborated the point that, if this prosecution succeeded, it would establish a precedent imperiling one literary giant after another. Horace, Virgil, Congreve, Shakespeare, Hume, Gibbon, Voltaire, Schiller, Lessing—no one would be safe from "Mr. Hetherington's revenge." A verdict of not guilty, Talfourd declared, would prevent the harassment of publishers, book vendors, and librarians, and would disappoint "only those who desire that cheap blasphemy should have free course." That astonishing conclusion vindicated Hetherington's worst suspicions by implying that costly publications should be exempt from the blasphemy laws, which should reach only the cheap press that sold to the poor and disreputable classes. In contrast with the prosecution, Talfourd spoke for hours, splendidly and passionately.[16]

Chief Justice Denman, summing up, complimented Talfourd for his "eloquent and animated address," but insisted that the court and the jury were bound by the law as handed down, not by the law as Talfourd wanted to amend it. Reading passages of *Queen Mab*, Denman reminded the jury that the poem cast insult on objects of Christian veneration. The jury had to decide whether that insult shocked the feelings of Christian readers. If so, the verses libeled God and Christian beliefs. Having said that, Denman expressed his personal opinion that "the best and most effectual method of acting in regard to such obnoxious doctrines, is to refute them by argument and reasoning . . . [rather] than prosecuting their authors." He concluded, however, that the jury had a duty under the law as he had explained it. The jury, to the astonishment of all connected with the case, returned a verdict of guilty. The government neglected to request the court to pronounce sentence, thereby dropping the case. Moxon returned to his business, and the prosecutions against the other respectable book-dealers were forgotten. Hetherington and his radical friends found satisfaction in the jury's verdict but had no desire to see the publishers of *Queen Mab* imprisoned; they too dropped the matter.[17]

We cannot know why the jury reached its verdict, but some explanation seems required. The verdict was not what Hetherington expected; it showed no double standard, although every previous prosecution for blasphemy, with the possible exception of Woolston's case, fueled Hetherington's expectation. The conviction of Moxon, a reputable publisher who sold the great books to the peers of the realm, was and remained unique in the history of blasphemy cases. The jury had every reason to acquit. The prosecutor himself announced that he would be pleased with a verdict that ended prosecutions for opinions on religion. The judge said he thought the best policy was not prosecutions but counterarguments. The defense counsel warned that, if Moxon was found guilty for publishing Shelley, no author, publisher, vendor, or librarian would be secure against a charge of blasphemy. Yet the jury convicted, even though Talfourd showed that the offensive lines taken in context indicated that Shelley, despite having fancied himself to be irreverent, "everywhere falters or trembles into piety." Talfourd showed too that the poem was published not by itself, to persuade or offend, but as merely a small part of the complete works of Shelley; indeed, Talfourd showed that the offensive lines were incidental, rather than part of a grand design to promote infidelity, and even the incidental lines, in context, were not necessarily shocking. The insult to God, for example, had been put into the mouth of Ahasuerus, the Jew who supposedly scoffed at Jesus and was condemned to wander the earth until the Second Coming. Talfourd had spoken convincingly for several hours, and yet failed to convince. Why?

The jury might really have been shocked by *Queen Mab*, however unlikely that seems. Or the jury might have reached its verdict with a Machiavellian cunning. The verdict could have been intended to signify that Talfourd had been right in one respect: Virgil, Shakespeare, Hume, and Gibbon were not safe as long as blasphemy remained a crime. In effect, the jury's verdict may have meant that, if the blasphemy laws were not scrapped, even the literary giants might fall victim. In fact, however, the courts did not alter the law of blasphemy, nor did Parliament, notwithstanding this verdict or the report of the 1841 commission. And, in fact, Shakespeare and company, and their publishers, had no reason to fear. Moxon's *Queen Mab* case was unique. The Libel Act of 1843 helped ensure that. It provided that, in the event of a prosecution for any criminal libel, the defendant was entitled to introduce evidence that the publication was made without his authority, consent, or knowledge.

The jury's verdict, with nearly equal cunning, might have signified that the law allowing prosecutions instigated by private accusation should be scrapped. Moxon's case was not unique in that respect. Many prosecutions for seditious libel had been instigated after 1819 by the reactionary Constitutional Association, and many prosecutions for blasphemous libel had been instigated by the equally reactionary Society for the Suppression of Vice. "Mr. Hetherington's revenge" could have become an epidemic. It did not. It remained, nevertheless, a means of bringing prosecutions for blasphemy down to the present time.[18] In the end, the conviction of Moxon was fruitless in every respect—fruitless and freaky.

The case of Charles Southwell was far more conventional, in the sense that he represented poverty and political radicalism. He was also an atheist, the first self-professed atheist to be prosecuted for his blasphemous publications. For centuries, the word "atheist" had been used to label anyone who disagreed with the majority's understanding of Christianity. It was a term of opprobrium used invidiously to blacken the reputation of all sorts of dissenters and heretics. The early Baptists and the early Quakers had been denounced as atheists, as had anti-Trinitarians of any kind. "Atheism" as a meaningless hate-word had been employed by pagan Romans against the early Christians, not so much for beliefs as for their attitude toward Roman gods. Christians reviled the Roman gods, with the result that the Romans, who tolerated almost all religions, regarded Christians as atheists; they were fit subjects for persecution as enemies to the peace of the empire—indeed, as blasphemers. Charles Southwell was the first genuine English atheist, one who denied the existence of God, to be tried for blasphemy. However, to say that he was prosecuted for his atheism, a statutory crime since 1698, would be misleading. He was prosecuted, rather, because he denounced and ridiculed the idea of God with a vehemence probably unmatched before his time. Atheists, like the early Christians on the subject of Roman gods, tend to have a propensity for calumny. They do not content themselves with mere denial of God.[19] Southwell did not. He belched animosity. If anyone ever deserved conviction for blasphemy, it was he.

He had been a radical bookseller, a soldier of fortune, an actor, and a popular lecturer. Politically, he had been a Chartist, an Owenite, and then a socialist. In Bristol on November 6, 1841, he published the first number of *The Oracle of Reason*, which he edited. The paper quickly attracted readers, about four thousand per copy. In the first issue, Southwell claimed that it was "the only exclusively *atheistical* print that has appeared in any age or country." Before the month was out, a grand jury had indicted him for blasphemy; he was arrested, and, being unable to pay bail, he was jailed. He spent seventeen days in jail before being released on bail. The indictment described his crime. He had compared Jesus Christ to Tom Thumb and Baron Munchausen, called religion a leprosy, denounced all religions as superstitious and founded on falsehoods, proclaimed flamboyantly that God did not exist, and elaborately denounced "that revoltingly odious Jew production, called BIBLE." Richard Carlile had also referred to "the Jew book," and many deists had employed language that sounded anti-Semitic, although they themselves probably were not; that is, their remarks about the Jews of the Old Testament did not govern their conduct toward Jews. Southwell, as an

actor, played Shylock most sympathetically, as a product of Christianity's ostracism, hatred, and ill-treatment. Because he was an atheist,
Southwell was as anti-Christian as he sounded anti-Semitic.[20] But not all
atheists shared Southwell's temperament, which he displayed in *The Oracle of Reason*. His successor as editor and as a victim of the blasphemy
laws, George Jacob Holyoake, described Southwell as "ill-worded, disparaging, sarcastic, biting, reproachful overbearing and disagreeable."[21]
Indeed, Southwell's blasphemous remarks beggar paraphrase.

He depicted the Bible as a history of lust, sodomies, slaughter, and
depravity. He called it "a concentration of abominations . . . the out-
pourings of some devil! . . . one of the most contemptible and brutalizing
books that ever was penned!" He found its heroes, from Moses to Peter
and Paul—"the last of the gang"—to be "canting, impudent impostors;
slaughtering fanatics, plundering judges, and abominable kings," and
found even the prophets to have "vomited . . . balderdash." He concluded his description by declaring that God must be a devil or demon,
"a monster made up of every conceivable enormity." Small wonder that
the Bristol authorities promptly charged Southwell with blasphemy.[22]

The prosecutor could have rested his case after reading the indictment. Instead, he misled and exaggerated. Southwell's remarks, he said,
inculcated opinions that "would produce deeds of violence." Southwell
had a right to his opinions on religion "if he keeps his opinions within his
own bosom." The law objected "not to his opinions, but only to the
publication of them," because they injured society. The press should not
be free for "scattering all kinds of error." Argument might counter argument, but "abuse" could not be answered. Atheism, by denying God's
existence, would "overturn the very foundations of society."

Southwell conducted his own defense—very badly, despite his rhetorical talents. Like the Lancashire Railway Company, he had no termi-
nal facilities. He rambled for nearly seven hours without finishing. The
judge had to continue the trial until the next day, when Southwell continued to stupefy the jury for several more hours. Excepting a few occasions, the prosecutor and judge did not interrupt his irrelevancies. He
spoke about the jury system, the biblical canon, socialism, the history of
the Quakers, Robert Owen, superstition, the differences between Catholicism and Protestantism, the philosophy of Aristotle, of Pascal, and
of others, the Bible as poetry, and the need of Christians to be critical of
the Bible. Whatever topics he touched, he relied on authorities, reading
aloud from dozens, especially critics of the Bible. He was long-winded,
derivative, and chaotic. The jury should have convicted Southwell of
inducing boredom. The court interrupted him a few times when he began
to read authorities, like Voltaire, who were "blasphemous." Sometimes
the interruptions seem comical. On one occasion, for example, when

Southwell sought to prove that prominent writers had questioned the existence of angels, the judge stopped him for attacking the existence of angels, "one of the truths of our holy religion."

Southwell simply had no idea how offensive his publications had been to religious readers. He thought he had merely "criticized" the Bible and the existence of God, and he argued that he was entitled to the same right of criticism as others. Although the prosecutor had quoted extensively from Francis L. Holt's *History and Digest of the Law of Libel* in an effort to instruct the jury on the meaning of blasphemy, Southwell insisted that blasphemy could not be defined. Holt had quoted and paraphrased the case law, but Southwell failed outright to understand that the legal authorities and precedents were against him. He repeatedly claimed that no evidence existed and that none had been introduced to show that he had blasphemed; and he denied that he had.

Southwell aspersed the prosecutor's limited presentation of the meaning of freedom of the press, but probably gained no support from the jurors when he alleged that freedom of the press protected his publications. To Southwell, freedom of the press meant that he had a right to publish whatever he pleased. The prosecution presented him as a persecutor of religion; he saw himself as a victim of religious intolerance. He demanded the same right to publish his opinions on religion as Christians and Jews were accorded. The prosecutor's charge that he had abused his freedoms prompted Southwell, properly, to declare that abuse and licentiousness were always charged by those in power who did not like publications with which they disagreed. To the claim that his remarks about God and the Bible were shocking, he responded that the prosecutor's remarks had shocked him, and that the Bible was still more shocking. To prove this, he read passages that he said shocked him—but not until the judge had given women an opportunity to leave the courtroom rather than be exposed to such salacious or repugnant passages as the story of Lot and his daughters. Finally, Southwell believed that, because truth would conquer error, as Milton had argued, the only proper way to treat his work was by answering it. At no point had Southwell confronted the reality of the case against him as a blasphemer.

Sir Charles Wetherall—the recorder of Bristol, who sat as Southwell's judge—instructed the jury by pronouncing bromides, pieties, and clichés. He converted Lord Hale's doctrine about Christianity as the law of the land into a proposition that Christianity was "the very basis, in fact, of our constitution and government." He emphatically decided that Southwell was guilty of blasphemy and that the jury must so find. A verdict of not guilty, he told the jurors, would reveal that they were "prepared to go along with the writer of these publications in the establishment of Atheism." Moreover, acquittal would mean "that there is no

Almighty Being—that Christianity is not truth, but the invention of the
devil." Indeed, the jury's verdict would show whether the jurors "will
become participators in the very wicked, blasphemous, and atrocious
objects of the defendant." The jury promptly did its duty, and the judge
as promptly sentenced Southwell to a year in the city jail plus a fine of
£100.[23] Southwell served his time and paid his fine, quarreled with col-
leagues in the radical movement, especially on the subject of how best to
present atheism to the public, and eventually emigrated to Australia and
New Zealand.

He quarreled fiercely with George Jacob Holyoake. Holyoake was
only twenty-four years old when he succeeded Southwell as editor of *The
Oracle of Reason* in late 1841. He too knew poverty and had been an early
convert to Owenism, Chartism, and socialism. Unlike Southwell and
Hetherington, who died early, Holyoake did not die until 1906, at the age
of eighty-nine, a great-grandfather of the movements for theological free
thought and political radicalism. He lacked Carlile's charisma, Hetherington's single-mindedness, and Southwell's offensiveness. He never became a commanding leader. But Holyoake possessed a trait that none of
his free-thought precursors had: he was engagingly likable. He was also
sensible, controlled, even moderate. Self-taught, he became broadly
educated in history, law, philosophy, religion, mathematics, and economics. He published over thirty little books of his own writing, in
addition to books, magazines, and newspapers that he had edited.
Among his works were the first biographies of Richard Carlile and
Henry Hetherington. Were it possible, Holyoake would have made
radicalism respectable.[24]

Under his editorship, *The Oracle of Reason* quickly underwent a change
in tone, even in substance. Billingsgate was the first to disappear; Holyoake abhorred vituperation. Religion was not even his foremost concern,
though he also edited an atheist journal. He made the *Oracle*'s pages focus
on the problem of poverty. Scientific developments and issues of political
and economic reform received his serious attention. When he presented
religious issues, he tried to be respectful, though radical. He was not even
an atheist, despite his description of himself as such. He would later call
himself a "secularist." Still later, in 1869, Thomas H. Huxley coined the
term "agnostic," which most accurately described Holyoake.[25]

Holyoake got into trouble with the law against blasphemy because of
an impromptu utterance. At the conclusion of a socialist lecture he gave
in Cheltenham on "Home Colonisation," in which he said nothing about
religion, a member of the audience, a local preacher, complained that,
although Holyoake had told them their duty toward man, he had said
nothing about their duty to God, and asked whether Holyoake believed
that there should be churches. In reply, Holyoake made what he later

called "an indecorous remark." He did not wish to mix religion with a secular subject, he observed, but the national debt hung "like a millstone round the poor man's neck," and religious institutions cost £20 million annually. "Worship being thus expensive," he declared, "I appeal to your heads and your pockets whether we are not too poor to have a God? If poor men cost the state as much [as God] they would be put like officers upon half-pay, and while our distress lasts I think it would be wise to do the same thing with deity." Not being religious, he added, he would not support churches. He believed in morality but not in God: "I do not believe there is such a thing as a God." And as long as Southwell remained imprisoned, Holyoake said, he fled the Bible "as a viper" would and revolted "at the touch of a Christian."[26]

Subsequently, on a trip to Bristol, Holyoake learned that the Cheltenham *Chronicle* accused him of blasphemy, of "devilism," and of being a socialistic, atheist "monster." To vindicate himself of the accusations, Holyoake promptly returned to Cheltenham, where he spoke again, monitored by the police. At the conclusion of his lecture, he was arrested, without a warrant, for his earlier blasphemous utterance. Three local magistrates, one of whom was a preacher, ruled that, because he had insulted God, he must be held for trial. After he had spent a night in a filthy, lice-ridden jail, the local authorities made him walk through Cheltenham in handcuffs, transported him to Gloucester, again paraded him publicly to humiliate him, and jailed him for sixteen days before accepting bail. Although Holyoake was a sweet-tempered man, he could not resist comments about Christian hospitality. "It was thought if I was chained like a felon and dragged through two towns, it would wound my feelings. If these are the ways in which the truths of Christianity are to be taught, I leave you to judge of them."[27]

Shortly after he was bailed out, his Cheltenham hosts, George and Harriet Adams, who sold radical publications, were also arrested for blasphemy. Their crime consisted in selling issues of *The Oracle of Reason*, which carried Southwell's aspersive articles. George Adams was subsequently convicted and sentenced to one month; the prosecution failed to bring his wife to trial. Their cases were disposed of soon after Holyoake's at the Gloucester Assizes, before a judge named Erskine, who had also presided over Holyoake's trial.[28]

On the day of Holyoake's trial, the Gloucester courthouse was packed from morning until the verdict late the same night. The indictment against the defendant charged him, in the usual inflated terms, of having blasphemously libeled God by making that remark about not believing in Him and recommending that He be put on half-pay. That was supposed to have been said "maliciously . . . to the high displeasure of Almighty God." The case for the prosecution concluded with the presentation of a single witness, who testified that he had heard Holyoake say the words quoted in the indictment. The prosecutor, a Mr. Alexander, did not even trouble to explain why those words should be considered blasphemous. Nor did he show malice, as Holyoake stated at the opening of his defense. Erskine ruled that the jury would decide whether the words were blasphemous or malicious. He did not explain either term.

Buoyed by the presence of that doughty champion of free speech Richard Carlile, who brought him refreshments and sat near him morning to night, Holyoake spoke for eleven hours. Carlile described his defense as "the most splendid of the kind ever delivered in this country. . . . I could scarcely restrain myself from jumping into the dock to embrace you on several occasions," he later wrote. Some of Carlile's shopmen had made better, much briefer defenses, probably written by Carlile himself, but Holyoake performed creditably if long-windedly. In his account of his trial, he praised his judge for fairness and patience, and modestly added, "I more deserved the sentence for the length of my defence than for the words for which I was indicted." Accounts of his trial omit the time-consuming quotations from more than thirty authors.[29]

Holyoake also quoted from the Cheltenham press to expose the class bias of the suit against him. The crowd in the courtroom tended to be fashionable; peers of the realm, merchants, clergymen, and their wives had turned out to see the "atheist" get his just deserts. Had he made the speech for which he was indicted before such an audience, Holyoake claimed, his remarks would have been privileged. His blasphemy resulted from speaking before uneducated workingmen in a "mechanics institute." He had injured no man's reputation or person, taken no one's property, breached no contract, taught no wickedness. He had "set only an example of free speaking. I was asked a question, and answered it openly. I am not even charged with declaring dogmatically, 'There is no God.' I only expressed an opinion." Judge Erskine remarked that the law allowed all men liberty of opinion if they spoke "seriously and decently." Holyoake insisted that he had, though he acknowledged that "decency" no doubt meant whatever those in authority believed to be proper. But the evidence did not show that his audience of workingmen had been unable to distinguish decency from indecency.

The press had described him as a monster, a bigot, a blasphemer, and an atheist. He therefore sought to explain himself. He did not assume that he was "right," he said. "Of all the *isms*," he believed that dogmatism was the worst. He did not judge others by the agreement of their opinions with his. He respected differences of opinion and asked for the same respect for his opinions. Neither a bigot nor a blasphemer, he had merely declared his disbelief and thought that was no crime. "There is a great difference between denial and disbelief. If I had said distinctly 'there is no God,' it would have been stating that I was quite sure of it. I could not have said that, because I am not sure of it. I saw reasons for disbelief, but did not assert denial. Disbelief is all I profess."[30]

Later, when he was imprisoned for blasphemy, the prison chaplain visited him, and Holyoake recorded a conversation that began as follows:

"Are you really an atheist, Mr. Holyoake?"

"Really I am."

"You deny that there is a God?"

"No; I deny that there is sufficient reason to believe that there is one."

"I am very glad to find that you have not the temerity to say that there is no God."

"And I am very sorry to find that you have the temerity to say there is one. If it be absurd for me to deny what I cannot demonstrate, is it not improper for you to assert so dogmatically what you cannot prove?"

"Then where would you leave the question of atheism?"

"Just where it leaves us both. It is a question of probability."[31]

Holyoake also explained to the jury that he had discoursed on socialism, not religion. He had not propagated his religious opinions. His reference to God occurred in his response to a question, and all he meant by saying that God should be put on half-pay was that the clergy cost far too much, especially when so much poverty existed. England paid five times as much as the rest of Christendom for its clergy. "I proposed a reduction of one-half for the benefit of the poor." Judge Erskine interjected that, if the jury believed that and believed that the defendant had not meant to insult God, they should acquit him. Holyoake replied that God could not be insulted; Christians might claim that their feelings had been shocked, but he was even more shocked that he should be prosecuted. Relying on Jonathan Edwards, the American theologian, Holyoake stressed that God could not be insulted, annoyed, or shocked, because he was a perfect being. Borrowing next from Thomas Jefferson, as had Southwell, Holyoake sought to show that a mistake in translation bottomed the doctrine that Christianity is part of the law of the land. It was a pedant's point, and an irrelevant one.[32]

Holyoake nevertheless made some penetrating observations about the law of blasphemy. It was a law inconsistently applied. In Moxon's case, "the *respectable* blasphemer" went free. "Blasphemy in guinea volumes it [the law] allows, but exhibits the holiest horror at it when in penny pamphlets." The law could also be barbarous, inflicting severe punishments for mere remarks. In Annet's case, an old man who had confessed his error was pilloried and imprisoned for a year at hard labor. The law was also capricious, because it meant one thing at one time and another thing later on, and for proof he observed that Protestantism had once been regarded as blasphemous, and later Quakerism was. Holyoake also characterized the law of blasphemy as disregarding equal justice. He found proof in the fact that Christians might blaspheme the faith of Mohammed or of other religions. Finally, he decried the law for debasing religion, which he believed should not be reduced to something narrower than the relation that human sentiments bore toward an infinitely perfect being. That was not just a criticism of the law; it was a criticism of Christianity, or of any organized religion. All connected faith with particular modes of belief and superstition. This solemn argument was not becoming in a man accused of jesting about God, whose existence he thought unknowable. In his conclusion, however, Holyoake returned to the point with which he had begun eleven hours earlier: he was not guilty of the malice necessary for the commission of this offense. "Surely," he thought, "it is not blasphemous to argue that human misery should be alleviated at the expense of spiritual pride."[33]

Judge Erskine instructed the jury to take the law as it existed. It allowed every difference of opinion short of "indecent reviling." The task of the jury was to decide whether Holyoake had uttered the words ascribed with the intention of bringing God into contempt. Although Holyoake should get the benefit of any doubt, if he used levity to treat the majesty of God contemptuously, his guiltless desire to cut clerical income became irrelevant. After a brief deliberation, the jury convicted Holyoake, though he recorded that one of its members "was a Deist, a professed friend of free speech." Erskine promptly sentenced Holyoake to six months in jail—not in prison, where felons were incarcerated. Erskine thought it a lenient sentence that assumed that the words of levity had been uttered "in the heat of the moment."[34]

The prosecution, conviction, and sentence showed, rather, that anyone might be found blasphemous, the disbeliever as well as the denier, the whimsical as well as the offensive, if his audience paid a penny rather than a pound. During his long winter in jail, Holyoake received from one of his arresting magistrates a copy of the famous book *Natural Theology* by William Paley, a gift intended to convert him. The prisoner read it and wrote a book of his own, *Paley Refuted*. That same winter, his young daughter "died the death of the poor" from cold and hunger, which exposed her to disease. Holyoake himself had a hard winter, because he was unable to buy the warmth, good food, and other comforts that money could have bought. The experience intensified his so-called socialism and atheism. Later, when told that his "persecution" should not be ascribed to Christianity, he responded that Christians had set a watch on him, informed against him, prejudiced the public against him, testified against him, found him guilty, and sentenced him. He had since studied the New Testament and concluded, "A man who believes that men need saving, that there is only one way whereby they can be saved, that *his* way is that way, and that it is better for a man to lose the whole world than to lose his own soul by missing that way, such a believer will inevitably coerce all he can into it." A "Freethinker" should fear falling into the hands of Christians, Holyoake thought. Nevertheless, he ceased thereafter to write or speak against Christianity. When he was first released, he wrote for *The Oracle of Reason* an essay on the values of "freedom of speech and liberty for all" and the equal rights of atheists and Christians. His theme was that a difference in faith ought not make a difference in rights. He also censured cruel jail conditions.[35]

In the history of the offense of blasphemy, victims had tended to be obstinate, unruly, intemperate Christians of an unpopular sect. Later, when anti-Christian deists became the victims, they were as obnoxious to conventional church and state authorities as blasphemers had ever been. Southwell's conviction fit the pattern; he deliberately sought to be as outrageous as he could. Holyoake's case, however, was quite different. By the standards of the law of blasphemy, he was as inoffensive as a disbeliever could have been. In effect, his case taught that mere disbelief constituted blasphemy.

That fact, however, did not stop Holyoake or other freethinkers from continuing to publish their opinions. Thomas Paterson, who succeeded Holyoake as editor of *The Oracle of Reason*, had Southwell's flamboyance and offensiveness. His inflammatory placards in the window of the periodical's offices attracted angry crowds and charges of blasphemy and obscenity. The atheists capitalized on his conviction and imprisonment by publishing his trial record under the title *God Versus Paterson: The Extraordinary Bow-Street Police Report* (London, 1843). In Edinburgh, the proprietors of a radical bookshop, Thomas Finlay and his son-in-law, Henry Robinson, suffered from a ruinous police raid that ended in their arrest and the confiscation of their stock. The London atheists saw a fresh means of publicizing the martyrdom of their fellows. Southwell and Paterson, fresh out of prison, went to Edinburgh to spread the atheist gospel. They were as zealotic as their religious counterparts had been when promoting new sects, whether Baptist, Presbyterian, Quaker, or Methodist. They felt a compulsion to witness, to proselytize, and to suffer for their cause.[36] In Edinburgh, Paterson established a new bookstore that he called a "Blasphemy Depot" and did a good business selling copies of the books that the police had confiscated in the Finlay-Robinson shop. In his thinking, he was bearding the bigots by satisfying an "immense demand for blasphemous works." He advertised them as exposures of the "absurdities" and "horrible effects springing from the debasing god-idea." He sold *The Oracle of Reason*, Holyoake's *Paley Refuted*, the report of his own trial, *God Versus Paterson*, a book entitled *Existence of Christ Disproved*, another on the Bible as "An Improper Book for Youth," Haslam's *Letters to the Clergy*, D. F. Strauss's *Life of Jesus* (which treated the Gospels as a fit subject for scholarly criticism), and books by Hume, Volney, Palmer, Paine, and Carlile. Blasphemy even spread to the village of Campsie, where John McNeile peddled copies of *The Oracle of Reason* and got arrested. Paterson, who had been bailed out, rushed to Campsie to exploit the situation.[37]

Paterson's trial for blasphemy before Lord Clerk, the chief judge of the High Court of Justiciary in Edinburgh, took place near the close of 1843. Until the recent atheist invasion, Scotland had not engaged in the blasphemy prosecutions that had plagued England since the close of the Napoleonic Wars. Like the English provinces, Scotland was supposed to be backward and intolerant compared with cosmopolitan London. In fact, however, London had been the scene of the most prosecutions. Paterson's in Edinburgh was the first of its kind for decades, and he made the occasion worthwhile.[38] He was a working-class journalist who seemed to have appeared on the freethinker scene out of nowhere in 1841, blazed like a comet, and disappeared in 1845, when he emigrated to America.[39]

Like other blasphemy defendants, Moxon excepted, Paterson represented himself and ended up in prison. The evidence against him for selling blasphemous books was overwhelming. The prosecutor called witnesses to prove the sales and read from the appendix to the indictment, exposing the jurors to the blasphemous passages of various books. Paterson defended himself by making a five-and-a-half-hour speech on the horrors of Christian history and the virtues of free thought. He was rhetorically splendid and utterly irrelevant. Contrary to his reiterated statements that he was the victim of bigots who could not stand differences of opinion, he was tried for maliciously reviling and bringing into contempt the Bible and Christianity. Utterly lacking in Holyoake's civility, he spoke with daring arrogance and insult. Having described God with abhorrence, he declared that humanity must renounce its idolatrous worship and the belief that sprang from it. He described Christianity as false, his own beliefs as truth, his motives as pure. He sounded much like the true believers whom he castigated. His professed atheism, however, proved to be much like Holyoake's; he disbelieved the existence of God as unknowable and beyond the capacity of man to understand; only God Himself, "if a God there be," could fathom the infinite, the immortal, the omniscient.[40]

Paterson was like a preacher, and he preached morality without a deity, confidently believing that, in an enlightened new age, Christianity would be rejected. The court let him preach even when he declared that God, if He existed, was more pleased with those who expressed their ignorance of Him than with the "noisy curs" who gave Him a character that Satan, if he existed, would be ashamed of. "Nor is it merely with respect to God that Christians are so outrageously absurd and horribly irrational; but their whole conduct in the matter of religion bears upon it 'the mark of the beast.'" Looking for God in the Bible was "downright lunacy," and Christianity was a "cunning fable," a compound of paganism that had plunged the world into an intellectual darkness for well over a thousand years. Not even he could describe "the scenes of animosity, malice, carnage, bloodshed, and torture, which the followers of Christ have practiced on each other, for the honour of Jesus, and the salvation of the Christian religion, from its commencement to the present. . . ."[41]

Only when Paterson sought to read from the Bible to prove that it deserved the character he ascribed to it did Justice Clerk stop him. Although Paterson had denied that his views were blasphemous by asserting that orthodoxy always regarded heterodoxy as blasphemous, Clerk warned him that he had failed to show that the indictment did not charge a crime. Unless he proved that the passages quoted in the indictment did not asperse God, the Bible, or Christianity, he was misconducting his defense. Paterson responded that he was "perfectly able" to show that the passages had a lawful meaning, but in fact he did not even try to do that, unless he understood himself to be doing so when he claimed that his freethinker propositions constituted a new revelation of truth. The judge disagreed. In his summation for the jury, Clerk stated that the passages in the indictment were blasphemous vilifications. The jury agreed, although they took about forty-five minutes to reach their verdict of guilty on all eleven counts. When sentencing Paterson to fifteen months in the penitentiary without "the least chance of getting any relief," Clerk observed that the prisoner's malice was beyond question. He had dared the authorities to prosecute him and welcomed the prosecution as an advertisement for his atheist books. He served his time in solitary confinement and was treated brutally.[42]

Hetherington published the report of Paterson's trial, introduced by Holyoake's "Dissertation on Blasphemy Prosecutions." Holyoake discerned two classes of people who supported such prosecutions. Those who believed that blasphemy was wicked and offensive acted out of religious motives; they were the bigots, foes of liberty. Those who thought that blasphemy was dangerous acted out of expediency, tolerating the prosecutions in order to protect religion and prevent change. Holyoake believed that the principle of fairness demanded equal treatment for Christians and atheists. Christian opinions were as offensive to atheists as their opinions were to Christians. Both opinions, right or wrong, offensive or not, should be allowed freedom of expression. To prosecute atheists conflicted, also, with professed Christian principles, not the least of which involved the responsibility of man to God. "But since those feel no responsibility who are not free to act, the Atheist who is deprived of the privileges of free expression, is left irresponsible." It was too precious a point, not nearly as true as his argument that prosecutions for blasphemy injured society by hampering the spread of "useful" opinions and by intimidating the heterodox. Roman Catholicism had viewed Protestantism as blasphemous, and every Protestant establishment of religion had regarded newer denominations as blasphemous. For every Carlile who offered successful opposition, a hundred others were silenced by prosecutions. Nevertheless, prosecutions—"persecutions," he said—often spread the truth, even as they hampered it. Holyoake resolved that apparent paradox by claiming that the best test of truth was open discussion, but that, "when persecution is employed to suppress opinion, the best friend of truth is he who bravely endures it." Someday, he hoped, juries would acquit defendants accused of blasphemy; in no other way would the law of intolerance be defeated.[43]

Despite Holyoake's hopes, no one was acquitted. Thomas Finlay, the aged bookseller, was convicted a month after Paterson, at a trial before the sheriff of Edinburghshire. Finlay and his son-in-law, Henry Robinson, who was also convicted, were charged with blasphemy for selling a satire on the Bible written by "Cosmopolite." The book was *The Bible, An Improper Book for Youth, and Dangerous to the Easily Excited Brain—with immoral and contradictory passages therefrom.* Each was imprisoned for two months.[44]

A month later, early in 1844, Matilda Roalfe received the same sentence from the same judge, Sheriff George Tait, whom Holyoake described as a gentleman noted for "his bland disposition, urbanity, learning, and impartiality as a judge."[45] Roalfe had been a Sunday-school teacher who found her way to freethought on discovering that she could not explain inconsistencies in the Bible. Like Paterson, she left London to challenge Edinburgh's "bigots" after Finlay and Robinson were arrested. She felt a duty to resist "tyranny." Taking over Paterson's "Blasphemy Depot," she circulated a manifesto announcing that she would sell atheist books whether or not they brought the Bible and Christianity into contempt. Her place was raided, her stock seized; she was imprisoned until she made bail. At her trial, she denied that she had acted with malicious intent, but the court thought otherwise. She cleverly cross-examined an officer who testified that she sold him *The Oracle of Reason.* He conceded that he had read the blasphemous periodical without its having any effect on his mind or his moral values. Proving that the periodical had no injurious effect did not, however, reduce its offensiveness or its illegality, according to the prosecution. Roalfe argued that atheists should have an equal right with Christians to publish their opinions on religion. She did not understand that the law, technically, did not deny that right; its sanctions supposedly applied only to the malicious reviling or ridicule of religion. Moreover, as the judge said, he was bound by "the example of the High Court" in Paterson's case. The report of Roalfe's trial concluded with the news item that, as soon as she was imprisoned, a Mr. Baker "of the United Order of Blasphemers, London," had arrived in Edinburgh to supervise the "Atheistical Depot" in the absence of Paterson and Roalfe.[46]

The atheists apparently sought to give the impression that the 1840s were a replay of the 1820s, and that their ranks included courageous martyrs comparable to Carlile's seemingly innumerable shopmen, who had volunteered their services to support the cause, despite certain imprisonment. For that very reason, the government finally wised up. Mr. Baker was not prosecuted; the prosecutions simply ended. There were no more martyrs, the sales of blasphemous literature declined, and so did the number of irreligious radicals or freethinkers.

The prosecutions had begun when the bishop of Exeter demanded enforcement of the law against the publishers of Haslam's *Letters to the Clergy*. Prosecutions had the effect of stimulating sales of banned books and magazines. Imprisonments radicalized victims and their sympathizers. Holyoake, a sort of deist, had become a self-professed atheist and militantly joined the atheist cause when Southwell was imprisoned. By 1844, all blasphemy victims had served their sentences and were free, unmolested, despite their taunts and provocations. As a result, Holyoake speedily became more moderate. *The Oracle of Reason* had died out by the close of 1843, and had been replaced by another radical periodical, *Movement*, edited by Holyoake; but it downplayed religious issues in favor of political and social ones, and soon died. The socialist movement, which had begun with Robert Owen and had spawned the atheist movement, had declined by the mid-1840s. It was disorganized, rent by schism, and financially bankrupt. The circulation of Owen's periodical, *New Moral World*, had fallen to about 750 by 1845, and it ceased publication. Holyoake started *The Reasoner* in 1846, but its initial circulation of about sixteen hundred quickly fell off by nearly one-third. The demise of socialism signaled the decline of the atheists. "Atheism" had triggered the prosecutions. The deists, beginning with Paine, had been anti-Christian but not antitheist. The atheists had been the first openly to repudiate God as well as the Bible and Christianity. By the mid-1840s, after prosecutions had ceased, the atheists, though they tried to be as noisy as ever, were going unnoticed and into a decline. James Watson, a leading freethought publisher and once a Carlile shopman, despairingly wrote to

Holyoake in early 1846, "All the pamphlets issued against superstition or religion for years past lay on the shelves like so much waste paper."[47]

Atheism, and free thought generally, never seriously threatened the respect for religion felt by Victorian Britain at the time. Prosecutions, by focusing media attention on its victims, increased the circulation of free-thinker periodicals to a maximum of five thousand copies per issue, at a time when the Chartist movement had over three million supporters and over seven million people attended church regularly. The Sabbath was strictly observed on Sunday by preaching and organized prayers, and other religious and scientific developments far exceeded in importance the rise and fall of free thought. The rise of paleontology, and Charles Lyell's *Principles of Geography*, which spoke of evolution and vitiated a literal interpretation of Genesis, were far more significant to Christianity than freethought. The same was true of the works of German scholars who specialized in biblical criticism. Schleiermacher and Strauss, translated into English, displayed reverence combined with an utter subversion of the inerrancy of the Bible. The continued spread of evangelical denominations outside of Anglicanism and the development of the High Church Tractarian movement, of the Oxford movement, and of the Evangelical Alliance of 1846 all outclassed atheism and freethought in significance. So did the rise of Christian Socialism, a passionate humanitarian reformism based on religious impulse. Indeed, freethought was important in the 1840s only because it provoked a flurry of prosecutions that were unwise, intolerant of intolerance, and subservient to orthodoxy's worst impulses. Prosecutions for blasphemy, even when focused on revilers, uselessly and needlessly limited the scope of freedom of the press and of conscience.[48]

CHAPTER TWENTY-ONE

Bible Burning and a Debate Revived

GREAT BRITAIN ignored freethinkers for well over a decade after the early 1840s. The circulation of their publications diminished, although, from the standpoint of devout Christians, all the towns of the kingdom were cesspools of licentiousness, because the crown allowed blasphemers to trumpet their opinions as they wished from press and platform. In Ireland, however, blasphemy took a new form of expression that smashed the limits of tolerance: Bible burning. Religious people regarded Bible burning as an unforgivably outrageous offense. Henry Hetherington had urged Bible burning in 1840 but had not added to his scandalous opinions by actually burning a Bible.[1] That did not become a practice or a form of blasphemy until the 1850s in Ireland. The defendant in the first case was, amazingly, not a freethinker but a member of a Roman Catholic order.

In Mayo County in 1852, John Syngean Bridgman, a Franciscan friar known as Brother John, was tried at the spring Assizes before the chief justice of the Queen's Bench for blasphemously burning a copy of the Authorized Version of the New Testament. Protestant missionaries had made concerted efforts to convert the Catholics of Mayo County. Those missionaries and Brother John had had several altercations. He retaliated by denouncing them and their missionary efforts. Assaulting their religious beliefs and their Bible, he climaxed his bad judgment by publicly burning the King James Version of the New Testament as he loudly proclaimed it to be not the word of God but the word of the devil "and the Devil's Book—Luther's Bible, or your Heretic Bible." Outraged Protestants made a criminal complaint and testified against him at his trial for blasphemy.

Baron Lefroy, the presiding judge, instructed the jury that, if the defendant had spoken the words attributed to him, he was guilty of blasphemy. Lefroy impartially declared that, although the Authorized

Version had been burned in this instance, the crime would have been the same if a Douay or Rhenish Version had been burned. Moreover, the mere burning of the Bible did not constitute the crime. If a man burned a Bible, any Bible, the judge said, "and if you believe that he did not intend any contempt, then you should acquit him." The crime existed only if the words spoken showed "a want of reverence for the Scriptures." A mixed jury of Protestants and Roman Catholics convicted. The sentence was light: Brother John was bound over to keep the peace and be of good behavior for seven years.[2]

Two years later, in 1854, a man named McTeague was tried and convicted in Londonderry in a similar case. He too had vilified the Bible while burning it. In both cases, therefore, the verbal element of the crime of blasphemy was present and crucial. The case of Vladimir Petcherine in 1855 was different.[3]

Petcherine's was an exceptional case. Notwithstanding the prosecution of Brother John, trying a Roman Catholic priest for blasphemy seemed shocking. And never before had the alleged blasphemy consisted exclusively of an overt act, Bible burning, unaccompanied by offensive language. And rarely before had an accused blasphemer been found not guilty.

Petcherine, who was about fifty at the time of his prosecution, was a Russian of high birth who had been a professor of Greek and a librarian at the University of Moscow. In 1840, he abandoned the Greek Orthodox church in favor of Roman Catholicism. The czar sentenced him to perpetual exile. He joined the Redemptorist Fathers, one of the church's most ascetic orders. Redemptorists were bound by vows of poverty and self-denial, and they were obligated to wander as missionaries to reclaim souls lost because of sinning.

Petcherine somehow reached Kingstown in Ireland, where he exhorted people to bring to him immoral and infidel publications so that he might destroy them. By "immoral," Petcherine meant lewd; by "infidel," irreligious. He instructed followers to burn such publications in the chapel yard. Among the people present in the chapel yard when the bonfire was lit were some Protestants who claimed to have seen their Bible thrown into the flames. One was a Methodist minister who stirred up animosities against Catholics, claiming that they hated the Authorized Version of the Protestant Bible. He charged that Petcherine had blasphemously burned it.

The government ordered the prosecution of Petcherine as a result of Protestant agitation against him. His counsel, at his trial, declared that public opinion had prejudiced his case. "The press has teemed with imputations of the foulest and fiercest kind against the person, the order, and the faith of the accused. The pulpit and the platform have rung with them to the echo."[4]

Five prosecutors, including Ireland's attorney general and solicitor general, were arrayed against the priest in the highest criminal court in Dublin, with two high-court justices on the bench. The event excited intense public interest. Reporters from London as well as provincial newspapers were present, along with clergymen of various denominations, lords and ladies, and people of all classes. The streets around the courthouse were jammed with persons awaiting news of the case.

The seven-count indictment, in the language of a critic, reduced to this: "A Popish, Russian priest tried for blasphemously burning the Holy Scriptures in Dublin."[5] Baron Greene, the presiding judge, summarized the indictment by saying that Petcherine stood charged of having "contemptuously, irreverently, and blasphemously" burned or caused to be burned the Authorized Version of the Bible of the established church, with the intent of spreading hatred of it, to the dishonor of Almighty God.[6] In fact, however, the testimony at the trial did not show that Petcherine ever said anything against any version of the Bible, or even that he knew the fire had consumed a Bible. It could have been placed there by a Protestant zealot or a misguided parishioner of the priest's. Unlike Brother John, Petcherine, who was not present when the fire was started, possessed no malicious intent to express hatred for the Authorized Version or bring it into contempt. The prosecution did not try to prove that he did. Nor did the prosecution show that his preaching against immorality in any way referred to the Protestant Bible. His attorney, Thomas O'Hagan, argued effectively that, even if the jury believed in the truth of the prosecution's evidence, it did not show Petcherine's complicity in blasphemy, not even if blasphemy meant Bible burning unaccompanied by contumelious remarks. The judges prevented O'Hagan from proving that in the defendant's sermons he had never aspersed or referred to any version of the Bible.

Baron Greene, in charging the jury, observed that the defense had not challenged the law of blasphemy. He stressed that Christianity was part and parcel of the law of the land, and therefore any publication or "any conduct tending to bring Christianity . . . into disrepute, or to expose it to hatred and contempt," was a high offense against the law and Christianity. Never before had a court described any sort of conduct as blasphemy. Petcherine's judges were making new law. By the old law, conduct insulting to Christianity could not be blasphemy, because during the centuries since its biblical origins—including the centuries since it had become a common-law crime—blasphemy had always been a purely verbal crime, a form of defamation. Desecrating a church or burning a Bible might be sacrilege but not blasphemy. The law as laid down in Petcherine's case was bad law, conflating different crimes against religion.

Baron Greene instructed the jury that, even if they believed that a Bible had been burned, they must hold the defendant not guilty unless they were convinced that he was responsible for its burning and that he had the blasphemous intent ascribed to him by the indictment. He must, that is, have burned it to show his hatred and contempt of it. The jury, consisting of both Protestants and Catholics, deliberated for about three-quarters of an hour. Its verdict of not guilty provoked "rapturous cheers" from the people in and outside the courtroom.

A year later, in the *Dublin Review*, an anonymous author, a Trinitarian Christian who fully accepted the law of blasphemy, wrote that it was "sheer nonsense" to say that Christianity was part and parcel of the law of the land, because Christianity signified so many different beliefs. No one could even say whether a belief in the Trinity or in incarnation or in revelation was essential to Christianity. Moreover, the writer fully quoted from Jefferson's letter to Major Cartwright to prove that authorities for the doctrine that Christianity was the law of the land had relied on a mistranslation from Justice Prisot's law French, making the term for "ancient writings" mean "holy scripture."[7]

The writer's primary complaint, however, was not that the law of blasphemy was ill-founded but that it was not directed against the real offenders of God's majesty: freethinkers. He was indignant that the attorney general would prosecute a clergyman yet allow atheism to "be as rampant as it pleases." Everyone knew that in cities throughout the realm "cheap infidel publications" flourished, and that in public halls lecturers assaulted God and sought to uproot Christianity with impunity. By way of proof, the writer supplied examples from "Secularist" periodicals such as Holyoake's *Reasoner*, blaring blasphemies that were patent and insulting. The writer concluded that the prosecution of Petcherine resulted from religious prejudice on the part of "the influential orange-faction." Possibly because of the verdict and the public disgust with the prosecution, blasphemy trials died out in Ireland. No others occurred there during the remainder of the century.[8]

In England, such trials had also become unusual. Indeed, Holyoake's was the last, in 1842, and the last in Great Britain as a whole had been the Edinburgh convictions of Southwell, Finlay, Robinson, and Roalfe, in 1843 and early 1844. Not surprisingly, then, the 1857 blasphemy trial of Thomas Pooley in Cornwall seemed almost shocking. Holyoake, in his *Reasoner*, editorially remarked that he had thought blasphemy prosecutions had become obsolete: "Bigotry has slept for sixteen years in England."[9] John Stuart Mill's *On Liberty* passingly noticed the Pooley case to make the point that penalties for opinions still existed as a matter of law and were still enforced, "even in these times." A man of unexceptional conduct, said Mill, was actually sentenced to twenty-one months' imprisonment "for uttering, and writing on a gate, some offensive words concerning Christianity." And within a month after, Mill added, two men, one of whom was Holyoake, were rejected as jurymen at Old Bailey for admitting that they had no theological beliefs.[10]

When Henry Thomas Buckle, the historian of civilization, read Mill, he denounced the prosecution of Pooley as "alien to the genius of our time," and believed that it could not have happened in London or anywhere other than in a "remote part of the kingdom" like the Bodmin Assizes in Cornwall.[11] In fact, however, the presiding judge at the Bodmin Assizes was not some provincial justice of the peace; he was one of England's great judges, Sir John T. Coleridge of the Queen's Bench, and the prosecutor, surprisingly, was his son, John Duke Coleridge, the future lord chief justice of England who was responsible for the liberalization of the law on blasphemy. Their involvement in Pooley's prosecution was coincidental, not, as Buckle and Holyoake believed, conspiratorial.

Thomas Pooley, who lived in the village of Liskeard, was a well-digger of eccentric beliefs. He thought the earth was a living, thinking animal, and he feared that, if he dug too deeply in it, he might penetrate its skin and wound vital parts. He professed a belief in one great and wise "Almighty Power," but experience with his fellow men taught him to dislike Christians and "Christian Bible tyranny." He did not, however, interfere with the Christian beliefs of his loving wife, or the Christian education of his children. One of his odd beliefs, which resulted in his imprisonment, was that burning all the Bibles and spreading their ashes over fields would cure potato rot. Although Pooley was an exemplary father and husband, and an industrious worker, he had a reputation for being mentally unbalanced and a village freethinker. But he was ignorant of freethought literature. Holyoake, who went to Cornwall to study his case, wrote solemnly that, if Pooley had "had the advantage of Freethinking books, he might now be of sound mind."[12]

For fifteen years, Liskeard and its environs had been annoyed by chalked inscriptions on walls and gates, expressing sentiments that offended religious people.[13] Pooley was thought to be the culprit, but no one ever saw him do the writing. One day, the *Cornish Times* ran this ad: "BLASPHEMY.—Any person who has seen a man writing blasphemous sentences on gates or other places in the neighbourhood of Liskeard, is requested to communicate immediately with Messrs. Pedler and Grylls, Liskeard, or with the Rev. R. Hobhouse, St. Ive Rectory."[14] Soon after, the Reverend Paul Bush filed a criminal complaint against Pooley, asserting that he had blasphemously libeled the Holy Scriptures, the Christian religion, and God. Pooley may have been guilty of chalking the messages, but not even Bush ever saw him do it; Pooley was only seen in the vicinity, and he believed in God. Bush, who was rector of Duloe, swore that he had read on a gate the words: "Duloe stinks with the monster Christ's Bible-Blasphemy—T. Pooley." Some children erased all but the first and last words. No proof was ever offered that the printing was in Pooley's hand, but these words on the gate constituted the first count in Pooley's indictment for blasphemy.[15]

A second count consisted of similar gate-writing. When Pooley was summoned before the Liskeard magistrates, he walked into court with a rope around his neck and told his judges to pull it "and have done with it." To the constable who took him off to jail to await trial Pooley angrily said, "If it had not been for the blackguard Jesus Christ, when he stole the donkey, the police would not be wanted, and . . . he [Christ] was the forerunner of all theft and whoredom."[16] That remark added the third count to his indictment for blasphemy. A fourth count derived from his often stated belief that the ashes of Bibles would cure potato rot.

Lacking counsel, Pooley defended himself before the Coleridges. He pleaded not guilty, rather than not guilty by reason of insanity. Neither the prosecutor nor the judge suspected that he was unhinged. Later they said that he conducted his defense ably. The prosecutor argued that the case did not involve freedom of opinion in any sense. Anyone had a right to express opinions, however erroneously, and maintain them with serious argument. But this was a case involving indecent and extremely offensive language about the Saviour, and the public had to be defended against such insults. The prosecutor conceded, as to the first count, that, because key words had been rubbed out, the charge ought to be withdrawn. As to the count involving Bible ashes and potato rot, the prosecutor volunteered that the remark might have been made in jest, and the judge put this view to the jury.[17]

Judge Coleridge's charge showed studied moderation, but he saw the law the same way his son did. Pooley should not be found guilty because he differed in opinions with Christians, not even if he injured their feelings in the course of declaring his opinions in good faith. But if the jury believed that the words ascribed to him were indeed his, he had blasphemed, because the words ascribed could have no purpose but to outrage or insult. Blasphemy resulted from the intent to give offense and outrage the opinions of others. The jury promptly convicted on all counts. Pooley made a brief, impassioned anti-Christian speech before hearing his sentence. For the words on the gate, Coleridge sentenced him to six months' imprisonment; for the remark about the potato rot, six months; and for the remark made to the constable, nine months.[18] The sentence was excessively harsh. Indeed, the prosecution was unwarranted.[19]

In an editorial, *The Spectator* of London summed up the case by saying that Pooley was no doubt guilty under the law but was probably insane and suffered a sentence of "undue severity." A matter of even greater importance was "that the authority of the law should not be damaged by applying its most solemn machinery to trifles, or to getting up a burlesque upon the Inquisition."[20]

The prosecution and sentence received adverse publicity. George Holyoake's *Reasoner* probably had no influence, although the freethinkers promoted petitions to Parliament, advertising the injustice of the case. Holyoake went to Cornwall, interviewed everyone, and published a booklet reporting the case. He was convinced that Pooley was mad. Buckle read Holyoake's report and excoriated the Coleridges in *Fraser's Magazine*. John Duke Coleridge replied at length, explaining himself and his father.

One atheist, Lionel H. Holdreth, sent angry letters to the Home Office, to the attorney general, to Judge Coleridge, and to several newspapers, including the London *Times*. Apart from his savage remarks about religious persecution and injustice, he observed that in London there existed "Atheistic propaganda, regularly organised," behind the weekly publication of tracts against Christianity. Prosecute their authors, he urged. Prosecute Holyoake for publishing *The Reasoner* every week. "Send me to prison for a year and nine months for the crime of defending my opinions in the press and on the platform; and then I say, if you act wickedly, at least you act like men," but not when persecuting a poor, ignorant, undefended man and "leaving us alone."[21]

One petition in behalf of Pooley, arguing that he was of unsound mind and should not have been convicted, went to the Home Office. Sir George Gray, the home secretary, wrote to Judge Coleridge, reporting the belief about Pooley's insanity and requesting the judge to supply the Home Office with his notes on the trial plus any comments he might have. Judge Coleridge explained that he had not doubted Pooley's sanity but saw no reason why Pooley should not be pardoned. When Gray received that letter, he pardoned Pooley, who had spent five months in prison.[22] The government continued to leave the atheists alone. Pooley's case, despite his conviction, had been turned into a triumph for freedom of expression and a black eye for blasphemy prosecutions. Another would not occur for a generation. But the question whether blasphemy prosecutions were in the public interest became a matter of public debate.

W. D. Lewis, Q.C. (Queen's Counsel), read a paper on the law of blasphemous libel before one of the semimonthly meetings of the Juridical Society. That organization consisted of the elite of the English bench and bar. The presiding officer was the president of the society, the lord high chancellor.

Numerous judges and barristers were present, including the attorney general of England. No one before Lewis had sought to give a systematic account of the law of England on the subject of blasphemy.[23] He sought to determine the reasons assigned in English law for holding blasphemy criminally punishable. He returned to the 1676 *Rex* v. *Taylor*, in which Lord Chief Justice Hale held that blasphemy or "reproach of the Christian religion" was a crime because, by offending God and religion, blasphemy offended Christianity, which was part of the law of England. In defense of that proposition, Hale offered only the point that blasphemy dissolved the obligations on which civil society was based. In *Rex* v. *Woolston* of 1729, Chief Justice Raymond restated Hale's proposition by saying that, because Christianity was part of the law of the land, it must be protected from blasphemy. The reason he offered was that "whatever strikes at the very root of Christianity, tends manifestly to a dissolution of the civil government." Later judges embellished these points, which led Lewis to conclude that there were five grounds for criminalizing blasphemy. First, because Christianity was part of the law of England, deriding it derided the law. Second, blasphemy endangered the foundation of government and society. Third, it tended to destroy or undermine the existing standard of morals, based on Christianity. Fourth, it annihilated the sanctity of oaths, which were indispensable to the administration of justice. Finally, "the honour of God requires such punishment."[24]

Lewis defended English law because he thought it allowed freedom of opinion in the interests of truth, even though it properly punished the contumely or scoffing of religion. Heresy, he observed, was no longer criminal. But he supported his point by quoting *Rex* v. *Woolston* to demonstrate that only when "the very root of Christianity itself is struck at" did the law interpose against what was said. The case disproved his assertion, for Woolston's interpretation of miracles as allegories was a form of heresy, a disagreement with the orthodox view. Moreover, whether opinion remained free and whether the root of Christianity had been struck by the defendant were highly subjective matters. From Lewis's standpoint, however, the manner in which the defendant made his remarks decided the point.

Lewis would not punish nonconformity or heresy, only blasphemy, which he defined as uttering sentiments opposed to the Christian religion "in a scoffing, railing, or irreverent manner." The defendant's malice made the difference. If he spoke or wrote from a reproachful disposition rather than simply for the purpose of propagating irreverent opinions, he should be found guilty of blasphemy. "Speculative honest argument, in other words, the law does not criminally repress, though it be opposed to Christianity; but indecent abuse of religion and profaneness, tending to practical results injurious to society, the law prohibits and declares to be a crime." Lewis acknowledged that "considerable difficulty" attended the distinction between fair argument and derision, "but any man of masculine understanding," he offered, "would be able to deal properly with all such cases."[25]

Lewis next inquired what particular words constituted blasphemy, and declared that the crime existed when a remark ridiculed any of "the fundamental principles of the Christian religion," such as the existence of God, the divinity of Christ, or the divine inspiration of the Holy Scriptures. Although the crime was strictly a verbal one, involving no physical act, the words used were punishable for their tendency to produce harm to others or to society or to government. "The subversion of civil order, of morals, and of oaths," as he had pointed out, was the danger resulting from vilification of Christianity.

Lewis had read the law reports and legal commentators, but he was otherwise substantially innocent of the literature on blasphemy. He did not know the work or arguments of John Wickliffe, Nathaniel Lardner, Philip Furneaux, W. J. Fox, John Search, or Joseph Blanco White. But he had read Henry T. Buckle and John Stuart Mill's *On Liberty*, though not Mill's older, extended treatment of blasphemy. From Buckle and Mill, Lewis mustered what little he understood of the argument against the law of blasphemy. He understood that Buckle championed the right to argue in any way, including ridicule or any language that did not result in an actual breach of the peace. He understood that God was powerful enough to avenge His own honor. He understood too that educated persons believed that the prosecution of Pooley perverted the law and resulted in oppression. Finally, he understood Mill's argument that, if sarcasm, invective, and contumely against Christianity were illegitimate, then, logically and morally, the same rhetorical devices against irreligion ought to be equally illegitimate. Lewis asserted that he agreed with Buckle and Mill in favoring freedom of opinion on all subjects and conceded that "this complete liberty belongs to all, whether Christians or not." He would not have the law persecute any opinion, prohibit any opinion, or enforce any opinion, "provided there be decorum and respect." He disagreed with all other arguments against blasphemy that he understood.

Nothing in infidelity or unbelief could be defamed, he argued. The man who rejected religion "has nothing to offer which can entitle him to put the Christian under terms." The offense, he believed, "is all on one side." On the other hand, the right to impose penalties on blasphemers derived from "the essential nature of Christian doctrine" and from history. He insisted that the "essence of Christian faith" required reverence and could not tolerate derision or reproach. And whereas "reverence is essential" to Christianity, infidelity was indifferent to it. Infidelity and Christianity thrived in different environments. "Irreverence and contempt . . . involve not merely an improper prejudice against Christian opinions, but poison the very atmosphere of those opinions." By way of proof, Lewis contended that the majority of the community, which consisted of "the young, the ignorant, and the labouring poor," were entitled to the state's protection in taking care that Christian beliefs reached them "in their true character, without any illicit interference or poisonous adulteration."[26]

Having argued that the state must shield weak and unprotected people from blasphemers, who distorted Christianity, Lewis failed to understand that he had laid waste his previous distinction between heresy and blasphemy, and had also undermined his insistent claim that he favored "absolute freedom of opinion on all subjects."[27] He saw nothing inconsistent in his explicit view that liberty of opinion should be protected, and that punishing blasphemy did indeed protect liberty of opinion by allowing Christian opinions to flourish. "Now, what I am contending for is, that the state may adopt and act upon the opinion that atheism is publicly and nationally pernicious—that when atheism assumes the form of blasphemy it may be punished—and that so to treat it involves no violation of true liberty of opinion."[28] History, he added, proved the validity of his viewpoint. He did not know that Protestanism had once been regarded as blasphemous and atheistic, as had anti-Trinitarianism (by Protestants as well as Catholics), Baptism, and Quakerism, as well as Unitarianism and deism. Lewis had his history upside down.

He wound up by summarizing the grounds on which the law should punish revilers of Christianity. The constitution and government of the kingdom were identified with religion. The system of justice depended on oaths, whose sanctity blasphemy destroyed. The national standard of morality depended on Christianity. Thus, the state had a warrant to protect religion from insult. Moreover, the "feelings" of Christians "constituted rights" that the infidel might be bound to respect without violating his "reasonable liberty." Finally, though blasphemy was purely a verbal crime, the punishment of words unaccompanied by criminal acts followed legitimate precedents, as in the cases of perjury and obscenity.

As a law journal reported, Lewis had attempted to write the first coherent analysis of the law of blasphemy, yet he "failed to convince the majority of those who heard his paper read," proving that his viewpoint was "not quite tenable."[29] Lord Chancellor John Campbell observed that, although speaking scornfully or insultingly of the Christian religion should be punishable, Lewis went much further; he would prosecute not only Paine but Gibbon and Hume. As one who had formerly been attorney general, Campbell stated that crown officers had to consider not only the character of an offense but also the prudence of prosecuting it.

J. G. Phillimore, Q.C., went further, saying that, if Lewis's argument was pushed to its legitimate conclusion, it would justify revocation of toleration acts. Baron Bromwell criticized Lewis for carelessly defining key concepts and failing to understand that infidelity, even heresy, had a positive side. Bromwell would punish anyone who indecently attacked any religion or sect, not just Christianity. Mr. Phinn, Q.C., criticized Lewis for denying skeptics the right to use ridicule as a weapon; Phinn believed that truth could not suffer from verbal attacks. He reminded his listeners that blasphemy was an accordionlike term that had been applied to Socrates and Jesus. Mr. Collier, Q.C., found Lewis's premises "totally false." Critics of Christianity had to be "decorous," whereas Christians could use sarcasm, wit, and ridicule. Collier was not afraid of Christianity's being subjected to any criticism, though mere ridicule seemed punishable as a nuisance. Mr. Daniel, Q.C., on the other side, opposed blasphemy prosecutions. "Let the infidel revile religion," he declared; "he would reply to him." He did not fear reviling or scoffing. Advocates of truth should not object when ridicule was used against them. Montague Chambers, Q.C., was the only listener who supported Lewis.[30]

In reply, Lewis redefined blasphemy as lampooning events and persons deemed sacred by Christians or treating irreverently that which is essential to Christian belief. Heresy, he said, was opinion or argument. Blasphemy was neither; it was vilification. The state should treat atheism and other forms of blasphemy as its enemy. "Is the State to be hampered in discharging its duties . . . by the mere flimsy pretext of liberty?"[31]

Editorially, *The Solicitors' Journal* observed that the argument that blasphemy must be prosecuted to safeguard the sanctity of oaths had no basis. The oath of a non-Christian, "and even of one who might be generally characterized as an infidel," had equal force with that of a Christian. Moreover, Lewis notwithstanding, morals were independent of religious dogmas, "so that there is no necessary connection between morality and any form of religious belief." The editors could not support the double standard proposed by Lewis. Christianity was entitled to no special favors from the law. Whatever standard of expression applied in politics or literature pertained to religion. The rule of law should not be dependent on the subject matter under discussion. All parties to controversy were entitled to the same rights, contrary to Lewis's rejection of equality of rights. Finally, the editors believed that, under existing law, heresy and blasphemy were not as distinguishable as Lewis thought. Blasphemy, they wrote insightfully, is "heresy plus invective," or intemperance of heretical expression.[32]

An unsigned article in *Law Magazine and Review* presented a still more libertarian viewpoint on "The Law Relating to Blasphemy." The author stressed that a review of the leading cases showed that the offense of blasphemy was so vague and elastic as to apply to whatever the legal system sought to punish. The cases also showed two distinct doctrines as to what constituted blasphemy. One was any attack on the received religion of the country, the other only indecent attacks. Despite all the talk about Christianity as the law of the land, the law protected only the Church of England.

The publication of heterodox opinions, contrary to those of the establishment, breached the law. Thus, heresy and blasphemy were "only different degrees of the same crime." Judges stressed that a blasphemous attack on religion was indecorous, scoffing, or contemptuous. That meant that heterodox opinions must not offend Christian feelings. Such judges, like Lewis, confidently assumed that they knew the essence of Christian beliefs that should be protected against blasphemers. Other Christians, however, might consider different essences to demand respect. In the Holy Land, Latin and Greek churchmen fought so vehemently about their respective essences that Mohammedan police had to keep the peace. Christian controversialists in Great Britain and in Ireland did not believe in the same essences. Nor did Protestant sectarians. Lewis was right, though, in declaring that the law regarded reviling or ridiculing the essence of Christian belief as blasphemy.

In that sense, the mode of attack, not the attack itself, constituted the offense. But the cases illustrated that whether the mode was criminal was wholly personal. In effect, the views of "respectable tea-tables of worthy village spinsters" or of "the rector's lady or the curate's wife" fixed the standard by which the mode of attack was deemed criminal. Between the two sorts of blasphemy—the attack on Christian belief or heterodoxy, and the mode of attack—little difference could be found in fact. Before any words could be found blasphemous, it was necessary to determine what must not be blasphemed: "*Heresy* must be defined before we can prosecute for *blasphemy*."[33]

As for the second sort of blasphemy, which depended on the mode of attack, it said, in effect, "reason, but don't ridicule." What that meant was that "Mr. Lewis and his friends want to have, at the same time, all the credit of being tolerant, and all the advantage of persecuting those who offend them. Like a bragging bully at school, these gentlemen are willing to fight . . . but their terms are, that they are not to be hit on their noses and adjacent features, which are very tender." Although they reviled so-called infidels or atheists, whom they confused, they must not be assailed in like manner.

Some, like Lord Chancellor Campbell, differed by wishing to exempt gentlemen like Hume and Gibbon, and their publishers and booksellers, from the law of blasphemy. But Campbell and his supporters could not extend equal freedom to the "rough, coarse, and ungenteel" scoffing of the Carliles, Hetheringtons, and Pooleys. "So it becomes a mere matter of taste." The poor, the ill-bred, and the ignorant, whom the law supposedly protected, had to speak and write according to different rules. The author concluded that he had expected to find the bigot and tyrant lurking under the mantle of sectarian zeal but was startled to see him clad in the robes of a judge or a juridical essayist.[34]

The debate on the law of blasphemy as well as the occasional enforcement of that law possessed an air of unreality. One would think that blasphemy actually affected or undermined Christianity, or that the churches, clergy, tithes, and Bible societies functioned a whit differently because of the existence of blasphemy. No one could doubt that free thought, skepticism, and irreligion existed in England, but not because of the influence of blasphemers. English translations of the works of the Protestant theologians of Germany's Tübingen school of higher criticism of the Bible were more responsible than Holyoake or Pooley. So too were Sir Charles Lyell and other geologists whose work discredited the account of Creation in the book of Genesis. Equally subversive were the zoological works of Alfred Wallace and Charles Darwin. Above all, perhaps, was the damage done to fundamentalist Christianity by scholars and divines of the established church itself.

In 1860, for example, a year after Darwin's *Origin of Species*, seven liberal Anglicans, including Rugby's headmaster and three celebrated Oxford scholars, all subscribers to the Thirty-nine Articles, published *Essays and Reviews*, the first important English book reflecting Tübingen's higher criticism. One of the seven was Dr. William Temple, later the archbishop of Canterbury. The seven argued against a literal interpretation of the Bible and against received interpretations of the Thirty-nine Articles, the "essence" of Anglicanism. Their book received condemnation from a church convocation; two of the authors, who were ordained, were convicted of heresy, a judgment by the ecclesiastical Court of Arches that the Judicial Committee of the Privy Council reversed. The same authority interposed again in 1865 to quash the excommunication from the Church of England of John W. Colenso, the bishop of Natal, a Cambridge mathematician of distinction who wrote a devastating critique of the Pentateuch; Colenso argued that Moses was mythical and that whoever wrote his books collected fables and stories not divinely inspired.[35] Bishop Colenso, Charles Darwin, and Benjamin Jowett of Oxford undermined Christianity far more than Carlile, Hetherington, and Pooley. So did Hume and Gibbon, whom the lord chancellor regarded as above the law of blasphemy.

One jaundiced observer of changed conditions was a legal commentator who signed himself "W.C.S." in an article entitled "Blasphemy" in 1873. He described as "astonishing" the changes that had taken place "in the feelings of the nation." Freedom of discussion in matters religious, as well as political, now existed, and "it would be difficult to state the limit beyond which theological speculation may not run." The old days, of "regular crusades against the whole race of freethinking booksellers," were gone. The "law has entirely abandoned the protection of the Christian religion." License, not liberty, existed far beyond what sober and rational discussion required. "It would rather seem that *carte blanche* has been given to atheism and infidelity. Every secularist lecturer is apparently entitled to heap abuse on the religion established by law, or to demonstrate the mortality of man's spiritual nature amid the coarse applause of a public meeting." W.C.S. reminded readers that, by law, to challenge or deny the authority of the Holy Scriptures or the providence of God in the governance of the world was a crime, though unfortunately the law moldered unused. He thought a "regular infliction of fine and imprisonment" of blasphemers would "put a salutary restraint upon the actual freedom of thought." But the public no longer believed that blasphemers were immoral or that any connection existed between religion and morality.[36]

Another legal conservative, the most distinguished in Victorian England, Sir James Fitzjames Stephen, had an entirely different view of the matter. Stephen had sought to codify the criminal law of England. His *Liberty, Equality, Fraternity* still stands as the pre-eminent conservative reply to Mill's *On Liberty*, and he would write a three-volume history of the criminal law that is still not superseded. From 1879 to 1891, Stephen would serve on the Queen's Bench. In 1875, he published an extraordinary essay on "The Expression of Religious Opinions," in which he advocated parliamentary abolition of the statutory and common law on blasphemy.[37]

As usual, a tough realism dictated Stephen's views. He was not one who got indignant against those who sought to deter people from the expression of views adverse to Christianity. He did not understand how a sincere believer in Christianity could act other than to wish the suppression of anti-Christian opinions. And he himself believed that some opinions might be so injurious to society as to merit suppression. Like W.C.S., Stephen declared that by statute anyone who denied God or the divine authority of the Bible or the truth of the Christian religion, even in private conversation, was guilty of blasphemy. "Ought this state of things to continue?" asked Stephen. "I am most earnestly of the opinion that it ought not."[38]

His reasons were commonsensical. First, he observed, everyone knew that the truth of Christianity, the divine authority of the Bible, the existence of God, and the possibility of a future life were matters denied by a large and increasing number of persons in good faith and "upon intelligible grounds." Another "notorious fact" was that England had "many conscientious and respectable atheists and infidels of different kinds." Moreover, the laws against blasphemy "have proved utterly incompetent" to prevent the spread of such opinions, which were systematically defied with impunity. If any attorney general sought to enforce the blasphemy laws, the ministry to which he belonged must either put him out of power or be turned out of power. A penal law that could not be enforced was a menace that should be repealed. Stephen compared it to a rusty old weapon: it might not do harm for years, but "any accident may cause it to go off, and if it does, it will in all probability hardly do anything but mischief." Blasphemy prosecutions did no good and produced results that no friend of Christianity could endorse.

Such prosecutions had been of two kinds, one against persons who had argued seriously and in good faith against Christianity, and the other against persons using coarse abuse against the sacred. Stephen had made the old distinction between prosecutions based on matter and those on manner, the attack *per se* or the mode of attack. He would not prosecute either case, he wrote, "unless indeed it is committed under circumstances likely to produce a breach of the peace, in which case I would deal with it on that ground only." Thus Furneaux's old overt-acts test received Stephen's endorsement. He believed that punishment simply encouraged additional coarseness of expression by producing "a mischievous irrational sensitiveness." A person of sense ought not to be offended by coarse abuse but should feel contempt for the abuser. Rational men, he thought, should feel the same way about blasphemy. Vulgar abuse of individuals was not punishable, nor should vulgar abuse of religion be punishable without breach of the peace. Stephen thus entirely dismissed the viewpoint of conservatives like W. D. Lewis as persecutory and irrational.[39]

Stephen invited his readers to review particular passages of Gibbon's account of the doctrine of the Trinity in the twenty-first chapter of *Decline and Fall*. Gibbon had produced a skepticism about the Trinity incomparably greater than coarse reviling. Yet to prosecute Gibbon or his book-sellers "would be perfectly monstrous" in the absence of a systematic persecution of all skepticism. Imprisoning a poor miserable laborer like Pooley for his offensive remarks about Christianity written on a gate, while allowing every educated man in the nation to buy and read Gibbon, "is like punishing the throwing of stones and rewarding systematic poisoning."[40]

Practically speaking, wrote Stephen, prosecutions for coarse and disrespectful expressions had the objective of suppressing serious arguments. The government resorted to prosecution not because a publication was blasphemous but because it was anti-Christian, "and to a devout believer in Christianity, every pointed denial of its doctrine, every exposure of the weak side of any common opinion, appears blasphemous" or insulting. Stephen was agreeing with the view that the real objective of a blasphemy prosecution was to punish heresy, which was not a crime punishable by secular authority. Stephen argued that in politics argument had to be "unbridled and unrestrained" or one could not do justice to one's political views; the same situation must prevail as to religious opinions. The time had come to recognize that blasphemy prosecutions invariably failed in the purpose of shielding Christianity.

Furthermore, the law so utterly opposed the state of public feeling that the law was rarely enforced, although critics of Christian beliefs expressed themselves with increasing energy, pertinacity, and candor. When books and periodicals to which persons of the highest eminence contributed, regularly published denials of the divine authority of the Bible and the truths of Christianity, "the laws which forbid such discussions may be said to have broken down, and ought to be repealed—to recur to my former illustration—on the principle on which it is prudent to unload a blunderbuss too rusty to be fired."[41]

Stephen's estimation of the practical results of blasphemy prosecutions reinforced his opinion. That prosecutions did not check the growth of skepticism or preserve the institutions that they were intended to protect was obvious. Prosecutions had an unintended contrary result. They popularized the views they meant to suppress, and they thrust the advocacy of such views into the hands of men who had nothing to lose—the Paines and Carliles. Prosecutions also "helped to complete the alliance between religious and political disaffection." Stephen thought that it was impossible "to imagine anything more paltry and wretched than the advantages which Christianity obtained by the law against blasphemous libels." Accordingly, Stephen recommended a short statute by which "the whole of the law which can possibly be applied to the punishment of the expression of religious opinions should be abolished."[42]

Not very different in viewpoint was the essay by Frederic Pollock, who became England's most distinguished academic lawyer, on "The Theory of Persecution." Reviewing centuries of heterodoxy that had been subjected to prosecution, Pollock concluded that prosecutions had been ineffectual and misconceived. They were founded in part on the supposition that objectionable and offensive remarks about religion had injurious results. But the foundations of morality had not been weakened; respect for both morality and law had not ceased; society was not on the brink of dissolution because of heterodoxy. Indeed, the world was as orderly, prosperous, and flourishing as ever, despite heresies and blasphemies. Orthodoxy could name only one evil consequence: unbelief increased. But it did no harm. Blasphemy laws, Pollock found, "do not work, and no harm appears to come of their not working."[43] Others, including William A. Hunter, a professor of jurisprudence at University College, London, and Charles Bradlaugh, a leading freethinker, had reached similar conclusions.[44] Apparently, the establishment in religion and government silently agreed, because after Pooley's case a quarter of a century passed before another prosecution occurred.

CHAPTER TWENTY-TWO

Bradlaugh, Foote, and Coleridge's Decency Test

TWENTY-FIVE years after Pooley's case, a Tory member of Parliament instigated a blasphemy prosecution against a man who had been elected to the House of Commons but was refused a seat because he would not swear the oath of office on the Bible. He was Charles Bradlaugh, who in 1882, when the indictment was returned, was England's leading freethinker, a radical politician, an orator equal in talent to William Gladstone, and a cunning lawyer with himself as his only client. No one in England was more litigious. No one was more notorious, for he was a republican as well as an atheist, an advocate of women's rights, and a man who had once been tried for obscenity in a sensational case involving a sex manual.[1] He was also the founder and president of the National Secular Society and the editor and publisher of a radical magazine, *National Reformer*; moreover, his Freethought Publication Company had published *Freethinker*, a militant journal that specialized in sleaze, ridicule, and hate.

Freethinker's directors were indicted with Bradlaugh: George William Foote, a close associate in the National Secular Society who was *Freethinker*'s editor, and William Ramsey, the publisher and manager of the Freethought Publication Company. In the first number of the penny weekly, Foote had written: "The *Freethinker* is an anti-Christian organ, and is therefore chiefly aggressive. It will wage relentless war against superstition in general, and against the superstition of Christianity in particular."[2]

The charge of blasphemy against Bradlaugh, Foote, and Ramsey was the first in London since the Hetherington, Moxon, and Southwell cases of 1842–43. The indictment against the defendants specified fourteen counts of blasphemous libels published in eight different issues of *Freethinker*. They described or depicted God as bloodthirsty, barbarous, and despotic.[3]

The lapse of forty years between blasphemy cases in London made the law of blasphemy seem like a relic of past ages of persecution. Even in Dublin, where there had been no cases since the Bible burnings of the 1850s, a law journal editorially condemned blasphemy prosecutions as unwise because they did more harm than good. The trial would give publicity to the people who courted it and to their views, accentuating breaches of good taste that otherwise would have been quickly forgotten. The object of the prosecution, to suppress blasphemous publications, would be defeated by widely advertising an otherwise obscure weekly. "To awaken the sleeping terrors of this half obsolete part of our law is to expose the community to the risk of ill-judged and, indeed, mischievous prosecutions. . . . Most of us have long ceased to believe that it is right to punish men for their convictions, however mistaken."[4] The home secretary, Sir William Harcourt, who controlled the police, had a similar opinion; he was reluctant to prosecute *Freethinker*. Foote, its editor, invited prosecution, so that he could be martyred like freethought heroes of the past; he believed that, if he suffered the fate of Carlile and Hetherington, he might become a celebrity like Bradlaugh.[5]

Sir Henry Tyler, a Tory M.P. from London, persuaded the attorney general to institute the suit as a means of compromising Bradlaugh. A trial might sap his energy and handicap him in pursuing several suits that he had begun against those, like Tyler, who refused to allow him to be seated in the Commons. If suits against Bradlaugh succeeded, he might be bankrupted and become ineligible for the seat to which Northampton had elected him. He might also become ineligible if convicted of blasphemy. If his association with Foote and *Freethinker* could be exposed, he might be discredited.[6]

In fact, *Freethinker* pained Bradlaugh, because, like Holyoake, he preferred civility of discourse. *Freethinker*, he believed, "was lowering the tone of Freethought advocacy and giving an unnecessary handle to its foes."[7] Foote, who in the privacy of his study was a well-read literary critic, believed that, as an atheistic editor, he must assault not only Christians and Jews but also "mealy mouthed Freethinkers, who want omelettes without breaking of eggs and revolutions without shedding of blood. . . ."[8] Foote relished being vulgar and vicious, and he was every bit as bigoted as the worst of those whom he savaged. When the Tory Tyler instigated the prosecution of Foote and Ramsey to bring down Bradlaugh, Foote happily anticipated an increase in subscriptions.

Bradlaugh, ever adept at using the system to his own advantage, obtained an order changing the place of the trial from Old Bailey to the Queen's Bench; Justice James Fitzjames Stephen issued the writ of certiorari that transferred the case.[9] That maneuver ensured that Bradlaugh would receive a fairer trial. It also delayed the prosecution by nine months. Then Bradlaugh petitioned for a trial separate from that of the other defendants. As the months passed without trial, Foote, the would-be martyr, decided that he would publish a special Christmas issue that would be "full from cover to cover of what the orthodox call blasphemy."[10] One of the articles satirized the New Testament by running a fictitious report of a trial for blasphemy against the four Gospel narrators, Matthew, Mark, Luke, and John. Their indictment specified that they had scurrilously and blasphemously vilified Almighty God by claiming that He had cohabited with a Jewish virgin named Mary, with the result that "an illegitimate son named Jesus was born." Jesus, *Freethinker* reported, blasphemously claimed to be God himself, overturned His law, and alleged that those who did not believe in him would suffer eternal torments, and that those torments "were especially prepared for the great mass of God's creatures on account of sins committed before they were born." The provocation was so great, including cartoons lampooning God, that Foote and Ramsey were indicted a second time, in early 1883. Their printer, Henry A. Kemp, was indicted with them. A separate prosecution was commenced against a Fleet Street bookseller, H. C. Cattell, for selling the Christmas issue and exhibiting the most notorious of the cartoons. It illustrated a biblical passage in which God "shows his backside" to Moses. Within a couple of months, and before the 1882 prosecution was scheduled for trial, the Christmas-issue defendants were tried at Old Bailey before Justice Ford North, who was a Roman Catholic.[11]

The trial took place on March 1, 1883. The prosecutor was Sir Hardinge Giffard, a former attorney general who would become Lord Chancellor Halsbury. He informed the jury that anyone might dispute Christian beliefs if he expressed himself with "a due regard for the feelings of others and without the intention of outrage and insult." No one indulging the latter intention had a right to claim freedom of the press or liberty of discussion. In this case, the outrage and insult were so gross and degrading that the prosecutor refused to repeat the blasphemies by reading the indictment. The defendants had flaunted their blasphemies in the Christmas number, admitting that it was blasphemous cover to cover. Giffard concluded his case by producing witnesses whose testimony connected the defendants with *Freethinker*.

Foote, defending himself, spoke interminably but well. He mistakenly thought that Giffard's remarks about his indecencies misled the jury, because the charge against him was not obscenity but blasphemy. He regarded the law of blasphemy as a relic of a persecuting age. *Freethinker* had been singled out, he contended, because it was cheap, just a penny. Blasphemy prosecutions, he accurately remarked, were never commenced against the rich or against writers of expensive books, but were always directed against poor men "who are speaking to the masses of people." Foote had read the section on blasphemy in Justice James Fitzjames Stephen's recently published *History of the Criminal Law of England*.[12] Stephen, he correctly reported, stated that the offense consisted in the matter published, not the manner of expression. That made the law repressive. Stephen opposed blasphemy prosecutions.

Foote contended that the evidence against him did not convict him of blasphemy. The indictment stipulated, for example, that *Freethinker* gave great displeasure to Almighty God, but the prosecution offered no proof of that, and, in any case, it was a matter for God to decide. The indictment also stipulated that he had published blasphemies "to the great scandal and reproach of the Christian religion." The evidence showed nothing of the sort, for no Christian offered testimony as to scandal and reproach; the prosecutor merely alleged it. Moreover, no one forced *Freethinker* on people who did not want it. It was published and sold by people who believed in it, for the benefit of others who also believed in it. The indictment also stipulated that the alleged blasphemies breached the queen's peace. No evidence whatever was offered to prove that, Foote declared, and he was accurate as to that too.[13]

Most of Foote's argument sought to prove that views similar to those expressed in his weekly could be found in works "by the leading writers of to-day." He read from Mill's *Autobiography* to show that James Mill had told his son that God was "the most perfect conception of wickedness which the human mind can devise." Foote also invoked T. H. Huxley and Matthew Arnold to prove that expensive books contained "the same kind of language" as his publication, but without incurring prosecutions for blasphemy. He elaborately defended ridicule as a form of argument, though it outraged some. Outraged feelings, he asserted, cut like a two-edged sword. No one but a freethinker was ever called on to consider the feelings of those who differed, and no one was ever prosecuted for offending the feelings of freethinkers.[14]

Foote also made some sophisticated points—for example, that if blasphemy was an offense it could only be an offense against the deity blasphemed, and it could be committed only by a believer in that deity. He emphasized the failure of prosecutions to achieve their desired effect. They had the opposite effect, of stimulating sales of the works stigmatized as blasphemous. His argument was too long and repetitive, but it was well reasoned. He made it over the frequent and hostile objections of Justice North.[15]

Ramsey defended himself in a brief yet strong speech. He reminded the jurors that blasphemy changed in meaning over time. Quakers were once deemed blasphemous, then Unitarians. Paine's works had been prosecuted, yet were now freely published and sold. Verdicts of blasphemy crippled free inquiry, he contended. The jury should not convict him for bad taste; that was for public opinion to decide. The prosecution sought to punish him as a criminal because his opinions and theology differed from the majority's, and his means of expressing himself offended. Yet he did not expose anyone to offensiveness, because no one bought and read his weekly except voluntarily.[16]

Justice North's charge to the jury was disgracefully biased and mistaken in its statement of the law of blasphemy. He laid down the law as it had existed when denial or ridicule of the doctrine of the Trinity was criminal. Blasphemy, he declared, was punishable because it strongly tended to subvert religion and morality and to interfere with the law itself—for which no proof existed. He clearly thought the evidence proved the prosecution's case. It was a hanging charge, concluding with the point that convicting the authors "of this infamous publication" would not violate freedom of the press, because "unbridled licence" was not entitled to protection.[17]

After the jury had deliberated for two hours, North brought them back into court to inquire whether they needed further clarification of the law. The foreman, to the judge's dismay, reported that the jury understood the law but was unalterably divided. North summarily discharged them, saying that he would try the case again before a different jury. He refused to allow bail for the defendants.[18]

On the Monday next, the second prosecution commenced. The courtroom was jammed, and the nearby streets were crowded with concerned people. The prosecution repeated its case, proving the connection between the defendants and the Christmas number of their weekly. Foote repeated his argument with some additions. He attacked the doctrine that Christianity was part of the law of the land: Jews and unbelievers now sat in the Commons, for instance. He demonstrated how Christian polemicists outraged the feelings of non-Christians and of one another. No one, whatever his religion, was called on to respect the feelings of anyone else; only freethinkers had to avoid expressions of outrage, insult, sarcasm, and hatred. He added to the list of intellectuals whose work differed little from his own yet who were not prosecuted, and he elaborated on the failure of the prosecution to show breach of peace. The Christmas number produced no tumult in the street, no disturbance of any kind. He even quoted from letters of Sir William Harcourt, to make the point that prosecutions for blasphemy were unwise and did more harm than good. For over three hours he spoke, often to the applause of the courtroom audience. But the jury, according to the report of the case, seemed inattentive.

After brief remarks by Ramsey, Judge North repeated his hanging charge. This time, the jury, obviously selected with greater care than the first one, did not even leave the box; after consulting "about two minutes," they found the defendants guilty. Spectators sympathetic to them burst "into a storm of hissing, groaning, and derisive cries." The judge cleared the courtroom, although the roar of the street crowd could still be heard. North then sentenced the prisoners. Foote had thought that if found guilty he would receive a token sentence. North sent him to prison for one year. He sentenced Ramsey to nine months and Kemp to three. Cattell, the bookseller who had been found guilty separately, was heavily fined.[19]

Public comment was decidedly hostile to the prosecution and the sentences. London's *Spectator* criticized the law for its ambiguity. Was it matter or manner that the law targeted? In either case, the law was repressive and unwise, because the press and taste should be free. When the law punished indecency or bad taste, it became a class weapon of the prosperous against the poor. The class that made and enforced the law had little sympathy for the different taste of the class that usually broke the law. No one prosecuted Matthew Arnold for his sarcasms against the Trinity in his *Literature and Dogma*. "It seems to us painfully clear that there must be something wrong in a law of blasphemy which punishes the vulgar man for saying in coarse language what it never thinks of punishing the refined man for saying in keen, sarcastic language." Punishing Foote for using a bludgeon, because he did not know how to use a rapier, was unjust.

Moreover, the law pretended to punish criminal intent or malice. Foote and men like him probably did not intend to outrage public opinion. Foul language from him was to be expected; it was a class matter. The status and education of a writer should be considered when determining his intent to insult public feeling; the malice was probably greater in a man of cultivated intellect. In any case, *Freethinker* had not been forced on anyone who did not wish to read it; finding malice seemed wrong.

If the law were applied equally to writers of all classes, that would be fairer but would return England to the days of widespread persecution of opinions in religious matters. The better policy was not to prosecute, or to impose a light sentence. Had North sentenced Foote to a fortnight's imprisonment, one might say that society was vindicated in making the point that the sacred feelings of the great majority should not be outraged.[20]

A week later, *The Spectator* editorialized again on "The Blasphemy Controversy" by speculating that the punishment of Foote, a sincere atheist, was really for his atheism as much as for his coarse expressions. If coarse ridicule was to be punished, fairness required that coarse attacks on "*any*body's faith are to be punished equally." Foote should be punished only if a Christian ridiculing "Mahommedanism or Mormonism" could be punished.[21] A time would come when that view, first proposed by John Stuart Mill, would become popular.

The Law Times of London claimed "there is probably no section of the nation which is not heartily convinced that the law which treats blasphemy as a criminal offence is a relic of bygone times which, having been forced into notice, must be totally destroyed." That was strong language from a stolid legal journal. The editors also criticized Judge North's biased conduct of the case.[22]

Similarly, some newspapers chided North for not being impartial in the best traditions of the English bench, while others castigated him for acting like an inquisitor. Bradlaugh's *National Reformer* published stenographic reports of the trials and numerous articles, letters, and press summaries about it.[23]

One long essay that was especially thoughtful, by a writer signing himself "M.A.," deplored *Freethinker*'s views and style but, after carefully analyzing the law of blasphemy, reluctantly concluded that *Freethinker* had to be endured as "part of the price which we must pay for free discussion." The writer lambasted English Liberals who convinced themselves that liberty of the press did not suffer from prosecutions supposedly directed only against ribaldry and ridicule of religion in the most indecent manner. To M.A., opinion in religious matters, as in all other matters, could not be free unless writers could express themselves as they pleased, however offensively. Like *The Spectator*, he saw a law that benefited the upper classes against the less privileged masses. He reminded readers that religious reformers used invective and ridicule; even Christ had done so against the orthodox of his time. Reform and strong language went together. Wisdom required that, however hateful was *Freethinker*, assuming it was also sincere, "it would be better to leave such people alone, and to trust the good sense of the public to condemn what was worthy of condemnation."[24]

Meanwhile, the law remorselessly if glacially pressed on with the prosecution of Bradlaugh, Foote, and the others, who had been indicted nine months before North sentenced the makers of the Christmas issue of *Freethinker*. At last, in April 1883, the case was tried by jury, before John Duke Coleridge, Pooley's prosecutor, now the lord chief justice of England, and as fair a judge as existed. Bradlaugh petitioned to be tried separately from Foote and the others. He asserted that, inasmuch as they already stood convicted of blasphemy, his case might be prejudiced if he were tried with them. Furthermore, he wished to call them as witnesses in his behalf. Giffard, the prosecutor, objected, but Coleridge ruled that Bradlaugh should be tried separately. His case came up before Foote's second trial.

Bradlaugh's defense was that he was not in any way responsible for *Freethinker*, and surely not for those issues charged with blasphemous libel: he had not been connected with that weekly since 1881. Giffard observed, though, that it was published by Bradlaugh's Freethought Publications Company in the same premises as Bradlaugh's *National Reformer*, in a building owned by Bradlaugh. Moreover, Ramsey, the present publisher of *Freethinker*, was an employee of Bradlaugh, who knew the character of the blasphemous paper. The testimony of Foote and Ramsey, as well as of Annie Besant, Bradlaugh's partner, proved that Bradlaugh had nothing to do with *Freethinker* or the issues condemned as blasphemous. He did not deny the blasphemy, only his liability for it.[25]

Charging the jury, Lord Coleridge declared that the case raised two questions: was Bradlaugh liable for the disputed issues of *Freethinker*, and were they blasphemous? The law on the first question clearly held that he must have distinctly authorized their publication, not that he might have prevented their publication or was morally responsible for them or was connected with the paper. On the second question, Coleridge declared that he disagreed with Justice North, who found blasphemous any publication that attacked any fundamental principles of Christianity and any discussion hostile to the divine inspiration of the Bible. That view of the law derived from the doctrine that Christianity was part of the law of the land. But, Coleridge reasoned, any part of the law of the land could be attacked, whether it was religion, the monarchy, primogeniture, or the laws of marriage.

The correct view of the matter had been described by Thomas Starkie in his treatise on libel law, in which he had said that anyone might publish his opinion on religious subjects, however foolishly or ignorantly, as long as he was honest and not acting maliciously. "The wilful intention to insult and mislead others by means of licentious and contumelious abuse offered to sacred subjects," Starkie stated, "is the criterion and test of guilt."[26] Thus, Coleridge concluded, blasphemy consisted only of language "intended to insult the feelings and the deepest religious convictions of the great majority of the persons amongst whom we live." He added, "We must not do things that are outrages" to the Christian majority.[27] In effect, Coleridge said that the judge in Pooley's case, his father, had been right. In saying so, he was casually changing the law of blasphemy. Two weeks later, when Foote and Ramsey were tried before him, he made the change explicit. In Bradlaugh's case, Coleridge's charge practically urged the jury to return a verdict of not guilty; the jury did that.[28]

The trial of Foote and Ramsey was a replay of the first Foote prosecution, in the sense that Giffard presented the prosecution and the defendants made their usual speeches. Foote admired his own oration so much he had it published separately under the title *Defence of Free Speech, Being a Three Hours' Address to the Jury in the Court of Queen's Bench before Lord Coleridge.*[29] In the preface, he praised Lord Coleridge's kindness and generosity, and he proudly declared that Coleridge had listened to him "with rapt attention" and told the jury it was a "very striking and able speech you have just heard." Foote cleverly contended that a writer could not know from the vague law of blasphemy whether he was guilty of the crime. Even his judges disagreed as to what constituted blasphemy. And Justice Stephen, he added, differed with both Justices North and Coleridge. Stephen thought that, except for cursing and swearing, blasphemy ought not be punished at all. The law of blasphemy, Foote insisted, meant that one's fate depended on who happened to be his judge and on the tastes of his jurors.[30] Foote was right.

Coleridge certainly made the difference at the second trial. Explaining the law of blasphemy, he declared that *Freethinker* would undoubtedly have been blasphemous "in old times," because of its aspersions on Christianity. But the old law could no longer be taken as "the law of the present day." Christianity was no longer the law of the land in the way that it had once been: a Jew might become lord chancellor. Accordingly, "to asperse the truth of Christianity cannot *per se* be sufficient to sustain a criminal prosecution for blasphemy." Candidly he acknowledged that "law grows" and must "be applied to the changing circumstances of the times." Nonbelief was not by itself criminal.

Starkie, he said again, had correctly explained the law as it now existed. He did not note that the Royal Commission on the Criminal Law of 1841, of which Starkie was a member, accepted Starkie's view, which was that, without malicious intent to insult others, blasphemy did not exist, but also endorsed the view that the matter, not the manner, was conclusive in any case involving denial of God's existence or the divine inspiration of the Bible.[31] Coleridge was not certain whether the law of blasphemy ought to exist, but it did in fact exist, he said, in the sense that he understood it. He reinterpreted leading precedents to make them conform to his understanding: not the matter or substance of what was said but the manner of saying it was the issue in a blasphemy case. "I now lay it down as law," he concluded, "that, if the decencies of controversy are observed, even the fundamentals of religion may be attacked without the writer being guilty of blasphemy."[32]

Thus did the lord chief justice modify the law of the land on blasphemy. In effect, he had abrogated the provision of the statute of 1698 which had made criminal the mere denial of God, however reverently or civilly stated. He also restructured the precedents and common law so that anything contrary to his new view was no longer good law. Malicious intent to insult, or the expression of uncivilized indecencies that offended, constituted the crime. The "decencies" of controversy to which Coleridge had referred meant that proprieties of expression should be observed. "Indecency" did not, however, refer to something obscene in a sexual or execrementary sense. To say that a blasphemer spoke indecently meant merely that he was bad-mannered or used strong language and that he was unnecessarily offensive in making a point. Yet Coleridge's expression about "the indecencies of controversy" was unfortunate and misleading. Thereafter, although "indecent" merely meant some language that a gentleman might not use, it carried the misleading implication of somewhat obscene or filthy language.

The law as Coleridge expounded it would become the law of blasphemy for over ninety years. (By 1978, intent had disappeared as an element of the crime.[33]) Without doubt, Coleridge liberalized the law of blasphemy by excluding from its ambit decent or temperate rejections of Christianity. Ironically, such rejections, based on serious or scholarly argument, subverted religion and shook beliefs far more than abusive insults, which were not likely to be convincing. Offensive language or manner became the mark of the crime. Coleridge apparently did not realize that manner and matter are not always distinguishable—indeed, that they can be closely related. Saying that Jesus was the illegitimate offspring of a passing Roman soldier is not much less offensive than calling him a "bastard" and his mother a "whore"—one of the conventional blasphemous statements. Coleridge also justified the prosecution of language that offended Christians but not the prosecution of language that offended non-Christians and nonbelievers. If indecent expression constituted the crime because it offended the feelings of Christians, indecent expression that offended the feelings of others seemed equally entitled to enjoy the protection of the law. Ridiculing a person's patriotism, savaging his race or national origins, or vilifying his Judaism or Hinduism, or even his atheism, might be as psychologically hurtful as scorning his Christianity. Indeed, members of minority groups stood more in need of the protection of their feelings than the members of the majority, who easily resorted to the law to punish those who abused them. In fact, as the history of blasphemy in Britain abundantly demonstrated, Christians attacked their enemies by prosecuting them; atheists could not attack Christians with impunity or resort to the courts when attacked by Christians. Coleridge failed to see many of the shortcomings of the law of blasphemy.

He was the sort of English Liberal whom "M.A.," the essayist in the *National Reformer*, had criticized for believing that the liberty of the press would be secure if only maliciously motivated expressions could be suppressed. M.A. contended that such Liberals did not realize that malice, insult, and offensiveness were subjective notions. The existence of malice was invariably inferred from the nature of a defendant's language; anyone shocked by that language would discover a malicious intent to offend. Coleridge's decency test, if enforced, would have convicted Luther, Calvin, and Fox, as well as Jesus.

Foote was right in contending that a writer's fate depended on the tolerance of his judge and jury. Indeed, he did not go far enough. Blasphemy was a unique crime in the sense that no one could know whether it had been committed until a jury rendered its verdict. With any other crime, the fact that the offense had been committed was never in doubt, only the culpability of the defendant. In the case of blasphemy, the defendant could be wholly unaware of his guilt until charged and convicted. In no other area of the criminal law did an acquittal mean that the offense had not been committed.

Foote was also right in claiming, as he did in his long defense of himself, that *Starkie on Libel* offered no security for a free press. Foote had quoted the same passage in Starkie as had Lord Coleridge and remarked: "I say it is not so, and that an overt act of crime is the broad boundary between right and wrong," not Starkie's or Coleridge's "malicious intention." "It seems to me," Foote added, "that Starkie's law of blasphemous libel is simply a noose round the neck of every man who writes or speaks on the subject of religion; and if he happens to be on the unpopular side, somebody will pull the string. . . ."[34]

In the case of Foote and Ramsey, however, Coleridge's law had the effect of producing a hung jury. The jurors deliberated "some hours" but could not agree on a verdict. Three members of the jury stubbornly held out against a conviction. Since the defendants had already been convicted of the crime in a previous trial, and securing another conviction had become more difficult because of Coleridge's new doctrine on blasphemy, the prosecution was dropped. *Freethinker*, which is still published, attained new circulation records in 1883, because of the notoriety attending the prosecutions. Bradlaugh's National Secular Society peaked too.[35]

The blasphemy prosecutions of 1883 touched off the most intense public debate on the subject that England had experienced. W. Blake Odgers, a legal scholar whose works included a treatise on libel law, delivered a paper on blasphemy before the National Association for the Promotion of Social Sciences. It received considerable attention and, despite its conservative slant, was reprinted in Bradlaugh's *National Reformer*.[36] Odgers asked whether the law of blasphemy needed to be amended. He defined the crime as "an outrage on men's religious feelings, tending to a breach of the peace." His review of the case law led him to conclude that all the publications that had been judged blasphemous contained offensive language. That allowed him to be content with the law, because it did not interfere with freedom of expression. Dissenters,

Unitarians, and Jews were protected in the advocacy of their doctrines, and punishment did not extend to any opinion sincerely held and temperately expressed. Lord Chief Justice Coleridge's charge to the jury in Foote's case, Odgers believed, had perfected the law of blasphemy. Coleridge had been most convincing on the crucial issue of "Matter v. Manner."

Justice James Fitzjames Stephen, Odgers recognized, had taken a different view, writing that "the true legal doctrine upon the subject is that blasphemy consists in the character of the matter published and not in the manner in which it is stated."[37] Odgers disagreed. He remarked that Stephen had earlier taken the view that both readings of the law were equally defensible; moreover, Stephen had presented the two views in parallel columns, noting, "There is authority for each."[38] Odgers read the same cases and believed that they taught that manner, not matter, made the difference in a blasphemy case. He therefore concluded that the law of blasphemy was not "harsh and illiberal as some have imagined." It did not obstruct the freest inquiry, because it allowed the frankest avowal of all opinions, "however heretical." The law interfered only "where our religious feelings are insulted and outraged by wanton and unnecessary profanity."[39]

In the discussion that followed among those who heard Odgers deliver his paper, opinion was mixed. Some thought the law of blasphemy should be abolished, either because it was too vague or indefinite, or because it was really a law against heresy, or because it led to unintended consequences. One speaker, for example, observed that *Freethinker's* circulation increased fivefold on the punishment of its editor and publisher. Others believed that Odgers and Coleridge were right. The president of the society, William Barber, Q.C., agreed with Odgers and urged support of a recommendation to amend the criminal law by an act that would exempt a person from prosecution for simply expressing a sincere opinion "in decent language," but would subject anyone to prosecution for reviling religion with an intent to offend others.[40] Odgers supported the same recommendation in another article on blasphemy.[41] An essay in *The Fortnightly Review* similarly praised Coleridge's interpretation of the law and criticized Stephen's.[42]

The lead essay in *The Westminster Review*, by an anonymous author who focused on the question whether manner or matter was the crucial factor, came to very different conclusions. Reviewing the case law, the author confidently declared that matter, as Stephen had indicated, was the crucial factor in the law of blasphemy. In practice, the writer conceded, the modern cases reached only indecent and outrageous expression. But the law itself clearly proscribed certain substantive remarks about Christianity, regardless of how decently expressed they were. That brought the writer to ask what should be done about the situation. Two possibilities existed, he thought. A statute might be enacted limiting blasphemy to words that insulted religion, or the law of blasphemy should be altogether abolished.[43]

The "great principle of religious equality" demanded that, if insult to religion should be punished criminally, every religion should be equally protected, without exception. The difficulty, however, was that such a proposal was not feasible. It was impossible to carry into effect, not simply because the law could not be so burdened with prosecutions, but because the religious feelings of some conflicted with those of others. The law could not protect and prosecute both. Moreover, no way existed to distinguish between legitimate argument and "insult." The only alternative, therefore, was abolition of the law of blasphemy. It had done no good, anyway; it did not really help religion or destroy irreligion. Rather, it brought Christianity into contempt.

Dr. Nathaniel Lardner had been right, the essayist claimed, when he had argued, in Woolston's time, that if men are allowed to write against the Christian religion "there must also be considerable allowance as to the manner likewise." The best way to treat scurrility was to scorn it, the essayist believed. He condemned outrageous, insulting attacks on the religious opinions of others, but would not treat breaches of good taste as criminal. Besides, one man's insult was another's good-faith opinion. Feelings were too personal to be the test of criminality. "After all," he concluded, "nobody need look at these 'blasphemous' publications unless he chooses."[44]

In *The Fortnightly Review* in early 1884, Justice Stephen defended himself against his critics and elaborated on the view, expressed in passing in his 1883 history, that the matter, not the manner, was the crucial factor in the law of blasphemy.[45] On reviewing the case law once again and savaging Starkie's presentation, Stephen insisted that Blackstone, not Starkie, had accurately described the law of blasphemy: it is blasphemy to deny God's being or providence, or to say anything contemptuous about Jesus Christ. Matter, not manner, was the law's target, regardless of whether actual prosecutions involved coarse expression.

"No one can dislike the law," Stephen wrote, "more profoundly than I do," and no one thought it more unfit for an age of freedom. The failure of the jury to convict in Foote's case showed that Coleridge's view of the law did not work. The "decencies of controversy" could not possibly have been violated more brutally than by *Freethinker*. Yet a jury might properly be influenced by the argument that, if society allowed coarse and vulgar people to discuss religion freely, they would express themselves insultingly to others. "You cannot really distinguish between substance and style," Stephen wrote. "You must either forbid or permit all attacks on Christianity. You cannot in practice send a man to gaol for not writing like a scholar and a gentleman when he is neither one nor the other, and when he is writing on a subject which excites him strongly."

Stephen instanced the case of Voltaire, who had written a play entitled *David*. No judge could apply Coleridge's view of the law should that play be prosecuted. The judge would have to inform the jury that the law permitted one to say that David "was a murderer, an adulterer, a treacherous tyrant who passed his last moments in giving directions for assassinations," but the judge must also say that the decencies of controversy must be observed. The crown would never have prosecuted Voltaire's publisher, however, so that the law would be enforced with "unequal justice, which is much the same as injustice."[46]

Stephen believed that equal justice also required the protection of all religions, not just the Church of England or all Christian denominations. He wondered, though, whether the law could prevent Protestants and Catholics from insulting one another, or Christians from insulting Muslims. Insult, he believed, was inherent in religious as well as in political controversy. "Heat, exaggeration, and fierce invective" characterized the history of Christianity and religion.

A wholly different consideration led him to believe that the law of blasphemy could be explained only by "its true principle—the principle of persecution." It persecuted unbelievers. If the law were impartial, it would also protect *their* feelings from Christians' insults. Yet no act of Parliament that punished the Salvation Army or the Methodists for their opinions of freethinkers could be enforced. Preachers of all sorts would defy it. The Gospel, after all, was not meant to please sinners but to terrify them. Christians were not true to themselves if they observed the decencies of controversy.

Yet, Stephen observed, the same sort of arguments might be used against Christians. If there is no hell and no God, and if Christianity is false, as freethinkers believed, no reason existed for attacks on Christianity to be expressed only in polite language. The reality, however, was that the law imposed no restraints on Christians, however offensive their views to those who rejected them, because, Stephen claimed, the law "is based on the principle that Christianity is true, and is to be protected against attacks. And this is persecution."[47]

Stephen concluded that the best solution to the problem was for Parliament to repeal its laws against blasphemy and to enact that blasphemy no longer was a common-law offense. That would secure "complete liberty of opinion" in matters of religion and prevent the irregular intervals of scandalous prosecutions that did no good, least of all for the cause they were intended to serve. Alternatively, Parliament should enact Coleridge's doctrine into law, making it apply equally to all opinions concerning religion, and should permit only the top crown officers to institute blasphemy proceedings.[48]

Stephen's essay touched off another round of articles on the subject. One lawyer ably supported Stephen, and another as ably criticized his views and endorsed those of Coleridge.[49] No one added anything fresh to the discussion. But a movement began to bring blasphemy prosecutions to an end. In 1883, following the Bradlaugh and Foote prosecutions, the Reverend William Sharman, a Unitarian minister, had formed an Association for the Repeal of the Blasphemy Laws. Religious radicals joined with political radicals, most of them supporters of the programs championed in the pages of Bradlaugh's *National Reformer*. The new association crowded the great St. James Hall "to suffocation" at a meeting to demand repeal and the release of Foote and Ramsey.[50] In 1886, a new member of Parliament, Professor Courtney Kenny of Cambridge University, introduced a bill "to abolish Prosecutions against Laymen for the Expression of Opinion on Matters of Religion." The bill had been proposed initially by Justice Stephen in an article he had published in *The Contemporary Review* in 1875, where the idea languished until Kenny resurrected it. The bill provided that no criminal proceedings should be begun under statute or common law for atheism, heresy, schism, or blasphemy, spoken or published.[51] *The Spectator* accurately predicted that the government would not find the time to discuss the bill, and the editors added that the bill deserved the fate of being ignored. Like Odgers and Coleridge, *The Spectator* believed that England enjoyed the utmost freedom of expression in matters of religion. Abolishing the blasphemy laws would simply disable society from protecting itself against hateful outrages against religion. *The Spectator* supported a bill that would incorporate Coleridge's decency test.[52]

Kenny introduced such a bill in 1887, exempting from blasphemy prosecutions any publications on religion expressed in good faith without intent to insult. The bill protected all religions against insult, by providing that the intentional wounding of the religious feelings of any person by word, gesture, or exhibit constituted a misdemeanor punishable by up to one year's imprisonment. Stephen had suggested such a bill in his 1884 essay.

The idea went back to a speech by Lord Macaulay during the debate in 1833 on a bill to abolish civil disabilities on Jews. An opponent of the bill declared that a Jew might become a judge and sit on a prosecution for blasphemy of Christianity. "It has been said," Macaulay replied, "that it would be monstrous to see a Jew judge try a man for blasphemy. In my opinion it is monstrous to see any judge try a man for blasphemy under the present law. . . . Every man, I think, ought to be at liberty to discuss the evidences of religion." He would not prosecute the most blasphemous work if it had been sold to one willing to buy it, but he did not believe in a liberty to force on an unwilling audience anything intentionally offensive. If a book dealer displayed a "hideous caricature" of an object of reverence by almost all passersby, or if a person publicly applied opprobrious epithets to those who were religiously venerated, severe punishment should be the response. Liberty should not be used to outrage the feelings of others, Macaulay believed. Were he a judge in India, he said, he would "have no scruple about punishing a Christian who should pollute a mosque." He became a legislator in India and framed a blasphemy act that imposed a year's imprisonment for any word, gesture, or sound deliberately intended to wound another person's religious feelings.[53] Stephen had popularized this provision in the Indian Penal Code on blasphemy, protecting any religion. It did little to defuse the expression of hatreds between Muslims and Hindus and, if it had become law in Britain, would have likely set Christian sects there against one another in the courts. Secularists generally opposed the bill protecting all religions, because their atheistic beliefs did not seem to come within its provisions. They preferred the outright abolition of all blasphemy laws, not their liberalization or extension. More significantly, the public seemed apathetic to any measure, nor could Parliament be aroused.[54]

Bradlaugh, who had been sworn in as a member of the House of Commons in 1886, offered his own outright repeal bill in 1889, based on the original version by Stephen but without the so-called Indian clause protecting everyone's religious feelings. That left Christians without legal recourse if blasphemers verbally assaulted them. Accordingly, when Bradlaugh's bill came to a vote, it lost by nearly three to one.[55] In 1894, a similar bill was proposed. A writer in *The Westminster Review* discoursed on the need to enact it, in an article on "Intellectual Liberty and the Blasphemy Laws," yet did not move the members of Parliament. The bill failed to get beyond its first reading.[56]

But prosecutions for blasphemy ceased in the nineteenth century. Atheists and secularists who got into trouble with the law after Foote's conviction were prosecuted for obscenity, not blasphemy, in connection with dissemination of birth-control literature. *Freethinker* has continued publication without a break—even to this day. In effect, Coleridge was right in saying that opinion in religious matters was free. The law as he construed it remained a loaded pistol, but it did not fire for a generation.

CHAPTER TWENTY-THREE

The Age of John W. Gott

I N 1912, *The Literary Guide*, a secularist publication, asserted that "we
have had more prosecutions for blasphemy during the past twelve
months than for the previous fifty years, and more prosecutions for spoken blasphemy during the past five years than in the whole of the previous hundred years."[1] However, few of the cases were memorable, and
none occasioned an argument or idea that significantly contributed to the
principle of freedom of opinion on religious matters or to intellectual
liberty in general.

After the 1883 cases of Foote, Kemp, and Ramsey, blasphemy prosecutions died out for twenty years. But in 1903 the police in Leeds,
probably prompted by clergymen, initiated prosecutions against John
William Gott, George Weir, and Ernest Pack. The three men proclaimed themselves to be atheists and socialists. Gott, a clothier from
Bradford in Yorkshire, was editor of *The Truthseeker*, a radical monthly
that he had founded in 1894 as the voice of the Freethought Socialist
League. The other two also wrote for the magazine, which was scurrilously antireligious. In 1903, *The Truthseeker* republished a notorious
cartoon, lifted from *Freethinker*, purporting to depict God showing His
rear end to the devil. The radicals also launched open-air meetings in
Leeds, antagonizing the city police, who regarded them as public men-
aces deserving imprisonment. However, the local judge disapproved of
the prosecution, which reeked of irregularities. Pack was fined only 3
shillings for his blasphemy, and the cases against Gott and Weir were
dropped.[2]

In 1908, a London street lecturer named Harry Boulter was convicted
for blasphemous remarks, on the complaint of a clergyman, but the court
dismissed Boulter on his promise to behave. The judge, Sir Robert Phillimore of King's Bench, delivered a learned charge on the subject of the
common law of blasphemy, endorsing the decency test of Lord Chief

Justice Coleridge in the case of Foote and Ramsey. When Boulter broke
his pledge and voiced his sentiments on Christianity, he was rearrested
and imprisoned for one month. In 1911, the prosecutions in Leeds were
revived, not because of the dangerous views of the radicals, said Ernest
Pack, but because their endeavors flourished. "So," he wrote, "the parsons and police conspired together to stay our propaganda." Thomas W.
Stewart and Gott were the main victims.[3]

Stewart's crime consisted in a sarcastic speech that attracted nearly a
thousand people, in which he depicted clean-living atheists being sent to
hell on Judgment Day, while murderers who acknowledged their faith in
God, Christ, and the Bible were admitted to heaven. Stewart also claimed
that the Bible showed God to be guilty of obscenities and cruelties;
therefore, He "was not a fit companion for a respectable man like me."
Stewart was summarily convicted and sentenced to three months' imprisonment for his blasphemy.

Gott's crime consisted of selling an anticlerical pamphlet at Stewart's
public meeting. The pamphlet, *Rib Ticklers or Questions for Parsons*, listed
dozens of puerile one-liners, such as: "Is it true that the Lord strikes
churches with lightning as a warning to Freethinkers not to enter therein?
. . . [Is it true] that when David saw Bathsheba bathing herself he thought
he would like to bath Sheba?" Such tame stuff hardly merited notice, but
as the editor of *The Truthseeker*, Gott was targeted for prosecution. He was
an advocate of birth control and seemed, to conservatives, to be vulgar
and obscene as well as blasphemous.[4]

He openly boasted of selling other atheist pamphlets, such as *Christ,
the Greatest Enemy of the Human Race* and *The Bible: Its Horrors and Imbe-
cilities*. He defended himself by arguing that he had been selling such stuff
for many years, only at socialist and atheist meetings. He claimed too that
a person who did not believe in God could not be guilty of blasphemy.
Gott also quoted leading freethinkers, including John Stuart Mill and
George Bernard Shaw. Shaw had claimed that the Gospels were fictions,
that Jesus was fictitious, and that the "blackest spot in English public life
is the cowardly dishonour in which our public men leave the Blasphemy
Laws unrepealed. . . ." Although Gott asked the jury to "strike a decisive
blow in the interests of freedom of speech and an unfettered press," the
jury returned a verdict of guilty without leaving the jury box. Gott
received a sentence of four months.[5]

The Stewart and Gott cases stirred a sensation. Labour M.P.'s protested the prosecutions, and hundreds of intellectuals denounced the law
of blasphemy and petitioned the home secretary for the release of the
prisoners. The petitioners included Arthur Conan Doyle, Israel Zan-
gwill, George Moore, G. K. Chesterton, Havelock Ellis, John Galswor-
thy, G. E. Moore, George Bernard Shaw, G. M. Trevelyan, A. E.

Housman, and H. Granville-Barker. Their petitions failed, as did efforts to repeal blasphemy laws.[6]

Hypatia Bradlaugh Bonner, Charles Bradlaugh's daughter and a leading freethinker, in a tract on *Penalties Upon Opinion*, believed that the blasphemers were punished because of their anti-Christian beliefs, not because they intemperately insulted Christians. That is, she accepted James Fitzjames Stephen's view that the matter, not the manner, constituted the crime. Offensiveness, she objected, was mere pretense, because it was a crime only when it related to Christianity, not when scurrilous insults were heaped upon freethinkers. "What exactly is the charge in the recent blasphemy cases," she asked, "and for what are the men imprisoned"—for vulgarity or blasphemy? If for vulgarity, they should have been indicted for it. "They ought not to be indicted for blasphemy, and then have it pretended to the world that they are punished not for the blasphemous opinions they hold, but for the vulgarity with which they expressed them." Nor should they be imprisoned for vulgarity when others equally coarse and offensive remained free.[7]

The numerous cases of the time were humdrum, repetitive affairs, despite the angry denunciations by opponents of blasphemy prosecutions. None of the cases were interesting until the 1914 prosecution of Thomas W. Stewart. On cross-examination, Stewart declared that he had been prosecuted "about twenty times for blasphemy." That surely constituted an individual record, albeit an exaggerated one. His 1914 case attracts attention for a few reasons. One is that it led to a recommendation by the prime minister and the attorney general that Parliament abolish its blasphemy statutes. Since all prosecutions had been based on the common law of blasphemy, rather than statutory law, the great fuss about repeal, which failed anyway, seems like a clamor without meaning. Another reason the 1914 prosecution of Stewart is arresting is that a third-generation justice, John Coleridge, tried the case.[8]

Stewart was charged with blasphemy for having attacked the truths of Christianity by ribaldry and indecency. The prosecution relied especially on statements that "the whole Christian religion is a lie," that Jesus said lies that a parrot could be trained to say, and that nobody "outside a lunatic asylum" believed that "Jesus saved the world."[9]

Justice Coleridge accepted the law as his grandfather and father had defined it. That Mohammedanism and Judaism could be attacked in the most blasphemous language he called "a curious thing," but the law was the law. It protected freedom of expression because its penal sanction applied only to attacks on Christianity that were indecently expressed or intended to outrage the faith of believers. If Stewart had asserted the truth as he understood it, even if vulgarly, the jury should acquit; but if they believed that he spoke to scandalize Christianity and insult the

faithful, he was guilty of blasphemy. The jury quickly returned a verdict
of guilty. When sentencing Stewart to four months' imprisonment, Coleridge said he was being "lenient" even though Stewart had used the most
coarse and distasteful language the judge had ever heard.[10] His life must
have been highly sheltered.

The Stewart case produced an uproar of protest and renewed efforts
to nullify blasphemy laws. Petitions swamped the Home Office and the
Commons. The press and intellectuals commented adversely on the re-
vival of blasphemy law. *The Nation and Athenaeum* alleged that indecency
could be prosecuted without needing to protect Christians from being
scandalized, and added that the only religion that the law of blasphemy
really protected was that of the established church. Gilbert Murray, the
great Oxford classicist, eloquently favored unfettered speech on the subject of religion; he keelhauled Home Secretary Reginald McKenna, who
refused to release Stewart or commute his sentence. Murray also attacked
Coleridge for leading the jury to believe that it must decide whether
Stewart spoke honestly or intended to outrage Christian feelings, when in
likelihood he meant to do both. W. M. Geldart, a professor of law at
Oxford, noted with regret that the recrudescence of blasphemy prosecutions showed that officials, especially the police, believed that the public
viewed with favor their opposition to free speech.[11]

The London *Times* printed petitions and letters for repeal of the blasphemy laws. So did the Manchester *Guardian*, which led the opposition
to those laws in the respectable (nonatheist) press. The belief that no
person should ever be punished for his opinions received considerable
support. The bishop of London, no less, favored abrogation of the blasphemy laws. He declared, "In the first place, they savour of religious
persecution, and seem to limit freedom of speech. Christianity can endure and survive abuse; it ceases to be of Christ so soon as it begins to
persecute and retaliate." He added that only his own church actually
received the protection of blasphemy laws, even though its doctrines
needed no such aid.[12]

Even Prime Minister Herbert Asquith, supported by Attorney General John Simon, urged repeal of the statutory offense of blasphemy. In
a formal memorandum on blasphemy, Simon concluded that Parliament
should provide that, in the absence of obscenity, no language should be
found blasphemous if intended in good faith. The slipperiness of that
view can be judged from the fact that Simon believed that Stewart's
"attack on orthodoxy was not bona fide."[13] To a delegation seeking
repeal, Asquith, who had supported Bradlaugh's abrogation bill of
1889, declared that the offense of blasphemy should disappear entirely.
He favored punishing only such language, religious or otherwise, that
was reasonably calculated to create a breach of peace. But the govern-

ment did little to persuade Parliament to abolish its own blasphemy laws, let alone supersede the common law. Geldart was very likely correct: despite the outcry by publicists, the public supported imprisonment of blasphemers.[14]

In 1917, in the case of *Bowman* v. *Secular Society Ltd.*, the high-court justices in the House of Lords, constituting England's supreme appellate court, handed down a decision that removed the civil disabilities from persons regarded as blasphemers. More accurately, the justices held that an atheistic society may receive a bequest whose purpose is to promote anti-Christian beliefs. To reach such a decision, the high court ruled that the decency test announced in 1883 by Lord Chief Justice Coleridge correctly stated the law of blasphemy. The 1917 decision definitively adopted that test, which Coleridge had announced in a charge to the jury in the case of Foote and Ramsey. Yet, because *Bowman* was a civil case, commentators in the law journals continued to debate whether judges were bound by the decency test in a criminal prosecution.[15]

In civil matters, however, the decision had an emancipating effect by overruling a line of cases beginning in 1754 that made void or voidable any legal instrument, such as a will, bequest, deed, contract, guardianship, copyright, or trust, if it promoted blasphemy or irreligion. In that 1754 case, Lord Chancellor Hardwicke held that a legacy for the maintenance of a yeshiva, or academy, for the reading of Jewish law and for the propagation of Judaism was illegal, because Judaism, by rejecting Jesus Christ as Saviour, rejected Christianity, which was "part of the law of England."[16] Similarly, Lord Chancellor Eldon ruled in 1819 that Jewish children had no right to participate in a town trust for the benefit of schoolchildren. The trust, dating back to the sixteenth century, made no reference to religion. However, Eldon declared that the town grammar school propagated Christianity, which was part of the law of England, thereby excluding Jews.[17]

Unitarians suffered from the same sort of intolerance. Eldon ruled that, when a trust had been established in the early eighteenth century to create a church for "the use of Protestant Dissenters," Unitarians, who rejected the divinity of Christ, could not have been included. In 1813, four years before Eldon's ruling, Parliament granted to Unitarians the same toleration enjoyed by other dissenters, but that statute, Eldon held, was irrelevant with respect to the civil rights of Unitarians, because the statute merely exempted them from the criminal penalties that the Blasphemy Act of 1698 had applied to their doctrines. Eldon declared that "the Common Law is left by the statute [of 1813] exactly as it was before the statute passed." The judicial doctrine was that a trust could not be held for a use that would have been illegal at the time of its establishment. Accordingly, a chapel that had been Unitarian for generations reverted to

Trinitarian possession.[18] As a result of this case, the title of Unitarian properties was put in jeopardy. In 1842, a judicial decree ended decades of controversy over the control of a rich endowment called Lady Hewley's Charity. The court held that the eighteenth-century bequest for the benefit of "godly preachers of Christ's holy Gospel" excluded Unitarians. That immediately threatened the title of extensive Unitarian properties, including over two hundred chapels once Trinitarian. An 1844 act of Parliament provided legislative relief for property titles that had been held for over twenty-five years.[19]

Persons regarded as blasphemers had no recourse to law. Thus, their work could not be copyrighted. In one case, a literary pirate profited from publishing a physician's lectures and prevented his obtaining injunctive relief on the ground that passages in his lectures showed hostility to revealed religion and denied the immortality of the soul. Eldon supposed that such views conflicted with the Bible.[20] Similarly, Shelley's *Queen Mab* and Lord Byron's *Cain* failed to receive copyright protection because they seemed blasphemous.[21] For the same reason, Shelley lost custody of his children.[22] Annie Besant, the prominent atheist associated with Charles Bradlaugh, lost custody of her daughter because of similar judicial intolerance.[23]

Briggs v. *Hartley*, decided in 1850, was a leading case on the civil disabilities imposed on persons regarded as blasphemers. Vice-Chancellor Shadwell invalidated a legacy left for the best essay on the "subject of Natural Theology, treating it as a Science." Shadwell reasoned, "I cannot conceive that it is at all consistent with Christianity."[24] *Cowan* v. *Milbourn*, an 1867 case on breach of contract, was probably the leading precedent. Milbourn rented a hall to Cowan for the purpose of lectures but canceled the contract on learning that they would be hostile to Christianity and the Bible. An advertisement promised that they would seek to prove that Christ's character was "defective," his teachings "misleading," and the Bible not divinely inspired. Lord Chief Baron Kelly of the Court of Exchequer reasoned that, because there "is abundant authority for saying that Christianity is part and parcel of the law of the land," the proposed lectures could not be delivered "without blasphemy." Given that the lectures were never delivered, the judgment that they would be blasphemous showed that the subject matter, not the manner of delivery, governed the court's understanding.[25]

As a matter of fact, no indecency or reviling or ribaldry featured in any of the cases in which civil disabilities were imposed on supposed blasphemers. Mere conflict with Christianity sufficed to justify depriving individuals of their contractual, custodial, copyright, or other entitlements. Simple opposition or denial, not abusiveness of language, or intent to insult, or breach of peace, resulted in deprivation of equal rights.

If Coleridge's decency test prevailed in criminal cases, these civil cases showed that language which was legal at criminal law or could not be prosecuted was nevertheless illegal civilly. If, on the other hand, these civil precedents constituted the law, Coleridge's decency test made little sense.

Bowman v. *Secular Society, Ltd.*, in 1917, altered all that. The justices, voting four to one, endorsed the decency test and concluded that language that was not criminally liable imposed no civil liability either. They decided that the fortune bequeathed to the atheistic society for the propagation of its views violated no law, because no evidence showed intemperance or vilification in expression. The society's objectives were to promote secularization, ban religious tests, exclude religious teaching from public schools, promote marriage as a purely civil contract, abolish Sunday laws and blasphemy laws, and "do all such other lawful things as are conducive or incidental" to the attainment of its objectives. The justices repudiated the notion that a civil denial of Christian beliefs constituted blasphemy or rendered the society incapable of acquiring property.

To reach such a conclusion, the court had to overrule *Briggs* v. *Hartley* and *Cowan* v. *Milbourn*. It also had to explain that Christianity was part of the law of the land in the sense that England was a Christian country, but not in the sense that a denial of Christianity exposed one to criminal or civil penalties, unless that denial was scurrilous or breached the peace because of its offensiveness. Lord Buckmaster insisted that the common law of England knew of no prosecution for mere opinions and that a society for the propagation of anti-Christian opinions was not illegal *per se*. Lord Sumner noted that opinions once regarded as unlawful had become lawful as the nation matured and became more secure, and that, as a result, reasonable men no longer apprehended "the dissolution or the downfall of society because religion is publicly assailed by methods not scandalous." The law changed, he asserted, as conditions did, "experience having proved dangers once thought real to be now negligible."[26] None of the justices considered whether abusive language that was calculated to offend justified apprehensions that religion or society faced extinction or any danger.

That the decency test did not strike the fetters from blasphemers was indicated by John W. Gott's further troubles with the law. Gott was as cantankerous an atheist as his friend Thomas W. Stewart. Like Stewart, Gott had multiple fracases with the law, for profanity, obstruction, obscenity, and other offenses as well as blasphemy. His most serious offense occurred in 1921, when he was convicted at Old Bailey, for the fourth time, for selling *Rib Ticklers* and for comparing Jesus to a circus clown because he rode into Jerusalem on the back of two donkeys, as depicted in Matthew 21:2–10. Justice Avory's summation encouraged a Christian

jury to convict. He failed to instruct them that the accused was entitled
to the benefit of any doubt, and he made doubt unlikely because of two
rules that he laid down. The first was that the jury should find Gott
guilty if they believed that his pamphlet was calculated to outrage believers and so provoke a possible breach of the peace. The breach, he
ruled, need not occur; it need merely be possible if a Christian might have
"the instinct to thrash" the author (although the most severe reaction
according to the evidence consisted of comments of "shame" and "disgusting"). Second, Avory referred to language calculated not only to
outrage the feelings of the community generally, but also to offend persons of "strong religious feelings." That test would make convictions
easy. Avory sentenced Gott to nine months at hard labor, the most severe
sentence for blasphemy since 1883.[27]

When the case was appealed to the highest court, the lord chief justice
ruled that, notwithstanding Gott's poor health and his promise to cease
both the publication and sale of *Rib Ticklers*, he could not be bailed out
pending appeal, because he was "dangerous." Unanimously, the court
sustained Avory. It declared that Gott's pamphlet was offensive enough
for even a mere sympathizer with Christianity, not just a strong Christian, to be provoked to breach of the peace. The bad tendency of the
language warranted a belief that a breach of the peace might have occurred, even if it did not and there had been no threat of it. The chief
justice thought that nine months was not excessive in the case of a person
who, given his three prior convictions for blasphemy, knew what he was
doing. Gott served his time and died immediately after.[28]

Solicitors' Journal chided the chief justice for exaggerating the danger-
ousness of the offense of blasphemy, especially because so much doubt
existed as to what constituted the offense. The Coleridge decency test,
which stressed manner rather than matter, left open the question whether
the manner offended good taste or threatened breach of the peace. The
journal maintained that good taste was none of the law's business. Bad
manners justified prosecution only if tending to cause a breach of the
peace. "That requires that the evidence should show that there was in fact
a danger of the public peace being disturbed, and we do not notice that
this evidence was given in the case in question."[29] The journal might have
added that no blasphemy prosecution had ever shown an actual breach of
the peace, or even imminent danger of such a breach. Moreover, if the
threat of a breach of the peace was the law's concern, outraging an
atheist's opinion, or a Catholic's, or a Jew's might provoke the breach, yet
the law of blasphemy concerned itself with breach of the peace only in
defense of Protestantism, if not just the Church of England.

Edward Shortt, the home secretary who had refused to pardon or
release Gott, claimed in 1922 that no repeal of the blasphemy laws was

necessary. The common law, he argued, made punishable only statements intended to insult or abuse the religious beliefs of most people. Accordingly, the common law "does not interfere with free expression of bona fide opinion." Presumably, freethinkers could not seriously and sincerely believe Christian beliefs to be impossible or ridiculous, and freethinkers had no feelings warranting respect. In any case, Shortt believed that Coleridge's decency test provided all the freedom that should exist. He understood that, although the act of 1698 threatened freedom of expression in the abstract, it was in effect a dead letter. *The Law Times of London* remarked on "the curious conservatism of English legislators, who have continually preferred to allow a bad or unpopular law to remain on the Statute Book and to become dormant rather than to repeal it."[30]

Chapman Cohen refused to acknowledge defeat. He was George William Foote's successor as the editor of *Freethinker* and as president of the National Secular Society. A tireless agitator, he continued to write and speak against prosecutions for blasphemy. In 1922, in the wake of Gott's case, Cohen published a little tract, *Blasphemy: A Plea for Religious Equality*. Because he did not argue that atheism was a form of religion, his choice of a subtitle was misleading. His plea, however, was for equality for all expression on matters of religion, and he made worthwhile points, edged in irony and bitterness. Blasphemy, he said, was a crime so vague in nature that no one could be sure of having committed it until a jury returned a verdict of guilty. The crime had become the use of immoderate language in controversy over religion, and the law of blasphemy had become a method of educating people in the use of sober language. Indecent or intemperate language in politics or any subject other than religion could not be the basis for a criminal prosecution. Even in matters of religious opinion, ribaldry, ridicule, and contumelious reproach had the protection of law unless used against Christianity, giving Christianity a measure of protection afforded nothing else.

Repudiating Coleridge's decency test, Cohen contended that no Christian would agree that a tribunal of Muslims should decide whether Christians spoke decently about Mohammedanism. "Blasphemy is an offence constructed by Christians, the law is administered by Christians. It is Christians who define its scope and determine its penalties. No one but a Christian has any standing—except in the dock." Christians would not even trust their liberty to one another, for no Catholic would wish a verdict about his religious opinions to be determined by a jury of Protestants, and no Protestant would wish to have a jury decide whether he had treated Catholicism with becoming respect. No Christian beliefs were protected except when shared in common with the established religion of the nation. Therefore, to justify blasphemy laws on the ground that they protected people's feelings ignored the fact that the feelings of

many, especially of freethinkers, were unprotected against indecent verbal assaults.

Cohen drew from this the proposition that the question of offended
feelings was irrelevant. He invoked James Fitzjames Stephen to support
his view that matter, not manner, constituted the real offense. The Christian views of the Church of England, he said in effect, received special
protection in blasphemy prosecutions, although blasphemy was an offense that could not, in Cohen's opinion, be committed by anyone except
a believer: "How," he asked, "can a man speak disrespectfully of something which he honestly believes does not exist?" Moreover, he concluded, the blasphemy of an atheist "can do one no real harm," because
it "cannot really affect the fact of God's existence or the truth of Christian
doctrines."[31] In effect, Cohen made a strong argument, in American
terms, against the laws of blasphemy because they violated the principle
of the equal protection of the laws. In England, however, the argument
made no sense, precisely because the Church of England was not equal
under the law: it was, rather, established by law and preferred above all
others.

The movement for repeal of the blasphemy laws continued in a des-
ultory fashion. In 1927, an attempt to abrogate the old statute of 1698 and
replace it with the decency test's tighter definition of blasphemy almost
succeeded, although the Society for the Abolition of Blasphemy Laws
opposed the measure. "What would be suitable language in Whitechapel
[a slum] might be unsuitable in Mayfair [upper class]," the society contended. Moreover, an intellectual could use deadly sarcasm or scathing
ridicule and escape the law. A poor, uneducated man would be victimized by it. The society observed that the proposed bill discriminated in
still another way. It offered no protection for the religious feelings of
Jews, Mohammedans, or even Roman Catholics on practices like the
Mass that did not conform with those of the established church. Despite
that opposition, a bill that passed its second reading defined blasphemy as
the verbal crime of bringing Christianity into contempt by ribald, scurrilous, or contumelious language taught or distributed to children aged
sixteen or less. The Conservative government of Stanley Baldwin was too
busy with its program to bring the bill to its final reading, so it died in
committee.[32] Without doubt, public opinion had become aware of the
injustice and repression that actual prosecutions had engendered. But
opponents of such prosecutions did not know how to settle for half a loaf
any more than party whips cared to find time for a bill restricting blasphemy laws.

In 1930, when Labour was in power again, the chance for repeal of the
blasphemy laws seemed bright. Bradlaugh's abrogation bill of 1889 was
revived and actually passed a second reading by a large majority. At that

point, traditionalists became alarmed. Sir Frederick Pollock, the great legal historian, wrote a letter to the London *Times* in which he recommended adoption of a bill comparable to the provision of the Indian Penal Code that criminalized insulting words or gestures used "with deliberate intention of wounding the religious feelings of any person." Pollock argued that such a provision found a midpoint between fair controversy and wanton insult. It liberalized the law of blasphemy by adopting the decency test, to replace the Blasphemy Act of 1698, and it extended the law's protection impartially to all religions.[33]

Wanton insult was precisely what traditionalists feared if the Bradlaugh bill passed. Home Secretary Clynes declared that, if it passed, "the most offensive utterances, calculated to hurt the feelings of a large number of people, would not be punishable at law even if such utterances were likely to provoke a breach of the peace." To Clynes, the bill seemed to offer immunity to the most abusive blasphemy imaginable. *The Law Times*, noting that "real danger," editorialized that experience had shown the need for protection from indecent and offensive attacks. The young and the ignorant particularly stood in need of protection.[34]

As a result of such fears, the government offered an amendment to the bill, based on the Indian Penal Code, thus preserving prosecutions for words "outraging" the religious convictions of any person of any faith. *The Law Times* seemed to approve of the protection extended by the government's amendment to Judaism and Islam, but, noting the amendment's lack of a definition of religion, asked, "what is to be said of so-called crank religions such as Spiritualism and Christian Science?" The editors believed that the status quo was preferable to the creation of new blasphemy offenses. The supporters of the Bradlaugh bill also rejected the government's compromise, agreeing that retaining the laws in force was the lesser evil. As a result, they withdrew their bill, killing chances for revision. *Solicitors' Journal* criticized the promoters of the bill for having "thrown it out" merely because the government wished to retain power "to prevent the coarse and scurrilous abuse and ridicule of religious belief." The editors lamented that the country was left with a law against blasphemy "founded on a religious intolerance."[35]

CHAPTER TWENTY-FOUR

The American Middle Period: 1880–1940

T HE FREQUENCY of blasphemy prosecutions in nineteenth-century America barely exceeded the number of boojums sighted on the high seas. Between Kneeland's 1838 conviction and the next case, forty-five years elapsed. In nineteenth-century England, there had been scores and scores of cases, although in both countries the number diminished in the second half of the century. In the United States, there were many profanity cases, but profanity, even if akin to blasphemy, constituted a different crime. Profanity did not involve reviling or ridiculing religion or sacred things, and it did not constitute an attack on the beliefs of Christians. Profanity did, however, involve an affront to delicate sensibilities that objected to cursing. As a matter of law, cursing does not mean dirty language; it means calling upon divine judgment.

In some jurisdictions, as in Pennsylvania, the offense of blasphemy might require a showing of profane scoffing or rejection, meaning irreverence or disrespect. "Profane blasphemy" is a really a redundancy. Profanity is a lesser crime than blasphemy, and one that was never a common-law crime unless the profanity was so violent or repeated so often as to constitute a public nuisance.

Profanity does not imply four-letter words. One commits profanity by taking the sacred name of God in vain, as when swearing ("By God . . .") in circumstances not called for by the law, or by invoking God's help to bring down a curse on someone ("God damn you"). Swearing connotes an oath, not an obscenity. Indeed, merely pronouncing an imprecation upon someone without mentioning God constituted profanity, because of the assumption that God had been called upon to enforce the curse. Sometimes profanity and blasphemy were treated almost as interchangeable, but the correct law on the matter clearly distinguished the two.[1]

Although profanity prosecutions were fairly frequent, blasphemy prosecutions were so uncommon that they were occasions for some public excitement. Yet they did not stir the intense controversies that agitated Britain. A *New York Times* editorial on the subject in 1879, triggered by news of an English prosecution, declared that the United States enjoyed a greater freedom of inquiry and discussion on religious matters than England. "Blasphemy is rightly punished by statute here, as well as there; but a far more tolerant spirit and rule in determining what is blasphemous prevail in American than in the English courts."[2]

In fact, *The New York Times* misled in its explanation that opinions, "however extreme," might be expressed here, "provided they are conscientiously entertained and promulgated with propriety." That was merely saying that the manner of expression rather than the matter constituted the determining factor in a blasphemy case. The American law on the subject did emphasize manner rather than matter, as had English law. In that there was no real difference, contrary to *The New York Times*. In fact, American judges claimed that matter or content made all the difference. The editorial approvingly quoted Chief Justice Shaw in the case of Abner Kneeland, saying that the law "does not prohibit the fullest inquiry and the freest discussion for all honest and fair purposes, one of which is the discovery of truth. . . . It does not prevent the simple and sincere avowal of disbelief in the existence and attributes of a supreme, intelligent Being upon suitable and proper occasions." Yet Kneeland, who claimed to believe in a supreme being, had merely denied believing in the God of the Universalists. And the remarks adjudged blasphemous in Updegraph's case in Pennsylvania were no more shocking or malicious.[3]

America was freer than England on the issue of freedom of expression in matters of religion very likely because the First Amendment prevented an alliance between church and state at the national level, and the last state establishment of religion had expired in the United States in 1833. By contrast, England still maintains an established church. On issues of obscenity, America was no freer than England. Comstockery had its English counterparts, but it was American through and through. Free expression in matters concerning sex and bodily functions was at least as constricted here as in England. On issues involving religion, however, the United States, despite Kent in *Ruggles* or Shaw in *Kneeland*, seemed as a matter of practice to follow the overt-acts test embodied in the great Virginia Statute of Religious Freedom. Jefferson held aloft the American standard. Thus, when the controversy developed in England between two great liberal jurists, Lord Chief Justice Coleridge and Lord Justice Stephen, *The New York Times*, no bastion of liberalism, editorially sided with Stephen: "Sir James Stephen is altogether of the opinion that this state of the law [as defined by Coleridge's decency test, which *The New York Times* had endorsed in 1879] is revolting and monstrous." Both "law and logic," declared the editorial, were on the side of Stephen, whereas "his chief has been misled by his emotions into perverting the law of the land." The editorial concluded that Parliament should abrogate the common law of blasphemy.[4]

The New York Times reported an unusual case that occurred in Paterson, New Jersey, in 1882. It was the first and only one in which a state indicted a Jew for blasphemy, as well as the first American case since Kneeland's. The Paterson complainant, a devout Catholic, testified that he could not stand by and see Jews like Wolf Hirsh Rosentrauch, the defendant, revile Christ and abuse his mother, Mary. On cross-examination, the complainant admitted that he had a criminal record—a conviction for murder. The defendant testified that he and his accuser had had a business dispute, and he had refused to advance him further credit. Rosentrauch, who also swore his admiration for Jesus as a teacher of morals, denied the language attributed to him and denied that he was capable of using such language. After deliberating for five minutes, the jury acquitted.[5]

Four years later, another New Jersey case, involving Charles B. Reynolds, a former Methodist minister who had lost his faith, resulted in a conviction. Reynolds had become an agnostic preacher with a zeal to proselytize. Traveling from town to town, he would distribute his freethought pamphlets, pitch his tent, and invite people to hear him denounce Christianity and the Bible. At a "freethought meeting" in Boonton, New Jersey, in the summer of 1886, his speech on the virtues of infidelity provoked a riot. A crowd of religious rowdies pelted him with rotten eggs, tore down his canvas tent, and sought to throw him into a pond, but he escaped. The following spring, he turned up in Morristown, New Jersey, a city that *The New York Times* described as "famed heretofore for its lunatic asylum." His freethought pamphlets angered some citizens, who influenced a grand jury; Reynolds was indicted for his oral blasphemies in Boonton and his printed blasphemies in Morristown.[6]

The indictment held Reynolds accountable for having been jocular and sarcastic about God and the Bible. God, said Reynolds, drowned the whole world in a mad fury, because it was much worse than He ever supposed it could be, though He was all-knowing according to the Bible. It depicted "the most foul and bestial instances of fornication, incest, and polygamy, perpetrated by God's own saints." It also described God as the infant offspring of a Jewish girl, who must have cried, squealed, kicked, and been spanked when he was naughty. The statute against blasphemy penalized profane scoffing and exposing God or Christ to contempt or ridicule.[7]

Reynolds's case became celebrated for two reasons. It was only the second of its kind in the history of New Jersey, though the statute penalizing blasphemy went back to the seventeenth century. And, Reynolds employed Colonel Robert G. Ingersoll to defend him. The son of a Congregational minister, Ingersoll was the nation's foremost freethinker— "the greatest of infidel orators," said *The New York Times*. In an age of purple oratory, he was the most grandiloquent of all public speakers. The Reverend Henry Ward Beecher, a pulpit rival who anathematized Ingersoll, believed that he was the most brilliant orator in any land or in any tongue. No lawyer was better known or drew bigger crowds. Ingersoll's critics frequently targeted him with accusations of blasphemy. In 1884, Chief Justice Joseph P. Comegys of Delaware, addressing a grand jury, noted that Ingersoll had spoken against religion in Wilmington, and Comegys promised that, if Ingersoll ever returned and blasphemed, he would be convicted for his crime. The grand jury described Ingersoll as an "arch-blasphemer and reviler of God and religion" who would be brought to trial if he attempted again to lecture in Delaware. In every way, Ingersoll was equipped to defend Reynolds.[8]

For the half-year before the case came to trial, "no topic was so interesting to the public as this," and when the day of trial arrived, lines of people surrounded and packed the courthouse in Morristown, bulging its facilities. Three judges presided. After the prosecution presented to the jury evidence that Reynolds had distributed the supposedly blasphemous pamphlets, Ingersoll announced that, although he had no witnesses, he might feel like making a few remarks after dinner. "There will be great disappointment if you don't," remarked Francis Child, the chief judge. Ingersoll's speech took several hours.[9]

The issue presented by the case, he declared, was whether a person in New Jersey had a right to freedom of speech. In his high-flown bombast, he extolled intellectual liberty and censured religious persecution. Although most of what he declaimed was quite irrelevant or transcended the case, he defended Reynolds ably enough on the blasphemy issue without offering any fresh thoughts on it. For the most part, he remained civil, only occasionally lapsing into a lightly irreverent tone about the Bible, as when remarking that the Old Testament, as Reynolds had said, condoned infamous practices such as polygamy. "Abraham," Ingersoll observed, "would have gotten into trouble in New Jersey—no doubt of that. Sarah could have obtained a divorce in this state—no doubt of that. . . . If Solomon were living in the United States today, we would put him in the penitentiary." Ingersoll quoted Reynolds's language and sought to prove that he had simply repeated what was in the Bible. Was it blasphemy, he asked, to quote from the Sacred Scriptures, or was it blasphemy simply because Reynolds did not believe the Bible?

What did "blasphemy" mean? No one knew, Ingersoll contended, but at any rate its meaning depended on time and place. What was blasphemy in one country might be religious exhortation in another. We sent missionaries abroad to tell other people that their religions were false, their gods myths, their saviors impostors. If a Turk came to Morristown and handed out a pamphlet saying that the Koran was the inspired word of God, Mohammed his prophet, the Bible false, and Christ a myth, Morristown would lock him up. That was wrong, however. It violated the principle of free speech as well as religious liberty. And, like the prosecution of Reynolds, it was foolish policy. Ingersoll explained in the simplest terms:

> Here comes a man to your town and circulates a pamphlet. Now if they had just kept still, very few would ever have heard of it. That would have been the end. But in order to stop discussion of that question, they indicted this man, and that question has been more discussed in this country since this indictment than all the discussions put together since New Jersey was first granted to Charles the Second's dearest brother James, the Duke of York. And what else? A trial here that is to be reported and published all over the United States, a trial that will give Mr. Reynolds a congregation of fifty millions of people. And yet this was done for the purpose of stopping a discussion of this subject. I want to show you that the thing is itself almost idiotic—that it defeats itself and that you cannot crush out these things by force.[10]

Ingersoll also analyzed the statute penalizing blasphemy, quite literally word by word, and concluded that it oozed bigotry and persecution, a relic from a dead age. He implored the Christian jury to acquit, because "it never can do any church any good to put a man in jail for the expression of opinion. Any church that imprisons a man because he has used an argument against its creed, will simply convince the world that it cannot answer the argument."[11]

After the prosecutor took a moment to remind the jury that the defendant was guilty of "terrible blasphemy," Judge Child summed up in much the same way as the prosecutor. Although Ingersoll, he said, had defended free speech "by words so beautiful and fine of sentiment as to send a thrill through the veins of his hearers, he has not offset evidence by evidence." The essence of freedom was law, prescribed by the people. Their statute against blasphemy was not at all obsolete, as Ingersoll would have the jury believe. It had been re-enacted several times, as recently as 1874, when it was incorporated in a revision of the state's laws. People could speak as they pleased on any subject, but not reproachfully or scoffingly about God or the Christian religion "in a manner calculated to wound the religious sentiment of the community."[12]

After deliberating a little over an hour, the jury returned a guilty verdict. Judge Child declared that he would be lenient because the law had never been enforced before. More likely, Child had the good sense not to create a martyr by imprisoning Reynolds. He merely fined him $25 and costs. The court clerk estimated that the fine and costs totaled $75, which Ingersoll immediately paid.[13]

The New York Times lamented that, after half a year of intense excitement, the case produced merely "a mouse" in the shape of a small fine. But at least New Jersey "had gone on record against blasphemy." Blasphemous literature, like obscene literature, should be "suppressed," and its promoters punished for "a violation of public decency." Ingersoll had admitted that his client was guilty of bad taste but contended that no one should be convicted for that. "We beg his pardon," said the newspaper. "That is precisely what the jury did in this case, and what every jury should do when the breach of taste amounts to a gross indecency, and when there is a statute under which it can be prosecuted." For all of Ingersoll's talk about free speech, concluded the editorial, limits existed on any sort of libel, especially when public decency had been offended.[14]

No way exists whereby to reconcile the editorials of *The New York Times* in 1884, when recommending the abolition of the offense of blasphemy, and those in 1886, when applauding the verdict in the case of Reynolds. The newspaper reflected a raging liberalism, though, compared with the minister who, in the pages of *The North American Review*, expressed the belief that people who "venture to deny the divinity of our Blessed Lord and the obligations of His sacraments" transgressed "the limits of legitimate religious discussion."[15]

Another opinion that was atypical but certainly in keeping with the actual practice of American law—turning a deaf ear and a blind eye to blasphemy—was delivered in 1894 by Judge Watts Parker in the case of *Commonwealth of Kentucky* v. *Charles C. Moore*.[16] Moore, a prohibitionist and an atheist, wrote and published a newspaper in Lexington, Kentucky, in which he treated with offensive levity the scriptural account of the conception and birth of Jesus; he topped off the usual points by calling blasphemous the Bible's supposed declaration that Jesus was the offspring of an adulterous relationship between God and Mary, "a Jew woman." Moore, refusing to give bond for his appearance at the next term of the court, spent three months in jail. Demurring to the indictment, Moore claimed that his language constituted no offense in Kentucky law. Judge Parker, whom Moore later described as "an infidel," sustained the demurrer, quashing the indictment.[17]

The case, declared Parker, was the first of its kind in Kentucky. No statute against blasphemy had been enacted, and the state's high court had never ruled on an issue of blasphemy. Accordingly, Parker turned to the common law, which he found in Blackstone and Kent's opinion in *Ruggles*, which cited the English precedents. But England had an established church, whereas in this country the church and state were divorced. Parker reasoned that he therefore could not accept the common law on blasphemy; Kent should have rejected it, because the "difficulties in reconciling religious freedom with the right to punish for an offense against any given religion are manifest." Kentucky's constitution declared that no preference should be given to any religion, and that no person's civil rights should be diminished "on account of his belief or disbelief of any religious tenet, dogma or teaching." For Parker, the language meant that no crime of blasphemy could coexist with the state constitution. In England, he said, the greatest concession made to religious liberty was the right to controvert religious points with decency. Prosecuting blasphemy had nothing to do with maintaining good order, only with preserving the faith accepted by the state as the true one. By contrast, in Kentucky, with no religion to foster and defend, "there is no place for the common law of blasphemy."[18] That was the first opinion in American history to hold a blasphemy act unconstitutional, although not in an officially reported case or in one decided by a court of last resort. It was also the last American blasphemy case until Michael X. Mockus spewed out his opinions on religion in Lithuanian when lecturing in Waterbury, Connecticut, in 1916.

Mockus was a blasphemer who beat his prosecutors in one case by relying on free speech, yet in another had to flee abroad to avoid imprisonment. He had once studied for the priesthood but became a sarcastic assailant of Roman Catholicism. All religions disgusted him. As an itinerant lecturer on the virtues of Marxism and atheism, he achieved notoriety for his encounters with the law in three states.

Invited in 1916 to give his series of lectures in Lithuanian before the Lithuanian Freethought Association of Waterbury, he infuriated church members who infiltrated the meeting. They complained to the police about his scurrilous remarks concerning God, Christ, the Trinity, the Virgin Mary, and the Bible. He was arrested under an 1821 statute that originated in a 1642 enactment that had fixed the death penalty for blasphemy. The re-enactment of 1821 made one year in prison and a fine of $100 the maximum sentence. Tried in the city court of Waterbury, Mockus was found guilty; as the first blasphemer in the state's history, he was sentenced to only ten days. He might have avoided the sentence either by pleading guilty or by agreeing not to appeal his conviction.[19]

Mockus spurned the offer and retained the services of Theodore Schroeder, a New York lawyer who had founded the Free Speech League in 1902. It was a precursor of the American Civil Liberties Union. Although distinguished liberals served on its board, "Schroeder *was* the

Free Speech League," remarked Roger Baldwin, long the director of the ACLU. [20] An indefatigable publicist and champion of First Amendment rights, Schroeder assailed any censorship of expression, whether for reasons of obscenity or blasphemy. To him, these were no crimes. He argued that Mockus's provocative remarks did not constitute a crime. The judge allowed a continuance that gave Schroeder time to write a massive defense of the constitutional rights of freethinkers to speak with impunity. He later published the defense as a book, but wasted all that work on the judge. Overruling all of the demurrers by which Schroeder had raised the constitutional questions, the judge admitted that he had not read Schroeder's argument and would not do so. During the delays, before Mockus lost his appeal, he was free on bond, getting into trouble elsewhere. He never served time in Connecticut, because he disappeared from its jurisdiction. [21]

In 1917, when still under indictment for blasphemy in Waterbury, he lectured to Lithuanians in Waukegan, Illinois, where he delivered his set speech on the impossibility of virgin birth, on the foolishness of regarding Jesus as divine, and on the evils of Roman Catholicism. Scoffingly he denied the existence of God, trashed the Bible, and added ribaldry to his insults. "That Mockus was not stoned unto death," the Waukegan *Daily Sun* said, was "miraculous," for he outraged members of St. Bartholomew's Church and their priests, who were in the audience. The police arrested him for disorderly conduct, although no actual breach of the peace had occurred, and a week later the prosecutor filed a charge of blasphemy against him. [22]

A jury consisting wholly of Protestants acquitted Mockus of the disorderly-conduct charge, after he was defended on free-speech grounds by his counsel, Frederick L. Main. The local newspaper editorialized that the jury believed that Mockus had a right to his opinions "in a country where free speech and free religious expressions and thought must prevail." [23]

Mockus's lawyer used the same free-speech defense to support a motion to quash the blasphemy accusation against Mockus. Judge Perry L. Persons of the county court, after hearing the prosecution support the charge of blasphemy, issued an extraordinary opinion. He regretfully quashed the accusation on the ground that no Illinois statute or ordinance against blasphemy existed, and the common law of blasphemy violated the state bill of rights. Judge Persons endorsed Jefferson's overt-acts test in matters of expression on religion. He failed to consider any of the usual arguments to the effect that blasphemous remarks insulted Christian beliefs and thus constituted an abuse of free speech. Although a majority of the people of the state were Christian, he declared, the law could not consider the validity or invalidity of opinions on religion. Under the state constitution, all people, the judge asserted, possessed the same civil rights and stood equal before the law, "the Protestant, Catholic, Mormon, Mahammedan, the Jew, the Free Thinker, the Atheist." Mockus had spoken "blasphemous words, which I do not care to repeat, maligning Jesus Christ," but, regardless of how "reprehensible" were the defendant's views, standing alone, "unaccompanied by acts of violence or other breach of peace," he had committed no crime.[24] Although Judge Persons could have strengthened his opinion by explaining his reasons for rejecting conventional arguments that accepted blasphemy as a common-law crime, his restraint and liberalism, so rare in blasphemy cases, command admiration. His was the first such opinion, sustaining a free-speech argument in a blasphemy case, since that of Judge Watts Parker in Moore's case in 1894.

Mockus's next encounter with the law ended in a ritualistically conventional opinion by Maine's highest court. In 1919, when xenophobia and the Red Scare began eating away at American freedoms, Mockus delivered his usual lectures before the Lithuanians of Rumford, Maine. His remarks on religion nettled the religiously orthodox, while his assault on the unholy trinity of government, religion, and capitalism angered traditionalists generally. By his third lecture, Catholic opponents mingled with freethinkers, and one of the policemen present, who understood Lithuanian, took notes. Mockus became the first and only defendant in the history of Maine as a state to be charged with blasphemy; the statutory crime dated back to the colonial period, when Maine was part of Massachusetts.

Mockus's two-day trial before Judge John Morrill ended in a conviction on eight counts of blasphemy. The local paper in Lewiston described the defendant's ridicule of religion as "unprintable," and the judge agreed. Mockus's attorney relied on freedom of expression in religious matters and the fact that Mockus's remarks did not breach the peace. The prosecutor, in an argument supported by the judge, contended that the jury should convict if they believed that the defendant's remarks tended to cause "a future outbreak against the peace." That was asking for a conviction for a crime that had not been committed and might never be. The prosecutor added that Mockus sought to destroy not only religion but the government. The judge's instructions to the jury reiterated the prosecutor's views. After the verdict of guilty, the judge asserted that no society could tolerate a malicious attempt to subvert religion. He described as "monstrous" the idea that "any such talk will be tolerated." After making derogatory remarks about immigrants, Judge Morrill sentenced Mockus to a term of one to two years in the state prison.[25]

The Maine Supreme Judicial Court unanimously sustained the conviction in an opinion that relied heavily on Chief Justice Shaw's in

Kneeland's case. Free expression did not extend to reviling religion, which was necessary for the stability of government. Christianity taught reverence toward God, Christ, and the Bible. Any exposure of them to ridicule and contempt constituted blasphemous breach of the peace.[26] Mockus, facing prison in both Connecticut and Maine, fled to Mexico. His encounters with the law had produced an unusual lower-court opinion sustaining his freedom in Waukegan and a knee-jerk reactionary opinion from Maine's high court in a case that was unique in that state. Mockus was guilty of robust free speech that revealed his religious prejudice; the state of Maine was simply guilty of religious prejudice.

In 1926, Mockus's prosecutor in Maine, Frederick R. Dyer, read news dispatches from Brockton, Massachusetts, about a Lithuanian communist agitator named Anthony Bimba who was on trial for blasphemy and seditious libel. Dyer wrote to the Brockton court to inquire further about Bimba, on the hunch that he might be the fugitive Mockus using an alias, but it turned out that Bimba was a much younger man, thirty-one at the time. He edited a communist publication in Brooklyn and was national secretary of the Lithuanian Communist Party. Bimba had spoken in Lithuanian at an indignation meeting in Brockton to protest the cruelties of Lithuania's protofascist government. What Bimba did not know was that factional enemies were present in the audience to ask questions that might expose him to criminal prosecution.[27]

On the day after Bimba's lecture, two of his listeners formally complained before the clerk of Brockton's Plymouth County court that Bimba had given a criminally libelous talk, both blasphemous and seditious. No one had been prosecuted under the Massachusetts blasphemy act since the decision in *Commonwealth* v. *Kneeland* in 1838. The charge of seditious libel was based on the provision of the state criminal-anarchy act of 1919, which penalized advocacy of "the overthrow of the Commonwealth or of the United States." The statute was not limited to advocacy of overthrow by force and violence. Mere advocacy sufficed, although, as to the charge of blasphemy, mere denial of God did not suffice; it had to be a willful or malicious denial, and Chief Justice Shaw had declared that a serious, decent denial was constitutionally protected.

According to the formal charges, Bimba declared that people had sweated under Christian rule for two thousand years, with the result that they had a government controlled by clerics and capitalists. "They tell us there is a God," he said. "Where is he? There is no such thing." Only fools believed in God or in the soul, he added, and Christ was "no more a God than you or I. He was just a plain man." That was his blasphemy. The charge of seditious utterance depended on Bimba's having declared that they were organizing "to overthrow the capitalistic government by revolution in the same way that they did in Russia, and to establish the same kind of government they now have in Russia." He added that he did not believe in the ballot and predicted that the red flag would fly over the Capitol in Washington.[28]

Unlike Mockus, who was tried in obscurity, Bimba benefited from the glare of considerable publicity. He was an extremely unpopular person, but the Red Scare and the Sacco-Vanzetti case had sensitized liberals to the injustice that was too easily present in the prosecution of alien radicals. The jail in Dedham, Massachusetts, where Sacco and Vanzetti awaited the results of their appeal was only fifteen miles from Brockton. Moreover, the Scopes trial in Dayton, Tennessee, during the preceding summer reinforced a widespread belief that the state should not penalize those who rejected religious orthodoxy.

Bimba had all the money and legal talent that he needed for his defense and for bail. The International Labor Defense Council of Chicago provided him with the legal services of the firm of Harry and Irving Hoffman, and the ACLU, having offered its assistance, stood by if needed. Professor Zechariah Chafee of Harvard Law School, the distinguished scholar of civil liberties, monitored Bimba's case; other civil libertarians offered their assistance, including Dudley Field Malone, who had been Clarence Darrow's partner in the Scopes trial. Moreover, the United Press, the Associated Press, and the International News Service had reporters in attendance at the trial, as did *The New York Times*, Boston's leading newspapers, and papers from other Massachusetts and New England towns. Alice Stone Blackwell, the noted feminist, was quoted widely when she described the prosecution of Bimba as "preposterous and absolutely indefensible." She was sorry that Bimba did not believe in God, but his expression of disbelief was no crime. If it were, she declared, some of the most prominent scientists would have to be jailed. And the doctrine that Jesus was not God but a man "is taught in all our Unitarian churches. If it were a legal offense, former President [Charles W.] Eliot [of Harvard] and a long list of distinguished Unitarians would be in prison. So would all the Jews." Nevertheless, Bimba and his supporters were unable to rent a lecture hall to hold a public rally; Boston and the surrounding towns shut down all facilities to the radicals in an attempt to suppress their viewpoint. The police hustled off the radical Scott Nearing and anyone else who tried to speak outdoors for Bimba.[29]

The trial without a jury opened on February 24, 1926, at the Brockton courthouse, with mounted police and state troopers surrounding the building and other officers guarding it within. Reporters and spectators competed for seats in the courtroom of Charles Carroll King, the fair-minded chief justice of the Plymouth County court. He rejected a defense motion to dismiss the charges as unconstitutional violations of Bimba's freedom of speech. Given the *Kneeland* precedent, King believed himself duty-bound to try the blasphemy charge, and he would not rule on the seditious-libel charge without first hearing the evidence. The city prosecutor, Manuel Rubin, presented the case against Bimba through the testimony of witnesses to his speech. Rubin sought to prove that Bimba had attacked the existence of God "and attempted to destroy and disrupt men's veneration for a religion."[30]

Defense witnesses presented a different Bimba. They testified that he had spoken of the tragedy of political prisoners imprisoned and tortured by the clerical government in Lithuania. In the context of his heartrending statement, Bimba had declared that he did not believe in God and that the priests did not either, or else they would not permit such atrocities. Every defense witness testified that Bimba had not mentioned Jesus Christ, had not spoken scornfully of God, and had said nothing about the red flag of communism flying over the Capitol. He had spoken of revolution and the need to overthrow the government only in connection with Lithuania. The prosecution witnesses were equally positive that he made the remarks attributed to him in the charges against him.[31]

The trial concluded after the fourth day. Prosecutor Rubin "did not stress the blasphemy charges in his summation," reported *The New York Times*. Earlier, the blasphemy charge had loomed largest in Rubin's arguments, but in the end he emphasized the charge of seditious utterance, because the evidence for that was far stronger than for blasphemy. For the defense, Harry Hoffman, summing up, again relied on freedom of speech. He confidently asserted that, if the court decided against his client on the blasphemy issue, he would win on an appeal, because, in the absence of proof of irreverence or of malicious intent, Bimba had not committed blasphemy. Hoffman sought to convince the juryless court that Bimba had made seditious remarks only against the government of Lithuania.[32]

A few days later, Judge King acquitted Bimba of the blasphemy charge but found him guilty of the political count. The judge decided that, although the defendant declared his disbelief in God, the evidence was unclear as to what he had actually said; he seemed to have expressed his personal belief "in a way allowed under the *Kneeland* decision." Despite equally contradictory evidence as to Bimba's political remarks and the fact that some members of the audience "were out to get him," he seems to have said that the red flag would wave over Washington as well as in Lithuania, and though he did not urge immediate overthrow, he seems to have counseled organization for the purpose of overthrow. As a result, the judge decided, Bimba had violated the criminal-anarchy act. But the country was at peace, and "radical activities are on the wane," so King imposed only a "meager" penalty, a fine of $100. Roger Baldwin of the ACLU immediately declared, "The conviction for sedition raises squarely the issue of free speeech. We are offering Bimba and his attorney the services of our lawyers in Massachusetts to carry the case to the Supreme Court if necessary."[33]

Press reaction favored the outcome. However, Providence newspapers recalled Rhode Island's tradition of dissent from the time of Roger Williams and invited Bimba to speak there. In Rutland, Vermont, a newspaper praised the free-speech tradition of Hyde Park, London, where anyone could speak as radically as he wished as long as he did not provoke a riot. *The New York Times* found irony in the fact that for Bimba's denial of God, which he admitted, he was acquitted, whereas for his seditious utterances, which he denied, he was convicted. The trial gave him a notoriety that made him "something like a national figure." Generally, the press complimented Judge King's handling of the trial. His calm and judiciousness prevented the sort of circus atmosphere that had characterized the Scopes trial in Tennessee. Judge King, reported a Boston paper, "conveniently let Massachusetts out of a somewhat embarrassing situation."[34]

Having appealed his conviction, Bimba was entitled under Massachusetts law to a retrial before a jury. Awaiting that retrial, he enjoyed his celebrity, lecturing to English-speaking audiences about Lithuania's plight, as well as continuing as editor of a communist paper. One year after his conviction, the district attorney of Plymouth County decided to drop the case. "Interests of public justice do not require further prosecution of this case," his office reported. "The issue is dead now and the offense is so trivial that I do not think it worth the time and heavy expense to prosecute." That remark applied with equal force to the original blasphemy charge, of which Judge King acquitted Bimba. Thus, he escaped even a small fine. In the same year, 1927, Bimba became an American citizen. He remained a communist and lived to see Lithuania become a constituent republic of the U.S.S.R. In 1962, the University of Vilnius in Lithuania awarded him an honorary degree in history.[35]

That another blasphemy case would arise in Massachusetts did not mean that the Commonwealth had learned nothing or was bent on suppressing caustic critics of the sacred. It showed, rather, how chancy and erratic a decision to prosecute may be. In mid-1927, even before the Bimba case reached its final resolution, Judge Devlin of Boston sentenced Warner M. Williams to six months because his book, *The Great Secret of Freemasonry*, contained a passage describing Jesus as "immoral." Williams appealed, entitling him to a trial by jury. The trial ended in a hung jury, and the case was dismissed.[36]

A Boston case that generated more excitement occurred in 1928, when a police officer obtained from Judge Michael J. Murray of the Municipal Court a warrant for the arrest of Horace Meyer Kallen on a charge of blasphemy. Kallen was a prominent lecturer and scholar, a founder of the New School for Social Research, the author of many books on philosophy, and the literary executor of William James. At a memorial meeting for Sacco and Vanzetti that drew an audience of two thousand people, Kallen declared that, if Sacco and Vanzetti had been anarchists, "so was Jesus Christ." The police who were present reported his remark to superiors, who obtained the warrant. The blasphemy charge was absurd, and Kallen was a formidable opponent who had the support of the Harvard and Manhattan intelligentsia. The next day, *The New York Times* ran these headings over its account: "BLAS-PHEMY CHARGE ON KALLEN HELD UP. Boston Judge Recalls Warrant. Plan to Drop Case Is Seen. Kallen Voices Disappointment." That told the entire story. The next issue of the paper noted that the warrant had been withdrawn "as an admission of fear and guilt on the part of Massachusetts authorities."[37]

LITTLE Rock, Arkansas, also in 1928, arrested Charles Smith of New York, the president of the American Association for the Advancement of Atheism. The initial charge of disorderly conduct was based on Smith's lobbying activities against a proposed state statute prohibiting the teaching of evolution in public schools. He had distributed antireligious tracts and placed a sign in his window: "Evolution is True. The Bible's a Lie. God's a Ghost." Police at first charged that he violated a city ordinance that outlawed reference to God except in "veneration and worship." Then, claiming that his literature was "calculated" to breach the peace, the police closed Smith's headquarters. At his trial, the judge refused to allow him to testify in his own behalf "because he would not take an oath on the Bible."[38]

When the ACLU protested Smith's treatment, the mayor of Little Rock declared that no atheist would be allowed in his city. Smith, having refused to pay the fine of $26.40, was jailed and went on a hunger strike. On the ninth day, the chief of police told a freethought reporter, "We don't want him in jail. Why, Mrs. Haldeman-Julius, I'll pay his fine myself, this minute, if he'll go away." Even the Baptist minister who was the prime mover of the antievolution statute announced that Smith should never have been imprisoned; the court, he declared, "violated the provision of the Constitution regarding the right of free speech." The authorities released Smith, but he refused to go away or to discontinue his activities. The police then rearrested him on a charge of blasphemy, based on the antibiblical nature of his literature. Summarily tried and convicted, he received a sentence of $100 and ninety days, but was released on bond pending appeal. Then the charges were quietly dropped and the case blew over.[39]

In 1937, in Windsor, Connecticut, a local court fined a speeding motorist $10 for his traffic violation and another $10 after summarily convicting him of blasphemy, because of remarks he made to the constable who arrested him. We do not know what he said, but undoubtedly his offense was profanity, not blasphemy.[40] A similar case occurred twenty years later in Mt. Clemens, Michigan, when a man was convicted of blasphemy for cursing an officer who was investigating a complaint concerning his abuse of his wife. The man pleaded guilty and was placed on probation for a year.[41]

Two years earlier, there had been a shocking blasphemy case in Canada. An Anglican priest was convicted in Roman Catholic Quebec for his moderate criticism of the Catholic church.[42] Canada had had few blasphemy prosecutions. The first, in 1900, resulted in a plea of guilty by the defendants.[43] The next case, in 1925, resulted in the reversal of a conviction, on the ground that an attack on the Roman Catholic clergy, however vitriolic, did not legally constitute an attack on religion.[44] In 1926, the only Canadian blasphemy prosecution outside of Quebec was brought against Ernest V. Sterry, the editor of an agnostic periodical in Toronto. He had poked fun at "touchy Jehovah," the Old Testament's depiction of God as mass murderer and megalomaniac. On conviction, the appellate court, following Coleridge's decency test, agreed with the prosecutor that language intended to insult the religious convictions of the great majority was intolerable. Sterry got sixty days.[45] In 1933, a court in Montreal reversed an earlier ruling when it held that an attack on the clergy constituted an attack on Roman Catholicism, because the clergy were an essential part of the religion.[46] Such was the state of the law when the Rahard case arose in 1935.

Victor Rahard, an Anglican priest in Montreal, publicly posted a critique of the Roman church and its priests, for which he was accused of blasphemy. He defended himself by arguing that he had not attacked God or Christianity, that he spoke in good faith and in decent language as a clergyman, and that his criticism of the Mass was part of the teaching of his own church. The chief judge of the Montreal Court of Sessions of the Peace rejected Rahard's motion to quash by ruling that his bad faith was "more than manifest" and that his language was so offensive and injurious to Roman Catholics as to pose a danger to the public peace—though no breach of the peace had occurred. The court held the accused guilty. No case could better illustrate the limitless subjectivity of the decency test and the danger it posed to freedom of expression. Fortunately, Canada has not again prosecuted blasphemy. Its precedents, however, allow the possibility of suppression even of normal sectarian controversy.

In the United States, there were no further blasphemy cases until

1968. By then, the Supreme Court had so radically expanded First Amendment freedoms that a state appellate court, in the landmark case of *Maryland* v. *Irving K. West*, held a blasphemy statute unconstitutional. That case marked the end of blasphemy prosecutions in the United States, but it was possible only because of the transformation of First Amendment law before 1968.[47]

CHAPTER TWENTY-FIVE

Modern America

W HEN the Maine Supreme Court decided the Mockus case in
1919, it correctly stated that the Constitution of the United
States was irrelevant to its decision.[1] That is, the First Amendment
restrained only the national government, not the states. A state could
introduce an inquisition or establish a state church without violating the
Constitution of the United States. That situation began to change in
1925, when the Supreme Court held that the Fourteenth Amendment's
guarantee that no state shall deny liberty without due process of law
meant that the First Amendment's protection of free speech applied to the
states as well as the United States. In effect, the due-process clause of the
Fourteenth Amendment incorporated the federal standard for freedom of
speech; thus, what the national government could not do was similarly
prohibited against state action.[2] Case by case, the Supreme Court na-
tionalized each of the rights guaranteed by the First Amendment to
protect each against violation by states.[3] In *Cantwell* v. *Connecticut*, 1940,
when the court made the free-exercise-of-religion clause a liberty protected against state infringement by the Fourteenth Amendment, the
court unanimously declared:

> In the realm of religious faith, and in that of political belief,
> sharp differences arise. In both fields the tenets of one man may
> seem the rankest error to his neighbor. To persuade others to his
> own point of view, the pleader, as we know, at times, resorts to
> exaggeration, to vilification of men who have been, or are, prom-
> inent in church or state. But the people of this nation have or-
> dained in the light of history that in spite of the probability of
> excesses and abuses, these liberties are, in the long view, essential
> to enlightened opinion and right conduct on the part of the citizens
> of a democracy. The essential characteristic of these liberties is,
> that under their shield many types of life, character, opinion and
> belief can develop unmolested and unobstructed. Nowhere is this

shield more necessary than in our own country for a people composed of many races and of many creeds.[4]

Notwithstanding that statement, two years later, in *Chaplinsky* v. *New Hampshire*, the Supreme Court unanimously declared, in an opinion by Justice Frank Murphy, that profanity lacked First Amendment protection. Chaplinsky, a Jehovah's Witness, had publicly denounced all religion as a "racket." Because the crowd he was addressing appeared restless, a policeman ordered Chaplinsky to move on. The Witness called the policeman "a God damned racketeer" and "a damned Fascist." The cop arrested him, and he was convicted because of his language. On appeal, the Supreme Court held that "certain well-defined and narrowly limited classes of speech" have no constitutional protection, among them "the lewd and obscene, the profane, the libelous, and the insulting or 'fighting' words—those which by their very utterance inflict injury or tend to incite to an immediate breach of the peace." Justice Murphy explained that such words are not an essential part of the exposition of ideas and are of "such slight social value as a step to the truth" that the social interest in order and morality outweighed any benefit to be derived from the words.[5]

The court said no more about profanity, but its doctrine applied equally to blasphemy. If "God damn" had no First Amendment protection, then cursing, reviling, or ridiculing God or religion would not seem to have a better claim. The court's opinion, however, was ill-considered. In the first place, "profanity" is not a well-defined concept. "Go to hell" is not profane, but "damn," even without the reference to God, *is* profane, on the supposition that only God can damn.[6] But, by the same reasoning, only God can consign a person to hell for eternity. And no reasoning will explain the notion of taking the Lord's name in vain, another form of profanity. "By God" is a criminal phrase according to the law of profanity, but the exclamation "Jesus Christ!" is not profanity. "Profanity" is in fact as nebulous a concept as "blasphemy." *Chaplinsky* and *Cantwell* are not easily reconciled. *Cantwell* allowed for exaggeration, vilification, and excess in order to protect freedom of speech.

Chaplinsky is also unconvincing, because the First Amendment should protect words that communicate strong feelings as well as ideas that are a step to the truth. Indeed, many ideas are no more steps to the truth than are feelings. Moreover, to exclude profanity from the First Amendment's protection violates the establishment clause of that amendment by favoring religious beliefs over nonreligious beliefs, and because it amounts to government endorsement of theological concepts. The idea that God is the source of damnation is purely theological in character, as is the idea of taking God's name in vain. The First Amendment, by banning the protection and advancement of religion, should safeguard an emotional utterance such as "damned Fascist," which, contrary to the court, conveys much by way of an idea as well as being epithetical. If, on the other hand, such language, when personally addressed to an individual, actually falls into the category of "fighting words," as the court held, the argument for its protection loses force.

The contention here is not against the court's fighting-words doctrine but against its claim that "profanity" is a well-defined class of words deserving no constitutional protection. The concern here is not simply freedom for profanity but also for "blasphemy," for what the court said about profanity applies as well to blasphemy. The prosecution of blasphemy and of profanity gives religion a preferential treatment, contrary to the establishment clause. Blasphemy that has no purpose other than to offend or express hate deserves no protection, but most blasphemy expresses ideas as well as feelings. Whether those ideas are steps to the truth is not for the Supreme Court to decide. Ours is an extraordinary system of government. We do not believe that government, including our highest court, has an obligation to keep citizens from lapsing into political or religious errors, or any other sort of error. We believe, rather, that citizens have the right and the duty of preventing the government from falling into error. The court's talk about protecting only language that is a step to the truth was Miltonian hokum that put it into a realm where it does not belong. For all we know, the officer in *Chaplinsky* may have been a "damned Fascist"; in any case, he should have offered Chaplinsky protection from the crowd as well as protection for his right to express himself about religion. The case occurred at a time when Witnesses were victims of persecution in the nation, in part because the court's first flag-salute decision conveyed the impression that the Witnesses were un-American.[7]

In keeping with the first flag-salute decision were a couple of lower-federal-court cases that dealt with blasphemy. In 1941, the United States Circuit Court of the Tenth Circuit sustained the constitutionality of an ordinance of Oklahoma City that punished profane, abusive, or insulting language and blasphemous language. One section of the ordinance made it unlawful to reproach or ridicule God, Jesus Christ, the Holy Ghost, the Bible, "or the Christian or any other religion." The ordinance had a supposed secular purpose: to prevent language calculated to breach the peace. That left the Witnesses to suffer the prejudices of public opinion expressed in a jury verdict. The court should have required in every case a showing of a real danger that a breach might result from speech. The ordinance protected religion, especially the Christian religion. It had been enacted to cope with the proselytizing of Jehovah's Witnesses. The federal court spoke ritualistically about "those who abuse these freedoms" by using the language prohibited. It announced, without any sort of reasoning, that the statute furnished sufficiently ascertainable standards of guilt. Having upheld the blasphemy ordinance, the court remanded the case for a determination as to whether the Witnesses had used language calculated to breach the peace.[8]

Two years later, a federal district court in Oklahoma confronted a nearly identical ordinance from Muskogee. Having observed that in the preceding eight months the police had made 204 arrests under the ordinance, the court held that the ordinance was not invalid, citing the Oklahoma City case as a precedent. However, the court also declared that the city authorities must be enjoined from enforcing the ordinance against Witnesses who offered their literature for sale or distribution "in a peaceable and courteous manner." That was a step in the right direction. In effect, the court was saying that, if no breach of the peace occurred or was imminent, the Witnesses should be left alone, regardless of whether the police thought their language was calculated to breach the peace.[9] No other blasphemy cases arose in the lower federal courts.

The Supreme Court has never decided a blasphemy case. It did, however, decide the case of *The Miracle*, involving "sacrilege," which a state court defined as if it meant substantially the same as blasphemy. This case, *Burstyn* v. *Wilson*, 1952, involved the censorship of a film, *The Miracle*, not a criminal prosecution. The movie, which had been made in Italy by Roberto Rossellini and starred Anna Magnani, depicted a young simple-minded peasant girl who is intoxicated and seduced by a man whom she believes to be St. Joseph. When she learns that she is pregnant, she thinks it is a miracle by God's grace. She is mocked by the housewives in her village and lives alone in a cave until her time comes; then she finds her way to an empty church, where she gives birth to her son.

The film critic of the Vatican newspaper did not in any way suggest that *The Miracle* was offensive to Roman Catholicism, but the Catholic Cinematographic Centre, a Vatican censorship agency, declared that the movie "constitutes an abominable profanation from religious and moral viewpoints." Yet it was not censored. It was freely shown in Italy, which has religious censorship. Then it played in New York City with English subtitles for several weeks, until a Catholic organization for film censorship, the National Legion of Decency, attacked it as "a sacrilegious and blasphemous mockery of Christian religious truth." Francis Cardinal Spellman of New York also condemned the movie.[10]

New York State had a film-censorship board, an agency of its Board of Regents. A state statute authorized the board to ban movies that were "obscene, indecent, immoral, inhuman, sacrilegious," or of such a character as to corrupt morals or incite to crime. After the public outcry against the film from Catholic sources, and despite favorable reviews by movie critics, the film board decided that the movie was "sacrilegious" and banned its further exhibition, because the "mockery or profaning" of the sacred religious beliefs of any portion of the state's citizens was "abhorrent to the laws" of the state. On review, the state's highest court upheld the censorship, ruling that "sacrilege," which meant "the act of violating or profaning anything sacred," was an adequately definite standard, although it defined "profane" as a synonym of "sacrilege." The state court declared that it meant "that no religion . . . shall be treated with contempt, mockery, scorn and ridicule." The court also found no violation of the First Amendment's guarantees and held that commercial motion pictures are not entitled to the protections of free speech and press. The U.S. Supreme Court unanimously reversed in an opinion by Justice Tom Clark.

Clark ruled that movies, which are a significant medium for the communication of ideas, *are* protected by the First Amendment. He declared that "sacrilegious" is so vague and indefinite as to offend due process of law. The New York statute also unconstitutionally abridged freedom of speech and press. Censorship constituted a form of prior restraint, which the First Amendment prohibited. The all-inclusive definition of "sacrilege" by the New York courts vested the censor with an unrestrained control over movies. The state, Clark stated, "has no legitimate interest in protecting any or all religions from views which are distasteful to them." He added, "It is not the business of government in our nation to suppress real or imagined attacks upon a particular religious doctrine," whether expressed in movies, speeches, or publications. Clark did not mention blasphemy.[11] In effect, however, what he said about sacrilege was completely applicable to blasphemy.

Justice Frankfurter, joined by two others, made that point explicitly in his concurring opinion. He regarded words such as "sacred," "profane," "sacrilegious," and "blasphemous" as impossibly vague, especially as used by the state film board and the state courts. Frankfurter observed that the basic meaning of "sacrilege" was "church robbing." In Roman Catholic thought, the word meant injurious acts against sacred places, persons, or things. "Blasphemy" coexisted with "sacrilege" as a religious crime in Catholic thought, but "blasphemy," like "heresy," applied to doctrine and dogma. In English law, "sacrilege" meant doing injury to the property of the established church. A summary of the meaning of "sacrilege" and "blasphemy" in dictionaries since 1651 occupied an eight-page appendix to Frankfurter's opinion. He concluded that the New York courts had construed "sacrilege" as if it meant "blasphemy," which he said was "a peculiarly verbal offense." If "sacrilege" meant more than physical abuse of sacred persons, places, and objects, it permitted censorship of religious opinions, just like the prosecution of blasphemous statements. "Blasphemy," Frankfurter declared, "was the chameleon phrase which meant the criticism of whatever the ruling authority of the moment established as orthodox religious opinion." To allow the state to censor on the basis of sacrilege or blasphemy would have stultifying consequences on the creative process and fetter the mind, in violation of the First Amendment.[12]

After the case of *The Miracle*, no state blasphemy act could survive the appellate process if challenged on free-speech grounds or even due-process grounds. And the strongest argument against the constitutionality of a blasphemy statute was not even involved in the case of *The Miracle*—namely, preferential treatment of Christianity, or the promotion of religion in violation of the First Amendment's establishment clause.

Such was the state of First Amendment law in 1968 when a blasphemy case occurred in Maryland. Because of the decision on *The Miracle*, Maryland's appellate courts voided the state's old statute on blasphemy, inaugurating a new age: the end of blasphemy convictions in the United States.

In Carroll County, Maryland, Charles J. Simpson, a magistrate who was not a lawyer, first became aware of Maryland's 1723 statute on blasphemy in 1968, when a state trooper accused three young men of that crime. They pleaded guilty before Simpson, who fined them $25 each. He relished the blasphemy statute, which punished anyone who blasphemed or cursed God or used profane words about Christ or the Trinity. Simpson did not understand that the statute criminalized blasphemy, not profanity, that it clearly discriminated against Unitarians and Jews, and that it gave preferential treatment to orthodox Christianity. He thought that the blasphemy statute allowed him to impose an additional sentence on people who were guilty of disorderly conduct. Accordingly, he urged police to bring a charge of blasphemy whenever they thought it appropriate. Like Simpson, the police in Westminster, Maryland, and elsewhere in Carroll County confused profanity with blasphemy.

When Irving K. West, a truckdriver, was arrested for disorderly conduct, he told the police officer to "get your God damn hands off me." Simpson sentenced West to thirty days in jail for his supposed blasphemy. The ACLU, on learning about West's case, filed an appeal challenging the constitutionality of the 1723 blasphemy statute, rather than explaining that the conviction should be reversed because West had not blasphemed when he cursed the officer. West, who had served three days in jail, was released on bail. But Simpson was not stymied. Another man, on being stopped for speeding by a state trooper, exclaimed "God damn" and found himself convicted of blasphemy as well as speeding. The enforcement of his sentence depended on the outcome of West's case.[13]

In May 1969, a Carroll County Circuit Court judge, Edward O. Weant, Jr., ruled that the "archaic" 1723 statute was unconstitutional. Weant reasoned that it violated the First Amendment's clause against establishments of religion as well as its free-speech clause. The state's attorney had argued that, despite its origins, the statute had lost its religious significance and merely connoted that indecent language in public should be punished. Judge Weant responded that the charge of blasphemy against West derived from the fact that the statute sought to protect Christianity, favoring it in a way that conflicted with the establishment clause. Weant reversed West's conviction. The state appealed, in the hope of getting Weant's opinion overruled.[14]

Two weeks later, in nearby Wilmington, Delaware, state police arrested two teenage boys, Matthew A. Bennett and William Bertolette, for blasphemy. The crime of the high-school seniors was the publication and sale of an underground newspaper, *Acid Flash*, in which they said that Jesus was born a "bastard." They faced a possible sentence of one year in prison as well as a fine, under the Delaware blasphemy statute, which had originated in 1682 and been revised and re-enacted in 1740 and 1826. The constitutionality of that statute had been sustained by the Delaware Supreme Court in 1837 in an opinion by Chief Justice John M. Clayton.[15] However, in 1967 a panel of lawyers seeking revisions in the state's criminal code urged abolition of the blasphemy statute. The panel believed that blasphemy should be tolerated, and that doubts existed about the propriety of the state's involvement "in a primarily religious area." The legislature did nothing. But when the two boys were charged with blasphemy in 1969 and jailed because they could not make a high bail, the Wilmington *Evening Journal* questioned the constitutionality of the old blasphemy statute and quoted from Judge Weant's recent opinion in Maryland.[16]

Because both boys had attorneys, the ACLU intervened only to file a brief in the case as a friend of the court. It determined to challenge the constitutionality of the statute. The next day, the two boys were released from jail awaiting trial. Delaware procrastinated, and then, four months after the original arrests, the state prosecutor informed the Superior Court that the state was withdrawing the blasphemy charges. When Judge Andrew D. Christie asked him whether the 143-year-old statute should remain on the books, the prosecutor replied: "It is the opinion of our office that it should be changed. Religious beliefs vary, and we feel everyone has a right to express their own religion and religious belief." Judge Christie responded that the attorney general would have difficulty administering the statute, which would likely be found unconstitutional.[17]

In 1970, the Court of Special Appeals of Maryland finally ruled in

Maryland v. *Irving K. West*. In a unanimous opinion, the five judges observed that the blasphemy statute of 1723 had its origin in an act of 1649, which imposed the death sentence. The later revision retained the substance of the original statute but required that the blasphemous language be maliciously used; it reduced the penalty to boring through the tongue for the first offense, burning the forehead with the letter "B" for a second offense, and death for the third offense. A revision of 1860 reduced those penalties to imprisonment and fine. But all versions of the statute, the court observed, were intended to preserve the sanctity of the Christian religion.

The First Amendment, the court stated, banned laws respecting an establishment of religion. Although even the Supreme Court had observed that "we are a religious people whose institutions presuppose a Supreme Being,"[18] the establishment clause prohibited not only preferring one religion over others but even aiding all religions and favoring believers over nonbelievers. Relying on Supreme Court decisions, the Maryland court reasoned that, whenever the power and prestige of government supports a particular religion or religious belief, the wall of separation between church and state has been breached. Government, state and federal, must assume a "neutral position" with respect to religion. The Supreme Court had held that, if the purpose and primary effect of an enactment is to advance religion, the enactment violates the First Amendment.[19]

Maryland had argued that the old blasphemy statute had gained a "secular aura" in an effort to avoid breach of the peace by persons who felt outraged by blasphemous statements. The court repudiated the validity of this contention, because neither the history of the statute nor its language justified relating its prohibitions to prevention of violence or breach of the peace. The statute categorically proscribed blasphemous statements under any and all circumstances. "Patently," the court observed, "the statute was intended to protect and preserve and perpetuate the Christian religion in this state." Therefore, it conflicted with both of the religion clauses of the First Amendment.[20]

The opinion in *West* was by no means definitive. It did not consider arguments that might be made on behalf of the blasphemy statute, especially those dealing with legitimate limitations on free expression. Criminal libels such as obscenity and blasphemy may be viewed as abuses of First Amendment liberties, especially if they employ language that shocks and insults. Although the Maryland court did not face the free-speech issue in *West*, if it had done so, the court might have held the statute unconstitutional on the ground that shock and insult, regardless of how sincerely felt, cannot be the measure of a constitutional liberty, for that would make the religious sensitivity of believers the test of their critics' freedom. Moreover, even if a blasphemy statute could be defended as not conflicting with the free-exercise and free-speech clauses, the Maryland court had presented an unanswerable objection to the constitutionality of prosecuting blasphemy: prosecution conflicted with the prohibition against laws concerning establishments of religion.

The coup de grâce against blasphemy prosecutions was not an opinion by the Supreme Court, and not even a state-court decision that gave fuller consideration to the issue than Maryland's *West* case. It was an incident in Pennsylvania, but not a decision by that state's high court to overrule *Updegraph* v. *Commonwealth*, the 1824 decision sustaining a blasphemy statute on the ground that Christianity was part of the state's common law. Rather, the incident simply involved the dropping of charges in a blasphemy prosecution.

Since the decision in 1824, Pennsylvania had had a history of supporting Christianity by various legal means. Regarding Sunday as "a holy and sacred day," the state criminalized working on that day "as a profanation of the Lord's day." The state high court sustained the conviction of a Seventh-Day Adventist for working on Sunday.[21] A later decision sustained Sunday laws on the ground that Christianity was part of the state's common law.[22] Pennsylvania regarded profanity as a crime and punished imprecations of divine vengeance and the taking of the Lord's name in vain.[23] Pennyslvania regarded as void a bequest that property should be used to establish and run "The Infidel Society of Philadelphia," the court observing that the bequest insulted the popular religion of the state.[24] The state court reaffirmed this decision in 1880, when ruling that no trust could be enforced if its object was to propagate atheism in contradiction of the public morals and truths of Christianity.[25] Given Pennsylvania's persistent support of laws favoring Christianity, despite a state constitutional ban on laws preferring one religion over others, the change of view is significant.

That change happened in 1971 in a case involving two Pittsburgh shopkeepers who were charged with blasphemy under a statute of 1794, because they displayed in the windows of their stores a "wanted" poster for Jesus Christ. A long-haired, hippie likeness of Jesus adorned the poster, which said: "Wanted for sedition, criminal anarchy, vagrancy and conspiracy to overthrow the established government. Dresses poorly; said to be a carpenter by trade; ill-nourished; associates with common working people, unemployed, and bums. Alien; said to be a Jew." The ACLU defended both shopkeepers at a preliminary hearing and attacked the constitutionality of the blasphemy statute. The county prosecutor asked the magistrate to drop the charges, and the case ended.[26] With it ended blasphemy prosecutions in the United States: there has not been one since 1971 in any state.

Periodically, however, religious organizations claim to be powerfully offended by some publication or movie and seek to suppress it or punish as blasphemers those responsible for it. They are fully justified in the expression of their opinions. But some prosecutor must decide whether to take legal action based on each complaint. No prosecutor has supported legal action in such a case since the Pittsburgh poster complaint. A few illustrations reinforce the generalization that no blasphemy prosecution is likely to succeed.

In 1976, *The Passover Plot*, a movie based on a book by Hugh J. Schonfield, disturbed Christian fundamentalists. The movie depicted Jesus as a revolutionary who plotted his own crucifixion to free Jews from Roman rule and faked his death in a plan that failed. The United States Catholic Conference rated the movie as "condemned," because it was repugnant to believing Christians. An Interfaith Committee Against Blasphemy, operating out of Glendale, California, sought to boycott the film and instigate a prosecution. Nothing happened. In Israel, however, the Film Censorship Board banned *The Passover Plot* because it was so offensive to the Christian minority.[27]

In 1977, NBC-TV braved fiery protests against the showing of Franco Zeffirelli's six-hour movie, *Jesus of Nazareth*, which featured an international cast of film stars. General Motors withdrew its sponsorship after various evangelical groups scorched the film as "blasphemous." The Reverend Bob Jones of Bob Jones University declared, "The blasphemy of humanizing Jesus and denying His deity will not help the image of General Motors." The most interesting aspect of that statement is that it refrained from demanding a prosecution.[28]

Religious people can become offended easily. Some fundamentalists, for example, protested that *Oh God!* was blasphemous. Hardly. It was an amusing and silly but reverent movie starring George Burns as God. By contrast, a 1979 film, *Life of Brian*, a gross burlesque of the life of Jesus by the British comedy group "Monty Python," seemed vicious and vulgar. The Roman Catholic church and Orthodox rabbis joined forces in assailing the movie as profoundly blasphemous. Without doubt, it mocked Judaism, the Bible, and Christianity in as offensive a manner as it could, yet it received some favorable reviews from important critics and played profitably all over the nation. Significantly, despite all the intemperate denunciation of the film, no one sought to ban it or prosecute those responsible for it.[29]

Probably the greatest hullabaloo over a supposedly blasphemous film occurred in 1988 because of the movie *The Last Temptation of Christ*. A boring and dreadful film, based on the novel of the same name by Nikos Kazantzakis, it caused consternation mainly because of a sequence in which a delirious Jesus on the cross imagined himself a normal human being who had loved and married Mary Magdalene and fathered her children. Although the director, Martin Scorsese, and most others connected with the film were not Jewish, it occasioned some ugly anti-Semitism, because the company that owned it had a Jewish chief executive. The film created controversy worldwide and was banned in several countries. Scorsese and the director of the Venice Film Festival were prosecuted for blasphemy in Rome but were acquitted. In the United States, despite all the intense condemnation of the film as blasphemous, especially by Roman Catholic authorities, nowhere except in one county in Florida was an attempt made to ban its exhibition.[30]

The day before *The Last Temptation of Christ* was scheduled to be shown in Escambia County, Florida, the Board of County Commissioners held a public hearing at which several citizens, none of whom had seen the film, demanded that its showing be prohibited. One woman was convinced that "a majority of Americans considered the movie to be blasphemous." Other witnesses gave similar testimony. The local prosecutor, who was the county attorney, declared that the First Amendment made banning the movie futile, because no ban could withstand constitutional challenges. He urged that the board merely pass a resolution stating its feelings about the showing of the movie. One member of the board, however, rejected that recommendation, on the grounds that Jesus himself would have taken more definitive action, that the film was blasphemous and should be challenged on that basis, and that it was time to stand up for laws based on the Bible. Another board member cautioned that a ban would merely play into the hands of the movie's producer by making people more curious to see it. The board had no more respect for her opinion than for the county attorney's. By a four-to-one vote, the board voted for an ordinance that prohibited the showing of the movie in Escambia County at risk of a penalty of sixty days in jail or $500 or both.[31]

A phone call from Scorsese's office in California to a Tampa, Florida, law firm prompted five people to work throughout the night and then board a 6:00 A.M. flight to Pensacola, where the United States District Court, presided over by Judge Roger Vinson, would hear their argument to enjoin the enforcement of the ban. Meanwhile, the ACLU had also intervened and commissioned a Pensacola attorney to appear as a friend of the court. The brief in the case for the injunction was overpowering. Judge Vinson's decision merely abridged the arguments presented to him against the ban.[32]

Judge Vinson issued the restraining order against the ban because it was clearly unconstitutional as a violation of the First Amendment. He described the ban as a "classic example of a prior restraint" on the showing of the film. The case was governed by the precedent of *The Miracle*.

Responding to the argument that the film offended many people on religious grounds, he noted that no one was required to see it. Moreover, government could not dictate what religious views should be endorsed or banned, nor could government favor one religion over another. If the county could interfere with the rights of citizens "by decreeing what can or cannot be read, heard, or viewed," freedom would be endangered.[33]

CHAPTER TWENTY-SIX

The Gay News *Case*

S EX AND religion are intimately related in pages of the Old Testament. Sexual images saturate Ezekiel and the Song of Solomon.
Christian thought also reflects sexual imagery. The depiction of Jesus
Christ as a bridegroom, the image of the church as the bride, the eroticism of Michelangelo's original Sistine frescoes, and the poetry of
seventeenth-century Anglo-Catholics suggest a union of spiritual and
physical love. For good reason, the law of obscenity originated as an
offshoot of the law of blasphemy, before splitting apart in the eighteenth
century as a separate branch of criminal libel. The virgin birth was
always a likely subject for blasphemous ridicule, from Taylor's mad
utterances in the seventeenth century, to Paine's sarcasms, to Yeats's
"Stick of Incense":

> Whence did all that fury come?
> From empty tomb or Virgin womb?
> St. Joseph thought the world would melt,
> But liked the way his finger smelt.[1]

Birth control and censorship were as close as sex and religion. From
the time of Richard Carlile, blaspheming freethinkers championed the
use of contraceptives and wrote shocking birth-control manuals. The
most famous of these manuals was *The Fruits of Philosophy: The Private
Companion of Young Married People* (1832), by Charles Knowlton, an American who acknowledged himself to be an infidel. Significantly, he was
associated with Abner Kneeland, whom Massachusetts condemned for
blasphemy, and Knowlton's work was published in England by James
Watson, one of Carlile's blasphemous shopmen, by George Holyoake,
and later by Charles Bradlaugh and Annie Besant.[2]

Prosecutions for obscenity were not only related to those for blasphemy but were sometimes government devices to maximize the likelihood of imprisoning a blasphemer who might otherwise escape. The

government's choice of the crime depended on its calculation of which was most likely to succeed with a jury.[3]

After Gott's case of 1921, the crime of blasphemy, however frequently committed, disappeared from courtrooms; prosecutions for obscenity, with or without religious overtones, became routine from the early twentieth century through the 1950s.[4] Even so, the bounds of toleration kept widening. As early as 1931, D. H. Lawrence published a story, "The Man Who Died," that depicted Jesus, having survived his crucifixion, as enjoying sexual intercourse with a priestess of Isis. But no scurrilous or ribald word marred the story, except for the play on words about the "risen" Christ, and it was left unnoticed by the law.[5] The law also turned its deaf ear and blind eye toward smutty gags about the Second Coming.

By the 1960s, England had become indifferent to blasphemy. In 1962, Kingsley Amis published an irreverent poem that presented Jesus as a failure. Amis contended that, in the event of a Second Coming, Jesus ought to stick around a while longer to get to know the world by experiencing it. He should fall in love, marry, have children, and risk feeling about life and its problems, rather than just hearing about them as before. "People have suffered worse / And more durable wrongs / Than you did on that cross," wrote Amis flippantly.

> So, next time, come off it,
> And get some service in,
> Jack, long before you start
> Laying down the old law:
> If you still want to then,
> Tell your dad that from me.[6]

Half a century earlier, Thomas Stewart had been imprisoned for saying that only crazy people believed that Jesus had saved the world.

A decade after Amis's poem, *Godspell*, a rock musical, attracted theatregoers for several years. Depicting Jesus as a circus clown, the exact crime for which Gott spent nine months in prison, *Godspell* dressed Jesus in a Superman shirt, a baggy costume, and a bulbous red nose. His history was told in circus tricks, in TV quiz-show parodies, and in cartoon voices. By 1976, John Updike's *Marry Me* could with impunity include the following lines:

> "Heaven," Jerry said one night, entering her as she crouched above him. Afterward, he explained, "I had this very clear vision of the Bodily Ascension, of me going up into this incredibly soft, warm, boundless sky: you."
> "Isn't that blasphemous?"

"Because it makes my prick Christ? I wonder. They both have this quality, of being more important than they should be. As Christ relates to the universe, my prick relates to me."[7]

What once had been flagrant blasphemy as well as obscenity had become just fiction. Small wonder that in 1967, with no fanfare, Parliament quietly revoked the Blasphemy Act of 1698 and other "obsolete" statutes. The revocation came in the Criminal Justice Act of 1967, adopted at the recommendation of a government law commission, which described the statute and related ones as obsolete. Said Lord Gardiner in 1978, "According to my recollection, no one spoke a word in their favour. It was the general belief that we had now abolished the laws of blasphemy."[8] The common law of blasphemy, however, slept undisturbed in old judicial opinions.

Limits therefore remained on opinions about religion, despite the difficulties in defining those limits. In the same year as the publication of Updike's novel, Jens Jorgen Thorsen, a Danish film director, flamboyantly announced his intention to come to England for the purpose of making a pornographic film about the sex life of Jesus. "Pornography," he announced, "is a fine old tradition in England, and I, for one, see nothing wrong with it." He meant to depict Jesus in explicit sexual scenes with John the Baptist, Mary Magdalene, and an Arab girl. From Rome, the pope, echoed by both the Catholic archbishop in England and the archbishop of Canterbury, denounced the "blasphemous outrage." Prime Minister James Callaghan declared that the film would be deeply offensive and warned Thorsen not to enter the country to make it. He did not.[9]

At about the same time, in June of 1976, *Gay News*, a British fortnightly journal aimed at a homosexual readership, published a poem, "The Love That Dares to Speak Its Name."[10] The author was James Kirkup, an English poet of some distinction who was then a visiting professor at Amherst College. His poem consisted of sixty-six lines of free verse, printed on one full page of the tabloid-size paper with a large drawing to one side, showing the Roman centurion, behind Jesus, removing his body from the cross. Jesus is drawn in full frontal nudity and, in the phrase of the poem, "well hung." The poem's title derived from Lord Alfred Douglas's poem of 1894, "Two Loves," which termed homosexuality "the love that dare not speak its name." Kirkup's theme was the opposite: homosexual love does in fact now dare to speak its name.

The poem provoked the first British blasphemy prosecution in fifty-six years, the first since Gott's case in 1921. A Roman centurion narrates the poem in the first person. He was the one who, standing at the foot of the cross, had pierced Christ with a lance to hasten his death. The centurion, in the discreet phrasing of an appellate judge, describes "in explicit detail acts of sodomy and fellatio with the body of Christ" immediately after his death.[11] The poem is a homosexual fantasy whose point is that love is both physical and spiritual, that the two are inseparable, at least from Kirkup's gay standpoint, and that because of such love the unbelieving centurion becomes a convert to Christ.

After the trial and conviction of the editor of *Gay News* and of its publishing company, Kirkup, who had been in Kyoto at the time of the trial, declared that he felt "persecuted" and would never return to Britain. He had written the poem, he explained, "to portray strong deep emotion and intense passion (in both senses of the word), to present a human, earthly, and imperfect Christ symbolising my own outcast state and that of all outcasts in the society." He had no intent to blaspheme, although he realized that his poem would "dismay and shock some people," but he thought turnabout was fair play.

He himself had been dismayed and shocked most of his life by aspects of Christianity, not least the "grisly, gory details" of the cruxifixion. Although he described himself as "a born unbeliever who yet longed to believe," and stated, "I was never a Christian," he had attended a Methodist Sunday school as a child. It was "a dreadful place," he wrote, "like all Christian churches ever since," filling him with gloom and despair. At the age of five, when he heard of the torments of the damned, he wet his pants. He could never take part in holy communion, "for the very thought of eating bits of Christ's dead flesh and drinking cups of his blood" sickened him.

As for his poem, his motives were pure. He wanted to "create a work of art," not to blaspheme. He meant to "see Christ anew in terms of modern sexual liberation" valid for all people. He saw Christ as "a real human being" who once lived on this earth with "the same lusts, failings, ecstasies and sexual equipment" as the rest of us. Yet he thought that anyone who interpreted the poem "on a literal level" was naïve, because it should be construed "on the spiritual and poetic and mystical level on which it was written." He wanted, finally, to express "passionate love" for Jesus with both "humour and realism." His own religious nature had inspired him, Kirkup insisted; his poem was about "the transforming power of human and divine love. It is about the mystery of miracles—the miracle of the conversion of the centurion Longinus, and the resurrection of the dead body of Jesus through our human, earthly loves and desires."[12]

Kirkup apparently was unaware that his view of the resurrection, and surely his depiction of it in the poem, mocked Christian beliefs. Indeed, the poem blasphemed Christianity in a variety of ways. No one without a copy is likely to understand that. Since the formal records of the case do not reprint the poem or even quote from it, future scholars and judges, working from those records, are likely to wonder why it stirred such a controversy or even incited the prosecution. They might think that its homosexual character constitutes the explanation, as many in the gay community wanted people to think. Yet Hugh Montefiore, a bishop of the Church of England, had said, without criminal repercussions, that Jesus might have been gay; the trial judge in the *Gay News* prosecution said that to depict Jesus as gay did not constitute blasphemy; and the prosecutor of record, Mary Whitehouse, summed up by recalling:

> Now, as Judge King-Hamilton pointed out, it is not blasphe-
> mous to say for example, as Bishop Montefiore said, that Christ
> may have been a homosexual. Since he expressed this view in a
> reasonable fashion it could not be regarded as blasphemous. It is
> only blasphemous if it is so offensive in its manner to Christians
> and sympathisers with the Christian faith that it would be liable to
> cause a breach of the peace.[13]

Homosexuals took for granted that the poem was prosecuted because it appeared in *Gay News*, as if there would have been no prosecution if it had appeared in the *Times* of London. But if the poem had appeared in a major newspaper, it would have shocked more readers. The circulation of *Gay News* was about twenty thousand, and its readership was primarily the gay community. The poem was overlooked for about three months after its publication, indicating that it did not shock or insult its readers, which was probably an excellent reason that it should not have been prosecuted. Even after a casual "straight" reader very belatedly discovered the poem, prosecuting it for blasphemy gave it maximum publicity that did nothing for the protection of Christian sensibilities.

The poem is unique. The centurion, alone with the warm body of Jesus, begins to make love to him. "For the last time / I had my lips around the tip / of that great cock, the instrument / of our salvation, our eternal joy." Fellatio with Jesus might not be blasphemous, but describing his penis as the instrument of salvation *is* blasphemous from a Christian standpoint. In view of the Bible's rejection of homosexuality, to depict Jesus as promiscuously gay invites shock. The centurion says, "I knew he'd had it off with other men," and he enumerates at least seventeen, including the twelve disciples, with whom Jesus had had sex "together and apart." Stripping off his uniform, the centurion grew hot with love and in every orifice of Jesus' body, including his wounds, "I came and came and came, / as if each coming was my last." Then a miracle occurred: "I felt him enter into me, and fiercely spend / his spirit's final seed within my hole. . . . He crucified me with him into kingdom come.

This is the passionate and blissful crucifixion same sex lovers suffer."

The poem is fantasy, granted, but even as a metaphor it blasphemes the crucifixion, from a Christian viewpoint. The depiction of Jesus engaged in anal intercourse and ejaculating becomes blasphemy when identified with the crucifixion, just as it is blasphemy to speak of the resurrection as "the horny paradise" of the entwined bodies. The poem ends with the centurion's conversion when, after three days, Jesus appears before him and "took me to him with the love that now forever dares to speak its name." That blasphemes the Christian concept of salvation, notwithstanding Kirkup's belief that he had expressed himself with "humour and realism" in the course of his "spiritual and poetic and mystical poem."

Mary Whitehouse, a woman in her upper sixties, learned about Kirkup's poem more than three months after its publication. Quickly she oiled the wheels of British justice to secure a prosecution for blasphemy. "I simply had to protect our Lord," she explained. As head of the National Viewers' and Listeners' Association, Whitehouse did everything possible to keep the presses, movie screens, and airwaves free from any materials that might be smutty or denigrate Christianity. Her enemies, especially at the BBC, regarded her as a female cross between Anthony Comstock and Joseph McCarthy, crusading for Christian evangelism. Without doubt, she made herself an effective censor of public morals.[14]

On reading Kirkup's poem, Mrs. Whitehouse wrote her lawyer to determine "if it was blasphemous, if we could take action under the law." She was fairly sure of her ground, explaining that the offense "lies in the attacking of Christianity in an indecent manner, with intent to bring religion into contempt, corrupt public morals and shock or insult believers." A prosecution, she added, if successful, "would kill the Thorsen film stone dead—and a good deal more!" She intended to institute a private prosecution for blasphemy.[15]

When the case was over, Whitehouse was asked why she had prosecuted, thus giving such publicity to the poem and defeating the purpose of protecting Christian feelings. She replied that, if *Gay News* got away with impunity, greater blasphemy on a wider scale would have resulted, for there was a "lobby which is out for the destruction of the Christian faith."[16] Her fears seem hysterical if they were sincere.

Private prosecutions for blasphemy, which had been prominent in the early nineteenth century, had all but died out. Probably the most famous private prosecution was Hetherington's against Moxon in 1840 for publishing *Queen Mab*. At the close of November 1976, Whitehouse issued a press statement indicating her intention to prosecute the June 1976 issue of *Gay News* for containing "a blasphemous and obscene poem" about Jesus. She acted in accordance with a statute of 1888 that required the approval of a judge before a prosecution for blasphemy or other criminal libel could be instituted. Accordingly, her solicitor appeared before a judge of the Queen's Bench for permission to bring the action. The solicitor for *Gay News* responded that Kirkup was a distinguished poet, that the paper had received only a few letters of complaint and no phone calls, and that the reactions could scarcely be described as an expression of public "outrage." The high-court judge first granted leave for the prosecution and then granted a bill of indictment, enabling the case to go to trial at Old Bailey without further preliminaries.[17] The case continued in the name of the crown: the Queen against Denis Lemon, who edited *Gay News*, and against Gay News Ltd., the publisher. The *Times* of London repeatedly stated that "the prosecution had been taken over by the Crown," yet it remained a private prosecution, with the counsel for the prosecution chosen by Whitehouse.[18]

She and her lawyers decided that the prosecution against the printer and the illustrator should be dropped and that none should be instituted against Kirkup. He was out of the country and, they reasoned, had written privately, or at least did not publicize the poem; only Lemon and his publisher committed that crime. Since the publisher was a company, Lemon, aged thirty-two, was the only person in the blasphemer's dock where Gott had last stood. Lemon owned a majority of the company's shares. He raised £21,000 for the trial, enough to buy the best defense. Lemon's barrister was John Mortimer, creator of "Rumpole of the Bailey," and the publisher's was Geoffrey Robertson, an eloquent specialist in obscenity cases. The prosecutor, soon to become a Queen's Counsel, was John Smyth, whom Whitehouse described as an "evangelical Christian."[19]

The indictment had only one count and almost none of the usual denunciatory overkill and redundancy that had characterized indictments in blasphemy cases in earlier generations. The defendants were charged with having "unlawfully and wickedly published . . . a blasphemous libel concerning the Christian religion, namely, an obscene poem and illustration vilifying Christ in his life and in his crucifixion."[20] That was terse.

In the spring of 1977, an administrator of the court system asked Judge Alan King-Hamilton to preside at the trial. In his autobiography, the judge wrote that he wondered "if it was because I was a Jew and could therefore be expected to be less offended by the poem than a practising Christian." King-Hamilton was president of his synagogue and a leader of reform Judaism in Britain. He recalled that the poem shocked him when he read it: "One didn't have to be a Christian to be revolted by it." Presumably one had to be heterosexual. In any case, King-Hamilton said that he accepted the assignment because he understood that a judge should never allow his own views to interfere with a fair trial. Appellate-court judges subsequently praised his "masterly" handling of the case.[21]

The case was tried July 4–12, 1977. Outside Old Bailey, pickets from the "Gay Lib Campaign," protesting against what they deemed an attack on homosexuals, depicted Whitehouse in their posters cheek by jowl with Hitler. At times the chant "Kill Whitehouse" was matched by "Kill a queer for Christ." The judge later wanted his readers to understand that the prosecution was not instituted because the paper spoke for homosexuals. "The offending matter was the poem, not the paper which published it." Whether the gay community or the radical one understood that is dubious. Anarchist and Marxist publications distributed leaflet reprints of the controversial page from *Gay News*. Liberals, intellectuals, and artists, who were extremely articulate, censured the prosecution, though far fewer defended the poem. Public opinion, which had been strongly opposed to the Thorsen film, was so divided in the *Gay News* case that Whitehouse could not persuade church leaders to speak out in support of the prosecution. She was convinced that the gay community had intimidated them. "What has happened," she explained, "is quite simply this, that the church has compromised where homosexuality is concerned and it was afraid to come out and say anything about the poem." Inside Old Bailey, wrote the judge, the courtroom was "absolutely packed" throughout the seven-day trial.[22]

About half that time was spent in legal arguments in the absence of the jury, which was sexually and racially mixed. The defendants, Lemon and Gay News Ltd., both used all their peremptory challenges to weed out as jurors people whose threshold of shock seemed low. Copies of the poem were distributed to the jurors, but the judge warned the press not to reprint it. Counsel for the defense then sought to quash the indictment on the unrealistic grounds that the offense of blasphemy had become obsolete and the charge should have been obscenity. Mortimer claimed that, because Britain had evolved into a tolerant, secular, pluralistic society, blasphemy no longer existed as a common-law offense. If Rumpole had made that point before a judge sitting without a jury, his purpose would have been to lay the foundation for an appeal. The House of Lords could change the common law, but the common law of blasphemy consists of judicial precedents from Taylor's case in 1676 to Gott's in 1921. That the House of Lords would overrule the common law was extremely unlikely.

Having noted that the indictment referred to "an obscene poem," Mortimer argued that the prosecution should have brought its charges under the Obscene Publications Act of 1959. Judge King-Hamilton later wrote that in the prevailing climate of permissiveness, which resulted in prosecutorial failures under the Obscene Publications Act, Lemon and his employer would likely have been acquitted if the charge had been obscenity rather than blasphemy. A charge of obscenity would have required proof that the poem taken as a whole tended to "deprave and corrupt" its readers. Moreover, the statute of 1959 allowed expert testimony on the question whether the publication served the interests of science, literature, art, learning, or other matters of public concern.[23]

Judge King-Hamilton, ruling against the motion to quash the indictment, observed that the essence of the offense was blasphemy, not obscenity, although the blasphemy took the form of an obscene poem. He also ruled that expert testimony was not required, because the poem spoke for itself. Smyth for the prosecution wanted expert theological testimony to prove that the poem blasphemed Christian beliefs and doctrines, but the judge disallowed that motion too. He did not want literary critics and theologians confusing the jury or bogging down the case with their controversies. It did not occur to him that the experts might have enlightened the jury. He believed that the jury was capable of deciding whether the poem was blasphemous without the advice of experts. Inconsistently, however, the judge allowed expert testimony on whether *Gay News* was a responsible paper of merit. Bernard Levin, a literary critic, and Margaret Drabble, a novelist, testified to the good character of the paper. The judge later conceded that he should not have allowed their testimony, because the paper's character was not at issue, only whether the poem it had published was blasphemous.[24]

Smyth opened for the prosecution with a slashing assault on the poem as a blasphemous libel whose "vileness" exceeded anything "the most perverted imagination" could conjure up. He defined the crime in this case as an attack on Christ in such indecent terms that it undermined Christianity and outraged the feelings of any Christian sympathizer. "You can say Christ was a fraud or deceiver, or that Christ may have been a homosexual, provided you say it in a reasonable, measured, reflective, decent way."[25] Smyth's statement indicates that Britain's threshold of toleration had advanced light-years in the little more than a half-century since Gott's time. Smyth's test was Coleridge's, of course, from 1883, when it was acknowledged that a decent denial of God, Christianity, or Christian doctrines did not constitute blasphemy, but never before had a British court heard a prosecutor concede that Christ could be decently described as a fraud or as a homosexual. Smyth nevertheless expressed shock and outrage because of the poem's equation of divine and sexual love. It "desecrated" Christ by portraying him as "utterly promiscuous" and having "performed buggery" with fifteen named people as well as in "orgies with the apostles" and other groups. The poem also "desecrated" the resurrection and salvation.[26]

The defense contended that the offense of blasphemy had not been committed without proof of (1) an intent to attack Christianity, (2) an intent to do so scurrilously, thereby shocking and insulting believers, and (3) an intent to cause a breach of the peace. The judge rejected all three contentions. He thereby wiped out criminal intent as an element of the crime. He also held that the publication need not intend to breach the peace but must just create a tendency toward such a breach; the mere possibility that it might exist, not the probability, sufficed.

Eliminating intent as an issue meant that Lemon could not be interrogated on his reasons for publishing the poem. He could not testify that he had not intended to publish a blasphemy, to insult or outrage Christians, or to attack Christ. Eliminating intent also made the prosecutor's task far easier and substantially broadened the offense of blasphemy, at a time when poetry, stage plays, musical comedies, dramas, novels, and television productions spewed out blasphemies such as Woolston, Paine, Carlile, Foote, and Gott had not dreamed of expressing. Not that art, literature, or other forms of expression were endangered by King-Hamilton's rulings. Even in far less permissive times, high-toned or serious writers such as Matthew Arnold, Algernon Swinburne, George Bernard Shaw, George Moore, and James Joyce never had to worry about blasphemy charges. Kirkup's "Love That Dares to Speak Its Name" was exceptional.

Nevertheless, King-Hamilton's rulings on criminal intent and breach of the peace stretched the law of blasphemy at a time when it should have been narrowly constricted in order to acknowledge the growth of actual freedom of expression. The history of the law of blasphemy seems to prove that criminal intent was an essential element of the offense. Yet in this very case appellate courts would resolve the point in King-Hamilton's favor. He acknowledged that the old cases and treatises, including *Starkie on Libel*, which Coleridge had quoted extensively in the case of Foote and Ramsey, stressed intent. But the defendants in that case had admitted their intention to attack the Christian religion by publishing an issue of their magazine that Christians would regard as blasphemous. King-Hamilton decided, therefore, that there was no knowing whether Coleridge approved of Starkie on intent in the passage that he quoted. Unlike King-Hamilton, Coleridge had clearly endorsed the entire passage.

Nevertheless, several modern authorities, including Halsbury's *Laws of England*, made no reference to intent. Accordingly, the judge defined blasphemy without reference to it: "The offence of blasphemous libel today occurs when there is published anything concerning God, Christ or the Christian religion in terms so scurrilous, abusive or offensive as to outrage the feelings of any members of or sympathizer with the Christian religion and [that] would tend to lead to a breach of the peace."[27] The *Gay News* case redefined the law, making it even more reactionary.

Defense counsel, Robertson and Mortimer, ably provided the arguments that their experts might have made, giving the jury a basis for reasonable doubt about the guilt of the defendants—if the jury were open-minded. Smyth presented the poem as an outrageous attack on Christianity, but defense counsel presented it as religious in nature. Aside from their platitudes about the poem as a reflection of "the artist's search for the truth," they argued that the poem was not blasphemous because, rather than attacking Christ, it glorified him by asserting Christian beliefs—crucifixion, resurrection, salvation—and by speaking of a love for him as understood and experienced by a homosexual man fantasizing about Christ. The poem was "no lavatory limerick" but a serious account of how "one man, a soldier and an unbeliever, found Christian love and salvation." Taken as a whole, the poem accepted Christianity and surely did not revile it. However idiosyncratic the poem might appear to heterosexuals, it was an account of how one man attained his conversion to Christianity and came to know God. Precedents galore, some from the Bible itself, had compared divine love with both human love and sexual love. Homosexuality was not criminal, and the poem simply presented a gay interpretation of Christ. It was published in a gay newspaper, intended mainly for gays, so it was not forced on the public, did not shock or outrage its readers, and would not tend to breach the peace. Robertson quoted Paul to the Corinthians: "I am made all things to all men that by all means I may save some" (1 Corinthians 9:22). Mortimer concluded with a strong plea for tolerance in support of Robertson's interpretation of the poem as a religious statement that did not blaspheme.[28]

KING-HAMILTON's charge strongly supported the prosecution's case. He thought that the poem was blasphemous "on its face" and that its words "spoke for themselves." The language was indecent, he thought. The jury had an obligation to determine whether the poem offended. They should ask themselves what their reactions to it were and whether it aroused feelings of anger or provoked a desire for revenge. The intent of the poem's author, editor, or publisher was irrelevant.

Repeatedly, King-Hamilton used the word "profanity" when describing the poem. To him, it meant something dirty or objectionable, but it is not a synonym for "blasphemy," and defendants were not charged with profanity, just as they were not charged with indecency. For the jury he offered a botched connection between profanity and blasphemy. Profanity of a living person, said the judge murkily, would provoke offense. "How much more offensive is it, and how much more likely to cause a breach of the peace if it is about Christ? Could Christianity have been founded upon the teachings of a man who behaved as alleged in the poem?" Little wonder that gays considered the case as an attack on them.

One wonders whether the judge would have delivered a similar charge if the facts explicitly described Jesus in heterosexual acts. Would such acts have been understood as profaning or vilifying him? As for the arguments in behalf of tolerance, the judge asked "what next?" if there were no limit on expression.

After deliberating for three hours, the jury asked for a fresh instruction on the matter of a tendency to breach of the peace. King-Hamilton repeated Justice Avory's ruling in Gott's case, to the effect that the blasphemy and the breach existed in contemplation of law if any person had an instinct to thrash the one who expressed the sentiments at issue. That too reflected outrageous bias. When the jury reported an hour later that it could not reach a unanimous verdict, King-Hamilton urged them to return a majority verdict of ten to two, or eleven to one, which would be sufficient to convict. Another hour later, the jury returned verdicts of guilty against both defendants, by a vote of ten to two. When the judge sentenced them the next day, he unburdened himself about his lack of doubt that the poem was "quite appalling and contains the most scurrilous profanity." What was appalling was King-Hamilton's persistent abuse of the word "profanity," which as a matter of law referred to the taking of God's name in vain or an imprecation calling on divine judgment. King-Hamilton mauled a legal term and employed it as if it connoted obscenity. For him, explicit homosexuality in connection with Jesus amounted to a crime. He could not understand how Kirkup could write and the paper publish the poem with such a reckless disregard for the feelings of Christians and their sympathizers. The judge then imposed a nine-month suspended sentence on Lemon, fined him £500, and ordered him to pay one-fifth of the prosecution costs; the remainder he assessed against Gay News Ltd., which he fined £1,000. Later the judge wrote that he had been "wrong" in sentencing Lemon and "regretted it." He confessed relief, however, that the Court of Appeal, which reversed Lemon's nine-month suspended sentence, upheld him in all other respects.[29]

The three-member Court of Appeal of the Queen's Bench, in 1978, spoke through a long-winded and discursive opinion by Lord Justice Roskill. Mortimer, on the appeal, had two major arguments. He contended that King-Hamilton should have informed the jury that the prosecution had an obligation to prove that the defendants intended to offend Christians, not just that they intended to publish a poem that the jury took as offensive. Second, he contended that the trial judge should have instructed the jury that the offense of blasphemy could not be committed unless the defendants attacked the Christian religion. (Kirkup's poem purported to be an acceptance of Christianity, not an attack upon it.)

Roskill, for the Court of Appeal, believing that Coleridge had properly enunciated the law of blasphemy in the 1883 prosecution of Ramsey and Foote, quoted his opinion. The lengthy passage began with Coleridge's quotation from *Starkie on Libel*, in which Starkie distinguished between mere denial (matter) and malicious statements (manner). Roskill continued Coleridge's quotation of Starkie as follows:

> It is the mischievous abuse of this state of intellectual liberty which calls for penal censure. The law visits not the honest errors of mankind. A wilful *intention* to pervert, insult, and mislead others, by means of licentious and contumelious abuse applied to sacred subjects, or by wilful misrepresentation or wilful sophistry, *calculated* to mislead the ignorant and the unwary, is the criterion and the test of guilt. A malicious and mischievous *intention*, or what is equivalent to such an *intention*, in law, as well as in morals—a state of apathy and indifference to the interests of society—is the broad boundary between right and wrong.

Coleridge then said: "Now that I believe to be a correct statement of the law." One would think that the court had endorsed Mortimer's point: there must be a showing of criminal intent to blaspheme. Indeed, Roskill added that the entire passage from Starkie should be seen in the context of the opening of the chapter in which the quoted language appeared, and he even quoted Starkie's first line: "The first grand offence of speech and writing is, speaking blasphemously against God, or reproachfully concerning religion, with an *intent* to subvert man's faith in God, or to impair his reverence of him."[30] Incredibly, Roskill then ignored all the quoted material as if it did not exist and declared, as if this were dispositive, that Coleridge had told the jury that, because Ramsey and Foote had admitted an intention to attack Christianity, the jury had to decide whether defendants had expressed themselves offensively or indecently. Coleridge did in fact stress manner over matter, but Roskill did not make his point about intent in the proper way; rather, Coleridge told the jury that intent was not an issue in that case, because the defendants had admitted that they had intended their publication to be an attack on Christianity.

Having misused Starkie and Coleridge on the issue of criminal intent, Roskill then confronted the question whether blasphemy could be committed in the absence of an attack on Christianity. He acknowledged that many early cases showed judges including in their charges to the juries the fact that the defendants must have had an intent to attack, and he acknowledged that, in the Boulter case of 1908 and in Gott's in 1921, the judges had referred to an intent to attack Christianity. However, Roskill insisted that a proper understanding of those cases revealed that the real question in each was whether the defendants had spoken offensively.

Even if one accepted that characterization, it did not alter the fact that the precedents showed "attack" to be an element of blasphemy, just as they showed criminal intent to blaspheme as another element.

According to Roskill, "attack," properly understood, meant a lack of moderation or of decency. Thus, any publication that insulted or aroused resentment was, in effect, an attack. In any case, "attack" did not merely connote hostility. One might shock or offend without attacking, as King-Hamilton had ruled. Roskill noted that neither Justice Coleridge in Foote's case, nor Justice Phillimore in Boulter's, nor Justice Avory in Gott's had instructed the jury that they should not convict unless the evidence proved an intent to blaspheme or to attack. Roskill also approved of King-Hamilton's rulings on the omission of an obscenity count, on the exclusion of expert testimony, and on the meaning of breach of the peace.

In conclusion, the Court of Appeal ruled that the trial judge had correctly informed the jury that they should convict if they believed that the publication vilified Christ even if it did not attack him; moreover, the prosecution did not have to establish any intention beyond one to publish material that the jury believed to be blasphemous. This left the crime of blasphemy anything that a jury found offensive.

A year later, in 1979, the case was appealed to Britain's highest court, the judicial section of the House of Lords, consisting of its law lords, who constitute the ultimate court of appeal, sitting in a bench of five. In the *Gay News* case, the five divided three to two in favor of the prosecution, with each of the five writing an opinion. Viscount Reginald Dilhorne's, on the majority side, most effectively presented its viewpoint. Although he acknowledged that James Fitzjames Stephen and William S. Holdsworth, two of the greatest legal historians, believed that the specific intentions of a libeler must be proved, Dilhorne disagreed with them. Criminal intent, he accurately observed, was almost always inferred from the natural consequences of one's acts. Not until the Criminal Justice Act of 1967 did courts and juries become free from the obligation to presume that a defendant intended or foresaw the results of his actions. That is, if a court or a jury reached the conclusion that certain language was blasphemous, an intent to blaspheme was inferred. So Dilhorne believed. His reasoning was faulty. Intent may validly be inferred from the consequences of one's acts, but not from one's words, unless one utters a threat or criminally incites. A person might express an opinion or write a poem with no intent whatever of shocking, insulting, or offending blasphemously, even though others may react in that unexpected manner.

Dilhorne attached considerable significance to the fact that in none of the leading cases did the trial judge instruct a jury that they must be satisfied with proof that the defendant had intended to blaspheme. (Why

else had Coleridge quoted to the jury Starkie on criminal intent?) Lord
Dilhorne did not answer the two dissenters in this case on the question
whether judges had instructed jurors on intent. But he concluded that
guilt for blasphemy did not depend on the accused's having an intent to
blaspheme, only on the blasphemous nature of his publication.[31]

On the same side, Lord Leslie Scarman wrote an imaginative opinion.
Not only did he believe that the common law of blasphemy served a
useful purpose; he recommended that Parliament should broaden it so
that every religion had the same benefit as Christianity: "I think there is
a case for legislation extending it to protect the religious beliefs and
feelings of non-Christians. The offence belongs to a group of criminal
offences designed to safeguard the internal tranquility of the kingdom. In
an increasingly plural society such as that of modern Britain it is necessary not only to respect the differing religious beliefs, feelings and practices of all but to protect them from scrutiny, vilification, ridicule and
contempt."[32] That revived the Macaulay-Stephen proposition that Britain's blasphemy laws should emulate India's.

Scarman did not bother to point out that India's blasphemy laws were
impotent and that no pluralistic society was more divided by religious
murders and hatred than India. Scarman thought that on the issue of
intent history seemed obscure, leaving the court free to adopt its own
view on the basis of principle. For him, the principle was that publications offending against religion were blasphemous. An intent to blaspheme did not matter, only an intent to publish the words found
blasphemous by a jury. The law, as Scarman would have it, made blasphemous any language about religion that caused a jury to be angry or
resentful.

Lords Kenneth Diplock and Edmund-Davies, dissenting, reviewed
the old cases and convinced themselves that the precedents showed a need
to prove criminal intent to blaspheme. The first Lord Coleridge explicitly
proved the point in Pooley's case, as did Stephen's *Digest of the Criminal
Law*. The second Lord Coleridge, in Bradlaugh's case, as well as in that
of Ramsey and Foote, also spoke about blasphemies as words "calculated
and intended to insult the feelings and the deepest religious convictions"
of Christians. Diplock and Edmund-Davies also construed Boulter's and
Gott's cases as additional proof that the jury must be satisfied with the
existence of an intention to blaspheme. Justice Phillimore in *Boulter* had
quoted Starkie on willful intent, and Justice Avory in *Gott* had, like
Coleridge, referred to a necessity for the words to be "calculated and
intended to insult the feelings" of believers. The three justices in the
majority in the *Gay News* case failed to confront the proofs adduced by the
dissenters about the precedents.

Diplock, dissenting, believed that, whatever justification had existed for inferring intent prior to the Criminal Justice Act of 1967, after 1967 the evidence of a defendant as to what he had intended had become admissible. The 1967 statute exempted courts and juries from the obligation to infer intent from the natural consequences of defendants' acts. Edmund-Davies concluded that "to treat as irrelevant the state of mind of a person charged with blasphemy would be to take a backward step in the evolution of a humane code." Similarly, Diplock regretted the majority's "retrograde step," which he believed unjustifiable. Diplock added that, although Lemon should have known that his publication of the poem would shock believers, "Mr. Lemon was entitled to his opportunity of sowing the seeds of doubt in the jury's minds."[33]

THE LAW of blasphemy emerged from the *Gay News* case as extremely suppressive in theory. Language having a remote bad tendency to hurt the feelings of believers constituted a breach of the peace, because it could inspire a vengeful impulse. Such language blasphemed, regardless of the intent of those who used it. Although manner, not matter, still counted most, the law became more reactionary than it had been.

In fact, however, not even secularists, freethinkers, or atheists suffered from the law of blasphemy. Gott was the last victim of that kind. The law in reality has had little to do with the law on the books or the law of judges. Modern Britain simply did not prosecute. The *Gay News* case was an anomaly—an effort to prevent Jesus from being kidnapped by the gays. Not even Whitehouse sought prosecution of *Socialist Challenge* and *Socialist Worker*, papers that flauntingly reprinted Kirkup's poem, or of The Free Speech Movement, which offered copies of it to anyone who sent a self-addressed stamped envelope—an offer that still stands.[34]

In the abstract, the law might sustain an inquisition, but it also might just as well have become obsolete, because it existed side by side with unprosecuted blasphemies. John Updike's *Marry Me*, as noted earlier, compared a character's penis to Christ and sexual intercourse to heaven, but the passage was incidental to a novel that was otherwise free of offensive matter. In the 1970s, a spate of books appeared that would have been condemned as blasphemous in earlier eras. One was by a comparative philologist and expert on myths, John Allegro, who traced the origins of Christianity to a cult that ate amanita mushrooms, which hallucinogenically inspired the worship of God as a "mighty penis in the sky ejaculating spermatozoa every time it rained." The book seemed like a scholarly hoax, but its blasphemous character is abundant. *The Jesus Hoax*, by a former nun; *The Myth of God Incarnate*, by Anglican churchmen and professors of theology; and the book from the film *Life of Brian*, by several humorists who call themselves "Monty Python," also escaped legal difficulties. Of all these, only Kirkup's poem was prosecuted for blasphemy, although Jens Jorgen Thorsen would surely have been prosecuted too if he had made the threatened porno film about Jesus.[35]

In sum, whatever the law of blasphemy means in a British court, outside of that court—and that includes the office of the director of public prosecutions—blasphemy is an offense that is no longer prosecuted. The law ticks away as if it were a time bomb that no longer detonates. Yet it is no dud; it is merely dormant and may go off again one day. The judges who dealt with the *Gay News* case ensured its vitality, as did do-nothing parliaments.

CHAPTER TWENTY-SEVEN

The Rushdie Affair:
Should All Religions Be Protected
or None?

AFTER the Lords sustained the convictions in the *Gay News* case, efforts were made to abolish the common law of blasphemy by an act of Parliament. All failed. The principal effort took place in the House of Lords, where Lord Willis, who called himself "a Humanist," introduced the abolition bill. He described the common law as unfair because it did not require proof of intent to blaspheme, did not allow expert witnesses, and did not protect any religion but Christianity. Yet the extension of the law to protect other religions would discriminate against those who, like Lord Willis, had "no particular religious beliefs."

The earl of Halsbury replied that blasphemy was "an act of violence to the deeply spiritual feelings" of believers. When the law of obscenity was relaxed, he claimed, obscenity mushroomed alarmingly; blasphemy would rage if not prosecutable. On the same side, Earl Ferrers argued that to permit a minority of unbelievers to provoke or insult the majority was "wrong." The bishop of Durham opposed abolishing the common law, because it protected deep-rooted values and reverential attitudes that benefited society. But he favored extending the law to protect all religions. The bishop of Leicester, claiming that Christianity, like God, did not require the support of the criminal law, believed that the law of blasphemy should be retained to protect people's feelings against scurrility and ridicule. Those were the main lines of argument in the course of a debate that took less than four hours. In the end, Willis withdrew his bill, because a government law commission was scheduled to review the law on blasphemy. He had known that before introducing the bill. The debate seemed pedestrian as well as futile.[1]

In 1981, that law commission produced a "working paper" that was the most cogently analytical discussion of blasphemy that Britain had ever seen. It was intended as an interim report designed to provoke an informed public discussion. After briefly sketching the history of the law of blasphemy, the commission described its defects in detail. The law was uncertain because its meaning kept changing with time. What was blasphemous in Gott's time, for example, had now become acceptable. However, no one could be sure, because, until a jury rendered a verdict, the question whether the offense had been committed remained unknown. Moreover, the jury's verdict depended on its subjective considerations of what was abusive, shocking, or offensive. No clear objective standards existed for defining the crime.

A century and a half earlier, when certain explicit denials were deemed blasphemous, the law seemed clearer. In those days, breach of the peace resulting from blasphemy meant a likelihood, or at least a fear, that society might be convulsed if religion lost popular respect; revolution was not then considered an impossibility. Breach of the peace did not then refer to individuals' becoming angry. As times changed, "blasphemy" came to mean language that angered Christians, whether or not a public disturbance occurred. Angry feelings, even if only possible, not probable, seemed sufficient to constitute breach of the peace. The offender need not have had an intent to stir up such feelings; his intent had become irrelevant. He or she might be someone with profound religious beliefs and sincere motives and yet have used language that a jury might find shocking. That all struck the commission as too vague.[2]

It found an anomaly or a shortcoming in the fact that the law of blasphemy narrowly protected only Christianity as the established church espoused it. Other denominations and sects were protected only if they shared the beliefs of the established church. The commission might have added that, as a result, the basic belief of Baptists in adult baptism could be blasphemed; so could the basic Quaker belief in the indwelling Christ.

The commission then inquired into the arguments for the maintenance of criminal sanctions against blasphemy. It believed that the argument that prosecutions were necessary to protect religion and society had lost validity, if it ever had any. The law penalized only the manner of expression, not the matter, notwithstanding that a rational and serious discussion might well induce outrage, even violence. The distinction between manner and matter, the commission declared, was not well founded. It observed that an offensive statement might be made decently—that is, calmly or soberly. Often, however, the argument itself, not the language in which it was couched, constituted the offense. Moreover, the serious, respectful phrasing might present an argument that subverted religion far more effectively than nasty language, which might anger yet not convince. In any case, the commission did not believe that the criminal law was "an appropriate means of enforcing respect for religious beliefs."[3]

Blasphemy prosecutions for the protection of public order seemed wholly unjustifiable. Disturbance of the peace could be dealt with if no crime of blasphemy existed. On the other hand, if there were no such crime, the law would provide no recourse for injury done to the feelings of individuals. The commission believed that "the most powerful" argument in behalf of retaining prosecutions for blasphemy "is the effect which it is alleged that insults to religious beliefs may have on those holding such beliefs." The argument assumed, however, that religious beliefs had some sort of pre-eminent position; no other sorts of beliefs were comparably protected. Presumably, the sacred nature of religious beliefs made them special, or made the feelings of their proponents more sensitive to abuse. But the commission found nothing to support an argument that religious beliefs stood in danger of attack, or of being undermined by attack. It also disputed the contention that other beliefs could not be held as deeply or be any less sensitive to assault from abusive or shocking criticism. Political beliefs relating to the flag or to the monarchy might well be as profoundly felt as religious ones. And non-Christian religious beliefs, or beliefs other than those shared by Christians, were as easily offended as Christian beliefs. What, then, justified the narrow scope of the law of blasphemy in England and Wales? Scotland and Northern Ireland managed to maintain society without having a law of blasphemy, and, although Christianity thrived as securely there as in England and Wales, there was no evidence that in Scotland and Northern Ireland religious sensibilities endured more insult than in England and Wales.[4]

Still, the commission professed concern for "public insults intentionally aimed at religious beliefs whose predominant purpose is to cause distress to believers in relation to their faith." It therefore considered alternatives to the unsatisfactory common law of blasphemy. No statute was needed to criminalize the publication of insulting matter likely to provoke a breach of the peace by outraging the religious convictions of others; the law had always penalized breach of the peace. Nor did the commission believe that a new statute was needed to make criminal the incitement to religious hatred. That was likely a weak contention by the commission, as was its claim that criminalizing incitement to religious hatred did not protect the feelings of individuals wounded by insults.

The commission then confronted the main issue: whether Parliament should enact a new statute to punish public insult to the feelings of all religious believers. It answered negatively, primarily because of its concern for free speech. The range of topics capable of causing offense to the feelings of some religious group seemed "so wide that it would constitute an unprecedented curb on freedom of speech." Open arguments about abortion, birth control, blood transfusions, and the use of drugs for medical treatment might be restricted, because all such matters concerned some religious beliefs that could be offended. Moreover, the commission claimed that some religious beliefs deserved to be attacked, such as that adulterers should be stoned to death. That observation returned the commission to its point that the feelings of religious people could be insulted or outraged by matter, cold-sober matter, not merely manner that abused or ridiculed. Accordingly, it advanced the idea that a new blasphemy statute should enable a defendant to show that, even if his remarks caused offense, this was "an ancillary effect irrelevant to his objective in publishing, and that the value of the publication in terms of that objective outweighed its capacity to wound or outrage."[5] The commission also believed strongly that, if a new statute were to replace the existing common law, it should require proof of specific intent to blaspheme.

Yet the commission advocated abolition of the common law without replacement by a new statute. It believed that any new statute ought to protect non-Christian religions as well as Christian ones, but the commission knew of no way to define religion and believed that a failure to do so would make a new statute even more dangerous to freedom of expression. It candidly opposed the extension of the law's protection to every group calling itself religious, contending that the public interest was advanced by attacks on certain practices and beliefs of some groups calling themselves religious. It alluded to the doctrine of mass suicide practiced in Jonestown, and it opposed the law's protection of the Church of Scientology and the Unification Church ("Moonies") as contrary to public policy. Suggesting that there were other religions equally undeserving, the commission discerned no satisfactory solution to the problem of protecting all religious beliefs or of legitimately distinguishing among them. It concluded, therefore, that, in the absence of evidence that religion stood in jeopardy, and in the presence of unacceptable consequences attending the protection of all religions, no new statute was advisable except one that repealed the common law of blasphemy.[6]

Four years passed before the law commission spoke again. It made its final report in 1985, urging complete abolition of the law on blasphemy. Taking account of "the exceptionally heavy response to the provisional proposals of our working paper," the commission observed that it had received reactions from eighteen hundred organizations, groups, and individuals, as well as more than 175 petitions bearing a total of 11,770 signatures. A majority of those who favored retention of the common law or opposed its abolition responded to organized campaigns, especially one led by Mary Whitehouse's National Viewers' and Listeners' Association. Only twenty-nine organizations and fifty-two individuals approved of the recommendation to abolish the common law without replacing it with a new offense of blasphemy. Those so minded included the Baptist Union, the Unitarians, and a division of the Methodists, as well as secularist and free-thought societies, and organizations of the legal profession, police chiefs, journalists, and writers. Those favoring retention of the common law included most Christian church groups as well as Jewish and Muslim societies. The commission also noted that several articles about its working paper had appeared in the law journals.[7] Politely the commission summarized objections to its working paper, without suggesting that it felt despair because those who opposed its views failed to consider its arguments: opponents repeated worn-out views as if the commission had never produced its 166-page analysis.

Most of the commission's final report, which was just forty-nine pages, repeated arguments in its working paper. This repetition seems attributable to the fact that opponents had not troubled to read the working paper. Once again, the commission explained the shortcomings of the common law of blasphemy and of the arguments in its behalf.

Although the commission, which consisted of five people, unanimously favored abolition by Parliament of the common law of blasphemy, only a three-member majority supported the view that Parliament should not enact a new statute preserving the offense. Two members—the chairman, Ralph Gibson, who subsequently became a high-court justice, and Brian Davenport, Q.C.—wrote a terse but compelling statement in dissent. They favored the enactment of a new statute that would be free of the defects of the common law, whose major shortcoming was its protection of one religion only.

The minority commissioners believed that all citizens had a duty in a pluralistic society "not purposely to insult or outrage the religious feelings of others." To abolish the common-law crime without replacing it would leave a legal gap not covered by existing laws against obscenity and breach of the peace, thereby allowing blasphemers deliberately to outrage religious feelings. The dissenters resorted to a poor example to make their point. They declared that discussions vilifying or ridiculing "the concepts of the body and blood of Christ in the Mass or Holy Communion" would cause grave offense to "Christians, and to non-Christians who have respect for Christian beliefs. . . ." But most Protestants other than those of the Church of England had small respect for the Mass or holy communion; the Reformation served as witness to that. James Kirkup had expressed a viewpoint probably shared by most Protestants when he said that "the very thought of eating bits of Christ's dead flesh and drinking cups of his blood made me sick."[8] Still, the gap in the law mentioned by the dissenting commissioners would have existed if the common-law crime had been abolished without replacement.

Except for waffling on the meaning of "religion," the two dissenters were extraordinarily careful in describing the provisions of the statute that they recommended to Parliament. The offense would consist of "grossly abusive or insulting material relating to a religion with the purpose of outraging religious feelings." Thus, they would extend the law's protection "to any religion," not just Christianity. They were willing to leave "religion" undefined, or let Parliament do the defining; they thought a practical solution might be to protect those religious groups having certified places of worship. They stressed that the problem was to safeguard against the deliberate outraging of religious feelings, not to define religion. But they sought also to safeguard against abuses of the new offense of blasphemy that they recommended.

They believed that they had cribbed and cabined the offense sufficiently to protect freedom of speech. Abuse or insult had to be "gross." Criminal intent should be restored to the law of blasphemy; it was "essential that the offence should not be capable of being committed in ignorance or inadvertence." A showing of blasphemous intent—"the deliberate causing of outrage"—would be required on the part of the prosecution. The dissenters would protect statements that attributed folly or evil to that which the religious held sacred, even though such statements knowingly caused outrage. They were not trying to insulate religion from sharp criticism or ridicule, only from publications whose chief purpose was to cause outrage by grossly abusive language. Aware of recriminations among sects, they claimed that religious disputation would not be considered blasphemous under their proposed law. Whether they were realistic in this regard is dubious. Those familiar with the views of Jehovah's Witnesses on Roman Catholicism would likely see grossly abusive language causing, and intended to cause, Catholic outrage. The dissenting commissioners, however, urged three restrictions on the operation of the proposed statute to prevent its misapplication: abolition of the private right of prosecution, as existed in the *Gay News* case; a requirement that the director of public prosecutions must give consent prior to prosecution; and a requirement that indictment by grand jury must also preface any prosecution. The minority concluded that abolition of the common law without replacement would signify that Parliament lacked respect for the reverence that religious people felt toward the sacred.[9]

The majority's statement weighed the minority's views. The majority denied that total abolition of the offense of blasphemy would, as critics charged, unloose a "flood of blasphemous material." No basis for the charge existed, it claimed. It similarly repudiated as groundless the charge that abolition would in effect suggest that Parliament condoned the blasphemies that had been subject to the common law. "Abolition of the common law would undoubtedly be seen, quite properly," said the majority, "as disapproval of an unsatisfactory and archaic offence."[10]

The majority's statement, though insisting on repeal without replacement, acknowledged that a requirement of proof of criminal intent would be beneficial if Parliament did adopt a replacement. The majority did not disagree with the minority's effort to improve the existing common law. Rather, the majority feared that even the minority's law on blasphemy would be unworkable and repressive. They feared that "a new offence, however restrictively drafted, would be used to a greater extent than the common law has been, particularly by adherents of religions who are exceptionally intolerant of criticism or who possess strongly heterodox views to which they wish to draw the attention of society."[11] Islam seemed to have been on the minds of the majority in that respect. They remained convinced that the proposed new offense would unduly restrict freedom of expression.

The restriction of the offense to "gross" abuse or insult did not appease the majority, because they believed that "gross" was as subjective as "abusive" or "insulting." Language regarded as acceptable by one religion could be regarded as grossly abusive or insulting by another: as ever, one person's free speech was another's blasphemy. The majority would not concede that the restoration of criminal intent to the definition of the offense adequately safeguarded liberty of expression. Free speech required that some religious tenets deserved exposure in the strongest terms, including abuse and offense. The critic's purpose, said the majority, "may indeed be to shock or outrage his readers by the use of abuse or insult, the better to realise the effect of that criticism."[12]

Once more the majority argued that too many practical obstacles existed to defining religion or deciding which religions deserved protection. Some did not; others were not regarded by outsiders as religious in nature. Some that were unquestionably religious did not desire protection (e.g., Buddhism and the Baptist Union). The minority's recommendation that all religions that owned certified places of worship should be protected seemed unsatisfactory. Certification by government authorities involved criteria not necessarily relevant or appropriate for defining a religious body that deserved protection against blasphemy. Moreover, no publicly available list existed of certified religions. Similarly, no reliance should be placed on the law of religious charities as a source of determining which religions deserved protection, for that law, as a legal expert had said, was in an "unholy mess." A bequest to an enclosed Roman Catholic convent, for example, was not charitable, because it was not for the public benefit, yet the Moonies were registered as a charity for the advancement of religion.

The majority felt forced to conclude that the definition of religion posed insuperable problems for blasphemy law. They believed that even the minority's proposed statute would result in an offense of "remarkable breadth which, it seems to us, would curb freedom of expression to an unacceptable extent." Besides, the majority contended that a new statute would be contrary to the interests of an increasingly pluralistic and secular society—exactly contrary to the minority view. Perhaps because the commission was divided and the minority had effectively presented its views, Parliament struck its usual pose: it did nothing. As a result, the common law remained as it had been, meaning whatever judges and juries preferred from case to case.[13]

In 1988, the Rushdie affair reignited the question whether the common law should be extended to protect other religions. Salman Rushdie, one of Britain's foremost novelists, published *The Satanic Verses*. The ensuing furor, conducted on an international scale, caused twenty-two persons to lose their lives and many scores to be injured in riots, a disruption in diplomatic relations between the West and Iran, book burning and book banning, and a price on the head of Rushdie as a blasphemer of Islam. The astounding sales of the book in Europe and America made him a multimillionaire who still lives in hiding, protected by the British government from some Muslim assassin who in turn stands to gain at least a million from Iran for murdering Rushdie on behalf of the good name of Allah.[14]

This man whose book constituted a pretext for such upheaval was born in Bombay to a Muslim family but was educated in England at Rugby and Cambridge University. After a couple of years in Karachi, Pakistan, to which his parents had moved, he returned to England. In London, his fiction soon made him prosperous, and his third-world politics made him a darling of left-wing intellectuals. Mocking and sneering at the West, especially the United States and Margaret Thatcher's administration in Britain, Rushdie found in all the world only Sandinista Nicaragua as a place he could commend. His novels reflected his prejudices. Foreign Secretary Geoffrey Howe declared that *The Satanic Verses* had not only deeply offended Muslims but was "extremely critical, rude about us. It compares Britain with Hitler's Germany."[15] Yet the book won the Whitbread Prize, worth £20,000. An earlier novel had won the Booker Prize, Britain's most prestigious literary honor, and Rushdie had been elected a fellow of the Royal Society of Literature.

The Satanic Verses seems to be a phantasmagoric, surrealistic, and absurdist book. It is huge, sprawling, opaque, nihilistic, and kaleidoscopic. It is crammed with esoterica, allegories, parables, metaphors, Arab words, and word plays. It is inventive, exuberant, and incoherent, if not crazy. Little in the book is as it seems, for a devil in one scene is an angel in the next, and heaven becomes hell. It seems to be a book about lost faith on the part of a marginal or alienated man living in a Western, secular, dynamic society who comes from an Asian, religious, traditional society. It is also about the problems of third-world immigrants in modern Britain. Shuttling between London and Bombay, and between the present and seventh-century Arabia, it has at least three different plots. Its language is sometimes "street-smart," but it is definitely not an obscene book, surely not in the disputed passages, Muslim assertions notwithstanding.

Given that Rushdie had been educated as a Muslim, had studied Islamic history at King's College, Cambridge, and had encountered religious censorship as a TV writer during his stay in Pakistan, he should have known that he might produce a sensation by criticizing or undermining the Koran (or Qur'an)—the sacred book of Muslims, believed by them to have been revelations made to Mohammed by God through the archangel Gabriel. Yet two chapters of *The Satanic Verses*, "Mahound" and "Return to Jahilia," contain remarks that even moderate Muslims, let alone fundamentalists, regarded as blasphemous.

When the book was published, Rushdie gave an interview to an Indian journal. Asked about the controversy that had immediately engulfed his book, he replied that no subjects were off limits, "and that includes God, includes prophets." Some people might get "upset" with his book because "it is not reverent," but he had a right to write about religion and revelation from a secular viewpoint. "Besides," he added, "Mohammed is a very interesting figure. . . . He is the only one [among prophets] about whom there is some half-established more-or-less factual historical information. That makes him a human being and doubly interesting."[16] The remark proves that the character Mahound is Rushdie's version of Mohammed, whose name is not mentioned in the novel.

Rushdie blasphemously gave to Islam's holiest figure, the revealer of the Koran, the name "Mahound," which Islam-hating medieval Christians had employed to describe Mohammed as a false prophet who was the agent of the devil, if not Satan himself. Rushdie called the holy city of Mecca "Jahilia," which means "darkness" or "ignorance." He depicted twelve prostitutes as taking the names and then the personalities of Mohammed's twelve wives, though he did not, contrary to the claims of his Islamic detractors, depict Mohammed's twelve wives as prostitutes. Even so, Muslims revere the prophet's wives as "mothers of believers," so that the mere association of them with prostitutes infuriated believers. There is nothing sexy, scatological, or obscene about that section of the book, but Muslims who had not read the book assumed otherwise. Seeming overeager to be offended, Muslims were also insulted that Rushdie had called the revered Abraham "a bastard" in the sense of having been born illegitimately. In the

offensive passage, however, Abraham's wife calls him "a bastard," meaning something like scoundrel, after he abandoned her.

   The worst blasphemies in the book are those that seem to attribute the
Koran, the revealed *ipsissima verba* of God, to Mohammed himself or,
worse still, to Satan. A character in the novel who has Rushdie's first
name serves as Mohammed's scribe, taking down the revelations. Salman
gets a "diabolic idea." He begins changing words surreptitiously: "Little
things at first. If Mahound recited a verse in which God was described as
all-hearing, all-knowing, I would write, *all-knowing, all wise*. Here's the
point: Mahound did not notice the alterations. So there I was, actually
writing the Book, or rewriting it, anyway, polluting the word of God
with my own profane language." Salman could only conclude that, if his
words could not be distinguished from the Revelation by God's own
messenger, the book lacked divine quality. "Now I was writing the Revelation and nobody was noticing." He began making more important
changes and got away with them too, although he recognized that he had
to be careful lest the prophet find out and execute him. Asked how he
knew he would be killed, Salman replies, in a wickedly comic line, "It's
his Word against mine."[17]

   In a different passage, Salman notices that Mahound, who had been
a merchant, received revelations that were to his advantage, making Salman wonder "what manner of God this was that sounded so much like a
businessman." When the faithful disputed Mahound's views on any question, "from the possibility of space travel to the permanence of hell, the
angel [Gabriel] would turn up with an answer, and he always supported
Mahound. . . ."[18]

   Attributing the Koran to human composition indisputably constituted
blasphemy as a matter of Islamic law.[19] Yet Rushdie went further, if
ambiguously, by allowing the inference that Satan was the real author of
the Koran, at least of some verses. The very title of the novel, *The Satanic
Verses*, as understood by literal-minded hostile Islamic critics, suggested
diabolic authorship of the holy word of God. Actually, "satanic verses"
referred to a brief passage that Mohammed subsequently deleted. A
disputed tradition exists for the allegation that, in order to obtain conversions from prosperous members of his tribe, Mohammed accepted
three idolatrous goddesses as divine intercessionaries. The verses in which
he does so are the "satanic verses." "Satan threw on his tongue" those
words of acceptance, which Gabriel subsequently induced him to repudiate. Merely recalling the disputed tradition constituted no blasphemy.

   But Rushdie's rendering of the incident makes Mohammed look self-
seeking. The satanic verses survived in just a couple of collections of old
traditions, which Rushie stated the orthodox would deny or rewrite.
However, Rushdie added a provocative point. Gabriel, whom he calls

"Gibreel," one of the principal characters in the novel, "knows one small detail, just one tiny thing that's a bit of a problem here, namely that *it was me both times* [accepting and rejecting the verses], *baba, me first and second also me.* From my mouth, both the statement and the repudiation, verses and converses, universes and reverses, the whole thing, and we all know how my mouth worked." What we know is that he cannot be trusted; he works for himself.[20] At the least, then, the Koran appears, from Rushdie's words, to be something of a fraud. This outraged Muslims as blasphemous. Rushdie seemed to acknowledge that he had blasphemed. At one point in the book, Mahound growls at the character with Rushdie's first name: "Your blasphemy, Salman, can't be forgiven. Did you think I wouldn't work it out? To set your words against the Words of God."[21]

Worse still, Muslims preferred to believe that the term "satanic verses" stood for the Koran generally, or, as one said, "Rushdie's use of the name of the devil responsible for the fraud is intended to indicate that the whole Koran is fraudulent and Mohammed a mean imposter; not a question of two verses spotted as such but all the 6,236 verses making up the entire book. In other words, the title is a *double entendre.*"[22] Of the entire book, the most horrifying thing was the title.

Very few of those who condemned the book had read it. They claimed that they did not have to. The man who successfully led the movement to ban the book from India declared, "I do not have to wade through a filthy drain to know what filth is." Excerpts and the opinions of those who had read the book satisfied him. Lest he be thought a wild-eyed fanatic, one should know that he also declared: "This is the legal system of a civilised society. We respect each other's religious beliefs. We do not intentionally outrage the religious feelings of others or insult their religion or ridicule the personalities to whom we are emotionally attached or mock our religious susceptibility."[23] Another critic observed that reading the book would not change anyone's mind. That was true: the blasphemies were not imagined, although they were exaggerated. Rushdie probably did not intend his title to apply to anything but the couple of verses about the goddesses, yet that incident hardly warranted the title for the entire book. The bulk of it, seven of nine chapters, was inoffensive, as readers might have determined. No basis existed for the claim that there was "hardly a single page which does not reflect insult."[24] Yet an Asian scholar writing in *The Political Quarterly*, a leading journal, expressed a common view: "Virtually every practising Muslim was offended by passages from the book and shocked that it was written by a Muslim. . . . The truth is that all the religious zealots had to do was simply quote from *Satanic Verses* for anger, shame and hurt to be felt." The book, he said, "was no more a contribution to literary discourse than pissing upon the Bible is a theological argument."[25]

Hysteria accounts for the widespread condemnation of the book as "the most offensive, filthy and abusive book ever written by any hostile enemy of Islam." The author of that statement, a Saudi who chaired the U.K. Action Committee on Islamic Affairs, demanded that all copies of the book be destroyed, that no others be printed, that Muslims of the world receive an "unqualified public apology . . . for the enormous injury to the feelings and sensibilities of the Muslim Community," and that damages be paid to an Islamic charity in Britain.[26]

Much of the hysteria in Britain was deliberately incited by an international network of extremists, underwritten by the Saudis, who used the book to exploit anti-Western feelings. Many ridiculous statements were made for propaganda purposes. Some of the outraged Muslims purported to see a Zionist conspiracy behind the whole affair. An Iranian leader stated that the furor was "not about the book" but "over the West trying to dictate to Islam." The Ayatollah Khomeini's infamous legal judgment that Rushdie and "all" involved in the book's publication "who were aware of its content, are sentenced to death" was part of this pattern. He too saw the book as Western enmity, supported by Zionism, against Islam.[27] Khomeini did far more damage to Islam than Rushdie's blasphemies, by demanding the murder of Rushdie and his publishers and putting an enormous price on their heads. But the riotings, book burnings and bannings, bomb threats against bookstores, state-sponsored terrorism, diplomatic crises, and death edicts command no attention here, only the blasphemy.

Britain has over a million Muslim residents, mostly recent émigrés from India and Pakistan. The Union of Muslim Organisations sought to get the book legally banned in Britain and its author prosecuted for blasphemy. An inflammatory Muslim letter written to Prime Minister Thatcher, whom *The Satanic Verses* had libeled as "Mrs. Torture" and "Maggie the Bitch," got nowhere. She replied that "there are no grounds" on which the government would consider banning the book. "It is an essential part of our democratic system that people who act within the law should be able to express their opinions freely." Appeals to the lord high chancellor, the attorney general, and the Home Office also failed. A group of Muslims who had employed a law firm to assist in getting a prosecution were advised that the law against blasphemy protected only Christianity. That did not appease Muslim outrage or sense of injustice. Nor did the judiciary's summary decision to reject a private blasphemy prosecution by a Mr. Choudhury against Rushdie and his publisher. The high court held that the law did not protect Islam against blasphemy.[28]

John Patten for the Home Office expressed the government's sympathy for the hurt that Muslims felt, but denied that Rushdie had violated any law. The government was guided by two principles: "the freedom of speech, thought and expression; and the notion of the rule of law." The same freedom that enabled Muslims to hold their protest meetings and marches against the book allowed Rushdie to say whatever he pleased short of breaking the law. The government had considered the claim that the law of blasphemy ought to be amended so that books such as *The Satanic Verses* would be outside the law's protection. For several reasons, however, an alteration of the law seemed unwise. No agreement existed on whether the law should be reformed or repealed. Second, the difficulties in redefining blasphemy were immense: "People hold with great passion diametrically opposing views on the subject." Nor did agreement exist on which religious groups should be protected—all, including the minor and obscure, or just the faiths believing in one God, or only the major or mainstream faiths? Even if agreement could be reached on such matters, practical difficulties would exist in enforcing a new blasphemy law. It might lead to "a rush of litigation which would damage relations between faiths." A new blasphemy law could become too divisive.[29] Minister Patten might have explained that a British jury would not likely have convicted Rushdie or his publisher for blasphemy. Had the law allowed a prosecution and it resulted in an acquittal, Muslims' sense of discrimination would merely be intensified, notwithstanding a reform of the law making it a crime to blaspheme Islam.

The Muslim effort to reform the law of blasphemy by having it extend to the protection of the major religions received respectful support from influential clergy. Dr. Robert Runcie, the archbishop of Canterbury, extended his sympathy to Muslims for the hurt they felt because of the book. "I understand their feelings and I firmly believe that offence to the religious beliefs of the followers of Islam or any other faith is quite as wrong as offence to the religious beliefs of Christians." Catholic leaders echoed such views. A joint statement by leaders of six very different religions, members of the World Conference on Religion and Peace, also deplored the hurt inflicted on Muslims, and supported a change in the law so that "all minority religions will be fully protected." Some Labour M.P.'s from Islamic districts abandoned the usual Labour opposition to blasphemy laws and campaigned for their extension to cover Muslims. But an Islamic political scientist at Exeter observed that a sort of unholy alliance was developing between Britain's Muslims and "extreme right-wing caucuses within the Tory party over social and moral issues." The "fringes" of the party supported the reform of the law to cover all religions. *The Economist* said: "Rabbis, priests and mullahs are, it seems, uniting to restrain free speech, lest any member of their collective flock should have his feelings hurt. . . . The Rushdie affair is showing not just that some Muslims do not understand the merits of free speech. It shows that many Western clerics do not either."[30] It showed still more. Religious leaders demanded government control of artistic freedom so that their beliefs could enjoy government protection. In effect, the various faiths were asking, in the name of tolerance, that the state's power be placed at their disposal on the question whether religion enjoyed special immunities. An able English Muslim scholar unwittingly showed the danger. Writing in a major journal, he insisted on extension of the law of blasphemy to cover all religions, claiming that anything less would mean a denial of equality for non-Christian religions. That was a reasonable conclusion, but his other point was unreasonable: "The group which feels hurt is the ultimate arbiter of whether a hurt has taken place."[31] If religion ever got the authority to decide what is blasphemous, freedom of expression would extend as far as the intolerance of sectarianism.

Of the various religious leaders sympathizing with the Muslims and criticizing Rushdie for his blasphemy, Lord Immanuel Jacobovits, the chief rabbi of England, made the most arresting statement. He readily protested against the publication of *The Satanic Verses*, on the ground that, in a civilized society, "we should generate respect for other people's religious beliefs and not tolerate a form of denigration and ridicule which can only breed resentment to the point of hatred and strife." But he declared that Jews should not support an extension of the blasphemy laws. "In any event," he wrote, "the Jewish definition of blasphemy is confined to 'cursing God' and does not include an affront to any prophet, not even Moses, in our case." Because they lived in a Christian society with an established church, Jews should leave the law on blasphemy as it was, "enshrining the national respect for the majority faith." What concerned him, however, was not religious offenses but socially intolerable conduct calculated to "incite revulsion or violence, by holding up religious beliefs to scurrilous contempt, or by encouraging murder." As for free speech, it was not an absolute. There were laws on pornography, libel, incitement of race hatred, subversion, and breaches of national security, as well as blasphemy. Experience had shown that words, "by poisoning the atmosphere, can be as lethal a threat to mankind as any physical pollution."[32]

Lord Jacobovits and the other religious leaders who denounced Rushdie did not think worth considering the argument that *The Satanic Verses* was fiction, that artistic integrity was at stake, that Rushdie had written a fantasy, or that the blasphemous sections were presented as the dreams of a demented character who imagined himself to be Gabriel. What mattered was that the book injured the feelings of Muslims to the point of outraging them. If a novel should present in attractive language the psychotic dreams of a Nazi demanding a "final solution" for Jews, or of a Klansman demanding that "niggers be sent back to Africa," proponents of free speech and artistic integrity would confront the problem that

Rushdie's book presented. That Rushdie did not necessarily believe in or advocate the opinions of his fictional characters, who sometimes took conflicting views, did not alter the emotional damage inflicted by his book. To contend that a novelist can depict murder, treason, or blasphemy without being a murderer, traitor, or blasphemer ignores the title of the book, which was a profound insult to the Koran, and the fact that Rushdie should and must have known that "Mahound," like the title, would do harm. A writer ought to use his freedom of speech and artistic license with some sense of civic responsibility.[33]

Such contentions, though strong and disturbing, bring to mind arguments used to justify past prosecutions for blasphemy. The Islamic reaction to *The Satanic Verses*, although shocking to Westerners of today, was quite similar to that of Calvin toward Servetus, of England toward Bartholomew Legate, and of Scotland toward Thomas Aikenhead: all were executed for blasphemy. What the centuries have taught should not be abandoned out of respect for a minority religion or the feelings of its believers, any more than out of respect for a majority religion or the feelings of *its* believers.

The arguments about the law of blasphemy stirred up by the Rushdie affair repeated the majority and minority arguments of the law commission's working paper of 1981. No one had anything fresh to say except Keith Ward, a minister of the established church and professor of the philosophy of religion at the University of London. Ward had been one of the three members of the bishop of London's committee assigned to define the establishment's position on the law of blasphemy. The committee had endorsed the minority report of the law commission, urging that the law of blasphemy be extended to all religions, on the supposition that the law would promote reverence and give a sense of protection to minority religions.[34] After the Rushdie affair, however, Ward confessed error and changed his mind about the law of blasphemy. To begin with, he narrowly defined blasphemy "from a religious point of view," as defaming the name of God. That seemed to return to the ancient Jewish definition, which was narrow. He saw irony in the fact that Christians should favor prosecutions for blasphemy when their own "founder" had been executed for that crime by "sincere, devout religious believers." Religion, he generalized, possessed "repressive tendencies," especially the religion of the established church. Yet dissent was "built deeply into the Christian tradition," and from that Ward developed a simple argument that placed him in the tradition of the Christian writers, like Busher, Furneaux, Fox, Lardner, and Blanco White, who opposed the law of blasphemy as a burden on religious liberty as well as freedom of expression. Ward also rejected the law of blasphemy as un-Christian.

He declared himself committed to the viewpoint that "it is profoundly *irreligious* to take offence when offence is offered." Christianity taught him that Christians "ought" to believe, "after reflection on the life and teaching of Jesus," that, if offense is deliberately inflicted on a believer, he or she should demonstrate belief by "*not* taking offence," even if offered abusively. When he was a member of the committee of the Church of England that supported extension of the blasphemy laws, he still hoped that the law might have an educative effect on the population and stimulate a sense of reverence. Further reflection convinced him that the law was not an effective instrument to reach those ends. "The most obvious way is to make it apparent that your religious faith is in fact admirable and estimable and is contributing to peace and reconciliation in the world. This is better than having a law which says, 'we are not going to let you insult us.' " Blasphemy was a sin, but sins should not be made crimes; only crimes that are crimes regardless of whether they are sins should be prosecuted. Moreover, the majority report of the law commissioners rightly declared that the undefinable character of religion made it an unsuitable object of support by prosecutions. "What is religion?" Ward asked, and though he claimed that as a professor of the philosophy of religion he had the "expertise" to answer, he could not. "I am supposed to know what a religion is, but I have to tell you that I have failed. . . ." Any definition that included God excluded Buddhism. How could Buddhism be included and scientology be excluded? Defining religion would probably include groups "you did not want to include." Some religions fundamentally conflicted in their beliefs. Ward thought that the Church of Scotland blasphemed Roman Catholicism by insulting it abusively.

Ward concluded that "the real defense of free speech is that it is for the sake of truth that we are prepared to put up with the abuses of it, because truth is so important that it is worth a few abuses in the hope of getting it." His previous view that the law of blasphemy should be extended to cover all religions now appeared to him to be "not a properly Christian view."[35] Ward's Christian view, spiced with a dash of John Stuart Mill on free speech, subverted the conventional claim that blasphemy required prosecution to avenge or ward off injury to the feelings of believers. The best consequence of the Rushdie affair was Ward's view of blasphemy.

The most recent invocation of the law of blasphemy occurred in 1989, when a censoring agency, the British Board of Film Classification, denied its imprimatur to a short video about the sixteenth-century Carmelite nun St. Teresa of Avila. There was no prosecution for the production of the video, which was called "Visions of Ecstasy." The board refused to allow it to be shown on British television, because it seemed blasphemous. That was the first time in seventy-seven years that the board had censored anything on the basis of blasphemy.

The makers of the film asserted their right to explore the relationship between mysticism and repressed sexuality. They did so by depicting St. Teresa's lesbian fantasies and her sexual attraction to Christ. The film board rejoined that the video showed "the mingling of religious ecstasy and sexual passion," a legitimate subject of art but not when its manner of presentation outraged the sacred. The board said that "the wounded body of the crucified Christ is presented solely as the focus of, and at certain moments a participant in, the erotic desire of St. Teresa, with no attempt to explore the meaning of the imagery beyond engaging the viewer in an erotic experience." Accordingly, the board believed that a jury might find the video to violate the criminal law of blasphemy. The makers of the film objected, on the ground that no reasonable person would take the video to be scurrilous or disparaging. Its subject was not Christ but Teresa's imagination. The board, holding fast, responded that the film's eroticism made it "soft-core" pornography whose distribution would insult the feelings of believing Christians.

The upshot of this division of opinion was a two-day quasi-judicial hearing before a five-member Video Appeals Committee, with formal arguments by both sides. Geoffrey Robertson, who had defended the publisher of *Gay News*, produced various expert witnesses. They praised the artistry and psychological validity of the video. Robertson argued that it did not outrage or insult, although he acknowledged that art might offend. Notwithstanding Robertson and his witnesses, the appeal committee in early 1990 sustained the refusal to give the video a certificate. A writer in the freethought journal that reported the case concluded that it demonstrated "the utter absurdity of the blasphemy law." Rather, the law, insofar as it protected Christians, operated with utter promiscuity, allowing whoever invoked it to censor on wholly subjective grounds.[36] Such is the present state of the law in Britain.

CHAPTER TWENTY-EIGHT

Conclusions

Most of history, being a register of inhumanities, is not fit to repeat. It includes prosecutions for blasphemy and its variant misnomer, heresy. Believing that their religion required intolerance to sustain it, Christians praised dead saints and persecuted living ones, making martyrdom sublime, grief ordinary. Example is always more efficacious than precept, terrifying examples the most efficacious of all. Because the rewards of religion were distant, Christians thought that punishment of irreligion or mistaken religion reinforced the faith.

The verdicts of time mock judgments and alter sensibilities. Socrates, Aristotle, Jesus, Michael Servetus, Giordano Bruno, George Fox, William Penn, and Tom Paine were condemned for blasphemy. In the sixteenth century, Protestantism seemed blasphemous to the Roman Catholic church; in the next century, Protestant countries punished Unitarians, Baptists, and Quakers as blasphemers. Beliefs that once staggered society achieved respectability as fighting faiths.

Historically, the word "blasphemy" has functioned as an epithet to aggravate or blacken an opinion on sacred matters that is objectionable to those in authority. They may genuinely feel that their religion has been assaulted, yet the "blasphemy" may exist only in their minds and not in the mind of the offender. In one respect, blasphemy, like any form of criminal libel, is a unique crime. In contrast to embezzlement, murder, or larceny, whose existence has objective reality, no one knows whether the crime of blasphemy has occurred until a jury returns a verdict of guilty. Even then the culprit is guilty of the crime as a matter of law, though he may never have intended to commit it and after his conviction may still believe that he has not done so. He is incapable of understanding that the orthodox, especially biblical literalists, cannot be placated or appeased unless they feel revenged for the abuse of their faith. Blasphemy is a horror to them, for, as an English lawyer of the seventeenth century said, it is "speaking Treason against the Heavenly Majesty, the belching out of execrable words against God, whereby the Deity is reproached." Similarly, a Scottish jurist in the same year, 1678, referred tersely to the crime of "divine laese majesty or treason," and he joined blasphemy to witch-craft and heresy as "treasons against God."[1] Prosecutions for blasphemy, however, have often been "treason" against intellectual liberty and free-dom of religion. Over the centuries, the sanctions against blasphemy have inhibited not only religious but artistic, political, scientific, and literary expression.

Blasphemy appears to be in a persistent vegetative state in America, and in a state of suspended animation in Great Britain. Perhaps we no longer live in a time that tries men's souls. In some ways, we have become a numb society. Today almost anything seems endurable, inevitable, or unscotchable. Yet what appears to be a debasing permissiveness may well be worth the freedom it affords in the various forms of human expression. Freedom is often a condition of enlightenment. Elders of today can recall when adolescents furtively read Joyce's *Ulysses* and Farrell's *Studs Lonigan* as dirty books. Unashamed and exploitive hard-core pornography has re-placed movies that were censored as "blue"—now a quaint term. By 1971, the Supreme Court of the United States, when reversing a conviction for offensive conduct, quipped that "one man's vulgarity is another's lyric." The case concerned a young man who had worn in public a jacket stenciled with the words "Fuck the Draft" to proclaim his contempt for our involve-ment in the war in Vietnam. The court understood that the First Amend-ment protects the emotive as well as the cognitive force of words. It did not, however, understand that some who were exposed involuntarily to the offensive words might have felt repulsion, shock, and even injury.[2]

Nothing seems offensive any longer in a constitutional sense. One may now openly say, without fear of prosecution, that Jesus was a bas-tard who entertained no notion that he was divine, or that the doctrine of the Trinity is unscriptural and breaches the unity of God. Celebrated theologians and New Testament scholars commonly profess beliefs that once provoked not only coercion of dissent but execution for the dissent-ers. Men were once hanged for saying something like Thomas Jefferson's remark about "the incomprehensible jargon of the Trinitarian arithmetic, that three are one, and one is three." Lincoln blasphemed by old stan-dards when he supposedly spoke of "the unsoundness of the Christian scheme of salvation and the human origin of the scriptures." People were once imprisoned for scourging Christianity as George Santayana did when he wrote that "Christianity persecuted, tortured, and burned. . . . It kindled wars, and nursed furious hatreds and . . . sanctified . . . ex-termination and tyranny." Alfred North Whitehead committed what was once a capital blasphemy when he declared that he considered "Christian theology to be one of the great disasters of the human race."[3] Remarks of this nature now are commonplace and, as far as the law and culture are concerned, not the least offensive.

To the Anglo-Catholic T. S. Eliot, such remarks showed the dominance of what is sometimes called secular humanism. In *After Strange Gods*, Eliot lamented that genuine blasphemy, "a symptom that the soul is still alive," is no longer within man's capability. When God is dead to man's religious perception, Eliot believed, blasphemy too is dead. He was not wholly wrong, for blasphemy could not exist in a society of atheists. Ours, however, has been a monotheistic society whose laws on both sides of the Atlantic still punished blasphemy when Eliot wrote. He knew little and cared less about criminal prosecutions; the law of blasphemy simply did not interest him. He used blasphemy like a compass, only to take a fix on the religious direction of our culture. When he claimed that modern society could no longer generate genuine blasphemy, he did not mean that our law protected outrageous defamations of God, the Bible, or Christianity. He meant, rather, that blasphemy is possible only in an age of reverent belief, for which he yearned: nostalgia for a more congenial past steeped his writing. In dead days, speaking evil of God or of things sacred provoked the genuine horror that used to be felt in the presence of spiritual corruption.

In the twentieth century, Eliot reflected, scorning God, even reviling Him, has become merely a breach of good taste, not of deep-seated faith. The logic is that a man who exclaims "Go to hell!" does not really curse if he does not believe in an afterlife. He may be offensive, but he does not profane the faith. Blasphemy should be "not a matter of good form but of right belief," Eliot thought. If people are still shocked "by any public impertinence towards a Deity for whom they feel privately no respect at all," the bad taste of the impertinence rather than the offense to right belief shocks them. The blasphemer, moreover, "unless he profoundly believes in that which he profanes," no more blasphemes than a parrot mimicking speech can really curse. "I am reproaching a world in which blasphemy is impossible," Eliot complained, adding maliciously that not even George Bernard Shaw could blaspheme.[4]

If Eliot had been right, the law would have held only the faithful accountable for the crime of blasphemy. In times past, the rejection of God by a heathen or of the divinity of Jesus by a Jew might unleash the hellhounds of persecution and a criminal prosecution. There never was a time when only a person raised as a Christian could commit the crime of blasphemy against Christianity by denying the Trinity or some Christian dogma. Even in Leviticus, the blasphemer was a non-Jew. In law and religion, only a believer could be a heretic, but anyone, even an unbeliever, could blaspheme. Historically, blasphemy has been a complex and protean offense whose dragnet has ensnared people of no or little faith as well as the unorthodox faithful. At various times in the past, blasphemy was nearly indistinguishable from the crimes of idolatry, sacrilege, heresy, obscenity, profanity, sedition, treason, and breach of the peace. The meaning of blasphemy has ranged from the ancient Hebrew crime of cursing the ineffable name of God to the modern crime of ridiculing Him or professing atheistic principles in a way that insults the religious feelings of others. Blasphemy is not just an irreligious crime; political considerations have often tinged prosecutions, as have considerations of public order and morality. Abner Kneeland, George Holyoake, and Charles Bradlaugh, for example, would never have been prosecuted if they had not been radical social reformers; nor would James Kirkup's poem have been prosecuted if it had depicted Jesus as a heterosexual.

Even though law held everyone, including nonbelievers, criminally responsible for blasphemy, Eliot seized an arresting thought: only a believer can blaspheme. In a skeptical age, blasphemy does become a breach of taste; the decency test itself suggests that. In the nineteenth century, which was swept by religious enthusiasm and the spread of atheistic publications, blasphemy prosecutions were revived. The irreverent twentieth century witnessed their decline. But blasphemy prosecutions are not stone-cold dead. In England, the law still penalizes blasphemy, though it is hardly enforced. In America, the constitutional law of the First Amendment renders blasphemy laws inoperative for practical purposes, yet never has the Supreme Court actually held unconstitutional a blasphemy law. The unthinkable is theoretically possible but realistically unlikely in the extreme, although the contemporary Supreme Court has been packed with conservatives. Not even they would sustain a blasphemy conviction.[5] A criminal law, however, even if only a vestigial relic, is never stone-cold dead until it is repealed or directly held unconstitutional.

As recently as 1977, the Massachusetts legislature, in deference to civic groups that commonly censure books and films as blasphemous, refused to repeal its blasphemy law of seventeenth-century origin.[6] That law ticks away on the books—once like a live time bomb, now more like a dud. When the right occasion and the right prosecutor happen to coincide and a jury does its duty toward religion, someone might be convicted. Should anyone be convicted anywhere in the United States, the probability is very great that an appellate court would reverse and be upheld by the Supreme Court if it honors its First Amendment principles.

American citizens have an obligation to prevent the government from falling into error; no longer is it the business of the government to decide whether citizens have fallen into errors of opinion, taste, or religion. Most Americans probably do not accept the view of Justice Oliver Wendell Holmes that the principle of the Constitution that most imperatively calls for our attachment is "not free thought for those who agree with us but freedom for the thought that we hate." Most, however, would agree with

Justice Robert Jackson's declaration: "If there is any fixed star in our constitutional constellation, it is that no official, high or petty, can prescribe what shall be orthodox in politics, nationalism, religion, or other matters of opinion or force citizens to confess by word or act their faith therein." Blasphemy is surely the expression of thought that we hate, and government, in seeking its suppression, enforces orthodoxy and forces citizens to stifle the expression of their beliefs about religion.

Blasphemy can, of course, be painfully offensive to the religious, just as desecration of the flag is offensive to our civil religion of patriotism. The offensiveness of antireligious language is the foremost reason for criminalizing blasphemy. But offensiveness is an insufficient basis for sustaining blasphemy laws. Religion is not entitled to a special protection against offensiveness that is not enjoyed by other matters of public concern. People are free to express themselves about such matters in ways that offend others, short of personally libeling them or engaging in provocative epithets addressed to specific individuals. Gritty, nasty language in any matter of public concern has constitutional protection. As the Supreme Court declared, in a case dealing with language of racial hatred, a "function of free speech under our system of government is to invite dispute. It may indeed best serve its high purpose when it produces a condition of unrest, creates dissatisfaction with conditions as they are, or even stirs people to anger. It may strike at prejudices and preconceptions and have profound unsettling effects as it presses for acceptance of an idea."[7] If one has a right to try to persuade others to abandon or change their religious beliefs, that right should include ridicule, raillery, and reproach, as it does with respect to other kinds of beliefs. The subject of religion is not entitled to unique immunity. Moreover, incisive rational argument, which the law protects, can be as offensive and subversive of religion as vituperation, sarcasm, and burlesque.

Those who demand blasphemy prosecutions to protect religion against offensive language turn a blind eye to the fact that religious leaders engage in the very vituperation that they wish to deny others. Some of the nastiest language imaginable characterized the statements of one religion about others, or about faiths deemed heretical, or about "infidels." Reproaching and reviling establishments of religion or a dominant faith commonly marked the religious expression of dissidents too. Inoffensive speech was not the hallmark of Elijah, Isaiah, or Jesus himself. Paul, Athanasius, Augustine, Luther, Calvin, Fox, and other champions of true faith pursued a tradition of vehement denunciation. Entrance into the kingdom of God was at stake. That is one reason that some of the greatest figures in Christian history were not tolerationists. Convinced that they were right about the only absolute that counted eternally, they believed that all who differed, being wrong, must therefore be offenders against religion. But persecutors acted out of choice, not necessity, because Christianity, from Jesus to Fox and Furneaux, also yielded a tradition of toleration.

Another conflict between blasphemy laws and the First Amendment derives from the fact that prosecutions implicitly strike at heretical expression. Heresy died as secular crime in the seventeenth century, yet no language can be found blasphemous without a prior understanding of what must not be blasphemed. In effect, blasphemy cannot be prosecuted unless some implicit standard of heresy exists, thus aggravating the abridgment of freedom of speech and religious liberty.

Religious liberty, which extends to irreligious liberty, and freedom of speech are not the only bases for holding unconstitutional the blasphemy laws that still exist in some states, and the common law of blasphemy that could be invoked in any of them. As the Ruggles case of 1811 and Gathercole's Case of 1838 explicitly held, blasphemy laws protect only Christianity. That gives Christianity a favored position. Such special protection violates the government neutrality embodied by the First Amendment between religion and irreligion; favoritism of one religion or any kind of special preference for it by law also constitutes a law respecting an establishment of religion. The offense of blasphemy was a side effect of the existence of an established church, which still exists in England; but there is no rationale for the offense in America, which separates church and state.

The primary purpose of a blasphemy law is to further religious ends, not secular ones. Discrimination in favor of Christianity denies the equal protection of the laws to other religions. The argument that the law protects against offensiveness is without merit, given the fact that non-Christians can be offended with impunity as far as blasphemy laws are concerned; moreover, religionists can savage agnostics and atheists without having the law be the least bit concerned for their feelings.

Blasphemy prosecutions also tend to violate the equal-protection clause, because they tend to reflect class discrimination. The prosecutions of Edward Moxon, the wealthy bookman, and of *Gay News* were exceptional; defendants have almost always been people of the lower class. Judges and prosecutors in dozens of cases had declared that irreverence and ridicule when addressed to the poor are blasphemous, although the same language in Voltaire or G. B. Shaw, generally read by the more educated classes, enjoyed immunity from prosecution. Different rules governed the couth and the uncouth. In effect, one law existed for the prosperous and well educated, another for the masses. What sold for a pound was acceptable satire; what sold for a penny was blasphemous reviling. Shakespeare had it right in *Measure for Measure* when Isabella says, "That in the captain's but a choleric word, which in the soldier is flat blasphemy." Equal protection of the laws requires the same standards of justice, which blasphemy prosecutions have violated.

Blasphemy laws are also so vague that the very issue in any prosecution is whether the crime has been committed. The jury, which reflects public prejudice, determines that issue. But if a person cannot know whether he has committed a crime until a jury returns a verdict, the law governing that crime should be held void for vagueness. If people of common intelligence must necessarily guess at the meaning of a criminal law and differ about its application, it is unconstitutional as a denial of due process of law. That is an old principle.[8]

Recent decisions of the Supreme Court reveal further evidence of the unconstitutionality of blasphemy prosecutions under the First Amendment. In the flag-burning cases of 1989 and 1990 and in the St. Paul cross-burning case of 1992, the court upheld the right to engage in so-called expressive conduct or symbolic speech that communicates messages of hatred and contempt—for the country, its government, or its officials in the flag-burning cases, and for black Americans or anyone categorized by race, religion, creed, or gender in the cross-burning case. One has a constitutional right to hate American foreign policy, blacks, or Jews. Whatever messages or opinions are communicated by flag burning or cross burning—that is, however expressive such conduct may be—it is a form of conduct, and not literally speech. If the First Amendment protects such conduct, it surely protects mere verbal expressions against religion, no matter how abusive or offensive such speech may be. If a statement is merely obnoxious and not threatening in the sense of inciting or advocating immediate violence, it constitutes free speech.[9]

In the cross-burning case, the court's opinion clearly bears other implications for the unconstitutionality of blasphemy prosecutions. The court believed that the St. Paul ordinance penalized only such fighting words as insulted, injured, or promoted violence on the basis of religion, race, creed, or gender. Other fighting words remained free under the ordinance. As the court said, "abusive invective, no matter how vicious or severe," was permissible unless addressed to "specified disfavored" topics such as religion. One might, for example, damn all anti-Catholic bigots, but those bigots could not damn Catholicism. The city of St. Paul, Justice Antonin Scalia wrote for the court, "has no such authority to license one side of a debate to fight freestyle, while requiring the other to follow Marquis of Queensberry Rules." The ordinance was, in effect, underbroad, or insufficiently inclusive. All fighting words, not just some, must be penalized.[10]

On such reasoning, a blasphemy prosecution, whether founded on statute or the common law, would be unconstitutional, because it punished only verbal abuse or hatred of Christianity. That is, it would fail to protect other religions from similar invective. The common law, of course, protects only Christianity, and no statute in the United States or Britain extends similar protection to other religions. Moreover, even if such a statute existed, protecting all religions alike, it would still remain unconstitutional, because it allowed religious believers to assail the irreligious. Not even a statute that equally protected every species of religion and irreligion from vitriolic criticism and ridicule could withstand First Amendment scrutiny. Such a statute would be void because it would muzzle, or at least have a chilling effect on, free expression on the subject of religion. No basis exists for giving to that subject an exemption from scuzzy language not enjoyed by other subjects of public interest such as art or politics.

Although the court was unanimous in holding unconstitutional the St. Paul cross-burning ordinance, Justice Scalia spoke for only a bare majority. The others concurred in the outcome on wholly different reasoning. Yet they too would clearly regard a blasphemy prosecution as an assault on the First Amendment. Justice Byron White, speaking for the four who concurred separately, observed that the "mere fact that expressive activity causes hurt feelings, offense, or resentment does not render the expression unprotected."[11] Nor would the four constitutionally endorse a majority policy that victimized the free speech of minorities.

Freedom of expression has never been freer than now, but it is not limitless. In matters of religion, atheists have the same rights as theists, but not everyone may worship as he pleases, let alone put his beliefs into practice. He might conceivably engage in the murderous rites of the goddess Kali, or unroll his prayer rug in the middle of highway traffic. Cultists who fondle venomous snakes to demonstrate the faith of the true believer (Mark 16:18, Luke 10:19, Acts 28:3–6) can be arrested, because public safety in this instance is a greater value than freedom of faith. One may not exercise one's religion at the expense of the public health, order, or welfare, nor plead conscientious objection to evade civic obligation. Caesar's conscription laws, for example, encompass all with such exceptions as only Congress may make. No one, however sincere, will prevail in alleging that his duty to God makes him decline the importunities of the Internal Revenue Service. Some who have claimed the immunity of their religious beliefs have been convicted of fortune-telling, breach of the peace, polygamy, draft evasion, nudity, the practice of medicine without a license, and blasphemy.[12]

Blasphemy is still a crime in many states of this country, although prosecutions, like Lenin's state, have withered and died away. In Great Britain, however, a country that values freedom of expression as highly as the United States does, but where Christianity is still part of the laws of the land, Jens Jorgen Thorsen's Danish film about the sex life of Jesus,

The Return, would be prosecuted for blasphemy if an attempt were made to show it or even to import it.[13]

That blasphemy is a highly subjective crime does not mean that it is an imaginary one, or that the orthodox are so unduly sensitive as to demand the censorship or prosecution of every artist or poet who offends. Even reactionaries should be able to make distinctions between a work that they find offensive in part and one that is outrageous enough to shock and repel throughout its pages. Liberals too often behave like Chicken Little, giving the impression that one case of suppression means the sky is falling and Shakespeare will be next. Blasphemy can really exist, and an argument could be made, on behalf of all religions, that prosecution under a law that attempts to define hard-core blasphemy might not be invalid. Hard-core blasphemy could be defined as fighting language of hate that is directed against any religion, is intended to outrage and injure, and, taken as a whole, is without redeeming social values.

Before me is a four-page pamphlet entitled *The Bethlehem Bastard*, written by "K.J." and published by The Kill Club in Boulder, Colorado. The pamphlet expresses its author's psychotic hatreds and rage. The mother of Jesus is "Mary the Whore," "a wanton slut," and Joseph angrily demands, "Which of you fuckers is this 'Holy Ghost'?" It concludes, "There is no God, and Jesus is a fraud. Kill Jesus before Jesus kills you!" The conviction of the author of this tract for hard-core blasphemy, however ill-advised the prosecution, would not have jeopardized the religious freedom of people who argue that God does not exist or that Jesus was not God. Nor would the suppression of the tract threaten the artistic or intellectual freedom of an Andrés Serrano. Serrano's work of "art" entitled *Piss Christ* depicts Christ on the cross submerged in and surrounded by Serrano's urine. Conceivably, Serrano might have been making a comment about the degradation of religion in modern society. *Piss Christ* was subsidized by the National Endowment for the Arts (NEA), which also granted an award assisting the creation of a collage that depicts Christ as an intravenous drug user. The artist of that piece, David Wojnarowicz, did another picture with public tax dollars showing a madonna with the baby Jesus holding a revolver. Another NEA grant sponsored a worthless musing, ostensibly by Lazarus, about his homosexual experience with Jesus. The story is accompanied by a sketch showing Jesus fondling Lazarus's penis.[14]

Prosecution of such "art" or poisonous tracts like *The Bethlehem Bastard* is unconstitutional and, even if not so, would be extremely inadvisable, if only because it would give the works a notoriety that would spread their scum and enhance their financial value; if ignored, they would likely stay unknown or be dismissed as trashy exhibitionism. But the prosecution of such works would not mean that avant-garde art has been thrust under a falling sky. Patrick Buchanan and Jesse Helms protest government funding of anti-Christian art and would probably welcome blasphemy prosecutions. As a result, defenders of freedom of expression reflexively feel obligated to champion it against the forces of darkness and censorship. Assuming that the First Amendment entitles any person to express herself as an artist in any way she pleases, no one has a right to have her art subsidized by the government.

Moreover, when the government underwrites a collage of Christ as a drug addict or the homosexual-Lazarus sketch, it employs its authority on the side of insult against the religious beliefs of most Christians, and non-Christians may feel the outrage too. The First Amendment ensures government neutrality in the arena of religion and irreligion, not government sponsorship of one side against the other. But, of course, government has always utilized tax dollars for religious art. Whether art is religious or antireligious, the First Amendment means also that it is free to circulate, even if it is scum.

The temptation to prosecute must be stilled, not only because revenge is an unworthy objective and exacts a high cost, but also because the fundamental law, as construed by the Supreme Court, commands toleration even of the repugnant. More important, human experience has shown that, even if distinctions can be made between garbage and art, once the garbage gets thrown into the maw of the disposal, distinctions lose force, and more than just garbage gets chewed up. To give an absurd example, the House Un-American Activities Committee once associated little Shirley Temple with those who served the purposes of the Communist Party. McCarthyism is a phenomenon that has been repeated intermittently throughout our history, from the time of the Sedition Act of 1798. The Federal Bureau of Investigation maintained files on scores of poets, novelists, playwrights, columnists, journalists, and other writers deemed subversive, including H. L. Mencken, Pearl Buck, Dale Carnegie, Gertrude Stein, Rex Stout, Tennessee Williams, Damon Runyon, E. B. White, F. Scott Fitzgerald, and William Inge. We should also bear in mind that special interests perennially seek the censorship of *The Merchant of Venice* and *Huckleberry Finn*. The other fellow is always the one who can't maintain the distinction. Whom can we trust to do so?[15]

More than three thousand years after the Mosaic injunction "You shall not revile God," we know that compliance with that command opens the way for prosecutions to become a sepulcher of hatreds and atrocities that shame a later age. For some eighteen centuries, prosecution of the offense of blasphemy victimized an incalculable number of Christians. The Jock of Broad Scotlands and John Taylors who spoke scurrilously about sacred matters were uncommon. Blasphemy laws netted, rather, the Servetuses, Brunos, Ketts, Legates, Biddles, Naylers, Emlyns, and Woolstons, who worshipped God and revered Christ as devoutly as their suppressors. Some of the victims rejected the authority of the pope or sacraments devised by the Roman Catholic church. Some thought that they had rediscovered the primitive church. Some followed the example of Jesus by accepting baptism only as adults. Some professed a Christ who was "so God" he was never truly human, and others a Jesus who was so human he was never God. Most repudiated the fourth-century doctrine of the Trinity as unscriptural. Some took the Bible too literally, others too symbolically. All these blasphemers were earnest and devout enthusiasts who believed differently from those in authority. Reproaching or reviling God or Christ or the Bible was as repugnant to them as to their persecutors. Of course, all this can be dismissed as "ancient history." The Inquisition is over, and things like that no longer happen. In fact, they continue to happen.

When Trinitarians finally accepted anti-Trinitarians in peace, together they turned on the deists. Skeptics and Unitarians manned the American courts, as well as evangelists, in finding that Christianity was part and parcel of the law of their states, nothwithstanding constitutions that banned preference of one religion over others or guaranteed freedom of the press and of opinion on matters of religion. By the time of Tom Paine and Elihu Palmer, deists, though reverent believers in God, had become irreligious in a conventional sense; they were anti-Christian as well as anti-Semitic, in the sense that they repudiated the Bible and the God it depicted, especially in the Old Testament. In time, though, even deists were indulged; in America, they were never even prosecuted.

Once deists gained their freedom, agnostics and atheists became the victims of blasphemy laws. Some were vituperative—as much even as Athanasius or Martin Luther or the first generation of Quakers. In the United States, and then in England, a legal fiction developed that only vituperation was blasphemous. That is, words that shocked, insulted, outraged, or offended were deemed blasphemous, even in America, but atheistic arguments temperately or moderately advanced came within the protections of freedom of expression. Coleridge's decency test, distinguishing manner from matter or style from substance, had its origins in the United States. It was a legal fiction, because the Jesus-was-a-bastard offense was uncommon, and because the very judges who hewed to the decency test, which presumably legitimated moderate denials, sustained convictions for moderate denials. Abner Kneeland, for example, did not rail and rant against God; he said only that Universalists believed in a God, in Christ, and in miracles, which he did not. George Holyoake also merely expressed disbelief. Gott's conviction for blasphemy based on his feeble one-liners in *Rib Ticklers* is representative, not exceptional.

Echoing little Peterkin in Southey's poem "The Battle of Blenheim," we may ask, "But what good came of it at last?" All was not lost, because even death teaches the value of life. Blasphemy, as either concept or crime, benefited mankind by engendering the claim to freedom of conscience that pious people, not skeptics, made. That freedom of conscience came at all to Christendom was probably the result of perpetual religious fission: the promptings of conscience that seized people to their innermost depths varied so much that freedom was possible for none unless for all.

Whether convictions and judicial rulings that sustain them are enlightened or benighted depends on whether one believes that the downfall of society, the subversion of government, or the dissolution of Christianity or of morality is at stake because of some disgusting literary gaucherie or a hateful publication. Reasonable people should have learned by now that morality can and does exist without religion, and that Christianity is capable of surviving without penal sanctions. The use of the criminal law to assuage affronted religious feelings imperils liberty—not greatly, to be sure, because blasphemy laws have become legal relics in the Anglo-American world. But they are reminders that a special legal preference for religion in general, or for Christianity in particular, violates the Constitution. They are reminders too that the feculent odor of persecution for the cause of conscience, which is the basic principle upon which blasphemy laws rest, has not yet dissipated.

Notes

Chapter 1   Origins of the Offense

1. The leading work is Eudore Derenne, *Les Procès d'impiété: Intentes aux philosophes à Athènes au Vme et au IVme siècles avant J.C.* (Liège and Paris, 1930; New York, 1976 reprint).

2. *Plutarch's Lives*, trans. Bernadotte Perrin (Cambridge, Mass., 1951, 11 vols.), vol. 3, *Nicias*, p. 291. Plato, *The Laws*, trans. A. E. Taylor (London, 1960), vol. 9, secs. 853–56, pp. 240–43; vol. 10, secs. 907–10, pp. 300–304.

3. Felix M. Cleve, *The Giants of Pre-Socratic Greek Philosophy* (The Hague, 1969, 2 vols.), vol. 1, pp. 168–328, has the best discussion of Anaxagoras. I have followed the chronology in A. E. Taylor, "On the Date of the Trial of Anaxagoras," *Classical Quarterly*, vol. 9 (1917), pp. 61–87. On Pericles, see Plutarch, *Cimon and Pericles*, trans. B. Perris (New York, 1910), ch. 32, p. 149; chs. 4–6, pp. 107–10; ch. 8, pp. 112–13, 226 n. 3. An excellent introduction is Donald Kagan, *Pericles of Athens and the Birth of Democracy* (New York, 1990).

4. Plutarch, *Cimon and Pericles*, chs. 31–32, pp. 147–49, 226 n. 3. C. M. Bowra, *Periclean Athens* (New York, 1971), pp. 191–94. E. F. Benson, *The Life of Alcibiades* (London, 1928), pp. 57–58, 96. A. R. Burn, *Pericles and Athens* (London, 1948), pp. 152–53. George Grote, *History of Greece* (New York, n.d., 4 vols.), vol. 2, p. 511.

5. Paul Decharme, *Euripides and the Spirit of His Dramas*, trans. James Loeb (New York, 1906), pp. 19–20, 72–73. Nicholas G. L. Hammond, *History of Greece to 322 B.C.* (Oxford, 1959), p. 404. Gilbert Murray, *Euripides and His Age* (New York, 1913), pp. 57, 188–89. Euripides, *Orestes*, line 418. Euripides, *Hippolytus*, line 612. Aristotle, *The Art of Rhetoric*, trans. John H. Freese (Cambridge, Mass., 1967), vol. 3, ch. 15, lines 7–8, pp. 440–41. On Aeschylus, see Murray, *Euripides*, p. 57; Leonard Woodbury, "The Date and Atheism of Diagoras of Melos," *Phoenix*, vol. 19 (1965), p. 199.

6. Thucydides, *History of the Peloponnesian War*, trans. Charles Forster Smith (London, 1921, 4 vols.), vol. 3, pp. 231–35, 275–77, 287–93. *Plutarch's Lives*, vol. 4, *Alcibiades*, pp. 53–61. Benson, *Life of Alcibiades*, pp. 152–68, 177–82. Andokides, *On the Mysteries*, ed. with intro. and commentary by Douglas MacDowell (Oxford, 1962), pp. 6–10, 166–76, 182–83, 192–93. R. C. Jebb, *The Attic Orators from Antiphon to Isaeos* (1875; New York, 1962, reprint, 2 vols.), vol. 1, pp. 73–79, 109–19, 281–83. For

background on Greek religion, see Jane Harrison, *Prolegomena to the Study of Greek Religion* (3rd ed. of 1922; New York, 1955 reprint), pp. 150–60, 539; Martin P. Nilsson, *Greek Popular Religion* (New York, 1940), pp. 42–64; W. K. C. Guthrie, *The Greeks and Their Gods* (Boston, 1955), pp. 277–94.

7. Diogenes Laertius, *Lives of Eminent Philosophers*, trans. R. D. Hicks (Cambridge, Mass., 1970, 2 vols.), bk. 9, ch. 8, secs. 49–55, in vol. 2, pp. 463–69. Morio Untersteiner, *The Sophists*, trans. Kathleen Freeman (Oxford, 1954), pp. 4–8.

8. Theodor Gomperz, *Greek Thinkers: A History of Ancient Philosophy*, trans. Laurel Magnus (London, 1901–12, 4 vols.), vol. 1, pp. 408, 577–78. C. H. Oldfather, trans., *Diodorus of Sicily* (Cambridge, Mass., 1950, 12 vols.), vol. 5, p. 141. Cicero, *De Natura Deorum*, trans. H. Rackham (Cambridge, Mass., 1951), pp. 61, 375. Woodbury, "Date and Atheism of Diagoras," pp. 178–211.

9. Benson, *Life of Alcibiades*, pp. 68–69, 110–11. A. E. Taylor, *Socrates: The Man and His Thought* (1933; New York, 1953 reprint), pp. 48–49. Dorothy Stephans, *Critias: Life and Literary Remains* (Cincinnati, 1939), pp. 40–50. Hammond, *History of Greece*, pp. 442–45.

10. The trial is reported in Plato's early dialogues, collected in the Lane Cooper ed., *On the Trial and Death of Socrates* (Ithaca, N.Y., 1941), and in *The Last Days of Socrates*, trans. Hugh Tredennick (Baltimore, 1954). The *Apology* is the chief source. See also Xenophon, *Memorabilia*, trans. E. C. Marchant (Cambridge, Mass., 1959). Anton-Hermann Chroust, *Socrates: Man and Myth* (London, 1957). See also Gregory Vlastos, ed., *The Philosophy of Socrates* (Garden City, N.Y., 1971); Karl Popper, *The Open Society and Its Enemies* (London 1957, 3rd ed., 2 vols.); Alan D. Winspear and Tom Silverberg, *Who Was Socrates?* (New York, 1960, 2nd ed.); A. E. Taylor, *Socrates*, pp. 100–116, and his *Varia Socratica* (Oxford, 1911), pp. 1–39; A. S. Ferguson, "The Impiety of Socrates," *Classical Quarterly*, vol. 7 (1913), pp. 157–75; I. F. Stone, *The Trial of Socrates* (Boston, 1988); Gregory Vlastos, *Socrates: Ironist and Moral Philosopher* (Ithaca, 1991), probably the best on the subject.

11. Socrates's final speech is in the *Apology;* his final days are reported in Plato's *Crito* and *Phaedo*, both reprinted in the Cooper and Tredennick editions.

12. Diogenes Laertius, *Lives*, bk. 5, chs. 5–10, in vol. 2, pp. 449–53. Alfred W. Benn, *The Greek Philosophers* (London, 1914, 2nd ed.), pp. 245–48. Anton-Hermann Chroust, *Aristotle* (Notre Dame, 1973, 2 vols.), vol. 1, pp. 145–54.

13. Herbert Chanan Brichto, *The Problem of "Curse" in the Hebrew Bible* (Philadelphia, 1963), p. 158, argues that the text in Exodus should be translated, "Do not act in disrespect of God nor bring under a ban an elected chieftain of your people," leaving no room for the possibility that the crime of blasphemy could be committed against a ruler. On the relation between God and ruler, see C. R. North, "The Old Testament Estimate of the Monarchy," *American Journal of Semitic Languages and Literatures*, vol. 47 (1931), pp. 1–19; Erwin R. Goodenough, "Kingship in Early Israel," *Journal of Biblical Literature*, vol. 48 (1929), pp. 33–48.

14. Leviticus 24:13–16. On sacrifice, see Johannes Pederson, *Israel: Its Life and Culture* (Oxford, 1940), vol. 4, pp. 299–375.

15. On Baal cults, see Pederson, *Israel*, vol. 4, pp. 503–23; E. Robertson Smith, *The Religion of the Semites* (New York, 1956, reprint ed.), pp. 92–108; William Foxwell Albright, *Yahweh and the Gods of Canaan* (Garden City, N.Y., 1968), pp. 115–45, 185–91, 226–64.

16. Accounts of Rab-Shakeh's blasphemy are in 2 Kings 18–19 and Isaiah 36–37.

17. Brichto, *The Problem of "Curse,"* pp. 1–12. Sheldon H. Blank, "The Curse, Blasphemy, the Spell, and the Oath," *Hebrew Union College Annual*, vol. 23 (1950–51),

pp. 73–95, 135–51. "Blessing and Cursing," *Encyclopedia Judaica* (Jerusalem, 1971), vol. 4, pp. 1084–87.

18. *The New English Bible with the Apocrypha* (New York, 1976) is a convenient collection. R. H. Charles et al., eds., *The Apocrypha and Pseudepigrapha of the Old Testament in English* (Oxford, 1913, 2 vols.), has valuable introductions and notes.

19. Brichto, *The Problem of "Curse,"* ch. 4. Emil Schürer, *The Literature of the Jewish People in the Time of Jesus*, ed. Nahum N. Glatzer (New York, 1972), and D. S. Russell, *Between the Testaments* (Philadelphia, 1960), are good introductions to the Septuagint and intertestamental literature. James H. Charlesworth, *The Pseudepigrapha and Modern Research* (Missoula, Mont., 1977), is a helpful guide to concordances and indexes that allow one to discover the uses of "blaspheme" and its variants. Ewin Hatch and Henry A. Redpath, *A Concordance to the Septuagint and the Other Greek Versions of the Old Testament* (Graz, Austria, 1954, 2 vols.), is invaluable.

20. For references to blasphemy, see Tobit 1:18; Wisdom of Solomon 1:6, 11; Bel and the Dragon 9:1; 1 Enoch 94:7, 11, 94:9, 96:7; Zedokite 7:12, 14:8.

21. Philo, a Greek-Jewish secular author, used "blasphemy" in the Greek sense, to mean any sort of slander or evil-speaking; see Flaccus, 33, and *The Special Laws*, vol. 4, p. 197. Philo seems to have meant by "blasphemer" one who "is profane and reviles things sacred"; he did not define blasphemy against God but gave the example of one who ascribed evil to God (*One Flight and Finding*, pp. 83–84). Philo thought the death penalty appropriate for anyone who blasphemed God or "even ventures to utter His Name unseasonably" (Moses, vol. 2, p. 206). All this is from *Philo*, trans. F. H. Colson and G. H. Whitaker (Cambridge, Mass., 1929–62, 12 vols.), vol. 5, p. 55; vol. 6, p. 551; vol. 8, p. 131; vol. 9, p. 321. In the Qumran literature, by contrast, a variety of words were used that could be translated as "blaspheme"—e.g., words for "curse," "reproach," "despise," and "insult"—but without exception they connote blasphemy only when referring to verbal abuse of God. The broadest Hebrew use of the concept of blasphemy that I have found occurs in the "Damascus Rule," where there is a reference to defilers speaking "with a blasphemy of the name of God" (William H. Brownlee, "The Dead Sea Manual of Discipline," *Bulletin of the American Schools of Oriental Research*, Supp. Studies, nos. 10–12, 1951, p. 28). Brownlee, formerly a colleague, generously searched Qumran texts for all usages of "blaspheme" and its variants.

22. Beginners interested in the Talmud should consult Moses Mielziner, *Introduction to the Talmud* (New York, 1968, 4th ed.); Hermann L. Strack, *Introduction to the Talmud and Midrash* (New York, 1959, 5th ed.); Jacob Neusner, *Invitation to the Talmud* (New York, 1973); George Horowitz, *The Spirit of Jewish Law* (New York, 1963); the introduction by Herbert Danby to his translation of *The Mishnah* (London, 1933); Salo Baron, *The Social and Religious History of the Jews* (New York, 1952–80, 16 vols.), vol. 2, pp. 215–321.

23. *The Babylonian Talmud: Sanhedrin*, ed. I. Epstein et al. (London, 1935–48, 34 vols.), 49b, vol. 1, p. 332, and 45b, vol. 1, p. 300 (cited hereafter as *Sanhedrin*). On the concept of the unity of God, see Ephraim E. Urbach, *The Sages* (Jerusalem, 1975, 2 vols.), vol. 1, pp. 19–36; Louis Jacobs, *A Jewish Theology* (New York, 1973), pp. 21–37.

24. *Sanhedrin*, 55b, vol. 1, p. 378; 56a, vol. 1, pp. 378, 381.

25. George Foot Moore, *Judaism in the First Centuries of the Christian Era* (Cambridge, Mass., 1927–30, 3 vols.), vol. 1, pp. 423–42. *Sanhedrin*, 90a, vol. 1, p. 602; 101a, vol. 1, p. 688. "Tetragrammaton," *Jewish Encyclopedia*, vol. 12, pp. 118–20. "Jehovah," ibid., vol. 7, pp. 87–88. Samuel S. Cohon, "The Name of God," *Hebrew*

Union College Annual, vol. 24 (1950–51), pp. 579–604. The Old Testament employed the tetragrammaton instead of the name with great frequency; by actual count, "YHVH" occurs 5,989 times. The New Testament invariably translates it as "the Lord." See also *Talmud, Sotah*, 37b, p. 186, and *Yoma*, 66a, p. 308. On the power of the name, see Urbach, *Sages*, vol. 1, pp. 124–34.

26. *Sanhedrin*, 56a, vol. 1, p. 378; 60a, vol. 1, pp. 407–9.

27. Ibid., 56a, vol. 1, p. 378; 60a, vol. 1, p. 407.

28. On the Sanhedrin, see Sidney B. Hoenig, *The Great Sanhedrin* (Philadelphia, 1953); Hugo Mantel, *Studies in the History of the Sanhedrin* (Cambridge, Mass., 1965). See also *Talmud, Makkoth*, 7a, p. 35; *Sanhedrin*, 41a, vol. 1, p. 267; 52b, vol. 1, pp. 352–53; 89a, vol. 1, p. 589. See also "Blasphemy," *Jewish Encyclopedia*, vol. 3, pp. 237–38; Horowitz, *Spirit of Jewish Law*, p. 185.

Chapter 2   The Jewish Trial of Jesus

1. On the Synoptic Gospels, see Frederick C. Grant, *The Growth of the Gospels* (New York, 1933); Vincent Taylor, *The Formation of the Gospel Tradition* (London, 1935, 2nd ed.); Martin Dibelius, *From Tradition to Gospel*, trans. B. I. Woolf (Cambridge, 1971); Rudolf Bultmann, *History of the Synoptic Tradition*, trans. John Marsh (New York, 1963, rev. ed.); Willi Marxsen, *Introduction to the New Testament*, trans. G. Buswell (Philadelphia, 1974, 3rd ed.); Werner Georg Kümmel, *Introduction to the New Testament*, trans. Howard C. Kee (Nashville, 1973, 17th ed.).

2. Hugo Mantel, *Studies in the History of the Sanhedrin* (Cambridge, Mass., 1965), pp. 268–73.

3. On John, see Rudolf Bultmann, *The Gospel of John: A Commentary*, trans. G. R. Beasley-Murray et al. (Philadelphia, 1971). Raymond E. Brown, ed., *The Gospel According to John* (Garden City, N.Y., 1966–70). Ch. H. Dodd, *Historical Tradition in the Fourth Gospel* (London, 1963).

4. James M. Robinson, *The Problem of History in Mark* (Naperville, Ill., 1957), p. 54. Bultmann, *Synoptic Tradition*, p. 374, says: "These works are completely subordinate to Christian faith worship. . . . The Gospel belongs to the history of dogma and worship." A. E. J. Rawlinson, *St. Mark* (London, 1925), p. 220, spoke of the Gospel as "Christian propaganda." The quotation on "propaganda material" in my text is from Robert Morgan, "Nothing More Negative," in Ernest Bammel, ed., *The Trial of Jesus* (London, 1970), p. 137. The use of "propaganda" in relation to the Gospels is not uncommon.

5. Hans Küng, *On Being a Christian*, trans. Edward Quinn (Garden City, N.Y., 1976), p. 327. On the obtuseness of the disciples and the mystery of Jesus' identity, see Theodore J. Weeden, *Mark—Traditions in Conflict* (Philadelphia, 1971), pp. 23–24.

6. Oscar Cullmann, *The State in the New Testament* (New York, 1956), p. 45. According to the *Catholic Encyclopedia* (1908), vol. 4, p. 520, Jesus was condemned for "sedition and tumult." Sedition was "open resistance, an uprising of a rather large group of persons with the use of—armed or unarmed—force against the magistrates, and the accused was tried under Caesar's law governing treason; the name of the crime was 'crimen maiestatis.' " Any affront to the emperor's authority, dignity, or honor was treason. See Adolph Berger, *Encyclopedia Dictionary of Roman Law*, in *Transactions*, American Philosophical Society, new ser., vol. 43, pt. 2 (1953), pp. 418, 695.

7. Rudolf Bultmann, *Primitive Christianity*, trans. R. H. Fuller (New York, 1956), pp. 71–72. On Jesus as a Jew, works by Jewish authors include Joseph Klausner, *Jesus of Nazareth*, trans. Herbert Danby (New York, 1944); Geza Vermes, *Jesus the Jew* (New York, 1973) and *Jesus and the World of Judaism* (Philadelphia, 1983); Jules Isaac, *Jesus and Israel*, trans. Sally Gran (New York, 1971); Samuel Sandmel, *We Jews and Jesus* (New York, 1973) and *A Jewish Understanding of the New Testament* (New York, 1974, rev. ed.).

8. Vincent Taylor, *The Names of Jesus* (New York, 1953), p. 25. See also Ferdinand Hahn, *The Titles of Jesus in Christology* (New York, 1969), pp. 15–42; Reginald H. Fuller, *The Foundations of New Testament Christology* (New York, 1965), pp. 34–43, 119–24; Vermes, *Jesus the Jew*, pp. 160–91; H. E. Todt, *The Son of Man in the Synoptic Tradition* (Philadelphia, 1965), reflecting Rudolf Bultmann, *Theology of the New Testament*, trans. K. Grobel (New York, 1951–55, 2 vols. in one), pp. 26–32.

9. Vincent Taylor, *Names of Jesus*, p. 199, and *Gospel According to Mark* (London, 1952), p. 563. Joseph Klausner, *The Messianic Idea in Israel* (New York, 1955), pp. 223–36, shows the political-religious context of Daniel.

10. On Son of Man, in addition to the works cited in n. 8 above, see Norman Perrin, *A Modern Pilgrimage in New Testament Christology* (Philadelphia, 1974); John R. Donahue, *Are You the Christ? The Trial Narrative in the Gospel of Mark* (Missoula, Mont., 1973), pp. 139–87; "Son of Man in Mark," in Samuel Sandmel, *Two Living Traditions* (Detroit, 1972), pp. 166–77.

11. Taylor, *Names of Jesus*, pp. 54–59, and see his chs. on each of the titles. See also Richard N. Longenecker, *The Christology of Early Jewish Christianity* (London, 1970), pp. 63–119; Hahn, *Titles of Jesus*, pp. 136–93, 279–333, 348–50. Fuller, *Foundations*, discusses each title three times, under Palestinian Judaism, Hellenistic Judaism, and Christian Hellenism. See Vermes, *Jesus the Jew*, pt. 2, "The Titles of Jesus." For an equation of the Son of God with a miracle worker or magus, see Morton Smith, *Jesus the Magician* (New York, 1978), pp. 39, 100–139, 177.

12. On Messiah, in addition to the works cited in n. 11, see Emil Schürer, *The History of the Jewish People in the Age of Jesus Christ*, new English ed. rev. and ed. Geza Vermes et al. (Edinburgh, 1973–79, 2 vols.), vol. 2, pp. 492–554; George Foot Moore, *Judaism in the First Centuries of the Christian Era* (New York, 1971 reprint, 2 vols.), vol. 2, pp. 323–76; Jacob Neusner et al., *Judaisms and Their Messiahs at the Turn of the Christian Era* (Cambridge, 1987).

13. Abba Hillel Silver, *A History of Messianic Speculation in Israel* (Boston, 1959), pp. 16–17, pointed out that messianic hopes were "rife" among Jews in Israel at the time of Jesus, not just because of the Roman occupation but also because the Jews believed that they were on the threshold of the millennium. Many people claimed to be the Messiah.

14. On the Davidic king or Son of David, see Hahn, *Titles of Jesus*, pp. 240–78; Vermes, *Jesus the Jew*, pp. 129–59; Klausner, *Messianic Idea*, pp. 519–31. On capitalization, see Floyd V. Filson, "Capitalization in English Translations of the Gospel of Matthew," in David E. Aune, ed., *Studies in New Testament and Early Christian Literature* (Leyden, 1972), pp. 25–30.

15. On John 11:47–53, see Paul Winter, *On the Trial of Jesus*, eds. T. A. Burkill and Geza Vermes (Berlin, 1974), pp. 54–55.

16. On Jesus and the Temple, see Donahue, *Are You the Christ?*, pp. 103–38; Werner Kelber, *The Kingdom in Mark* (Philadelphia, 1974), pp. 99–116; Donald Juel, *Messiah and Temple* (Missoula, Mont., 1977), pp. 130–36; Walter Schmithals, *Paul and*

James (Naperville, Ill., 1965), p. 21; Lloyd Gaston, *No Stone on Another: Studies in the Significance of the Fall of Jerusalem in the Synoptic Gospels* (Leyden, 1970).

17. Schürer, *History of the Jewish People*, vol. 2, pp. 225–26. Herbert Danby, "The Bearing of the Rabbinical Criminal Code on the Jewish Trial Narratives in the Gospels," *Journal of Theological Studies*, vol. 21 (1919), pp. 51–76. Klausner, *Jesus of Nazareth*, pp. 334–41. Mantel, *History of the Sanhedrin*, pp. 268–90. Haim Cohn, *The Trial and Death of Jesus* (New York, 1977), pp. 71–141, 340.

18. On the un-Jewishness of the question, see Klausner, *Jesus of Nazareth*, p. 342. Cf. Rawlinson, *St. Mark*, p. 222; Josef Blinzler, *The Trial of Jesus* (Westminster, Md., 1959), pp. 102–3.

19. On tearing clothes, see, e.g., Genesis 44:13. Numbers 14:6, Joshua 7:6.

20. Schürer, *History of the Jewish People*, vol. 1, pp. 330–35. *Josephus*, trans. H. St. J. Thackeray et al. (Cambridge, Mass., 1950–67, 9 vols.), vol. 2, pp. 323–53; vol. 8, pp. 489–511; vol. 9, pp. 400–401.

21. Brown, ed., *Gospel According to John*, pp. 850–51, 877. Winter, *On the Trial*, pp. 90–102. Joseph N. Baumgarten, "Does TLH in the Temple Scroll Refer to Crucifixion?," *Journal of Biblical Literature*, vol. 91 (1973), pp. 472–81. Martin Hengel, *Crucifixion*, trans. J. Bowden (Philadelphia, 1977).

22. D. E. Nineham, *The Gospel of St. Mark* (New York, 1976, rev. ed.), p. 402. Hahn, *Titles of Jesus*, p. 147. On Stephen, see Schmithals, *Paul and James*, pp. 13–37; Marcel Simon, *St. Stephen and the Hellenists in the Primitive Church* (London, 1958).

23. *Palestine Talmud, Taanith* 65b, quoted in R. Travers Herford, *Christianity in Talmud and Midrash* (London, 1903), p. 62.

24. On the dating of the Gospels, see John A. T. Robinson, *Redating the New Testament* (Philadelphia, 1976), for the thesis that all the Gospels were written before A.D. 70, because none mentions the destruction of the Temple in that year. But dozens of details become unintelligible if the composition of the Gospels occurred between A.D. 40 and 65. Robinson did not discuss, let alone solve, any of the problems created by his reading. One may as well argue that the Synoptic Gospels were written after A.D. 70, when the Sadducees had disappeared, because Mark, Matthew, and Luke did not mention them and did not know them. The word "rabbi," used in Matthew 23:7 and several times in John, did not come into use until after 70. John 9:22 refers to the Jews having expelled from their synagogues anyone who confessed Jesus to be Christ, but the date of that event, although uncertain, is not earlier than 80 or 85, and perhaps as late as 125. See Douglas R. A. Hare, *The Theme of Jewish Persecution of Christians* (Cambridge, 1967), pp. 38–39, 48–55; J. Louis Martyn, *History and Theology in the Fourth Gospel* (New York, 1968), pp. 17–41. For the generally accepted dating, see Robinson, *Redating*, p. 7. Mark was composed between 65 and 75, Luke and Matthew between 80 and 90, and John between 90 and 100.

25. Gerard S. Sloyan, *Jesus on Trial*, pp. 48–59, especially 48. Donahue, *Are You the Christ?*, p. 223.

26. Blinzler, *Trial*, pp. 117–21.

27. Ibid., pp. 105–8. Catholic priests since Vatican II have rejected Blinzler. See Dominic M. Crossan, "Anti-Semitism and the Gospel," *Theological Studies*, vol. 26 (1965), pp. 189–214; Tibor Horvath, "Why Was Jesus Brought to Pilate?," *Novum Testamentus*, vol. 11 (1969), pp. 178–84; Bruce Vawter, "Are the Gospels Anti-Semitic?," *Journal of Ecumenical Studies*, vol. 5 (1968), pp. 473–87; Jeffrey G. Sobosan, "The Trial of Jesus," *Journal of Ecumenical Studies*, vol. 10 (1973), pp. 70–90; Raymond E. Brown et al., *The Jerome Biblical Commentary* (Englewood Cliffs, N.J., 1968);

Brown, ed., *Gospel According to John;* Sloyan, *Jesus on Trial;* Donahue, *Are You the Christ?*

28. David R. Catchpole, *The Trial of Jesus: A Study in the Gospels and Jewish Historiography from 1770 to the Present Day* (Leyden, 1971), pp. 131–32.

29. Ibid., pp. 141, 200, 271.

30. J. Duncan Derrett, *Law in the New Testament* (London, 1970), pp. 407, 424, 425, 448, 453–54.

31. Küng, *On Being a Christian*, pp. 320–21, 328–30, 337–39.

32. Marcel Simon, *Jewish Sects at the Time of Jesus*, trans. J. H. Farley (Philadelphia, 1967). J. W. Lightley, *Jewish Sects and Parties in the Time of Jesus* (London, 1925). Charles Guignebert, *The Jewish World in the Time of Jesus* (New Hyde Park, N.Y., 1959, reprint), pp. 161–261. Jacob Neusner, *The Rabbinic Traditions About the Pharisees Before 70* (Leyden, 1971, 3 vols.). Louis Finkelstein, *The Pharisees* (Philadelphia, 1962, 3rd ed., rev. 2 vols.). On heresy in Jewish law and thought, see Herford, *Christianity in Talmud and Midrash*, pp. 125–37, 360–90.

33. Hare, *Theme of Jewish Persecution*, pp. 24, 26.

34. J. C. O'Neill, "The Charge of Blasphemy at Jesus' Trial Before the Sanhedrin," in Bammel, ed., *Trial of Jesus*, pp. 72–74.

35. Ibid., pp. 75, 77.

36. C. H. Dodd, *More New Testament Studies* (Manchester, 1968), pp. 98, 99.

37. Hans Conzelmann, *Jesus* (Philadelphia, 1973), p. 86. See also Cullmann, *The State*, p. 42.

38. Robinson, *Problem of History*, p. 12. Werner Kelber, Anitra Kolenkow, and Robin Scroggs, "Reflections on the Question: Was There a Pre-Markan Passion Narrative?," report prepared for the Markan Task Force of the Society of Biblical Literature, Oct. 1971, 107th Annual Meeting, *Seminar Papers* (3 vols.), vol. 2, pp. 505–85, especially p. 565.

39. S. G. F. Brandon presents this viewpoint in his books, *The Fall of Jerusalem and the Christian Church* (London, 1954), *Jesus and the Zealots* (New York, 1967), and *Trial of Jesus* (New York, 1968). See also Rawlinson, *St. Mark*, p. 220; Hans Conzelmann, *The Theology of St. Luke* (New York, 1961), pp. 83–93; William R. Wilson, *The Execution of Jesus* (New York, 1970), pp. 75–84. On persecution, see Robert J. Getty, "Nero's Indictment of the Christians in A.D. 674," in Luitpold Wallach, ed., *The Classical Tradition* (Ithaca, N.Y., 1966), pp. 285–92; Paul Winter, "Tacitus and Pliny: the Early Christians," *Journal of Historical Studies*, vol. 1 (1967), pp. 31–40; Robin Lane Fox, *Pagans and Christians* (New York, 1986), pp. 419–92.

Chapter 3   *Christianity Transforms Blasphemy*

1. *Shepherd of Hermas*, in Kirsopp Lake, trans., *The Apostolic Fathers* (London, 1932–33, 2 vols.), vol. 2, p. 271.

2. On early Christianity, see Philip Schaff, *History of the Christian Church* (New York, 1910, 5th ed., 8 vols.), vols. 1–3; J. F. Bethune-Baker, *An Introduction to the Early History of Christian Doctrine* (London, 1942, 7th ed.); Hans Lietzmann, *A History of the Early Church*, trans. B. L. Woolf (London, 1950–51, 4 vols.); Maurice Goguel, *The Birth of Christianity*, trans. H. C. Snape (London, 1954); Hans Conzelmann, *History of Primitive Christianity*, trans. J. E. Steely (Nashville, 1973); F. J. Foakes-

Jackson, *The History of the Christian Church (to 451)* (New York, 1933); Jaroslav Pelikan, *The Emergence of the Catholic Tradition* (Chicago, 1971); Walter Bauer, *Orthodoxy and Heresy in Earliest Christianity*, ed. R. A. Kraft and G. Krodel (Philadelphia, 1971).

3. On the diversity in the New Testament, see Gunther Bornkamm, *The New Testament: A Guide to Its Writings*, trans. R. H. Fuller (Philadelphia, 1973); Willie Marxsen, *Introduction to the New Testament*, trans. G. Buswell (Philadelphia, 1968). For conflicting views on early Jewish Christianity, see S. G. F. Brandon, *The Fall of Jerusalem and the Christian Church* (London, 1957); George Strecker, "On the Problem of Jewish Christianity," in Bauer, *Orthodoxy and Heresy*, pp. 241–85; Hans-Joachim Schoeps, *Jewish Christianity*, trans. D. R. A. Hare (Philadelphia, 1969); Jean Danielou, *The Theology of Jewish Christianity*, trans. J. A. Baker (London, 1964).

4. The fullest work is Karl Joseph Hefele, *A History of the Councils of the Church*, trans. H. N. Oxenham (Edinburgh, 1871–95, 5 vols.), rev. and expanded in a French edition by Henri Leclercq. See also Henry M. Gwatkin, *Studies of Arianism* (London, 1882); J. N. D. Kelly, *Early Christian Creeds* (New York, 1972, 3rd ed.).

5. On the councils, see works cited in n. 4 above; on the council of 359, see Hefele, *History of Councils*, vol. 2, pp. 246–70.

6. Walter Schmithals, *Paul and James* (Naperville, Ill., 1965), pp. 16–37. Marcel Simon, *St. Stephen and the Hellenists in the Primitive Church* (London, 1958). Schoeps, *Jewish Christianity*, p. 43.

7. On *minim*, see R. Travers-Herford, *Christianity in Talmud and Midrash* (Clifton, N.J., 1966 reprint), pp. 125–37, 360–90.

8. Tertullian, *Treatise on Penance*, trans. W. P. LeSaint (Westminster, Md., 1959), pp. 88–89, 247 n. 353.

9. *First Epistle of Clement*, in Lake, trans., *Apostolic Fathers*, vol. 1, pp. 89, 91. *Second Epistle of Clement*, in ibid., p. 149. Robert M. Grant, *The Apostolic Fathers: An Introduction* (New York, 1964), pp. 138–42.

10. "Mathetes" (Disciple) is a pseudonym; see *Epistle of Mathetes, to Diognetus* (ca. 130), in Alexander Roberts and James Donaldson, eds., *The Ante-Nicene Fathers* (New York, 1911–19, 10 vols.), vol. 1, p. 26 (cited hereafter as *Ante-Nicene Fathers*). *Epistle of Polycarp to the Philippians* (ca. 150), in ibid., pp. 34, 41. *The First Apology of Justin*, in ibid., vol. 1, pp. 160, 164, 173.

11. James A. Kleist, ed., *The Epistles of St. Clement of Rome and St. Ignatius of Antioch* (Westminster, Md., 1961), includes the quotation on Docetic blasphemy at p. 92.

12. Danielou, *Theology of Jewish Christianity*, pp. 9–10. Justin, *Dialogue with Trypho, a Jew*, in *Ante-Nicene Fathers*, vol. 1, pp. 268, 270.

13. R. M. Grant, *Gnosticism and Early Christianity* (New York, 1966, 2nd ed.). Hans Jonas, *The Gnostic Religion* (Boston, 1958). G. Quispel, "Gnosticism and the New Testament," and Hans Jonas, "Response," in J. Philip Hyatt, ed., *The Bible in Modern Scholarship* (Nashville, 1965), pp. 252–71, 279–93.

14. Justin, *Dialogue with Trypho*, in *Ante-Nicene Fathers*, vol. 1, p. 212. Adolf Harnack, *History of Dogma*, trans. N. Buchanan (London, 1905, 3rd ed., 7 vols.), vol. 1, pp. 267–68.

15. Irenaeus, *Against Heresies*, in *Ante-Nicene Fathers*, vol. 1, pp. 314, 317, 352, 409, 428, 435.

16. Tertullian, *Prescription*, in *Ante-Nicene Fathers*, vol. 3, pp. 245–46, 263–65. See also Tertullian, *Against Marcion*, in ibid., pp. 272, 299, 341, 345; Jean Danielou, *The Origins of Latin Christianity*, trans. D. Smith and J. Baker (London, 1977), pp. 139–75, 263–73.

17. S. L. Greenslade, *Schism in the Early Church* (New York, 1952), attempts distinctions between schism and heresy. On persecution under Decius and the rise of Novatianism, see W. H. C. Frend, *Martyrdom and Persecution in the Early Church* (Oxford, 1965), ch. 13. Dionysius of Alexandria is in *Ante-Nicene Fathers*, vol. 6, p. 103.

18. Dionysius of Rome, *Against Sabellians*, in *Ante-Nicene Fathers*, vol. 6, p. 365.

19. Kelly, *Early Christian Creeds*, p. 13, for "slogans and tags." J. N. D. Kelly, *Early Christian Doctrines* (New York, 1960), pp. 117, 119.

20. On modal monarchianism and Sabellius, Bethune-Baker, *Introduction to Christian Doctrine*, pp. 96–112; Kelly, *Early Christian Doctrines*, pp. 119–23; Pelikan, *Emergence*, pp. 176–81. On Hippolytus, *Ante-Nicene Fathers*, vol. 5, p. 125. On Dionysius and Athanasius, Philip Schaff and Henry Wace, eds., *A Select Library of Nicene and Post-Nicene Fathers* (New York, 1890–1900), 2nd ser., vol. 4, pp. 168, 186.

21. Hans Lietzmann, *From Constantine to Julian* (London, 1953, 2nd ed., vol. 3 of *History of the Early Church*), pp. 94–102. Kelly, *Early Christian Doctrines*, p. 118.

22. Eusebius, *The Life of Constantine*, in *Nicene and Post-Nicene Fathers*, vol. 1, p. 490. Eusebius, *The Ecclesiastical History*, trans. Kirsopp Lake and J. E. Oulton (Cambridge, Mass., 1963, 2 vols.), vol. 2, pp. 395, 397. Ramsay MacMullen, *Constantine* (New York, 1969), pp. 73, 83–86, 110–20.

23. *Ante-Nicene Fathers*, vol. 6, pp. 291–99.

24. Lietzmann, *Constantine to Julian*, pp. 94–136. Gwatkin, *Studies of Arianism*. Arius is in Athanasius, *Defense of the Nicene Definition*, in *Nicene and Post-Nicene Fathers*, 2nd ser., vol. 4, p. 154, also pp. 70, 457–58.

25. The only extant pre-Nicene statement by Arius was reported by Alexander, in *Ante-Nicene Fathers*, vol. 6, p. 297. See also Athanasius, *De Synodis*, in *Nicene and Post-Nicene Fathers*, 2nd ser., vol. 2, p. 6; Sozomen, *Ecclesiastical History*, in ibid., p. 252.

26. Socrates Scholasticus, *Ecclesiastical History*, in *Nicene and Post-Nicene Fathers*, 2nd ser., vol. 2, pp. 6–7. Hefele, *History of Councils*, vol. 1, pp. 231–439, on Council of Nicaea. See also Gwatkin, *Studies of Arianism*, pp. 17–51; Schaff, *History*, vol. 3, pp. 618–32.

27. The creed is in *Epistola Eusebii*, in *Nicene and Post-Nicene Fathers*, 2nd ser., vol. 4, pp. 74–76. For discussion see Kelly, *Early Christian Creeds*, pp. 205–30; Pelikan, *Emergence*, pp. 200–210.

28. On the various meanings of the creed to different Christians, see Kelly, *Early Christian Creeds*, pp. 231–62, and Kelly, *Early Christian Doctrines*, pp. 231–51. Socrates, *Ecclesiastical History*, in *Nicene and Post-Nicene Fathers*, 2nd ser., vol. 2, pp. 12, 14; Sozomen, *Ecclesiastical History*, in ibid., p. 255; ed. pref. to *Select Writings of Athanasius*, in ibid., p. xix.

29. Socrates, *Ecclesiastical History*, p. 27. Lietzmann, *Constantine to Julian*, pp. 211–35. Hefele, *History of Councils*, vol. 2, pp. 177–270. Gwatkin, *Studies of Arianism*, pp. 156–65. For the "blasphemy of Sirmium," see Athanasius, *Writings*, in *Nicene and Post-Nicene Fathers*, 2nd ser., vol. 4, pp. lxxviii, 450; Sirmium is now Mitrovica, Yugoslavia. Kelly, *Early Christian Doctrines*, p. 238, quotes Jerome.

30. Hefele, *History of Councils*, vol. 2, pp. 246–339. "Every pitch of blasphemy" is in Athanasius, *Writings*, p. 454.

31. Athanasius, *Writings*, pp. 93–95, 106, 436.

32. Ibid., pp. 150–54, 159–60, 168–70, 177, 234, 293–94, 458–67.

33. Hanson, intro. to Jean Danielou et al., *Historical Theology*, trans. Hanson (Baltimore, 1969, 3 vols.), vol. 2, p. 17; see pp. 131–40 for A. H. Coutrain on liturgy. See also Kelly, *Early Christian Doctrines*, p. 233.

34. On the creeds of 381–451, see Kelly, *Early Christian Creeds*, pp. 296–331; Hefele, *History of Councils*, vol. 2, pp. 340–51; vol. 3, pp. 285–383.

35. The act of 380 is quoted in Schaff, *History*, vol. 3, p. 142. For a variant translation, see bk. 16, tit. 1, no. 2, reprinted in Clyde Pharr, trans., *The Theodosian Code and Novels* (Princeton, 1952), p. 440, and, at pp. 450–63, the sixty-six laws. See also William K. Boyd, *The Ecclesiastical Edicts of the Theodosian Code* (New York, 1905), pp. 33–70; Henry Charles Lea, *A History of the Inquisition* (New York, 1955 reprint, 3 vols.), vol. 1, pp. 219–24.

36. If Julian "the apostate" was correct, as quoted in S. L. Greenslade, *Church and State from Constantine to Theodosius* (New York, 1954), p. 57, the execution of the Priscillianists in 385 was not the first instance of capital punishment for heresy, as most historians state; but nothing in Athanasius's *Writings* supports Julian, nor does Socrates or Sozomen record the executions that Julian mentioned. The Priscillian episode is in Schaff, *History*, vol. 3, pp. 963–67; Foakes-Jackson, *History of the Church*, pp. 408–13, 428. On Hypatia, see Schaff, *History*, vol. 3, pp. 66–67; Socrates, *Ecclesiastical History*, p. 160.

37. Rufinus, *Apology*, in *Nicene and Post-Nicene Fathers*, 2nd ser., vol. 3, pp. 465–66.

Chapter 4   Compelling Heretics

1. On Augustine, see his *Confessions*, any edition.

2. W. H. C. Frend, *The Donatist Church: A Movement of Protest in Roman North Africa* (Oxford, 1952), is superb. Geoffrey Grimshaw Willis, *Saint Augustine and the Donatist Controversy* (London, 1950), is a defense of Augustine. See also Frederick W. Dillistone, "The Anti-Donatist Writings," in Roy W. Battenhouse, ed., *A Companion to the Study of St. Augustine* (New York, 1956), pp. 175–202.

3. Saint Augustine, *Letters*, trans. Wilfrid Parsons (New York, 1951–56, 6 vols.), vol. 1, pp. 187, 203, 368. I have also used the variant translations of letter 76 in Dillistone, "Anti-Donatist Writings," p. 186. See also Augustine's "Homilies on the Gospel of John," in Philip Schaff and Henry Wace, eds., *A Select Library of the Nicene and Post-Nicene Fathers of the Christian Church* (New York, 1886–90, 14 vols.), vol. 7, pp. 79–80. See also Willis, *Saint Augustine*, p. 130.

4. On the relationship between blasphemy and treason, see Floyd S. Lear, "Blasphemy in the Lex Romana Curiensis," *Speculum*, vol. 6 (1931), pp. 445–59. On Augustine's thought on church and state, see John Neville Figgis, *The Political Aspects of S. Augustine's "City of God"* (London, 1921), pp. 51–80. Augustine, *Letters*, vol. 1, p. 182.

5. Augustine, *Letters*, vol. 1, pp. 1, 186; vol. 2, p. 20; vol. 4, p. 186. Augustine's letters are usually cited by number and section, so that one may consult any edition. His principal letters on persecution are numbers 87, 93, 173, and above all 185, which in the edition I used is in vol. 4, pp. 141–90. His "letters" are often elaborate essays.

6. Ibid., vol. 5, pp. 146, 149 (letter 228).

7. Ibid., vol. 2, pp. 59, 61, 63–4 (letter 93).

8. Ibid., vol. 2, pp. 64–65; vol. 4, pp. 150–52.

9. Ibid., vol. 4, pp. 154–60.

10. Ibid., pp. 161, 165.

11. Ibid., pp. 165, 170.

12. Frend, *Donatist Church*, pp. 258, 263–64, 269, 298–309, 403–11, 435.

13. *Corpus Juris Civilis*, Novel 77, ed. Wilhelm Kroll (Berlin, 1900–1905, 3 vols.), vol. 3 (trans. R. Scholl), p. 382. Zeger Bernard van Espen, *Jus Ecclesiasticum Universum* (Cologne, 1715, 3 vols.), vol. 2, pp. 256–58. John Godolphin, *Reportorium Canonicium; or An Abridgment of the Ecclesiastical Laws of This Realm Consistent with the Temporal* (London, 1678), p. 559.

14. On heresy in the Middle Ages, see Malcolm D. Lambert, *Medieval Heresy: Popular Movements from Bogomil to Hus* (London, 1977); Jeffrey B. Russell, *Dissent and Reform in the Early Middle Ages* (Los Angeles, 1965); R. I. Moore, *The Origins of European Dissent* (New York, 1977), and Moore's collection of documents, *The Birth of Popular Heresy* (New York, 1975); Gordon Leff, *Heresy in the Later Middle Ages* (Manchester, 1967, 2 vols.); Robert E. Lerner, *The Heresy of the Free Spirit in the Later Middle Ages* (Berkeley, 1972); and Walter L. Wakefield and Austin Evans, eds., *Heresies of the High Middle Ages* (New York, 1969), an invaluable and comprehensive collection of primary sources. Blasphemy was so unimportant a subject in the Middle Ages that historians of heresy, with the exception of Leff, fail to notice it. Wakefield and Evans do not list "blasphemy" in their index, though I found about forty references to it in their documents; these show that church authorities declared that heretics are blasphemers against God and the faith of the church and describe particular doctrines as blasphemous, but every person who died for religious opinion was condemned for heresy, not blasphemy.

15. On the Cathars and on the Albigensian Crusade, see Henry Charles Lea, *A History of the Inquisition of the Middle Ages* (1887; New York, 1955 reprint, 3 vols.), vol. 1, pp. 89–208; vol. 2, pp. 1–112. See also Austin P. Evans, "The Albigensian Crusades," in *The Later Crusades*, ed. Robert Lee Wolff and H. W. Hazard (Philadelphia, 1962), pp. 277–324; Joseph R. Strayer, *The Albigensian Crusade* (New York, 1971); Steven Runciman, *Medieval Manichee* (Cambridge, 1955); Walter L. Wakefield, *Heresy, Crusade and Inquisition in Southern France 1100–1250* (London, 1974).

16. The *"Summa Theologica" of St. Thomas Aquinas*, trans. Fathers of the English Dominican Province (London, 1912–29, 22 vols.), vol. 9, pp. 148–53 (available in any edition as pt. 2, 2nd pt., under question 11, "Of Heresy," arts. 1–2).

17. Ibid., pp. 164–69, question 13, "Of Blasphemy," arts. 1–3.

18. Ibid., pp. 153–54, 168–69. The final quotation is from Aquinas's commentaries on the work of Peter Lombard, available only in Latin as *Scripture Super Sententiis Magistri Petri Lombardi*, ed. Marie Fabien Moos (Paris, 1947–56, 4 vols. in 3), vol. 4, d. 13, question 2, art. 3, no. 160, p. 569.

19. *"Summa Theologica,"* vol. 9, pp. 154–55.

20. Ibid., pp. 168–69.

21. Modern Catholic theologians still follow Thomas Aquinas. Arthur Preuss's revision of Anton Koch, *Handbook of Moral Theology* (St. Louis, 1925), distinguishes between immediate blasphemy (against God) and mediate (against revealed religion, the church, or the saints); between direct and indirect blasphemy, depending on whether dishonor to God is intended; and between heretical blasphemy ("if it involves heresy") and imprecative blasphemy; in any case, blasphemy is "a crimen laesae maiestatis, the most grievous sin a man can commit" (ibid., pp. 181–82). John A. McHugh and Charles J. Callan, *Moral Theology*, rev. Edward P. Farrell (New York, 1958, 2 vols.), after defining heresy as "an error opposed to faith," distinguishes between heretical blasphemy and the nonheretical; the former affirms about God

something false or denies something true, whereas the latter "affirms or denies something about God according to truth, but in a mocking or blaming way" (vol. 1, p. 348). The references to "God" mean also the church, the Virgin, saints, the sacraments, the crucifix, the Bible, "etc." Bernard Häring, *The Law of Christ*, trans. E. G. Kaiser (Westminster, Md., 1963, 2 vols.), vol. 2, pp. 205–6, is virtually identical in substance.

22. For references to Jews as blasphemers, see the papal letters reprinted in Solomon Grayzel, *The Church and the Jews in the Thirteenth Century* (New York, 1966), pp. 107, 109, 115, 127, 129, 157, 173, 205, 251, 253, 309, 311; see also pp. 337, 341–43.

23. Salo Wittmayer Baron, *A Social and Religious History of the Jews* (New York, 1952 ff., 2nd rev. ed., 16 vols. to date), vol. 9, pp. 6–7, on Alexander. "*Summa Theologica*," vol. 9, p. 143. See also Grayzel, *Church and Jews*, p. 12.

24. For "The Policy of Degradation," see Grayzel, *Church and Jews*, ch. 7. On the legal status of Jews in the Middle Ages, see also Baron, *Social and Religious History*, vol. 9, ch. 40, on "Serf of the Chamber"; vol. 11, ch. 47, "Citizen or Bondsman." On the massacres, which are all too familiar, one might refer to Heinrich Graetz, *History of the Jews* (New York, 1927, 6 vols.), and almost say passim. On 1096, see Baron, *Social and Religious History*, vol. 4, pp. 89–106, 124–47, Baron, ibid., vol. 11, p. 270, concludes his account of the slaughters in Germany in 1348–49 by saying that about three hundred German communities were annihilated. For an unusual analytical account, see Norman Cohn, *The Pursuit of the Millennium* (New York, 1971, rev. ed.), pp. 69–139.

25. Grayzel, *Church and Jews*, pp. 29–32, 251. Baron, *Social and Religious History*, vol. 9, pp. 63–67, 93–96. Graetz, *History of Jews*, vol. 3, pp. 573–79. William Popper, *The Censorship of Hebrew Books* (New York, 1969), pp. 7–12.

26. The quotations are from Baron, *Social and Religious History*, vol. 9, pp. 56–79, 273 n. 18. See also ibid., pp. 57, 62, 69–70, 87, 272 n. 15; vol. 14, pp. 30–31, 56–57, 81, 127–28, 158; Graetz, *History of Jews*, vol. 3, pp. 585–86; vol. 4, pp. 213–15; Popper, *Censorship*, pp. 3, 16, 31–37, 46–48.

27. On the Free Spirit movement, see Cohn, *Pursuit*, pp. 148–86; and especially Leff, *Heresy*, vol. 1, pp. 308–407. See also Robert E. Lerner, *Heresy of the Free Spirit*.

28. Cohn, *Pursuit*, pp. 153–55.

29. Ibid., pp. 172–74.

30. Quoted in ibid., p. 180. Leff, *Heresy*, vol. 1, pp. 373, 377–78.

31. Leff, *Heresy*, pp. 314, 318, 327, 358, 364–65.

32. For the bull of 1418 and Jerome of Prague, see John Foxe, *The Acts and Monuments of John Foxe* (1563), ed. George Townshend (New York, 1965 reprint, 8 vols.), vol. 3, pp. 523, 528. Lea, *Inquisition*, vol. 2, organizes the data by country, dispersing the discussion of the Waldensians throughout; for their origins in France, see ibid., pp. 145–61. Lea covers the Hussites in his chapter on Bohemia (pp. 427–505), and in the last chapter (pp. 506–67) discusses the Hussites topically and stresses their union with the Waldensians. On the Waldensians, see also Leff, *Heresy*, vol. 2, pp. 448–71; Lambert, *Medieval Heresy*, pp. 67–91, 151–64. Lambert, pp. 272–334, provides a modern account of the Hussites. For briefer accounts of the Inquisition, see A. S. Turberville, *Medieval Heresy and the Inquisition* (London, 1920); and G. G. Coulton, *Inquisition and Liberty* (London, 1938), both of which discuss the Waldensians and Hussites; an apologetic Catholic account purporting to correct Lea is E. Vacandard, *The Inquisition*, trans. B. L. Conway (London, 1908). Albert C. Shan-

non's *Popes and Heresy in the Thirteenth Century* (Villanova, Pa., 1949) is more critical but limited to the origins of the Inquisition.

Chapter 5 Protestantism Rediscovers Blasphemy

1. Earl Morse Wilbur, *A History of Unitarianism: Socinianism and Its Antecedents* (Cambridge, Mass., 1945), pp. 3–112, covers the early Arians of the first half of the sixteenth century and their relationship to the Anabaptists, some of whom were anti-Trinitarians. The definitive book on the background of this chapter is George Huntston Williams, *The Radical Reformation* (Philadelphia, 1972), which comprehensively covers all the sixteenth-century sectarian movements to the left of the conventionally major Protestant churches throughout Europe.

2. The best book on the Anabaptists is Williams, *Radical Reformation.* See also F Belfort Bax, *Rise and Fall of the Anabaptists* (1903; New York, 1970 reprint); Claus-Peter Clasen, *Anabaptism: A Social History, 1525–1618* (Ithaca, N.Y., 1972); William R. Estep, *The Anabaptist Story* (Grand Rapids, Mich., 1975); Cornelius Krahn, *Dutch Anabaptism* (The Hague, 1968).

3. Bax, *Rise and Fall*, pp. 117–256.

4. Roland H. Bainton, "The Development and Consistency of Luther's Attitude Toward Religious Liberty," *Harvard Theological Review*, vol. 22 (1929), pp. 118–19. Joseph Lecler, *Toleration and the Reformation*, trans. T. L. Westow (New York, 1960, 2 vols.), vol. 1, pp. 161–63. See *Luther's Works*, ed. Jaroslav Pelikan and Helmut T. Lehmann (St. Louis and Philadelphia, 1955–76, 55 vols.), vol. 13, pp. 61–67; on Psalm 82:5, pt. 4 (1530).

5. *Luther's Works*, vol. 2, p. 60. Bainton, "Development and Consistency," pp. 111, 119, 121, 148. Heinrich Graetz, *History of the Jews* (New York, 1927, 6 vols.), vol. 4, pp. 549–52. See also Salo Wittmayer Baron, *Social and Religious History of the Jews* (New York, 1952 ff., 2nd rev. ed., 16 vols. to date), vol. 13, pp. 216–27.

6. *Luther's Works*, vol. 2, pp. 60–61, 334; vol. 4, pp. 31–32, 294, 334, 399; vol. 41, pp. 211, 279, 299, 330. In vol. 41, see also pp. 11, 13, 80, 81, 172, 234–36, 279, 285, 298, 300, 302, 309, 311, 321, 323, 328, 330, 331, 333, 339, 340, 342, 344, 349, 352, 357, 359, 360, 369, 370.

7. Ibid., vol. 1, p. 179; vol. 2, pp. 49, 110; vol. 3, pp. 162, 173; vol. 13, p. 61; vol. 14, p. 95; vol. 41, p. 81; vol. 49, pp. 141, 233.

8. On Calvin, I have relied mainly on the old-fashioned and sympathetic biography by Paul Henry, *The Life and Times of John Calvin*, trans. Henry Stabbing (New York, 1854, 2 vols.). See also Thomas H. Dyer, *The Life of John Calvin* (New York, 1855); Williston Walker, *John Calvin* (New York, 1906); Georgia Harkness, *John Calvin* (New York, 1931); John T. McNeill, *History and Character of Calvinism* (New York, 1954); T. H. L. Parker, *John Calvin* (Philadelphia, 1975). Harkness, *John Calvin*, p. 109, quotes the passage on predestined infants.

9. "Traitors to God" (*"traistres à Dieu"*) is from a 1555 sermon on Deuteronomy 15, in John Calvin, *Opera Quae Superaunt Omnia*, ed. Wilhelm Baum et al. (New York, 1964 reprint, 59 vols.), vol. 27, p. 245. The French phrase is from Henry, *Life and Times*, vol. 1, p. 353. On dishonoring God, see Calvin, *Opera*, vol. 24, p. 360. Harkness, *John Calvin*, pp. 101–13, discusses Calvin on blasphemy and heresy.

10. Henry, *Life and Times*, pp. 11, 42–49, 57–59, 64–68.

11. Sebastian Castellio, *Concerning Heretics: Whether They Are To Be Persecuted and How They Are To Be Treated*, trans. with intro. by Roland H. Bainton (New York, 1935), pp. 38–41.

12. Robert Wallace, *Antitrinitarian Biography* (London, 1850, 3 vols.), vol. 1, pp. 412–17, 139; vol. 2, pp. 1–3. Wilbur, *Unitarianism*, pp. 283–84. Richard Copley Christie, *Etienne Dolet: The Martyr of the Renaissance* (London, 1880), pp. 446–47.

13. The best introductions to Servetus are Roland H. Bainton, *Hunted Heretic: The Life and Death of Michael Servetus* (Boston, 1953), and the first third of Wilbur, *Unitarianism*. I relied most on R. Willis, *Servetus and Calvin* (London, 1877), which quotes at length from or reprints the important documents in English translation. The primary source is Calvin, *Opera*, vol. 8, pp. 458–871, containing the Calvin-Servetus correspondence, the trial records, and invaluable supplementary material.

14. *De Trinitatis Errorisbus*, in *The Two Treatises of Servetus on the Trinity*, trans. E. M. Wilbur (Cambridge, Mass., 1932), p. 50. Bainton, *Hunted Heretic*, p. 52, quoted Oecolampadius. Willis, *Servetus and Calvin*, pp. 33–34, quoted Zwingli. Wilbur, *Unitarianism*, p. 58, and Bainton, *Hunted Heretic*, p. 53, quoted Bucer. See also the statement by Calvin in Willis, p. 433.

15. On Servetus as Dr. Villaneuve, see Willis, *Servetus and Calvin*, pp. 79–156; Wilbur, *Unitarianism*, pp. 114–31; Bainton, *Hunted Heretic*, pp. 75–127.

16. For summaries of the *Restitutio*, see Willis, *Servetus and Calvin*, pp. 191–230; Bainton, *Hunted Heretic*, pp. 128–42.

17. Willis, *Servetus and Calvin*, p. 168; pp. 157–90 cover the Servetus-Calvin correspondence. See also Wilbur, *Unitarianism*, p. 134, and Stefan Zweig, *The Right to Heresy*, trans. E. Paul (London, 1951), p. 263, for English translations of Calvin's letter to W. Farel, Feb. 13, 1547, in Calvin, *Opera*, vol. 12, p. 283. The Cerberus quotation is from Bainton, *Hunted Heretic*, p. 147, and Willis, *Servetus and Calvin*, p. 359.

18. Quoted in Willis, *Servetus and Calvin*, p. 346.

19. Willis, *Servetus and Calvin*, pp. 304–479, recounts the trial, reprinting all vital trial records.

20. For Calvin's letters and the replies of the Swiss cities and churches, see Willis, *Servetus and Calvin*, pp. 428–60. For the reply of Schaffhausen, see Bainton, *Hunted Heretic*, p. 203.

21. Bainton, *Hunted Heretic*, pp. 207–9, for the verdict and the execution. See also Willis, *Servetus and Calvin*, pp. 480–87; Henry, *Life and Times*, vol. 2, pp. 221–22.

22. *Defensio Orthodoxae Fidei*, vol. 8, p. 476. On Alesius, see Wilbur, *Unitarianism*, p. 192.

23. Bainton, intro. to Castellio, *Concerning Heretics*, p. 6 for the first quotation. See also Roland H. Bainton, "Sebastian Castellio and the Toleration Controversy," in *Persecution and Liberty: Essays in Honor of George Lincoln Burr* (New York, 1931, no. ed.), pp. 183–209; the quotation is at p. 184. Zweig, *Right to Heresy* (originally entitled *Castellio Against Calvin*), is the fullest narrative on Castellio. For an excellent brief account by a liberal Jesuit, see Lecler, *Toleration*, vol. 1, pp. 337–64. See Henry M. Baird, *Theodore Beza* (New York, 1889), pp. 61–69, for a summary of Beza's tract replying to Castellio's *Concerning Heretics*.

24. Bainton, intro. to Castellio, *Concerning Heretics*, p. 114. W. K. Jordan, *The Development of Religious Toleration in England* (Cambridge, Mass., 1932–40, 4 vols.), vol. 1, p. 310. On Acontius, see ibid., pp. 303–65; his *Satanae Stratagemata* (*Satan's Stratagems*) is available in modern translation by Charles D. O'Malley (San Francisco,

1940), published by the California State Library for the WPA in bound multilith pages. See Baird, *Theodore Beza*, pp. 63–68; Zweig, *Right to Heresy*, pp. 317–23. See also Walter Rex, "Blasphemy in the Refuge in Holland and in the French Enlightenment," in *Studies on Voltaire and the Eighteenth Century*, ed. Theodore Besterman, *Transactions of the Second International Congress on the Enlightenment*, vol. 57 (1967), pp. 1307–11.

25. Castellio, *Concerning Heretics*, p. 129.

26. Ibid., pp. 132–33, 137, 139, 248, 280–81.

27. Ibid., pp. 139, 264, 266.

28. Ibid., p. 284.

29. Ibid., pp. 229, 280, 283–84, 286.

30. Ibid., pp. 10, 265. Zweig, *Right to Heresy*, pp. 323–66.

31. Wilbur, *Unitarianism*, chh. 6–8, 15, 17. Lecler, *Toleration*, vol. 1, pp. 365–80. Wallace, *Antitrinitarian Biography*, vol. 2, p. 106.

32. The fullest account of Gentile and his trials is Benedictus Aretius, *A Short History of Valentinus Gentilis the Tritheist* (London, 1696), pp. 1–134, originally published in Bern in 1567, by a supporter of Beza. See also Castellio, *Concerning Heretics*, pp. 30–31, 40, 42–44, and 55–63.

33. Joshua Toulmin, *A Dialogue Between a Dutch Protestant and a Franciscan Friar* (London, 1784), pp. 3–7.

34. Earl Morse Wilbur, *A History of Unitarianism in Transylvania, England and America* (Cambridge, Mass., 1952), pp. 22, 26, 38 (cited hereafter as *Unitarianism* II). On the name "Unitarian," first used in Transylvania in 1568 but not the formal designation of the denomination until 1600, see ibid., p. 47 n. 12. On David, see ibid., pp. 23–80; Wallace, *Antitrinitarian Biography*, vol. 1, pp. 245–63; William C. Gannett, *Francis David* (London, 1914).

35. William Boulting, *Giordano Bruno* (London, 1914), p. 57. J. Frith, *Life of Giordano Bruno*, rev. M. Carriere (London, 1887). John Owen, *Skeptics of the Italian Renaissance* (London, 1893), pp. 245–343.

36. Boulting, *Bruno*, p. 141.

37. Ibid., p. 142. John Herman Randall, *Making of the Modern Mind* (Boston, 1940), p. 243.

38. The quotation is from Boulting, *Bruno*, pp. 270, 276, 277. On Bruno before the Inquisition at Venice, see ibid., pp. 254–79; and Frith, *Life of Bruno*, pp. 238–83, invaluable for reprinting English translations of the important documents, including the accusations for blasphemy on pp. 262–65.

39. For the trial in Rome, see Frith, *Life of Bruno*, pp. 284–302, which includes the sentence. The statement of the witness is in Owen, *Skeptics*, pp. 328–29.

40. For "the images of God," see Ludwig von Bar, *History of Continental Criminal Law* (Boston, 1916), p. 281. See ibid., pp. 184, 228, 280–81, for various statutes punishing blasphemy.

41. Wilbur, *Unitarianism* II, pp. 444–47. Wallace, *Antitrinitarian Biography*, vol. 2, pp. 528–30.

42. Owen, *Skeptics*, pp. 345–419, covers Vanini.

43. Carl E. Jarcke, *Handbuch des gemeinen Deutschen Strafrechts* (Berlin, 1827–30, 3 vols.), vol. 2, pp. 27–46, covers blasphemy in Germany from 1500 to 1800. In eighteenth-century Prussia, the penalty was imprisonment for six months. In Austria and Bavaria, Catholic areas, death remained a penalty but the law seemed to be a dead letter. By 1787, Austria sent blasphemers to "the madhouse."

Chapter 6   The Fires of Smithfield

1. Account by William of Newburgh, trans. in W. O. Hassall, ed., *Medieval England as Viewed by Contemporaries* (New York, 1957), pp. 81–82. Assize of Clarendon, 1166, in George B. Adams and H. Morse Stephens, eds., *Select Documents of English Constitutional History* (New York, 1929), p. 17.

2. Henry Charles Lea, *A History of the Inquisition of the Middle Ages* (1887; New York, 1955 reprint, 3 vols.), vol. 1, pp. 113–14.

3. W. R. W. Stephens, *The English Church from the Norman Conquest to the Accession of Edward I* (London, 1904), p. 49. Felix Makower, *The Constitutional History and Constitution of the Church of England* (London, 1895), pp. 384–464. Sir William Holdsworth, *A History of English Law* (London, 1903–38, 16 vols.), vol. 1, pp. 614–32. Sir Frederic Pollock and Frederick William Maitland, *The History of English Law before the Time of Edward I* (Cambridge, 1899, 2nd ed., 2 vols.), vol. 1, pp. 124–32. Sir James Fitzjames Stephen, *A History of the Criminal Law of England* (London, 1883, 3 vols.), vol. 2, pp. 404–13.

4. Pollock and Maitland, *History of English Law*, vol. 2, p. 548. Frederick William Maitland, "The Deacon and the Jewess," in *Roman Canon Law in the Church of England* (London, 1898), pp. 158–79. Lea, *Inquisition*, vol. 1, p. 486. John Foxe, *The Acts and Monuments of John Foxe* (*The Book of Martyrs*, 1563), ed. George Townshend (New York, 1965 reprint, 8 vols.), vol. 1, p. 486. *The Mirror of Justices*, ed. William Joseph Whittaker, intro. by F. W. Maitland (London, 1895), pp. 59, 135.

5. Thomas Wright, ed., *A Contemporary Narrative of the Proceedings Against Dame Alice Kyteler* (Camden Society, 1843), pp. ix, 1–4, 42–45. *Dictionary of National Biography*, ed. Sir Leslie Stephen and Sir Sidney Lee (London, 1885–1905, 63 vols.), vol. 14, p. 1231 (cited hereafter as *D.N.B.*).

6. Foxe, *Acts and Monuments*, vol. 3, pp. 4, 5, 21, 23. Wycliffe's case is also reported in Thomas B. Howell, comp., *A Complete Collection of State Trials and Proceedings for High Treason and Other Crimes* (London, 1809–28, 34 vols.), vol. 1, pp. 67–90 (cited hereafter as *State Trials*).

7. Foxe, *Acts and Monuments*, vol. 3, p. 23.

8. Stephen, *History of Criminal Law*, vol. 2, pp. 443–44. H. G. Richardson, "Heresy and the Lay Power under Richard II," *English Historical Review*, vol. 51 (1936), pp. 1–28. Foxe, *Acts and Monuments*, vol. 3, pp. 38, 100.

9. Foxe, *Acts and Monuments*, vol. 3, pp. 110, 116, 118, 125, 127, 286–87.

10. Maitland, *Roman Canon Law*, pp. 174–77. Stephen, *History of Criminal Law*, vol. 2, pp. 445–48. Foxe, *Acts and Monuments*, vol. 3, pp. 221–29. *State Trials*, vol. 1, pp. 163–75. "The Royal Writ for the Burning of Sawtre," in Henry Gee and William John Hardy, eds., *Documents Illustrative of English Church History* (London, 1896), p. 139.

11. Stephen, *History of Criminal Law*, vol. 2, pp. 447–50. Foxe, *Acts and Monuments*, vol. 3, pp. 239–40, 353–55. "Act De Haeretico Comburendo, p. 1401," Gee and Hardy, eds., *Documents*, pp. 133–37.

12. For the number of burnings I have relied on the incidents related in vols. 3–5 of Foxe, *Acts and Monuments*, for the period 1401–1534, not counting those that seem uncertain. John A. F. Thomson, *The Later Lollards* (New York, 1965), was also helpful. Foxe, *Acts and Monuments*, vol. 4, pp. 217–46, covers the inquisition in Lincoln. Philip Hughes, *The Reformation in England* (London, 1950–54, 3 vols.), vol. 1, pp. 128–29, gives the figure of 342. On John Huss and Jerome of Prague, see Foxe, *Acts and Monuments*, vol. 3, pp. 523, 558. On Joan's case, which I could not confirm,

see H. J. W. Coulson, "The Law Relating to Blasphemy," *Law Magazine and Review*, 4th ser., vol. 9 (1883–84), p. 161.

13. J. V. Bullard and H. Chalmer Bell, eds., *Lyndewood's Provinciale* (London, 1929), pp. 127, 131–32, bk. V, tit. V, chs. 2 and 4.

14. On the rise of Protestantism and the Henrician Reformation in England, see Thomson, *Later Lollards;* James Gairdner, *Lollardy and the Reformation in England* (London, 1908, 4 vols.); Sir Maurice Powicke, *The Reformation in England* (London, 1941).

15. E. Belfort Bax, *Rise and Fall of the Anabaptists* (1903; New York, 1970 reprint), pp. 332–34. Thomas Fuller, *Church History of Britain*, ed. J. S. Brewer (Oxford, 1845, 6 vols.), vol. 3, p. 175. Edward Bean Underhill, *Struggles and Triumphs of Religious Liberty* (New York, 1858), p. 98.

16. John Stow, *The Annales of England faithfully collected out of the most authenticall authors, records and other monuments of antiquitie* (1592), p. 965.

17. Ibid., p. 973.

18. Foxe, *Acts and Monuments*, vol. 4, pp. 628, 630, 632, 655.

19. Ibid., pp. 697–705. Elizabeth F. Rogers, ed., *The Correspondence of Sir Thomas More* (Princeton, 1947), p. 558, letter to M. Roper, June 3, 1535.

20. Gairdner, *Lollardy and the Reformation*, vol. 1, pp. 453–61. Thomas Wright, ed., *Three Chapters of Letters Relating to the Suppression of Monasteries* (London, 1843), pp. 13–34. James Anthony Froude, *History of England from the Fall of Wolsey to the Death of Elizabeth* (New York, 1865, 10 vols.), vol. 1, pp. 294–316; vol. 2, pp. 205–11.

21. W. K. Jordan, *The Development of Religious Toleration in England* (Cambridge, Mass., 1932–40, 4 vols.), vol. 2, p. 43. Hughes, *Reformation in England*, vol. 2, p. 12, reported only twenty-seven burnings of Anabaptists during the same period.

22. Foxe, *Acts and Monuments*, vol. 5, p. 704.

23. Hughes, *Reformation in England*, vol. 2, pp. 105, 114, 128–29, 141, 150–59, 262.

24. John Strype, *Memorials of the Most Reverent Father in God Thomas Cranmer* (1694; Oxford, 1840 reprint, 2 vols.), vol. 1, pp. 255–57. Robert Wallace, *Antitrinitarian Biography* (London, 1850, 3 vols.), vol. 1, p. 6; vol. 2, pp. 122–24.

25. John Bruce, ed., *The Works of Roger Hutchinson* (Cambridge, 1842), pp. ii–v. *D.N.B.*, vol. 2, pp. 748–49. John Strype, *Ecclesiastical Memorials, Relating Chiefly to Religion . . .* (1721; Oxford, 1822, 3 vols.), vol. 2, p. 335. Gilbert Burnet, *The History of the Reformation of the Church of England* (1680), rev. Nicholas Pocock (Oxford, 1865, 7 vols.), vol. 2, pp. 203–4. For a copy of Joan of Kent's sentence, see B. Evans, *The Early English Baptists* (London, 1862–64, 2 vols.), vol. 1, pp. 242–43. On Anne Askew, see Foxe, *Acts and Monuments*, vol. 5, pp. 536–50.

26. John Proctor, *The Fal of the Late Arrian* (1549), quoted by George T. Buckley, *Atheism in the English Renaissance* (Chicago, 1932), pp. 56–57.

27. Stow, *Annales of England*, p. 605. Wallace, *Antitrinitarian Biography*, vol. 1, pp. 12–14; vol. 2, pp. 124–27.

28. Hughes, *Reformation in England*, vol. 2, p. 255. Protestant accounts give 288 as the number burned and 419 to 739 when adding those who died in prison; see Evans, *Early English Baptists*, vol. 1, p. 119.

29. Hughes, *Reformation in England*, vol. 2, pp. 259–62.

30. Foxe, *Acts and Monuments*, vol. 6, pp. 598, 602.

31. Ibid., vol. 8, pp. 45, 52, 59, 65, 69–71.

32. Ibid., vol. 7, p. 636. For Philpot's accusations of blasphemy, ibid., pp. 634, 636, 646, 648, 658, 664, 679, 680.

33. Ibid., vol. 4, pp. 427, 442; vol. 7, pp. 47, 103, 355.

34. Ibid., vol. 7, p. 631.

35. *An Apology of John Philpot, Written for spitting on an Arian: With an Invective against the Arians*, reprinted in Strype, *Ecclesiastical Memorials*, vol. 3, pp. 363–80. Foxe, *Acts and Monuments*, vol. 7, p. 626.

36. On the Elizabethan Reformation, see A. G. Dickens, *The English Reformation* (New York, 1964); W. H. Frere, *The English Church in the Reigns of Elizabeth and James I* (London, 1904); Hughes, *Reformation in England*, vol. 3; J. B. Black, *The Reign of Elizabeth, 1558–1603* (Oxford, 1959, 2nd ed.); M. M. Knappen, *Tudor Puritanism* (Chicago, 1939); Arnold Oskar Meyer, *England and the Catholic Church under Elizabeth*, trans. J. R. McKee (London, 1916).

37. David Laing, ed., *The Works of John Knox* (Edinburgh, 1846–64, 6 vols.), vol. 5, pp. 207–8, 222–24, passim.

38. Ibid., pp. 224–25.

39. Ibid., p. 228.

40. Ibid., p. 231.

41. Herbert John McLachlan, *Socinianism in Seventeenth Century England* (London, 1951), p. 31. *D.N.B.* on Nicholas, vol. 14, pp. 426–31. Thomas Price, *A History of Protestant Nonconformity in England from the Reformation Under Henry VIII* (London, 1836–38, 2 vols.), vol. 1, p. 293. John Lingard, *History of England from the First Invasion by the Romans to 1688* (London, 1883, 10 vols.), vol. 6, p. 344. The uncertain sixth case might be that of William Hacket, a wheelwright of Northamptonshire who, about 1601, claimed to be Jesus Christ. Hacket's apostles proclaimed him in the streets of London, causing a "great hurly burly in the City." Hacket was hanged in Cheapside "for his odious blasphemies against God, and high Treason against Queen Elizabeth," and two of his apostles died in jail. (John Taylor, *Ranters of Both Sexes* [London, 1651], pp. 6–7. No other source, primary or secondary, mentions the case.)

42. Copies of the recantation are printed in Price, *History of Protestant Nonconformity*, vol. 1, p. 294; and Francis Blomefield, *An Essay Towards a Topographical History of the County of Norfolk* (London, 1805–10, 11 vols.), vol. 3, p. 292. The writs De Haeretico Comburendo are printed in Hughes, *Reformation in England*, vol. 3, pp. 411–13. The fullest reports of the case are in Underhill, *Struggles and Triumphs*, pp. 179–92; and in Evans, *Early English Baptists*, vol. 1, pp. 151–64.

43. Foxe's letter, in translation from the Latin, is in Price, *History of Protestant Nonconformity*, vol. 1, pp. 294–95. For Elizabeth's opinion, see Fuller, *Church History of Britain*, vol. 4, p. 390.

44. All quotations are from Underhill, *Struggles and Triumphs*, pp. 184, 189, 193.

45. On David Georg, whose Latin pen name was Joris, see Wallace, *Antitrinitarian Biography*, vol. 3, pp. 544–51; Sebastian Castellio, *Concerning Heretics*, trans. with intro. by Roland H. Bainton (New York, 1935), pp. 305–9. On Vittel, see *D.N.B.*, vol. 20, pp. 375–76. On the Familists, see Bax, *Rise and Fall of the Anabaptists*, pp. 338–66; Fuller, *Church History of Britain*, vol. 4, pp. 407–13; John Strype, *Annals of the Reformation and Establishment of Religion* (Oxford, 1824, 4 vols.), vol. 2, pp. 282–89.

46. William Burton, *David's Evidence* (1590), pp. 124–25.

47. Stow, *Annales of England*, pp. 1173–74.

48. Blomefield, *Topographical History of Norfolk*, vol. 3, pp. 292–93. Wallace, *Antitrinitarian Biography*, vol. 1, pp. 37–38; vol. 2, p. 366.

49. *D.N.B.*, vol. 9, pp. 74–75. Burton, *David's Evidence*, p. 125.

50. Alexander B. Grosard, *The Life and Works of Robert Greene* (New York, 1964 reprint), pp. 259–60.

51. Burton, *David's Evidence*, p. 125.

52. "The Cases of Bartholomew Legate and Edward Wightman," in *State Trials*, vol. 2, pp. 727–42. Wallace, *Antitrinitarian Biography*, vol. 2, pp. 530–34. *D.N.B.*, vol. 2, pp. 846–47.

53. Speech to Parliament, March 1609, in Charles H. McIwain, ed., *The Political Works of James I* (Cambridge, Mass., 1918), p. 307.

54. *State Trials*, vol. 2, p. 727.

55. Ibid., p. 734.

56. Archbishop Abbott to Lord Ellesmere, Jan. 21, 1612, Jan. 22, 1612, in J. Payne Collier, ed., *The Egerton Papers* (Camden Society, 1840), pp. 447, 448.

57. *State Trials*, vol. 2, p. 730.

58. Quoted in Wallace, *Antitrinitarian Biography*, vol. 2, pp. 534–39. See also *D.N.B.*, vol. 21, pp. 195–96.

59. Bishop Richard Neile's report, in "The Trendall Papers," Congregational History Society, *Transactions*, vol. 1 (1902), pp. 199–200.

60. Ibid., and *State Trials*, vol. 2, pp. 735, 738.

61. "The Trendall Papers," vol. 1, p. 200.

62. Ibid., and *State Trials*, vol. 2, p. 731.

63. *State Trials*, vol. 2, p. 731.

64. Edward Cardwell, ed., *The Reformation of the Ecclesiastical Laws as Attempted in the Reigns of King Henry VIII, King Edward VI and Queen Elizabeth* (Oxford, 1850), pp. 28–29.

65. Bacon, "Of Atheism," quoted in Buckley, *Atheism in the English Renaissance*, p. 50.

66. *Smith* v. *Martin* (1632), in Samuel Rawson Gardiner, ed., *Reports of Cases in the Courts of Star Chamber and High Commission* (Westminster, 1886), p. 152.

Chapter 7   Socinian Anti-Trinitarians

1. Wilbur K. Jordan, *The Development of Religious Toleration in England* (Cambridge, Mass., 1932–40, 4 vols.), vol. 2, p. 32.

2. For James on Arminius, see James O. Halliwell, ed., *The Autobiography and Correspondence of Sir Simonds D'Ewes* (London, 1845, 2 vols.), vol. 1, p. 82. On Vorst, see Charles R. Gillett, *Burned Books* (New York, 1932, 2 vols.), vol. 1, pp. 98–101; Jordan, *Religious Toleration*, vol. 2, pp. 31–32, 335–37.

3. Herbert John McLachlan, *Socinianism in Seventeenth-Century England* (London, 1951), pp. 36–37. Earl Morse Wilbur, *A History of Unitarianism* (Cambridge, Mass., 1946–52, 2 vols.), vol. 1, p. 411. The name "Unitarian" was first used in an English tract in 1673 and appeared in a title for the first time in 1687, by which time it was common. See Wilbur, *Unitarianism* II, pp. 199, 216; McLachlan, *Socinianism*, pp. 294, 302, 310–13, 320.

4. On Socinianism as it emerged in the Racovian Catechism, see Wilbur, *Unitarianism*, pp. 29–32. On Baptism, see Thomas Crosby, *The History of the English Baptists* (London, 1738–39, 2 vols.), vol. 1, pp. i–lxi, 1–139; Joseph Ivimey, *A History of the English Baptists* (London, 1811, 4 vols.), vol. 1, pp. 1–126; W. T. Whitely, *A History of the British Baptists* (London, 1932, 2nd ed.), pp. 17–58.

5. Jordan, *Religious Toleration*, vol. 2, p. 32.

6. Ibid., pp. 35–36, 38, 148, 153. Whitely, *British Baptists*, p. 29.

7. Jordan, *Religious Toleration*, vol. 2, pp. 262–66.

8. See ibid., pp. 258–314, for a review of early Baptist works on liberty of conscience. For the quote from Helwys, see ibid., p. 283. Edward Bean Underhill, ed., *Tracts on Liberty of Conscience and Persecution, 1614–61* (London, 1846), pp. 3–81, reprints Busher's work.

9. Murton's tract of 1615, *Objections Answered by Way of Dialogue*, is in Underhill, ed., *Tracts on Liberty of Conscience*, pp. 85–180, as it was reprinted in 1620 and 1662 under the title *Persecution for Religion Judg'd and Condemn'd*. For the references to blasphemy, see ibid., pp. 120–24.

10. On Laud, see Hugh R. Trevor-Roper, *Archbishop Laud, 1573–1645* (London, 1962, 2nd ed.); Jordan, *Religious Toleration*, vol. 2, pp. 129–65 passim. On Laud's period as primate, see also Samuel Rawson Gardiner, *History of England from the Accession of James I to the Outbreak of the Civil War, 1603–42* (London, 1883–84, 10 vols.), vols. 7–9.

11. "The Trendall Papers," Congregational Historical Society, *Transactions*, vol. 1 (1902), pp. 194–202.

12. *Att.-Gen.* v. *Fisher* (1596), in John Hawarde, *Les Reportes del Cases in Camera Stellata*, ed. William P. Baildon (London, 1894), pp. 41–42. See also ibid., p. 54, for Wheeler's case. *Att.-Gen.* v. *Miles* (1606), in ibid., p. 301. Vicar's case (1631), in Samuel R. Gardiner, ed., *Reports of Cases in the Courts of Star Chamber and High Commission* (London, 1886), pp. 232–34. No good scholarly book on the Star Chamber exists; the best primary source is William Hudson, *A Treatise of the Court of Star Chamber* (ca. 1635), in Francis Hargrave, ed., *Collectanea Juridica: Consisting of Tracts Relative to the Law and Constitution of England* (London, 1791–92, 2 vols.), vol. 1, pp. 1–240.

13. Cawdrey's case (1591), with Coke's additions of 1605, in 5 Coke's Reports 8b, 9a, 40a, 40b. Attwood's case (1618), in Henry Rolle, *Abridgment des Plusieurs Cases et Resolutions del Common Ley* (1668), reprinted in Hargrave, ed., *Collectanea Juridica*, vol. 2, p. 78.

14. See Roland G. Usher, *The Rise and Fall of the High Commission* (Oxford, 1913); Leonard W. Levy, *Origins of the Fifth Amendment* (New York, 1968), chs. 4–9.

15. Lane's case (1631), in Gardiner, ed., *Reports of Cases*, pp. 188–94.

16. On Bastwick, see Jordan, *Religious Toleration*, vol. 2, p. 159; vol. 3, pp. 279–80. On Burton, see ibid., vol. 2, pp. 253–54; vol. 3, pp. 358–61. On Prynne, see ibid., vol. 2, p. 210. On the trials, see Gardiner, *History of England*, vol. 8, pp. 226–32; Samuel R. Gardiner, ed., *Documents Relating to the Proceedings against William Prynne, in 1634 and 1637* (London, 1877); William Prynne, *A New Discovery of the Prelates Tyranny* (1641), pp. 33–60; *State Trials*, vol. 3, pp. 711–70.

17. On the abortive canons of 1640, see Robert Wallace, *Antitrinitarian Biography* (London, 1850, 3 vols.), vol. 1, pp. 65–68. On the mob of Brownists, see Usher, *Rise and Fall of High Commission*, p. 333; Gardiner, *History of England*, vol. 9, p. 215.

18. Quotations from Steuart, Pagitt, and Bastwick are in Jordan, *Religious Toleration*, vol. 3, pp. 274–81 passim.

19. Wallace, *Antitrinitarian Biography*, vol. 1, pp. 69–70. *Journals of the House of Commons* (cited hereafter as *Journals H.C.*), vol. 4, p. 206 (July 14, 1645). *Journals of the House of Lords*, vol. 6, p. 494, July 12, 1645.

20. On Best, see McLachlan, *Socinianism*, pp. 149–62; Wilbur, *Unitarianism* II, pp. 322–27; Wallace, *Antitrinitarian Biography*, vol. 3, pp. 161–67.

21. Alex F. Mitchell and John Struthers, eds., *Minutes of the Sessions of the West-*

minster Assembly of Divines (Edinburgh, 1874), p. 101. D. Laing, ed., *Letters and Journals of Robert Baillie* (Edinburgh, 1841–42, 3 vols.), vol. 2, p. 280.

22. *Minutes of Westminster Assembly*, pp. 101–2, 114, 170, 175, 214. *Journals H.C.*, vol. 4, p. 284, Sept. 24, 1645.

23. *Journals H.C.*, vol. 4, p. 420 (Jan. 28, 1646).

24. Ibid., p. 493, March 28, 1646. *Minutes of Westminster Assembly*, p. 214.

25. *Journals H.C.*, vol. 4, p. 500 (April 4, 1646). On the five members and their views, see Jordan, *Religious Toleration*, vol. 3, pp. 56, 329–31, 371–76.

26. Jordan, *Religious Toleration*, vol. 3, p. 278. Ibid., p. 280. Wilbur Cortez Abbott, *The Writings and Speeches of Oliver Cromwell* (Cambridge, Mass., 1937–47, 4 vols.), vol. 1, p. 278. Thomas Carlyle, ed., *Oliver Cromwell's Letters and Speeches* (London, 3 vols.), vol. 1, p. 176. Laing, ed., *Letters and Journals of Robert Baillie*, vol. 2, p. 280.

27. Thomas Edwards, *Gangraena or a catalogue and discovery of many of the errours, heresies, blasphemies and pernicious practices of the sectaries of this time, vented and acted in England in these four last years* (1646), pt. 1, pp. 1–39. On Edwards, see Jordan, *Religious Toleration*, vol. 3, pp. 281–87. For the recorder of the Westminster Assembly, see Laing, ed., *Letters and Journals of Robert Baillie*, vol. 2, p. 361.

28. *Journals H.C.*, vol. 4, pp. 506, 515, 518, 524, 527, 540, 556, 563, 586; vol. 5, p. 296. Paul Best, *A Letter of Advice unto the Ministers assembled at Westminster* (1646), p. 8. See also Jordan, *Religious Toleration*, vol. 3, p. 92; McLachlan, *Socinianism*, p. 153 n. 6.

29. Paul Best, *Mysteries Discovered* (London, 1647), p. 4 (misnumbered p. 1). "Heads of Proposals," Aug. 1, 1647, in Samuel Rawson Gardiner, ed., *The Constitutional Documents of the Puritan Revolution, 1625–1660* (Oxford, 1906), p. 321. See also Jordan, *Religious Toleration*, vol. 3, pp. 95–104. On Selden, see John Towill Rutt, ed., *Diary of Thomas Burton* (London, 1828, 4 vols.), vol. 1, p. 65. On Goodwin, see Edwards, *Gangraena*, pt. 2, pp. 22, 26–27, 123; pt. 3, p. 65.

30. Best, *Mysteries Discovered*, pp. 4–5, 10–11, 14–15.

31. *Journals H.C.*, vol. 5, p. 257 (July 24, 1647); p. 296 (Sept. 8, 1647). McLachlan, *Socinianism*, pp. 160–62. Joshua Toulmin, *A Review of the Life, Character and Writings of the Rev. John Biddle* (London, 1789), p. iii.

32. Carlyle, ed., *Cromwell's Letters and Speeches*, vol. 3, p. 63, for "conspicuous Heresiarch."

33. McLachlan, *Socinianism*, p. 169. The basic source on Biddle is [John Farrington], *A Short Account of the Life of John Biddle*, reprinted in English from the Latin edition of 1682, in *Unitarian Tracts* (London, 1691–1701, 5 vols.), vol. 1 (1691). See also Anthony à Wood, *Athenae Oxonienaes, an Exact History of All the Writers and Bishops who Have Had Their Education in the University of Oxford*, ed. P. Bliss (Oxford, 1813–20), vol. 2, pp. 330–32; Wilbur, *Unitarianism* II, pp. 192–208; McLachlan, *Socinianism*, pp. 164–217; Wallace, *Antitrinitarian Biography*, vol. 3, pp. 173–206.

34. Wood, *Athenae*, vol. 2, p. 331, on Ussher's reaction. John Biddle, *Twelve Arguments Drawn Out of the Scripture; Wherein the commonly received Opinion touching the Deity of the Holy Spirit is clearly and fully refuted* (1647), pp. vii–xiv, for the petition to Vane, April 1, 1647.

35. *Journals H.C.*, vol. 5, p. 184 (May 26, 1647); pp. 293, 296 (Sept. 6 and 8, 1647).

36. Gillett, *Burned Books*, vol. 1, p. 330. McLachlan, *Socinianism*, p. 176 n. 5. Wilbur, *Unitarianism*, vol. 2, p. 196. Wallace, *Antitrinitarian Biography*, vol. 1, p. 3; vol. 3, pp. 158–61.

37. The statute is in C. H. Firth and R. S. Rait, *Acts and Ordinances of the*

Interregnum, 1642–1660 (London, 1911, 3 vols.), vol. 1, pp. 1133–36. See also Jordan, *Religious Toleration*, vol. 3, pp. 111–13.

38. On Baptist thought, see Jordan, *Religious Toleration*, vol. 3, pp. 452, 542. The tracts touching the problem of blasphemy are Samuel Richardson, *The Necessity of Toleration in Matters of Religion* (1647), reprinted in Underhill, ed., *Tracts on Liberty of Conscience*, pp. 235–85; Samuel Richardson, *An answer to the London ministers letter* (1649); Henry Danvers, *Certain quaeries concerning liberty of conscience* (1649); Anon., *A Short Discovery of his Highness that Lord Protector's Intentions* (1651), reprinted in Ivimey, *History of English Baptists*, vol. 1, pp. 220–29.

39. *The Petition of Divers Gathered Churches, And others wel affected, in and about the City of London, for declaring the Ordinance of the Lords and Commons, for punishing Blasphemies and Heresies, Null and Void* (1651), pp. 2–4.

40. McLachlan, *Socinianism*, pp. 172, 178, 180. See also David Underdown, *Pride's Purge* (Oxford, 1971).

41. Toulmin, *Review*, p. 74. Wood, *Athenae*, vol. 2, p. 301. McLachlan, *Socinianism*, p. 184.

42. Wood, *Athenae*, vol. 2, p. 360. On Fry, see McLachlan, *Socinianism*, pp. 239–49; Gillett, *Burned Books*, pp. 344–51; *D.N.B.*, vol. 7, pp. 737–38; Wallace, *Antitrinitarian Biography*, vol. 3, pp. 206–10.

43. *Journals H.C.*, vol. 6, pp. 123, 125, 131.

44. John Fry, *The Accuser Sham'd* (1649), pp. 12, 14–16. McLachlan, *Socinianism*, pp. 241–42.

45. On Cheynell, see *D.N.B.*, vol. 4, pp. 222–24; Wood, *Athenae*, vol. 2, pp. 358–61; Gillett, *Burned Books*, vol. 1, pp. 351–53; Wallace, *Antitrinitarian Biography*, vol. 1, pp. 72–77.

46. John Fry, *The Clergy in Their Colours* (1650), pp. 14–17, 28, 64.

47. *Journals H.C.*, vol. 6, pp. 536–37, 539–40 (Feb. 20 and 22, 1651). Wood, *Athenae*, vol. 2, p. 361. *D.N.B.*, vol. 7, p. 738.

48. Toulmin, *Review*, pp. 78–81. McLachlan, *Socinianism*, p. 185.

49. On Rakow and the Racovian Catechism, see Wilbur, *Unitarianism* 11, pp. 408–19, 449–55. *Journals H.C.*, vol. 7, pp. 113–14. Gillett, *Burned Books*, vol. 1, pp. 354–55. McLachlan, *Socinianism*, pp. 187–93.

50. Wilbur, *Unitarianism* 11, pp. 204–5, for the Calvinist scholar and Owen. McLachlan, *Socinianism*, p. 197, for the London Presbyterian. Gillett, *Burned Books*, vol. 1, pp. 355–56, for Poole.

51. John Biddle, *The Apostolic and True Opinion Concerning the Holy Trinity* (1653), and Biddle, *A Twofold Catechism: The One simply called A Scripture-Catechism; The Other, a brief Scripture-Catechism for Children. Wherein the chiefest points of the Christian Religion, being Question-wise proposed, resolve themselves by pertinent Answers taken word for word out of the Scripture, without either Consequences or Comments. Composed for their sakes that would fain be meer Christians, and not of this or that Sect.*

52. Biddle, *A Twofold Catechism*, preface passim.

53. *Journals H.C.*, vol. 7, p. 400 (Dec. 12 and 13, 1654).

54. Ibid., p. 416 (Jan. 15, 1655).

55. On the licensing laws, see William K. Clyde, *The Struggle for the Freedom of the Press from Caxton to Cromwell* (London, 1934), pp. 187–88, 299, 314–18.

56. Ibid., pp. 225–29, 232–37, 314, 334–35.

57. Goodwin, *Fresh Discovery of the High Presbyterian Spirit* (1655), reprinted in ibid., pp. 328–37.

58. Toulmin, *Review*, pp. 117–19. David Masson, *The Life of John Milton* (Lon-

don, 1859–94, 7 vols.), vol. 5, pp. 14, 64. For the quotation, *A True State of the Cause of Liberty of Conscience in the Commonwealth of England, Together with a True Narrative of the Cause, and Manner, of Mr. John Biddle's Sufferings* (1655), pp. 2–3.

59. *The Spirit of Persecution Again broken loose, by an Attempt to put in Execution against Mr. John Biddle . . . an abrogated Ordinance . . . for punishing Blasphemies and Heresies. Together with, A full Narrative of the whole Proceedings upon that Ordinance against the said Mr. John Biddle* (1655), pp. 2–6.

60. Ibid., pp. 4–6.

61. Ibid., pp. 19–20. *A True State.*

62. The Instrument of Government, quoted in *Spirit of Persecution*, p. 9, is reprinted in Gardiner, ed., *Constitutional Documents*, p. 416.

63. *Spirit of Persecution*, pp. 6, 8–9.

64. *A True State*, pp. 5–12; material quoted on p. 10.

65. McLachlan, *Socinianism*, p. 210. Louise Fargo Brown, *The Political Activities of the Baptists and Fifth Monarchy Men in England during the Interregnum* (Washington, D.C., 1912), pp. 90–91. Clyde, *Struggle for Freedom*, p. 255. For Cromwell's order of Aug. 28, 1655, ibid., pp. 323–27. The Anabaptist tract is reprinted in Ivimey, *History of the English Baptists*, vol. 1, pp. 220–29.

66. Toulmin, *Review*, p. 120. McLachlan, *Socinianism*, p. 209. James Bradley Thayer, *A Preliminary Treatise on Evidence at the Common Law* (Boston, 1898), pp. 75–80. Sir James Fitzjames Stephen, *A History of the Criminal Law of England* (London, 1883, 3 vols.), vol. 1, pp. 209–300.

67. *Publick Intelligencer*, Sept. 29, 1655. Masson, *Life of Milton*, vol. 5, pp. 65–66. Wilbur, *Unitarianism*, vol. 2, pp. 216–17. McLachlan, *Socinianism*, p. 209. On Firmin, see Wallace, *Antitrinitarian Biography*, vol. 3, pp. 372–89. *D.N.B.*, vol. 7, pp. 46–49.

68. Quoted in Brown, *Baptists and Fifth Monarchy Men*, pp. 91–92. Clyde, *Struggle for Freedom*, pp. 255–56. McLachlan, *Socinianism*, p. 210.

69. Wilbur, *Unitarianism*, vol. 2, p. 206. Toulmin, *Review*, pp. 122–23.

70. Rutt, ed., *Diary of Thomas Burton*, vol. 3, pp. 118, for the quotation. McLachlan, *Socinianism*, pp. 210–17. Toulmin, *Review*, pp. 124–30. *A Short Account of the life of John Biddle*, pp. 8–9.

Chapter 8   The Ranters

1. Laurence Clarkson, *The Lost Sheep Found* (1660), p. 27. (All seventeenth-century tracts cited in this chapter were published in London.) A. L. Morton, *The World of the Ranters: Religious Radicalism in the English Revolution* (London, 1970), ch. 5, is a study of Clarkson; ch. 4 is on the Ranters generally. Christopher Hill, *The World Turned Upside Down: Radical Ideas During the English Revolution* (New York, 1973), ch. 9, treats the Ranters. Jerome Friedman, *Blasphemy, Immorality, and Anarchy: The Ranters and the English Revolution* (Athens, Ohio, 1987), is comprehensive and disappointing. Norman Cohn, *The Pursuit of the Millennium: Revolutionary Millenarians and Mystical Anarchists of the Middle Ages* (New York, 1970, rev. ed.), has a valuable appendix containing extracts from Ranter and anti-Ranter documents, pp. 287–330. Robert Barclay, *The Inner Life of the Religious Societies of the Commonwealth* (London, 1876), appendix to ch. 5, includes abbreviated Ranter documents by Joseph Salmon and Jacob Bauthumley. Nigel Smith, ed., *A Collection of Ranter Writings from the 17th*

Century (London, 1983), contains works by Abiezer Coppe, Laurence Clarkson, Joseph Salmon, and Jacob Bauthumley.

2. On the Diggers, see introduction, George H. Sabine, ed., *The Works of Gerrard Winstanley* (Ithaca, N.Y., 1941); David W. Petegorsky, *Left-Wing Democracy in the English Civil War* (London, 1940), ch. 4. On Clarkson's tract of 1647, see Morton, *World of the Ranters*, p. 132; Perez Zagorin, *A History of Political Thought in the English Revolution* (London, 1954), pp. 31–32. For Cromwell, see Wilbur Cortez Abbott, *Writings and Speeches of Oliver Cromwell* (Cambridge, Mass., 1937–47, 4 vols.), vol. 3, p. 435. The Winstanley quotation is from *A New-Yeers Gift for the Parliament and the Armie* (1650), in Sabine, ed., *Works of Winstanley*, pp. 389–90.

3. Gertrude Huehns, *Antinomianism in English History* (London, 1951), unfortunately dismissed the Ranters with a paragraph (p. 109), but is otherwise instructive. The Grindletonians, an obscure sect named after the place of their origin in Yorkshire, believed in universal grace, the indwelling Christ, and the possibility that sin does not exist for Christians; see Hill, *World Upside Down*, pp. 65–68. The Behmenists, a similarly mystical sect, were named for the founder of their movement, Jacob Boehme; see Rufus M. Jones, *Spiritual Reformers of the 16th and 17th Centuries* (1914; Boston, 1959 reprint), which is mainly about Boehme and his English followers, including the Seekers, so named because they looked for the true church, found none, and joined none. On the Familists, see this book, ch. 6, pp. 91–93. Unlike the Familists and Behmenists, the Seekers did not form a sect. Hill, *World Upside Down*, pp. 148–58, treats the Seekers, as does Rufus M. Jones, *Studies in Mystical Religion* (London, 1909), pp. 449–500, which includes, with little understanding, some references to Ranters.

4. Gilbert Roulston, *The Ranters Bible. Or, Seven Several Religions by Them Held and Maintained* (1650), pp. 1–6.

5. *Copps Return to the Wayes of Truth* (1651) describes his upbringing; his account of his conversion is in his first *A Fiery Flying Roll* (1649), preface. For a similar account of a conversion, see George Foster, *The Sounding of the Last Trumpet* (1651), pp. 1–10.

6. Anthony à Wood, *Athenae Oxoniensis* (London, 1721, 2nd ed., 3 vols.), vol. 2, p. 501. *Routing of the Ranters* (1650), p. 3. *The Ranters Ranting* (1650), p. 2.

7. *Fiery Flying Roll*, vol. 1, pp. 1–5 passim, and, for the long quotation, pp. 6–7.

8. Ibid., pp. 6–8.

9. Ibid., vol. 2, pp. 2–4, 13–15, 19. Sabine, ed., *Works of Winstanley*, p. 262.

10. Cohn, *Pursuit of the Millennium*, and Jones, *Studies in Mystical Religion*, cover the Middle Ages. Jones, pp. 428–48, is good on Familism, and on p. 445 quotes Ainsworth; on p. 455, Murton. See also Barclay, *Inner Life*, for background on religious mysticism and belief in the indwelling Christ, ch. 5, pp. 9–10. Champlin Burrage, *Early English Dissenters* (Cambridge, 1912, 2 vols.), vol. 1, pp. 212–14, reprints Jessop. Roulston, *Ranters Bible*, p. 2, describes Ranters as Familists. John Tickell wrote *The Bottomless Pit Smoaking in Familisme* (1651).

11. The 1644 quote is from Thomas Clarkson, *A Confutation of the Anabaptists* (1644), p. 4. Hill, *World Upside Down*, p. 81, quotes Case; Hill is best on the emergence of radical ideas, but he tends to exaggerate and selects evidence, sometimes out of context, to suit his political interpretation.

12. Thomas Edwards, *Gangraena: or a Catalogue and Discovery of many of the Errours, Heresies, Blasphemies and pernicious Practices of the Sectaries of this time* (1646), p. 116.

13. Ibid., no. 32, p. 22; no. 11, p. 20; no. 77, p. 26; no. 165, p. 35; no. 176, p. 36.

14. Ibid., no. 13, p. 20 (quoting *The Bloudy Tenet of Persecution*); no. 166, p. 35.

Joseph Salmon, *A Rout, A Rout* (1649), pp. 1–11 passim; pp. 3, 4, 11 for the quotations.

15. On the Ranter theme, see Coppe, *Fiery Flying Roll*, vol. 1, p. 10; Foster, *Last Trumpet*, pp. 7–10, 14, 17–19; Salmon, *A Rout*, pp. 2–4. Morton, *World of the Ranters*, p. 84. The Leveller was Richard Overton, *The Hunting of the Foxes* (1649), reprinted in Don M. Wolfe, ed., *Leveller Manifestoes of the Puritan Revolution* (New York, 1944), p. 371.

16. Hill, *World Upside Down*, pp. 47, 75, quotes Dell, and, p. 31, Overton. The other Leveller quote is in Abbott, *Writings of Cromwell*, vol. 2, p. 69, and the royalist in G. P. Gooch, *English Democratic Ideas in the Seventeenth Century* (1898; New York, 1959 reprint), p. 167.

17. The seditious tract was *The Second Part of England's New Chaines* (1649), reprinted in William B. Haller and Godfrey Davies, eds., *The Leveller Tracts, 1647–1653* (New York, 1944), p. 177 ff. "The Third Agreement" is in Wolfe, ed., *Leveller Manifestoes*, p. 397 ff. See also Pauline Gregg, *Free-born John: A Biography of John Lilburne* (London, 1961), pp. 207–84; H. N. Brailsford, *The Levellers and the English Revolution* (London, 1961), pp. 481–522. Coppe, *Fiery Flying Roll*, vol. 1, p. 11.

18. Louise Fargo Brown, *The Political Activities of the Baptists and the Fifth Monarchy Men in England during the Interregnum* (Washington, D.C., 1912), pp. 11–18. B. S. Capp, *The Fifth Monarchy Men* (London, 1972), pp. 14, 20–22, 50–58. The "Fifth Monarchy" was to be the successor of the four "beasts" or empires mentioned in Daniel's vision (Daniel 7:1–14), which millenarians of the seventeenth century construed as Babylon, Assyria, Greece, and Rome. The Fifth Monarchists of England expected the imminent kingdom of Christ on earth and claimed the religious duty of taking up arms against Cromwell and Parliament in order to usher in the millennium.

19. John Holland, *Smoke of the Bottomlesse Pit* (1651), pp. 1–2. Jacob Bauthumley, *The Light and Dark Sides of God* (1650), p. 17. Edward Hide, *A Wonder Yet No Wonder* (1651), pp. 36–37. Lodowick Muggleton, *The Acts of the Witnesses of the Spirit* (1699), reprinted in Joseph Frost and Isaac Frost, eds., *The Works of John Reeve and Lodowicke Muggleton* (London, 1831, 3 vols.), vol. 3, p. 56, where Muggleton said: "So that the Life of a Dog, Cat, Toad, or any venomous Beast, was the Life of God: Nay That God was in a Table, Chair, or Stool. This was the Ranters God, and they thought there was no better God at all." Muggleton, who had known Ranters personally and was briefly attracted to their movement at its outset, wrote *Acts of the Witnesses* in 1677. All books and tracts in *Works of Reeve and Muggleton* contain the pagination of the original editions or, in some instances, of their eighteenth-century reprints. The table of contents is detailed, making it easy to locate any item, even though the three volumes do not have continuous pagination or an index. See also Coppin, *Divine Teachings* (1649), pp. 8–9; Coppe, *Fiery Flying Roll*, vol. 2, p. 18.

20. Clarkson, *Lost sheep*, p. 33.

21. Holland, *Smoke*, pp. 3–5. J.M., *The Ranters Last Sermon* (1654), pp. 4, 7. Clarkson, *Lost sheep*, p. 28. Bauthumley, *Light and Dark Sides*, pp. 28–31. *The Arraignment and Tryall with a Declaration of the Ranters* (1650), p. 4. *Routing of the Ranters*, p. 2.

22. "To the pure all things are pure" is from Titus 1:15, quoted by Coppe, *Fiery Flying Roll*, vol. 1, p. 8, and Clarkson, *Lost Sheep*, p. 25. See also Laurence Clarkson, *A Single Eye*, pp. 7–9, 11, 15–16, and *Lost Sheep*, pp. 26–27. The long quotation is from M. Stubs, *The Ranters Declaration* (1650), p. 2. *Arraignment and Tryall*, p. 3. *The Ranters Religion* (1650), p. 5. Roulston, *Ranters Bible*, p. 5. *Strange Newes from Newgate and the Old Baily* (1651), pp. 3–4. *Routing of the Ranters*, pp. 4–5.

23. Clarkson, *Lost sheep*, p. 28. Ephraim Pagitt, *Heresiography* (1654, 5th ed.), p. 144. *Strange Newes from Newgate*, pp. 2–3. *Ranters Religion*, p. 8, also reported the travesty.

24. Clarkson, *Lost sheep*, p. 25. *Ranters Last Sermon*, p. 3.

25. Holland, *Smoke*, p. 4. *Routing of the Ranters*, p. 6. Winstanley, *A Vindication*, in Sabine, ed., *Works of Winstanley*, pp. 400–401. Bauthumley, *Light and Dark Sides*, p. 26.

26. John Taylor, *Ranters of Both Sexes* (1651), p. 4. Sheppard's prologue to his *The Joviall Crew* (1651), opposite the title page, is: "Bedlam broke loose? Hell is open'd too. / Mad-men & Fiends, & Harpies to your view / We do present: but who shall cure the Tumor? / All the world now is in the Ranting Humor." Hotham is quoted in *The Journal of George Fox*, ed. John T. Nickalls (Cambridge, 1952), p. 90. Salmon, *A Rout*, p. 1. Clarkson, *Lost sheep*, pp. 24–25. Morton, *World of the Ranters*, pp. 87, 112. Stubs, *Ranters Declaration*, pp. 5–6.

27. Holland, *Smoke*, p. 1, used "Atheistical," and Taylor, *Ranters of Both Sexes*, p. 1, "irreligious." Roulston, *Ranters Bible*, p. 4, used "Marcions." "Gnosticks" appears in *Ranters Religion*, p. 4. *Reliquiae Baxterianae, or . . . Baxter's Narrative*, ed. M. Sylvester (London, 1696), pp. 76–77. *The Journal of George Fox*, ed. Norman Penney (Cambridge, 1911, 2 vols.), vol. 1, p. 47.

28. Winstanley, *Vindication*, in Sabine, ed., *Works of Winstanley*, pp. 399–403.

29. *Journals H.C.*, vol. 6, p. 354 (Feb. 1, 1650). *Journal of Fox*, ed. Penney, vol. 1, p. 47.

30. *Journal of Fox*, ed. Penney, vol. 1, p. 90. Joseph Salmon, *Heights in Depths and Depths in Heights* (1651), title page for quotation. Coppe, *Fiery Flying Roll*, vol. 2, pp. 13, 14. Salmon clearly recanted, but *Heights in Depths*, pp. 37–54, is unorthodox on God, heaven, hell, sin, and the Trinity.

31. Salmon, *Heights in Depths*, p. A4 in preface ("To the Reader"), p. 52. Tickell, *Bottomless Pit*, pp. 37–38.

32. Clarkson, *A Single Eye*, p. 14. *Journals H.C.*, vol. 6, p. 427 (June 21, 1650).

33. *Journals H.C.*, vol. 6, pp. 430 (June 21), 437 (July 5), 440 (July 12), 443–44 (July 19). "A Declaration of the Army," July 19, 1650, in Abbott, *Cromwell*, vol. 2, p. 286. On the Blasphemy Act of 1650, see above, pp. 156–57.

34. C. H. Firth and R. S. Rait, eds., *Acts and Ordinances of the Interregnum, 1642–1660* (London, 1911, 3 vols.), vol. 2, pp. 409–12. *Journals H.C.*, vol. 6, p. 453. John Milton, "Of Civil Power," in *The Works of John Milton*, ed. Frank Allen Patterson (New York, 1931–38, 18 vols.), vol. 6, p. 11.

35. "An Act for Relief of Religious and Peaceable People," in Firth and Rait, eds., *Acts and Ordinances*, vol. 2, pp. 423–25.

36. *Journals H.C.*, vol. 6, p. 475 (Sept. 27, 1650). Clarkson, *Lost sheep*, pp. 30–31.

37. *Weekly Intelligencer*, Oct. 1–8, 1651, quoted in William M. Clyde, *Freedom of the Press from Caxton to Cromwell* (London, 1934), p. 206, and Morton, *World of the Ranters*, p. 103. *Routing of Ranters*, p. 2. *Journals H.C.*, vol. 6, p. 475 (Oct. 1, 1650). Coppe's book was reprinted in Jan. 1650; the House ordered it burned in Feb.; the committee examined him in Sept., more than six months after the offense.

38. *A Remonstrance of the sincere and zealous Protestation of Abiezer Coppe* (1651). *Copps Return to the Wayes of Truth*, pp. 14, 19–21. Tickell, *Bottomless Pit*, p. 38.

39. Humphrey Ellis, *Pseudochristus: Or, A true and fanciful Relation of the Grand Impostures, Horrid Blasphemies, Abominable Practices* (1650), pp. 33–38, 42–51.

40. George Foster's *Sounding of the Last Trumpet* (1651) sounds like the work of an antinomian Seeker, not a Ranter. Cohn, *Pursuit of the Millennium*, p. 303, reported

that Bauthumley's tongue was bored. I could not verify the fact from a primary source; Morton, *World of the Ranters*, p. 96, and Hill, *World Upside Down*, p. 176, retail the same incident. Samuel Rawson Gardiner, *History of the Commonwealth and Protectorate* (London, 1894–1901, 3 vols.), vol. 1, p. 396; Jones, *Studies in Mystical Religion*, p. 479 n. 2; and Morton, *World of the Ranters*, pp. 104–5, describe the treatment of Ranters in the army. See also *Arraignment and Tryall*, p. 4; *The Ranters Recantation* (1650), p. 5; *Routing the Ranters*, pp. 2–3; *Ranters Last Sermon*, pp. 6–7; *Strange Newes from Newgate*, p. 6.

41. Stubs, *Ranters Declaration*, p. 4. John Cordy Jeafferson, ed., *Middlesex County Records* (London, 1886–92, 7 vols.), vol. 3, p. 204. *A List of some of the Grand Blasphemers and Blasphemies* (1654), broadsheet. *The Ranters Creed, Being a true copie of the Examination of a blasphemous lot of people called Ranters* (1651), pp. 1–6. Taylor, *Ranters of Both Sexes*, pp. 2–3.

42. *List of Grand Blasphemers. A Declaration of John Robins, the false prophet*, by G.H., an Ear-witness (1651), pp. 1–6, includes statements by Robins in which he exalted himself as the "third Adam," who was divinely inspired, but denied being God or immortal. *Ranters Creed*, pp. 1–6. Taylor, *Ranters of Both Sexes*, pp. 1–6, alleged, in the subtitle and elsewhere, that Robins "doth Accuse himselfe to be the great God of Heaven." See also Lodowick Muggleton, *Acts of the Witnesses*, in Frost and Frost, eds., *Works of Reeve and Muggleton*, vol. 3, pp. 20–23, 45–48; the quotation is on p. 21.

43. Muggleton, *Acts of the Witnesses*, in Frost and Frost, eds., *Works of Reeve and Muggleton*, vol. 3, pp. 20, 42–45. Tany, *The Nations Right in Magna Charta discussed with the Thing called Parliament* (1651) and *Theaurau John his Aurora* (1651). *D.N.B.* on Tany, vol. 19, pp. 363–64.

44. Norwood wrote the preface to Tany's *Theaurau John his Aurora*. See also *The Case and Trial of Capt. Robert Norwood* (1651) and *A Brief discourse made by Capt. Robert Norwood . . . upon an indictment . . . in Old Bayly* (1652); *List of Grand Blasphemers*. Norwood denied the charges of blasphemy and professed Christianity, yet he was anticlerical and said, "Verily I cannot but abhor the Doctrines and Principles of most Christians," which he condemned as "Doctrines of devils." He embraced antinomianism, and declared we sin "by oppression, by injustice, and by deceit" (*Case and Trial*, pp. 7, 13, 15, 17).

45. Herbert John McLachlan, *Socinianism in Seventeenth Century England* (London, 1951), pp. 226–37, is good on Erbury; see also Hill, *World Upside Down*, pp. 154–59. The primary source is *The Testimony of William Erbury* (1658), which includes his encounter with Cheynell and his denunciation of the Ranters, pp. 3–18, 315–37. On Walker, see *Middlesex County Records*, vol. 3, p. 215, May 25, 1653.

46. Frost and Frost, eds., *Works of Reeve and Muggleton*, contains books, pamphlets, and letters. Alexander Gordon, who did the *D.N.B.* essay on Muggleton (and those on Reeve, Coppe, Tany, and Robins), published two lectures which constitute all the scholarship on Muggletonianism: "The Origin of the Muggletonians," paper read before the Liverpool Literary and Historical Society, April 5, 1869, and "Ancient and Modern Muggletonians," paper read before the same society a year later. The only other writings on the subject are James Hyde, "The Muggletonians and the Document of 1729," *New-Church Review*, vol. 7 (1900), pp. 215–27; George Charles Williamson, *Lodowick Muggleton: A Paper Read before Ye Sette of Odd Volumes* (London, 1919), which derives wholly from Gordon.

47. T. B. Macaulay, *The History of England, from the Accession of James II* (London, 1849–65, 5 vols.), vol. 1, p. 164.

48. Muggleton, *Acts of the Witnesses*, in Frost and Frost, eds., *Works of Reeve and Muggleton*, vol. 3, pp. 38–39.

49. Ibid., pp. 47–48. The Reeve quotation is from his *A Transcendent Spiritual Treatise* (1652), in ibid., vol. 1, pp. 1–2, reprinted the 2nd ed. of 1756. My description of the Reeve-Muggleton theology is from this work.

50. The imprisonment and trial of 1653 are reported in ibid., vol. 3, pp. 67–78. *A Remonstrance*, in ibid., vol. 1, pp. 15–22.

51. *Journal of Fox*, pp. 182, 195. Morton, *World of the Ranters*, pp. 97, 138. Hill, *World Upside Down*, p. 176. R. Forneworth, *Ranter Principles and Deceits Discovered*, p. 19. Richard Hickcock, *Testimony against the People call'd Ranters*, pp. 2–4. Fox referred to "Ranters" as late as 1668 (*Journal*, ed. Nickalls, p. 622), but he meant rude, disruptive people, a standard by which Fox and all Quakers of the 1650s were Ranters (see ch. 9 of this book).

52. On Coppin, see *D.N.B.*, vol. 9, pp. 1117–18. For his earlier beliefs on the indwelling God, see his *Divine Teachings*, pp. 8–9. His *Truth's Testimony* (1654), p. 25, reports his rejection of Ranters; that tract describes his later beliefs and five blasphemy prosecutions in which he ably defended himself.

53. Kelsey to Cromwell, 1653, in T. Birch, ed., *A Collection of State Papers of John Thurloe* (London, 1742, 7 vols.), vol. 4, p. 486.

54. Historical Manuscripts Commission, *Report on Manuscripts in Various Collections* (London, 1901), vol. 1, pp. 132–33.

55. Kelsey in Birch, ed., *Thurloe Papers*, vol. 4, p. 486. *Mercurius Politicus*, June 26–July 3, 1656, reported the case of Jock of Broad Scotland, reprinted in David Masson, *The Life of John Milton* (London, 1859–94, 7 vols.), vol. 5, pp. 92–94.

Chapter 9   The Early English Quakers

1. *The Journal of George Fox*, ed. Norman Penney (Cambridge, 1911, 2 vols.), vol. 1, pp. 249–50. This edition is the unexpurgated text, *verbatim* and *literatim*. But both it and *The Short Journal and Itinerary Journals of George Fox*, ed. Norman Penney (Cambridge, 1925), are extremely difficult to read, because Fox's style and eccentricities in spelling compound the problems presented by seventeenth-century orthography. *The Journal of George Fox*, ed. John T. Nickalls (Cambridge, 1952), presents in modern English most but not all of the 1911 *Journal* with valuable additions from the 1925 *Short Journal*. As a convenience to the reader, I have used, whenever possible, Nickall's 1952 edition and hereafter cite it as *Journal* (1952). On occasion, the earlier, definitive editions by Penney, which contain invaluable scholarly notes, must be used.

2. Burrough's remarks are from his intro. to George Fox, *The Great Mistery of the Great Whore Unfolded* (1659), reprinted in *The Works of George Fox* (Philadelphia, 1831, 3 vols.), vol. 3, p. 14; and Edward Burrough, *A Word of Reproof* (1659), quoted in Christopher Hill, *The World Turned Upside Down* (New York, 1973), p. 197. Hill's eagerness to turn the early Quakers into "political radicals" (p. 195) turns the matter upside down; they were nonpolitical and wholly religious. Dewsbury's statement of 1665 is in William C. Braithwaite, *The Beginnings of Early Quakerism* (London, 1912), p. 280. Braithwaite's is the classic treatment for the period to 1660. Hugh Barbour, *The Quakers in Puritan England* (New Haven, 1964), is the only modern monograph that adds anything of value to Braithwaite.

3. *Journal* (1952), pp. 14, 27, 68. On lamenting the army's failure, see Mabel Richmond Brailsford, *A Quaker from Cromwell's Army: James Nayler* (London, 1927), p. 24. Nayler's *Lamb's War Against the Man of Sin* (1657) is in his *A Collection of Sundry Books, Epistles and Papers*, ed. George Whitehead (London, 1716), pp. 375–400.

4. *Journal* (1952), pp. 182, 244–45. Braithwaite, *Beginnings*, pp. 195, 446.

5. *Journal* (1952), pp. 36, 92, 242–49. *Journal*, ed. Penney (1911), vol. 1, pp. 217–19. Braithwaite, *Beginnings*, pp. 486–99.

6. Barbour, *Quakers*, pp. 257–58, quotes Audland. Braithwaite, *Beginnings*, p. 136, and, on the woman, p. 199. For the Fox quote, Braithwaite, *Beginnings*, p. 451; *Journal* (1952), p. 280, gives a variant quotation.

7. *Journal* (1952), pp. 24, 39–40, 51. Braithwaite, *Beginnings*, pp. 444–45.

8. *Journal* (1952), p. 35. Barbour, *Quakers*, p. 211, gives the quotations; his ch. 8 on persecution of Quakers is very good.

9. *Journal* (1952), pp. 7, 8, 11, 19–20. Barbour, *Quakers*, pp. 154–57.

10. On Fox's railing as love, see *Journal*, ed. Penney (1911), vol. 1, pp. 90–92, 116. For the first Baxter quote, Braithwaite, *Beginnings*, p. 284; for the second, *Reliquae Baxterianae* (London, 1696), p. 77. On vituperative conduct, see Braithwaite, *Beginnings*, ch. 12.

11. Proclamation of 1655, reprinted in Samuel R. Gardiner, *History of the Commonwealth and Protectorate* (London, 1903, 4 vols.), vol. 3, pp. 260–61.

12. *Reliquae Baxterianae*, p. 77. *Journal*, ed. Penney (1911), vol. 1, p. 89. *Journal* (1952), pp. 15, 18, 27. On going naked "for a sign," see Braithwaite, *Beginnings*, pp. 148–51.

13. On the name "Quaker," *Journal*, ed. Penney (1911), vol. 1, pp. 5–9; vol. 2, p. 395. Robert Barclay, *Apology for the Quakers* (1675), proposition xi, sec. 8, of any edition; I used the 8th ed. (Providence, 1940), p. 359. Braithwaite, *Beginnings*, p. 57. For the quote on Nayler, see James Gough, *Memoirs* (Dublin, 1781), p. 56.

14. *Journal* (1952), pp. 8, 10–28.

15. *Diary of Thomas Burton*, ed. John Towill Rutt (London, 1828, 4 vols.), vol. 1, p. 62 (cited hereafter as *Diary of Burton*). On the social backgrounds of the early Quakers and their geographic strengths, see Barbour, *Quakers*, ch. 3. On religious precursors, see generally Rufus M. Jones, *Spiritual Reformers of the 16th and 17th Centuries* (1914, Boston, 1959 reprint), and *Studies in Mystical Religion* (London, 1909); Robert Barclay, *The Inner Life of the Religious Societies of the Commonwealth* (London, 1876), ch. 5, pp. 9–10. See also my n. 3 to ch. 8, above.

16. *Journal*, ed. Penney (1911), vol. 1, p. 2. *Journal* (1952), pp. 51–52.

17. For Fox on the Ranters, *Journal* (1952), pp. 47, 81, 181–83, 195. For the tract of 1652 and More's statement, see Braithwaite, *Beginnings*, pp. 40, 58. G.H., *The Declaration of John Robins* (London, 1651), vol. 1, p. 6, identified Ranters as Shakers. J.M. (a former Ranter), *The Ranters Last Sermon* (London, 1654), p. 6, referred to "Ranters, Quakers, Shakers, and the rest of their atheistical crew." See also *The Ranters Creed* (1651), p. 6. R. Forneworth, *The Ranters Principles* (London, 1654), a Quaker tract censuring Ranters, was written to distinguish Quakers from Ranters. On Hotham, *Journal* (1952), pp. 75, 90. On the identification of Hotham, *Short Journal*, ed. Penney (1925), p. 277. Dr. Robert Gell made a statement similar to William Penn's about the Quakers' having prevented England from being overrun by the Ranters; see Jones, *Studies in Mystical Religion*, p. 481. The "leveller" remark, and many like it, are in *Diary of Burton*, vol. 1, p. 169. On the grand jury, Hill, *World Upside Down*, p. 192; Hill, p. 195, calls the Quakers "political radicals" to make them fit his ideological straitjacket.

18. *Journal* (1952), p. 61.

19. Braithwaite, *Beginnings*, p. 6. *Journal* (1952), pp. 73, 100–101. Brailsford, *Quaker from Cromwell's Army*, pp. 38–39, 41–42, 46–48, 67. Nayler, *Collection of Sundry Books*, p. 12, for the quote on his call.

20. *Reliquae Baxterianae*, p. 76. Braithwaite, *Beginnings*, p. 241. Alexander Gordon, on Nayler, *D.N.B.*, vol. 14, p. 133.

21. *Journal* (1952), pp. 129–30. On Fell, see Braithwaite, *Beginnings*, pp. 105–6. See Barbour, *Quakers*, p. 148, for Nayler on Fox and Fox's reply to a judge.

22. On Fox's blasphemy case of 1652, see *Journal* (1952), pp. 129–39. For "Sonne of God," see *Short Journal*, ed. Penney (1925), pp. xx, 5, 17, 479 n. 2. For "My Father and I are one," see *Journal*, ed. Penney (1911), vol. 1, p. 66; for Penney's comments, ibid., p. 425.

23. *Journal* (1952), pp. 132–39. *Journal*, ed. Penney (1911), vol. 1, pp. 62–67. On the petition, *Short Journal*, ed. Penney (1925), pp. 283–84; Braithwaite, *Beginnings*, pp. 108–9; and especially Fox, *The Great Mistery*, in *Works*, vol. 3, pp. 585–97.

24. Nayler, *Divers Particulars of the Persecutions of James Nayler, by the Priests of Westmoreland* (1652), reprinted in *Collection of Sundry Books*, pp. 1–10.

25. *The Examination of James Nayler, upon an Indictment for Blasphemy, at the Sessions at Appleby*, in *Collection of Sundry Books*, pp. 11–16. On Pearson, see Brailsford, *Quaker from Cromwell's Army*, pp. 28–29; Braithwaite, *Beginnings*, pp. 112–13.

26. *Journal* (1952), pp. 158–59. *Short Journal*, ed. Penney (1925), pp. 32–33.

27. *Journal* (1952), p. 160.

28. Ibid., pp. 160–64. On Cromwell and the Quakers, see W. K. Jordan, *The Development of Religious Toleration in England (1640–1660)*, vol. 3, pp. 176–79; Braithwaite, *Beginnings*, ch. 17, on Quaker "Relations with the State." On the Nominated Parliament of 1653, see Gardiner, *Commonwealth and Protectorate*, vol. 2, pp. 272–92.

29. *Journal* (1952), p. 233. Brailsford, *Quaker from Cromwell's Army*, pp. 85–89. Braithwaite, *Beginnings*, pp. 170–200. Emilia Fogelklou, *James Nayler* (London, 1931), pp. 131–37.

30. Brailsford, *Quaker from Cromwell's Army*, p. 76. Braithwaite, *Beginnings*, pp. 172–73, 178–80, 446. Gardiner, *Commonwealth and Protectorate*, vol. 3, p. 263. For Fox's account, *Journal* (1952), pp. 191–99.

31. *Journal* (1952), pp. 242–66.

32. Ibid., pp. 267–69. Braithwaite, *Beginnings*, pp. 245–48. Brailsford, *Quaker from Cromwell's Army*, pp. 93–100, includes the Fox letter on "unclean spirits" on p. 97. For an eyewitness account of the Fox-Nayler schism at Exeter, see Hubberthorne's letter reprinted in Fogelklou, *James Nayler*, pp. 164–67.

33. James Deacon, *The grand Impostor examined, Or, the Life, Trial, and Examination of James Nayler* (1656), reprinted in *State Trials*, vol. 5, pp. 826–42, of which pp. 830–32 include some of the letters to Nayler. Deacon was an interrogator at the Bristol examination. In addition to his account, other eyewitness reports are Ra[lph] Farmer, *Sathan Inthron'd in his Chair of Pestilence* (1657) and William Grigge, *The Quakers Jesus* (1658). Grigge took the shorthand notes of the Bristol interrogation, ibid., epistle, ans. 2. Farmer's *Sathan Inthron'd*, pp. 4–10, includes a good selection of the letters. Another valuable primary source is Anon., *A True Narrative of the Examination, Tryall, and Sufferings of James Nayler* (1657). Anon., *Memoirs of the Life, Ministry, Tryal and Sufferings of that Very Eminent Person James Nailer, the Quaker's Great Apostle* (1729), is a later collection of the documents of the case, but unique because the long preface is favorable to Nayler and the documents are studded with notes pointing out

distortions in the presentation of the evidence against him; the author also reprinted some eloquent letters by Nayler on his religious beliefs (pp. 71–80).

34. On the Dorcas Erbury incident, see Deacon, *Grand Impostor*, in *State Trials*, vol. 5, pp. 834, 837. Henry J. Cadbury, *Fox's Book of Miracles* (Cambridge, 1948), is best on "miraculous" cures by Quaker preachers. There are some 150 entries on cures attributed to Fox; on Howgill and the lame boy, ibid., p. 12. See also Braithwaite, *Beginnings*, pp. 247, 341. Fox's letter is in Farmer, *Sathan Inthron'd*, pp. 9–10.

35. Most of the primary sources mentioned in n. 33 above include accounts of the entry into Bristol. Fogelklou, *James Nayler*, pp. 157–73, contains an excellent account of the Fox-Nayler schism and its effect upon Nayler. See also Brailsford, *Quaker from Cromwell's Army*, pp. 116–18. On Fox's recommendations to the Bristol Quakers, see *Journal* (1952), pp. 281–82.

36. The primary sources for the Bristol examination are referred to in n. 33 above. In "Proceedings in the House of Commons Against James Nayler for Blasphemy and Misdemeanours," *State Trials*, vol. 5, pp. 801–20, p. 806 refers to Nayler's resemblance to Jesus. On the same point, see Grigge, *Quakers Jesus*, pp. 68–69; Farmer, *Sathan Inthron'd*, pp. 25–27. *A True Narrative*, pp. 1–28, reproduces the complete record of the parliamentary committee's interrogations and report. For judgments that Nayler was mad, see the account by David Hume, quoted in *State Trials*, vol. 5, p. 804; David Masson, *The Life of John Milton* (London, 1859–94, 7 vols.), vol. 5, p. 68; Thomas Carlyle, *Oliver Cromwell's Letters and Speeches* (London, 1904, 3 vols.), vol. 3, p. 213; Barclay, *Inner Life*, p. 427; Charles H. Firth, *The Last Years of the Protectorate* (London, 1909, 2 vols.), vol. 1, p. 96; Jordan, *Religious Toleration*, vol. 3, pp. 221, 223, 226; Theodore A. Wilson and Frank J. Merli, "Nayler's Case and the Dilemma of the Protectorate," University of Birmingham *Historical Journal*, vol. 10 (1965–66), pp. 46, 47; and, to a lesser extent, Fogelklou, *James Nayler*, pp. 163, 172, 176, 179–80.

37. The Bristol examinations are reprinted in Grigge, *Quakers Jesus*, pp. 4–6. Barbour, *Quakers*, p. 185, quotes the Fell letter in the context of the prevailing Quaker apocalyptic view.

38. Deacon, *Grand Impostor*, in *State Trials*, vol. 5, pp. 832, 834. For a variant report of the same interrogation, see Grigge, *Quakers Jesus*, p. 7.

39. *State Trials*, vol. 5, p. 834. The woman supposedly called "mother" was Martha Symonds; for her examination, ibid., pp. 835–36. On her, see Fogelklou, *James Nayler*, pp. 151–55. Farmer, *Sathan Inthron'd*, pp. 9–10, for Fox's letter to Nayler about her.

40. For the Bristol examinations of Nayler's companions, see Deacon, *Grand Impostor*, in *State Trials*, vol. 5, pp. 833–38.

41. *Journals H.C.*, vol. 7, p. 448 (Oct. 31, 1656). *State Trials*, vol. 5, p. 805.

42. *State Trials*, vol. 5, pp. 805–15. *Journals H.C.*, vol. 7, p. 448.

43. The Instrument of Government is reprinted in Samuel R. Gardiner, ed., *Constitutional Documents of the Puritan Revolution* (London, 1906, 3rd ed.), pp. 405–17; the religion clauses, p. 416. My summary of the religious policy of the protectorate is from Jordan, *Religious Toleration*, vol. 3, pp. 144–202.

44. Jordan, *Religious Toleration*, vol. 3, pp. 164–65; ibid., pp. 450–51, on the growth of Congregationalism.

45. Ibid., pp. 156–58; for the quote from the ambassador, p. 171.

46. *Journals H.C.*, vol. 7, p. 399. Jordan, *Religious Toleration*, vol. 3, pp. 166, 170.

47. Firth, *Last Years*, vol. 1, pp. 11–21. Jordan, *Religious Toleration*, vol. 3, pp. 188–90. The constitution of 1657 was "The Humble Petition and Advice," reprinted in Gardiner, ed., *Constitutional Documents;* see pp. 454–55 for the religious clause. For

the political situation leading to the new constitution, see Firth, *Last Years*, vol. 1, pp. 128–200.

48. Carlyle, *Cromwell's Letters and Speeches*, vol. 3, p. 213.

49. *Rex* v. *Taylor*, 3 Keble 607 (1676), and 1 Ventris 293 (1676).

50. Instrument of Government, in Gardiner, ed., *Constitutional Documents*, pp. 405–17. *Diary of Burton*, vol. 1, pp. 29, 112, 118, 123, 141.

51. *Diary of Burton*, vol. 1, pp. 25, 59, 68, 88, 90, 97. On the no-law theme, ibid., pp. 38, 58, 87, 120–21, 125, 128, 152, 163, 174. On the omnipotence of Parliament, pp. 58, 108, 125. For Howard, p. 78. For Sydenham, p. 86. For Strickland, p. 88, and see also Wolsey, p. 89. For Kelsey, p. 164. Some claimed that the jurisdiction of the defunct ecclesiastical courts devolved upon Parliament (pp. 35, 108, 125, 141–42).

52. On vindicating the honor of God and blasphemy as treason against God, ibid., pp. 25–26, 39, 48, 51, 55, 59–60, 63, 68, 86, 89, 96, 109, 114, 122, 125, 132, 139, 150. On "merciful," p. 90. On Richard Cromwell, p. 126.

53. Ibid., pp. 62–63.

54. Ibid., pp. 25, 49–50, 63, 107. On Skippon, see Firth, *Last Years*, vol. 1, pp. 86, 92.

55. For examples of biblical speeches by major generals, see *Diary of Burton*, vol. 1, pp. 99–100 (Packer), pp. 101–4 (Walley), pp. 108–10 (Goffe), pp. 113–14 (Boteler), pp. 122–24 (Kelsey). A note showing references to the Bible during the course of the debates would have to read ibid., pp. 25–150 passim. On Smith, ibid., p. 87; and Masson, *Life of Milton*, vol. 5, p. 92.

56. *Diary of Burton*, vol. 1, pp. 170, 173, 174. Grigge, *Quakers Jesus*, p. 35.

57. *Diary of Burton*, vol. 1, pp. 98, 97, 108–9, 86, 124, 146, 169, in the sequence for the quotations in my text. For other anti-Quaker remarks, see pp. 70, 76, 128, 132, 137 ("they will level the foundations of all government"), 170. Farmer, *Sathan Inthron'd*, p. 28, called Quakerism a "medly of Popery, Socinianism, Arianisme, Arminianisme, Anabaptisme, and all that is nought."

58. For statements sympathetic to Quakers, see *Diary of Burton*, vol. 1, pp. 56, 62–63, 65, 69, 86, 88, 99, 120. For Baynes, White, and Goffe, pp. 59, 60, 110.

59. Ibid., pp. 88, 120.

60. Ibid., p. 33.

61. Ibid., pp. 46–48. Burton's prejudice shows up even in the reporting of the debate. In addition to his omission of Nayler's orthodox answers and his stating that Nayler had confessed, Burton omitted a tolerationist speech with the comment that the member, Walther Waller, "said a good deal more to extenuate the crime but I minded it not" (p. 152). At another point, Burton gave a few terse lines to several tolerationist speeches, saying it was too dark to take notes, but still later that night he gave ample space to a "very large and handsome speech" by Bampfield against "the merciful men," in which Bampfield advocated death (pp. 90–92). The fullest analysis of the debate by a historian is in Jordan, *Religious Toleration*, vol. 3, pp. 221–43. Jordan's four volumes are in many respects invaluable and definitive, but he was wholly uninterested in the subject of blasphemy and never treated it as a special problem. To Jordan, blasphemy was merely an aspect of heresy, although he never distinguished the two. He reported the opinions of an extraordinary range of people and sects on toleration, but omitted Quaker opinions. His account of Nayler's case was unreliable and ununderstanding. He simplistically identified the revengers as the Presbyterians, never mentioning Congregationalists and Independents, without whom the revengers would not have been a political force. Jordan gave the impression that the government stood for toleration against the dominant Presbyterian party in

Parliament. The government, in fact, was divided, as were Oliver and Richard Cromwell. The protector, having taken no position during the debate, offered no leadership; his councilors who sat in Parliament represented every viewpoint on every question during the Nayler debate. Jordan declared that the Nayler case was of great importance to the development of religious toleration, but, without understanding early Quakerism and the differences between heresy and blasphemy, he could not understand the reasons. He regarded Nayler as "obviously mad," "obviously demented," and "plainly unbalanced," and said that he had "messianic delusions." He also said that Nayler had been worshipped "as" the Lamb, rather than that the worship had been directed to the Lamb in Nayler. The distinction is crucial. Jordan declared that Nayler offended "all religious men," yet some who defended him were not offended. More to the point, Nayler himself was a devout Christian, as religious as any member of Parliament, and so were his followers. Jordan saw Nayler as an undoubted blasphemer and claimed that his blasphemy was "universally admitted." Yet many of Nayler's defenders in Parliament denied that he was guilty of blasphemy. Like Burton, Jordan thought that Nayler was "determined to hang himself. He confessed to all the committee's charges against him. . . ." Jordan stated that insanity was not a defense to the charge of blasphemy; but Nayler did not plead insanity; it *was* a defense under the act of 1650, and it was a defense even in Scotland, where the Presbyterians were in complete control. The Scottish Act Against Blasphemy of 1661 exempted anyone "distracted in his wits" (Baron David Hume, *Commentaries on the Law of Scotland, Respecting the Description and Punishment of Crimes* [Edinburgh, 1797, 2 vols.], vol. 2, p. 514). Without considering the cursing of God or atheistic denial and contempt of God, Jordan declared that "no severer test for the principle of religious toleration could have been devised by a satanic mind." Such a statement, from a specialist on toleration, was exaggerated as well as wrong. Firth, *Last Years*, vol. 1, pp. 83–106, treats the Nayler case without glaring error; Firth was not interested in the subject of blasphemy. Braithwaite, *Beginnings*, pp. 241–78, has a fascinating account of the Nayler case within the context of early Quaker thought; Braithwaite too was uninterested in blasphemy as a problem for religious toleration or as a legal or religious concept. He cared about the Quaker mind and the impact of the case on subsequent Quaker behavior and development. The biographers of Nayler stressed colorful details, such as the entrance into Bristol and the execution of the punishment, but they were innocent of any concern for procedure, jurisdiction, or the substantive offense.

62. *Diary of Burton*, vol. 1, pp. 53, 79.

63. Ibid., pp. 118–19. See also p. 123.

64. Ibid., pp. 56, 59–61.

65. Ibid., pp. 128–31, much of which consists of notes by Rutt, the editor of the *Diary of Burton*, from *State Trials*. Whitelocke's speech of Dec. 12 is fully reported in *State Trials*, vol. 5, pp. 821–28.

66. *Diary of Burton*, vol. 1, pp. 47, 65.

67. Ibid., pp. 66–68, 74, 101–4, 124, 132, 151, 164, for the revengers. For Cooper and Packer, pp. 96–97, 99–101.

68. *Journals H.C.*, vol. 7, pp. 468–69 (Dec. 16, 1656). *Diary of Burton*, vol. 1, pp. 152–58. Both sources include the vote and the sentence, but Burton provided additional detail on the debate concerning the lesser sentence. *Diary of Burton*, pp. 161–63, also includes the debate giving the rationale for Parliament's choosing to act judicially rather than legislatively. Boring through the tongue with a hot iron, however cruel, was a humane refinement of the ancient punishment of cutting the tongue off. See

John Godolphin, *Reportorium Canonicum; or An Abridgment of the Ecclesiastical Laws of This Realm Consistent with the Temporal* (London, 1678), p. 559. During the Nayler debate, a Major Audley said that boring through the tongue "is an ordinary punishment for swearing [profanity], I have known twenty bored through the tongue" (*Diary of Burton*, vol. 1, p. 154).

69. *Diary of Burton*, vol. 1, pp. 163, 167, 246.

70. Ibid., pp. 38, 137, 247. For the lashing scene, see *A True Narrative*, pp. 34–38, written before Nayler underwent the last third of his punishment in Bristol. See also "The Testimony of Rebecca Travers," in *Memoirs of the Life, Ministry, Tryal and Sufferings*, pp. 58–59.

71. *Diary of Burton*, vol. 1, pp. 167–73. *Journals H.C.*, vol. 7, p. 470 (Dec. 18, 1656). On this toleration issue and the constitution of 1657, see above, p. 190 and n. 47.

72. *Diary of Burton*, vol. 1, pp. 182–83, 217–21. *State Papers Domestic, Commonwealth and Protectorate*, vol. 131, no. 45 (Dec. 20, 1656). *Journals H.C.*, vol. 7, p. 471. *A True Narrative*, pp. 49–56, includes the petitions of the one hundred to Parliament and to Cromwell, prefaced by a plea for religious liberty for Nayler and all Quakers. A copy of the petition to Cromwell, endorsed by him on Dec. 25, 1656, is reprinted in Norman Penney, *Extracts from State Papers Relating to Friends, 1654 to 1672* (London, 1913), pp. 21–23, bearing eighty-eight signatures, including: Joshua Sprigge, a former New Model Army chaplain; Giles Calvert, the printer of Ranter, Leveller, and Quaker tracts; and Edward Bushell, one of the minor heroes in the history of English liberty. In 1670, Bushell was the foreman of the jury that refused, against fierce judicial browbeating, to return a verdict of guilty in the trial of Penn and Mead for inciting a riot—practicing their religion in violation of the act against conventicles. Bushell and his jury were fined, refused to pay, and were sent to jail, where they stayed some months before a higher court ruled in favor of the right of the jury to return an honest verdict. See William S. Holdsworth, *A History of English Law* (London, 1938–66, 6th ed., rev., 16 vols.), vol. 1, pp. 344–46.

73. *Journal*, ed. Penney (1911), vol. 1, p. 266. *A True Narrative*, p. 55. *Diary of Burton*, vol. 1, pp. 217–18, 263. Grigge, *Quakers Jesus*, pp. 16–18.

74. *Diary of Burton*, vol. 1, pp. 265–66. *A True Narrative*, p. 42, for the size and behavior of the crowd and for Rich's conduct at the branding.

75. Grigge, *Quakers Jesus*, pp. 19–22.

76. On Nayler's change of attitude, see his "Confessions" written from Bridewell Prison, 1658, in Whitehead's introduction to Nayler's *Collection of Sundry Books*, pp. xxv–xxxix; the words quoted are on p. xxxv.

Chapter 10   Christianity Becomes the Law of the Land

1. For general background, see David Ogg, *England in the Reign of Charles II* (Oxford, 1955, 2 vols., rev. ed.), which is superficial on religion and law; Sir George Clark, *The Later Stuarts* (Oxford, 1956, 2nd ed.).

2. A. A. Seaton, *The Theory of Toleration Under the Later Stuarts* (1910; New York, 1972 reprint), is excellent. H. F. Russell-Smith, *The Theory of Religious Liberty in the Reigns of Charles II and James II* (Cambridge, 1911), is inferior.

3. Charles's Declaration of Breda, April 4, 1660, reprinted in Henry Gee and

W. J. Hardy, eds., *Documents Illustrative of English Church History* (London, 1896), pp. 585–88. For Charles's promise to the Quakers, Clark, *Later Stuarts*, p. 20. On the Quaker Act, William C. Braithwaite, *The Second Period of Quakerism* (London, 1919), pp. 22–25.

4. On the various statutes, see Gee and Hardy, eds., *Documents*, pp. 594–640; C. Grant Robertson, ed., *Select Statutes: Cases and Documents to Illustrate English Constitutional History, 1660–1832* (London, 1904), pp. 10–42. The Conventicles Act of 1664 was renewed and made permanent in 1670. For statistics, Clark, *Later Stuarts*, p. 27.

5. On the state of the Anglican church during the Puritan supremacy, see R. S. Bosher, *The Making of the Restoration Settlement: The Influence of the Laudians, 1649–1662* (New York, 1951), especially pp. 5–18; William Arthur Shaw, *A History of the English Church During the Civil Wars, 1640–1660* (London, 1900, 2 vols.), an unsympathetic account; William Holden Hutton, *The English Church from the Accession of Charles I to the Death of Queen Anne* (London, 1903), pp. 122–78. On Quakers, see Braithwaite, *Second Period*, pp. 109–15, which includes the estimate that five thousand of the sixty thousand who were imprisoned died in prison. Daniel Defoe, in his intro. to Thomas Delaune, *A Plea for Nonconformists* (London, 1706, 7th ed.), estimated eight thousand. William Penn, *Good Advice* (London, 1687), stated that "more than five thousand persons died under bonds for matters of mere conscience to God" since 1660, in *The Select Works of William Penn* (London, 1825, 3 vols., no ed.), vol. 2, p. 585. The estimates of the number who died in prison seem inflated, because a disproportionate number of Quakers were imprisoned, yet only about 450 Quakers died in prison; at the time, Quakers constituted about 17 percent of the Protestant dissenter population. Gerald R. Cragg, *Puritanism in the Period of the Great Persecution, 1660–88* (Cambridge, 1957), gives no statistics, but see ch. 2, "The Pattern of Persecution," and ch. 4, on jail conditions. See also Daniel Neal, *The History of the Puritans, or Protestant Nonconformists* (London, 1822, 5 vols., rev. ed.), vol. 5, pp. 19–20. For Baxter, *Reliquae Baxterianae*, ed. M. Sylvester (London, 1696), pt. 2, p. 436.

6. Charles's Declaration of Indulgence is reprinted in Robertson, ed., *Select Statutes*, pp. 42–44. For the evolution of the Indulgence, its impact, and the reasons for its withdrawal, see Frank Bate, *The Declaration of Indulgence, 1672* (London, 1908), chh. 5–6.

7. On the Anglican church during the Restoration, see Hutton, *English Church*, pp. 179–215. On the High Church party, see Bosher, *Making of the Restoration Settlement*, ch. 4; George Every, *The High Church Party, 1688–1718* (London, 1956), pp. 1–18. On the latitudinarians, see Seaton, *Theory of Toleration*, pp. 45–51, 66–72, 84–92, 205–19; he deals with the High Church men at pp. 107–13, 116–21, 132–41, 154–67, 172, 182, 188–94.

8. Seaton, *Theory of Toleration*, p. 153.

9. Ibid., pp. 205–18.

10. For the act of 1677, 29 Ch. II ch. 9, *Statutes at Large* (1763), vol. 7, p. 417. See Sir James Fitzjames Stephen, *A History of the Criminal Law of England* (London, 1883, 3 vols.), vol. 2, p. 468; Sir William Holdsworth, *A History of English Law* (London, 1938–66, 16 vols., 6th ed., rev.), vol. 1, pp. 616–21.

11. Seaton, *Theory of Toleration*, p. 153.

12. Ibid., pp. 146, 183–86.

13. Seaton reviews tolerationist and antitolerationist tracts throughout his *Theory of Toleration*. For tolerationist arguments stressing the secular theme, see especially ibid., pp. 144–52; Charles F. Mullett, "Toleration and Persecution in England, 1660–89," *Church History*, vol. 18 (1949), pp. 30–31. Penn's major tolerationist tracts are

reprinted in vol. 2 of his *Select Works*, as follows: *The Great Case of Liberty of Conscience* (1671), pp. 128–64; *England's Present Interest Discovered* (1675), pp. 269–320; *A Persuasive to Moderation* (1686), pp. 504–42. For his secularist position, presented in the works of 1675 and 1686, see also his *Great and Popular Objection against the Repeal of the Penal Laws* (1688), pp. 12–13, and *Three Letters* (1688), pp. 4–5, available only in the originals. As good as Penn but stressing the religious reasons for toleration is Robert Barclay, *An Apology for the True Christian Divinity* (London, 1676; Providence, 1840 reprint, 8th ed.), proposition 14, pp. 486–512. Barclay's *Apology* is the masterpiece of Quaker theology, marking the transition from Fox's feverish evangelism to the cool and placid quietism that would become more characteristic of Quakerism. On Barclay, see Rufus Jones's introduction to Braithwaite, *Second Period*, pp. xxx–xliv.

14. *The Works of John Bunyan*, ed. George Offer (Glasgow, 1856, 3 vols.), vol. 1, pp. 47, 56–57, 62, 64. See also John Brown, *John Bunyan* (London, 1928, rev. Frank Mott Harrison), pp. 132–50, 176–78; William W. Whitely, "Bunyan's Imprisonments: A Legal Study," *Transactions*, Baptist Historical Society, vol. 6 (1918–19), pp. 1–24; G. Lyon Turner, "Bunyan's License Under the Indulgence," ibid., pp. 129–37; Joyce Godber, "The Imprisonment of John Bunyan," *Transactions*, Congregationalist Historical Society, vol. 16 (1949), pp. 23–32. On Mead, see Cragg, *Puritanism in the Great Persecution*, p. 229; Bosher, *Making of the Restoration Settlement*, pp. 201–2.

15. Attwood or Adwood's case, Michaelmas term, Jan. 15 (1618), is reported in Henry Rolle, *Un Abridgment des plusieurs cases et resolutions Del Common Ley* (London, 1668), vol. 2, p. 78. On seditious libel, see Holdsworth, *History of English Law*, vol. 8, pp. 334–46 and, for its application to religious offenses, 402–8. Generally, see Leonard W. Levy, *Emergence of a Free Press* (New York, 1985), ch. 1; Frederick Seaton Siebert, *Freedom of the Press in England, 1476–1776* (Urbana, Ill., 1952), ch. 13. Field's case is reported in 1 Siderfin 69 and 1 Keble 175, 194, 209, 233.

16. Charles Ripley Gillett, *Burned Books* (New York, 1932, 2 vols.), vol. 2, pp. 443–45.

17. Ibid., pp. 449–54. Benjamin Evans, *The Early English Baptists* (London, 1862–65, 2 vols.), vol. 2, pp. 334–37.

18. The best account of Baxter's trial is in William Orme, *The Life and Times of Richard Baxter* (London, 1830, 2 vols.), vol. 1, pp. 443–68; also reported in *State Trials*, vol. 11, pp. 493–502.

19. For "best gay lyric poets," Albert C. Baugh et al., *A Literary History of England* (New York, 1948), p. 744. For "preached Blasphemy," see Anthony à Wood, *Athenae Oxonienses* (London, 1721, 2nd ed., 3 vols.), vol. 2, p. 1000, whose account Stephen, *History of Criminal Law*, vol. 2, p. 470, accepts. G. D. Nokes, *A History of the Crime of Blasphemy* (London, 1928), p. 44, is less certain about the blasphemy issue, because the law reports, mentioned in n. 20 below, do not refer to it. The Pepys quotations are from *The Diary of Samuel Pepys*, ed. Robert Latham and William Matthews (London, 1970 ff., 9 vols. thus far), vol. 4, p. 269.

20. 1 Keble 620 (1663); 1 Fortescue, 99, 100; 1 Siderfin 168. For the obscenity, Wood, *Athenae*, vol. 2, p. 1000. Obscenity was not squarely held punishable by the common law until *Rex v. Curll*, 2 Strange 788 (1727); see also *State Trials*, vol. 17, p. 153; Norman St. John-Stevas, *Obscenity and the Law* (London, 1956), pp. 22–24.

21. Lodowick Muggleton, *The Acts of the Witnesses* (1696), reprinted in *Works of John Reeve and Lodowick Muggleton*, ed. John Frost and Isaac Frost (London, 1831, 3 vols.), vol. 3, pp. 86–105. A Samuel Sears was charged with blasphemy in 1666 for saying that he was "really Christ and that he should [obscenity deleted] Kings, Princes, and Magistrates" (John Cordy Jeafferson, ed., *Middlesex County Records* [Lon-

don, 1886–92, 7 vols.], vol. 3, p. 371); I could not ascertain the disposition of the case.

22. Stephen, *History of Criminal Law*, vol. 2, p. 467.

23. *Diary of Pepys*, vol. 5, p. 446. *The Diary of John Evelyn*, ed. E. S. DeBeer (Oxford, 1955, 6 vols.), vol. 3, p. 521. The *London Newsletter* called *Sandy Foundation* "an infamous and blasphemous pamphlet" (Harry Emerson Wildes, *William Penn* [New York, 1974], p. 49). Catherine Owens Peare, *William Penn* (Philadelphia, 1957), p. 80, quotes Penn on the doctrine of the Trinity. The best account of this episode in Penn's life, reprinting extracts from primary sources, is John Bruce, "Observations upon William Penn's Imprisonment in the Tower of London," *Archaeologia*, vol. 30 (1853), pp. 70–90, where the quote from Vincent appears on p. 81. *Sandy Foundation* is reprinted in Penn's *Select Works*, vol. 1, pp. 129–56.

24. Bruce, "Penn's Imprisonment," pp. 78–79, reprints Arlington's order of arrest and the confirmatory order of the Privy Council. Penn blamed Henry Henchman, the bishop of London, but Bruce proves that only Arlington, the king himself, and the council were responsible for Penn's imprisonment.

25. William Penn, *Innocency with Her Open Face Presented. By Way of Apology for the Book Entitled The Sandy Foundation Shaken* (London, 1669), p. 4, for "noise of Blasphemy," reprinted in *Select Works*, vol. 1, pp. 157–72. "Thou mayest tell my father . . ." in *A Collection of the Works of William Penn*, ed. Joseph Bessie (London, 1726, 2 vols.), vol. 1, p. 6. On Stillingfleet's mission, *Callendar of State Papers, Domestic, 1668–9*, p. 146 (Jan. 4, 1669). On Stillingfleet, see Seaton, *Theory of Toleration*, pp. 86–92.

26. For Penn to Stillingfleet, see Bruce, "Penn's Imprisonment," p. 88. For Penn to Secretary of State Arlington, *Works of Penn*, ed. Bessie, vol. 1, p. 154. For the full text of Penn's letters to Arlington, see Norman Penney, ed., *Extracts from State Papers Relating to Friends, 1654–1672* (London, 1913), pp. 279–86. Bruce, "Penn's Imprisonment," p. 90, reprints the order of the council freeing Penn, July 28, 1669. On the intercession of the duke of York, see Robert Wallace, *Antitrinitarian Biography* (London, 1850, 3 vols.), vol. 1, p. 165.

27. On Firmin, see *D.N.B.*, vol. 7, pp. 46–49; Wallace, *Antitrinitarian Biography*, vol. 1, pp. 153–78 passim; vol. 3, pp. 272–89; Alexander Gordon, *Addresses, Biographical and Historical* (London, 1922), pp. 93–119. See also Herbert John McLachlan, *Socinianism in Seventeenth Century England* (London, 1951), pp. 306–7, for a concise summary of Penn's later account of his rejection of Socinianism and Firmin's response.

28. Penn, *Innocency with Her Open Face*, p. 13. Wallace, *Antitrinitarian Biography*, vol. 1, pp. 166–69.

29. McLachlan, *Socinianism*, p. 312, quotes Hedworth; ibid., pp. 299–315, for the best treatment of Hedworth.

30. On Muggleton's 1670 troubles, see *Acts of the Witnesses*, in *Works of Reeve and Muggleton*, vol. 3, pp. 133–36. For Muggleton to Fox, Muggleton, *Looking Glass for George Fox* (London, 1668), p. 76. *Looking Glass* (1756, 2nd ed.) is reprinted in *Works of Reeve and Muggleton*, vol. 2, with the original pagination of that edition, p. 88 for the quotation. Vol. 2 includes all of Muggleton's anti-Quaker tracts. Muggleton reproved Fox and the Quakers "for rejoicing in my sufferings, and beeing sorry magistrates did not punish me" (*Looking Glass*, in ibid., vol. 2, p. 86). On Muggleton, see Alexander Gordon, "Ancient and Modern Muggletonians," paper read before the Liverpool Literary and Historical Society, April 4, 1870. On Firmin, see Wallace, *Antitrinitarian Biography*, vol. 1, pp. 176–77.

31. *Journals of the House of Lords*, vol. 12, p. 688, May 11, 1675; p. 691, May 14; pp. 700–701, May 20.

32. Ibid., vol. 13, p. 26, Nov. 17, 1675. *Rex* v. *Taylor*, 3 Keble 607, 621 (1676) and 1 Ventris 293 (1676).

33. The indictment is reprinted in John Tremaine, *Pleas of the Crown* (Dublin, 1793), pp. 226–27.

34. Ibid., p. 227. 3 Keble 607, 621. 1 Ventris 293.

35. 3 Keble 607, 621. 1 Ventris 293.

36. H. L. Stephen, ed., *State Trials, Political and Social* (London, 1899, 2 vols.), vol. 1, pp. 211–35, for Hale's witchcraft case. See also J. F. Stephen, *History of Criminal Law*, vol. 2, pp. 432–35. For an excellent discussion of the question whether Hale invented a new crime and whether he was right in holding that Christianity was part of the law of the land, see Nokes, *History of the Crime of Blasphemy*, pp. 49–66, the best part of his little treatise. I shall treat these matters as they arise chronologically.

37. My account of Muggleton's 1677 trial is from Nathaniel Powell, *A True Account of the Trial and Sufferings of Lodowick Muggleton*, reprint of 1808, in Frost and Frost, eds., *Works of Reeve and Muggleton*, vol. 3, pp. 1–15. Also, *Acts of the Witnesses* (Muggleton's autobiography, written 1677, first published 1699) in ibid., vol. 3, pp. 153–71 (all items in *Works of Reeve and Muggleton* contain the pagination of the original tracts of the eighteenth-century reprints). Vol. 2 contains the tract against Penn.

38. The sources for the three certain blasphemy cases are (1) *News from Newgate: or the female Muggletonian being an account of apprehensions and commitment of a certain fanatical woman charged with speaking several horrid blasphemous words* (1678); (2) *The Tryal and Condemnation of Several Notorious Malefactors . . . Also the Tryal of Joseph Hindmarsh, who printed and published the Blasphemous Pamphlet, Entitled, The Presbyterian Pater Noster* (1681); (3) *A Full and True Account . . . of Susan Fowls . . . As also, Of her Tryal and Sentence . . . for Blaspheming Jesus Christ, and Cursing the Lord's Prayer* (1698); *The Second Part of the Boy of Bilson: Or, A True and Particular Relation of the Imposter, Susannah Fowles* (1698). Nokes, *History of the Crime of Blasphemy*, pp. 147–48, 162, lists on his charts sixteen other common-law convictions in Old Bailey for the period 1678–98, all "for offences in relation to religious opinion." All were for seditiousness, but perhaps none for blasphemy between 1678 and 1682. There were four cases during that period, none of which I could verify. I would bet that none involved blasphemy. Several pamphlets with the same title, *The Proceedings in* [or *of*] *the Old Bailey* [various spellings], cover the cases of 1683–98. None involved blasphemy, contrary to Nokes. For example, he lists the cases of Delaune and Baxter along with those of Taylor and Muggleton, making no distinctions between seditiousness and blasphemousness. His tables include many cases of the post-1698 period that I know were not prosecutions for blasphemy (Nokes, apps. B, C). Distinctions, when possible, should be made. Sir William S. Holdsworth, like Nokes, was of the opinion that offenses against religion were seditious because they were simultaneously offenses against the state, but Holdsworth carefully differentiated the separate branches of the law of criminal defamation (*History of English Law*, vol. 8, pp. 33, 337).

39. Robertson, ed., *Select Statutes*, pp. 249–52, reprints the Declaration of Indulgence of 1687. The leading authority on the reign of James II is still Thomas B. Macauley, *The History of England from the Accession of James II*, ed. Charles H. Firth (London, 1913–15, 6 vols.). On the declaration and its background, see ibid., vol. 2, pp. 664–72, 734–58, 862–86, 955–64.

40. Macauley, *History of England*, vol. 2, pp. 990–1038. Vol. 3 covers the flight of James and the accession of William and Mary. For the Anglican church under James II, see Hutton, *English Church*, pp. 217–33. For a political overview, see Clark, *Later*

Stuarts, pp. 116–43. For the trial of the seven bishops, see *State Trials*, vol. 12, pp. 183–524.

41. Braithwaite, *Second Period*, p. 190. On the expiration of the licensing laws on the press, see Siebert, *Freedom of the Press*, pp. 260–63. For the Toleration Act, see Robertson, ed., *Select Statutes*, pp. 70–75, or Gee and Hardy, eds., *Documents*, pp. 654–64.

42. On the 1710 report, see George Macauley Trevelyan, *The English Revolution, 1688–89* (London, 1938), p. 160, concluding with a good discussion of the Toleration Act. The most vivid and provocative treatment is Macauley, *History of England*, vol. 3, pp. 1385–92, although his remark that dissenters got as much liberty as under a statute framed by Jefferson was ridiculous.

43. H. S. Q. Henriques, *The Jews and the English Law* (Oxford, 1908), pp. 147–50, 154. The Toleration Act was extended to Catholics in 1778, to Unitarians in 1813, and to Jews in 1846 (ibid., p. 161).

44. On Firmin, see n. 27 above. On Unitarianism within the English church, see Wallace, *Antitrinitarian Biography*, vol. 1, p. 252; Earl Morse Wilbur, *A History of Unitarianism* (Cambridge, Mass., 1946–52, 2 vols.), vol. 2, ch. 12. On Milton, see Herbert McLachlan, *The Religious Opinions of Milton, Locke, and Newton* (Manchester, 1941), pp. 22–66. On real and nominal Trinitarians, Wallace, *Antitrinitarian Biography*, vol. 1, pp. 340–42, 362–64.

45. McLachlan, *Socinianism*, pp. 140, 313, 318, for Marvell, Hedworth, and Ashwell, and p. 326 for Firmin's circle. See also McLachlan, *Religious Opinions*, pp. 117–72, on Newton; Wilbur, *Unitarianism* II, pp. 219–26; Wallace, *Antitrinitarian Biography*, vol. 1, pp. 371–75, on Nye, and vol. 3, pp. 362–71, on Clerke. On the subject generally, McLachlan, *Socinianism*, chs. 15–16.

46. Wallace, *Antitrinitarian Biography*, vol. 1, pp. 183–84, 196–204. Gillett, *Burned Books*, vol. 2, pp. 533–38. Every, *High Church Party*, ch. 5, sympathetically traces "the High Church hunt for heretical latitude on the doctrine on the Trinity."

47. Wallace, *Antitrinitarian Biography*, vol. 1, pp. 218–360, describes each of the Unitarian tracts and many of the orthodox replies. Herbert McLachlan, *The Story of a Non-Conformist Library* (Manchester, 1925), pp. 53–87, also reviews the Unitarian tracts.

48. Wallace, *Antitrinitarian Biography*, vol. 1, pp. 214–15, 236, 258, 327–31, 352; vol. 3, p. 389. Wilbur, *Unitarianism* 11, pp. 227–31. Every, *High Church Party*, pp. 79–80.

49. Quoted in Wallace, *Antitrinitarian Biography*, vol. 1, pp. 259–61, 275–79. Every, *High Church Party*, pp. 77–78. Wilbur, *Unitarianism* 11, p. 229. McLachlan, *Socinianism*, p. 335.

50. The quotations are from Wallace, *Antitrinitarian Biography*, vol. 1, pp. 233–34, 253. See also McLachlan, *Socinianism*, p. 334, and, on the Arian movement, Wilbur, *Unitarianism* 11, pp. 236–70.

51. On Locke's religious beliefs, see McLachlan, *Religious Opinions*, pp. 69–114; H. R. Fox Bourne, *The Life of John Locke* (London, 1876, 2 vols.), vol. 1, pp. 165–94, 305–11; vol. 2, pp. 31–41, 180–87, 281–93, 404–39, which includes his controversy with Edwards. On the latter, see also Wallace, *Antitrinitarian Biography*, vol. 1, pp. 306–20. For a concise summary, see McLachlan, *Socinianism*, pp. 326–30, which includes Locke's reply to the bishop of Worcester.

52. For Clerke to Baxter, see McLachlan, *Socinianism*, p. 324. For Calamy, see Wallace, *Antitrinitarian Biography*, vol. 1, p. 233.

53. On Scotland during the Restoration, see Clark, *Later Stuarts*, ch. 12.

54. George Mackenzie, *The Laws and Customs of Scotland in Matters Criminal* (Edinburgh, 1678), tit. 3, sec. 1, p. 25; tit. 10, sec. 2, p. 85. David Hume, *Commentaries on the Law of Scotland respecting the Description and Punishment of Crimes* (Edinburgh, 1797, 2 vols.), vol. 2, p. 514.

55. Bortwick's case is reported in *State Trials*, vol. 13, pp. 938–40.

56. Anon., "Mr. Macauley's Account of Thomas Aikenhead," *The Christian Reformer*, vol. 12 (1856), pp. 37–38, reprints the statement made by Lorimer in the introduction to an untitled sermon that he published in 1697, defending himself against accusations of being responsible for Aikenhead's death. Macauley's own account of Aikenhead's case is in his *History of England*, vol. 6, pp. 2699–2700, in which he said, "The preachers were the boy's murderers."

57. Aikenhead's pretrial petition and Anstruther's letter of Jan. 26, 1696, eighteen days after the execution, are in "Proceedings against Thomas Aikenhead, for Blasphemy," 1696, in *State Trials*, vol. 13, pp. 921–23, 930. Emphasis in Anstruther's comment added.

58. I have followed Lorimer's account; Macauley's differs. Lorimer claimed that the chancellor favored a reprieve; Macauley claimed that the chancellor cast the deciding vote against a reprieve. (*The Christian Reformer*, vol. 12, pp. 37–38; Macauley, *History of England*, vol. 6, p. 2700.)

59. The account in *State Trials*, vol. 13, pp. 917–40, includes all pertinent documents except Lorimer's statement. John Gordon, *Thomas Aikenhead* (London, 1856), and *Supplement to "Thomas Aikenhead"* are virulently anticlerical tracts in defense of Macauley's account.

60. *State Trials*, vol. 13, pp. 926–27, for the evidence of Mungo Craig; pp. 917–18, 925–29 for Locke.

61. "The Trial of Patrick Kinnymount, for Blasphemy," 1697, in *State Trials*, vol. 13, pp. 1273–82. See Hume, *Commentaries on the Law of Scotland*, vol. 2, pp. 40–41.

62. Wallace, *Antitrinitarian Biography*, vol. 1, pp. 384–85, on stopping the presses. On Toland, see Robert E. Sullivan, *John Toland and the Deist Controversy* (Cambridge, Mass., 1982); Sir Leslie Stephen, *History of English Thought in the Eighteenth Century* (3rd ed. of 1902; New York, 1949 reprint, 2 vols.), vol. 1, pp. 101–19. See also John Orr, *Deism: Its Roots and Fruits* (Grand Rapids, Mich., 1934), pp. 116–24. For Toland's reception in Ireland, see *Journal of the House of Commons of the Kingdom of Ireland* (Dublin, 1763, 2nd ed.), vol. 2, pp. 903–4 (Sept. 9, 1697).

63. Wallace, *Antitrinitarian Biography*, vol. 1, pp. 376–77. Every, *High Church Party*, p. 81. For the case of Susan Fowls, see n. 38 above.

64. Wallace, *Antitrinitarian Biography*, vol. 1, p. 385.

65. For the act of 1698, see *Statutes of the Realm* (London, 1812–28, 11 vols.), vol. 7, p. 409, 9 Gul. III ch. 35.

66. John Godolphin, *Reportorium Canonicum; or An Abridgment of the Ecclesiastical Laws of this Realm consistent with the Temporal* (London, 1678), pp. 559–61.

Chapter 11   Early Colonial America

1. "For the Colony in Virginea Britannica. Lawes Divine, Morall and Martiall" (London, 1612), in Peter Force, ed., *Tracts and Other Papers Relating Principally to the*

Origin, Settlement, and Progress of the Colonies in North America (1844; Gloucester, Mass., 1963 reprint, 4 vols.), vol. 3, no. 2, pp. 9–10.

2. For the 1624 cases, H. R. McIlwaine, ed., *Minutes of the Council and General Court of Colonial Virginia* (Richmond, 1924), p. 14. Susie M. Ames, ed., *County Court Records of Accomack-Northhampton, Virginia* (Charlottesville, 1973), pp. 202 (cases of John Holloway and John Wilkins), 212 (case of Edward Douglas), 236 (case of Robert Warren), and 265 (1643 case of Liven Denwood). Ames, p. 234 (case of Lewis Whyte), for the profanity.

3. Proceedings of Oct. 11, 1670, in McIlwaine, ed., *Minutes*, p. 226. Mattie E. Parker, ed., *The Colonial Records of North Carolina: North Carolina Higher Court Records, 1670–1696* (Raleigh, 1968), p. xliii. William L. Saunders, ed., *The Colonial Records of North Carolina* (Raleigh, 1886–90, 10 vols.), vol. 1 (1662–1712), pp. 313–17, 326–27. Extracts from Norfolk County Records, case of Thomas Newhouse, Aug. 15, 1683, *William & Mary Quarterly*, 1st ser., vol. 2 (1893–94), pp. 178–79.

4. William W. Hening, ed., *Statutes at Large Being a Collection of All the Laws of Virginia (1619–1792)* (Richmond, 1809–23, 13 vols.), vol. 2, p. 333; vol. 4, pp. 468–69.

5. Madison to William Bradford, Jan. 24, 1774, in *The Papers of James Madison*, ed. William T. Hutchinson (Chicago, 1962), vol. 1, p. 106.

6. John Cotton, "A Reply to Mr. Williams" (1647), quoted in Perry Miller, *Orthodoxy in Massachusetts, 1630–1650* (Boston, 1959), p. 160.

7. "The Simple Cobler of Aggawam" (1647), in Perry Miller and Thomas H. Johnson, eds., *The Puritans* (New York, 1938), pp. 230, 232.

8. Cotton quoted in Philip F. Gura, *A Glimpse of Sion's Glory: Puritan Radicalism in New England: 1620–1660* (Middletown, Conn., 1984), p. 193.

9. George Lee Haskins, *Law and Authority in Early Massachusetts* (New York, 1960), pp. 32–37. Nathaniel B. Shurtleff, ed., *Records of the Governor and Company of Massachusetts Bay* (Boston, 1853–54, 6 vols.), vol. 2, pp. 93–94 (1644).

10. Shurtleff, ed., *Records of the Governor*, vol. 1, p. 88. J. Noble and J. F. Cronin, *Records of the Court of Assistants of the Colony of Massachusetts Bay* (Boston, 1901–28, 3 vols.), vol. 2, p. 16.

11. *[John] Winthrop's Journal "History of New England," 1630–1649*, ed. James Kendell Hosmer (New York, 1908, 2 vols.), vol. 1, p. 64. James Savage, ed., "Gleanings for New England History," in *Collections of the Massachusetts Historical Society*, 3rd ser., vol. 8 (1843), p. 323. Thomas Morton, *New English Canaan*, ed. Charles Francis Adams (Boston, 1883), pp. 318–19. The blasphemous language was: "the Divell was the setter of their church."

12. On Harvard, see Samuel Eliot Morison, *The Intellectual Life of Colonial New England* (Ithaca, N.Y., 1956), p. 45. For the Old Testament influences on Massachusetts colonial law, see Haskins, *Law and Authority*, pp. 124–26, 141–62.

13. Thomas Hutchinson, ed., *A Collection of Original Papers Relative to the History of Massachusetts Bay* (Albany, 1865, 2 vols.), vol. 1, p. 196.

14. On "Moses His Judicials," see Haskins, *Law and Authority*, pp. 106, 124–25; Worthington C. Ford, "Cotton's 'Moses His Judicials,' " *Proceedings*, Massachusetts Historical Society, vol. 36 (1902), pp. 274–84.

15. Body of Liberties, Capital Laws, sec. 94, cl. 3, in Richard L. Perry, ed., *Sources of Our Liberties: Documentary Origins of Individual Liberties in the United States Constitution* (Chicago, 1959), p. 158. On the blasphemy provision in the code of 1648, see Thomas Hutchinson, *The History of the Colony and Province of Massachusetts-Bay*, ed. Lawrence S. Mayo (Cambridge, Mass., 1936, 3 vols.), vol. 1, p. 372.

16. Shurtleff, ed., *Records of the Governor*, vol. 2, pp. 176–78.

17. Nathaniel B. Shurtleff, ed., *Records of the Colony of New Plymouth in New England* (Boston, 1856–61, 12 vols.), vol. 1, p. 44.

18. Ibid., pp. 160–61, 252, 254, 261–62, 312, 336.

19. Guppi's case of 1640 is reported in "Salem Quarterly Court Records and Files, 1637–1659," *The Essex Antiquarian*, vol. 3 (1899), p. 191; "Essex County Court Records, 1636–1641," *Essex Institute Historical Collections*, vol. 7, p. 125; *Records and Files of the Quarterly Courts of Essex County, 1636–1683* (Salem, Mass., 1911–21, 8 vols.), vol. 1, p. 25. None of the accounts describe the blasphemy.

20. On the Antinomian Controversy, see Emory Battis, *Saints and Sectaries: Anne Hutchinson and the Antinomian Controversy in Massachusetts Bay Colony* (Chapel Hill, N.C., 1962); Charles Francis Adams, *The Antinomian Controversy* (New York, 1976), part of his *Three Episodes in Massachusetts History*. For the primary sources, an excellent compilation is David H. Hall, ed., *The Antinomian Controversy: 1636–1638: A Documentary History* (Durham, 1990, 2nd ed.). It lacks extracts from Winthrop's *Journal*, but includes his *Short Story*, the trial of Wheelwright, and the various examinations of Hutchinson. Wilson's remark about blasphemy is in Hall, p. 388.

21. Shurtleff, ed., *Records of the Governor*, vol. 4, pt. 2, p. 256.

22. Gorton's statement of his religious views may be found in his tract, *Simplicities Defence against Seven-headed Policy* (London, 1646, 116 pp.), reprinted in Force, ed., *Tracts*, vol. 4, no. 6, separately paginated. The best modern treatment of Gorton's religious views is Gura, *Glimpse of Sion's Glory*, pp. 276–303, an excellent book, though Gura tends to exaggerate both the radicalism and the varieties of dissidents. See also Kenneth W. Porter, "Samuell Gorton: New England Firebrand," *New England Quarterly*, vol. 7 (1934), pp. 405–44. Another good narrative of Gorton's career, though poor on his religious views, is Robert Emmet Wall, Jr., *Massachusetts Bay: The Crucial Decade, 1640–1650* (New Haven, 1972), pp. 121–56.

23. On Gorton's obscure meanings, see his remarks in *Simplicities Defence*, in Force, ed., *Tracts*, vol. 4, no. 6, pp. 47, 71. See also *Samuel Gorton's Letter to Nathaniel Morton* (1669), in ibid., vol. 4, no. 7.

24. Edward Winslow, *Hypocrisie Unmasked by a True Relation of the Proceedings of the Governour and Company of Massachusetts against Samuel Gorton . . .* (London, 1646, 2nd ed. 1649).

25. Gorton's account is in his *Letter to Morton*, pp. 7–8. His prosecutors' accounts are in Winslow, *Hypocrisie Unmasked*, pp. 1–2, 54–55, 66–68. Williams's letter to Winthrop is reprinted in Wall, *Massachusetts Bay*, pp. 122–23. See also Winslow's use of the letter in *Hypocrisie Unmasked*, p. 56. For the Ranter description, ibid., p. 58; Shurtleff, ed., *Records of the Governor*, vol. 4, pt. 2, p. 256.

26. Gorton, *Simplicities Defence*, pp. 17–21. Winslow, *Hypocrisie Unmasked*, pp. 2–3. Wall, *Massachusetts Bay*, pp. 124–25.

27. The documents describing these matters, excepting Holden's insulting letter for the Gortonites, are in Gorton's *Simplicities Defence*, pp. 45–60; the quotation from Winthrop is at p. 56. Holden's letter of Sept. 24, 1643, is in Rhode Island Historical Society, *Collections*, ed. William Staples, vol. 2 (1835), pp. 262–69. *Simplicities Defence* is also available in the same volume, pp. 21–190.

28. Gorton, *Simplicities Defence*, in Force, ed., *Tracts*, vol. 4, no. 6, pp. 61–75. Winthrop, *Journal*, vol. 2, p. 149.

29. Winslow, *Hypocrisie Unmasked*, pp. 1–2, 54–55.

30. The word "Puritan" can be used in its most comprehensive sense to include Congregationalists, Presbyterians, Independents, Seekers, Gortonites, Quakers, An-

tinomians, Ranters, and Socinians. So used, the word loses meaning. I use the term "Puritan" at this point to mean the Congregational authorities.

31. Winslow, *Hypocrisie Unmasked*, pp. 5, 7, 47–50. Shurtleff, ed., *Records of the Governor*, vol. 4, pt. 2, pp. 256–60.

32. Winthrop, *Journal*, vol. 2, p. 160. Wall, *Massachusetts Bay*, pp. 141–56.

33. Case of Richard Smith, 1645, in "Ipswich Court Records," *The Essex Antiquarian*, vol. 8 (1904), p. 7. The bestiality case involved George Spencer, in Charles J. Hoadley, ed., *Records of the Colony and Plantation of New Haven, 1638–1649* (Hartford, 1857), pp. 62–73. Ibid., p. 262, for Pawquash; p. 255 for Mrs. Moore; p. 293 for King; p. 308 for Smoolt.

34. Francis Fane, *Reports of the Laws of Connecticut*, ed. Charles M. Andrews (Hartford, 1915), p. 63. *The Code of 1650, Being a Compilation of the Earliest Laws and Orders of the General Court of Connecticut* (Hartford, n.d.), p. 28.

35. Act for Felonies, 1639, in W. F. Browne et al., *Archives of Maryland* (Baltimore, 1883–), vol. 1, p. 71; Act Concerning Religion, in ibid., pp. 244–46. On Maryland, see Albert W. Werline, *Problems of Church and State in Maryland* (South Lancaster, Mass., 1948), pp. 1–10; William Warren Sweet, *Religion in Colonial America* (New York, 1965), pp. 167–84.

36. Browne, ed., *Archives of Maryland*, vol. 10, p. 184 (case of Susan Warren, 1652). Franklin B. Dexter and Z. J. Powers, eds., *New Haven Town Records, 1649–1769* (New Haven, 1917–62, 3 vols.), vol. 1, pp. 88–89, for Howe, 1651. For Crossman, 1851, see Shurtleff, ed., *Records of the Governor*, vol. 3, p. 257; vol. 4, p. 73.

37. Shurtleff, ed., *Records of New Plymouth*, vol. 3, pp. 4 (Allen and Kerbey, 1652), 111–12 (Katherine Aines, 1656). Dexter and Powers, eds., *New Haven Town Records*, p. 331 (Jeremiah Johnson, 1657). Charles J. Hoadley, ed., *Records of the Colony or Jurisdiction of New Haven* (Hartford, 1858), pp. 311–13, for East. A. J. F. Van Laer, ed., *Minutes of the Court of Fort Orange, 1652–1660* (Albany, 1920–23, 2 vols.), vol. 2, p. 225 (Corneilis T. Bosch).

38. John Noble, ed., *Records of the Court of Assistants of the Colony of Massachusetts Bay, 1630–1692* (Boston, 1904, 3 vols.), vol. 3, pp. 34–38, for Saucer. The 1655 case, Richard Nason's, is in Shurtleff, ed., *Records of the Governor*, vol. 4, pt. 1, p. 245.

39. Shurtleff, ed., *Records of the Governor*, vol. 4, p. 204. On Pynchon, see Herbert J. McLachlan, *Socinianism in Seventeenth Century England* (London, 1951), pp. 234–39. Gura, *Glimpse of Sion's Glory*, pp. 304–22, concedes that Pynchon's prosecutors did not charge him with Socinianism yet identifies him, mistakenly, as an anti-Trinitarian.

40. On Baptists, see Thomas E. Buckley, "Church and State in Massachusetts Bay: A Case Study of Baptist Dissenters, 1651," *Journal of Church and State*, vol. 23 (1981), pp. 309–21; William G. McLoughlin, *New England Dissent, 1630–1833: Baptists and the Separation of Church and State* (Cambridge, Mass., 1971, 2 vols.), vol. 1; Sweet, *Religion in Colonial America*, pp. 120–42; Carla Gardina Pestana, *Quakers and Baptists in Colonial America* (Cambridge, 1991).

41. Shurtleff, ed., *Records of the Governor*, vol. 4, p. 78.

42. After the Glorious Revolution of 1689, Protestants in Maryland again turned on the Catholics, and by 1700 an act established the Church of England in Maryland. See Albert W. Werline, *Problems of Church and State in Maryland* (South Lancaster, Mass., 1948), pp. 6–12, 20–21.

43. Browne, ed., *Archives of Maryland*, Provincial Court Proceedings, 1658, vol. 41, pp. 202–3; Matthew P. Andrews, *The Founding of Maryland* (Baltimore, 1933), pp. 156–57. E. Milton Altfeld, *The Jew's Struggle for Religious and Civil Liberty in Maryland* (Baltimore, 1924), pp. 1–5.

44. Rufus M. Jones, *The Quakers in the American Colonies* (1911; New York, 1966 reprint), pp. 26–40. This is the standard work on the subject. Its martyrology borrows heavily from a Quaker book by George Bishop, *New England Judged by the Spirit of the Lord* (1661), first published in 1703, and reprinted in Philadelphia in 1885. See Bishop, pp. 9–16. See also Shurtleff, ed., *Records of New Plymouth*, vol. 10, p. 158; Shurtleff, ed., *Records of the Governor*, vol. 4, pp. 415–16; Pestana, *Quakers and Baptists*, pp. 25–43.

45. "Trials of the Quakers," in Peleg Chandler, ed., *American Criminal Trials* (Boston, 1844, 2 vols.), vol. 1, p. 38.

46. Jones, *Quakers*, pp. 45–70. Bishop, *New England Judged*, pp. 55–58. Shurtleff, ed., *Records of the Governor*, vol. 4, pp. 308–9. John R. Bartlett, ed., *Records of the Colony of Rhode Island, and Providence Plantations* (Providence, 1856–65), vol. 1, pp. 374–80.

47. Bishop, *New England Judged*, pp. 239–40, 244, 273, 329, 473, 476. Jones, *Quakers*, p. 108. Hutchinson, *History*, vol. 1, p. 174. For the act of 1658, Shurtleff, ed., *Records of the Governor*, vol. 4, pp. 344–45.

48. *New Haven Town Records*, March 10, 1658, pp. 339–43. Jones, *Quakers*, pp. 61–62, 71–72. Bishop, *New England Judged*, pp. 58, 61–62, 125, 137, 156, 403.

49. *The Complete Writings of Roger Williams* (New York, 1963, 7 vols.). Vol. 5 consists of Williams's book of 1674, *George Fox Digg'd Out of His Burrowes*, a 503-page assault on the Quakers. Quotations are from ibid., pp. 101–2, 165, 234, 260, 419. On Williams, see Edmund S. Morgan, *Roger Williams: The Church and the State* (New York, 1967); Perry Miller, *Roger Williams: His Contributions to the American Tradition* (New York, 1962).

50. Jones, *Quakers*, pp. 76–89.

51. Shurtleff, ed., *Records of the Governor*, vol. 4, pt. 1, pp. 450–52.

52. Ibid., pp. 2–3, for the act of 1661. Jones, *Quakers*, pp. 90–120.

Chapter 12　America from 1660 to 1800

1. Case of John Newland, 1660, in *Plymouth Court Records*, vol. 3, p. 190. Case of Abigail Bets, 1663, *Records of the Particular Court of Connecticut, 1639–1663*, in Connecticut Historical Society, *Collections* (Hartford, 1928), vol. 22, p. 268. Case of Elizabeth Seger, July 2, 1663, Hartford County Court MSS, 1st ser., vol. 1, pp. 5, 36, 38, Connecticut Archives, Crimes and Misdemeanors, Connecticut State Library, Hartford. Case of Hannah Hackleton, June 15, 1665, in ibid., pp. 34–35, 38, 52–53. Case of William Thomas, 1666, in *Plymouth Court Records*, vol. 4, p. 112. Case of John Andrews, 1666, in Charles T. Libby et al., *Province and Court Records of Maine* (Portland, 1928–64, 5 vols.), vol. 1, p. 264. Case of Abraham Sutliffe, 1667, in ibid., vol. 4, p. 168. Case of Andrew Haly, 1667, in ibid., vol. 1, p. 288. Case of Goodman Hall, Feb. 25, 1668, in Hartford County Court MSS, vol. 1, pp. 28–29. Case of Phillip Read, in Nathaniel B. Shurtleff, ed., *Records of the Colony of New Plymouth in New England* (Boston, 1856–61, 12 vols.), vol. 5, p. 9.

2. Case of Edward Vickars, 1671, in Franklin B. Dexter and Z. J. Powers, eds., *New Haven Town Records, 1649–1769* (New Haven, 1917–62, 3 vols.), vol. 2, pp. 275–76. Cases of Robert Marshall and Barefootes Bond, 1672, in Zechariah Chafee, Jr., and Samuel Eliot Morison, eds., *Records of the Suffolk County Court, 1671–1680*, in Colonial Society of Massachusetts, *Collections* (Boston, 1930), vol. 1, pp. 86–87.

Phillip Reade of Concord, in ibid., pp. 114–15; also in J. Noble and J. F. Cronin, eds., *Records of the Court of Assistants of the Colony of Massachusetts Bay* (Boston, 1901–28, 3 vols.), vol. 3, p. 211. Case of B. Bond, in ibid., pp. 211–12. Case of Samuel Forman, 1674, in E. T. Corwin, ed., *Ecclesiastical Records of the State of New York* (Albany, 1901–6, 6 vols.), vol. 1, p. 646. Samuel Eliot Morison, *Harvard in the Seventeenth Century* (Cambridge, Mass., 1936), p. 405. William Brigham, ed., *The Compact with the Charter and Laws of the Colony of New Plymouth* (Boston, 1836), p. 244, for the act of 1671. N. Bouton, ed., *The New Hampshire State Papers* (Concord, 1867), vol. 1, p. 383, for the act of 1679.

3. Case of William King, 1681, in Noble and Powers, eds., *Court of Assistants*, vol. 1, p. 201; complaint of Thomas Maule against King, July 6, 1681, depositions of Aug. 22, 1681, and trial record, in MS Suffolk County (Mass.) Court Files, vol. 24, pp. 135–38, no. 2021; see also Carla Gardina Pestana, "The Social World of Salem: William King's 1681 Trial," *American Quarterly*, vol. 41 (1989), pp. 308–27, an examination of antipathies between Quaker factions and between the townspeople and the magistrates. Case of Timothy Isles, 1682, in Otis G. Hammond, ed., *New Hampshire State Papers* (Concord, 1943), vol. 40, p. 392. Case of William Scrivine, 1682, in Libby et al., *Province and Court Records of Maine*, vol. 3, p. 165. A. J. Van Laer, ed., *Court Minutes of Albany, Rensselaerswyck, and Schenectady, 1668–1685* (Albany, 1926–32, 3 vols.), vol. 3, pp. 195–98. Case of Joseph Gatchell, 1684, in Noble and Powers, eds., *Court of Assistants*, vol. 3, pp. 253–54. Pennsylvania act of 1682, in Samuel Hazard, ed., *Annals of Pennsylvania* (Philadelphia, 1850), pp. 619–21.

4. MS Suffolk County Court Files, vol. 1, pp. 254, 260–62 (1685). Appeal in ibid., vol. 29, no. 2400, pp. 1–3.

5. John R. Bolles and Anna B. Williams, *The Rogerenes* (Boston, 1904), is the fullest treatment. Useful material on Rogers also appears in Frances M. Caulkins, *The History of New London Connecticut* (New London, 1895), pp. 201–22. A brief, perceptive treatment is in William G. McLoughlin, *New England Dissent, 1630–1833: Baptists and the Separation of Church and State* (Cambridge, Mass., 1971, 2 vols.), vol. 1, pp. 249–52.

6. Bolles and Williams, *Rogerenes*, p. 178.

7. Rogers related the story in his book, *A Midnight Cry* (1706), extracts of which appear in Bolles and Williams, *Rogerenes*, pp. 44–46.

8. Ellen Starr Brinton, "The Rogerenes," *New England Quarterly*, vol. 16 (1943), pp. 3–17.

9. "Trial of Thomas Maule," in Peleg W. Chandler, ed., *American State Trials* (Boston, 2 vols.), vol. 1, pp. 143–49. See also Matt Bushnell Jones, "Thomas Maule, the Salem Quaker, and Free Speech in Massachusetts Bay," *Essex Institute Historical Collections*, vol. 72 (1936), pp. 1–42.

10. William H. Browne, ed., *Proceedings and Acts of the General Assembly of Maryland* (Baltimore, 1883–1926), vol. 19, pp. 440, 475–82; vol. 20, pp. 489–94, 561–65. H. R. McIlwaine and W. L. Hall, eds., *Executive Journals of the Council of Colonial Virginia* (Richmond, 1925–45, 6 vols.), vol. 1, pp. 361, 404–5, 416, 418–19. The Virginia warrant for Coode's arrest gives this extraordinary description: "he being of a Middle Stature a deformed person, his face resembling that of a Baboon or munckeys, Club-footed his feet standing inwards one to the other and a Notorious Coward."

11. Case of Ebeazar Fitch, 1701, in MS Connecticut Archives, "Crimes and Misdemeanors, 1662–1789," vol. 1, docs. 248–56. Act for Suppressing Blasphemy and Profanity, 1703, in Thomas Cooper and D. J. McCord, eds., *The Statutes at Large of South Carolina* (Columbia, S.C., 1836–41, 10 vols.), vol. 2, pp. 196–97.

12. On Tallman, see Paul M. Hamlin and Charles E. Baker, eds., *The Supreme Court of Judicature of the Province of New York, 1691–1704* (New York, 1959, 3 vols.), vol. 1, pp. 358–59; vol. 2, pp. 332–33.

13. Leon De Lainger and John Biggs, eds., *Court Records of Kent County, Delaware, 1680–1705* (Washington, D.C., 1959), pp. 328–29. Case of Arabella in "Trivia," *William and Mary Quarterly*, vol. 16 (1959), pp. 581–82 (from Colonial Office Series 5, vol. 717, nos. 19, 19i; vol. 721, no. 10, Public Record Office, London). Maryland's blasphemy act of 1694 was re-enacted in 1704, 1715, and 1723 (*Archives of Maryland*, vol. 17, p. 19; vol. 22, p. 523; vol. 26, p. 321; vol. 30, pp. 243–44; vol. 34, pp. 733–34).

14. Libby et al., *Province and Court Records of Maine*, vol. 5, pp. 129–30. *Acts and Laws of His Majesty's Province of New Hampshire* (Portsmouth, 1761), p. 14. William L. Saunders, ed., *The Colonial Records of North Carolina*, vol. 2, pp. 400–401, 405, 412–13, 437, 447, 470.

15. In 1745 occurred the case of Jabez Dexter, whose words were repeated in his indictment; he seems never to have come to trial (*Acts and Resolves* [of Massachusetts], vol. 13, p. 384). Rhodes's case, Nov. 10, 1757, Minute Book of the Superior Court of Judicature of the Province of Massachusetts Bay, Suffolk County, Office of the Clerk, State House, Boston. Petition of 1770 for relief of wife of Michael Hodge, who fled prosecution for blasphemy, *Acts and Resolves*, vol. 18, p. 407.

16. Connecticut Archives, "Crimes and Misdemeanors, 1662–1789," ser. 1, vol. 9, docs. 163–167. *Massachusetts Gazette & Boston News Letter*, Feb. 18, 1768, p. 2, for the story of Baldwin's case, datelined Hartford.

17. *Virginia Gazette*, May 4, 1769, p. 2. Theron Metcalf, ed., *General Laws of Massachusetts, from the Adoption of the Constitution to February, 1822* (Boston, 1823), p. 65; act of 1782, ch. 8. *General Statutes of the State of Connecticut, Revision of 1875* (Hartford, 1875), p. 512. William Slade, ed., *Vermont State Papers* (Middlebury, 1823), p. 355. Act of 1779, amended 1787 (*Statutes of the State of Vermont* [Bennington, 1791], p. 75), and again in 1797 (*Laws of the State of Vermont, 1797–1807* [Burlington, 1808, 2 vols.], vol. 1, p. 339). William Paterson, ed., *The Laws of New Jersey* (New Brunswick, 1800), p. 211, for the act of 1796.

18. See Leonard W. Levy, *The Establishment Clause: Religion and the First Amendment* (New York, 1985).

19. "Trial for Blasphemy," *Notes and Queries*, 1st ser. (1994), pp. 315–16, citing *The Oracle of Dauphin* (Harrisburg), Sept. 17, 1799.

20. Virginia act of 1699 in William W. Hening, ed., *Statutes at Large: Being a Collection of All the Laws of Virginia (1619–1792)* (Richmond, 1809–23, 13 vols.), vol. 3, pp. 168–69, copied by South Carolina in 1702 (Cooper and McCord, eds., *Statutes at Large of South Carolina*, vol. 2, pp. 196–97). For the manuals, see *Conductor Generalis or the Office, Duty, and Authority of Justices of the Peace* (Philadelphia, 1722), p. 36; George Webb, *The Office and Authority of a Justice of the Peace* (Williamsburg, 1736), pp. 61–62; William Simpson, *The Practical Justice of the Peace of South Carolina* (Charlestown, 1761), p. 48; James Parker, *Conductor Generalis* (Woodbridge, N.J., 1764), pp. 72–73; Richard Burn, *An Abridgment of Burn's Justice of the Peace* (Boston, 1773), pp. 69–72; J. Davis, *Office and Authority of the Justice of the Peace* (Newbern, N.C., 1774), p. 73; Richard Starke, *The Office and Authority of the Justice of the Peace* (Williamsburg, 1774), pp. 50–51; *Conductor Generalis* (New York, 1788), pp. 64–65; John Grimke, *The South Carolina Justice of the Peace* (Philadelphia, 1796), p. 83.

21. Act for Repealing Certain Laws, 1700, ch. 8, in *Maryland Archives*, vol. 24, p. 104.

22. William Warren Sweet, *Religion in Colonial America* (New York, 1965 reprint), pp. 271–72, 334–36.

23. Herbert M. Morais, *Deism in Eighteenth Century America* (New York, 1934), pp. 90–94, 156. Stiles is quoted in G. Adolph Koch, *Republican Religion: The American Revolution and the Cult of Reason* (New York, 1933), pp. 240–41.

24. Morais, *Deism*, pp. 61–69, 86. Koch, *Republican Religion*, pp. 187–209.

25. Koch, *Republican Religion*, pp. 131–46, 221–36. Morais, *Deism*, pp. 52, 126–27.

26. Koch, *Republican Religion*, pp. 82–84.

27. Morais, *Deism*, pp. 8–9, 17, 72, 90–94, 100–103, 120–27, 156. The case decided by Kent was *People* v. *Ruggles*, 8 Johns. (N.Y.) 290 (1811).

28. Morais, *Deism*, pp. 128–33, 137. Koch, *Republican Religion*, pp. 51–73, 96, 107.

29. Koch, *Republican Religion*, p. 239.

30. Shaw's opinion was delivered in *Commonwealth* v. *Kneeland*, 37 Mass. 206 (1838), discussed in ch. 18 below, as is Kent's opinion in the Ruggles case, cited in n. 27 above.

Chapter 13   England's Augustan Age of Toleration

1. Sollom Emlyn, *Memoir of the Life and Writings of Mr. Thomas Emlyn* (London, 1746, 4th ed., 3 vols.), vol. 1, pp. xviii–xxi.

2. Herbert S. Skeats, *History of the Free Churches of England* (London, 1869, 2nd ed.), p. 184.

3. Thomas Emlyn, *A True Narrative of the Proceedings Against Mr. Thomas Emlyn*, in S. Emlyn, *Memoir*, vol. 1, p. 17.

4. Ibid., pp. 17–20.

5. Ibid., pp. 45–49.

6. Ibid., p. 53.

7. *A Humble Inquiry into the Scriptural Account of Jesus Christ* (1702), the book for which Emlyn was criminally prosecuted, was the only English Unitarian book reprinted in America in the eighteenth century (Boston, 1756 and 1790). It was again reprinted in Boston when Unitarianism peaked there, in Jared Sparks, ed., *Collection of Essays and Tracts in Theology* (Boston, 1824, 4 vols.), vol. 4, pp. 209–66.

8. Sparks, ed., *Essays and Tracts*, pp. 217–18.

9. Emlyn, *True Narrative*, pp. 27–28, for the indictment. George Matthews, *An Account of the Trial, on the 14th of June 1703, Before the Court of the Queen's Bench, Dublin, of the Reverend Thomas Emlyn* (Dublin, 1839), is a Trinitarian account hostile to Emlyn, yet Matthews pronounced his prosecution "a disgrace to every party concerned" (p. 36).

10. Emlyn, *True Narrative*, p. 26.

11. See above, pp. 219–22, and n. 33 to ch. 10.

12. Emlyn, *True Narrative*, p. 53.

13. Ibid., p. 35.

14. See above, pp. 232–34.

15. Thomas Emlyn, *A Vindication of the Worship of the Lord Jesus Christ on Unitarian Principles* (1706), *The Supreme Deity of God the Father Demonstrated* (1707), and other tracts, in S. Emlyn, *Memoirs*, vol. 1.

16. Benjamin Hoadly, *Works*, ed. John Hoadly (London, 1773, 3 vols.), vol. 1, p. 537.

17. Paul O'Higgins, "Blasphemy in Irish Law," *Modern Law Review*, vol. 23 (1960), p. 157.

18. John Asgill, *An Argument Proving . . . the Covenant of Eternal Life . . .* (London, 1700), pp. 47–48.

19. Tresham D. Gregg, *The Covenant of Eternal Life* (New York, 1875), pp. 31–33, reprints the records from the Irish House of Commons.

20. Asgill, *Argument*, p. 8.

21. *Journal of the English House of Commons*, Nov. 26–Dec. 18, 1707, vol. 15, pp. 440–74 passim. *Mr. Asgill's Defense upon his Expulsion from the House of Commons of Great Britain in 1707* (London, 1712) contains the charges and Asgill's answers to each.

22. *Mr. Asgill's Defense*, pp. 43, 49.

23. Gregg, *Covenant of Eternal Life*, pp. 34–55, contains most of the documents on the Asgill case from the English House of Commons.

24. William Cobbett, ed., *Cobbett's Parliamentary History of England* [1066–1803] (London, 1806–20, 36 vols.), vol. 6, pp. 331–35 (March 17, 1704).

25. O'Higgins, "Blasphemy in Irish Law," pp. 157–60.

26. Norman Sykes, *William Wake: Archbishop of Canterbury, 1657–1737* (Cambridge, 1857, 2 vols.), vol. 2, pp. 170–71.

27. Norman Sykes, *Church and State in England in the XVIIIth Century* (Cambridge, 1934), p. 33.

28. On "atheism," see John Redwood, *Reason, Ridicule, and Religion: The Age of Enlightenment in England, 1660–1750* (Cambridge, Mass., 1976), a book that takes too seriously contemporary charges that England was becoming godless and irreligious.

29. On Arianism, see J. Hay Colligan, *The Arian Movement in England* (Manchester, 1913).

30. On deism, see John Orr, *English Deism* (Grand Rapids, Mich., 1934); Roland Stromberg, *Religious Liberalism in the Eighteenth Century* (London, 1954); Margaret Jacob, *The Newtonian and the English Revolution, 1689–1720* (Ithaca, N.Y., 1976); Sir Leslie Stephen, *History of English Thought in the Eighteenth Century* (New York, 3rd ed. of 1902; New York, 1949 reprint, 2 vols.).

31. Quoted in Stromberg, *Religious Liberalism*, p. 9.

32. Quoted in Jacob, *The Newtonian and the English Revolution*, p. 144.

33. Ibid., p. 23.

34. I have relied on Sir George Clark, *The Later Stuarts, 1660–1714* (Oxford, 1956, 2nd ed.), and the pertinent statutes and parliamentary records in Andrew Browning, ed., *English Historical Documents, 1660–1714* (New York, 1953).

35. The quotations from Queen Anne and Dr. Sacheverell are from the note in the anonymously edited book by Defoe, *The Shortest Way with the Dissenters and Other Pamphlets*, in the Shakespeare Head Edition of *The Novels and Selected Writings of Daniel Defoe* (Oxford, 1927), pp. 251–52.

36. Ibid., pp. 124–29 passim. The text of *The Shortest Way* covers pp. 113–33. For a good summary, see Walter Wilson, *The Life and Times of Daniel Defoe* (London, 1830, 3 vols.), vol. 2, pp. 51–54.

37. Quoted in John Robert Moore, *Daniel Defoe: Citizen of the Modern World* (Chicago, 1958), p. 111.

38. *Cobbett's Parliamentary History*, vol. 6. p. 822.

39. Ibid., p. 824.

40. *The Tryal of Dr. Henry Sacheverell Before the House of Peers for High Crimes and*

Misdemeanors (London, 1710), published by order of the House of Lords, is the official transcript. March 6 was the day of the blasphemous readings. For an easily available anthology of the official transcript, see *Cobbett's Parliamentary History*, vol. 6, pp. 806–91. The indispensable scholarly work is Geoffrey Holmes, *The Trial of Dr. Sacheverell* (London, 1973).

41. Richard Burridge, *Religio Libertini: Or, the Faith of a Converted Atheist. Occasionally set forth by Mr. Richard Burridge, Who was lately Convicted of Blasphemy Before the Right Honourable Sir Thomas Parker, Lord Chief Justice of England* (London, 1712); the account of the trial is on pp. 20–34, the quotation on p. 21; the tract is eighty pages.

42. A full report of the Whiston case is in "Proceedings against William Whiston, for publishing divers Tenets contrary to the Established Religion," 1711, in Thomas Bayly Howell, ed., *A Complete Collection of State Trials* (London, 1809–28, 34 vols.), vol. 15, pp. 703–15, which includes documents from the proceedings against Whiston by the university and by the convocation, as well as an extract from Burnet's *History of My Own Time* (London, 1724–34, 2 vols.).

43. Sykes, *William Wake*, vol. 2, pp. 154–60, covers the subject thoroughly.

44. Robert E. Sullivan, *John Toland and the Deist Controversy* (Cambridge, Mass., 1982), pp. 159–60, 168–69, 183. Frederick S. Siebert, *Freedom of the Press in England, 1476–1776* (Urbana, Ill., 1952), p. 318.

45. Matthew Tindal, *Reasons Against Restraining the Press* (London, 1704), pp. 4, 9–10.

46. Matthew Tindal, *A Letter to a Friend: Occasioned by the presentment of the grand jury for the county of Middlesex, of the author, printer and publisher of a book entitled the rights of the christian church asserted* (London, 1708), and *A Second Defence of the Rights of the Christian Church Occasion'd by two late Indictments* (London, 1708).

47. On theories of the freedom of the press, see Leonard W. Levy, *The Emergence of a Free Press* (New York, 1985).

48. J. M. Robertson, *A Short History of Freethought* (London, 1915, 3rd ed., rev., 2 vols.), vol. 1, p. 7.

49. Anthony Collins, *A Discourse concerning Ridicule and Irony in Writing* (London, 1729), pp. 5, 24, 75–76.

50. P. vi of the "Apology," which appears as a preface, pp. iii–lxii, to Anthony Collins, *A Discourse of the Grounds and Reasons of the Christian Religion* (London, 1724).

51. Ibid., p. liii.

52. James O'Higgins, *Anthony Collins: The Man and His Works* (The Hague, 1970), p. 78.

53. Anthony Collins, *Letter to Dr. Rogers . . . Concerning the Necessity of Divine Revelation* (London, 1727), pp. 63–64. On the overt-acts test, see Levy, *Emergence of a Free Press*, pages referred to in the index under "Overt acts test."

Chapter 14   Blasphemy and Obscenity

1. The Occasional Conformity Act and the Schism Act are reprinted in Andrew Browning, ed., *English Historical Documents, 1660–1714* (New York, 1953), pp. 406–10. See Basil Williams, *The Whig Supremacy*, 2nd ed. rev. C. H. Stuart (Oxford, 1962), ch. 4, "Religion and the Churches"; Norman Sykes, *Church and State in England in the XVIIIth Century* (Cambridge, 1934).

2. Sykes, *Church and State in England*, pp. 292–96.

3. Norman Sykes, *William Wake: Archbishop of Canterbury, 1657–1737* (Cambridge, 1957, 2 vols.), vol. 2, pp. 125–26.

4. Ibid., p. 150, letter of February 1718.

5. Ibid., p. 152, letter of July 5, 1717.

6. Ibid., p. 172, letter of April 7, 1729.

7. *The Charge of Whitlocke Bulstrode, Esq. to the Grand Jury, And other Juries, of the County of Middlesex* (London, 1718). The first tract dated the charge at April 21, 1718; *The Second Charge*, by a different printer, bears the date Oct. 9, 1718.

8. Roger Thomas, "The Non-Subscription Controversy Amongst Dissenters in 1719; The Salters' Hall Debate," *Journal of Ecclesiastical History*, vol. 4 (1958), pp. 162–86. J. Hay Colligan, *The Arian Movement in England* (Manchester, 1913), pp. 44–60. R. W. Dale, *History of English Congregationalism* (London, 1907, 2nd ed.), pp. 528–43. George Berkeley, "An Essay Towards Preventing the Ruin of Great Britain," in *The Works of George Berkeley*, ed. Alexander C. Fraser (Oxford, 1901, 4 vols.), vol. 4, pp. 322–23.

9. *Journals of the House of Lords*, vol. 21, pp. 229–32 (Feb. 12, 15, 17, 18, 1720). The offending tract was entitled *A Sober Reply to Mr. Higg's Merry Arguments from the Light of Nature for the Tritheistick Doctrine of the Trinity* (London, 1720). The technical appeal is reported in *Rex* v. *Hall*, 1 Strange 416 (1720). "The Case of Edmund Curll" (1727), in *State Trials*, vol. 17, p. 156, indicates the long period of imprisonment.

10. Sykes, *William Wake*, vol. 2, p. 165.

11. Ibid., pp. 135–38.

12. William Cobbett, ed., *Cobbett's Parliamentary History of England* (London, 1806–20, 36 vols.), vol. 7, pp. 894–95.

13. Sykes, *William Wake*, vol. 2, p. 138.

14. Ibid., vol. 2, p. 161. Charles R. Gillet, *Burned Books* (New York, 1932, 2 vols.), vol. 2, pp. 590–91.

15. Bernard Mandeville, *The Fable of the Bees: Private Vices, Publick Benefits*, ed. F. B. Kaye (New York, 1957 reprint, 2 vols.), vol. 1, pp. 385–87, footnotes quoting *Journals of the House of Lords*, vol. 21, pp. 231–32, and citing issues of *The British Journal*. Clinton Rossiter, *Seedtime of the Republic* (New York, 1953), p. 141. Da Capo Press of New York reprinted a facsimile version of the four-volume 6th ed. of *Cato's Letters* in 1971, under the general editorship of L. W. Levy, bound in two volumes. On *Cato's Letters* as a libertarian document, see Leonard W. Levy, *Emergence of a Free Press* (New York, 1985), pp. 109–18.

16. For Cato on the Trinity, see *Cato's Letters*, essay of March 16, 1723; other essays singled out by the grand jury are those of May 18, May 25, and June 15, 1723, in the Da Capo ed., vol. 2, pp. 118–25, 197–215, 236–46. For the charges, see John Wickliffe, *Remarks Upon two late Presentments of the Grand-Jury of the County of Middlesex* (London, 1729), pp. 1–3, reprinting "The Presentment of the Grand-Jury of the County of Middlesex, 1723."

17. Wickliffe, *Remarks Upon two late Presentments*, reprints the two grand-jury presentments at pp. 1–6. The first presentment appears in Mandeville, *Fable of the Bees*, vol. 1, pp. 383–86, which includes the 6th and final rev. of 1729.

18. Mandeville, *Fable of the Bees*, vol. 1, pp. 14, 402, 404–6. Kaye's edition is a work of splendid scholarship with a lengthy introduction on Mandeville and his book, pp. vii–cxlvl.

19. Edward Elwell, *The Triumph of Truth: Being an Account of the Trial of Mr. Elwell, for Heresy and Blasphemy, at Stafford Assizes* (1726), reprinted in Joseph Priestley,

Theological and Miscellaneous Works, ed. John Towill Rutt (London, 1817, 2 vols.), vol. 2, pp. 417–29, preface to trial by Priestley. See also *Memoir of Mr. Edward Elwell. To Which Is Added The Triumph of Truth: Being an Account of the Trial* (Birmingham, 1817); the *Memoir* has been ascribed to Joshua Toulmin.

20. Sykes, *William Wake*, vol. 2, p. 171.

21. Elwell, *Triumph of Truth*, pp. 422, 423.

22. Ibid., p. 425.

23. For a discussion of *Rex* v. *Taylor*, see above, pp. 219–22. On the history of English libel law, see William Holdsworth, *A History of English Law* (London, 1937, 2nd ed., 13 vols), vol. 8, pp. 333–46.

24. Frederick Seaton Siebert, *Freedom of the Press in England, 1476–1776* (Urbana, Ill., 1952), ch. 12. The statute, 14 Charles II. ch. 33, is reprinted in Siebert's *Documents Relating to the Development of the Relations Between Press and Government in England* (East Lansing, Mich., n.d.), sec. v, p. 1, a collection of privately printed documents.

25. Norman St. John-Stevas, *Obscenity and the Law* (London, 1956), pp. 16–20. Donald Thomas, *A Long Time Burning: The History of Literary Censorship in England* (New York, 1969), pp. 22–24.

26. *Rex* v. *Sedley* (1663), in *State Trials*, vol. 16, p. 155.

27. *Queen* v. *Read* (1708), Fortescue's Reports 98; reported also in "Case of Edmund Curll" (1727), *State Trials*, vol. 17, pp. 155, 157; Holt and Powell at p. 157.

28. See "Edmund Curll" in *D.N.B.*, vol. 5, pp. 868–73.

29. "The Case of Edmund Curll, Bookseller, in the King's Bench, for publishing a Libel," in *State Trials*, vol. 17, pp. 153–60. *King* v. *Curl*, 1 Barn. K.B. 20 (1727).

30. William H. Epstein, *John Cleland: Images of a Life* (New York, 1974), pp. 75–83.

31. *King* v. *Gallard*, Kelynge's English Crown Cases 163 (1733).

32. *Rex* v. *Cruden*, 2 Campbell's Nisi Prius Reports 89 (1809).

33. Anon., *Life of Thomas Woolston, with an Impartial Account of His Writings* (London, 1733), p. 31.

34. Ibid., pp. 22, 26, 29–30.

35. Thomas Woolston, *Whether the People Called Quakers do not the nearest, of any other Sect in Religion, resemble the primitive Christians in Principles and Practice* (London, 1720).

36. Thomas Woolston, *Defense of the Apostles and primitive Fathers of the Church, for their allegorical Interpretation of the Law of Moses, against the Ministers of the Letter, and literal Commentators of this Age* (London, 1721).

37. Sir Leslie Stephen, *History of English Thought in the Eighteenth Century* (New York, 3rd ed. of 1902, 1949 reprint, 2 vols.), vol. 1, pp. 228–37, for Stephen's treatment of Woolston.

38. Adam S. Farrar, *A Critical History of Free Thought* (London, 1862), p. 137.

39. John Orr, *English Deism* (Grand Rapids, Mich., 1934), p. 140.

40. John M. Robertson, *A Short History of Freethought* (London, 1915, 3rd ed. rev. and expanded), p. 312.

41. Norman L. Torrey, *Voltaire and the English Deists* (New Haven, 1930), pp. 59, 71.

42. Thomas Stackhouse, *A Fair State of the Controversy between Mr. Woolston and his Adversaries* (London, 1730), pp. 52, 294.

43. Thomas Woolston, *A Free Gift to the Clergy* (London, 1722), p. 50.

44. Thomas Woolston, *Defense of the Thundering Legion* (London, 1726), p. iv.

45. Anon., *A Moderator Between an Infidel and an Apostate* (London, 1725).

46. Anon., *Life of Woolston*, pp. 10–12.

47. Easily available in a photo-offset edition of the original London edition of

1727–30 reprinted as Thomas Woolston, *Six Discourses on the Miracles of Our Saviour and Defense of His Discourses* (New York, 1979), separately paginated.

48. For his professions of Christian faith, see *First Discourse*, p. 7; *Second Discourse*, p. 16; *Third Discourse*, pp. iv, 66; *Fourth Discourse*, p. 68; *Fifth Discourse*, p. 66; *Sixth Discourse*, p. 66. Also, Thomas Woolston, *Mr. Woolston's Defense of His Discourses on the Miracles of Our Saviour* (London, 1729), pt. 1, p. 15; pt. 2, pp. 7, 15, 65.

49. *Sixth Discourse*, pp. 5, 28.

50. Stackhouse, *A Fair State*, p. 294. Voltaire, who was aware of only the first three editions, stated in his *Letters on Rabelais* (1767) that each edition sold ten thousand copies, a figure he later inflated to twenty thousand for each edition (*Oeuvres Complètes de Voltaire: Nouvelle Edition* [Paris, 1883–85, 52 vols.], vol. 26, p. 485; *The Works of Voltaire* [Paris, 1901, 42 vols.], vol. 25, p. 485; vol. 20, p. 86; article on "Miracles" in his *Philosophical Dictionary* [1771], vol. 11, sec. 10, pp. 288, 291).

51. Anon., *Life of Woolston*, p. 14.

52. Letter to Prof. Turrettini, Nov. 28, 1728, quoted in Sykes, *William Wake*, vol. 2, pp. 170–71.

53. Anon., *An Account of the Trial of Thomas Woolston, B.D., Sometime Fellow of Sidney College, in Cambridge, on Tuesday the Fourth of March 1729, at the Court of the King's-Bench, in Guildhall, on Four Several Informations for Writing, Printing, Publishing, Four Blasphemous Books, On the Miracles of Our Saviour* (London, 1729), p. 3.

54. Ibid., pp. 3–6. A slightly different version of the trial is available in *Celebrated Trials and Remarkable Cases of Criminal Jurisprudence* (London, 1825, 6 vols.), vol. 3, pp. 432–33. Raymond's charge to the jury is better reported in *Rex v. Woolston*, case no. 11, Pasch. 2 Geo. II, Fitzg. R. 64–66 (1729), and Barn. K.B. 162–63 (1729).

55. *Fifth Discourse*, pp. 5, 28; *Sixth Discourse*, p. 27.

56. For a summary of the immense anti-Woolston literature, see John Hunt, *Religious Thought in England* (London, 1870–73, 3 vols.), vol. 2, pp. 416–31.

57. Stephen, *English Thought*, vol. 1, p. 237.

58. *Sixth Discourse*, pp. 58, 64–66.

59. Woolston, *Defense of His Discourses*, pt. 2, pp. vi, 67.

60. Waddington to Lardner, Nov. 14, 1729, and Lardner to Waddington, Nov. 22, 1729, reprinted in *The Works of Nathaniel Lardner*, ed. Andrew Kippis (London, 1815, 5 vols.), vol. 1, pp. xxxv–xxxvi.

61. John Disney, *A View of Ancient Laws against Immorality and Profaneness* (Cambridge, 1729).

62. Wickliffe, *Remarks Upon two late Presentments*.

63. Ibid., pp. 8–11.

64. Ibid., pp. 12–15.

65. Ibid., pp. 16–18.

66. Ibid., pp. 19–28.

67. Sollom Emlyn, intro. to 1730 ed. of *State Trials*, vol. 1, pp. xxx–xxxi.

Chapter 15   The "Age of Reason"?

1. William Bates, "Mr. Peter A N-T [Annet]," *Notes and Queries*, vol. 8 (Nov. 3, 1877), p. 351.

2. Both quoted in Nicholas Hans, *New Trends in Education in the Eighteenth Century* (London, 1951), pp. 169–70.

3. Bates, "Mr. Peter A N-T," p. 350.

4. *D.N.B.*, vol. 10, pp. 414–15.

5. Bates, "Mr. Peter A N-T," p. 350.

6. Peter Annet, *History and Character of St. Paul* (undated but after 1747), in Annet's *Collection of the Tracts of a certain Free Enquirer noted by his sufferings for his opinions* (London, n.d., possibly posthumous; Annet died in 1769).

7. "Reflections on Civil and Religious Liberty," *Gentleman's Magazine*, vol. 32 (Dec. 1762), p. 559.

8. "Two Original Letters from Peter Annet," *Gentleman's Magazine*, vol. 54 (April 1784), p. 251.

9. Thomas Starkie, *A Treatise on the Law of Slander and Libel* (London, 1813), ed. Henry Coleman Folkard (London, 1897, 6th ed.), p. 617.

10. 96 Eng. Rept. 224 (1762).

11. On Wilkes and his seditious libel, see Raymond Postgate, *That Devil Wilkes* (New York, 1929); George Nobbe, *The North Briton* (New York, 1939); Robert E. Rea, *The English Press in Politics, 1760–1774* (Lincoln, Neb., 1963); George Rudé, *Wilkes and Liberty* (New York, 1962).

12. *An Essay on Woman, And Other Pieces . . . by the Right Hon. John Wilkes, Preceded by an introductory narrative . . . connected with the prosecution of the author in the House of Lords, Digested and Compiled from contemporary writers* (London, 1871), a work anonymously edited by John Camden Hotten, contains documentary evidence of great value, including the affidavit of Wilkes's printer, Wilkes's statement, and Warburton's speeches, as well as the offensive poems.

13. See *Essay on Woman*, pp. 122, 162–66, 179–82, 185, 194–95, 202–8.

14. On outlawry, see L. W. Levy, *Jefferson and Civil Liberties* (Cambridge, Mass., 1963), pp. 192–93 n. 31; Telford Taylor, *Grand Inquest* (New York, 1955), pp. 301–5, 339–41.

15. Wilkes's story may be followed in the books cited in n. 11 above and in the old but fullest biography, Horace Bleackley, *Life of John Wilkes* (London, 1917), pp. 113–203; Bleackley's appendix, pp. 437–44, confirms Wilkes's authorship of *Essay on Woman*, as does the earlier work by Eric R. Watson, "John Wilkes and 'The Essay on Woman,' " *Notes and Queries*, 11th ser., vol. 9 (1914), pp. 121–23, 143–45, 162–64, 183–85, 203–5, 222–23, 241–42. For his trials, see "Proceedings in the Case of John Wilkes on Two Informations for Libels, King's Bench and House of Lords, 1763–1770," in *A Complete Collection of State Trials*, ed. Thomas B. Howell (London, 1809–28), vol. 19, pp. 1075–1138.

16. Earl Morse Wilbur, *A History of Unitarianism in Transylvania, England and America* (Cambridge, Mass., 1952), pp. 236–70, quotation at p. 262.

17. Ibid., pp. 274, 283.

18. Richard Burgess Barlow, *Citizenship and Conscience: A Study in the Theory and Practice of Religious Toleration in England during the Eighteenth Century* (Philadelphia, 1962). Anthony Lincoln, *Some Political and Social Ideas of English Dissent, 1763–1800* (1938; New York, 1971 reprint).

19. Pp. 41–65 of the 1769 1st London ed. of *Commentaries on the Laws of England* (4 vols.).

20. Blackstone, *Reply to Dr. Priestley's Remarks on the Fourth Volume of the Commentaries* (London, 1769), reprinted in *Palladium of Conscience; or, the Foundation of Religious Liberty* (Philadelphia, 1773; New York, 1974 reprint, gen. ed. Leonard W. Levy), p. 40.

21. *Palladium of Conscience* includes Philip Furneaux, *Letters to the Honourable Mr.*

Justice Blackstone, Concerning His Exposition of the Act of Toleration (London, 1770), and an *Appendix*, which includes judicial opinions and Mansfield's speech in the sheriff's case, *Allen Evans* v. *Sir Thomas Harrison, Chamberlain of London* (1762), affirmed in the Lords in 1767 (letter 1, pp. 10–12), and *Appendix*, pp. 112–55. For Mansfield's exceptions, see pp. 151, 152.

22. See Leonard W. Levy, *Emergence of a Free Press* (New York, 1985), p. 152 and additional references indexed under "overt acts."

23. Furneaux proposed the overt-acts test in *Palladium of Conscience*, letter 3, pp. 31–43.

24. Ibid., letter 4, pp. 44–76, continues the argument on the scope of expression for reviling, affronts, and indecencies.

25. *Regina* v. *Lemon* (C.A.), 3 Weekly Law Rev. 404, 412 (Aug. 11, 1978).

26. Lincoln, *Some Political and Social Ideas of English Dissent*, a book with a misleading title, proves that English dissent was nearly devoid of social ideas.

27. Thomas Chubb, "Remarks on the Scriptures," *Posthumous Works* (London, 1748, 2 vols.), vol. 1, pp. 2–65; quotation at p. 64.

28. Edmund Burke, *Reflections on the French Revolution*, intro. by A. J. Grieve (London, 1967), p. 27.

29. Eric Foner, *Tom Paine and Revolutionary America* (New York, 1976), pp. 220–49, quotation at p. 220. E. P. Thompson, *The Making of the English Working Class* (New York, 1964), pp. 89–98; quotation at p. 90. See also David Freeman Hawke, *Paine* (New York, 1974), pp. 230–50; Alfred Owen Aldridge, *Man of Reason: The Life of Thomas Paine* (Philadelphia, 1959), pp. 134–43, 161.

30. *Rex* v. *Paine*, in *State Trials*, vol. 22, p. 357 (1792).

31. Sir James Fitzjames Stephen, *A History of the Criminal Law of England* (London, 1883, 3 vols.), vol. 2, pp. 362–63, for the cases.

32. Thomas Erskine May, *The Constitutional History of England Since the Accession of George III, 1760–1860* (New York, 1880, 2 vols.), vol. 2, p. 142 n. 2.

33. *Speeches of Thomas Lord Erskine*, ed. Edward Walford (London, 1870, 5 vols.), vol. 1, p. 313. For a discussion of Erskine's views on the press, see Levy, *Emergence of a Free Press*, pp. 282–89. See also Stephen Parks, ed., *The Friends to the Liberty of the Press: Eight Tracts, 1792–93* (New York, 1974), facsimile reprints, paginated separately, for Erskine's speeches on the scope of political expression.

34. *Rex* v. *Williams*, in *State Trials*, vol. 26, p. 654 (1797).

35. Paine to Adams, Jan. 1, 1803, in *Complete Writings of Thomas Paine*, ed. Philip S. Foner (New York, 1945, 2 vols.), vol. 2, pp. 1434, 1436.

36. *The Age of Reason*, in *Complete Writings of Paine*, vol. 1, p. 600.

37. Ibid., pp. 466–67.

38. Ibid., p. 468.

39. Ibid., pp. 550, 553, 555, 570, 572, 574. "Blasphemously obscene" is at p. 570.

40. Ibid., pp. 571–82.

41. Ibid., pp. 576–77.

42. Ibid., p. 508.

43. Ibid., pp. 574–76.

44. Ibid., p. 471.

45. Ibid., p. 604.

46. Ibid., pp. 518, 537.

47. Ibid., p. 596.

48. Ibid., pp. 464, 482–83, 484, 498, 504.

49. *Rex* v. *Thomas Williams*, in *State Trials*, vol. 26, pp. 653, 660 (1797). On special juries and Williams, see *The Autobiography of Francis Place*, ed. Mary Thale (Cambridge, 1972), appendix, pp. 159–72.

50. *State Trials*, vol. 26, pp. 653, 664, 697.

51. Ibid., p. 705.

52. Ibid., p. 664.

53. Ibid., p. 668.

54. May, *Constitutional History*, vol. 2, pp. 156–59. Arthur E. Sutherland, "British Trials for Disloyal Association During the French Revolution," *Cornell Law Quarterly*, vol. 34 (1949), pp. 316–28.

55. *State Trials*, vol. 26, pp. 671–95.

56. Ibid., pp. 705–20.

Chapter 16   Eaton to Carlile

1. Samuel H. Romilly, *Memoirs*, ed. by his sons (London, 1840, 3 vols.), vol. 2, p. 90.

2. On Stone's case, see the Unitarian journal *Monthly Repository of Theology* (London), vol. 1 (1806), pp. 450–51, 490–91, 528–31; vol. 2 (1807), pp. 565–66; vol. 3 (1808), pp. 28–31, 129, 210–13, 243–44, 273–77, 282–84, 374, 412, 518; vol. 4 (1809), pp. 404, 536–37.

3. *Rex* v. *Eaton*, in *State Trials*, vol. 31, pp. 927–58 (1812). Daniel L. McCue, Jr., "Daniel Isaac Eaton," in *Biographical Dictionary of Modern British Radicals, 1770–1830*, ed. J. O. Baylen and N. J. Gossman (Sussex, 1979), pp. 140–44.

4. Letter to Lord Ellenborough, n.d., in *The Complete Writings of Percy Bysshe Shelley*, ed. Roger Ingpen and W. E. Peck (New York, 1926–30, 10 vols.), vol. 5, pp. 283–94.

5. Kenneth Neill Cameron, *The Young Shelley: Genesis of a Radical* (New York, 1950), pp. 180, 186, 405 n. 127.

6. See Richard W. Davis, *Dissent in Politics, 1780–1830: The Political Life of William Smith M.P.* (London, 1971), especially ch. 11, pp. 181–211, on the "Emergence of Unitarianism." Davis also wrote the sketch of Smith in *Biographical Dictionary of Modern British Radicals*, pp. 447–50.

7. William Smith to Jeremy Bentham, Feb. 16, 1818, in Jeremy Bentham, *Church-of-Englandism and Its Catechism Examined* (London, 1818), preface, pp. xviii–xxi. See also Smith's letter to Norfolk *Chronicle*, July 24, 1813, quoted in Davis, *Dissent in Politics*, p. 194.

8. Bentham to Smith, Jan. 24, 1818, and Feb. 1818, in Bentham, *Church-of-Englandism*, pp. xiv–xviii, xxv–xlii. Davis, *Dissent in Politics*, omits Bentham's attack on Smith. Bentham was as unrealistic as he was long-winded.

9. 53 Geo. III, ch. 160.

10. Thomas Hansard, ed., *Parliamentary Debates*, new ser., vol. 25, pp. 1147–48 (May 5, 1813).

11. Ibid., vol. 26, p. 1222 (July 20, 1813).

12. *Attorney General* v. *Pearson*, 3 Merivale's Chancery Reports 353, 407–9 (1817).

13. 2 Swanston's Chancery Reports 470, 527 (1819).

14. William Holdsworth, *A History of English Law* (London, 1943, 16 vols.), vol. 6, p. 241.

15. Arthur Aspinwall, *Politics and the Press, 1780–1850* (London, 1949), pp. 8–13. Collett D. Collett, *History of the Taxes on Knowledge* (London, 1933 reprint), pp. 5–22. G. D. H. Cole, *The Life of William Cobbett* (London, 1927), pp. 201–7. S. Maccoby, *English Radicalism, 1786–1832* (London, 1955), pp. 322, 324–29. E. P. Thompson, *The Making of the English Working Class* (New York, 1964), pp. 633–39. See especially William H. Wickwar, *The Struggle for the Freedom of the Press, 1819–1832* (London, 1928), an excellent book.

16. *The Speech of Earl Grey in the House of Lords, May 12, 1817 on Lord Sidmouth's Circular* (London, 1817), pp. 3–9, 38–39, 67. Maccoby, *English Radicalism*, pp. 324–29. On Sidmouth, see Philip Ziegler, *Addington: A Life of Henry Addington, First Viscount Sidmouth* (London, 1965).

17. "Return to an Address of the House, dated 19th March 1823;—for a Return of the Individuals who have been Prosecuted either by Indictment, or other Process, for Public Libel, Blasphemy, and Sedition . . . from 1812 . . . to 1823," *Journals H.C.*, vol. 88 (1823), pp. 1082–1101.

18. Robert Aspland, *An Inquiry Into the Nature of the Sin of Blasphemy and Into the Propriety of Regarding It as a Civil Offence* (London, 1817), pp. 62, 68–80 (derived from July sermons).

19. Thompson, *English Working Class*, p. 639.

20. *Speech of Earl Grey*, pp. 74–79, 82–85. R. Brook Aspland, *Memoir of the Life Works and Correspondence of the Reverend Robert Aspland* (London, 1850), p. 378. Davis, *Dissent in Politics*, pp. 200–201.

21. "Return to an Address," pp. 1082–1101.

22. *On the Law of Libel; with Strictures on the Self-Styled "Constitutional Association"* (London, 1823), an anonymous book, discusses bail in libel cases on pp. 24, 58–71.

23. See Frederick W. Hackwood, *William Hone: His Life and Times* (London, 1912); pp. 133–53 describe his arrest and imprisonment.

24. "Trial by Jury and Liberty of the Press: The Proceedings at the Public Meeting, December 29, 1817, at the City of London Tavern [for] William Hone," in William Tegg, ed., *The Three Trials of William Hone, for Publishing Three Parodies* (London, 1876, reprinting the work of the same title printed by Hone in 1818); quotations at pp. 194, 203.

25. Tegg, ed., *The Three Trials*, pp. 8–10, 66, 75–76.

26. Ibid., pp. 73–82, 140–43. The three were Lords Eldon, Sidmouth, and Castlereagh. Eldon exhibited sealed bags of supposedly damning documents. Sidmouth's father was a doctor. Castlereagh represented Down, was the son of Lord Londonderry, and favored flogging as a punishment—with the culprit tied to a "triangle."

27. Ibid., pp. 86, 96.

28. Ibid., pp. 162–63, 90.

29. All facts derive from ibid. On common jurors and special jurors, see *On the Law of Libel*, pp. 31–50.

30. Tegg, ed., *The Three Trials*, p. 210.

31. Carlile's article in *The Republican*, vol. 11 (Jan. 28, 1825), pp. 97–109, is an autobiographical account. Joel H. Wiener, *Radicalism and Freethought in Nineteenth-Century Britain: The Life of Richard Carlile* (Westport, Conn., 1983), is the first scholarly biography of Carlile. Wickwar, *Struggle for Freedom of the Press*, is concise on

Carlile but reliable. G. D. H. Cole, *Richard Carlile, 1790–1843* (London, 1943), is a booklet, as is George Jacob Holyoake, *The Life and Character of Richard Carlile* (London, 1849), by a convicted blasphemer who knew Carlile. Theophilia Carlile Campbell, *The Battle of the Press* (London, 1899), is filiopietistic and discursive. Guy A. Aldred, *Richard Carlile: Agitator* (Glasgow, 1941), is a mercifully brief left-wing tract. J. Ann Hone, *For the Cause of Truth: Radicalism in London, 1796–1821* (Oxford, 1982), provides the context and background of Carlile's agitation.

32. *The Republican*, vol. 7 (May 30, 1823), p. 683.

33. Ibid., and vol. 11 (Jan. 28, 1825), p. 102.

34. Ibid., vol. 2 (March 2, 1820), pp. 226–27; vol. 7 (May 30, 1823), p. 675; vol. 11 (Jan. 28, 1825), pp. 102–4; vol. 14 (July 14, 1826), pp. 2–13.

35. Ibid., vol. 7 (May 30, 1823), pp. 675–76.

36. See Leonard W. Levy, *Emergence of a Free Press* (New York, 1985), pp. 93–100.

37. *The Republican*, vol. 4 (Dec. 29, 1820); vol. 7 (May 30, 1823), pp. 676–77, 683.

38. Ibid., vol. 12 (November 25, 1825), pp. 643–44.

39. Thompson, *Making of the Working Class*, p. 700.

40. Wickwar, *Struggle for Freedom of the Press*, p. 315. The total figures are Wickwar's, based on his counts of cases listed in various reports, which he described as "inaccurate."

41. John Macdonell, ed., *Report of State Trials*, new ser. (London, 1888–98, 8 vols.), vol. 1, p. 1386.

42. Ibid., vol. 1, p. 1385. Appendix to *Persons prosecuted for Libels, Blasphemy and Sedition* (1821), in *House of Commons Papers, General Index to the Accounts and Papers, Reports of Commissioners Estimates . . . 1801–1852* (London, 1854), p. 399. Wickwar did not use either of these sources.

43. Macdonell, ed., *Report of State Trials*, new ser., vol. 1, p. 1388.

44. Carlile's eyewitness report, in a public letter to Lord Sidmouth dated Aug. 18, 1819, is reprinted in Campbell, *Battle of the Press*, appendix 2, pp. 307–15. See also Thompson, *Making of the Working Class*, pp. 669–89; Maccoby, *English Radicalism*, pp. 355–65; Donald Read, *Peterloo: The "Massacre" and Its Background* (Manchester, 1958); Robert J. Walmsley, *Peterloo: The Case Re-Opened* (Manchester, 1969).

45. *The Republican*, vol. 2 (Jan. 14, 1820), p. 2.

46. Ibid., vol. 1 (Oct. 12, 1819), pp. 97–98.

47. The eighteen-page "Introduction" to Carlile's report of his *Mock Trials* is a documentary collection of his pretrial conduct: *The Report of the Proceedings of the Court of King's Bench, in the Guildhall, London, on the 12th, 13th, 14th, and 15th Days of October: Being the Mock Trials of Richard Carlile, for alleged Blasphemous Libels*, published in 1819 and then as a book in 1822. But it covers only Oct. 12, despite its title. See also *The Speech of John Gale Jones Delivered at the British Forum* (London, 1819).

48. Carlile, *Mock Trials*, p. 7.

49. Ibid., p. 13.

50. Ibid., p. 14.

51. Ibid., p. 4.

52. Wickwar, *Struggle for Freedom of the Press*, p. 85, citing manuscript correspondence between Francis Place and Carlile.

53. *The Republican*, vol. 8 (Nov. 7, 1823), p. 545.

54. Carlile, *Mock Trials*, p. 29.

55. "Trial of Mr. Carlile," *British Press*, Oct. 14, 1819, in Campbell, *Battle of the*

Press, appendix 1, pp. 265–315, reprints the proceedings of the second day, Oct. 13. Carlile's argument based on the act of 1813 is at pp. 275–76, 284–86, 292, 301.

56. *The Republican*, vol. 4 (Nov. 3, 1820), p. 336; vol. 5 (March 1, 1822), p. 275; vol. 7 (May 16, 1823), p. 624; vol. 7 (May 30, 1823), p. 678.

57. "Trial of Mr. Carlile," in Campbell, *Battle of the Press*, pp. 276, 282.

58. Ibid., p. 283.

59. Ibid., pp. 281, 284, 289, 291, 293, 295.

60. Ibid., p. 295.

61. Ibid., pp. 297–305.

62. William Hone, letter to *Morning Chronicle*, Oct. 15, 1819, in ibid., pp. 4–5.

63. *The Republican*, vol. 11 (July 1, 1825), p. 818.

64. *Rex v. Carlile*, in Macdonell, ed., *Report of State Trials*, new ser., vol. 1 (1819), p. 1387; vol. 4 (1819), pp. 1423–26. *Rex v. Carlile*, 3 Barn. and Alder. King's Bench Reports 161 (1819).

65. *The Republican*, vol. 7 (May 30, 1823), p. 678; vol. 6 (Dec. 13, 1822), p. 903.

66. *King v. Eaton*, in *State Trials*, vol. 31, p. 930 (1812).

67. Campbell, *Battle of the Press*, pp. 51, 285, 295.

68. Wickwar, *Struggle for Freedom of the Press*, pp. 136–41.

69. *The Trial of Joseph Russell* (Birmingham, 1819), pp. 14–15, 50.

70. *The Republican*, vol. 1 (Oct. 1, 1819), pp. 93, 95; vol. 2 (Jan. 21, 1820), pp. 47–51.

71. Hansard, ed., *Parliamentary Debates*, new ser., vol. 41, pp. 343, 988. Wilberforce to Milton, 1819, in Robert I. Wilberforce and Samuel Wilberforce, *The Life of William Wilberforce* (Philadelphia, 1841, 2 vols.), vol. 2, p. 222.

Chapter 17   Carlile's Shopmen and Free Expression

1. Wilbur D. Jones on Joseph Gale Jones in *Biographical Dictionary of Modern British Radicals, 1770–1830*, ed. J. O. Baylen and N. J. Grossman (Sussex, 1979), pp. 269–73.

2. *Substance of the Speeches of John Gale Jones, Delivered at the British Forum, March 11, 18, & 22, 1819* (London, 1819).

3. Shelley to Leigh Hunt, Nov. 3, 1819, in *The Complete Writings of Percy Bysshe Shelley*, ed. Roger Ingpen and W. E. Peck (New York, 1926–30, 10 vols.), vol. 10, p. 105. The printed letter on Carlile's case is fourteen pages.

4. On Fox, see Richard Garnett, *The Life of W. J. Fox* (New York, 1910). My quotations are from one of Fox's best-known sermons: *The Duties of Christians Toward Deists* (London, 1819), p. iv. Fox later became a radical journalist and member of Parliament.

5. Fox, *Duties of Christians*, pp. vi, viii–ix.

6. Ibid., pp. xii, 26–31.

7. Ibid., pp. 33–37.

8. Ibid., pp. 37–40.

9. Ibid., pp. 40–46.

10. Frederick Fox, *Constitutional Remarks Addressed to the People of Great Britain Upon the Subject of the Late Trial of Robert Carlile* (London, 1819), pp. 29–37.

11. Robert Hall, *Apology for the Freedom of the Press, and for General Liberty*, re-

printed in *The Miscellaneous Works and Remains of the Reverend Robert Hall*, ed. John Foster (London, 1846), pp. 159–243. The quotation is from p. 172.

12. "Hall's Reply," in ibid., p. 238.

13. "Modern Infidelity Considered," in ibid., pp. 277–94.

14. Christophilus, *Vindiciae Britanniicae. Christianity Interested in The Dismissal of Ministers. A Vindication of the People from the Charge of Blasphemy, and a Defence of the Freedom of the Press* (London, 1871), cited hereafter as *A Vindication.*

15. Ibid., pp. 41–54.

16. Ibid., pp. 110, 115.

17. Ibid., pp. 118, 139–42, 151–55.

18. James Mill, "Liberty of the Press," suppl. to *Encyclopaedia Britannica*, 5th ed., reprinted in Mill, *Essays on Government, Jurisprudence, Liberty of the Press, and the Law of Nations* (1825; New York, 1967), essays separately paginated; the material relevant to freedom of opinion on religion derives from pp. 30–34.

19. John Stuart Mill, "On Religious Persecution," *Westminster Review*, July 1824, reprinted in John Stuart Mill, *Prefaces to Liberty*, ed. Bernard Wishy (Boston, 1959), p. 68.

20. Ibid., pp. 73–76.

21. Ibid., pp. 76–77.

22. Ibid., pp. 76–77.

23. Ibid., pp. 81–84.

24. Ibid., pp. 84–85.

25. Ibid., pp. 85–90.

26. Ibid., p. 91.

27. Ibid., p. 99.

28. Erasmus Perkins, ed., *The Trial of the Rev. Robt. Wedderburn, a Dissenting Minister of the Unitarian Persuasion, for Blasphemy* (London, 1820).

29. Ibid., pp. 8–19.

30. Ibid., p. 19.

31. Erasmus Perkins, ed., *The Address of the Rev. R. Wedderburn to the Court of King's Bench, Westminster, on appearing to receive judgement for Blasphemy* (London, 1820).

32. *The Republican*, vol. 2 (Sept. 8, 1820), pp. 38–41; vol. 6 (Dec. 13, 1822), p. 897; vol. 7 (May 16, 1823), pp. 615, 617–18.

33. Ibid., vol. 2 (March 3, 1920), pp. 229–30; vol. 4 (May 19, 1820), pp. 113–14; vol. 5 (Jan. 4, 1822), pp. 14–17.

34. Ibid., vol. 4 (Nov. 3, 1820), p. 352.

35. Quoted in ibid., p. 353; pp. 353–60 cover the "Trial of Mr Davison," which Carlile assembled from newspaper reports. I have not been able to find a copy of *The Trial of Thomas Davison, for a Blasphemous Libel in the Deist's Magazine* (London, 1820), but the report in *The Republican* is accurate, though abbreviated, and on all points of law corresponds with *King v. Davison*, 4 Barn. and Alder. King's Bench Reports 958–62 (1821), the case on appeal.

36. *The Republican*, vol. 4 (Nov. 17, 1820), pp. 418–27, reports Cooper's argument in detail and the judges' opinions briefly. The official report at 4 Barn. and Alder. abbreviates Cooper but fully reports the judicial opinions.

37. Joel H. Wiener has a short sketch of Davison in *Biographical Dictionary of Modern British Radicals*, pp. 114–16.

38. *The Republican*, vol. 4 (Oct. 27, 1820), pp. 295–98; vol. 5 (Jan. 4, 1822), pp. 14–20. *Report of the Trial of Mrs. Carlile* [for seditious libel] (London, 1821).

39. *The Republican*, Dec. 29, 1820.

40. *Report of the Trial of Mary Anne Carlile for Publishing a New Year's Address to the Reformers of Great Britain, Written by Richard Carlile* (London, 1821).

41. "King against Carlile: Trial of Mary Anne Carlile for a Blasphemous Libel," in John Macdonnell, ed., *Report of State Trials*, new ser. (London, 1888–98, 8 vols.), vol. 1, pp. 1034–37.

42. Ibid., pp. 1037–42.

43. Ibid., pp. 1043–48.

44. *Suppressed Defence: The Defence of Mary-Anne Carlile, to the Vice Society's Indictment, against the Appendix to the Theological Works of Thomas Paine* (London, 1821), reporting the entire trial as well.

45. Macdonell, ed., *Report of State Trials*, pp. 1048–50.

46. Carlile to H. V. Holmes, Jan. 15, 1822, reprinted in Theophilia Carlile Campbell, *The Battle of the Press* (London, 1899), p. 86.

47. Ibid.

48. *The Republican*, vol. 7 (May 16, 1823), pp. 609–22, for the petition and inventory of seizures.

49. Ibid., pp. 623–30, where Carlile quoted the debates in the House of Commons and articles from the London *Morning Chronicle* written, I think, by young John Stuart Mill.

50. *Report of the Trial of Humphrey Boyle . . . As One of the Shopmen of Mr. Carlile . . . To Which Is Attached the Trial of Joseph Rhodes* (London, 1822).

51. *Report of the Trial of William Vamplew Holmes, One of Mr. Carlile's Shopmen . . . At Old Bailey, March 1st, 1822* (London, 1824).

52. *Report of the Trial of Mrs. Susannah Wright* (London, 1822).

53. *King* v. *Samuel Waddington* (1822), in Macdonell, ed., *Report of State Trials*, vol. 1, pp. 1339–44, 1368.

54. *King* v. *Tunbridge* (1823), in ibid., vol. 1, pp. 1368–69.

55. Mill, "On Religious Persecution," p. 83.

56. Thomas Hansard, ed., *Parliamentary Debates*, new ser., vol. 8 (May 26, 1823), pp. 709–16. On Hume, see the sketch by Gilbert Cahill, in *Biographical Dictionary of Modern British Radicals*, pp. 241–44.

57. Hansard, ed., *Parliamentary Debates*, new ser., vol. 8, pp. 716–35.

58. *The Republican*, vol. 7 (May 19, 1823), pp. 594–602, reports Watson's trial. See also W. J. Linton, *James Watson: A Memoir of the Days of the Fight for a Free Press in England* (Manchester, 1880), pp. 18–20 (in 1879 ed., pp. 16–17).

59. *The Republican*, vol. 8 (Oct. 31, 1823), pp. 532–44, reports Trust's trial. See ibid., vol. 8, pp. 478–80, 548–50, on the prosecution of John Jones.

60. Ibid., vol. 6 (July 19, 1822), p. 226; vol. 8 (June 11, 1824), pp. 759–62.

61. Ibid., vol. 9 (June 11, 1824), pp. 737, 742, 759–66.

62. Ibid., vol. 9 (June 4, 1824), pp. 706–7.

63. *The Reports of the Trials of William Campion, Thomas Jefferies, Richard Hassell, John Clarke, William Haley, William Cochrane, and Others for the Sale of Anti-Christian Publications in the Shop of Richard Carlile, 84 Fleet St., London, Tried at the Old Bailey Sessions for June, 1824, Before Newman Knowlys, the Recorder* (London, 1824).

64. Wickwar, *Struggle for Freedom of the Press*, p. 239, quoting *Black Dwarf*, and p. 245, quoting *Newgate Monthly*.

65. "To Robert Peel," *The Republican*, vol. 9 (June 11, 1824), pp. 737–38. Wickwar, *Struggle for Freedom of the Press*, pp. 253–59.

66. Hansard, ed., *Parliamentary Debates*, new ser., vol. 13, pp. 1015–18. *The Republican*, vol. 11 (June 17, 1825), pp. 737–49.

67. *The Republican*, vol. 11 (May 6, 1825), pp. 561–64.

68. Joel H. Wiener, *Radicalism and Freethought in Nineteenth-Century Britain* (Westport, Conn., 1983), pp. 109–12, 135–36. David Berman, *A History of Atheism in Britain* (London, 1988), pp. 202–6.

69. *Infidelity Punished. Report of a Remarkable Trial: The King vs. The Rev. Robert Taylor, a Minister of the Established Church of England. For a Blasphemous Discourse Against Our Lord Jesus Christ* (London, 1827); the "Vampire" quotation is at p. 7. On Taylor, see sketches in *D.N.B.*, *Biographical Dictionary of Modern British Radicals*, and, above all, Wiener, *Radicalism and Freethought*, pp. 130–34, 149–51, 155–70, 184–86.

70. "The Law of Blasphemy," *London Magazine*, vol. 19 (Nov. 1827), pp. 361–62.

71. *Quarterly Review*, Jan. 1831, p. 300, quoted in Simon Maccoby, *English Radicalism, 1832–1852* (London, 1935), pp. 23–24. Wiener, *Radicalism and Freethought*, pp. 140–70, for the "Infidel Tours."

72. H. Cutner, *The Devil's Chaplain* (London, n.d.), pp. 26–30, a sixty-eight-page essay printed at the back of a reprint of Taylor's crazy book *The Diegesis; Being a Discovery of the Origin, Evidences, and Early History of Christianity* (1829, Boston, 1894). Cutner, an atheist, praised the book as an enduring contribution to "free thought." On Taylor's second trial for blasphemy, see also Guy Aldred, *The Devil's Chaplain* (Glasgow, 1942), pp. 26–27. Aldred, also an atheist, came at the material from a Marxist perspective; his pamphlet on Taylor is thirty-two pages. See also Wiener, *Radicalism and Freethought*, pp. 179–80, based on the account of the trial in Carlile's journal *The Prompter*, July 23, 1831.

73. On Carlile's trial for seditious libel, see Wickwar, *Struggle for Freedom of the Press*, pp. 293–98; Wiener, *Radicalism and Freethought*, pp. 174–77.

74. G. D. H. Cole, *Richard Carlile, 1790–1843* (London, 1943), p. 26. George Jacob Holyoake, *The Life and Character of Richard Carlile* (London, 1870), p. 25. See also Wiener, *Radicalism and Freethought*, p. 185.

75. Cole, *Carlile*, p. 25.

76. Ibid., p. 30. The best coverage of Carlile's years following his last imprisonment is Wiener, *Radicalism and Freethought*, pp. 190–260.

Chapter 18   Early American State Cases

1. See Leonard W. Levy, *The Establishment Clause: Religion and the First Amendment* (New York, 1986), pp. 22–65.

2. *People* v. *Ruggles*, 8 Johns. (N.Y.) 290 (1811).

3. James T. Horton, *James Kent: A Study in Conservatism, 1763–1847* (New York, 1939), is a good biography.

4. Francis Newton Thorpe, comp., *The Federal and State Constitutions* (Washington, D.C., 1909, 7 vols.), vol. 6, pp. 2635–38.

5. Horton, *Kent*, p. 153.

6. *People* v. *Ruggles*, 8 Johns. 290, 292–97.

7. *Bloom* v. *Richards*, 2 Ohio 392 (1853).

8. Gathercole's Case, 2 Lewin 237 (1838).

9. Nathaniel H. Carter et al., *Reports of the Proceedings and Debates of the Convention of 1821, Assembled for the Purpose of Amending the Constitution of the State of New York* (Albany, 1821), pp. 462–63.

10. Ibid., pp. 463–64.

11. Ibid., pp. 464–65.

12. Ibid., pp. 574–76.

13. Ibid., pp. 576–77.

14. Jay's opinion is reprinted in full in *Speech of Abner Kneeland, Delivered Before the Full Bench of Judges of the Supreme Court, in His Own Defence, for the Alleged Crime of Blasphemy* (Boston, 1836), p. vii, and certified by Jay to be accurate at p. viii, reprinted in Leonard W. Levy, ed., *Blasphemy in Massachusetts: Freedom of Conscience and the Abner Kneeland Case, a Documentary Record* (New York, 1973), pp. 381–82.

15. "Trial of Jared W. Bell, 1821," in John W. Lawson, ed., *American State Trials* (St. Louis, 1921, 20 vols.), vol. 3, pp. 558–61. "In re Bell," 6 City Hall Records, N.Y.C., cited in *American Digest. Centennial Edition*, vol. 7, p. 2714.

16. *People* v. *Porter*, 2 Park Criminal Reports (N.Y.) 14 (1823).

17. Adams to Jefferson, Jan. 23, 1825, in *The Adams-Jefferson Letters*, ed. Lester J. Cappon (New York, 1971), pp. 607–8.

18. 11 Serg. & Rawl. (Pa.) 394 (1824).

19. Ibid., pp. 399–400.

20. Ibid., pp. 400–408.

21. Jefferson to Cartwright, June 5, 1824, in *The Writings of Thomas Jefferson*, ed. Albert Ellery Bergh (Washington, D.C., 1907, 20 vols.), vol. 15, pp. 48–51. In the appendix to his *Reports of Cases Determined in the General Court of Virginia* (Charlottesville, 1829), a posthumous publication, Jefferson expanded his letter to Cartwright into a "disquisition" on Christianity and the common law, pp. 137–41, and see preface, p. vi.

22. Story to Edward Everett, Sept. 15, 1824, in William Wetmore Story, *The Life and Letters of Joseph Story* (Boston, 1851, 2 vols.), vol. 1, p. 430.

23. Ibid., pp. 431–33, reprints Story's piece.

24. Story to Everett, Sept. 15, 1824, in ibid., p. 430.

25. *Vidal* v. *Mayor of Philadelphia*, 2 Howard 127, 198 (1844).

26. *State* v. *Chandler*, 2 Harr. (Del.) 553 (1837).

27. Ibid., pp. 554–63, which includes the section on Jefferson.

28. "Lynch law" at ibid., p. 570.

29. Ibid., p. 572 for the quotation on blasphemy, pp. 575–77 for the material on Furneaux.

30. 37 Mass. 206 (1838).

31. Samuel Gridley Howe, "Atheism in New England," *The New England Magazine*, vol. 7 (Dec. 1834), pp. 500–509, vol. 8 (Jan. 1835), pp. 53–62.

32. John Barton Derby, *Political Reminiscences, Including a Sketch of the Origin and History of the "Statesman Party" of Boston* (Boston, 1835), p. 144.

33. [Samuel D. Parker,] *Report of the Arguments of the Attorney of the Commonwealth at the Trials of Abner Kneeland for Blasphemy, January and May, 1834. Collected and published at the request of some Christians of various denominations* (Boston, 1834), pp. 13, 16. Thacher's charge is available in Lawson, ed., *American State Trials*, vol. 13, pp. 495–512.

34. *Commonwealth* v. *Kneeland*, 37 Mass. 206–46 (1838).

35. Kneeland to Lemuel Shaw, June 1, 1838, Shaw Papers, Boston Social Law Library Manuscript Collections.

36. Act Against Blasphemy, Mass. Statutes 1782, ch. 8. In fact, the act of 1782 ameliorated earlier punishments, which included hanging and boring through the tongue with hot irons.

37. Lawson, ed., *American State Trials*, vol. 13, p. 453.

38. [Parker,] *Report*, p. 60.

39. Derby, *Political Reminiscences*, pp. 12–15, 44, 82, 143.

40. The following account of and quotations from Parker's argument are based on his *Report*.

41. Putnam's charge is in Lawson, ed., *American State Trials*, vol. 13, pp. 533–35. On Greene, see Derby, *Political Reminiscences*, p. 145.

42. Lawson, ed., *American State Trials*, vol. 13, pp. 536–37 notes.

43. A Cosmopolite [David Henshaw], *Review of the Prosecution Against Abner Kneeland for Blasphemy* (Boston, 1835), p. 1.

44. Lawson, ed., *American State Trials*, vol. 13, p. 575.

45. William H. Allison, "Abner Kneeland," *Dictionary of American Biography*, vol. 10, pp. 457–58.

46. John W. Chadwick, *William Ellery Channing* (Boston, 1903), pp. 277, 285–86.

47. *Speech of Abner Kneeland Delivered Before the Full Bench of Judges of the Supreme Court, In His Own Defence, for the Alleged Crime of Blasphemy, Law Term, March 8, 1836* (Boston, 1836), p. 30.

48. Ibid., pp. 17–18, 42. *Speech of Abner Kneeland Delivered Before the Supreme Court of the City of Boston in His Own Defence, on an Indictment for Blasphemy, November Term, 1834* (Boston, 1834), p. 16.

49. *William Lloyd Garrison, 1805–79: The Story of His Life, Told by His Children* (New York, 1885, 4 vols.), vol. 2, p. 142. Henry Steel Commager, *Theodore Parker* (Boston, 1936), pp. 64–69. Chadwick, *Channing*, pp. 277, 285–86. William Henry Channing, *The Life of William Ellery Channing* (Boston, 1899), p. 506.

50. *Commonwealth v. Kneeland*, 37 Mass. 206 (1838); Shaw's opinion is at pp. 211–25.

51. Charles Francis Adams, *Richard Henry Dana* (Boston, 1891, 2 vols.), vol. 1, p. 354.

52. 37 Mass. 206, 213, 216–17. Emphasis added.

53. *Speech of Kneeland, November Term, 1834*, pp. 3–4. *Speech of Kneeland, Law Term, March 8, 1836*, p. 10.

54. *People v. Ruggles*, 8 Johnson's Reports (New York) 290 (1811).

55. On freedom of the press, see Leonard W. Levy, *Emergence of a Free Press* (New York, 1985), pp. 12–13, 38–44. For the Massachusetts Declaration of Rights, see Francis Newton Thorpe, comp., *The Federal and State Constitutions* (Washington, D.C., 1909, 7 vols.), vol. 3, p. 1892.

56. *Commonwealth v. Kneeland*, 37 Mass. 206, 210 (1838).

57. Ibid., p. 221.

58. Preamble to statute of 1786 in 12 Hening (Va.) *Statutes* 84.

59. On Furneaux, see above, pp. 327–30.

60. Morton's opinion is at 37 Mass. 206, 225–46.

61. Kneeland to Shaw, June 1, 1838, Shaw Papers, Boston Social Law Library.

62. Parker to George Ellis, quoted in Franklin B. Sanborn and William T. Harris, *A. Bronson Alcott: His Life and Philosophy* (Boston, 1893, 2 vols.), vol. 1, p. 281.

63. On Kneeland's later life, see Mary R. Whitcomb, "Abner Kneeland: His Relations to Early Iowa History," *Annals of Iowa*, 3rd ser., vol. 6 (1904), pp. 340–63.

Chapter 19   England Reconsiders the Law of Blasphemy

1. Joseph Blanco White, *The Law of Anti-Religious Libel Reconsidered* (Dublin, 1834).

2. See Richard Whatley, *Letters on the Church, by an Episcopalian* (London, 1826), especially p. 112.

3. See Leonard W. Levy, *Emergence of a Free Press* (New York, 1985), pp. 92–93, 152.

4. John Search, *Considerations on the Law of Libel, as Relating to Publications on the Subject of Religion* (London, 1833), pp. 1–2.

5. *Report of a Remarkable Trial: The King vs. The Reverend Robert Taylor* (London, 1827), p. 37. Search, *Considerations*, p. 9, cited the *Morning Chronicle*, Oct. 25, 1827, which quoted Tenterden as follows: "Every man in this country had a right of private judgement upon every subject: and however injurious those opinions might prove either to himself or others, so long as he continued to keep those opinions to himself, the laws of his country could take no cognizance of his offence."

6. Search, *Considerations*, p. 12.

7. Ibid., pp. 13–14.

8. Ibid., p. 18.

9. For harsh observations by Search on the judges and lawyers, see his *Considerations*, pp. 53–81 in particular. William Hawkins, *A Treatise on Pleas of the Crown*, first published in 1713, was an influential work on criminal law, frequently reprinted. Thomas Starkie, *A Treatise on the Law of Slander and Libel*, first published in 1813, was the most respected book on the subject.

10. Search, *Considerations*, p. 23.

11. Ibid., pp. 39–42, 44–45.

12. Ibid., pp. 50–51.

13. White, *Law of Anti-Religious Libel*, pp. 10–12, 22. On White, see Martin Murphy, *Blanco White: Self-banished Spaniard* (New Haven, 1989). Murphy's splendid book barely mentions White's *Law of Anti-Religious Libel*.

14. White, *Law of Anti-Religious Libel*, pp. 25–36.

15. Ibid., pp. 36–39, 73–75.

16. 1 Timothy 13.

17. White, *Law of Anti-Religious Libel*, pp. 47–48, 64–67.

18. Ibid., pp. 68, 70–71.

19. Ibid., pp. 72, 76–77.

20. Ibid., pp. 80–82.

21. Ibid., pp. 90–95.

22. Sir William Holdsworth, *A History of English Law*, ed. A. L. Goodhart and H. G. Hanbury (London, 1965, 16 vols.), vol. 15, pp. 143–45. Leon Radzinowicz, *A History of English Criminal Law and Its Administration from 1750* (London, 1948–68, 4 vols.), vol. 4, pp. 310–11, includes the names of the commissioners. Radzinowicz treats the death penalty at length, criminal libels not at all.

23. *British Parliamentary Papers, Report from the Royal Commission on the Criminal Law, 1834–1841, Sixth Report of Her Majesty's Commissioners on the Criminal Law, Dated the Third Day of May, 1841* (London, 1841), p. 628 (cited hereafter as *Sixth Report*).

24. Ibid., pp. 628–30.

25. White, *Law of Anti-Religious Libel*, p. 39.

26. Radzinowicz, *History of English Criminal Law*, abounds in statistics on a variety of crimes, excluding criminal libels of any kind. His figures on various sorts of

crimes show no increases during the years when Paine's religious works sold cheaply and Carlile was a thorn to the government.

27. *Whitney* v. *California*, 274 U.S. 357, 376 (1927).
28. *Sixth Report*, p. 628.
29. Ibid., pp. 630–32.
30. Ibid., pp. 632–33.
31. Ibid., p. 637.
32. Gathercole's Case, 2 Lewin 237, at 254 (1838).

Chapter 20   English Prosecutions of the 1840s

1. *Queen* v. *Hetherington* (1840), in John E. P. Wallis, ed., *State Trials*, new ser. (London, 1892), vol. 4, p. 569 (cited hereafter as *State Trials* [new ser.]). No sketch of Haslam appears in any reference work, not even in Gordon Stein, ed., *Encyclopedia of Unbelief* (Buffalo, 1985, 2 vols.). Edward Royle, *Victorian Infidels: The Origins of the British Secularist Movement, 1791–1866* (Manchester, 1974), p. 50, mentions Haslam as an Owenite officer in Manchester in the 1830s. In a biographical appendix, Royle has four lines on Haslam derived from an obituary notice. He seems to have been an obscure chemist who escaped the government's bloodhounds. (Ibid., p. 311.)

2. *Queen* v. *Hetherington*, in *State Trials* (new ser.), vol. 4, p. 566.

3. Ibid., pp. 598–99. Patricia Hollis, *The Pauper Press* (London, 1970), pp. 309–10. The report of Hetherington's trial in *State Trials* (new ser.) gives Heywood's first name as "Henry." The title page of Haslam's book referred to "A. Heywood." Abel Heywood was a leader of the radical movement in Manchester. See ibid., pp. 586, 598. On Philpotts, see "Speech of the Right Reverend the Lord Bishop of Exeter," *Quarterly Review*, vol. 66 (1840), pp. 484–527, especially pp. 507ff.

4. Ambrose G. Barker, *Henry Hetherington* (London, n.d. [ca. 1938]), an atheistic tract, is the only modern study.

5. Hollis, *Pauper Press*, pp. vii, 122, 310–11.

6. Collet Dobson Collet, *A History of the Taxes on Knowledge* (London, 1933), pp. 14–24.

7. *Queen* v. *Hetherington*, in *State Trials* (new ser.), vol. 4, pp. 566–69.

8. Ibid., pp. 570–80.

9. *The Full Report of the Trial of Henry Hetherington* (London, 1840), p. 28.

10. *Queen* v. *Hetherington*, in *State Trials* (new ser.), vol. 4, pp. 588–94.

11. Ibid., pp. 594–600, for the proceedings on the appeal. W. J. Linton, *James Watson: A Memoir* (London, 1879), p. 64.

12. *Queen* v. *Hetherington*, in *State Trials* (new ser.), vol. 4, pp. 575–76.

13. Quoted in H. Buxton Forman, *The Vicissitudes of Shelley's "Queen Mab"* (London, 1887), p. 17.

14. Robert Mortenson, "The Copyright of Byron's *Cain*," *Bibliographical Society of America*, vol. 63 (1969), pp. 5–13. Newman I. White, "Literature and the Law of Libel: Shelley and the Radicals of 1840–1842," *Studies in Philology*, vol. 22 (1925), pp. 34–47. Linton, *James Watson*, pp. 49–52.

15. *Queen* v. *Moxon* (1841), in *State Trials* (new ser.), vol. 4, pp. 694–95.

16. Ibid., pp. 715, 719. Talfourd's speech covers pp. 695–719.

17. Ibid., pp. 719–22, for Denman's instructions to the jury. See also Linton,

James Watson, p. 52; "The Laws Against Blasphemy: Mr. Serjeant Talfourd's Defence of Moxon," *Law Magazine or Quarterly Review* (London), vol. 26 (1841), pp. 139–42.

18. The *Gay News* case of 1977, discussed below, pp. 534–50, was privately instigated.

19. Robin Lane Fox, *Pagans and Christians* (New York, 1987), pp. 424–30, 551–52. *The Trial of Charles Southwell, Editor of "The Oracle of Reason," for Blasphemy* (London, 1842), pp. 75–76, for Southwell's reliance on authorities showing Roman reaction to Christians as atheists.

20. On Southwell, see his *Confessions of a Freethinker* (London, 1850). Harry H. Pearce, "Charles Southwell in Australia and New Zealand," *New Zealand Rationalist*, vol. 18 (July 1957), p. 10, for Southwell as Shylock.

21. *New Zealand Rationalist*, vol. 18 (Aug. 1957), p. 11.

22. For extracts from *The Oracle of Reason* and the indictment, see *Trial of Southwell*, pp. 2–7.

23. Ibid., pp. 99–102, for the charge to the jury.

24. George Jacob Holyoake, *Sixty Years of an Agitator's Life* (London, 1892), is a disappointing series of sketches and anecdotes. Lee E. Grugel, *George Jacob Holyoake: A Study in the Evolution of a Victorian Radical* (Philadelphia, 1976), is a good, brief biography.

25. See articles on agnosticism, atheism, and secularism in Stein, ed., *Encyclopedia of Unbelief*.

26. George Jacob Holyoake, *The History of the Last Trial by Jury for Atheism in England* (London, 1851), p. 5.

27. Ibid., pp. 5–16, 37.

28. Ibid., pp. 15–20.

29. Ibid., pp. 64–65, 67–71. Grugel, *Holyoake*, p. 26. Oddly, Grugel disposes of the blasphemy trial in a paragraph.

30. Holyoake, *History of the Last Trial*, pp. 31, 33, 41.

31. Ibid., pp. 80–81.

32. Ibid., pp. 37–38, 44–45, 51–55.

33. Ibid., pp. 55–60.

34. Ibid., pp. 61–64.

35. Ibid., pp. 73–100.

36. Royle, *Victorian Infidels*, pp. 83–85.

37. *The Trial of Thomas Paterson, for Blasphemy, Before the High Court of Justiciary, Edinburgh* (London, 1844), pp. 10–11.

38. The judge of the high court, when sentencing Paterson, stated that his case was the first of its kind "for a long term of years" (ibid., p. 57.)

39. I could not find any sketch of Paterson. Royle relies on Southwell's *Confessions* for his references to Paterson (*Victorian Infidels*, p. 314), and Stein, ed., *Encyclopedia of Unbelief*, has no entry on Paterson; nor is there any reference to him in Marshall E. Brown and Gordon Stein, eds., *Freethought in the United States: A Descriptive Bibliography* (Westport, Conn., 1978), in Albert Post, *Popular Freethought in America, 1825–1850* (New York, 1974), or in Sidney Warren, *American Freethought, 1860–1914* (New York, 1966).

40. *Trial of Thomas Paterson*, pp. 26–32.

41. Ibid., pp. 38–45, 53.

42. Ibid., pp. 48–58.

43. Ibid., pp. 3–8.

44. *Trial of Thomas Paterson* includes *The Trials of Thomas Finlay and Miss Matilda*

Roalfe (For Blasphemy), in the Sheriff's Court (London, 1844), pp. 61–74 for Finlay, p. 75 for a reference to Robinson.

45. Ibid., p. 61.

46. Ibid., pp. 75–80.

47. Royle, *Victorian Infidels*, p. 92.

48. Ibid., pp. 13–23, 74–76, 90–92, 107–25, 302–3. Grugel, *Holyoake*, pp. 29–49.

Chapter 21   Bible Burning and a Debate Revived

1. Hetherington wrote, "I would advise the human race to burn every Bible they have got" (quoted in Anon., "Bible Blasphemy," *Dublin Review*, vol. 40 [March 1856], p. 235).

2. P. M'Loskey, *The Trial and Conviction of a Franciscan Monk, at Mayo Spring Assizes, 1852* (Dublin, 1852); the indictment is at p. 13, the charge to the jury at pp. 26–27.

3. James Doyle, ed., *A Special Report of the Trial of the Rev. Vladimir Petcherine, (One of the Redemptorist Fathers), in the Court House, Green Street, Dublin, December 1855, On an Indictment Charging Him With Burning the Protestant Bible* (Dublin, 1856), pp. 16–17, from the attorney general's introductory remarks. Also, *Regina* v. *Petcherine*, in *State Trials* (new ser.), vol. 8, pp. 1086, 1087.

4. Doyle, ed., *Trial of Petcherine*, p. 34.

5. Anon., "Bible-Blasphemy," p. 201. This article of over fifty pages purports to be an essay review of Doyle's edition of Petcherine's trial.

6. *Regina* v. *Petcherine*, 7 Cox, Criminal Law Cases 79, 84 (1855).

7. Anon., "Bible-Blasphemy," pp. 221–23.

8. Ibid., pp. 235–47.

9. *The Reasoner: Journal of Freethought* (London), Aug. 26, 1857, p. 170.

10. John Stuart Mill, *On Liberty*, ed. David Spitz (New York, 1975), p. 30.

11. Henry Thomas Buckle, "Mill on Liberty," *Fraser's Magazine*, vol. 59 (May 1854), p. 56.

12. George J. Holyoake, *The Case of Thomas Pooley, the Cornish Well-Sinker: A Report Made at the Instance of the Secularists* (London, 1857), quoted at p. 14; Holyoake listed Pooley's delusions at p. 13.

13. John Duke Coleridge, "Mr. Buckle and Sir John Coleridge," *Fraser's Magazine*, vol. 59 (June 1854), p. 637.

14. Holyoake, *Case of Pooley*, p. 12.

15. Ibid., p. 21.

16. Ibid., p. 14.

17. Coleridge, "Mr. Buckle," pp. 634–40.

18. Holyoake, *Case of Pooley*, p. 31. Coleridge, "Mr. Buckle," p. 641.

19. James Fitzjames Stephen, *A Digest of the Criminal Law* (London, 1877), art. 161, p. 97 n. 1.

20. *The Reasoner* of Oct. 7 1857, p. 219, reprinted in its entirety the *Spectator* editorial of Aug. 8, 1857.

21. *The Reasoner*, Aug. 19, 1857, pp. 161–62, reprinting Holdreth's letters.

22. Coleridge, "Mr. Buckle," pp. 642–45.

23. Editorial, "The Law of Blasphemous Libel," *Solicitors' Journal & Weekly Reporter*, vol. 4 (Dec. 10, 1859), p. 76, commenting on the speech.

24. Although *Solicitors' Journal & Weekly Reporter* reported Lewis's speech in its Nov. 26, 1859, issue, I have cited the more easily readable and available reprint in *Papers Read Before the Juridical Society, 1858–1863* (London, 1859–63, 2 vols.), vol. 2, pp. 250–81; the quotation is at p. 254.

25. Ibid., pp. 259–60.

26. Ibid., pp. 271–73.

27. Ibid., p. 270.

28. Ibid., p. 277.

29. *Solicitors' Journal & Weekly Reporter*, Dec. 10, 1859, p. 76.

30. Ibid., pp. 48–49, 84–85.

31. Ibid., p. 145.

32. Ibid., pp. 76–77.

33. Anon., "The Law Relating to Blasphemy," *Law Magazine and Review*, vol. 8 (1860), pp. 246–80; the remark about heresy and blasphemy is on p. 274.

34. Ibid., pp. 274–79.

35. *Essays and Reviews* (London, 1860; 12th ed., 1865). George William Cox, *The Life of John William Colenso* (London, 1888, 2 vols.), vol. 2, pp. 428–87.

36. W.C.S., "Blasphemy," *Journal of Jurisprudence and Scottish Law Magazine*, vol. 17 (1873), pp. 582–89.

37. James Fitzjames Stephen, "The Laws of England as to the Expression of Religious Opinions," *Contemporary Review*, vol. 25 (Feb. 1875), pp. 446–75.

38. Ibid., p. 468.

39. Ibid., pp. 468–69.

40. Ibid., p. 470.

41. Ibid., pp. 470–71.

42. Ibid., pp. 471–75.

43. Frederic Pollock, "The Theory of Persecution," in his *Essays in Jurisprudence and Ethics* (London, 1882), pp. 165–66.

44. W. A. Hunter, *The Past and Present of the Heresy Laws* (London, 1878), a tract of twenty-three pages. Charles Bradlaugh, *The Laws Relating to Blasphemy and Heresy: An Address to Freethinkers* (London, 1878), a tract of thirty-two pages.

Chapter 22   Bradlaugh, Foote, and Coleridge's Decency Test

1. *Regina* v. *Charles Bradlaugh and Anne Besant*, 14 Cox Criminal Cases 68 (1878). See S. Chandrasekhar, *"A Dirty, Filthy Book": The Writings of Charles Knowlton and Annie Besant on Reproductive Physiology and Birth Control and an Account of the Bradlaugh-Besant Trial* (Berkeley, 1981).

2. *Freethinker*, vol. 1 (May 7, 1883), p. 1.

3. *Regina* v. *Bradlaugh and Others*, 15 Cox Cr. Cases 217, pp. 218–19 (1883).

4. Anon., "Blasphemous Publications," *Irish Law Times*, vol. 17 (July 29, 1882), pp. 362–63. See also *The Law Times* (London), vol. 78 (July 22, 1882), p. 210.

5. *Verbatim Report of the Two Trials of G. W. Foote, W. J. Ramsey and H. A. Kemp for Blasphemous Libel in the Christmas Number of the Freethinker* (London, 1884), p. 93, quoting two letters by Harcourt. Arthur Calder-Marshall, *Lewd, Blasphemous & Obscene* (London, 1972), p. 181, quoting Foote.

6. *Verbatim Report of the Two Trials*, pp. 90–91.

7. Quoted by Walter L. Arnstein, *The Bradlaugh Case: A Study in Late Victorian Opinion and Politics* (Oxford, 1965), p. 250.

8. Quoted in Calder-Marshall, *Lewd*, p. 179.

9. G. W. Foote, *Reminiscences of Charles Bradlaugh* (London, 1891), p. 28.

10. Quoted in ibid., p. 184.

11. *Freethinker*, vol. 2 (Dec. 25, 1882), pp. 322–25.

12. Sir James Fitzjames Stephen, *A History of the Criminal Law of England* (London, 1883, 3 vols.), vol. 2, pp. 474–76.

13. *Verbatim Report of the Two Trials*, pp. 13–18.

14. Ibid., pp. 18–29.

15. Ibid., pp. 31–33.

16. Ibid., pp. 35–39.

17. Ibid., pp. 39–46.

18. Ibid., p. 46.

19. Ibid., pp. 47–108.

20. *The Spectator* (London), vol. 55 (March 10, 1883), pp. 313–14.

21. Ibid., March 17, 1883, pp. 348–49.

22. "The Offence of Blasphemy," *The Law Times*, vol. 74 (March 10, 1883), p. 331.

23. *The National Reformer*, vol. 41, issues of March and April 1883.

24. "Prosecution for Blasphemy," a three-part essay, in *National Reformer*, vol. 41 (April 8, 15, and 23, 1883), pp. 230–31, 246–47, 299.

25. *Regina v. Bradlaugh and Others*, 15 Cox Criminal Cases 217–23 (1883). See also Annie Besant, "How They Tried Charles Bradlaugh for Blasphemy," *National Reformer*, vol. 41 (April 22, 1883), pp. 290–91; Arthur H. Nethercot, *The First Five Lives of Annie Besant* (Chicago, 1960), pp. 187–92.

26. Thomas Starkie, *The Law of Slander and Libel* (London, 1830, 2nd ed.), vol. 2, p. 130.

27. *Regina v. Bradlaugh*, 15 Cox Cr. Cases 217, 225–26, 230–31.

28. For press comment on the Bradlaugh case, see *National Reformer*, vol. 41 (April 22, 29; and May 13, 1883).

29. George William Foote, *Defence of Free Speech, Being a Three Hours' Address to the Jury in the Court of Queen's Bench Before Lord Coleridge* (London, 1889).

30. Ibid., pp. 17–20. *Regina v. Ramsey and Foote*, 15 Cox Cr. C. 213, 234.

31. See ch. 19 above, pp. 431–33.

32. *Regina v. Ramsey and Foote*, 15 Cox Cr. C. 213, 234–38.

33. *Regina v. Lemon*, 3 Weekly Law Reports 404 (Aug. 11, 1978).

34. Foote, *Defence of Free Speech*, pp. 39–40.

35. On the divided jury, see Foote, *Reminiscences of Bradlaugh*, p. 34. Edward Royle, *Radicals, Secularists and Republicans: Popular Freethought in Britain, 1866–1915* (Manchester, 1980), pp. 34, 36, 333.

36. W. Blake Odgers, "Should the Existing Law As to Blasphemy Be Amended, and, If So, in What Direction?," *National Reformer*, vol. 42 (Oct. 14, 1883), pp. 244–46; (Oct. 21), pp. 260–62.

37. Stephen, *History of Criminal Law*, vol. 2, p. 474.

38. James Fitzjames Stephen, *A Digest of Criminal Law* (London, 1877), art. 161, pp. 97–98.

39. W. Blake Odgers, in *Transactions, 1857–1883*, National Association for the Promotion of Social Science, vol. 27 (1884), pp. 127–43.

40. William Barber, in *Transactions*, vol. 27 (1884), pp. 143–49.

41. W. Blake Odgers, "The Law Relating to Heresy and Blasphemy," *Modern Review*, vol. 4 (1883), pp. 586–608.

42. John Macdonell, "Blasphemy and the Common Law," *The Fortnightly Review*, June 1883, pp. 776–89.

43. Anon., "Blasphemy," *The Westminster Review*, vol. 239 (July 1883), pp. 1–11.

44. Ibid., pp. 9–11.

45. James Fitzjames Stephen, "Blasphemy and Blasphemous Libel," *The Fortnightly Review*, new ser., vol. 207 (March 1, 1884), pp. 289–318.

46. Ibid., pp. 315–16.

47. Ibid., pp. 317–18.

48. Ibid., p. 318.

49. H. J. W. Coulson, "The Law Relating to Blasphemy," *Law Magazine and Review*, vol. 9, 4th ser. (1883–84), pp. 158–73. Lindsey Middleton Aspland, *The Law of Blasphemy: Being a Candid Examination of the Views of Mr Justice Stephen* (London, 1884), tract of forty-eight pages.

50. *National Reformer*, vol. 41, issues of May 27, July 22, Aug. 5, 1883.

51. James Fitzjames Stephen, "The Laws of England As to the Expression of Religious Opinions," *The Contemporary Review*, vol. 25 (Feb. 1875), pp. 474–75.

52. "Repeal of the Blasphemy Laws," *The Spectator*, April 10, 1886, pp. 476–77.

53. Courtney Kenny, "The Evolution of the Law of Blasphemy," *Cambridge Law Journal*, vol. 1 (1922), pp. 127–42, at p. 130. Indian Penal Code, sec. 298. *The Works of Lord Macaulay*, ed. Lady Trevelyan (London, 1866, 8 vols.), vol. 8, speech of April 17, 1833, pp. 104–5.

54. *National Reformer*, issues of March 6, 13; Feb. 27, 1887.

55. Ibid., April 14, 21, 1889. Kenny, "Evolution of Law of Blasphemy," p. 138.

56. E. G. Taylor, "Intellectual Liberty and the Blasphemy Laws," *The Westminster Review*, vol. 143 (1894), pp. 117–39.

Chapter 23   *The Age of John W. Gott*

1. Hypatia Bradlaugh Bonner, "Another Blasphemy Case," *The Literary Guide* (London), Sept. 1, 1912, p. 140.

2. Ernest Pack, *The Trial and Imprisonment of J. W. Gott* (Bradford, 1912), pp. 26–27, reprinting the complaint for blasphemy because of the cartoon, which appeared in the Oct. 1903 issue of *The Truthseeker*.

3. *Freethinker*, March 1, 8, 22, 1908, June 20, 1909. *Rex* v. *Boulter*, Feb. 8, 1908, reported in *The Justice of the Peace*, vol. 72 (1908), pp. 188–89. See also Edward Royle, *Radicals, Secularists and Republicans: Popular Freethought in Britain, 1866–1915* (Manchester, 1980), pp. 277–79; Pack, *Trial of J. W. Gott*, p. 27.

4. Pack, *Trial of J. W. Gott*, pp. 24–34, which covers Stewart's trial too, and pp. 64–66, reprinting extracts from *Rib Ticklers*.

5. Pack, *Trial of J. W. Gott*, pp. 36–44, 72–74.

6. Ibid., pp. 115–23.

7. Hypatia Bradlaugh Bonner, *Penalties Upon Opinion: or Some Records of the Laws of Heresy and Blasphemy* (London, 1912), pp. 106–7.

8. *The Literary Guide*, issues of Jan.–May 1914. *Freethinker*, March 29, April 5, 1914.

9. Hypatia Bradlaugh Bonner, "The Latest Trial for Blasphemy," *The Literary Guide*, Jan. 1, 1914, pp. 3–4.

10. Ibid., pp. 4–5.

11. Ibid., p. 5. Hypatia Bradlaugh Bonner, "The Press on the Blasphemy Case," ibid., Feb. 1914, pp. 20–21.

12. Ibid., pp. 20–21.

13. Simon's memorandum is reprinted in Louis Blom-Cooper and Gavan Drewery, eds., *Law and Morality* (London, 1976), pp. 252–53.

14. Robert S. W. Pollard, *Abolish the Blasphemy Laws* (London, 1957), thirteen-page pamphlet, pp. 9–10 for Asquith.

15. *Bowman v. Secular Society, Ltd.*, Appeals Cases, House of Lords 406 (1917). "Twofold Aspect of the Law of Blasphemy," *Solicitors' Journal & Weekly Reporter*, vol. 66 (July 8, 1922), p. 629. "Blasphemy," *The Law Times*, vol. 153 (Feb. 11, 1922), p. 153.

16. *De Costa v. De Paz* (1754), best reported in *In re Bedford Charity*, 2 Swanston 470, 487 n. a (1819).

17. *In re Bedford Charity*, 2 Swanston 470 (1819).

18. *Attorney General v. Pearson*, 3 Merivale's Chancery Reports 353 (1817).

19. See Earl Morse Wilbur, *A History of Unitarianism* (Cambridge, Mass., 1946–54, 2 vols.), vol. 2, pp. 356–62, especially for the discussion of the case of Lady Hewley's Charity (1842).

20. *Lawrence v. Smith*, Jacobs English Chancery Reports 471 (1822).

21. *Shelley v. Westbrooke*, ibid., 266 (1817). *Murray v. Benbow*, ibid., 474 n. (1822).

22. Kenneth Neill Cameron, *The Young Shelley: Genesis of a Radical* (New York, 1950), pp. 180, 186, 405 n. 127.

23. E. G. Taylor, "Intellectual Liberty and the Blasphemy Laws," *The Westminster Review*, vol. 143 (1894), pp. 117–22. *In re Besant*, 11 Chancery Division Law Reports 508 (1879).

24. *Briggs v. Hartley*, 19 Law Journal Reports 2 Ex 230 (1850).

25. *Cowan v. Milbourn*, 2 Bulwer's Court of Exchequer Law Reports 230, 234 (1867).

26. *Bowman v. Secular Society, Ltd.*, Appeals Cases 406, at 466–67, 475–77.

27. 16 Cohen's Criminal Appeal Reports 86 (1921). See also *Freethinker*, Jan. 8, 1922, p. 28; Jan. 29, 1922, pp. 75, 91; Feb. 12, 1922, p. 109.

28. 16 Cohen's Cr. Ap. R., pp. 87–90.

29. "Prosecutions for Blasphemy," *Solicitors' Journal & Weekly Reporter*, vol. 66 (Jan. 28, 1922), p. 228. See also ibid., July 8, 1922, pp. 629–30.

30. *The Law Times*, vol. 153 (Feb. 11, 1922), p. 106.

31. Chapman Cohen, *Blasphemy: A Plea for Religious Equality* (London, 1922), pp. 16–27. Cohen's book *Almost An Autobiography* (London, 1940) detailed his leadership of the secularist movement in the Bradlaugh tradition, combining political radicalism with atheism.

32. Extract from 1927 tract by the Society for the Abolition of the Blasphemy Laws, in Blom-Cooper and Drewery, eds., *Law and Morality*, pp. 255–56. "Seditious and Blasphemous Teaching," *The Law Times*, vol. 163 (April 2, 1927), p. 302. See also G. D. Nokes, "The Future of Blasphemy Laws," *The Nineteenth Century and After* (London), vol. 108 (March 1930), p. 396.

33. "Blasphemy," *Solicitors' Journal & Weekly Reporter*, vol. 74 (Feb. 22, 1930), p. 111.

34. "The Real Danger," *The Law Times*, vol. 169 (Feb. 8, 1930), p. 125.

35. "The Blasphemy Bill," ibid. (March 1, 1930), p. 169. "The Law As to Blasphemy," *Solicitors' Journal & Weekly Reporter*, vol. 74 (March 15, 1930), p. 160. For the defense of a bill adopting the provision of the Indian Penal Code, see Nokes, "Future of Blasphemy Laws," pp. 391–401.

Chapter 24   The American Middle Period

1. The following cases are a highly selective sampling of state decisions that seem accurate and either define profanity or distinguish it from blasphemy: *Holcomb* v. *Cornish*, 8 Conn. 375 (1831); *Johnson* v. *Barclay*, 16 N.J. 1 (1837); *Ex parte Delaney*, 43 Cal. 478 (1872); *State* v. *Moser*, 33 Ark. 140 (1878); *Gaines* v. *State*, 75 Tenn. 410 (1881); *State* v. *Lafayette Chrisp*, 85 N.C. 528 (1881); *Commonwealth* v. *Linn*, 158 Pa. 22 (1893); *Bodenhamer* v. *State*, 60 Ark. 10 (1894); *State* v. *Wiley*, 76 Miss. 282 (1898); *Sanford* v. *Miss.*, 91 Miss. 158 (1907); *Orf* v. *State*, 147 Miss. 160 (1927); *Commonwealth* v. *Brown*, 67 Pa. D.&C. 151 (1948).

2. *New York Times*, Sept. 11, 1879, p. 4.

3. Ibid., June 15, 1884, p. 8.

4. Ibid.

5. Ibid., May 24, 1882, p. 3.

6. Ibid., May 20, 1887, p. 8.

7. "The Trial of Charles B. Reynolds, for Blasphemy," in John D. Lawson, ed., *American State Trials* (St. Louis, 1921, 20 vols.), vol. 16, pp. 795–857, reports the case.

8. See Clarence H. Cramer, *Royal Bob: The Life of Robert G. Ingersoll* (Indianapolis, 1952), p. 168. See also Wilmington *Evening Journal*, May 27, 1969, p. 1, for Comegys.

9. *New York Times*, May 20, 1887, p. 8. Most of the report of the trial in Lawson, ed., *American State Trials*, consists of Ingersoll's speech, which was reprinted in pamphlet form and is also available in *The Works of Robert G. Ingersoll* (New York, 1907), vol. 11, pp. 54–117.

10. Lawson, ed., *American State Trials*, vol. 16, p. 807.

11. Ibid., p. 853.

12. The quoted words, not in Lawson, are from an anonymous pamphlet, *The Great Jersey Heresy Case: In Full and Complete, Speech in the Trial of the Rev. Charles B. Reynolds for Blasphemy* (Chicago, 1887), p. 11.

13. Ibid., pp. 12–13.

14. *New York Times*, May 21, 1887, p. 4.

15. The Right Rev. Leighton Coleman, "The Limits of Legitimate Religious Discussion," *The North American Review*, vol. 156 (Jan. 1893), pp. 9–17, quotation at p. 16.

16. The case is reported only in the autobiography of Charles C. Moore, *Behind the Bars: 31498* (Lexington, Ky., 1899), pp. 290–91, reprinting the report in *Free-thought Magazine* (Chicago), April 1895.

17. Ibid., p. 216, for "a Judge known to be an infidel."

18. Ibid., pp. 291–93.

19. Theodore Schroeder, *Constitutional Free Speech Defined and Defended in an Unfinished Argument in a Case of Blasphemy* (New York, 1919). This inaccurate, sometimes incoherent, disorganized, yet useful book purports to be Schroeder's defense of

Mockus. The sparse facts of the case are at pp. 13, 454. See also *The Outlook*, vol. 115 (Jan. 17, 1917), pp. 96–97.

20. Quoted in David Brudnoy, "Liberty's Bugler: The Seven Ages of Theodore Schroeder," unpublished Ph.D. dissertation, Brandeis University, 1971, p. 145.

21. Schroeder, *Constitutional Free Speech*, p. 455.

22. Waukegan *Daily Sun*, Jan. 22, 24, 26, 29, 1917. Hardly an issue of the paper did not carry a story on Mockus right through the middle of March 1917.

23. Ibid., Feb. 1, 1917, p. 4.

24. Ibid., March 3, 1917, reprinting the opinion of the court.

25. Lewiston *Evening Journal*, Oct. 25, 27, 30, 1919.

26. *State* v. *Michael X. Mockus*, 120 Maine 84–98 (1921).

27. William Wolkovich, *Bay State "Blue" Laws and Bimba* (Brockton, Mass., 1973), pp. 19–27, 98.

28. *New York Times*, Feb. 19, 1926, p. 3.

29. The quotation from Blackwell is in ibid., Feb. 22, 1926, p. 3. See also Wolkovich, *Bay State*, pp. 53–55, 62–64, 79–80.

30. *New York Times*, Feb. 25, 1926, p. 23; Feb. 26, 1926, p. 3.

31. Ibid., Feb. 27, 1926, p. 3.

32. Ibid., Feb. 28, 1926, p. 9.

33. Ibid., March 3, 1926, p. 25. Wolkovich, *Bay State*, devotes a large part of his little book to an effective coverage of the trial, pp. 72–117.

34. Wolkovich, *Bay State*, pp. 119–25, surveys the press.

35. Ibid., pp. 126–29; p. 21 for the degree.

36. *New York Times*, June 15, 1927, p. 6. Zechariah Chafee, Jr., *The Inquiring Mind* (New York, 1928), p. 114 n. 8. I could not find additional information about the case.

37. *New York Times*, Aug. 28, 1928, p. 26; Aug. 29, 1928, p. 8.

38. Ibid., Oct. 18, 1928, p. 1; Oct. 29, 1928, p. 23. Marcet Haldeman-Julius, "Is Arkansas Civilized?," *The Debunker*, vol. 9 (Dec. 1928), pp. 3–16, 113–20.

39. *New York Times*, Nov. 15, 1928, p. 60. Rand School, *American Labor Year Book*, vol. 10 (1929), p. 204.

40. *New York Times*, Oct. 14, 1937, p. 29.

41. Ibid., Jan. 9, 1957, p. 24.

42. *Rex* v. *Rahard*, 3 Dominion Law Reports 230 (1935).

43. *Queen* v. *Pelletier*, 6 Revue Légale 116 (1900).

44. *Rex* v. *Kinler*, 63 Rapports Judiciaires de Québec 483 (1925).

45. *Rex* v. *Ernest V. Sterry*, 5 Canadian Law Rev. 362–65 (1927), reporting the trial. See also "Annotation on Blasphemy," 48 Canadian Crim. Cases 1–22 (1927); "Libeling God in Canada," *The Literary Digest*, vol. 193 (April 9, 1927), p. 30.

46. *Rex* v. *St.-Martin*, 40 Rev. de Jur. 411 (1933).

47. *Maryland* v. *West*, 9 Md. App. 270 (1970).

Chapter 25   Modern America

1. *State* v. *Michael X. Mockus*, 124 Me. 84, 97 (1919).

2. *Gitlow* v. *New York*, 268 U.S. 652, 665 (1925).

3. *Stromberg* v. *Cal.*, 283 U.S. 359 (1931). *Near* v. *Minn.*, 283 U.S. 697 (1931).

Hamilton v. *Regents of University of Cal.*, 293 U.S. 245 (1934). *De Jonge* v. *Ore.*, 299 U.S. 353 (1937). *Cantwell* v. *Conn.*, 310 U.S. 296 (1940). *Everson* v. *Bd. of Ed.*, 330 U.S. 1 (1947).

4. *Cantwell* v. *Conn.*, 310 U.S. 296, 310 (1940).

5. *Chaplinsky* v. *New Hamp.*, 315 U.S. 568 (1942).

6. *Johnson* v. *Barclay*, 16 N.J. 1 (1837). *Sanford* v. *Miss.*, 91 Miss. 158 (1907). *Torrington* v. *Taylor*, 59 Wyo. 109 (1943).

7. *Minersville School District* v. *Gobitis*, 310 U.S. 586 (1940). See David R. Manwaring, *Render unto Caesar: The Flag-Salute Controversy* (Chicago, 1962), pp. 163–86, on "The Persecution of Jehovah's Witnesses."

8. *Oney* v. *Oklahoma City*, 120 F. 2d 861 (1941).

9. *Lynch* v. *City of Muskogee*, 47 F. Supp. 589 (E.D. Okla.) (1942).

10. The facts of the case are best presented in the concurring opinion of Justice Felix Frankfurter in *Burstyn* v. *Wilson*, 343 U.S. 495, 507–16 (1952).

11. Ibid., pp. 497–506.

12. Ibid., pp. 517–40.

13. Baltimore *Sun*, July 22, 23, Aug. 9, Sept. 12, 1968.

14. Ibid., May 9, 1969. *Time*, vol. 93 (May 16, 1969), p. 72.

15. *State* v. *Chandler*, 2 Del. 553 (1837).

16. Wilmington *Evening Journal*, May 26, 27, 1969, p. 1 both days. *The New York Times* also reported the case, May 29, 1969, p. 41.

17. Wilmington *Evening Journal*, Sept. 30, 1969, p. 1. *New York Times*, Oct. 1, 1969, p. 26.

18. *Zorach* v. *Clauson*, 343 U.S. 346, 313 (1952).

19. *Abingdon School Dist.* v. *Schempp*, 374 U.S. 203 (1963).

20. 9 Md. App. 270, 263 Atlantic Rep., 2nd ser. 602–5.

21. *Specht* v. *Commonwealth*, 8 Pa. 312 (1848).

22. *Sparhawk* v. *Union Passenger Ry.*, 54 Pa. 401 (1867).

23. *Commonwealth* v. *Linn*, 158 Pa. 22 (1893).

24. *Zeisweiss* v. *James*, 63 Pa. 465 (1870).

25. *Manners* v. *Philadelphia Library Co.*, 93 Pa. 165 (1880).

26. *New York Times*, April 25, 1971, p. 60. *Civil Liberties* (published by the ACLU), Sept. 1971.

27. Los Angeles *Times*, Nov. 17, 1976, p. 1. I have an undated four-page tract of the Interfaith Committee Against Blasphemy, signed by W. S. McBirnie, a Protestant fundamentalist connected with a theology school in Glendale. Allan E. Shapiro, "On Blasphemy," Jerusalem *Post*, Feb. 10, 1984.

28. *New York Times*, March 16, 1977.

29. Ibid., Aug. 28, 30, 1979. Los Angeles *Times*, Aug. 27, 31, 1979.

30. *New York Times*, July 13, 15, 21, 24, 25, Aug. 5, 8, 1988, ran articles on the controversy about the movie before it opened in New York. After it opened on Aug. 11, the paper's coverage was intensive: Aug. 11, sec. 1, p. 25; Aug. 12, sec. 1, p. 26, sec. 3, pp. 1, 4; Aug. 13, sec. 1, p. 1; Aug. 14, sec. 1, p. 36; Aug. 15, sec. 3, p. 74; Aug. 18, sec. 3, p. 2; Aug. 21, sec. 2, p. 21; Aug. 24, sec. 1, p. 15; Aug. 26, sec. 3, p. 19; Aug. 26, sec. 1, p. 17; Sept. 6, sec. 3, p. 19; Sept. 8, sec. 3, p. 17; Sept. 11, sec. 1, p. 34.

31. I have had the cooperation of all parties to the incident; they supplied me with the records of the case. I have a transcript of the minutes of the Sept. 8, 1988, meeting of the Board of County Commissioners of Escambia County, Fla., pp. 17–27; a copy of Ordinance 88-9 imposing the ban; the briefs of the attorneys employed by

Plitt Theatres Inc. and Martin Scorsese as well as by the ACLU; and a copy of the records pertaining to a federal-district-court injunction against the county commissioners' ban.

32. I am especially grateful to Mr. Gregg Thomas of Holland & Knight, who presented the principal brief, and to Mr. Daniel M. Soloway of McKenzie, Millsap & Soloway, for the ACLU; Mr. Charles J. Kahn, Jr., of Levin, Middlebrooks et al.; and Mr. William P. Buztrey, county attorney, Escambia County. I have their letters describing the incident and their documents.

33. *Plitt Theatres Inc. and Martin Scorsese* v. *Escambia County, Fla.*, Case No. 88-30303-RV, U.S. District Court, Northern District of Florida, Pensacola, a ten-page photocopy of a typescript opinion by Judge Roger Vinson, Sept. 9, 1988.

Chapter 26   *The* Gay News *Case*

1. W. B. Yeats, "Stick of Incense," ca. 1931, in *The Poems of W. B. Yeats*, ed. Richard J. Finneran (New York, 1983), p. 341.

2. See S. Chandresekhar, *"A Dirty, Filthy Book": The Writings of Charles Knowlton and Annie Besant on Reproductive Physiology and Birth Control and an Account of the Bradlaugh-Besant Trial* (Berkeley, 1981), which reprints Knowlton's text at pp. 87–147.

3. See the section on "Profanity, Obscenity and Blasphemy," in Edward Royle, *Radicals, Secularists and Republicans: Popular Freethought in Britain, 1866–1915* (Manchester, 1980), pp. 271–83.

4. See Norman St. John-Stevas, *Obscenity and the Law* (London, 1956); Arthur Caler-Marshall, *Lewd, Blasphemous & Obscene* (London, 1972), pp. 193–232.

5. D. H. Lawrence, "The Man Who Died," in *The Short Novels of D. H. Lawrence* (London, 1956, 2 vols.), vol. 2, p. 43 for the sex scene.

6. Kingsley Amis, "New Approach Needed," in Philip Larkin, ed., *The Oxford Book of Twentieth-Century English Verse* (Oxford, 1973), p. 530.

7. John Updike, *Marry Me: A Romance* (New York, 1976), p. 153.

8. Thomas Hansard, ed., *Parliamentary Debates (Lords)*, 5th ser., vol. 389 (Feb. 23, 1978), p. 282. On the abolition of the 1698 statute, see The Law Commission, *Working Paper No. 79: Offences Against Religion and Public Worship* (London, 1981), pp. 28–29.

9. Bernard Nossiter, "X-Rated Life of Christ?," Los Angeles *Times*, Sept. 25, 1976.

10. James Kirkup, "The Love That Dares to Speak Its Name," *Gay News*, No. 96, June 3–16, 1976, p. 26.

11. Lord Roskill, in *Regina* v. *Lemon*, and *Regina* v. *Gay News Ltd.*, 3 *Weekly Law Reports* 404, 405 (Aug. 11, 1978).

12. Robin Lustig, " 'Sunday School Terrified Me,' says *Gay News* Poet," *The Sunday Observer* (London), July 17, 1977, p. 3.

13. Ingrid Anderson and Pamela Rose, "Who the Hell Does She Think She Is?: PLR Interviews Mary Whitehouse," *Poly Law Review*, vol. 3 (1980), p. 15.

14. Ibid., pp. 13–18. Michael Tracey and David Morrison, *Whitehouse* (London, 1979), a detailed and hostile book. The quotation is in Corinna Adam, "Protecting Our Lord," *New Statesman and Nation*, new ser., vol. 94 (July 15, 1977), p. 74.

15. Tracey and Morrison, *Whitehouse*, pp. 3–4, quotes her letters of Nov. 1 and 9, 1976, to her lawyer.

16. Anderson and Rose, "Who the Hell Does She Think She Is?," p. 14.

17. Tracey and Morrison, *Whitehouse*, pp. 5–9. London *Times*, Dec. 10, 1976, p. 2.

18. London *Times*, July 9, 1977, p. 2; July 12, 1977, p. 1.

19. Tracey and Morrison, *Whitehouse*, pp. 9–11.

20. *Regina* v. *Lemon*, 3 *Weekly Law Reports* 404, 405 (Aug. 11, 1978).

21. Alan King-Hamilton, Q.C., *And Nothing But the Truth* (London, 1982), pp. 172–74.

22. " 'Gay News' Crucified," *Socialist Challenge*, July 14, 1977, p. 1. Tracey and Morrison, *Whitehouse*, pp. 12–17. King-Hamilton, *And Nothing But the Truth*, p. 174.

23. Law Commission, *Working Paper No. 79*, pp. 53–54.

24. My account of the trial, whose transcript has not been published, is based on reports in the London *Times*, July 4–13, 1977; on the references to the trial in appellate proceedings; on King-Hamilton, *And Nothing But the Truth*, pp. 172–85; and on Nicolas Walter, *Blasphemy in Britain: The Practice and Punishment of Blasphemy, and the Trial of "Gay News"* (London, 1977), a sixteen-page essay by an eyewitness to the trial and a leader of the campaign to abolish all blasphemy laws. Walter's little book of ninety-six pages, *Blasphemy Ancient and Modern* (London, 1990), is an expansion of his essay but abbreviates the report of the trial.

25. Walter, *Blasphemy in Britain*, p. 11.

26. London *Times*, July 5, 1977.

27. King-Hamilton, *And Nothing But the Truth*, pp. 177–78. Earl of Halsbury, *The Laws of England* (London, 1976, 4th ed.), vol. 11, para. 1009.

28. London *Times*, July 9, 10, 12, 1977.

29. Ibid., July 11, 12, 13, 1977. King-Hamilton, *And Nothing But the Truth*, pp. 179–80. Walter, *Blasphemy in Britain*, p. 16. Adam, "Protecting Our Lord," p. 74.

30. *Regina* v. *Lemon*, *Regina* v. *Gay News Ltd.*, 3 W.L.R. 404, 414–15 (1978), in which Roskill quoted Coleridge's opinion in *Rex* v. *Ramsey and Foote*, 15 Cox C.C. 231, 236 (1883); it was in *Rex* v. *Ramsey and Foote* that Coleridge quoted *Starkie on Libel*, to which Roskill added the opening quotation from Starkie, 3rd ed. (1869), p. 583. Emphasis added.

31. *Regina* v. *Lemon*, *Regina* v. *Gay News Ltd.*, 143 *Justice of the Peace and Local Government Review Reports*, 315, 323–30 (1979).

32. Ibid., p. 343.

33. Ibid., pp. 315–23 for Diplock, pp. 330–42 for Edmund-Davies.

34. London *Times*, July 14, 1977, p. 4. Walter, *Blasphemy Ancient and Modern*, p. 78.

35. Phyllis Graham, *The Jesus Hoax* (London, 1974). John Hick, ed., *The Myth of God Incarnate* (Philadelphia, 1977). John Allegro, *The Sacred Mushroom and the Cross* (Garden City, N.Y., 1970), p. 190; see also pp. xi, 28, 61, 105–6, 111, 125.

Chapter 27   The Rushdie Affair

1. Thomas Hansard, ed., *Parliamentary Debates* (Lords), vol. 389 (Feb. 23, 1978), pp. 279–350.

2. The Law Commission, *Working Paper No. 79: Offences against Religion and Public Worship* (London, 1981), pp. 72–82.

3. Ibid., pp. 92–98.

4. Ibid., pp. 98–111.

5. Ibid., pp. 121, 124.

6. Ibid., pp. 128–40, 163–64.

7. The Law Commission, *Criminal Law: Offences against Religion and Public Worship* (London, 1985), pp. 5–6. In the same year appeared a dreadfully dull little novel about Mary Magdalene and her love affair with Jesus, whom she called her "husband," but, the sexual relationship notwithstanding, nothing in the book is in the least sexy or blasphemous. (Michele Roberts, *The Wild Girl* [London, 1985].)

8. Law Commission, *Criminal Law*, pp. 41–42. For Kirkup, see Robin Lustig, " 'Sunday School Terrified Me,' Says *Gay News* Poet," *Sunday Observer* (London), July 17, 1977, p. 3.

9. Law Commission, *Criminal Law*, pp. 43–45.

10. Ibid., p. 24.

11. Ibid., p. 25.

12. Ibid., p. 26.

13. Ibid., pp. 25–28.

14. The best introduction is Daniel Pipes, *The Rushdie Affair: The Novel, the Ayatollah, and the West* (New York, 1990). The book itself is Salman Rushdie, *The Satanic Verses* (London, Penguin, 1988).

15. Pipes, *Rushdie Affair*, p. 32.

16. Shrabani Basus, "Interview with Salman Rushdie," *Sunday* (India), Sept. 18–24, 1988, reprinted in Lisa Appignanesi and Sara Maitland, eds., *The Rushdie File* (Syracuse, 1990), pp. 32–33. *The Rushdie File* is an invaluable compilation of primary sources without editorial comment.

17. Rushdie, *Satanic Verses*, pp. 367–68.

18. Ibid., p. 364.

19. Carl W. Ernst, "Blasphemy: Islamic Concept," in Mircea Eliade, ed., *The Encyclopedia of Religion* (New York, 1988, 16 vols.), vol. 2, pp. 242–45.

20. Rushdie, *Satanic Verses*, p. 123. Pipes, *Rushdie Affair*, pp. 56–62, is excellent on the "satanic verses" issue.

21. Rushdie, *Satanic Verses*, p. 374.

22. London *Times*, Feb. 28, 1989, quoted in Pipes, *Rushdie Affair*, p. 117.

23. Syed Shahabuddin, "You Did This with Satanic Forethought, Mr. Rushdie," *Times of India*, Oct. 13, 1988, in Appignanesi and Maitland, eds., *Rushdie File*, pp. 39–40.

24. Statement by a mosque official of Bradford, England, in ibid., p. 54.

25. Tariq Modood, "British Asian Muslims and the Rushdie Affair," *The Political Quarterly*, vol. 90 (1990), pp. 143–60; quotation on p. 154.

26. U.K. Action Committee on Islamic Affairs, Oct. 28, 1988, in Appignanesi and Maitland, eds., *Rushdie File*, p. 47.

27. Pipes, *Rushdie Affair*, pp. 127–28, 131, 166; p. 128 for the first quotation. On the ayatollah's edict, ibid., pp. 26–30, 87–105. For the document, see Appignanesi

and Maitland, eds., *Rushdie File*, pp. 74–76. On the Saudis, Pipes, *Rushdie Affair*, pp. 20, 60, and *Rushdie File*, p. 60.

28. London *Times*, in Appignanesi and Maitland, eds., *Rushdie File*, p. 46.

29. London *Times*, July 5, 1989, p. 13, for the text of Patten's speech. On p. 1, the *Times* headlined the story "Government Rejects Changes in Blasphemy Law."

30. *Independent*, Feb. 21, 22, 1989, in Appignanesi and Maitland, eds., *Rushdie File*, pp. 100–102, for the archbishop. The joint statement is in ibid., pp. 125–26. Aziz Al-Azmeh, who wrote for *New Statesman & Society*, Jan. 20, 1989, is in ibid., p. 57. Pipes, *Rushdie Affair*, pp. 165 180–81, for campaigning of Labour M.P.'s and for *The Economist*.

31. Tariq Modood, "Religious Anger and Minority Rights," *The Political Quarterly*, vol. 90 (1989), p. 284.

32. London *Times*, March 9, 1989, in Appignanesi and Maitland, eds., *Rushdie File*, pp. 197–99.

33. For amplification of this viewpoint, see Richard Webster, *A Brief History of Blasphemy: Liberalism, Censorship, and "The Satanic Verses"* (Southwold, Eng., 1990). The subtitle of this little book is accurate; the title is utterly misleading.

34. For extracts from the "Report to the Archbishop of Canterbury," see *Law, Blasphemy and the Multi-Faith Society*, intro. Bhikhu Parekh (London, 1990), pp. 80–82.

35. Keith Ward, "Third Introductory Paper," in ibid., pp. 30–38.

36. Jim Herrick, "Visions of Censorship," *New Humanist: Bimonthly Journal of the Rationalist Press*, Jan. 1990, pp. 5–9. Los Angeles *Times*, Dec. 28, 1989.

Chapter 28　　Conclusions

1. John Godolphin, *Reportorium Canonicum; or An Abridgment of the Ecclesiastical Laws of This Realm* (London, 1678), pp. 559–60. George MacKenzie, *The Laws and Customs of Scotland in Matters Criminal* (Edinburgh, 1678), tit. iii, 1, p. 25; tit. x, 2, p. 85.

2. *Cohen* v. *California*, 403 U.S. 15 (1971).

3. Jefferson to T. Pickering, Feb. 27, 1821, in *The Writings of Thomas Jefferson*, ed. Albert E. Bergh (Washington, D.C., 1907, 20 vols.), vol. 15, p. 323. George Santayana, *Reason in Science* (New York, 1983, reprint of 1906 ed.), p. 285. *Dialogues of Alfred North Whitehead*, ed. Lucien Price (Boston, 1954), p. 174.

4. T. S. Eliot, *After Strange Gods* (New York, 1934), pp. 55–57.

5. See discussion of the flag-burning and cross-burning cases, above, pp. 574–75, and n. 9 below.

6. Boston *Globe*, Nov. 30, 1977, p. 3.

7. *Terminiello* v. *Chicago*, 337 U.S. 1, 4 (1949).

8. See Anthony Amsterdam, "The Void-for-Vagueness Doctrine in the Supreme Court," 109 *U. Pa. L. Rev.* 67 (1960); Note, "The First Amendment Overbreadth Doctrine," 83 *Harvard L. Rev.* 844 (1970).

9. The flag-burning cases are *Texas* v. *Johnson*, 109 S. Ct. 2533 (1989), and *United States* v. *Eichman*, 110 S. Ct. 2404 (1990). The cross-burning case is *R.A.V.* v. *City of St. Paul*, 112 S. Ct. 2538 (1992).

10. *R.A.V.* v. *City of St. Paul*, 112 S. Ct. 2538, 2548.

11. Ibid., p. 2559.

12. See William G. Torpey, *Judicial Doctrines of Religious Rights in America* (Chapel Hill, N.C., 1948), pp. 37–81.

13. San Francisco *Chronicle*, March 12, 1992, p. D-5.

14. Gary J. Moes, "The Separation of Culture and the State: Should Government Endow the Arts?," *Rutherford Institute Journal*, Jan. 1992, pp. 1, 6–7, 10. John Whitehead, "Art as Propaganda: A Prelude to Persecution," ibid., p. 5. The picture of Christ engaged in homosexual activity appears in a publication called *Performance Journal 3*, produced by Movement Research of New York City. A remarkable interview with Franky Schaeffer appears on pp. 8–9 of the same issue of the *Rutherford Institute Journal* as the Moes and Whitehead articles, in which Schaeffer criticizes fundamentalists and television preachers for greater "blasphemy" in commercializing Christianity; he says that if he had to choose between "so-called conservative Christians" and homosexual artists, he "would prefer the honesty of the overtly anti-Christian art."

15 On Shirley Temple, see August R. Ogden, *The Dies Committee: A Study of the Special House Committee for the Investigation of Un-American Activities, 1938–1944* (Washington, D.C., 1945), pp. 64–65, 69, 104. On the FBI, Natalie Robins, *Alien Ink: The FBI's War on Freedom of Expression* (New York, 1992).

Index